# Innovative Perspectives on Public Administration in the Digital Age

Aroon P. Manoharan
*University of Massachusetts - Boston, USA*

James McQuiston
*Kent State University, USA*

A volume in the Advances in Electronic Government, Digital Divide, and Regional Development (AEGDDRD) Book Series

IGI Global
DISSEMINATOR OF KNOWLEDGE

Published in the United States of America by
IGI Global
Information Science Reference (an imprint of IGI Global)
701 E. Chocolate Avenue
Hershey PA, USA 17033
Tel: 717-533-8845
Fax: 717-533-8661
E-mail: cust@igi-global.com
Web site: http://www.igi-global.com



Library of Congress Cataloging-in-Publication Data

Names: Manoharan, Aroon, 1979- editor. | McQuiston, James, 1983- editor.
Title: Innovative perspectives on public administration in the digital age / Aroon P. Manoharan and James McQuiston, editors.
Description: Hershey, PA : Information Science Reference, 2018. | Includes bibliographical references.
Identifiers: LCCN 2017058882| ISBN 9781522559665 (hardcover) | ISBN 9781522559672 (ebook)
Subjects: LCSH: Internet in public administration. | Social media--Political aspects.
Classification: LCC JF1525.A8 I485 2018 | DDC 352.3/802854678--dc23 LC record available at https://lccn.loc.gov/2017058882

This book is published in the IGI Global book series Advances in Electronic Government, Digital Divide, and Regional Development (AEGDDRD) (ISSN: 2326-9103; eISSN: 2326-9111)

British Cataloguing in Publication Data
A Cataloguing in Publication record for this book is available from the British Library.

# Advances in Electronic Government, Digital Divide, and Regional Development (AEGDDRD) Book Series

Zaigham Mahmood
University of Derby, UK & North West University, South Africa

ISSN:2326-9103
EISSN:2326-9111

Mission

The successful use of digital technologies (including social media and mobile technologies) to provide public services and foster economic development has become an objective for governments around the world. The development towards electronic government (or e-government) not only affects the efficiency and effectiveness of public services, but also has the potential to transform the nature of government interactions with its citizens. Current research and practice on the adoption of electronic/digital government and the implementation in organizations around the world aims to emphasize the extensiveness of this growing field.

**The Advances in Electronic Government, Digital Divide & Regional Development (AEGDDRD)** book series aims to publish authored, edited and case books encompassing the current and innovative research and practice discussing all aspects of electronic government development, implementation and adoption as well the effective use of the emerging technologies (including social media and mobile technologies) for a more effective electronic governance (or e-governance).

Coverage

- E-Government in Developing Countries and Technology Adoption
- Urban Development, Urban Economy
- E-Governance and Use of Technology for Effective Government
- Issues and Challenges in E-Government Adoption
- ICT within Government and Public Sectors
- Knowledge Divide, Digital Divide
- Frameworks and Methodologies for E-Government Development
- Adoption of Innovation with Respect to E-Government
- Online Government, E-Government, M-Government
- Emerging Technologies within the Public Sector

IGI Global is currently accepting manuscripts for publication within this series. To submit a proposal for a volume in this series, please contact our Acquisition Editors at Acquisitions@igi-global.com or visit: http://www.igi-global.com/publish/.

The Advances in Electronic Government, Digital Divide, and Regional Development (AEGDDRD) Book Series (ISSN 2326-9103) is published by IGI Global, 701 E. Chocolate Avenue, Hershey, PA 17033-1240, USA, www.igi-global.com. This series is composed of titles available for purchase individually; each title is edited to be contextually exclusive from any other title within the series. For pricing and ordering information please visit http://www.igi-global.com/book-series/advances-electronic-government-digital-divide/37153. Postmaster: Send all address changes to above address. 

## Titles in this Series

*For a list of additional titles in this series, please visit: www.igi-global.com/book-series*

*Handbook of Research on Modernization and Accountability in Public Sector Management*
Graça Maria do Carmo Azevedo (University of Aveiro, Portugal) Jonas da Silva Oliveira (ISCTE – Instituto Universitário de Lisboa, Portugal) Rui Pedro Figueiredo Marques (University of Aveiro, Portugal) and Augusta da Conceição Santos Ferreira (University of Aveiro, Portugal)
Information Science Reference • copyright 2018 • 539pp • H/C (ISBN: 9781522537311) • US $285.00 (our price)

*Knowledge-Based Urban Development in the Middle East*
Ali A. Alraouf (Qatar Urban Planning, Qatar)
Information Science Reference • copyright 2018 • 310pp • H/C (ISBN: 9781522537342) • US $185.00 (our price)

*Nationalism, Social Movements, and Activism in Contemporary Society Emerging Research and Opportunities*
Emily Stacey (Swansea University, UK)
Information Science Reference • copyright 2018 • 135pp • H/C (ISBN: 9781522554332) • US $155.00 (our price)

*Handbook of Research on Sustainable Development and Governance Strategies for Economic Growth in Africa*
Kassa Teshager Alemu (Ethiopian Civil Service University, Ethiopia) and Mulunesh Abebe Alebachew (Bahir Dar University, Ethiopia)
Information Science Reference • copyright 2018 • 621pp • H/C (ISBN: 9781522532477) • US $325.00 (our price)

*Political Mediation in Modern Conflict Resolution Emerging Research and Opportunities*
José Pascal da Rocha (Columbia University, USA)
Information Science Reference • copyright 2018 • 246pp • H/C (ISBN: 9781522551188) • US $150.00 (our price)

*Proliferation of Open Government Initiatives and Systems*
Ayse Kok (Bogazici University, Turkey)
Information Science Reference • copyright 2018 • 231pp • H/C (ISBN: 9781522549871) • US $195.00 (our price)

*Socio-Economic and Education Factors Impacting American Political Systems Emerging Research and Opportunities*
Pamela Hampton-Garland (University of the District of Columbia, USA) Lisa Sechrest-Ehrhardt (University of the District of Columbia, USA) and Benson George Cooke (University of the District of Columbia, USA)
Information Science Reference • copyright 2018 • 191pp • H/C (ISBN: 9781522538431) • US $145.00 (our price)

IGI Global
DISSEMINATOR OF KNOWLEDGE

701 East Chocolate Avenue, Hershey, PA 17033, USA
Tel: 717-533-8845 x100 • Fax: 717-533-8661
E-Mail: cust@igi-global.com • www.igi-global.com

# Table of Contents

# Detailed Table of Contents

When a disaster strikes, nonprofit organizations face the need to mobilize resources as quickly as possible in a limited time frame. Given its characteristics to instantly spread information to masses of people, social media is considered one of the most effective ways for nonprofits to publicize opportunities to take voluntary actions. Despite the envisioned use, little has been examined about the effectiveness of social media in encouraging people to give. This chapter takes the case of earthquake, tsunami, and nuclear threat that struck Japan in 2011 to examine whether the use of social media was effective in nonprofit fundraising. Analyzing data collected in an original online survey, the authors find that the use of social media both before and after the disaster has a positive impact on the amount of donations that nonprofits raise. Use of social media during non-disaster times is the key for successful fundraising in times of disaster.



Electronic government (e-gov) has not been implemented as extensively in many developing countries as in developed countries, especially in certain fields, such as occupational safety and health (OSH). This chapter considers e-gov that is effected through the websites of leading OSH bodies in a developing country, Trinidad and Tobago, and two developed nations, the USA and UK. Using a content analysis and comparison exercise, OSH e-gov shortcomings and opportunities in T&T are noted. Improvement recommendations include development of a strategy and strategy execution plan to boost stakeholder recognition of the value of the OSH agency and OSH e-gov in T&T; partnership-building to make resources available for OSH e-gov enhancement; enhanced accessibility and utility via a wider range of media formats to users; better stakeholder responsiveness via engagement with social media and better online support; and increased data collection and analysis in order to drive continual improvement.



Investments in criminal justice have been expanding over the decades especially as specific outcomes have been sought to address the issues surrounding crime and public safety. Reducing crime and the rate of imprisonment can both significantly impact public safety and cost savings, as well as address outcomes for the justice-involved population in reducing the rate of return to imprisonment, or recidivism. Lessening sentences for non-violent crimes and expanding drug courts as an alternative to incarceration,

# Preface

Public administration has evolved and adapted to the changing technological environment and a tech-savvy citizenry. The collection of chapter in *Innovative Perspectives on Public Administration in the Digital Age* discusses a wide array of innovative approaches that are being utilized in the provision of e-government services to their citizens. As the general public increasingly finds itself online, stakeholders, businesses, and citizens expect more from their governments. Accordingly, this volume examines and discusses how public institutions can be more responsive, efficient, and transparent through e-government technologies.

In Chapter 1, "Designing a Semantic Tool to Evaluate Web Content of Government Websites," Manoj Thomas and Samaa Elnagar propose a method for stakeholders, government officials, and researchers to ontologically evaluate the content of government websites. By standardizing the metric by which this content is evaluated, connections to other domains including records management and human resources training can be made. Making use of an ontology-based approach to web content ensures that the quality of material presented on these sites as well as the happiness level of citizens is high. The authors strongly recommend that a data-gathering process precede any attempt to establish programs, as locating best cases will increase the potential success rates of new programs. The system proposed in the chapter will increase the automation of online content and analysis of larger data.

In Chapter 2, "Foundations' Civic Engagement With Stakeholders: Leveraging Social Media Strategies," Sarah Maxwell and Julia Carboni explore the relationships that independent, corporate, and community groups have with their stakeholders utilizing Relationship Management Theory. The authors identify that community groups are using social media services like Facebook significantly more often in their calls to action to members. Where there has also been considerable usage of social media by public organizations, there has not been a monitoring of the analytics that are available from these services. The authors establish a tripartite typology that make it easier for managers of each group to review the communication strategies that they currently utilize and leverage social media activity for their greatest benefit.

In Chapter 3, "In Prosperity Prepare for Adversity: Use of Social Media for Nonprofit Fundraising in Times of Disaster," Aya Okada, Yu Ishida and Naoto Yamauchi find evidence that social media users are more supportive of organizations during periods of extreme duress, such as during natural disasters or public health concerns. By analyzing the tsunami, earthquake, and nuclear accident that occurred in Japan in 2011, the authors find evidence that donations made to nonprofits increased significantly in the period after the event; however, there will be a non-zero effect on donations in the long-term. The authors propose that nonprofit organizations benefit from the interactive nature of social media websites to establish dialogue and increase the overall quality of service provision to those impacted by natural disasters.

In Chapter 4, "E-Government of Occupational Safety and Health: Improvement Prospects for a Developing Nation," Marcia Nathai-Balkissoon and KF Pun delve into the occupational safety and health situation with a qualitative case analysis of Trinidad and Tobago's TTOSHA bureaucracy. The e-government services of Trinidad and Tobago's occupational safety concerns are compared to institutions in other small island developing states as well as similar bureaucracies in the United States and the United Kingdom. The authors specifically compare the level of accessibility and support information, the provision of technical information, and the breadth of electronic media resources that the organization offers. The chapter describes a set of best practices from developed nation-states that can be adopted for developing countries wishing to establish e-government services. The study concludes with a set of policy prescriptions that the TTOSHA should adopt to decrease response times, increase transparency, and bolster citizen satisfaction with the organization.

In Chapter 5, "States' Budget Investments in Technology and Improving Criminal Justice Outcomes," Deborah Spigner and Lois Warner focus on the actions taken by California, Hawaii, and New Jersey to decrease incarceration rates, as well as state investments in criminal justice technologies. The authors discuss the programs available from the Office of Justice Programs to facilitate the adoption of new technologies by states and territories. They also examine he usage of evidence-based policymaking as a contributing factor to reduce the proportion of citizens incarcerated; strategic planning by cities, states, and the national government have led to considerable investments in new technology. Discussing the specific actions in each case study, the authors provide best practices for those administrators that aim to decrease the amount of resources utilized in the incarceration of citizens.

In Chapter 6, "The eXtensible Business Reporting Language: A Digital Tool to Enhance Public Sector Accountability," Andrea Fradeani and Michela Soverchia provide readers with a detailed analysis about the eXtensible Business Reporting Language, and how the freeware tool can be utilized to increase government responsiveness, accountability, and transparency. A number of countries have voluntarily taken up the standard but this chapter represents the first substantive analysis of the tool in public administration literature. The authors discuss the experience of the Italian Court of Auditors, who used XBRL during a three-year trial period before adopting it for all financial statements made by public organizations in 2016. The benefits of utilizing the framework are numerous for public organizations as costs will be decreased, and other organizations can easily make sense of the data, including the private sector.

In Chapter 7, "How to Migrate Citizens Online and Reduce Traffic on Traditional Channels Through Multichannel Management: A Case Study of Cross-Organizational Collaboration Surrounding a Mandatory Self-Service Application," Christian Østergaard Madsen and Pernille Kræmmergaard conduct a case study about Payments Denmark (Udbetaling Denmark) with an eye toward how the organization provided services with much smaller expenditures than the prior program of municipalities providing public benefits. The authors propose that organizations can move away from traditional avenues of service and move towards e-government modes of service provision. The authors identify that all stakeholders in public and private organizations should agree to share costs and revenue at a point before multichannel collaboration is started. Results indicate that there is a rebound effect observed; traditional modes of content (including phone calls) are utilized when users are unclear about how to navigate and make usage of e-government services. Although e-government services can be deemed mandatory for users, organizations must maintain some traditional channels for those citizens that require face-to-face interactions.

In Chapter 8, "The Impact of Digital Health on Traditional Healthcare Systems and Doctor-Patient Relationships: The Case Study of Singapore," Ching Yuen Luk, present the development trajectory of digital health in Singapore since 1980 through a historical perspective and secondary data collected from government documents, literature, newspaper clips and survey reports. Singapore has over 30 years of experience in developing digital health, and has initiated several initiatives to improve productivity in health care and enhance the patient experience. These include MediNet, the Electronic Medical Record (EMR) System, the National Electronic Health Record (NEHR) System and related online health portals. The chapter studies the benefits brought by different digital health programmes, the views of doctors and citizens on digital health and the impact of digital health on the current health care system and doctor-patient relationship. It also examines the implications of digital health in Singapore for other countries.

In Chapter 9, “The Evolution of Self-Organized Social Solidarity (SoSS) Initiatives in Greece and Their Relationship to Online Media: A Longitudinal Research,” Dimitris Gouscos and Eleni-Revekka Staiou show the evolution of SoSS initiatives through a longitudinal research for the period 2014-2016, and provide an understanding of the relationship between these initiatives and the online media. Citizens felt the urge to self-organize and take action based on their own strengths as the only practical solution to fill in the gaps left by the state’s absence of intervention. Rooted in the country’s economic crisis, Greek citizens’ self-organized social solidarity (SoSS) initiatives have been focused on acting and innovating rather than protesting. Specifically, the chapter examines how the citizens utilized the internet and the social media for their communication during the same period of time, using data obtained from updating the platform Organosi 2.0, in the summer of 2017.

In Chapter 10, “Motivational Factors and Barriers for Technology-Driven Governance: An Indian Perspective,” Ankit and Deepika Dhamija make the case that the substantive technology barriers that exist in the developing world, which are numerous, are definitely surmountable. The chapter examines the barriers and constraints that are faced by developing nations globally, and addresses the specific contact surrounding the implementation of e-governance in India. The chapters also present some of the successful e-governance initiatives in India, as well as the motivational factors for their implementation. The authors finally suggest a holistic approach to study and incorporate the needs of the stakeholders, understand the capacities of government organizations, and their processes and structures.

In Chapter 11, “A Central Asian View of E-Government Services Adoption: Citizens’ Trust and Intention to Use E-Services,” Rita Ismailova, Gulshat Muhametjanova, and Bahtiyar Kurambayev examine the development of e-government services in the context of Central Asian Kyrgyz Republic. The growing internet penetration in developing countries has led to the increasing focus on e-government services and its potential for efficiency in the public sector. Recent studies have also shown rapid adoption of new technologies in various parts of Asia and South America. However, Kyrgyzstan and other countries in Central Asian region still remain largely understudied as the internet technologies are still in their nascent stages in the region. Accordingly, this chapter examines seven research questions related to e-government services in Kyrgyz Republic, along with examining citizens’ intention to use government websites based on their perceived usefulness.

In Chapter 12, “Mobile Governance for Affordability and Profitability/Feasibility,” Vinay Sharma and Anita Sengar examine the application of ‘E’ and Mobile mode for governance, and more specifically among the ‘Health Care’ system and ‘Changing Market Scenario’ in rural areas. The chapter indicates that the rural people of India desire for better ‘Health Care’ services and ‘market scenario’ through alternative means, and are also willing to pay for such enhanced level of services. Thus E-Governance and M-Governance platforms have emerged as important mediums for governments to provide such improved services, as well as build citizen trust and bridge the digital divide.

In Chapter 13, “Embodiment and Gameplay: Situating the User in Crowdsourced Information Production,” Karin Hansson and Love Ekenberg discuss the handling of user data in tools for crowd sourced data production and suggest a framework for describing the socio-technical setting for the production of data, and thereby the detectability of bias patterns in collaborative information production. This framework combines the concept embodiment, to describe the situated perspective of the user belonging to a certain material reality, with the concept gameplay, describing the data gathered on user activity on the platform.

In Chapter 14, "Friending and Funding Through Facebook: Social Media Use of Regional Nonprofit Organizations," Debika Sihi addresses the networking aspect of social networking services among nonprofit organizations. The use of social media by nonprofits provide a cost-effective means to share information among stakeholders and help in fundraising activities, which are very particularly essential for regional organizations. The chapter specifically addresses two important objectives with regard to nonprofits: 1) assess the impact of leadership and strategic emphasis on the use of social media for information transmission, and 2) study the utilization of social media tools for crowdfunding by nonprofits.

# Chapter 1
# A Semantic Approach to Evaluate Web Content of Government Websites

**Manoj A. Thomas**
*Virginia Commonwealth University, USA*

**Samaa Elnagar**
*Virginia Commonwealth University, USA*

## ABSTRACT

*Government agencies rely on websites to disseminate large volumes of information to the citizens. As public information changes over time due to changes in laws and regulations, maintaining currency and consistency of the web content becomes acutely important. Government agencies have to regularly evaluate the web content (WC) to ensure high quality of information available to the citizens, businesses, and public administrators. Currently there exists no standardized approach for monitoring and maintaining WC. In this chapter, the authors propose a WC ontology for the systematic and formal representation of the concepts and functions associated with the evaluation of web content on government websites. An ontology-based evaluation tool is proposed that can be used to improve the quality of web content and efficiency of the evaluation process. The ontological approach holds promising features and benefits including information sharing, reducing time and paperwork during evaluation, assuring more accurate results, and communicating evaluation results to knowledge engineers, public administrators, evaluators, and decision makers engaged in e-government initiatives.*

DOI: 10.4018/978-1-5225-5966-5.ch001

## 1. INTRODUCTION

Openness, transparency, and accountability in the public sector are increasingly important to establish trust in public authorities. Many jurisdictions have introduced e-government initiatives and information policies on public services to facilitate these functions and to enhance the effectiveness of public authorities in meeting these obligations (Shepherd, Stevenson, & Flinn, 2010). E-government is fundamental to the modernization of any government (Lin, Fofanah, & Liang, 2011). It enables citizens and businesses to access government services and information through the use of Internet and other channels of communication (Lin et al., 2011; Valdés et al., 2011; Wimmer, 2002).

E-government initiatives provide enormous volume of information via online content and offers numerous benefits to the public and to other government agencies. Content made available through e-government websites include texts, images, scripts, and different types of documents. Information disseminated through government websites educate citizens, elevate the level of government transparency (Hernon & Relyea, 1995), and reduce mailing and paper printing costs (Fountain, 2002; Relyea, 2002). Moreover, it maximizes efficiency, effectiveness, speed, productivity and service delivery of government services (Sarantis, Charalabidis, & Askounis, 2011; Wimmer, 2002),

In addition to textual content, web content (WC) includes the presentation and layout of information and functions on the website (Santos, 2003). Web content management can be defined as the process of creating, storing, publishing, and updating the web content of organizational websites to communicate with the internal and external stakeholders (Qin, 2004). However, managing government web content is complex for several reasons (Eschenfelder, 2004). 1) E-Government initiatives are centralized, yet distributed in nature (Landsbergen Jr & Wolken Jr, 2001). So, it requires extensive oversight and co-ordination to ensure compliance with policies and standards. 2) Maintaining currency of the content is difficult as public information changes when legislations change over time (e.g., goals, objectives, practices, etc.) 3) The employees who create and maintain content are usually spread throughout the organization and report to different managers. In addition, legislative requirements have to be adhered during the management of web content.

Government agencies have unique requirements that make the evaluation of WC different from commercial agencies. First and foremost, the government agencies have to undertake regular WC evaluation to ascertain that the content delivered is accurate and consistent and offers the desired benefits at an acceptable cost. Second, the evaluation enables continuous refinement of the website content and related processes based on the evolving needs of stakeholders. Third, web content evaluation is important to ensure that government websites meet the standards of governmental and legislative requirements.

Many frameworks and models have also been proposed to assess e-government research and practice (Ramaprasad, Sánchez-Ortiz, & Syn, 2015), yet there exists no standardized process for evaluating e-government WC. To address this gap, many government agencies have independently developed evaluation tools, manuals, and questionnaire-based guidelines for WC evaluation. For example, the government of Alberta in Canada (Govt. of Alberta, 2004) has developed a comprehensive guide to manage and assess web content. The Australian government has an online web guide to monitor and evaluate government websites[1]. American agencies rely on HowTo.gov guide to assess their WC[2]. Thus, in many cases, agencies develop and follow their own internally developed guidelines for WC assessment. More recently, content management systems have emerged to assist in the designing, managing, and monitoring web content of e-government projects (Joha & Janssen, 2010). They provide capabilities such as decentralized authoring, workflow management, and separation of content from presentation. However, challenges such as usability and interoperability (Souer, Honders, Versendaal, & Brinkkemper, 2008), and minimal support for content evaluation highlight the need for improved solutions by which public officials and web content evaluators may conduct the assessment of WC.

A review of published e-government literature also indicates a crucial gap in published research related to the assessment of WC. Although the evaluation of WC has clear benefits, and is important to the government agencies, research in this area lags practice. While literature suggests many methods to assess the quality of website portals (Ziemba, Jankowski, Wątróbski, & Becker, 2015), none cater to the unique needs of government agencies. The construction of a knowledge repository based on ontologies would enable the formal specification of content lifecycle management, methods of assessment, and other influencing factors such as legal and privacy requirements. An ontology provides specific vocabulary to describe domain knowledge, and implementable in machine readable format using ontology web language (OWL). The ontological form of knowledge representation (Ziemba et al., 2015) can be used to systematically map the state-of-practice in WC assessment by encapsulating the main concepts and related norms. So, a shift in the strategy from technology-based conceptualizations to a systemic one that is based on ontologies would not only aid in bridging the practical gaps in WC management, but also contribute to the knowledge base related to e-government research (Ramaprasad et al., 2015).

The objective of this paper is to demonstrate the use of an ontology-based evaluation tool that can assist users in the complex WC evaluation scenarios. In this research paper, we focus only on the evaluation of WC in an e-government environment. We contend that utilizing an ontology-based approach to assess the WC holds promises and benefits. The ontology presented in this paper serves as the foundation to build a semantic tool that government agencies can use to assess their WC. Evaluating WC by using an ontology-based solution will not only improve efficiency of the assessment process by reducing the time and the paper work required for evaluation, but also assure more accurate results. Using ontology as the semantic underpinning offers benefits to stakeholders by providing a platform for sharing organizational knowledge across the myriad users and agencies. By explicitly specifying the shared understanding of the domain, ontological descriptions help to enhance the accuracy and reliability of complex information gathering and assessment exercise. An organization's WC is a subset of its organizational domain, and the quality of the WC and information presented therein can be significantly improved when the domain knowledge is represented in a shared ontology. Using ontology as the enterprise model for information will thus help improve information consistency, reusability, interoperability, and knowledge sharing (Ding & Foo, 2002). Developing an ontological perspective for evaluating WC is a novel approach that has not been sufficiently investigated.

The rest of the paper is organized as follows. In section 2 we provide a review of literature related to evaluation approaches and ontologies used for WC management. In this section, we also discuss the role of ontologies, related application areas and justify the design principles for building the WC ontology. We explain our WC ontology in section 3. In section 4 we discuss the implementation architecture of the ontology-based evaluation system. Practical implications, contributions to research, and policy implications are discussed in Section 5. We outline the limitations and future research directions in section 6. Finally, section 7 concludes the paper by summarizing the strengths and weaknesses of the proposed ontology-based approach for WC evaluation.

## 2. BACKGROUND

### 2.1. Related Literature

Web content management is an important field of research (Alalwan, Thomas, & Weistroffer, 2014; Freeman & Yin, 2005). It has been utilized and investigated in different application domains such as e-government, e-commerce, e-libraries, enterprise portals, and software content management (Goodwin & Vidgen, 2002). WC management allows controlling the content and design of websites, and includes many functions such as creating new content, editing existing information, and administrating web presentation.

A few studies have discussed the evaluation of e-government WC using ontologies. Magoutas et al. (2007) presented a three-layer quality ontology called Quality of e-government Services (QeGS) that was partially developed using Protégé, an open source ontology editor[3]. The QeGS formalized knowledge for the realization of a multi-perspective and adaptive evaluation of e-government services. Each layer of the ontology maintains a different level of abstraction concerning the modeled concepts and relations among concepts. The top layer is the most abstract, the middle layer is less abstract, while the third one is application specific. The system evaluated the services based on three different perspectives: the customer, the service provider, and the objective perspective. The system thus offers a 360-degree assessment of quality and validates the knowledge needed to realize an adaptive approach.

Ziemba et al. (2015) used five conceptualization methods including: eQual, Ahn, SiteQual, Web Portal Site Quality and Website Evaluation Questionnaire to evaluate the quality of e-government websites. Each conceptualization method was evaluated in the form of a domain ontology. In the evaluation process, a reasoner was used to classify concepts by checking the answers to questions of the competence ontology. The ontology reasoner generated the hierarchy of concepts to be consistent with each method. This evaluation process allowed the reuse and sharing of knowledge contained in the individual methods.

Sheng and Lingling (2011) developed an ontology-based system structure that enhances data sharing while modeling an e-government's system by adding an ontology presentation layer between the traditional e-government supporting platform and e-government application system. The authors used ontology engineering methods for conceptual design and ontology modeling. They segmented the ontology modeling process into three aspects: conceptual entity, conceptual property, and relationship between concepts which corresponds with class, property and axiom in OWL language respectively.

Fonou-Dombeu & Huisman (2013) presented an adaptive strategy for searching and selecting domain. The strategy relies on ontology-based and generic search engines, and predefined ontology features to locate existing domain ontologies and related data sources. The researchers used a set of criteria including semantic coverage, codification language, and modularity to select the best reusable set of ontologies for a domain. Their approach may be used as a pre-investigative task for semi-automatic and automatic ontology reuse solutions as it enables the ontology engineer to search and retrieve existing domain ontologies along with their data sources. However, reusing ontologies is far from an automatic process and requires significant effort from the knowledge engineer.

Santoso (2016) implemented a focused crawler to aggregate information automatically over e-government portals using an ontological approach. The crawler consists of two modules, i.e., a multi-tread downloader and a scheduler. The authors used Model-Driven Engineering (MDE) to implement the crawler model. The crawler used a set of rules based on content, link structure, URL, and anchor text in the aggregation processes. In terms of the number of relevant documents from which information was aggregated, the authors found that the use of ontology in the focused crawler produced more effective results as compared to the Breadth First Search (BFS) approach. The main advantage of the crawler was that information was retrieved only from relevant web pages, instead of the whole website. This approach saved time, reduced complexity, and enhanced relevancy. Table 1 shows a summary of WC evaluation approaches using ontologies.

A few other approaches have been proposed to evaluate e-government WC. By adopting a Delphi method and analytic hierarchy process (AHP), Zhu et al. (2007) designed an assessment criteria system for Chinese e-government websites. They used an online questionnaire designed to collect feedbacks and expert opinions, and different weights were given for each criterion. The AHP used a more reasonable exponential scale than the traditional 1~9 proportional scale. Their study found that the online Delphi method overcame deficiencies of subjective judgment, shortened the cycle of the investigation, and saved costs. In another study, Siskos et al. (2014) implemented a multi-criteria methodology to evaluate e-government using a system of eight criteria based on the principles and tools of multi-criteria decision analysis (MCDA). The methodology adopted four viewpoints: infrastructures, investments, e-processes, and users' attitude. The overall evaluation of e-government was obtained through an additive value model and multi-criteria ordinal regression approach. The study concluded that e-government evaluation process is an independent procedure controlled by the evaluator with the possibility of implementing new and different considerations and criteria.

From the literature review, we conclude the following. First, only few studies have evaluated e-government websites or portals, of which two studies (Siskos, Askounis, & Psarras, 2014; Ziemba et al., 2015) developed conceptualizations to address the quality of e-government websites, one study used a crawler to aggregate information automatically over e-government portals (Santoso, Zeniarja, 2016), and one study used ontologies to assess quality of e-government services (Magoutas, Halaris, & Mentzas, 2007). None of the studies reviewed developed a comprehensive approach for WC evaluation. Evaluating WC of e-government websites is a complex process that has to take into consideration several interacting factors including social, technical, and legal issues. Second, the current approaches to evaluate the WC of e-government websites are mostly based on questionnaires and guidelines. There are no automated or semi-automated methods available. If information provided by e-government services are to be beneficial to the citizens and government agencies, WC evaluation has to be carried out in a manner that ensures currency, consistency, and legislative adherence. Third, using ontologies to describe the main concepts of the WC domain can help to ensure reusability of information, interoperability with other government agencies, knowledge sharing with citizens, and improvements in the efficiency of the WC evaluation processes. An ontology approach thus provides additional advantages over other approaches such as AHP and MCDA for WC evaluation of e-government.

## 2.2. Ontologies

Ontologies help foster knowledge sharing among users with different roles and different organizational functions. Gruber (Gruber, 1993) defines ontology as "a formal, explicit specification of a shared conceptualization." *Conceptualization* refers to the abstract model of a phenomena in the world and the relevant concepts of that phenomena; *explicit* implies that there are clear definitions of the concepts and the constraints; *formal* means that the ontology is machine readable; and *shared* implies that the ontology captures consensual knowledge that is acceptable to all stakeholders. The Ontology Web Language (OWL) is commonly used to express ontologies. OWL is developed as part of the Semantic Web initiatives from W3C and has evolved as the popular open standard for semantic knowledge representation.

*Table 1. Summary of reviewed literature on WC evaluation using ontologies*

| Research | Contribution | Limitations |
|---|---|---|
| Fonou-Dombeu & Huisman, 2013. | Adaptive strategy for searching and selecting domain ontologies. | Lack of automation. Need active participation of the knowledge engineer. |
| Magoutas, Halaris, & Mentzas, 2007. | Three-layer quality ontology called Quality of e-government Services (QeGS). | Not applied to develop an ontology based system. |
| Santoso, Zeniarja, 2016. | A focused crawler to collect information automatically from e-government portals using an ontological approach. | Web crawling in the domain of e-government needs further study. |
| Li, Liu, 2011. | Developed an ontology-based system by inserting a resource ontology expression layer into the traditional e-government system structure. | Completeness of ontology depends on domain experts' analysis and extraction of domain knowledge before construction |
| Siskos, Askounis, & Psarras, 2014. | A multi-criteria methodology to evaluate e-government using eight evaluation criteria using MCDA. | The use of mid-weight estimations is usually not robust. The UTAII linear programming problem does not guarantee a single criteria weighting. |
| Ziemba et al., 2015. | Five conceptualization methods to evaluate the quality of websites and enhance the reuse and knowledge sharing in each individual method. | Need to combine ontologies to integrate data from different assessment methods.<br>No assessment of the performance of each method. |
| Sánchez et al., 2015. | A semantic variance intuitive measure to quantify the degree of semantic dispersion of the taxonomic structure of an ontology. The measure can also be used as an automatic ontology evaluation score. | Other semantic evidences need to be incorporated into the assessment of the ontology accuracy such as, the concepts informativeness coherency with respect to their actual usage. |

As a knowledge representation language for expressing the domain knowledge in a machine-readable format, OWL describes concepts (*class*), properties of concepts (*attributes* in the *class*) and restrictions on properties (*axioms*) using the normative RDF/XML structure. Ontologies represented in OWL can provide context representation and semantic reasoning capabilities (Thomas & Redmond, 2011). Ontologies are extensively used in different application domains ranging from collaborative knowledge acquisition systems (van der Aalst & Kumar, 2003) to Geographic Information Systems (Visser, Stuckenschmidt, Schuster & Vögele, 2002), and semantic information search and retrieval (LePendu & Dou, 2011; Thomas, Redmond, Yoon & Singh, 2005).

To develop the ontological descriptions for the WC domain, the first decision we took was to modularize the concepts into small and homogeneous groups that are readily understandable. To re-use existing ontologies, and vocabularies of relevance, we conducted a thorough search of the publicly available ontology repositories. The search did not reveal any information models or ontologies that dealt with WC evaluation. However, ontologies from other application domains were identified that could be utilized in developing our ontology. For example, the privacy ontology (Hecker, Dillon, & Chang, 2008; Jutla & Xu, 2004) can be used to describe the privacy concepts applicable to the e-government website. Similarly, the security ontology developed by Tsoumas and Gritzalis (2006) is of interest to describe the security concepts related to e-government web content. Records management is an important function of e-government. Therefore, we link the records management ontology designed by Alalwan and Thomas (2011) to describe those parts of the domain related to creating and modifying online records. We also utilize the organization ontology that is discussed in Fox et al. (1996) for the personnel functions of web content management. Tapping into these established ontologies helped strengthen our ontology model as described later in the paper.

To identify and extract the main concepts of WC assessment domain, we conducted a detailed review of three popular WC evaluation guidelines. We first reviewed the Australian Web Guide (Govt. of Australia, 2013) developed by The Australian Government Information Management Office (AGIMO) in the Department of Finance and Deregulation. We then analyzed the Canadian Government of Alberta WC Guide (Govt. of Alberta, 2004). The third evaluation system reviewed was the US government guide that is available at the howto.gov website[4]. The analysis of these WC guidelines revealed numerous processes for web content management involving multiple redundant concepts. They elaborate human involvement in interpreting and using guidelines and procedures. Furthermore, a major hurdle in operationalizing the guidelines is that the data gathering is entirely a manual process that requires the interpreter to develop, organize and administer the various questionnaires. Implementing the processes can be time consuming and synthesizing the results can be tedious. Thus, removing all redundant concepts and keeping only the related and unique ones was the first step we adopted in constructing the ontology.

A systemic review of the guidelines affirmed an important postulate. Similarities in the concepts from the three different sources indicated that a semantic model is ideal to represent the domain of interest – i.e., the evaluation of WC in an e-government domain. The three sets of guidelines provided a uniform representation of the domain concepts with common attributes. The similarities of concepts also reinforced the benefit of using ontologies for modeling domains where concepts overlap and concept relationships are comparable. Therefore, we developed an ontology called the Web Content (WC) Ontology. Implementing an information system (IS) based on the WC ontology will be useful for building applications where selected aspects of the evaluation of web content in an e-government domain can be automated or semi-automated.

## 3. THE WC ONTOLOGY

Ontology development is an iterative process and requires the researcher to gain a thorough understanding of the problem domain. During the development process it is a common practice to check whether there exists ontologies that describe the problem domain and verify their suitability by testing against well-defined use cases (H. L. Chen, 2004; Firat, Madnick, & Grosof, 2004). Available ontologies can be extended to improve design or new ontologies can be created if one does not exist. After gaining a thorough understanding of the evaluation requirements of the WC in an e-government domain, an exhaustive search of the ontology repositories and related literature was conducted to identify any previous ontology that could be used or extended for this research. Although no ontologies were identified that specifically addressed the research problem, the exercise was fruitful in identifying other useful ontologies, specifically the security ontology (Tsoumas & Gritzalis, 2006), the privacy ontology (Hecker et al., 2008), the organization ontology (Fox et al., 1996), and the records management ontology that can augment the WC ontology (Alalwan & Thomas, 2011). The Protégé Knowledge Acquisition System (Protégé, 2017) was used to model and build the WC ontology (Horridge, Knublauch, Rector, Stevens, & Wroe, 2004).

Two domain experts and one practitioner familiar with WC evaluation were consulted to verify the concepts definitions, logical axioms, and the relationships between the concepts identified from the three WC assessment guidelines. They also helped fill in the gaps to enhance the richness and condition the ontology for applicability and extensibility. The selection of concept names and relationships used in the ontology directly correlates to the terminology defined in the three evaluation guidelines and the collective acumen of the domain experts overseeing the development process. Although changes to the base ontology were rare once the knowledge experts agreed on the final design choice, fine adjustments were made throughout the development process, especially in cases where scenario-based testing revealed minor weaknesses and concerns. Based on our evaluation of the three WC assessment tools, we identified three main upper-level concepts: *Web Content Management*, *Training*, and *Personnel*. The green solid boxes in Figure 1 represent the upper-level concepts. The white solid boxes represent the sub-level concepts. In the interest of brevity and space, only the most relevant concepts are shown in Figure 1 and described in the following sections. In the rest of the paper, ontology specific terms are shown in *Italics* (e.g., concept names, relationship, etc.) For more information on ontology, interested readers may refer to Smith, et al. (Smith, 2001). Readers may also refer to Horridge et al. (Horridge et al., 2004) for a more detailed description of the OWL syntax.

## 3.1 Concept: Web Content Management

The *Web Content Management* concept is the first of the three-main upper-level concepts in the WC ontology. This concept has two sub-level concepts: *Type of Website* concept and *Guide of Web Content* Management concept. *Type of Website* concept characterizes the *Intranet* and the *Extranet* sub-level concepts and incorporates both internal and external users. *Users* concept, including the *Internal* and *External* users concept, is associated with the *Type of Website* concept using the *hasAccess* relation. Figure 2 shows the OWL snippet for the *hasAccess* relationship between *Users* and *Type of Website* sub-concepts.

*Figure 1. The WC ontology for web content evaluation*

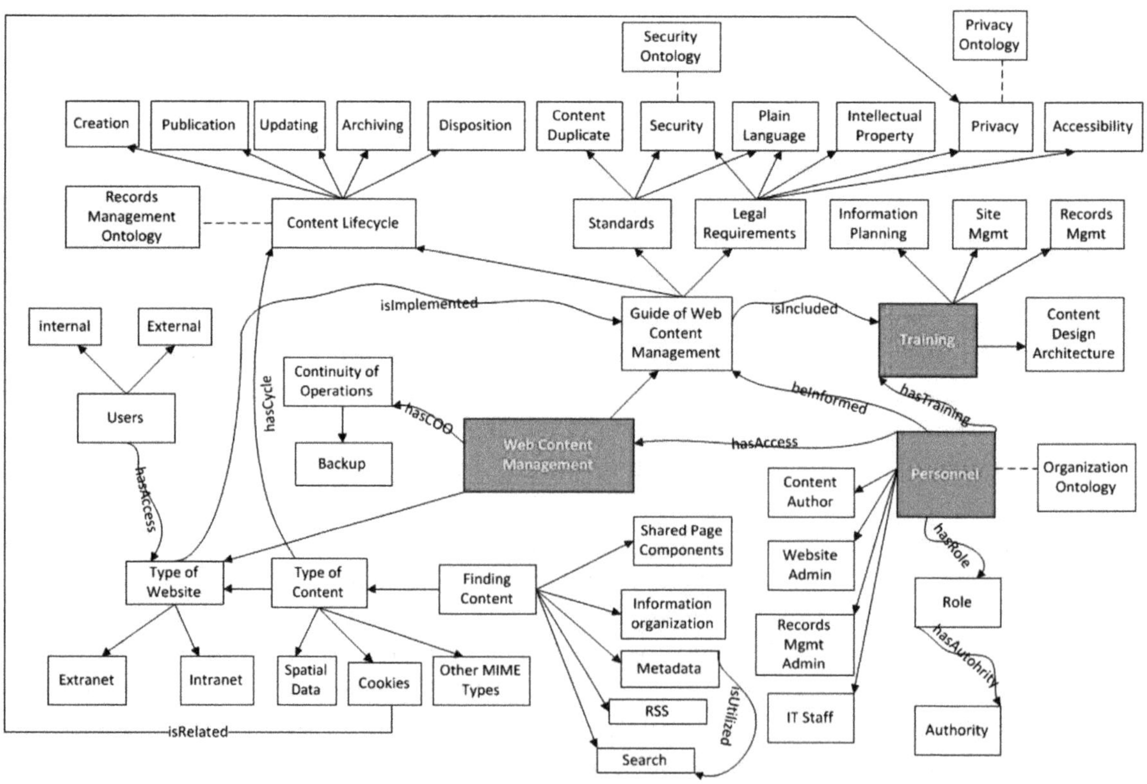

*Figure 2. OWL snippet for hasAccess relationship*

```
</owl:ObjectProperty>
<owl:ObjectProperty rdf:ID="hasAccess">
    <rdfs:domain rdf:resource="Users"/>
    <rdfs:range rdf:resource="Type of Website"/>
```

The *Type of Content* is an essential sub-level concept of the *Type of Website* concept. It represents the main content types relevant to e-government websites such as portable document format (PDF), video, spatial data, cookies, and other multipurpose internet mail extensions (MIME) types. The enumerated list of *Types of Content* shown in Figure 1 is not comprehensive, but it is an example of the most common types of content that government websites have to manage. In government websites, PDF files should be linked to one or more PDF reader applications (e.g., Adobe, eReader, and Evince). To play video files, embedded video players on the government website may be used, or the video files can be linked to a third-party site. Spatial data is used for different purposes related to GIS applications, enterprises, and jurisdictions. Cookies enable the website to gather information about the users. Since privacy requirements relevant to the e-government website involve the use of cookies, the *isRelated* object property is used to represent the relationship between the *Cookies* and *Privacy* concepts. For example, the Australian government agencies must comply with the Privacy Act 1988 that sets standards for collecting personal information through the use of cookies[5]. The OWL code snippet depicting this relationship is shown in Figure 3.

The *Finding Content* concept in the ontology facilitates searching, locating, and finding content on the website. It has the following sub-level concepts: *Shared Page Components*, *Information Organization*, *Metadata*, *RSS* (really simple syndication), and *Search*. The *Shared Page Components* concept identifies the different navigation elements in the website. Examples include: site maps, search pages, filter pages, and contact pages. *Information Organization* concept represents the structuring of the web content in a way that enables users to navigate through the website. For example, classification is one approach to organize the website content. *Metadata* concept is data used to describe other data. Instances (ontology individuals) of the *Metadata* concept enable the identification and retrieval of information more effectively. Really Simple Syndicate (RSS) is a commonly used approach to disseminate content updates over the Internet directly to the subscribers. Conceptually speaking, RSS notifies subscribers when the existing content is revised or new content is added. The *RSS* concept represents all instances of the web content that are communicated to the e-government website subscribers. As the volume of information on the e-government website increase, a semantically driven search and retrieval function will be more useful in locating the relevant content (Thomas & Redmond, 2011). The *Search* concept works in conjunction with the *Metadata* concept and the *Information Organization* concept as shown by the *isUtilized* relation.

*Figure 3. IsRelated relationship*

```
</owl:ObjectProperty>
<owl:ObjectProperty rdf:ID="isRelated">
    <rdfs:domain rdf:resource="Cookies"/>
    <rdfs:range rdf:resource="Privacy"/>
```

Another important concept related to the *Web Content Management* concept is the *Guide of Web Content Management* concept. Three sub-level concepts fall under the *Guide of WC Management* namely, *Legal Requirements*, *Standards*, and *Content Lifecycle*. E-government websites have to comply with many legislative requirements related to accessibility, privacy management, security specifications and language support. *Accessibility*, *Privacy*, *Intellectual Property*, *Security*, and *Plain Language* are the sub-level concepts to characterize these requirements of e-government websites. The Disability Discrimination Act 1992 specified by the Australian agencies, and the Freedom of Information Act 1982 of the United States to ensure that people with disabilities have the same privileges to access information are examples of the *Accessibility* concept. Similarly, the American government agencies have to adhere to the Privacy Act of 1974, and the Canadian agencies in Alberta have to adhere to the Freedom of Information and Protection of Privacy Act. These are examples of instantiations (ontology individuals) that fall under the *Privacy* concept. For the *Intellectual Property* sub-level concept, examples of OWL individuals include the specifications defined by the U.S. Patent Law, the Copyright Law, and the Digital Millennium Copyright Act. We link the *Privacy* concept to the privacy ontology proposed by Hecker et al. (2008) to manage the complexity of the interrelated privacy policies.

The Plain Writing Act of 2010 of the United States requires the "federal government to write all new publications, forms and publicly distributed documents in a 'clear, concise, well-organized' manner"[6]. The *Plain Language* concept represents the stipulations that should be followed by the government agencies. The Plain Language specifications for the Canadian government of Alberta, and the Australian agencies fall under the *Standards* sublevel concept rather than *Plain Language* sub-level concept of the *Legal Requirements* concept since there are no Canadian or Australian legislations that enforce the use of plain language on their government websites. The *Content Duplication* concept is used to ensure that the content in one section is not unnecessarily duplicated on another section. The Cross Government Internet Committee protocol is established in Alberta to eliminate any content duplication. "Create once, use many times" is the principle adopted by the Australian agencies to manage content duplication.

The *Security* concept represents the security standards and protocols that should be followed while implementing and using the e-government websites. In the U.S., the e-government websites have to adhere to the security requirements specified by the Federal Information Security Management Act. In Australia, the *Security* concept relates to the *Standards* concept since the Australian Government Protective Security Policy Framework (Govt. of Australia, 2013) is used to control the security requirements of the government websites. Similarly, for the government of Alberta, the *Security* concept is related to the *Standards* concept because certain standardized security measures have to be followed to ensure records accessibility and alteration (Govt. of Alberta, 2004, p. 29). To deal with the complexity of the security protocols and standards, we augment the *Security* concept by linking it to the security ontology designed by Tsoumas and Gritzalis (2006).

A thorough analysis of the three e-government website guidelines indicated that the lifecycle of the web content spans five stages. They are, *Creation*, *Publication*, *Maintenance*, *Archiving*, and *Disposition*. We provide OWL concept representations for each of the five stages. To enable a reasoner to infer the lifecycle stage of the web content, the *hasCycle* relation links the *Type of Website* concept to the *Content Lifecycle* concept. The OWL syntax for this relationship is shown in Figure 4. The web content lifecycle is closely related to the records management process. For example, creating and updating online records are integral parts of the website content management. Therefore, we link the *Content Lifecycle* concept to the *Records Management* ontology proposed by Alalwan and Thomas (2011). The *Backup* concept characterizes the various backup procedures such as storing offsite copies of organizational content, continuity of operation and disaster recovery plans.

## 3.2 Concept: Personnel

The second main upper-level concept in the WC ontology, *Personnel* describes how employees interact with the website content. *Personnel* has sub-level concepts such as *Content Author*, *Website Administrator*, *Records Management Administrator*, and *IT Staff* that describe the different types of employees who create or alter the website content. The list of sub-level employee concepts is not comprehensive and can be extended to include other types of users who interact with the website content during its lifecycle. The *Authority* concept describes the rights that an employee has to perform a certain action. For the sake of simplicity, the levels of interaction are limited to an enumerated list of five different actions – create, view, modify, publish, or delete. The role of the employee in performing these actions is defined by the *Role* concept. The *hasRole* relationship links the *Role* concept to the *Personnel* concept. The *hasAuthority* links the *Role* and the *Authority* concepts. The OWL code snippet depicting these relationships is shown in Figure 5.

Employees interact with the web content for its management, and the rules of interaction are informed by the web content management guidelines. Employees also receive training in the management of web content (discussed in the next section). Extensions to the ontology to include other organizational activities can be accomplished by linking the ontology to the organization ontology developed by Fox et al. (1996).

## 3.3 Concept: Training

The third main upper-level concept is *Training*. Employees require training since lack of staff training is recognized as one of the main obstacles to the success of website content management (Dawes et al., 1999; J. E. Fountain, 2004). Training is imparted to the employees to match the *Role* and *Authority* of each employee. The web content guidelines indicate that employees should receive training related to the

*Figure 4. hasCycle relationship*

```
</owl:ObjectProperty>
<owl:ObjectProperty rdf:ID="hasCycle">
    <rdfs:domain rdf:resource="Type of Website"/>
    <rdfs:range rdf:resource="content Lifecycle"/>
```

*Figure 5. hasRole and hasAuthority relationships*

```
</owl:ObjectProperty>
<owl:ObjectProperty rdf:ID="hasRole">
    <rdfs:domain rdf:resource="Personnel"/>
    <rdfs:range rdf:resource="Role"/>
</owl:ObjectProperty>
<owl:ObjectProperty rdf:ID="hasAuthority">
    <rdfs:domain rdf:resource="Role"/>
    <rdfs:range rdf:resource="Authority"/>
```

different aspects of the *Guide of Web Content Management* such as *Legal Requirements*, *Standards*, and *Content Lifecycle*. For example, the training for the content management staff may include topics such as content design and architecture, information planning, site management, and records management. The *Training* concept in the ontology allows classification of known facts related to an employee's training requirements (for example, the current level of employee training). A reasoner in conjunction with the ontology can then assert exceptions and infer the necessary training requirements for employees based on their roles and authority. The OWL code snippet in Figure 6 shows the *Training* concept relationship to the *Guide of Web Content Management* concept using the *isIncluded* axiom.

## 4. IMPLEMENTATION ARCHITECTURE

To use the ontology-based evaluation tool, an evaluator first uses a web-based interface to enter the baseline scenario of all the criteria for evaluating the WC. The criteria can include legislative acts and related standards, content lifecycle, employee roles and authorities, employee training requirements, web content formats, and the methods used for searching the web content. These baseline entries are stored in a central repository. The repository can be a relational database or an application that translates the data to an XML compliant format. The implementation architecture is shown in Figure 7.

*Figure 6. isIncluded relationship*

```
</owl:ObjectProperty>
<owl:ObjectProperty rdf:ID="isIncluded">
    <rdfs:domain rdf:resource="Guide of Web Content Management"/>
    <rdfs:range rdf:resource="Training"/>
```

*Figure 7. Implementation architecture for ontology-based web content evaluation*

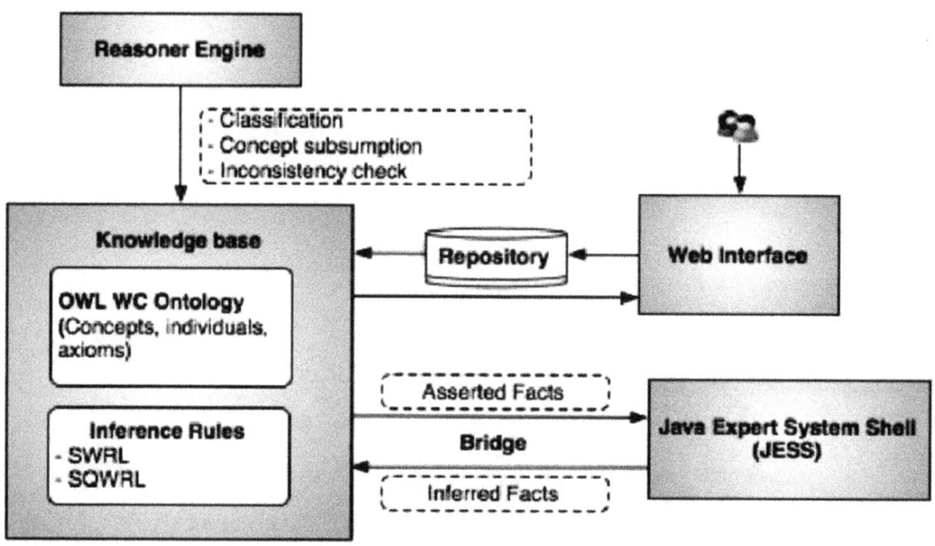

The architecture for ontology based reasoning typically involves the use of a rule based expert system (e.g., Java Expert System Shell), a reasoner (e.g., RacerPro or Pellet), and a knowledge base. Design science researchers and knowledge engineers commonly employ this architecture in application areas such as finance, eCommerce, and medicine (Bak, Jedrzejek, & Falkowski, 2009; Bouamrane, Rector, & Hurrell, 2009; O'Connor, Shankar, Nyulas, Tu, & Das, 2008). Their utility for knowledge representation (Bera, Burton-Jones, & Wand, 2011; Y.-J. Chen, 2010; Garcia-Crespo, Ruiz-Mezcua, Lopez-Cuadrado, & Gonzalez-Carrasco, 2011), concept classification (Álvarez Sabucedo, Anido Rifón, Corradini, Polzonetti, & Re, 2010; Fauzi & Belkhatir, 2013; Vandic, Van Dam, & Frasincar, 2012), inconsistency detection (LePendu & Dou, 2011) and semantic reasoning (Beimel & Peleg, 2011; Y.-J. Chen, 2010; Sourouni, Kourlimpinis, Mouzakitis, & Askounis, 2010) is well documented. We use similar architectural components in our implementation architecture (see Figure 7).

When the system is initiated for evaluating WC, the reasoner classifies the data (known facts) in the repository as asserted individuals in the WC ontology. The reasoner also performs concept inconsistency checks, automated concept subsumption, and reclassification of ontology instances (OWL individuals). In addition to the asserted individuals (known facts), the knowledge base contains the inference rules that are used for the reasoning process. The rules are interpreted by the Java Expert System Shell (JESS). The JESS rule engine uses the Rete algorithm based pattern matcher to deductively (forward chaining) or inductively (backward chaining) reason inferred facts from the known facts and inference rules (Forgy, 1982; Peuschel & Schäfer, 1992). When the inference process is completed, the inferred facts are transferred to the knowledge base and the reasoner is recalled to perform a consistency check of the knowledge base and the ontology. The inference rules are developed by the knowledge engineer and implemented in Semantic Web Rule Language (SWRL). Semantic queries are structured using the Semantic Query Web Rule Language (SQWRL). The rules and queries are triggered by JESS by matching the asserted OWL individuals in the ontology. The inference rules and the WC ontology, along with the JESS rule engine and the reasoner serve to infer the evaluation outcome of the WC. The inferred facts are returned to the user via the web-based interface. The results presented to the user indicate the evaluation criteria of the WC that matches or diverge from the baseline evaluation scenario.

## 4.1 Evaluation

The WC ontology proposed above is designed to capture as much essence of the WC evaluation as possible. The design and implementation of the artifact is in itself an experiment from which we learn about the nature of the problem, its utility in a given environment and possible solutions (von Alan, March, Park, & Ram, 2004).

Descriptive evaluation comprising of scenario based testing and functional analysis by domain experts are used to validate the quality of the concepts, utility of the ontology and usability in evaluating WC.

### 4.1.1 Scenario-Based Testing

To demonstrate the utility of the semantic approach, we describe a scenario that is commonly encountered during WC evaluation. Consider the case of an agency that uses the Australian Web Guide. The web content evaluator first starts by entering the baseline requirements for the three upper-level concepts, namely *Web Content Management*, *Personnel*, and *Training*. For example, the *Legal Requirements* (e.g., Freedom of Information Act 1982), *Accessibility* requirements (e.g., the Disability Discrimination Act

1992), *Privacy* (e.g., the Privacy Act of 1988), and *Intellectual Property* (e.g., Copyright Act 1968) specifications are entered by the evaluator via the web interface to the repository. The required baseline of *Standards* for *Plain Language*, *Content Duplication*, and *Security* (e.g. Australian Government Protective Security Policy Framework) are also entered. Based on the Australian Web Guide, the *Creation*, *Publication*, *Updating*, *Archiving*, and *Disposition* concepts for the *Content Lifecycle* are derived from the Archives Act 1983.

The Australian government websites can be classified into two types - Intranet and Ministerial, and Departmental websites. Certain requirements such as the Public Service Act 1999, and the Financial Management and Accountability Act 1997 should be entered as instances of the *Type of Website* concept. The desired baseline for the *Finding Content* concept is specified in the Australian Web Guide. For instance, the *Search* concept criteria should assist in conducting the agency search service, and should be based on the Funnelback documentation for Agencies[7]. Requirements for the different *Type of Content* should be entered to the repository. For example, *Cookies* concept should comply with the Information Privacy Principles under the Privacy Act. Furthermore, the evaluator should also enter the desired criteria for the *Personnel* concept (i.e. roles and authorities) and *Training* concept to the repository.

After entering the baseline scenario, the evaluator then enters the current state of the WC. Similar to the baseline scenario, this phase includes entering data for the three upper-level concepts (*Web Content Management*, *Personnel*, and *Training*), and the sub-level concepts shown in Figure 1. Examples of the data entered include the content lifecycle stage of information available on the website, the type of content available on the website and its purpose, and the training courses attended by the employees. This data will be also stored in the repository.

Once all entries are completed, the reasoner is invoked to classify the asserted facts for the upper level concepts and sub-level concepts. The application heuristic then transfers the asserted facts to the fact base, following which the matching SWRL rules in the rule base are triggered by the expert system (JESS). For example, Figure 8 shows the SWRL rule to identify the training requirement (OWL individual *z*) that the personnel (OWL individual *x*), who has a specific role (OWL individual *y*) needs to complete. The inferred facts (outcome of JESS rule execution) are returned to the knowledge base. Finally, the user interface displays the results comparing the evaluation outcome of the WC to the specified baseline criteria. The evaluator can then analyze the results to determine whether the agency matches the requirements of the Australian Web Guide. The results also serve as a benchmark for the agency to improve the effectiveness of the web content management on e-government websites.

### 4.1.2 Domain Experts Analysis

Developing the ontologies and the concept definitions therein is a complex iterative process. The WC ontology is the outcome of subjective tradeoffs and objective goals. Subjective decisions focused on the

*Figure 8. SWRL rule to determine the training of personnel with a specific role*

```
EvaluationWCM    EvaluationWCM:Personnel(?X) ∧ EvaluationWCM:hasRole(?X,?Y) ∧
EvaluationWCM    EvaluationWCM:hasTraining(?X,?Z)-->
EvaluationWCM    EvaluationWCM:Training(?Z)
```

degree of detail in the characterization of concepts. Objective goals addressed how the application can benefit from the use of the WC ontology.

Since there exists no widely accepted formal methodology for ontology evaluation (Weinberger, Te'eni, & Frank, 2008), inputs from knowledge engineers and e-government domain experts were regularly solicited to ensure the semantic correctness of the ontology. Seeking active involvement of domain experts is a commonly applied method to evaluate ontologies (Baker et al., 2013; Edgington, Raghu, & Vinze, 2005). Open discussions and regular reviews helped raise competency questions and identify weaknesses in the ontology. The domain experts verified the ontology characteristics such as consistency, clarity, coherence, generality and minimal bias (Du & Zhou, 2012; Edgington et al., 2005; Weinberger et al., 2008). To ensure that the concepts were accurate representations of the real world, scenario based testing (such as the one described above) was conducted with the domain experts. Asserted facts correctly classified by the reasoner and the inferred facts generated by the expert system (JESS) demonstrated that the ontology is useful in evaluating e-government websites.

## 5. DISCUSSION

E-government transforms government structures and improves the quality of government services to citizens, businesses, and public authorities (Gil-García & Pardo, 2005). An effective e-government system should be reliable, economical and easy to maintain (Hashemi, Monfaredi, & Masdari, 2013). For citizens and businesses, e-government facilitates efficient delivery of information, access to government services (Lin et al., 2011), and empowerment to participate in government (Valdés et al., 2011). For public authorities, e-government provides opportunities to increase operational efficiency by reducing costs (Gil-García & Pardo, 2005) and integrate services provided by the various public agencies (Valdés et al., 2011).

E-government in the digital age can be characterized by two contrasting trends. On one hand, new policies increasingly rely on e-government platforms to provide services to citizens. The platforms, therefore, have to be oriented around individualized digital user experiences and market-style provision. They should be designed and managed in a way that enables citizens to navigate the information rich websites with ease. On the other hand, due to political polarization and budget cuts, government agencies are constrained for resources to undertake policies in a client-centered manner (Tummers & Rocco, 2015). Yet, e-government initiatives are more than just the delivery of online services (Valdés et al., 2011), and requires planning and coordination of goals, policies, processes and technologies (Koh, Prybutok & Zhang, 2008). Unlike any IS implementation, e-government managers face numerous additional technological, organizational, legal, and environmental challenges (Gil-García & Pardo, 2005). Significant technological challenges faced by the e-government website managers include balancing the complexity of web content and integrating technology newness and quality assurance (Shepherd et al., 2010). Organizational challenges include aligning e-government goals and objectives of multiple public agencies, and gaining strong, consistent, and active support of the political leadership (Rose & Grant, 2010; Shepherd et al., 2010). Top management support plays an important role in e-government initiatives to guide the allocation of resources, integration of services, and re-engineering of business processes. Legal and regulatory challenges include adherence to policies and standards and assurance of privacy (Rocheleau, 2000). Lastly, environmental challenges to e-government initiatives arise from coercive pressure exerted by citizens and businesses, political pressure from legislative bodies, and public-private partnerships.

In order to overcome technological challenge in e-government, two factors that influence the adoption of technologies must be taken into consideration - system usefulness and ease of use (Gil-García & Pardo, 2005). Organizing training presentations, and online videos and tutorials that demonstrate the use of an ontology-based knowledge sharing system, would enhance perceived usefulness and ease of use of e-government websites. Organizational and cultural changes are often more difficult to address than technological challenges (Furuholt & Wahid, 2008). Therefore, identifying structural changes to ensure the effective adoption of e-government objectives, and applying a gradual change plan is crucial (Al-Sebie, 2014). Although changing institutionalized rules or practices is not easy, executive and legislative support from legislators and other policy makers can help make the transition easier (Gil-García & Pardo, 2005). An ontology-based approach for WC evaluation can assist in addressing public policy problems by ensuring that governing laws presented to the citizens are updated and maintained consistently, while providing legitimacy to online information disseminated by government agencies. Overcoming environmental challenges should include reforming existing processes by simplifying legal regulations and procedures (Almarabeh & AbuAli, 2010). An ontology base approach for WC management can provide solutions to address some environmental concerns. For example, the integration of privacy ontology (see section 2.2) can address the coercive pressures of citizens and businesses to adhere with established privacy standards. Similarly, personnel and web content management concepts within the ontology would address citizen requests for limiting the storage and use of personally identifiable information. Integrating *fair information practices* (Almarabeh & AbuAli, 2010) in the WC ontology can ensure that the collection and retention of personal information is kept to a minimum.

As e-government initiatives mature, and the concept becomes more evolved, policies and programs oriented towards integration of public services and advancing online services for citizens become essential. To respond to pressure for expanded e-government services, and to incorporate advances in information technology, decision makers should seek a more broadly-based understanding of the interaction among technology, agencies, and citizens (Gil-García & Pardo, 2005). The ontology based tool for web content evaluation presented in this paper is one such application grounded in the latest IS research and practice. The solution utilizes a modernistic approach to improve the quality of web content and efficiency of the evaluation process. The design rationale of the solution relies on the WC ontology for the systematic and formal representation of the domain knowledge. By providing structure and organization to the complex e-government information management functions, the ontology serves as an enabler for information sharing among the stakeholders involved in e-government initiatives. For e-government initiatives to be successful, the information disseminated must be of good quality, reliable, homogenous and accurate. The solution approach described in this research reduces the time and paper work required for the evaluation of web content and assures more accurate results. It provides a stronger impetus for ownership, version control, privacy, security and change management associated with the web content evaluation by public officials and evaluators. Although the complexity and newness of technology are factors that may constrain the adoption (Gil-García & Pardo, 2005) of the evaluation tool, IS researchers can assist practitioners by examining the challenges, building artifacts, evaluating utility, developing strategies and documenting findings.

## 5.2 Contribution to Research

Construction of high quality e-government solutions is essential to the coordination of activities that the citizens and businesses demand from the government. In our research, we analyzed the guidelines of three government organizations to identify the concepts and functions that can be integrated in the WC ontology for web content evaluation. As an enterprise model, the ontology provides a foundation for developing a knowledge-rich environment for organizing, evaluating and improving web content in e-government initiatives. Knowledge engineers, semantic web researchers, and e-government decision makers will benefit from the knowledge gained from the development and use of ontology for web content evaluation. Our research will also benefit those researchers conducting interdisciplinary studies in semantic systems and e-government.

In our research, we also identified a set of reference ontologies and their extensions that are applicable to e-government. They may serve as a template for practitioners, domain experts and researchers for the development of other ontology based applications. Our research thus contributes to the body of scholarship by proposing technological solutions to ensure the delivery of reliable and consistent information via e-government websites. As ontology based representational formalisms become more popular, related toolsets and methodologies that enable rapid configuration, data exploration and knowledge sharing will be crucial. Avenues for extending our study will include further research to advance the understanding of the usability of such tools and their diffusion in the e-government initiatives.

## 5.3 Policy Implications

An effective e-government should maximize the effectiveness, speed, productivity and delivery of public services and information (Sarantis et al., 2011; Wimmer, 2002). The need for intensive and generalized use of ICT to provision public services and enhance managerial efficiency of public servants is well recognized (Gil-García & Pardo, 2005). To achieve this goal, the utilization of new and innovative technological approaches become essential (Rose & Grant, 2010).

Building e-government capabilities facilitate and strengthen the public service infrastructure available to the community. Examples of e-government capabilities include provisioning agency specific information, conducting financial transactions, and enabling citizen participation in policy development (Rose & Grant, 2010). As public information changes over time (due to policy updates, regulatory changes or collaboration between agencies for delivering composite services), maintaining the currency and consistency of the web content becomes important. In this paper, we demonstrated how digital information related to e-government can be monitored and maintained using the WC ontology. The ontology-based approach addresses some of the challenges in disseminating consistent, reliable and accurate information that accompany policy revisions and regulatory updates. Knowledge engineers should be mindful that continuous improvement to the WC ontology would be necessary to accommodate the updates to policy changes. When change is necessitated, a timely and systematic response will be required to ensure consistency of the ontology and the applications that utilize it.

As public agencies create new policies and programs, we recommend that the government strategy first evaluate the organizational and structural model of existing e-government initiatives. Doing so will help to identify areas where new and innovative technology can serve to improve operational efficiency, integrate services of multiple agencies, reduce cost, and enhance service quality. Change management that highlights the added value of technology, would help overcome the stigma of viewing technology as a deterrent to implementation success (Gil-García & Pardo, 2005. Corresponding policy changes should also be made to the regulatory environment to allow and support the adoption of new and emerging technologies (Gil-García & Pardo, 2005). Only then a detailed roadmap should be formulated to further the reach of e-government initiatives.

## 6. LIMITATIONS AND FUTURE RESEARCH

The proposed ontology is not without limitations. First, the ontology design is based on the analysis of only three web content management guidelines for government organizations, namely the Government of Alberta guideline, the Australian guidelines, and the American guidelines. The Government of Alberta guidelines are at the province level, whereas the other two are country-level agency guidelines. Investigating additional national-level evaluation guidelines can help further confirm the concept generality presented in the ontology. Currently, the proposed model only aligns with the specific requirement of web content management of government agencies. Business functions pertinent to commercial organizations such as supply chain management, human resources, and marketing need to be considered to make the ontology applicable to private organizations. This represent opportunities for future research.

We also do not specify how other purposeful ontologies such as the organization (Fox et al., 1996), records management (Alalwan & Thomas, 2011), security (Tsoumas & Gritzalis, 2006), and privacy (Hecker et al., 2008) ontologies are integrated in our WC ontology. To realize the true benefits of semantic interoperability, the particulars and challenges of integrating the WC ontology to the external ontologies need a thorough and elaborate discussion. In this research, we only presented a scenario-based evaluation of the ontology based WC approach. Evaluating the ontology based solution in a real-world setting may not only help to assess the validity of the proposed solution, but also determine how it may impact user experiences.

## 7. CONCLUSION

Various new and emerging knowledge engineering technologies (e.g., ontologies, and expert systems) and tools (e.g., OWL, and SWRL) are now widely deployed (Ding & Foo, 2002; Garcia-Crespo et al., 2011) to improve knowledge sharing, reusability of information, and interoperability of systems. The study calls for wider adoption and inclusion of these technology advances in e-government initiatives. It will serve to further the coordination of activities between the citizen and the government and enhance e-government service provisions.

In this paper, we discuss the importance of evaluating web content and the drawbacks of the traditional evaluation method in the context of e-government. Evaluation of WC is essential to ensure accuracy of content, and to meet legislative standards. By focusing mainly on e-government we analyze the guidelines of three legislative bodies to determine the main concepts and functions of web content evaluation. We develop the WC ontology for the formal representation of the evaluation concepts and process. We discuss the implementation of an ontology-based evaluation tool and demonstrate its utility through scenario based testing and expert analysis.

The ontology based evaluation approach described in this paper offers many advantages. It semantically links content lifecycle activities to domain-specific concepts such as *Legal Requirements*, *Training* and *Records Management*. The standardization offered by the ontology will enable most legislative bodies to evaluate their web content. In addition, the ontology-based approach allows knowledge sharing among the governmental agencies, which is essential to disseminate information that is reliable, accurate and homogenous. The solution thus serves to address the currency, consistency and legislative requirements needed to ensure high quality of web content and efficiency of the evaluation process. The ontology-based evaluation approach presented in this paper may not be viewed as a fully automated system. Nevertheless, in comparison to the largely manual approaches that are currently in place, the solution presented in this paper serves as an improvement and as a more effective alternative for the management and evaluation of web content on e-government websites.

## REFERENCES


Al-Sebie, M. (2014). Organizational challenges facing integrating e-government systems: an empirical study. *European Scientific Journal, 10*(10).

Alalwan, J., & Thomas, M. (2011). *Designing ERM Ontology to Evaluate Records Management System.* Paper presented at the System Sciences (HICSS), 2011 44th Hawaii International Conference on. 10.1109/HICSS.2011.149

Alalwan, J. A., Thomas, M. A., & Weistroffer, H. R. (2014). Decision support capabilities of enterprise content management systems: An empirical investigation. *Decision Support Systems, 68*, 39–48. doi:10.1016/j.dss.2014.09.002

Alberta, G. o. (2004). *Managing Web Content: applying the information management framework to web resources.* Government of Alberta.

Almarabeh, T., & AbuAli, A. (2010). A general framework for e-government: Definition maturity challenges, opportunities, and success. *European Journal of Scientific Research, 39*(1), 29–42.

Álvarez Sabucedo, L. M., Anido Rifón, L. E., Corradini, F., Polzonetti, A., & Re, B. (2010). Knowledge-based platform for eGovernment agents: A Web-based solution using semantic technologies. *Expert Systems with Applications, 37*(5), 3647–3656. doi:10.1016/j.eswa.2009.10.026

Australia, G. o. (2013). *Protective Security Framework: Securing government business.* Academic Press.

Bak, J., Jedrzejek, C., & Falkowski, M. (2009). *Usage of the Jess engine, rules and ontology to query a relational database. In Rule Interchange and Applications* (pp. 216–230). Springer.

Baker, T., Bechhofer, S., Isaac, A., Miles, A., Schreiber, G., & Summers, E. (2013). Key choices in the design of Simple Knowledge Organization System (SKOS). *Journal of Web Semantics, 20*, 35–49. doi:10.1016/j.websem.2013.05.001

Beimel, D., & Peleg, M. (2011). Using OWL and SWRL to represent and reason with situation-based access control policies. *Data & Knowledge Engineering, 70*(6), 596–615. doi:10.1016/j.datak.2011.03.006

Bera, P., Burton-Jones, A., & Wand, Y. (2011). Guidelines for designing visual ontologies to support knowledge identification. *Management Information Systems Quarterly, 35*(4), 883–908. doi:10.2307/41409965

Bouamrane, M.-M., Rector, A., & Hurrell, M. (2009). *A hybrid architecture for a preoperative decision support system using a rule engine and a reasoner on a clinical ontology. In Web Reasoning and Rule Systems* (pp. 242–253). Springer.

Chen, H. L. (2004). *An intelligent broker architecture for pervasive context-aware systems* (PhD Dissertation). University of Maryland, Baltimore County.

Chen, Y.-J. (2010). Development of a method for ontology-based empirical knowledge representation and reasoning. *Decision Support Systems, 50*(1), 1–20. doi:10.1016/j.dss.2010.02.010

Dawes, S. S., Pardo, T. A., & DiCaterino, A. (1999). Crossing the threshold: Practical foundations for government services on the World Wide Web. *Journal of the American Society for Information Science, 50*(4), 346–353. doi:

Ding, Y., & Foo, S. (2002). Ontology research and development. Part 1-a review of ontology generation. *Journal of Information Science, 28*(2), 123–136.

Du, J., & Zhou, L. (2012). Improving financial data quality using ontologies. *Decision Support Systems, 54*(1), 7686. doi:10.1016/j.dss.2012.04.016

Edgington, T., Raghu, T. S., & Vinze, A. (2005). Knowledge Ontology: A Method for Empirical Identification of'AsIs' Contextual Knowledge. *System Sciences, 2005. HICSS'05. Proceedings of the 38th Annual Hawaii International Conference on.* 10.1109/HICSS.2005.377

Eschenfelder, K. R. (2004). Behind the Web site: An inside look at the production of Web-based textual government information. *Government Information Quarterly, 21*(3), 337–358. doi:10.1016/j.giq.2004.04.004

Fauzi, F., & Belkhatir, M. (2013). Multifaceted conceptual image indexing on the world wide web. *Information Processing & Management, 49*(2), 420–440. doi:10.1016/j.ipm.2012.08.001

Firat, A., Madnick, S. E., & Grosof, B. (2004). *Contextual alignment of ontologies for semantic interoperability*. Social Science Research Network Electronic Paper Collection.

Fonou-Dombeu, J. V., & Huisman, M. (2013). *Adaptive search and selection of domain ontologies for reuse on the Semantic Web*. Academic Press.

Forgy, C. L. (1982). Rete: A fast algorithm for the many pattern/many object pattern match problem. *Artificial Intelligence, 19*(1), 17–37. doi:10.1016/0004-3702(82)90020-0

Fountain, J. (2002). *Developing a basic research program for digital government: information, organizations, and governance. National Center for Digital Government, Kennedy School of Government.* Harvard University.

Fountain, J. E. (2004). *Building the virtual state: Information technology and institutional change.* Brookings Institution Press.

Fox, M. S., Barbuceanu, M., & Gruninger, M. (1996). An organisation ontology for enterprise modeling: Preliminary concepts for linking structure and behaviour. *Computers in Industry*, *29*(1), 123–134. doi:10.1016/0166-3615(95)00079-8

Freeman, R. T., & Yin, H. (2005). Web content management by self-organization. *Neural Networks. IEEE Transactions on*, *16*(5), 1256–1268. PMID:16252831

Furuholt, B., & Wahid, F. (2008). E-government Challenges and the Role of Political Leadership in Indonesia: the Case of Sragen. *Hawaii International Conference on System Sciences, Proceedings of the 41st Annual*. 10.1109/HICSS.2008.134

Garcia-Crespo, A., Ruiz-Mezcua, B., Lopez-Cuadrado, J. L., & Gonzalez-Carrasco, I. (2011). Semantic model for knowledge representation in e-business. *Knowledge-Based Systems*, *24*(2), 282–296. doi:10.1016/j.knosys.2010.09.006

Gil-García, J. R., & Pardo, T. A. (2005). E-government success factors: Mapping practical tools to theoretical foundations. *Government Information Quarterly*, *22*(2), 187–216. doi:10.1016/j.giq.2005.02.001

Goodwin, S., & Vidgen, R. (2002). Content, content, everywhere... time to stop and think? The process of Web content management. *Computing & Control Engineering Journal*, *13*(2), 66–70. doi:10.1049/cce:20020202

Gruber, T. R. (1993). A translation approach to portable ontology specifications. *Knowledge Acquisition*, *5*(2), 199220. doi:10.1006/knac.1993.1008

Hashemi, S., Monfaredi, K., & Masdari, M. (2013). Using cloud computing for e-government: Challenges and benefits. *International Journal of Computer, Information. Systems and Control Engineering*, *7*(9), 596–603.

Hecker, M., Dillon, T. S., & Chang, E. (2008). Privacy ontology support for e-commerce. *IEEE Internet Computing*, *12*(2), 54–61. doi:10.1109/MIC.2008.41

Henriksson, A., Yi, Y., Frost, B., & Middleton, M. (2007). Evaluation instrument for e-government websites. *Electronic Government, an International Journal*, *4*(2), 204-226.

Hernon, P., & Relyea, H. C. (1995). Government publishing: Past to present. *Government Information Quarterly*, *12*(3), 309–330. doi:10.1016/0740-624X(95)90021-7

Horridge, M., Knublauch, H., Rector, A., Stevens, R., & Wroe, C. (2004). A practical guide to building OWL ontologies using the Protégé-OWL plugin and CO-ODE Tools. University of Manchester.

Howto.gov. (2014). *Federal laws and regulations for government websites*. Retrieved from http://www.usa.gov/webcontent/reqs_bestpractices/laws_regs/index.shtml

Joha, A., & Janssen, M. (2010). *Content management implemented as shared service: a public sector case study. In EGovernment, E-Services and Global Processes* (pp. 138–151). Springer.

Jutla, D., & Xu, L. (2004). *Privacy agents and ontology for the semantic web*. Academic Press.

Koh, C. E., Prybutok, V. R., & Zhang, X. (2008). Measuring e-government readiness. *Information & Management*, *45*(8), 540–546. doi:10.1016/j.im.2008.08.005

Kuzma, J. M., & Price, C. (2009). Analysis of UK Parliament Web Sites for Disability Accessibility. *Proceedings of the 8th European Conference on Information Warfare and Security.*

Landsbergen, D. Jr, & Wolken, G. Jr. (2001). Realizing the promise: Government information systems and the fourth generation of information technology. *Public Administration Review, 61*(2), 206–220. doi:10.1111/0033-3352.00023

LePendu, P., & Dou, D. (2011). Using ontology databases for scalable query answering, inconsistency detection, and data integration. *Journal of Intelligent Information Systems, 37*(2), 217–244. doi:10.100710844-010-0133-4 PMID:22163378

Lin, F., Fofanah, S. S., & Liang, D. (2011). Assessing citizen adoption of e-Government initiatives in Gambia: A validation of the technology acceptance model in information systems success. *Government Information Quarterly, 28*(2), 271–279. doi:10.1016/j.giq.2010.09.004

Magoutas, B., Halaris, C., & Mentzas, G. (2007). An ontology for the multi-perspective evaluation of quality in e-Government services. Electronic Government, 318-329.

O'Connor, M. J., Shankar, R. D., Nyulas, C., Tu, S. W., & Das, A. K. (2008). *Developing a Web-Based Application using OWL and SWRL.* Paper presented at the AAAI Spring Symposium: AI Meets Business Rules and Process Management.

Peuschel, B., & Schäfer, W. (1992). Concepts and implementation of a rule-based process engine. *Proceedings of the 14th international conference on Software engineering.*

Protégé. (2012). Protégé Editor and Knowledge Acquisition System. Author.

Protégé. (2017). Retrieved from http://protege.stanford.edu/

Qin, J. (2004). *Web content management.* John Wiley & Sons.

Qin, J. (2004). Article. *Management Information Systems Quarterly, 28*(1), 75–105. doi:10.2307/25148625

Ramaprasad, A., Sánchez-Ortiz, A., & Syn, T. (2015). *An ontology of egovernment.* Paper presented at the International Conference on Electronic Government.

Relyea, H. C. (2002). E-gov: Introduction and overview. *Government Information Quarterly, 19*(1), 9–35. doi:10.1016/S0740-624X(01)00096-X

Rocheleau, B. (2000). Prescriptions for Public-Sector Information Management A Review, Analysis, and Critique. *American Review of Public Administration, 30*(4), 414–435. doi:10.1177/02750740022064759

Rose, W. R., & Grant, G. G. (2010). Critical issues pertaining to the planning and implementation of e-government initiatives. *Government Information Quarterly, 27*(1), 26–33. doi:10.1016/j.giq.2009.06.002

Santos, J. (2003). E-service quality: A model of virtual service quality dimensions. *Managing Service Quality, 13*(3), 233–246. doi:10.1108/09604520310476490

Santoso, H., Zeniarja, J., Luthfiarta, A., & Wijaya, B. (2016). An Ontological Crawling Approach for Improving Information Aggregation over eGovernment Websites. *Journal of Computational Science, 12*(9), 455–463. doi:10.3844/jcssp.2016.455.463

Sarantis, D., Charalabidis, Y., & Askounis, D. (2011). A goal-driven management framework for electronic government transformation projects implementation. *Government Information Quarterly*, *28*(1), 117–128. doi:10.1016/j.giq.2009.10.006

Sheng, L., & Lingling, L. (2011, November). Application of Ontology in E-Government. In *Management of e-Commerce and e-Government (ICMeCG), 2011 Fifth International Conference on*. IEEE.

Shepherd, E., Stevenson, A., & Flinn, A. (2010). Information governance, records management, and freedom of information: A study of local government authorities in England. *Government Information Quarterly*, *27*(4), 337–345. doi:10.1016/j.giq.2010.02.008

Siskos, E., Askounis, D., & Psarras, J. (2014). Multicriteria decision support for global e-government evaluation. *Omega*, *46*, 51–63. doi:10.1016/j.omega.2014.02.001

Smith, A. G. (2001). Applying evaluation criteria to New Zealand government websites. *International Journal of Information Management*, *21*(2), 137–149. doi:10.1016/S0268-4012(01)00006-8

Souer, J., Honders, P., Versendaal, J., & Brinkkemper, S. (2008). A Framework for Web Content Management System Operations and Maintenance. *Journal of Digital Information Management*, *6*(4), 342–347.

Sourouni, A.-M., Kourlimpinis, G., Mouzakitis, S., & Askounis, D. (2010). Towards the government transformation: An ontology-based government knowledge repository. *Computer Standards & Interfaces*, *32*(1), 44–53. doi:10.1016/j.csi.2009.06.002

Thomas, M., & Redmond, R. (2011). A Framework for Analyzing User Interaction in Digital Spaces. In V. Sugumaran (Ed.), Intelligent, Adaptive and Reasoning Technologies: New Developments and Applications (pp. 23-25). Hershey, PA: IGI Global.

Thomas, M., Redmond, R., Yoon, V., & Singh, R. (2005). A semantic approach to monitor business process. *Communications of the ACM*, *48*(12), 55–59. doi:10.1145/1101779.1101809

Tsoumas, B., & Gritzalis, D. (2006). *Towards an ontology-based security management.* Paper presented at the Advanced Information Networking and Applications, 2006. AINA 2006. 20th International Conference on. 10.1109/AINA.2006.329

Tummers, L., & Rocco, P. (2015). Serving clients when the server crashes: How frontline workers cope with E-government challenges. *Public Administration Review*, *75*(6), 817–827. doi:10.1111/puar.12379

Valdés, G., Solar, M., Astudillo, H., Iribarren, M., Concha, G., & Visconti, M. (2011). Conception, development and implementation of an e-Government maturity model in public agencies. *Government Information Quarterly*, *28*(2), 176–187. doi:10.1016/j.giq.2010.04.007

Van der Aalst, W. M. P., & Kumar, A. (2003). XML–Based Schema Definition for Support of Interorganizational Workflow. *Information Systems Research*, *14*(1), 23–46. doi:10.1287/isre.14.1.23.14768

Vandic, D., Van Dam, J.-W., & Frasincar, F. (2012). Faceted product search powered by the Semantic Web. *Decision Support Systems*, *53*(3), 425–437. doi:10.1016/j.dss.2012.02.010

Visser, U., Stuckenschmidt, H., Schuster, G., & Vögele, T. (2002). Ontologies for geographic information processing. *Computers & Geosciences*, *28*(1), 103–117.

von Alan, R. H., March, S. T., Park, J., & Ram, S. (2004). Design science in information systems research. *Management Information Systems Quarterly*, *28*(1), 75–105.

Weinberger, H., Te'eni, D., & Frank, A. J. (2008). Ontology-based evaluation of organizational memory. *Journal of the American Society for Information Science and Technology*, *59*(9), 1454–1468. doi:10.1002/asi.20859

Wimmer, M. A. (2002). A European perspective towards online one-stop government: The eGOV project. *Electronic Commerce Research and Applications*, *1*(1), 92–103. doi:10.1016/S1567-4223(02)00008-X

Zhu, Q., Du, J., & Han, X. (2007). *The establishment and application of evaluation criteria systems for Chinese egovernment websites.* Paper presented at the Wireless Communications, International Conference on Networking and Mobile Computing, 2007. WiCom 2007.

Ziemba, P., Jankowski, J., Wątróbski, J., & Becker, J. (2015). *Knowledge management in website quality evaluation domain. In Computational collective intelligence* (pp. 75–85). Springer. doi:10.1007/978-3-319-24306-1_8

## ENDNOTES

1 http://webguide.gov.au/

2 http://www.howto.gov/web-content

3 https://protege.stanford.edu/

4 http://www.howto.gov/web-content

5 http://webguide.gov.au/types-of-content/cookies/

6 http://www.usa.gov/webcontent/reqs_bestpractices/laws_regs/plain-writing-act.shtml

7 https://agency-admin.funnelback.com/search/admin/agencies_help/

# Chapter 2
# Foundations' Civic Engagement With Stakeholders:
## Leveraging Social Media Strategies

**Sarah Maxwell**
*University of Texas at Dallas, USA*

**Julia Carboni**
*Syracuse University, USA*

## ABSTRACT

*Nonprofit organizations often adopt social media such as Facebook to encourage stakeholders to engage in the organizational mission. Calls to action via social media tend to reach subscribers who "like" or follow the organization via one-way communication. Researching effective approaches to dialogic communication, which asks followers to engage rather than observe, the authors focus on relationship management theory (RMT). RMT stresses organizational-stakeholder dynamic interactions. Using a quantitative modeling approach, the authors examine Facebook posts made by three different types of foundations (community, corporate, and independent) to determine how foundations call for stakeholder engagement. To date, few studies focus directly on types of posts and the response, or lack of response, to organizational messages via social media. Civic engagement requires action on the part of the stakeholder to address social problems. Defining participation and engagement varies by field and types of interaction. This research contributes to literature examining the "digital citizen."*

## INTRODUCTION

Civic engagement, encouraged through various forms of social media, is expanding rapidly in recent literature. Given the nature of foundations in the public and nonprofit realms as funders and policy-leaders, calling stakeholders to action by foundations remains lacking in exploration. What is the role of private, community, and corporate foundations in encouraging participation beyond their grantees? Broadly, civic engagement refers to citizen participation in their communities with the purpose of improving the community (Adler and Goggin, 2005; Carboni, McNeely, & Maxwell, 2015). Specifically,

DOI: 10.4018/978-1-5225-5966-5.ch002

civic engagement in social media is a process that "involves moving an individual away from disinterest, distraction, ignorance, and apathy towards education, understanding, motivation, and action" (Obar, Zube, & Lampe, 2012).

Although civic engagement is often applied to political participation, the term also relates to individual and collective action through civil society. Civil society includes the institutions and organizations with which individuals voluntarily associate to advance common interests (Anheier 2005; Skocpol & Fiorina 1999). Civil society is distinct from government and business and includes nonprofit organizations, which are rarely studied in this context. Wallace (2012), for example notes that information and communication technologies, rather than contributing to the breakdown of society, encourage "new forms of connectedness and community and a form of 'knowledge commons' that creates a public space for deliberative democracy" (p. 112).

In the United States, nonprofit foundations are an important vehicle for civic engagement as they provide organizational mechanisms for individuals to improve communities. Nonprofit foundations typically provide grant funding to nonprofits, individuals and communities for scientific, educational, cultural, religious, or other charitable purposes. Foundations act as intermediaries, funding nonprofits in tandem or independently of government (Riely & Kraft, 2010). Although most are not in formal relationships with government, foundations often serve an agenda-setting role in targeting social problems and proposing solutions for ameliorating community and larger social ills (Duan-Barnett, Wangelin, & Lamm, 2012).

Increasingly, foundations use social media to engage with citizens and other stakeholders. While some literature exists on social media usage among nonprofits generally, and foundations specifically, limited evidence exists regarding online stakeholder engagement with social media. Online stakeholders are those who converse via social media with organizations. They may or may not be active in additional organizational activities. Eikenberry (2012) suggests that collaborative social networking is often missed in practical terms, as organizations typically focus on one-way communication. Additionally, many organizations lack a cohesive plan for adoption of social media. Offering an example of local health departments, Renmin (2016) finds that age and backgrounds of top executives, as well as organizational factors, such as size contribute to the adoption of social media usage.

Social media can be viewed as a tool for relationship management, facilitating civic engagement with online stakeholders. Are foundations simply posting information on social media sites such as Facebook, or is there a conversation taking place between the organization and its stakeholders? Engagement via social media sites such as Facebook is defined differently from use in this context. Simply having a social media site does not mean users or stakeholders are actively *engaged* with the organization that manages the social media platform. Are foundations' stakeholders responding to foundation Facebook posts? Are they civically engaged in an online conversation about their communities?

High asset corporate, private, and community foundations are analyzed to determine how foundations use social media to engage online stakeholder citizens. While all foundations serve charitable purposes, corporate and non-corporate, or private foundations are typically funded by an endowment or principal fund, often with a single source. Conversely, community foundations are nonprofit organizations with public charity status that receive funding from numerous sources. To maintain public charity status, they must seek funds from diverse sources. Given this fiscal arrangement, community foundations are hypothesized to be more likely to promote online civic engagement through social media than their corporate and private counterparts because of the need to secure diverse streams of funding. We also predict that online stakeholders will be more engaged with community foundation social media than with corporate or private foundations.

Civic engagement assumes a level of two-way dialogue, as engagement is not listening; it entails a response of those who are interested in making a difference. Social media engagement is defined as responses from foundation stakeholders on "social media sites" or social networking sites. This study focuses on Facebook as the social media site due to the overwhelming adoption of Facebook by the nonprofit sector. Foundations fall within the nonprofit sector, encompassing private, corporate, or community foundations whose missions are generally to help ameliorate social problems within their communities (Bennett, 2014). In a study of advocacy organizations, Obar, Zube, and Lampe (2012) find that advocacy organizations interact with social media frequently. Foundations are situated to adopt social media techniques used by advocacy organizations, incorporating various Facebook, Twitter, or other social media sites to engage their stakeholders.

This chapter proceeds as follows: First, a review of extant scholarship on social media and civic engagement is presented. Next, the chapter turns to foundations and their role in civic engagement. We present Relationship Management Theory in the following section, linking social media engagement to the development of civic engagement by foundation stakeholders. We then present the research methodology and quantitative analysis of organizational Facebook post content, indicating which foundation posts elicit responses by stakeholders. The conclusion offers practical ideas for foundations, working in partnership with public agencies to promote civic engagement through social media strategies.

## SOCIAL MEDIA AS CIVIC ENGAGEMENT

Civic engagement receives considerable attention in volunteerism, youth development, democracy, and community engagement scholarship (Carboni, McNeely, Maxwell, 2014; Cruce and Moore 2012; Putnam 2001; Wuthnow 1998). Civic engagement, touted as a positive attribute within communities, is less studied as a means for "expand[ing] opportunities, information, and experiences available to participants" (Carboni, et al, 2014. p. 137). With the adoption of social media sites, as well as apps, civic engagement potentially embraces active communication via these burgeoning web-and mobile-based technologies. We ask how do foundations contribute to civic engagement via social media? Civic engagement is not simply volunteering or assuming activist roles. It entails belief systems, which suggest that a person considers himself or herself interested and engaged in larger societal problems (Ehrlich, 2000). "An individual is willing to see the moral and civic dimensions of issues, to make and justify informed moral and civic judgments, and to take action when appropriate" (Ehrlich, 2000, p. *xxvi*). Additionally, civic engagement "means promoting the quality of life in a community, through both political and non-political processes" (Ehrlich, 2000). Thus, civic engagement assumes the form of action, but also of discourse, which prompts online stakeholders to share or respond (Rheingold, 2008). In a 2104 study, Guo and Saxton found that public education and grassroots lobbying via Twitter among nonprofits comprised the majority of advocacy practices. Public education is also the most widely used hashtag in social media advocacy efforts (Saxton, Niyirora, Guo, & Waters 2015).

Scholarship regarding social media *engagement* remains limited in comparison to social media *use* among public administrators and their third sector counterparts. Guo and Saxton (2014), in reference to scholarship on social media engagement, state: "... most of these studies only examine the prevalence of social media, or *whether* advocacy organizations use social media; they barely touch on *how* they use them, and when they do, have merely looked at static profile information" (p. 2). Eikenberry (2012) also notes the challenges facing government and nonprofit agencies in identifying social networking tools to adequately engage their constituents. We use the industry definition for "social media engagement" defined as total likes, comments, and shares per Facebook post (Facebook, 2015; Wall Street Journal, 2015). Bridging the gap between public and privately funded organizations, we analyze civic engagement, or citizen participation in community and political discourse, to assess high-asset foundations' effectiveness in sparking citizens to engage in foundation discourse.

Foundations play a role in civic engagement in a variety of ways, which includes acting as intermediaries, including: active participation in government service delivery through public-private partnerships and mission-based activities designed to ameliorate social problems. Both require action on the part of foundation stakeholders. The Charles Stewart Mott Foundation serves as an example, funding programs that "seek to increase the nonprofit and philanthropic sector's responsiveness and capacity to address social and community needs" (Charles Stewart Mott Foundation, 2015).

"Grant-giving foundations are intermediaries between the individual donors who fund them and the various social enterprises that they, in turn, support. But if foundations serve only as passive middlemen, as mere conduits for giving, then they fall far short of their potential and of society's high expectations. Foundations can and should lead social progress" (Porter & Kramer, 1999). One of the first articles to suggest that foundations must "create value" was Porter's and Kramer's (1999) Harvard Business Review, which pointed directly to foundations' work in agenda setting through advancing the state of knowledge. Foundations have been, and remain intermediaries "free from political pressures" in furthering the knowledge base surrounding change and solutions (Porter & Kramer, 1999). Thus, foundations and their stakeholders participate in civic engagement, using Ehrlich's (2000) definition, through improving the quality of life in communities. "Civic engagement means working to make a difference in the civic life of our communities and developing the combination of knowledge, skills, values and motivation to make that difference" (p. vii). Social media provide an avenue for foundations to participate in and promote civic engagement.

## SOCIAL MEDIA USE OF NONPROFIT FOUNDATIONS

Facebook provides a forum for foundation stakeholders to engage in discussions related to grant implementation, or programs that serve members of the community. Applying stakeholder relationship concepts from Bortree & Seltzer (2009) and Sweetser & Lariscy (2008), we contend that stakeholders meet government, nonprofit, and foundation decision makers in a space that accommodates all groups' interest, allowing them to engage in discourse on areas of mutual concern. "Government 2.0" is now discussed as collaborative, participatory, and open (Reddick and Aikins, 2012). In other words, dialogic communication on Facebook is possible, and its potential for civic engagement among foundations is explored in this paper. Although dialogic communication is possible, Waters, Burnett, Lamm, and Lucas (2009) found through a comprehensive Facebook content analysis that few nonprofits make effective use of available Facebook offerings. These scholars find that nonprofits do not take full advantage of potential interactions with their stakeholders (Waters, Burnett, Lamm, & Lucas, 2009). Acknowledging this finding, we analyze the content of organizational Facebook posts from high-asset foundations to see what types of Facebook post content elicit the most engagement by users and whether there are differences by foundation type.

Improving the quality of communities and ameliorating social problems sustain nonprofit foundation missions, suggesting that dialogic communication inspiring action is preferable for effective civic engagement over one-way communication. Social media use is now common among the public and nonprofit sectors. Although nonprofits report email usage as their preferred form of communication, Facebook is the most common form of social media used by nonprofits (Auger, 2013; M+R NTEN, 2012). The Nonprofit Technology Network (NTEN) is a membership network of nonprofits, which produces respected reports of social media usage among nonprofits. NTEN found that Facebook is almost as universally accepted by nonprofits as email (NTEN, 2015). Within NTEN's report, nonprofit survey respondents noted multiple challenges to social media use with one of the most daunting tasks as proving Return on Investment (ROI) to the organization (NTEN, 2015). ROI requires engagement among the organization and its stakeholders, but nonprofits have yet to adopt social media analytical and evaluation strategies in a comprehensive manner. Nonprofits report having almost 200 Facebook subscribers for every 1000 email subscribers (M+R NTEN, 2014). Nonprofits with higher assets also report greater Facebook usage (M+R NTEN, 2014). Scholarly literature supports these findings, and suggests Facebook and Twitter as platforms more readily embraced than other social media sites such as Google + (Obar, 2014). Obar (2014) also finds that advocacy groups are enthusiastic about social media potential for outreach, but advocacy groups "remain cautious of unproven techniques that may divert resources from strategies known to work" (p. 211)

Increasingly, foundations among other nonprofits and advocacy groups rely on social media to communicate their mission effectively. Obar, Zube, and Lampe (2012) state, "Web 2.0 refers to the software platform that gave birth to the technology that we currently understand as social media" (p. 7). We follow Obar, Zube, and Lampe's (2012) terminology to investigate social media engagement by high-asset foundations to determine if foundations are engaging citizens through two-way, or dialogic communication. We also reference O'Reilly (2005) in developing a definition for social media sites: 1) users are viewed as "co-developers," 2) collective intelligence is created and 3) as more people use the sites, the engagement is enhanced. Reddick & Aikins (2012) also note that Web 2.0 is focused on democratic governance. Social media in this sense can be linked to personalized service delivery and feedback loops as well as decision-making that involves stakeholders.

Social media use by foundations is not heavily studied as a purposeful communication strategy (Räth, Smolnik, Urbach, & Zimmer, 2009; Treem & Leonardi, 2012). In other words, although social media use may be highly visible and active, social media as a strategic planning tool, especially between foundations and government has not been thoroughly reviewed. Rather, scholarship often considers social media *use,* as opposed to social media as an engagement tool with community members or differing groups of strategic stakeholders. Nonprofits readily acknowledge that social media are not viewed as components of overall strategic plans, and Facebook and other forms of social media fall into the hands of interns and others who are not active participants in the strategic planning process (Ragan Communications and NASDAQ, 2013; Westcott, 2007;). Indeed, of the companies with interns, 78% report using interns for Facebook. Foundations tend to share the social media duties, with 40% of foundation communication staff reporting that they personally interact with social media on the job (Switzer, 2011). Yet an ongoing misconception by nonprofits is that posting one-directional information or simply having a Facebook account implies "engagement" (Maxwell & Carboni, 2014; Auger, 2010).

Recent surveys offer a glimpse into the Web 2.0 foundation world. Similar to nonprofits generally, foundations are shown to post on social media platforms, lacking strategic purpose (Foundation Center, 2014). Only 30 percent of foundations acknowledge social media as part of their overall formal strategy (Foundation Center, 2014). The Foundation Center's Glass Pockets project, which is a survey of national foundations, reports that less than half of foundations employ any Web 2.0 platforms. When used, social media are generally only adopted for one-way communication, simply to inform communities about their work (Foundation Center, 2014). Overwhelmingly, foundations report that they do not find social media to be beneficial (Foundation Center, 2010). A recent study of social media use among German foundations reports that the number of likes on foundations' Facebook pages is strongly correlated with the number of comments, photos, and links (BÜrger, 2015). In this study, information and public education comprised the advocacy tactics used most frequently by foundations to engage their stakeholders, while surprisingly, 38.7% of foundation posts did not attempt any type of advocacy.

## CIVIC ENGAGEMENT THROUGH RELATIONSHIP MANAGEMENT

Incorporation of citizen and community stakeholders in foundation-work presents the potential to solicit advice, comments, and various forms of participation. Relationship Management Theory (RMT) emphasizes an organization's dynamic interactions with stakeholders (Ledingham 2003). The mission of an organization is related to its relationship with the organization's public, or stakeholders (Dozier, Gruning, & Gruning, 1995). Civic engagement is the discourse that arises from dynamic interaction between the organization and its stakeholders regarding action related to a social problem. Interactions with stakeholders under RMT emphasize reciprocal exchanges, which in turn, help to advance the organizational goals and strategies (Ledingham, 2003; Carboni, et al, 2014). The management of relationships is key to RMT. Stakeholders tend to select organizations with which they would like to engage often based on previous interaction with the organization (Hung 2005; Waters, 2008). Facebook posts offer dialogic communication opportunities, or what Kent and Taylor (1998) refer to as the "negotiated exchange of ideas" (p. 325). More recently, the term "digital citizen" reflects the changing relationship between citizen and government (Falk, 2011). Specifically, citizens engage through Facebook and other social media in the forms of social movements, co-production (i.e., relying directly on engagement from citizens as well as civil society-organizations), and connected government (ie., "transform[ing] interaction with citizens and public service delivery" (Falk, 2011).

Reddick and Aikins (2012) refer to the enhancement of knowledge management (p. 3), while others investigate dialogic and improved two-way communication, both indicating social-media-engagement between an organization and its stakeholders (Maxwell & Carboni, 2014; Carboni & Maxwell, 2014; Bortree & Seltzer, 2009). We attempt to address gaps in identifying effective use of social media through Relationship Management Theory. Applied to foundations' "effective" use of Facebook to improve dialogic, or two-way communication, we conduct Facebook content analyses for three types of foundations --- community, corporate, and non-corporate private grant making foundations—whereby we assess effective civic engagement discourse, i.e., public dialog on social or community issues, between organizations and their stakeholders. Although some scholars argue that social media platforms such as Facebook cannot contribute to civic engagement (Hand & Ching, 2011), we suggest stakeholders *are potentially effective* in informing the discourse, especially through the management and implementation of programs at the local levels. We must understand how stakeholders are engaging with social media as a precursor to understanding potential effectiveness. This new approach bridges the communications and public management fields.

The emerging communications literature continues to show that online communication differs from traditional forms of communication (Obar, 2012; Maxwell & Carboni, 2014; Treem & Leonardi, 2012). Traditional forms of civic engagement require participation, including examples such as town meetings

(Vogt, Förster, Kabst, 2014). However, traditional forms of organizational interaction with stakeholders are often restrictive, limiting attendance as a result of location or time (Vogt, Förster, Kabst, 2014).

This study approaches civic engagement through social media sites in the broader sense of community improvement and stakeholder engagement. Generally, community stakeholders hold an active interest in the work of the foundations they follow on Facebook; they may or may not be activists for a particular cause. We purport the adoption of participation via Facebook using dialogic communication is a useful adaptation of civic engagement strategies for foundations. Using likes, comments, and shares is a form of engagement that may or may not promote action in the typical conception of activism. Civic engagement can assume the form of education, information sharing, and discourse. Demonstrating action, beyond the slacktivism debate, is an important concept for advocacy groups; it therefore is noted here, but also distinguished from RMT and the concept of civic discourse in light of foundations and their general mission to ameliorate social problems. In this sense, foundations play a specialized intermediary role in civic engagement, as they are more likely to engage stakeholders in discourse than inciting action or activism beyond volunteer recruitment for local nonprofits or discourse about how to best solve community issues.

## FOUNDATION TYPES, MISSION, AND CIVIC ENGAGEMENT

Using the three main categories of foundations in the United States (corporate, private, and community), we review the differences foundations may exhibit in civic engagement via social media. Foundation type serves as an important factor in determining civic engagement, as Fernandez and Hager (2014) suggest that the type of foundation indicates differing interactions with stakeholder groups or government. Specifically, "To the extent that foundations are conceived of and consider themselves as *private*, they will act in a way that shields operations from public view, participation, and critique" (Fernandez & Hager, 2014, p. 409) . Thus, foundations are not a monolithic group. Private, family-operated foundations are potentially more likely to work quietly, not necessarily hoping for high-level interactions with those who are not directly engaged in the work of the foundation. The Foundation Center Glass Pockets, which is a survey of national foundations, tracks social media usage, finding that community, corporate, and private-family foundations use social media sites at 88%, 55%, and 34% respectively (Foundation Center 2014). Given the findings of Fernandez & Hager, 2014, we suggest that community and corporate foundations play a stronger role in actively pursuing civic engagement through social media.

## RESEARCH METHODOLOGY

Civic engagement as dialogic discourse is measured through engagement with stakeholder post content on foundation Facebook pages from a random sample of 100 high asset foundations (> $10 million) in three categories: community, private-family, and corporate foundations. Data were collected through commercially available programs. Guidestar provided the initial list of foundations in addition to detailed organizational information, such as assets. After downloading all foundations in the three categories greater than $10 million in assets, Excel was used to randomly generate 100 foundations in each of the categories. Publically available Facebook content is available through a multitude of programs, allowing any user to gather posts within a given time frame. We collected the Facebook content for the total 300 foundations and separated them by category.

In comparing across the three types of foundations, we collect data from a commercially available program. Hundreds of social media analytics programs found on the Internet (e.g., Trackur) that allow any visitor to view analytics for various social media platforms such as Facebook, Twitter, Google+, and others. Since Facebook is the most widely used Web 2.0 platform among nonprofits and foundations, we choose to review Facebook content. We also selected Facebook for its discourse reciprocity via comments, and by proxy, also likes and shares among its users (Saxton & Waters, 2014). Commercially available programs have inherent limitations, including the amount of time users can track content. Therefore, Facebook data were collected over a two-week period in February 2015. Two-week analyses are consistent with methodological procedures of other media studies (Weare, Loges, & Oztas 2007). February was also selected as the month is an average month for engagement via social media. The M+R NTEN Benchmarks study (2014) reports that December is the most active month for online nonprofit messages, but the response rate tends to be lower in December. February is similar to other non-holiday months. Of these 300 foundations, 106 foundations had at least one Facebook post during the time period studied. This included 72 community foundations, 11 private foundations, and 23 corporate foundations. This finding is supportive of our prediction that community foundations are more likely to have an online social media presence.

To further compare social media engagement of foundations, we provide summary statistics and chi-squared analysis to determine whether specific types of post content resulted in user engagement by foundation type. We detail differences in post engagement by post type (status, link, photo, video). By engagement, we mean the total number of likes, shares and comments per post. Social media "engagement" refers to the responses by organizational stakeholders to posts on Facebook made by the organization. These are defined primarily by likes, comments, and shares related to each organizational post on Facebook (Pletikosa Cvijikj & Michahelles, 2013). The end user's response defines the level and type of engagement (Facebook, 2015; Wall Street Journal, 2015). Specifically, literature is emerging from social networking journals, in addition to mass communication scholarship, demonstrating the technical definition of social media engagement. In addition to likes, comments, and shares, scholars also include interaction duration (Pletikosa Cvijikj & Michahelles, 2013). Commercial social media programs also define engagement as *likes + comments + shares* (Facebook, 2015). In addition to industry standards and technical scholarship, social science has also recently defined engagement using these parameters with reference to nonprofits (Saxton and Waters, 2014; Carboni and Maxwell, 2015). Saxton and Waters (2014), for example, use *likes*, *shares*, and *comments* to evaluate organizational stakeholders' response to Facebook content. Responses to posts are also shown to differ by post type (e.g., photo, video, or comment), vividness of the post, content type, or time of day (Pletikosa Cvijikj & Michahelles, 2013). Engagement can be assessed by organizations, enabling them to further develop those relationships through continued online dialogue using techniques shown to be successful through the literature.

Specifically, we examine whether the content type of a post resulted in user engagement. We examine five types of post content: organization information post; other information post; question post; request action with post; and request other action. Organization information posts gave information about the organization. Other information posts gave information about something other than the organization. Question posts included a question for social media stakeholders. Requests for actions with post posts included a request for users to engage with the post. Request for other action posts requested some other action of social media stakeholders other than interacting with the post (e.g.- asking stakeholders to vote). Individual posts were coded by two people to fall into these categories. Categories are not mutually exclusive. Details for each post content type are given in Table 1 along with Cronbach's alpha to indicate intercoder reliability. Cronbach's alpha scores range from 0.972 to 1.00. Summary statistics for all variables are given in Table 2.

## ANALYSIS

As indicated in Table 3, we find that community foundations are less likely to generate Facebook posts than their private or corporate foundation counterparts are. For community foundations, 72 organizations made 664 posts during the study period for an average of 9.22 posts per organization. The 11 private

*Table 1. Post content coding*

| Post Content Type | Description | Coding Scheme | Cronbach's Alpha |
|---|---|---|---|
| organization information | The post shares information about the organization. | 0=no<br>1=yes | 0.9746 |
| other information | The post shares information about something other than the organization (e.g.- community event, news). | 0=no<br>1=yes | 0.9896 |
| question | The post asks a question. | 0=no<br>1=yes | 1.000 |
| request action with post | The post requests user to interact with post. | 0=no<br>1=yes | 0.9927 |
| request other action | The post requests user take action other than interacting with post. | 0=no<br>1=yes | 0.9720 |

*Table 2. Summary statistics*

| Variable | Mean | SD | Min | Max |
|---|---|---|---|---|
| total engagement with post | 72.057 | 371.051 | 0 | 7672 |
| organization information | 0.552 | 0.498 | 0 | 1 |
| other information | 0.820 | 0.385 | 0 | 1 |
| question | 0.147 | 0.354 | 0 | 1 |
| request action with post | 0.032 | 0.176 | 0 | 1 |
| request other action | 0.322 | 0.467 | 0 | 1 |
| post type: status | 0.094 | 0.292 | 0 | 1 |
| post type: link | 0.424 | 0.494 | 0 | 1 |
| post type: photo | 0.421 | 0.494 | 0 | 1 |
| post type: video | 0.061 | 0.239 | 0 | 1 |
| foundation type: community | 0.586 | 0.493 | 0 | 1 |
| foundation type: private | 0.140 | 0.347 | 0 | 1 |
| foundation type: corporate | 0.274 | 0.446 | 0 | 1 |

*Table 3. Number of posts by post type and foundation type*

| | Link | Photo | Status | Video | Total |
|---|---|---|---|---|---|
| community foundation | 293 | 275 | 59 | 37 | 664 |
| community foundation percentage | 44% | 41% | 9% | 6% | 100% |
| private foundation | 77 | 60 | 12 | 10 | 159 |
| private foundation percentage | 48% | 38% | 8% | 6% | 100% |
| corporate foundation | 111 | 142 | 36 | 22 | 311 |
| corporate foundation percentage | 36% | 46% | 12% | 7% | 100% |
| Total | 481 | 477 | 107 | 69 | 1,134 |
| total percentage | 42% | 42% | 9% | 6% | 100% |
| | | | | | |
| Pearson chi2(6)= | 9.979 | | Pr= | 0.126 | |

foundations made 159 posts during the study period for an average of 14.45 posts during the study period and the 23 corporate foundations made 311 posts during the study period for an average of 13.52 posts per organization. This contradicts our prediction that community foundations would have higher Facebook usage.

We also find lower average engagement for all community foundation posts than for private or corporate foundations. Community foundation posts had an average of 11.82 engagements per post while private foundations had an average of 155.21 engagements per post, and corporate foundations had an average of 158.16 engagements per post. As previously stated, engagement includes likes, share, and comments for each post. Engagement rates indicate that private and corporate foundations are much more successful in eliciting stakeholder engagement.

As indicated in Table 3, we did not find significant differences in post types (link, photo, status, video) among foundation types in a chi squared analysis. This indicates that observed frequencies in the data did not significantly deviate from the null hypothesis that foundations would use social media in similar ways. Among all foundations, links and photos were the most popular post type followed by a status without multimedia. Videos were used least frequently. In terms of engagement, multimedia posts with photos and videos were mostly likely to elicit stakeholder engagement for all foundation types. Average total engagement by post type for all foundation types is included in Table 4.

*Table 4. Average total engagement by post type*

| | Community | Private | Corporate |
|---|---|---|---|
| Link | 9.000 | 91.494 | 73.541 |
| Photo | 17.000 | 210.633 | 273.046 |
| Status | 2.661 | 1.167 | 6.556 |
| Video | 10.189 | 498.100 | 91.682 |

Table 5 demonstrates that foundations post different types of content. Slightly more than half of posts for all foundation types included information about the organization. All three types of foundations were likely to post information about something other than the organization though private and corporate foundations were more likely to post this type of information. Private and corporate foundations were also more likely to post questions and less likely to post requests for action than their community foundation counterparts. In line with the predicted outcome, this indicates that community foundations are more likely to use social media as a platform to get people engaged with the organization or some external issue.

## DISCUSSION

In this study, contrary to expectations, we found that private and corporate foundations were more likely to use social media on average than their community foundation counterparts were. We predicted community foundations would be more likely to utilize social media in order to reach diverse stakeholders that might be tied to funding sources. Although community foundations' unique mission lead to this supposition, findings paint a very different picture. However, it makes sense that private and corporate foundations might have a larger social media presence, as they are more likely to have professional staff to manage communications (Obar, Zube and Lampe 2012). Reliance on a single or small number of funding sources also reduces the pressure to spend less on overhead faced by many nonprofits that rely on public support. This reduced pressure may mean that private and corporate foundations can spend more on strategic communications than their publicly supported counterparts can. It is highly likely that community foundations' reliance on multiple funding streams may make them inherently more beholden to the bottom line. Community foundations may find that they need to keep overhead low, as they are subjected to considerable more scrutiny than a family foundation, for example. We also found that private and corporate foundations were more likely to create stakeholder engagement with posts than community foundations. This finding warrants further analysis about how foundations employ social media as part of strategic communications.

*Table 5. Posts by foundation type and content type*

| | Information About Organization | | Other Information | | Question | | Post Action | | Other Action | |
|---|---|---|---|---|---|---|---|---|---|---|
| | No | Yes | No | Yes | No | Yes | No | Yes | No | Yes |
| Community foundation | 295 | 369 | 139 | 525 | 579 | 85 | 637 | 27 | 413 | 251 |
| Private foundation | 69 | 90 | 23 | 136 | 135 | 24 | 155 | 4 | 121 | 38 |
| Corporate foundation | 152 | 159 | 46 | 265 | 255 | 56 | 305 | 6 | 238 | 73 |
| | Pearson chi2(2) = 2.0199 Pr = 0.364 | | Pearson chi2(2) = 7.1914 Pr = 0.027 | | Pearson chi2(2) = 4.6596 Pr = 0.097 | | Pearson chi2(2) = 3.3914 Pr = 0.183 | | Pearson chi2(2) = 25.4866 Pr = 0.000 | |

Finally, we found that community foundations are more likely to use Facebook posts as a call to action than private or corporate foundations, but less likely to have online stakeholder engagement with posts. This finding is puzzling in light community foundation missions, which lend themselves to civic engagement and interaction with community stakeholders more than private or corporate foundation counterparts. This finding warrants further analysis.

## CONCLUSION

Within the larger framework of civil society, the public and private sectors provide spaces for transparency, discourse, and accountability via social media. Foundations serve a special purpose in the voluntary sector. Similar to nonprofits, foundations work in partnership with other community-based organizations to improve local communities. However, foundations also play an intensified role in civil society, similar to government, as they seek to transform society, working in public-private partnership to ameliorate larger scale social problems. High-asset foundations are uniquely positioned in their civic-engagement roles, as they fund and help set the agenda for the programs and services provided by the nonprofit sector. Foundations are fundamental players in the collective work of civil society and offer a potential avenue for improved discourse with stakeholders.

Given Relationship Management Theory, our findings suggest that, on a practical level, foundations should review their communication strategies and assess outcomes. Are they engaging in discourse that results in a response from stakeholders? In other words, are stakeholder exchanges dynamic between organization and stakeholder? Does that response result in engagement with the Facebook post? Individually, foundations can use online commercially available programs to analyze their social media dialogue. Is it working? Are stakeholders responding? Beyond Facebook posts, do calls for action via social media result in stakeholder participation in person? These are questions that can only be answered by the foundations themselves, but hint that social media may offer new ways to assess implementation of organizational strategies.

Civic engagement is fostered by active involvement in social issues. Social media as the civic engagement messenger not only has the potential to prompt action, but also discourse. We sought to assess Facebook as a form of civic engagement development by high-asset foundations. These results provide an important first step for understanding how post content influences user engagement. Further analysis, including regression models that account for organizational and foundation type characteristics is warranted to understand fully the relationship between post content type and user engagement.

Additionally, foundations with differing missions might share their individual findings. For decades, government-funded programs have reported "what works" in their quarterly reports they submit to their funding agency. Foundations have participated in the evolution of "best practices" or "evidence-based practices" through numerous reports published typically by subject area (e.g., best practices in youth employment or independent living). The time is ripe for foundations to begin sharing best practices in social media engagement. How and when can foundations bring communities together via social media sites and what types of posts or content work best for the intended response. Rather than posting the work of the foundation in random posts, foundations can begin to strategically post content with expected results. Measuring and sharing those results are the start of a new paradigm in best practices research and evaluation. Given the findings presented here, further debate about "slacktivism" is also warranted. When are dialogic responses simple responses and when do they produce change or action?

Foundations, government, and the nonprofit sector offer civic engagement opportunities to a new generation of eager social media enthusiasts. Foundation leaders are poised to take a leadership role with social media and improving civic engagement. Continued public-private partnerships can embrace social media as a communications strategy for social change. Employing social media analytics by the foundation, allows leaders and staff to assess targeted best practices in achieving their unique missions.

## REFERENCES

Alan, A., Soskis, B., & Toepler, S. (2012). *Public Philanthropic Partnerships in the U.S.: A Literature Review of Recent Experiences*. Washington, DC: Council on Foundations.

Anheier, H. (2005). *Nonprofit Organizations: Theory, Management and Policy*. New York: Routledge.

Auger, G. A. (2010). Using dialogic website design to encourage effective grantor –grantee Relationships. *Prism, 7*(2). http://praxis.massey.ac.nz/prism_on-line_journ.html

Auger, G. A. (2013). Fostering democracy through social media: Evaluating diametrically opposed nonprofit advocacy organizations' use of Facebook, Twitter, and YouTube. *Public Relations Review, 39*(4), 369–376. DOI: 10.1016/j.pubrev.2013.07.013

Bennett, S. (2014). 86% of charities and nonprofits use Twitter, 71% say social useful for donations. *Social Times*. Retrieved August 5, 2015 from http://www.adweek.com/socialtimes/charity-nonprofit-social-media-study/499579

Bortree, D., & Seltzer, T. (2009). Dialogic strategies and outcomes: An analysis of environmental advocacy groups' Facebook profiles. *Public Relations Review*, *35*, 317-319. 10.1016/j.pubrev.2009.05.002

Bürger, T. (2015). Use of digital advocacy by German nonprofit foundations on Facebook. *Public Relations Review*, *41*(4), 523–525. doi:10.1016/j.pubrev.2015.07.007

Carboni, J. L., & Maxwell, S. P. (2015). Effective social media engagement for nonprofits: What matters? *Journal of Nonprofit and Public Affairs*, *1*(1), 18–28. doi:10.20899/jpna.1.1.18-28

Carboni, J. L., McNeely, C. L., & Maxwell, S. P. (2014). Community Engagement as a Predictor of Higher Education Matriculation. In T. Bryer (Ed.), *National service and volunteerism: Achieving impact in our communities*. Lanham, MD: Lexington Books.

Charles Stewart Mott Foundation. (2015). *Funding interests*. Retrieved from http://www.mott.org/FundingInterests/programs/civilsociety/us July 14, 2015.

Council on Foundations. (2011). *Community foundations: Snapshots of public-philanthropic partnerships*. Washington, DC: Council on Foundations.

Council on Foundations. (2015). *Public-Private Partnerships.* Retrieved from http://www.cof.org/content/public-philanthropic-partnerships

Cruce, T. M., & Moore, J. V. III. (2012). Community Service during the Frist Year of College: What is the Role of Past Behavior? *Journal of College Student Development*, *53*(3), 399–417. doi:10.1353/csd.2012.0038

Dozier, D. M., Grunig, L. A., & Grunig, J. E. (1995). Manager's guide to excellence in public relations and communication management. Mahwah, NJ: Lawrence Erlbaum Associates, Inc.

Duan-Barnett, N., Wangelin, J., & Lamm, H. (2012). Models of Social Change: Community Foundations and Agenda Setting. *The Foundation Review*, *4*(4), 7. doi:10.4087/FOUNDATIONREVIEW-D-12-00030.1

Ehrlich, T. (2000). *Civic Responsibility and Higher Education*. Phoenix, AZ: Orynx Press.

Eikenberry, A. M. (2012). Social networking, learning, and civic engagement: New relationships between professors and students, public administrators and citizens. *Journal of Public Affairs Education*, *3*(18), 449–466.

Facebook. (2015). *How is engagement rate defined?* Retrieved from https://www.facebook.com/help/178043462360087 July 7, 2015.

Falk, S. (2011). The rise of the digital citizen. *Policy Advice and Consulting*, *4*(4), 157–161.

Fernandez, K. M., & Hager, M. A. (2014). Public and private dimensions of grantmaking foundations. *Public Administration Quarterly*, *38*(3), 405–439.

Foundation Center (2010). *Are Foundation Leaders Using Social Media?* Washington, DC: The Foundation Center.

Foundation Center. (2014). *Foundations Today Tutorials.* Retrieved from http://foundationcenter.org/getstarted/tutorials/ft_tutorial/what.html

Foundation Center. (2014). *Infographic: What's trending with foundations and social media.* Retrieved from http://glasspockets.org/glasspockets-gallery/foundations-and-social-media-infographic#sthash.kj7wkbMv.dpuf

Guo, C., & Saxton, G. D. (2014). Tweeting social change: How social media are changing nonprofit advocacy. *Nonprofit and Voluntary Sector Quarterly*.

Hand, L. C., & Ching, B. D. (2011). "You have one friend request": An exploration of power and citizen engagement in local governments' use of social media. *Administrative Theory & Praxis*, *33*(3), 362–382. doi:10.2753/ATP1084-1806330303

Hung, C. F. (2005). Exploring types of organization public relationships and their implications for relationship management in public relations. *Journal of Public Relations Research*, *17*(4), 393–42. doi:10.12071532754xjprr1704_4

Kent, M., & Taylor, M. (1998). Building dialogic relationships through the World Wide Web. *Public Relations Review*, *24*(3), 321–334. doi:10.1016/S0363-8111(99)80143-X

Ledingham, J. (2003). Explicating relationship management as a general theory of public relations. *Journal of Public Relations Research*, *15*(2), 181–198. doi:10.1207/S1532754XJPRR1502_4

Ledingham, J., & Bruning, S. D. (1998). Relationship management in public relations: Dimensions of an organization-public relationship. *Public Relations Review, 24*(1), 55–65. doi:10.1016/S0363-8111(98)80020-9

Ledingham, J., & Bruning, S. D. (2000). *Public relations as relationship management: A relational approach to the study and practice of public relations*. Mahwah, NJ: Lawrence Erlbaum & Associates, Inc.

Lee, Y. H., & Hsieh, G. (2013, April). Does slacktivism hurt activism?: the effects of moral balancing and consistency in online activism. In *Proceedings of the SIGCHI Conference on Human Factors in Computing Systems* (pp. 811-820). ACM. 10.1145/2470654.2470770

Ma, L. (2016). What drives the adoption of social media applications by the public sector? Evidence from local health departments. *International Journal of Public Administration in the Digital Age, 4*(3), 76–93. doi:10.4018/IJPADA.2016100106

Maxwell, S. P., & Carboni, J. L. (2014). Stakeholder communication in Service Implementation Networks: Expanding Relationship Management Theory in the voluntary sector. *International Journal of Nonprofit and Voluntary Sector Marketing*. doi:10.1002/nvsm.1506

Milward, H. B., & Provan, K. G. (2000). Governing the hollow state. *Journal of Public Administration: Research and Theory, 10*(2), 359–379. doi:10.1093/oxfordjournals.jpart.a024273

Milward, H. B., & Provan, K. G. (2003). Managing the Hollow State: Collaboration and contracting. *Public Management Review, 5*(1), 2–18. doi:10.1080/1461667022000028834

Milward, H. B., & Provan, K. G. (2006). *A manager's guide to choosing and using collaborative networks*. IBM Center for the Business of Government.

M+R & NTEN. (2012). *eNonprofit Benchmarks Study: An analysis of online messaging, fundraising, advocacy, social media, and mobile metrics for nonprofit organizations*. Retrieved from http://www.e-benchmarksstudy.com/

M+R & NTEN. (2014). *eNonprofit Benchmarks Study: An analysis of online messaging, fundraising, advocacy, social media, and mobile metrics for nonprofit organizations*. Authors.

M+R & NTEN. (2015). *eNonprofit Benchmarks Study: An analysis of online messaging, fundraising, advocacy, social media, and mobile metrics for nonprofit organizations*. Authors.

O'Reilly, T. (2005) *What is Web 2.0? Design patterns and business models for the next generation of software*. Retrieved from http://www.oreilly.com/pub/a/web2/archive/what-is-web-20.html

Obar, J. A. (2014). Canadian advocacy 2.0: An analysis of social media adoption and perceived affordances by advocacy groups looking to advance activism in Canada. *Canadian Journal of Communication, 39*(2), 211–233. doi:10.22230/cjc.2014v39n2a2678

Obar, J. A., Zube, P., & Lampe, C. (2012). Advocacy 2.0: An analysis of how advocacy groups in the United States perceive and use social media as tools for facilitating civic engagement and collective action. *Journal of Information Policy, 2*, 1–25. doi:10.5325/jinfopoli.2.2012.0001

Pletikosa, C. I., & Michahelles, F. (2013). Online engagement factors on Facebook brand pages. *Social Network Analysis and Mining*, *3*(4), 843–861. doi:10.100713278-013-0098-8

Porter, M., & Kramer, M. (1999). Philanthropy's new agenda: Creating value. *Harvard Business Review*, *77*(6). PMID:10662001

Putnam, R. D. (2001). *Bowling Alone*. New York: Simon and Schuster.

Raeth, P., Smolnik, S., Urbach, N., & Zimmer, C. (2009). Towards assessing the success of social software in corporate environments. *AMCIS 2009 Proceedings*. Retrieved from http://aisel.aisnet.org/amcis2009/662

Ragan Communications and NASDAQ. (2013). *Structuring a social media team*. Raglan Communications.

Reddick, C. G. (2014). Citizens and Mobile Government Adoption: A Comparison of Activities and Uses. *International Journal of Civic Engagement and Social Change*, *1*(1), 13–26. doi:10.4018/ijcesc.2014010102

Reddick, C. G., & Aikins, S. K. (2012). Web 2.0 Technologies and Democratic Governance: Political, Policy and Management Implications. New York, NY: Springer.

Reddick, C. G., & Ponomariov, B. (2013). The Effect of Individuals' Organization Affiliation on their Internet Donations. *Nonprofit and Voluntary Sector Quarterly*, *42*(6), 1197–1223. doi:10.1177/0899764012452670

Saxton, G. D., Niyirora, J. N., Guo, C., & Waters, R. D. (2015). # AdvocatingForChange: The Strategic Use of Hashtags in Social Media Advocacy. *Advances in Social Work*, *16*(1), 154–169.

Saxton, G. D., & Waters, R. D. (2014). What do stakeholder like on Facebook? examining public reactions to nonprofit organizations' informational, promotional, and community-building messages. *Journal of Public Relations Research*, *26*(3), 280–299. doi:10.1080/1062726X.2014.908721

Skocpol, T., & Fiorina, M. (Eds.). (1999). *Civic engagement in American democracy*. Brookings Institution Press.

Sweetser, K. D., & Lariscy, R. W. (2008). Candidates make good friends: An analysis of candidates' uses of Facebook. *International Journal of Strategic Communication*, *2*(3), 175–198. doi:10.1080/15531180802178687

Treem, J. W., & Leonardi, P. M. (2012). Social Media Use in Organizations: Exploring the Affordances of Visibility, Editability, Persistence, and Association. *Communication Yearbook*, *36*, 143-189. Available at SSRN: http://ssrn.com/abstract=2129853

United Nations. (2013). *The role of philanthropic organizations in the post-2015 development agenda setting*. New York: United Nations.

Vogt, S., Förster, B., & Kabst, R. (2014). Social Media and e-Participation: Challenges of Social Media for Managing Public Projects. [IJPADA]. *International Journal of Public Administration in the Digital Age*, *1*(3), 85–105. doi:10.4018/ijpada.2014070105

Wall Street Journal. (2015). *Buzz, engagement, and reach performances of the Wall Street Journal on social media*. Retrieved from http://www.talkwalker.com/en/academy/academy/industries/media-publishers/social-media-analytics-for-the-wall-street-journal/

Wallace, C. (2012). Can information and communications technology enhance social quality? *The International Journal of Social Quality, 2*(2), 98–117. doi:10.3167/IJSQ.2012.020207

Waters, R. D. (2008). Applying relationship management theory to the fundraising process for individual donors. *Journal of Communication Management, 12*(1), 73–87. doi:10.1108/13632540810854244

Waters, R. D. (2009). Measuring stewardship in public relations: A test exploring impact on the fundraising relationship. *Public Relations Review, 35*(2), 113–119. doi:10.1016/j.pubrev.2009.01.012

Waters, R. D. (2011). Redefining stewardship: Examining how Fortune 100 organizations use stewardship with virtual stakeholders. *Public Relations Review, 37*(2), 129–136. doi:10.1016/j.pubrev.2011.02.002

Waters, R. D., Burnett, E., Lamm, A., & Lucas, J. (2009). Engaging stakeholders through social networking: How nonprofit organizations are using Facebook. *Public Relations Review, 35*(2), 102–106. doi:10.1016/j.pubrev.2009.01.006

Waters, R. D., & Feneley, K. L. (2013). Virtual stewardship in the age of new media: Have nonprofit organizations' moved beyond Web 1.0 strategies? *International Journal of Nonprofit and Voluntary Sector Marketing, 18*(3), 216–230. doi:10.1002/nvsm.1469

Waters, R. D., & Jamal, J. Y. (2011). Tweet, tweet, tweet: A content analysis of nonprofit organizations' Twitter updates. *Public Relations Review, 37*(3), 321–324. doi:10.1016/j.pubrev.2011.03.002

Weare, C., Loges, W. E., & Oztas, N. (2007). Email effects on the structure of local associations: A social network analysis. *Social Science Quarterly, 88*(1), 222–243. doi:10.1111/j.1540-6237.2007.00455.x

Westcott, S. (2007). Face time: Charities flock to social-networking Web sites to reach out to new people, spark discussion, and help raise money. *The Chronicle of Philanthropy, 19*(7).

Wuthnow, R. (1998). *Loose Connections*. Boston: Harvard University Press.

# Chapter 3
# In Prosperity Prepare for Adversity:
## Use of Social Media for Nonprofit Fundraising in Times of Disaster

**Aya Okada**
*Kanazawa University, Japan*

**Yu Ishida**
*Miyagi University, Japan*

**Naoto Yamauchi**
*Osaka University, Japan*

## ABSTRACT

*When a disaster strikes, nonprofit organizations face the need to mobilize resources as quickly as possible in a limited time frame. Given its characteristics to instantly spread information to masses of people, social media is considered one of the most effective ways for nonprofits to publicize opportunities to take voluntary actions. Despite the envisioned use, little has been examined about the effectiveness of social media in encouraging people to give. This chapter takes the case of earthquake, tsunami, and nuclear threat that struck Japan in 2011 to examine whether the use of social media was effective in nonprofit fundraising. Analyzing data collected in an original online survey, the authors find that the use of social media both before and after the disaster has a positive impact on the amount of donations that nonprofits raise. Use of social media during non-disaster times is the key for successful fundraising in times of disaster.*

DOI: 10.4018/978-1-5225-5966-5.ch003

## 1. INTRODUCTION

Nonprofit organizations today are one of the key actors in disaster relief, response, and reconstruction (Kapucu *et al.*, 2011). Not only are they active as first responders, but also essential organizations that facilitate recovery while working closely with organizations in both public and private sectors (Kapucu, 2007).

Disasters are times when nonprofit organizations face the need to mobilize resources as quickly as possible in a limited time frame. Once a nonprofit decides to engage in response activities, the organization uses multiple communication channels to send out information to mobilize people for financial donations, in-kind giving, and/or volunteering. These opportunities become chances for people willing to help those suffering from the tragedy to take actions. Solnit (2009) described the emergence of such highly motivated population as "A Paradise Built in Hell." Nonprofit organizations play an important role in transforming the desires of these people into actual actions (Okada & Yamauchi, 2014).

Given its characteristic to instantly spread information to masses of people, social media is considered one of the most effective ways for nonprofit organizations to publicize opportunities of voluntary actions in critical situations. Social media refers to "interactive online technologies and practices that people use to share opinions, insights, experiences, and perspectives with each other" (Haddow & Haddow, 2014, p.242). Examples include Facebook, Twitter, and YouTube, just to name a few. Mayfield (2006) sees participation, openness, conversation, community, and connectedness as key features that distinguish social media from traditional media.

Despite the envisioned use, little has been documented about how nonprofit organizations use social media in times of disaster to mobilize the public towards voluntary actions. Much less known is whether the use of social media is effective in encouraging people to give or to volunteer. In this paper, we take the case of earthquake, tsunami, and nuclear threat that struck Japan n March 11, 2011 to examine the effectiveness of social media in nonprofit fundraising. To what extent did nonprofits use social media to mobilize the public towards voluntary actions? Did the use of social media change overtime from response to recovery phase? More importantly, was the use of social media effective in encouraging people to make financial contributions? We analyze these questions using an original data collected through an online survey and find that use of social media both *before* and *after* the disaster has a positive impact on the amount of donations that nonprofits raise. The paper thus argues that use of social media during non-disaster times is the key for successful fundraising in times of disaster.

The paper is organized as follows. We first review literature related to impact of nonprofits' social media use in times of disaster and clarify the contributions of this paper to the existing body of knowledge. The paper then draws three hypotheses on effectiveness of social media in the aftermath of disasters from existing studies. Following a brief description of the context of the study - the 2011 Japan disaster – we elaborate the survey design and present the analysis results. The paper concludes with implications drawn from the findings and future research agenda.

## 2. SOCIAL MEDIA, DISASTERS, AND NONPROFITS

As an emerging new tool, social media has attracted much attention in both disaster studies and nonprofit studies. In this section, we review the literature in these bodies of work and highlight our contributions.

## 2.1. Social Media in Disaster Studies

Literature on disasters have explored wide range of possibilities that utilization of social media might bring about in disaster situations. Studies on crisis communication, in particular, highlight the potential use of social media in emergencies (Hughes & Palen, 2009). Assuming the effectiveness of social media to share and spread information in the aftermath of disasters, both scholarship and practitioners have identified tips for its successful usage as part of organizational communication strategies (e.g. Haddow & Haddow, 2014; Veil *et al.*, 2011). Social media enable all types of organizations engaged in relief activities to put out information instantly to the public, therefore giving earliest possible warnings and collecting the most up-to-date information from the ground. These new tools are also used to share information and to facilitate communication as well as collaboration among different types of organizations engaged in response activities (Gao *et al.*, 2011).

Studies also document and analyze the use of social media in actual cases of disasters. Researches conducted in Japan, for example, examine wide use of social media in the aftermath of the 2011 disaster (see Section 4 for the details of the disaster). Sekiya (2012) analyzed the purposes of Twitter use after the 2011 disaster. Kawai and Fujishiro (2013) analyzed how people used Twitter to obtain disaster-related information, and Yamamoto *et al.* (2012) examined the influence of Twitter use on people's perception of "safety" and "anxiety" following the disaster.

## 2.2. Social Media in Nonprofit Studies

Ever since the introduction of social media, nonprofit organizations have looked into how they might adopt and utilize these tools. Given such trend, researchers have examined various ways for nonprofits to use social media. For example, Lovejoy and Saxton (2012) examined Twitter utilization among 100 largest nonprofit organizations in the United States and identified three types of Tweet functions: information, community (e.g. giving recognition and thanks, acknowledgment of current and local events), and action (e.g. promoting an event, donation appeal, selling a product, call for volunteers and employees, lobbying and advocacy, encouragement to join another site, to vote for organization, and to learn how to help). Svensson *et al.* (2015) particularly highlighted the use of social media for nonprofits to disseminate information, to build engagement, and to facilitate action. Briones *et al.* (2011) conducted a case study of American Red Cross to document the use of social media to build strong and lasting relationships with potential supporters.

Not all nonprofits are in favor of adopting and facilitating the use of social media. Studies have identified obstacles that prevent nonprofit organizations from utilizing these new tools. In the context of New Zealand, Zorn *et al.* (2013) found that nonprofits have limited familiarity with the use of social media. Size and complexity of the organization may hinder its adoption among nonprofits, as well as age-based digital divides (Eimhjellen *et al.*, 2013). Curtis *et al.*, (2010) further elaborated that organizational structure, such as lack of independent public relations department, as potential obstacle. As Briones *et al.* (2011) noted, the obstacle may simply be lack of staff and time. Given these challenges, Nah and Saxton (2013) highlighted the following key drivers of organizational adoption and use of social media: organizational strategies, capacities, governance features, and external environment. Waters *et al.* (2009) further discussed that careful planning is needed for effective use of social media in nonprofit organizations. While strategic use of social media, such as targeting audience and spending more time managing the sites, facilitates connections between nonprofits and stakeholders (Hu & Shi,

2017), more financial investments in social media may in some cases result in less strategic use of these communication tools (Sihi, 2017).

Once a nonprofit organization decides to adopt social media as part of its communication strategy, the next question is to think about how best to utilize the new tools to achieve their goals. Examining 145 advocacy organizations in the United States, Guo and Saxton (2017) found that nonprofits who send out information more frequently and those that join more conversations online have a better chance of attracting more attention among social media users. Another tactic is to carefully select the content of information and frame them in a certain way, as Guo and Saxton (2014) showed on nonprofit advocacy. Auger (2014) went further to test what types of messages are effective. The study conducted a rhetorical analysis on Tweets made by nonprofits and found that positively framed messages tend to persuade supporters to take actions for the cause that these organizations advanced. In the context of the United Kingdom, Lucas (2016) argued that adopting strategies such as encouraging supporters to gain public recognition for their action or presenting efficacy of one's support, facilitates social media users to share nonprofits' work to their friends and peers.

## 2.3. Nonprofits' Social Media Use in Disaster Contexts

In what ways can nonprofit organizations use social media in times of disaster? Studies on crisis communication encourage nonprofits to utilize these new communication channels as they are today perceived as a credible source of information. For example, Austin *et al.* (2012) argued that during a crisis, people use social media for insider information and to check in with family and friends.

Studies suggest that using social media as a medium of communication may also bring benefits to nonprofit organizations. Schultz *et al.* (2011) found that use of social media enhances organizational reputation, encourages people to talk more about the crisis, and facilitates people's willingness to react to the crisis (e.g. to boycott). Confirming these findings, Utz *et al.* (2013) found that Facebook and Twitter increase an organization's reputation than traditional media. Social media also allows nonprofit organizations to communicate directly with the public, without going through interpretation of journalists in traditional media (Pavlik, 2001).

Studies also imply that nonprofits should not simply use social media, but be strategic about matching messages to its characteristics. Liu *et al.* (2011), for example, highlighted the importance of strategically matching information form and source among multiple communication streams in responding to crisis. Strategies of media mix may also be the key to successful use of social media. Waters and Tindall (2011) discussed the importance of being strategic in using multiple communication tools including mass media such as televisions and newspapers. They analyzed charitable giving in response to the December 2004 Asian tsunami and found that media coverage impacted traditional giving, i.e. donations made directly to nonprofit organizations, as well as e-philanthropy through third party outlets such as Amazon.com and eBay auctions. They encouraged nonprofit organizations to strategically use traditional mass media as well as digital media in approaching the public.

## 2.4. Contribution of This Study

This study joins the body of literature looking at nonprofits' use of social media in disaster times while making two key contributions. First, we bring in the case of triple disasters of earthquake, tsunami, and nuclear threat that struck Japan in 2011. Little has been studied about nonprofits' use of social media in countries outside North American and European contexts. As we discuss in section four, this particular disaster was the first large-scale disaster that Japan experienced with a wide-spread use of social media. We thus believe that the case is worth exploring in detail to draw implications for regions that face similar risks.

Second, we move beyond simple documentation of how nonprofits use social media, and statistically examine its effectiveness in encouraging people to give. Most studies that look into the effectiveness of social media, as we discuss in the next section, have been limited to case studies. We believe that findings from analysis using quantitative methodology will add to these rich set of descriptive studies.

## 3. USE OF SOCIAL MEDIA IN FUNDRAISING: HYPOTHESES

Among multiple purposes that nonprofit organizations aim to achieve using social media, this paper focuses on fundraising. Upon a decision to engage in disaster relief and response, nonprofit organizations face the need to secure sufficient financial resources to implement activities. To begin with, nonprofits today operate in an environment where securing financial resources and achieving financial stability is a huge challenge. Nonprofits are struggling through economic downturns and cuts in government funding (Burt & Taylor, 2003; Hackler & Saxton, 2007).

### 3.1. Hypotheses

How does using social media contribute to fundraising efforts of nonprofit organizations in times of disaster? In this section, we draw three hypotheses to test in the context of Japan from studies that examined the effectiveness of social media on disaster fundraising.

First of all, several studies to date have found that social media use is *in general* effective. For example, a detailed case study by Brengarth *et al.* (2015) found Facebook as useful tool in selling T-shirts for donation during a wildfire crisis. Similarly, Adler and Carpenter (2015) documented the effectiveness of Facebook in peer-to-peer fundraising campaign, and Muralidharan *et al.* (2011) found its effectiveness in raising funds for relief activities in the aftermath of the 2010 Haiti Earthquake. Saxton and Wang (2014) explained that *social network effect* is what makes Facebook an effective tool for fundraising: "organisations' fans reaching expanding circles of online friends in their own social networks, which ultimately increases charitable contributions (pp.862-863)." Saxton and Guo (2014) called such expanding scope of influence *social media capital*, and argued that nonprofits should target stakeholders in their communication strategies to increase such social capital. Given these findings, we draw and test the following hypotheses using variables that simply capture whether an organization uses Facebook and/or Twitter (named "use of Facebook/Twitter" in our dataset).

**Hypothesis 1:** Use of social media is effective in nonprofit fundraising in times of disaster.

Second, simply sending out information through social media may not enable the organization to use these innovative tools to its full potential. Being strategic about *when* to use social media may also be a key in encouraging people to give. Our second and third hypotheses thus go beyond simple usage of social media to *timing* of such use. To meet the emerging needs and to take advantage of rising interests towards the disaster, nonprofit organizations often begin asking for donations immediately after a particular disaster strikes. In the wildfire case, the first social media message to raise money was sent in less than 24 hours after the fire had surrounded houses (Brengarth *et al.*, 2015). Similarly, 82 percent of the nonprofits under study were using Facebook to seek for donations within two weeks after the initial shake in Haiti (Muralidharan *et al.*, 2011). We thus draw the following hypothesis using a variable that represents Facebook/Twitter use immediately after the disaster (labeled "use of Facebook/Twitter after 3.11" in our dataset).

**Hypothesis 2:** Use of social media is effective in nonprofit fundraising when used *immediately after* the disaster.

A related hypothesis is on continuous use of social media *before* and *after* the disaster. One can assume that if a nonprofit had used Facebook/Twitter to encourage people to make donations, "friends" or "followers" of the organizations may be *educated* before the disaster to take action immediately after the event. We test the following hypothesis three using a variable that captures continuous usage of social media before and after the event (labeled "use of Facebook/Twitter before and after 3.11" in our dataset).

**Hypothesis 3:** Use of social media is effective in nonprofit fundraising when used continuously both *before* and *after* the disaster.

## 4. CONTEXT: 2011 JAPAN DISASTER

On March 11, 2011, a magnitude 9.0 earthquake struck off the coast of Northeastern Japan. This historic earthquake generated a series of tsunami along a coastline of 450 km, reaching as high as 40.5 meters in some locations (Cabinet Office of Japan, 2011). These tsunamis triggered failure of reactors' cooling system at Fukushima Daiichi Nuclear Power Plant, leading to a release of radioactive materials. These triple disasters came to be known as the 2011 Japan disaster or 3.11, causing 15,894 deaths, and 2,546 missing as of December 8, 2015 (National Police Agency of Japan, 2017).

In response to the catastrophe, people all across Japan stood up to take voluntary actions for those suffering from the tragedy. A survey by the Japan NPO Research Association found that 75.6 percent of the respondents took some sort of voluntary actions including making donations, purchasing products of affected regions, sending/delivering goods to affected regions, and volunteering (see Figure 1). In another post-disaster survey by the Cabinet Office of Japan (2012), 59.5 percent of the respondents had taken some sort of voluntary actions in the aftermath of the 2011 triple disasters.

The irony of studying disasters is that we cannot assess or test what works and what doesn't until a disaster actually happens. Because the 2011 Tohoku disaster was the first large-scale disaster that Japan experienced under a wide-spread use of social media, we believe studying this case is worthwhile in drawing lessons for future disasters not only for Japan but also for other societies facing similar risks. Figure 2 shows the percentage of social media users as of March 2011. The result shows that at the time of the disaster, 75.2 percent of the respondents had access to social networking services such as mixi[1] and Facebook, and 50 percent to Twitter.

In the more recent years, the number of social media users are increasing constantly. According to the most recent survey by the Ministry of Internal Affairs and Communications (2017), percentage of the Japanese population using social media including Facebook, Twitter, and LINE increased from 41.4

*Figure 1. Voluntary actions taken in the aftermath of the 2011 disaster*
*Source: Japan NPO Research Association (2012).*

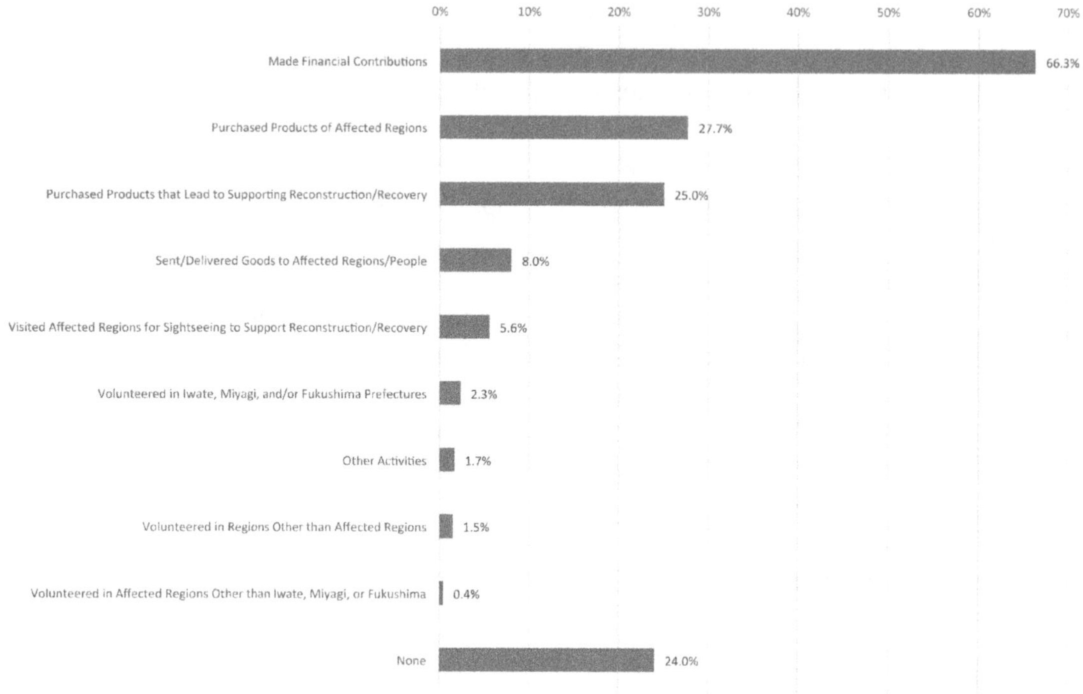


*Figure 2. Percentage of social media users in March 2011*
*Source: Ministry of Internal Affairs and Communications (2011).*

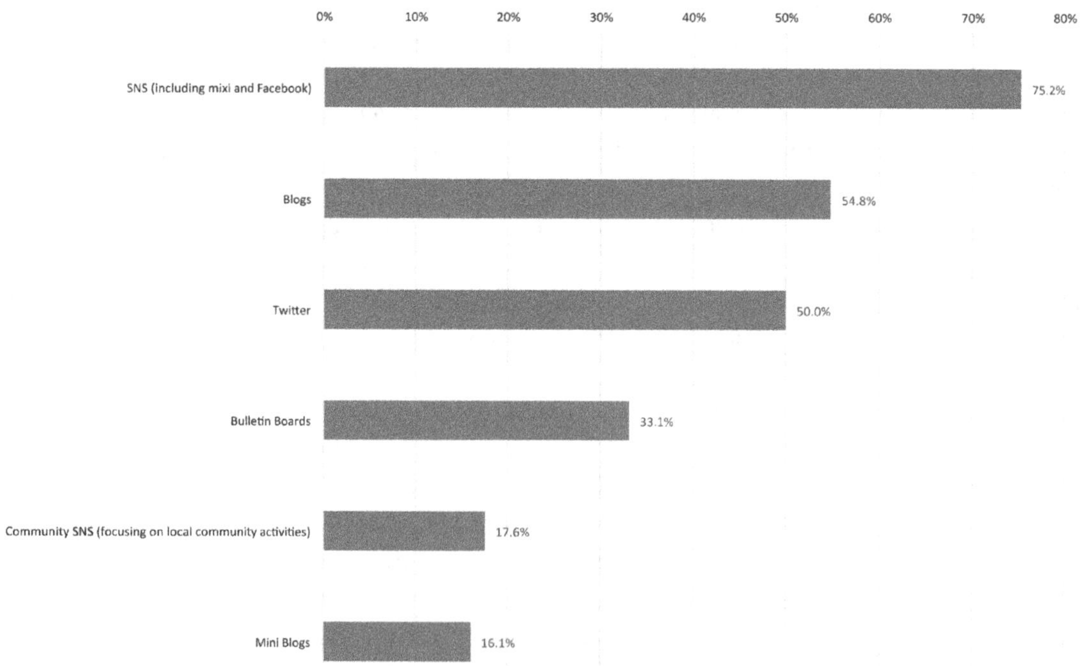

percent in 2012 to 71.2 in 2016[2]. Despite the image that social media are for younger generations, those in their 40s and 50s are also active social media users today (see Figure 3). Assuming that these conditions represent a global trend of expanding use of social media, we expect our findings to have implications for all nonprofit organizations with the possibility of facing crisis situations across the globe.

## 5. SURVEY DESIGN

In order to examine how nonprofit organizations used social media to mobilize the people towards voluntary actions after the 2011 Japan disaster, we developed a dataset collected through an original online survey. The objective of this survey was to understand how nonprofit organizations disseminated information about opportunities of voluntary actions[3].

Target organizations were selected using a list of nonprofit organizations that made active relief efforts in responding to this particular disaster. We first referred to a list of organizations participating in Japan Civil Network for Disaster Relief in the East Japan (JCN). JCN is "a broad coalition of Japanese NPOs, NGOs, CBOs[4], and private enterprises providing disaster relief, formed in order to support those affected by the March 11, 2011 East Japan Earthquake" (JCN, 2014). We believe that member organizations of JCN are the best possible list of nonprofit organizations that were active in responding to the 2011 Japan disaster. From this list, we identified nonprofit organizations that have one of the following legal status in Japan: "specified nonprofit corporation," "public interest incorporated association," "public interest incorporated foundation," "general incorporated association," and "general incorporated foundation." A request for survey participation was sent to 434 organizations whose active email address was identifiable by the research team. Included in the message was a link to the survey constructed using SurveyMonkey.

*Figure 3. Use of social media across generations in 2016*
*Source: Ministry of Internal Affairs and Communications (2017).*

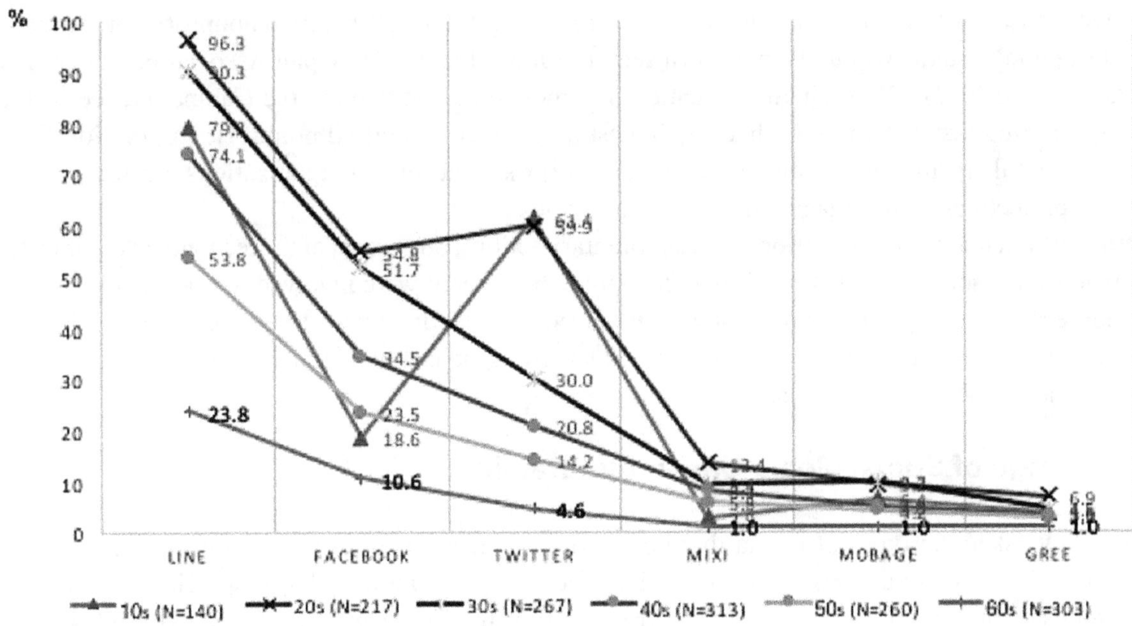

We opened the site between February 3, 2014 and March 24, 2014. A total of 143 organizations provided answers, resulting in a collection rate of 32.9 percent.

Table 1 lists questions in the survey that we use for analysis in this paper. While not examined in detail in this paper, the survey also asked nonprofit organizations reasons for choosing a specific communication media, emphasized message(s) in disseminated information, as well as perceived effectiveness of used communication channels[5].

Using the dataset developed from survey responses, we test the aforementioned hypotheses. Following an analysis of how nonprofit organizations used social media to mobilize the public towards voluntary actions, we employ ordered probit models to identify relationships between usage of social media and performance of mobilization. We estimate the impact of social media use on fundraising outcomes after controlling institutional attributes.

## 6. ANALYSIS RESULTS

### 6.1. Basic Statistics

Among the 143 nonprofit organizations that responded to our survey, 80 percent had the legal status of "specified nonprofit corporation," registered under the 1998 Act on Promotion of Specified Non-profit Activities (for details, see Pekkanen, 2000). Twenty percent had the status of "public interest corporation", including "general incorporated association" and "public interest incorporated association." These two legal status were distinguished following the Public Interest Corporation Reform in December 2008.

Looking at the respondent organizations by location of main office, we find that 47 percent were based in Kanto region, in and around the capital Tokyo. Following Kanto was the three most affected prefectures in Tohoku region, which accounted for 32 percent: Iwate prefecture (10 percent), Miyagi prefecture (13 percent), and Fukushima prefecture (9 percent).

We believe our sample decently represents nonprofit organizations that were active in responding to damages caused by the 2011 triple disasters. In terms of legal status, "specified nonprofit corporation" is the most popular status within the nonprofit sector in Japan today (The Japan Association of Charitable Organizations, 2012). With regard to location, the most recent survey by the Cabinet Office of Japan (2015) reported that Tokyo by far had the largest number of "specified nonprofit corporations" (19.1 percent of total organizations nationwide). It is no surprise that several organizations located within the affected prefectures were engaged in response activities[6].

Turning attention to mobilization towards voluntary actions, 88 percent of the respondent organizations had made some sort of efforts to mobilize the public. 63 percent were involved in fundraising, while 64 percent recruited volunteers. 54 percent were involved in collecting goods to be sent to affected regions. 37 percent of the organizations were engaged in soliciting other types of activities and 12 percent did not make any mobilization efforts.

### 6.2. Change of Social Media Use in Fundraising

The survey asked the types of media that nonprofit organizations used to transmit information about opportunities of voluntary actions. Figure 4 lists the top 12 media used by nonprofit organizations to raise funds during the first three months after the initial shake on March 11, 2011. We find that many

*Table 1. Questions asked in the survey*

<table>
<tr><td rowspan="5">Types of Solicited Voluntary Actions</td><td>Financial Giving</td></tr>
<tr><td>Volunteer Recruitment</td></tr>
<tr><td>In-Kind Giving</td></tr>
<tr><td>Did Not Solicit Voluntary Actions</td></tr>
<tr><td>Others</td></tr>
<tr><td rowspan="24">Medium/Communication Channels Used for Fundraising (multiple selection)<br>* Nonprofits were asked to answer this question for the following five time periods: before the 2011 Japan disaster, first three months (March to June 2011), second three months (July to September 2011), between first six months and the first anniversary (October 2011 to March 2012), between first and second anniversaries (April 2012 to March 2013).</td><td>Organizational Website</td></tr>
<tr><td>Organizational Newsletters and Magazines</td></tr>
<tr><td>Listserv</td></tr>
<tr><td>Flyers and Posters</td></tr>
<tr><td>Organizational Blogs</td></tr>
<tr><td>Held Events</td></tr>
<tr><td>Citizens Media</td></tr>
<tr><td>Facebook</td></tr>
<tr><td>Twitter</td></tr>
<tr><td>LINE</td></tr>
<tr><td>Other Internet Use</td></tr>
<tr><td>Television (Articles)</td></tr>
<tr><td>Television (Commercials)</td></tr>
<tr><td>Television (Others)</td></tr>
<tr><td>Radio (Articles)</td></tr>
<tr><td>Radio (Commercials)</td></tr>
<tr><td>Radio (Others)</td></tr>
<tr><td>Newspaper (Articles)</td></tr>
<tr><td>Newspaper (Advertisement)</td></tr>
<tr><td>Newspaper (Others)</td></tr>
<tr><td>Magazine (Articles)</td></tr>
<tr><td>Magazine (Advertisement)</td></tr>
<tr><td>Magazine (Others)</td></tr>
<tr><td>Other Media</td></tr>
<tr><td rowspan="5">Amount of Funds Raised (in 5 levels)</td><td>1 to 1 million Japanese Yen</td></tr>
<tr><td>1 million to 10 million Japanese Yen</td></tr>
<tr><td>10 million to 100 million Japanese Yen</td></tr>
<tr><td>100 million to 500 million Japanese Yen</td></tr>
<tr><td>500 million Japanese Yen and over</td></tr>
</table>

organizations tended use "in-house" media that the organization can use rather freely and easily, such as organizational website, newsletters and listserv. Looking at use of social media during the first three months after the disaster, we learn that Twitter was used by 27.3 percent and Facebook was used by 25.0 percent of the sample organizations.

How did the use of these different types of media change over time, from relief, recovery, to reconstruction phases? Figure 5 shows the rate of change observed in the usage of respective media, considering its usage before the disaster as the basis. Media are listed from high to low rate of change observed between the first and second anniversaries of the disaster. We find that "organizational website" and "organizational newsletters and magazines," both with high rate of use before the disaster, continued to be used by many organizations in the aftermath of the disaster. The rate of increase from relief to reconstruction phases was about 10 percent.

"Newspaper (Articles)", "Twitter" and "Organizational Blogs" showed the most rapid increase in usage during the relief period, within three months after the disaster. The rate of change was 50 percent, 33 percent, and 27 percent, respectively. Usage of "Facebook", "Twitter" and "Television (News)" increased rapidly between the first and second anniversaries of the disaster, during the reconstruction phase. We find that during this period, some organizations began to use media that they had not used before the disaster. For instance, while only 22.7 percent of the respondent organizations had used Facebook for fundraising before the disaster, the number almost doubled to 40.9 percent by the second anniversary.

Also worth noting is the decline of usage rate in several media around the second three months period (July to September 2011). Usage rate of "Facebook" "Events" and "Televisions (News)" increased rapidly again by the first anniversary. Rate of usage of several media dropped yet again by the second

*Figure 4. Media used during the first three months for fundraising*[7]

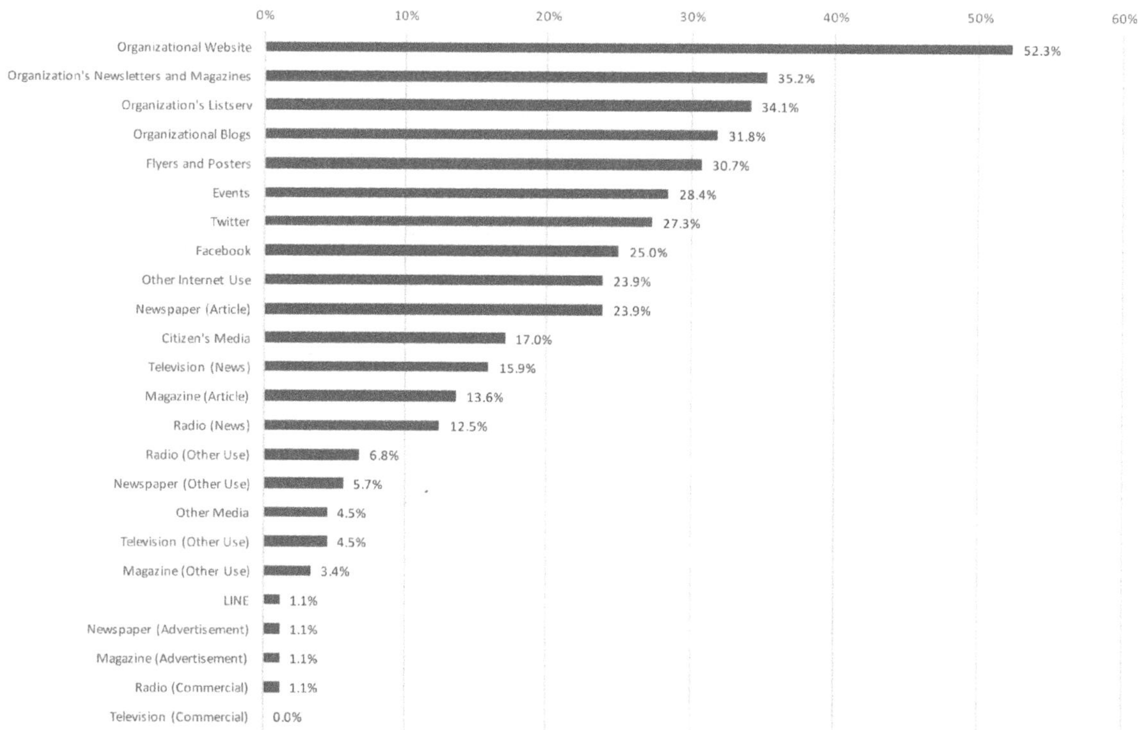

*Figure 5. Rate of change in use of respective media after the disaster (basis: media usage before the disaster)*

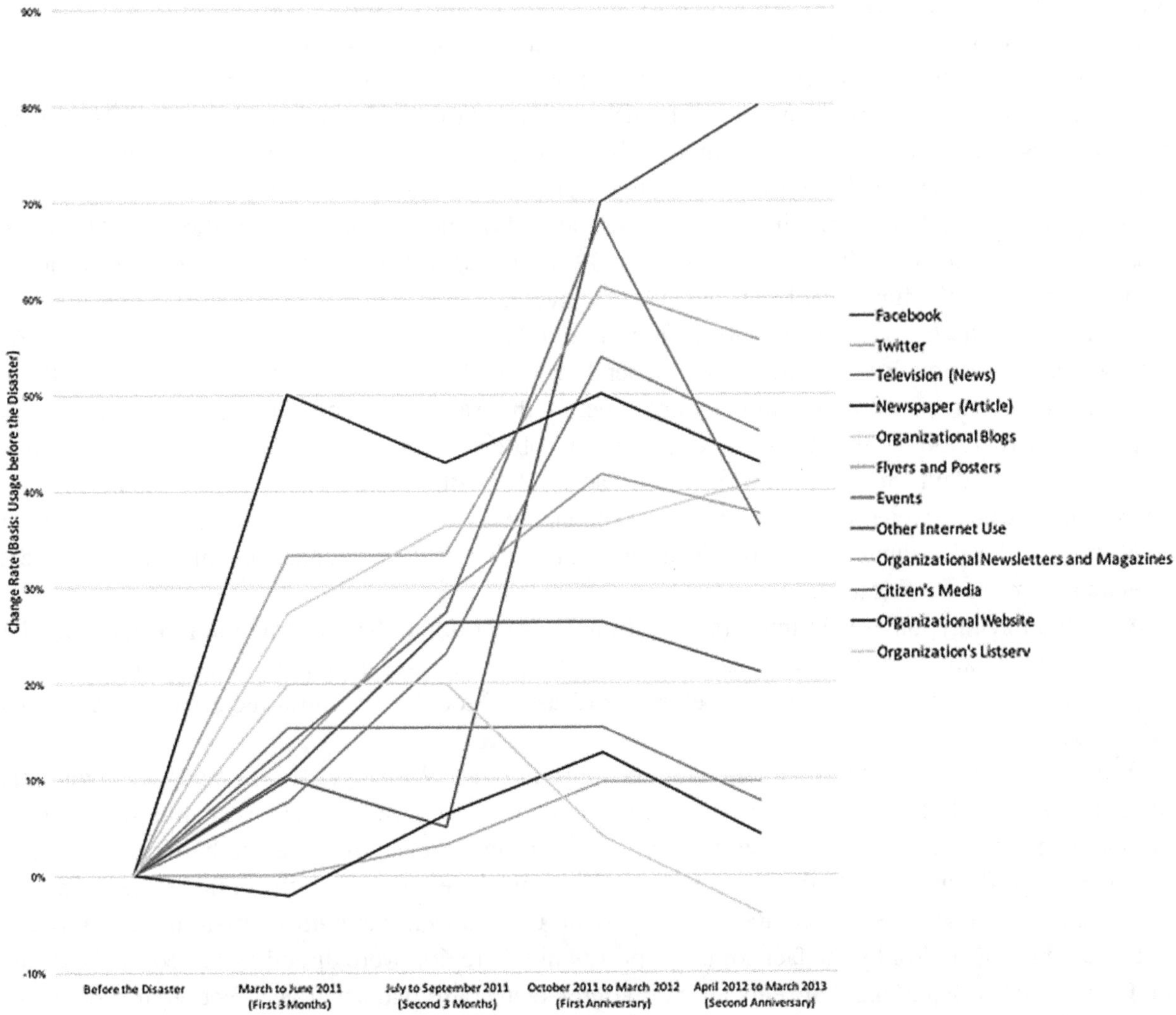


anniversary. There is a possibility that fundraising efforts had calmed down after a year, with the initial round of donations coming to an end.

Summarizing the changes of social media use, we find that Facebook experienced the largest increase through relief, recovery, and reconstruction phases. The number of organizations that used Facebook increased moderately during the first three months and decreased slightly during the second three months. The rate then jumped towards the first anniversary and continued to increase as affected regions carried forward various reconstruction efforts. Changes in the use of Twitter were slightly different. As noted before, the use of Twitter increased by about 30 percent during the relief period. It did not increase during the second three months, but jumped again by another 30 percent towards the first anniversary. Interestingly, usage of Twitter has declined slightly towards the second anniversary.

## 6.3. Effectiveness of Social Media in Fundraising

As shown on Figure 5, the number of nonprofit organizations that used Facebook and Twitter increased over time in the aftermath of the 2011 Japan disaster. Was the use of social media effective in achieving the objective of raising funds? In this section, we show the results of multiple regression models.

Our dependent variable is the amount of funds raised. As shown in Table 1, we had asked responding organizations to choose the amount of funds raised using five categories. Given the available sample size, we have re-categorized these five into three categories for analysis in estimation models: under one million Japanese Yen (approximately 10 thousand USD), one million to 100 million Yen (10-1,000 thousand USD), and over 100 million Yen (over 1,000 thousand USD). We apply the ordered probit models to estimate the function of this dependent variable.

Table 2 lists these variables with its definition and descriptive statistics. We were able to use 69 observations for estimation. Looking at the dependent variable, or the amount of funds raised, 30 observations or 43 percent of these samples were under 10 thousand USD, followed by 25 observations or 38 percent in 10-1,000 thousand USD category, and 13 observations or 19 percent raised over 1 million USD. For independent variables, we use "use of Facebook/Twitter" as well as "use of in-house media." To examine the effectiveness of timing of use, we break these variables into before and after the disaster on March 11. We also input legal status, location of office, years since foundation[8], and annual current revenue as control variables.

With the three hypotheses in mind (see Section 3), we examine three estimation models. Model 1 includes only variables on organizational attributes. Model 2 analyzes estimates on use of in-house media, which majority of the sample used before the disaster. Model 3 examines the effect of Facebook/Twitter use.

Table 3 presents the results of estimated fundraising outcomes. With regard to effects of organizational attributes, we find that the amount raised by "specified nonprofit corporations"[9] is smaller than organizations with other legal status. Having its main office in three prefectures affected by the disaster was negatively significant, but only in the base model. This may be explained by the unfavorable economic environment of these three prefectures in comparison to organizations with its main office in Tokyo metropolitan area, and/or by the fact some nonprofits in this region were directly affected by the disaster. Our estimates also found that years after obtaining legal status had negative effect on the amount of funds raised after the disaster. In other words, the longer the organization is in operation, the less money they raise. This analysis result was rather counter-intuitive, as one would imagine that an organization would obtain more trust among the public and thus be an attractive destination for people's donation in times of disasters. Findings from prior studies in Japan may help explain this result. Studies have found that organizations operating for longer term in Japan tend to strengthen its financing through development of program-based revenue, with a decrease in percentage of income from commissioned projects or subsidiary projects of central and local governments (Ishida, 2008; JILPT, 2007). We also find that the outcome of fundraising is significantly smaller for organizations with smaller current revenue size, particularly when compared against organizations with annual revenue of 1,000 thousand USD and over . This shows a clear scale merit. In order to raise funds, nonprofit organizations must invest resources.

Our estimates reveal that social media use is effective for nonprofit fundraising, supporting hypothesis one on overall usage of social media. The analyses also reveal several other findings. First, we find that Facebook/Twitter use *after* the disaster, referring to the first three months after disaster, may have a positive impact on the amount of money raised, as shown in model 3 (at ten percent significance level).

*Table 2. Definition and descriptive statistics of variables*

| Variable | Variable Type | Definition of Variable | Obs. | Mean | Std. Dev. | Min. | Max. |
|---|---|---|---|---|---|---|---|
| Outcome of fundraising | category | under 10 thousand USD, 10-1,000 thousand USD, 1,000 thousand USD and over | 69 | 1.75 | 0.76 | 1 | 3 |
| Legal status | dummy | Specified Nonprofit Corporation=1, Public Interest Corporation=0 | 69 | 0.74 | 0.44 | 0 | 1 |
| Duration after obtaining legal status | count | years | 69 | 11.88 | 20.30 | 1 | 109 |
| Current revenue: low | dummy | Under 10 thousand USD | 69 | 0.30 | 0.46 | 0 | 1 |
| Current revenue: middle | dummy | 10-1,000 thousand USD | 69 | 0.38 | 0.49 | 0 | 1 |
| Current revenue: high | dummy | 1,000 thousand USD and over | 69 | 0.32 | 0.47 | 0 | 1 |
| Location of office | dummy | 3.11 affected area=1, otherwise=0 | 69 | 0.29 | 0.46 | 0 | 1 |
| Use of in-house media: neither before nor after 3.11 | dummy | Yes=1, no=0: Reference group | 69 | 0.20 | 0.41 | 0 | 1 |
| Use of in-house media: only before the disaster | dummy | Yes=1, no=0 | 69 | 0.26 | 0.44 | 0 | 1 |
| Use of in-house media: only after 3.11 | dummy | Yes=1, no=0 | 69 | 0.14 | 0.35 | 0 | 1 |
| Use of in-house media: both before and after 3.11 | dummy | Yes=1, no=0 | 69 | 0.39 | 0.49 | 0 | 1 |
| Use of Facebook/Twitter: neither before nor after 3.11 | dummy | Yes=1, no=0: Reference group | 69 | 0.54 | 0.50 | 0 | 1 |
| Use of Facebook/Twitter: only before 3.11 | dummy | Yes=1, no=0 | 69 | 0.20 | 0.41 | 0 | 1 |
| Use of Facebook/Twitter: only after 3.11 | dummy | Yes=1, no=0 | 69 | 0.10 | 0.30 | 0 | 1 |
| Use of Facebook/Twitter: both before and after 3.11 | dummy | Yes=1, no=0 | 69 | 0.16 | 0.37 | 0 | 1 |

Our hypothesis two is thus supported. We did not find the same relation for in-house media examined in model 2.

Second, we find that organizations that continuously used Facebook/Twitter *before* and *after* the disaster raised more money than those that did not. Given that continuous use of in-house media around the initial shake were not statistically significant in affecting the amount of funds raised, we find that although using Facebook and Twitter may be effective in disseminating information, their usage in non-disaster times have a larger impact on fundraising. One can assume that the "friends" or "followers" of nonprofit's social media accounts are educated to receive information from the organization and are thus more likely to respond to a request to make donations once a disaster strikes. Hypothesis three is thus supported.

*Table 3. Estimation results of amount of funds raised (ordered probit model)*

| | Model 1 | Model 2 | Model 3 |
|---|---|---|---|
| | Basic Model | Timing of Media Use | |
| | Organizational Attributes | Use of In-House Media | Use of Facebook/Twitter |
| Legal status | -1.119*** | -1.174*** | -1.263*** |
| | (0.396) | (0.412) | (0.386) |
| Duration after obtaining legal status | -0.018*** | -0.019*** | -0.022*** |
| | (0.006) | (0.007) | (0.007) |
| Current revenue: under 100 thousand USD | -2.065*** | -1.969*** | -2.124*** |
| | (0.479) | (0.509) | (0.496) |
| Current revenue: 100-1,000 thousand USD | -2.187*** | -2.138*** | -2.406*** |
| | (0.538) | (0.544) | (0.574) |
| Location of office: affected area | -0.739* | -0.648 | -0.518 |
| | (0.419) | (0.416) | (0.441) |
| Use of in-house media: only before 3.11 | | -0.034 | |
| | | (0.491) | |
| Use of in-house media: only after 3.11 | | 0.276 | |
| | | (0.634) | |
| Use of in-house media: both before and after 3.11 | | 0.272 | |
| | | (0.483) | |
| Use of Facebook/Twitter: only before 3.11 | | | -0.139 |
| | | | (0.440) |
| Use of Facebook/Twitter: only after 3.11 | | | 0.97*8 |
| | | | (0.549) |
| Use of Facebook/Twitter: both before and after 3.11 | | | 1.095** |
| | | | (0.458) |
| Cut1. Constant | -3.131 | -2.986 | -3.163 |
| | (0.577) | (0.739) | (0.660) |
| Cut2. Constant | -1.212 | -1.049 | -1.012 |
| | (0.466) | (0.663) | (0.503) |
| Obs. | 69 | 69 | 69 |
| Log Likelihood | -48.349 | -44.328 | -44.328 |
| Wald | 40.260*** | 45.510*** | 45.511*** |
| McFadden's Adjusted $R^2$ | 0.232 | 0.195 | 0.246 |

Note: Standard errors are shown in parentheses.

***, **, * indicate statistically significant in 1%, 5%, and 10% level, respectively.

Reference group: "public interest corporation", 1,000 thousand USD and over, not located in affected prefecture, not using in-house media/Facebook/Twitter both before and after 3.11 disaster

Given that our hypothesis two and three were supported, we estimated the marginal effects of Facebook/Twitter use on the amount of funds raised. We find that continuous use of Facebook/Twitter *before* and *after* the disaster increased the probability to raise more than 10 thousand US dollars by 29.3 percent, and 25.9 percent for its use only *after* the disaster. Thus, using social media both *before* and *after* the disaster may enhance the chances of receiving donations of large amount or of having more number of donors, compared to using social media only *after* the disaster. Nonetheless, with both variables having fairly large marginal effects, we find that social media use have considerable impact on fundraising.

It is interesting to note that only about 20 percent of nonprofits used social media only *before* the disaster. Our findings imply that had those nonprofits combined usage *after* the disaster, they may have achieved higher fundraising outcomes. What prevented other organizations from encouraging people to give through Facebook and Twitter? A hint in answering this question was provided by a nonprofit practitioner, who shared with us the experience of intentionally *not* using social media after the disaster (Okada & Yamauchi, 2014) [10]. While this nonprofit was aware that using Facebook and Twitter would bring in more funds, they were also aware that the organization does not have the capacity to respond to expected volume of responses. This organization therefore refrained from using Facebook and/or Twitter after the disaster.

## 6.4. Interaction Effects of Organizational Attributes

Our estimates show that organizational attributes might influence the effect of social media use on nonprofit fundraising. To further analyze this point, we estimated the predicted probabilities of the amount of funds raised using legal status and Facebook/Twitter usage, holding other variables at their means. Table 4 shows that "specified nonprofit corporations" are less likely than "public interest corporations" to raise more money to ranges of "1,000 thousand USD and over." The probability of organizations with legal status of "public interest corporations" raising more money is higher. "Public interest corporations" have over a hundred years of history, and because its founding was approved by authorities before the aforementioned 2008 reform, both financial and human resources are secured to a certain extent. This also explains why the sign for duration after obtaining legal status was negative. Even though the predicted probability for "specified nonprofit corporations" to raise over 1,000 thousand USD is lower, the probability to raise money in the range of "10-1,000 thousand USD" is 0.72. Thus, we find that their use of social media is effective in raising funds to finance activities for disaster relief.

*Table 4. Predicted probabilities of fundraising outcome by legal status and Facebook/Twitter usage*

| Facebook/Twitter: Use of Both Before and After 3.11 | Under 10 Thousand USD | 10-1,000 Thousand USD | 1,000 Thousand USD and Over |
|---|---|---|---|
| Specified nonprofit corporation | 0.14 | 0.72 | 0.15 |
| Public interest corporation | 0.01 | 0.41 | 0.58 |
| Difference | 0.13 | 0.31 | -0.44 |

## 7. CONCLUSION AND FUTURE CONSIDERATIONS

Given the advantage of instantly spreading information to mass public, social media is assumed to be an effective communication channel for nonprofit organizations in times of disaster, when they need to mobilize the public towards financial contribution, in-kind giving, and/or volunteering. This paper examined the use of Facebook and Twitter by nonprofit organizations during the 2011 Japan disaster and found that such use was indeed effective in raising funds.

The key implication for nonprofits' communication strategies is that using social media both *before* and *after* the disaster is effective in mobilizing the public towards financial donations. Communication practices in non-disaster times, therefore, are critical for nonprofit organizations. Our study also found that the use of social media is effective in raising more money than in-house media such as organizational websites and blogs.

The findings of this paper raise further questions to be examined. First, this paper has primarily focused on whether the respondent organizations used social media or not, and not on the types of media mix adopted by respective organizations. Most, if not all, nonprofits use multiple communication channels and are often very strategic about the combination of media to use. Future research should ask the types of media mix that are effective in raising funds in times of disaster.

Second, future study should further examine the effect of continuous media usage on mid- to long-term donation. In multiple disasters around the world, we have seen empirically that donations tend to concentrate *immediately after* the disaster and fade away as time passes. A series of national household surveys in Japan found that while average donation was around 3,000 Japanese Yen (about 30 USD) per year, thus 250-300 Yen (about 2.5-3 USD) per month, the average for the month of March 2011, when the disaster struck Northeastern Japan, was 2,083 Yen (about 20 USD, Ministry of Internal Affairs and Communication Statistics Bureau, 2011). This was almost ten times more than non-disaster times. The following April 2011 was 1,580 Yen (about 16 USD), followed by 622 Yen (about 6 USD) in May, and 242 Yen (about 2.5 USD) in June. We therefore see that nonprofit organizations may collect considerable amount of donation during the first three months but experience significant drop afterwards. The trend for the first three months for the Kobe Earthquake in 1995 was 1,841 Yen (about 18 USD), 1,018 Yen (about 10 USD), and 217 Yen (about 2 USD), respectively. Future research should examine the possibility of using social media to strengthen the outcomes of mid- to long-term fundraising.

Third, the findings of our paper have not touched on one of the key characteristics of social media - its interactive nature. Unlike traditional media, these new tools enable two-way communication. Theoretically, nonprofit organizations are not only transmitters of information, but receivers of information. How such dialogic interactions lead to encouragement of voluntary actions is thus our next inquiry. Studies have found that despite such interactive nature, the way nonprofit organizations use social media so far has mainly been one-way (Svensson *et al.*, 2015), failing to capitalize on the innate two-way communication nature of social media (Muralidharan *et al.*, 2011). However, when nonprofits do pursue dialogic communication, the outcomes are favorable. Not only are social media users more likely to "like" and comment on dialogic messages (Saxton and Waters, 2014), they will also engage in more dialogic activities (Bortree & Seltzer, 2009). In the context of Japan, Okada *et al.* (2016) explored practices of nonprofit organizations that responded to the 2011 disaster and found that nonprofits that sent out more dialogic messages on Facebook and/or Twitter had raised more funds. Consequence of utilizing dialogic nature of social media on nonprofits' performance is a topic that awaits further research.

Finally, we need to take into consideration that nonprofits not only disseminate information about voluntary actions, but also other information that are not directly intended to encourage the audience to give or to volunteer. These may be information about the disaster *per se* or about the organization's relief efforts. Because this study used a dataset where responding nonprofit practitioners were asked to share their experience of social media use specifically for fundraising, we were not able to delve deeper into these different types of information that nonprofits present to the general public. Future studies should broaden the scope of information disseminated by nonprofits to enhance our understanding of nonprofit organizations as a sender of information.

## ACKNOWLEDGMENT

We appreciate all nonprofit organizations that took the time to participate in our online survey. We also thank the two anonymous reviewers for their insightful suggestions and comments for publication of earlier version of this article in *International Journal of Public Administration in the Digital Age* (Okada *et al.*, 2017). This research is a part of the project "The Private Aid Initiatives in the Great East Japan Earthquake" co-organized by the Japan NPO Research Association (JANPORA) and the Japan NPO Center (JNPOC), supported by "Takeda Inochi to Kurashi Saisei Program Grant." Part of this work was also supported by Japan Society for the Promotion of Science (JSPS) KAKENHI Grant "Impact of Disaster Related Policies on Public Service Provision by Nonprofit Organizations (15K11981)" and "Strategic Information Transmission of Nonprofit Organizations (16K17247)."

## REFERENCES

Adler, S., & Carpenter, H. (2015). Peer-to-peer fundraising success: paws with a cause. In H. Asencio & R. Sun (Eds.), *Cases on Strategic Social Media Utilization in the Nonprofit Sector*. Hershey, PA: Information Science Reference. doi:10.4018/978-1-4666-8188-0.ch002

Auger, G. A. (2014). Rhetorical framing: Examining the message structure of nonprofit organizations on Twitter. *International Journal of Nonprofit and Voluntary Sector Marketing*, *19*(4), 239–249. doi:10.1002/nvsm.1499

Austin, L., Liu, B. F., & Jin, Y. (2012). How audiences seek out crisis information: Exploring the social-mediated crisis communication model. *Journal of Applied Communication Research*, *40*(2), 188–207. doi:10.1080/00909882.2012.654498

Bortree, D. S., & Seltzer, T. (2009). Dialogic strategies and outcomes: An analysis of environmental advocacy groups' Facebook profiles. *Public Relations Review*, *35*(3), 317–319. doi:10.1016/j.pubrev.2009.05.002

Brengarth, L. B., Mujkic, E., & Millar, M. A. (2015). Social media in crisis: how social media created a npo and relief during a wildfire crisis. In H. Asencio & R. Sun (Eds.), *Cases on Strategic Social Media Utilization in the Nonprofit Sector*. Hershey, PA: Information Science Reference. doi:10.4018/978-1-4666-8188-0.ch001

Briones, R. L., Kuch, B., Liu, B. F., & Jin, Y. (2011). Keeping up with the digital age: How the American Red Cross uses social media to build relationships. *Public Relations Review*, *37*(1), 37–43. doi:10.1016/j.pubrev.2010.12.006

Burt, E., & Taylor, J. (2003). New technologies, embedded values, and strategic change: Evidence from the U.K. voluntary sector. *Nonprofit and Voluntary Sector Quarterly*, *32*(1), 115–127. doi:10.1177/0899764002250009

Cabinet Office of Japan. (2011). *White Paper Disaster Management* (in Japanese). Retrieved February 23, 2015, from http://www.bousai.go.jp/kaigirep/hakusho/h23/index.htm

Cabinet Office of Japan. (2012). *Survey on disaster volunteer activities on the Great East Japan Earthquake* (in Japanese). Retrieved September 10, 2014, from http://www.bousai.go.jp/kyoiku/volunteer/pdf/120625jittaichousa.pdf

Cabinet Office of Japan. (2015). *2014 Survey on specified nonprofit corporations and citizens' social contributions* (in Japanese). Retrieved July 24, 2015 from https://www.npo-homepage.go.jp/uploads/h26_shimin_chousa_all.pdf

Curtis, L., Edwards, C., Fraser, K. L., Gudelsky, S., Holmquist, J., Thornton, K., & Sweetser, K. D. (2010). Adoption of social media for public relations by nonprofit organizations. *Public Relations Review*, *36*(1), 90–92. doi:10.1016/j.pubrev.2009.10.003

Eimhjellen, I., Wollebaek, D., & Stromsnes, K. (2013). Associations online: Barriers for using web-based communication in voluntary organizations. *Voluntas*, *25*(3), 730–753. doi:10.100711266-013-9361-x

Gao, H., Barbier, G., & Goolsby, R. (2011). Harnessing the Crowdsourcing Power of Social Media for Disaster Relief. *Cyber-Physical Social Systems*. Retrieved April 29, 2015 from http://oai.dtic.mil/oai/oai?verb=getRecord&metadataPrefix=html&identifier=ADA581803

Guo, C., & Saxton, G. D. (2014). Tweeting social change: How social media are changing nonprofit advocacy. *Nonprofit and Voluntary Sector Quarterly*, *43*(1), 57–79. doi:10.1177/0899764012471585

Guo, C., & Saxton, G. D. (2017). Speaking and being heard: How nonprofit advocacy organizations gain attention on social media. *Nonprofit and Voluntary Sector Quarterly*, 1–22.

Hackler, D., & Saxton, G. D. (2007). The strategic use of information technology by nonprofit organizations: Increasing capacity and untapped potential. *Public Administration Review*, *67*(3), 474–487. doi:10.1111/j.1540-6210.2007.00730.x

Haddow, G. D., & Haddow, K. S. (2014). *Disaster Communication in a Changing Media World*. Waltham, MA: Elsevier Inc.

Hu, Q., & Shi, W. (2017). Understanding nonprofit organizations' use of social networking sites: An examination of management factors. *International Journal of Public Administration in the Digital Age*, *4*(1), 19–34. doi:10.4018/IJPADA.2017010102

Hughes, A. L., & Palen, L. (2009). Twitter adoption and use in mass convergence and emergency events. *International Journal of Emergency Management*, *6*(3/4), 248–260. doi:10.1504/IJEM.2009.031564

Ishida, Y. (2008, January). Financial Basis of Nonprofits Supported by the Society (in Japanese). *Komei*, 52-57.

Japan Civil Network for Disaster Relief in the East Japan (JCN). (n.d.). *Profile*. Retrieved July 10, 2014, from http://www.jpn-civil.net/2014/english/about_us/

Japan NPO Research Association (JANPORA). (2012) *Report on awareness survey on donation and volunteering after the Great East Japan Disaster* (in Japanese). Retrieved July 10, 2014 from http://www.osipp.osaka-u.ac.jp/janpora/shinsaitokubetsuproject/seika/seika1208.pdf

Kapucu, N. (2007). Non-profit response to catastrophic disasters. *Disaster Prevention and Management*, *16*(4), 551–561. doi:10.1108/09653560710817039

Kapucu, N., Yuldashev, F., & Feldheim, M. A. (2011). Nonprofit organizations in disaster response and management: A network analysis. *European Journal of Economic and Political Studies*, *4*(1), 83–112.

Kawai, T., & Fujishiro, H. (2013). Use of Twitter in the disaster information after the Great East Japan Earthquake. *Corporate Communication Studies*, *17*, 118–128.

Liu, B. F., Austin, L., & Jin, Y. (2011). How publics respond to crisis communication strategies: The interplay of information form and source. *Public Relations Review*, *37*(4), 345–353. doi:10.1016/j.pubrev.2011.08.004

Lovejoy, K., & Saxton, G. D. (2012). Information, community, and action: How nonprofit organizations use social media. *Journal of Computer-Mediated Communication*, *17*(3), 337–353. doi:10.1111/j.1083-6101.2012.01576.x

Lucas, E. (2017). Reinventing the rattling tin: How UK charities use Facebook in fundraising. *International Journal of Nonprofit and Voluntary Sector Marketing*, *22*(2), e1576. doi:10.1002/nvsm.1576

Mayfield, A. (2006). Social media…the hunted can become the hunter. *Public Relations Quarterly*, *52*(4), 9–12.

Minister of Internal Affairs and Communication. (2017). *White Paper Information and Communications in Japan* (in Japanese). Retrieved September 8, 2017 from http://www.soumu.go.jp/johotsusintokei/whitepaper/index.html

Ministry of Internal Affairs and Communication. (2011). *Research on possibilities of next-generation ICT society* (in Japanese). Retrieved April 28, 2015, from http://www.soumu.go.jp/johotsusintokei/linkdata/h23_05_houkoku.pdf

Ministry of Internal Affairs and Communication Statistics Bureau. (2011). *Impact of the Disaster on Results of Household Survey (with two or more people): Shift in Amount of Donation* (in Japanese). Retrieved April 29, 2015 from http://www.stat.go.jp/info/shinsai/pdf/ka1106-2.pdf

Muralidharan, S., Rasmussen, L., Patterson, D., & Shin, J. (2011). Hope for Haiti: An analysis of Facebook and Twitter usage during the earthquake relief efforts. *Public Relations Review*, *37*(2), 175–177. doi:10.1016/j.pubrev.2011.01.010

Nah, S., & Saxton, G. E. (2013). Modeling the adoption and use of social media by nonprofit organizations. *New Media & Society*, *15*(2), 294–313. doi:10.1177/1461444812452411

National Police Agency of Japan. (2017). *Updated information on victims and policy responses to earthquakes off the coast of Pacific Ocean in northeast Japan* (in Japanese). Retrieved December 13, 2017, from https://www.npa.go.jp/news/other/earthquake2011/pdf/higaijokyo.pdf

Okada, A., Ishida, Y., & Kikuchi, R. (2016). *"Dialogue" in Social Media: Implications for Strategic Communication of Nonprofits*. Association for Research on Nonprofit Organizations and Voluntary Action (ARNOVA) *45th Annual Conference*, Washington, DC.

Okada, A., Ishida, Y., & Yamauchi, N. (2017). Effectiveness of Social Media in Disaster Fundraising: Mobilizing the Public towards Voluntary Actions. *International Journal of Public Administration in the Digital Age*, *4*(1), 49–68. doi:10.4018/IJPADA.2017010104

Okada, A., & Yamauchi, N. (2014). *Role of information in mobilizing the public towards voluntary actions in times of disaster*. Japan NPO Research Association Discussion Paper Series. Retrieved February 23, 2015, from http://www.osipp.osaka-u.ac.jp/janpora/dparchive/papers/2014004E.pdf

Pavlik, J. V. (2001). News framing and new media: digital tools to re-engage an alienated citizenry. In Framing Public Life: Perspectives on Media and Our Understanding of the Social World. Mahwah, NJ: Lawrence Erlbaum Associates, Inc.

Pekkanen, R. (2000). Japan's new politics: The case of the NPO law. *Journal of Japanese Studies*, *26*(1), 111–148. doi:10.2307/133393

Pekkanen, R. (2006). *Japan's Dual Civil Society: Members without Advocates*. Stanford, CA: Stanford University Press.

Saxton, G. D., & Guo, C. (2014). Online stakeholder targeting and the acquisition of social media capital. *International Journal of Nonprofit and Voluntary Sector Marketing*, *19*(4), 286–300. doi:10.1002/nvsm.1504

Saxton, G. D., & Wang, L. (2014). The social network effect: The determinants of giving through social media. *Nonprofit and Voluntary Sector Quarterly*, *43*(5), 850–868. doi:10.1177/0899764013485159

Saxton, G. D., & Waters, R. D. (2014). What do stakeholders Like on Facebook? Examining public reactions to nonprofit organizations' informational, promotional, and community-building messages. *Journal of Public Relations Research*, *26*(3), 280–299. doi:10.1080/1062726X.2014.908721

Schultz, F., Utz, S., & Goritz, A. (2011). Is the medium the message? Perceptions of and reactions to crisis communication via twitter, blogs, and traditional media. *Public Relations Review*, *37*(1), 20–27. doi:10.1016/j.pubrev.2010.12.001

Sekiya, N. (2012). The Great East Japan Earthquake and social media [in Japanese]. *Journal of Disaster Information Studies*, *12*, 29–36.

Sihi, D. (2017). The influence of leadership and strategic emphasis on social media use of regional nonprofit organizations. *International Journal of Public Administration in the Digital Age*, *4*(1), 1–18. doi:10.4018/IJPADA.2017010101

Solnit, R. (2009). *A paradise built in hell: The extraordinary communities that arise in disaster*. New York, NY: Penguin Books.

Svensson, P. G., Mahoney, T. Q., & Hambrick, M. E. (2015). Twitter as a communication tool for nonprofits: A study of sport-for-development organizations. *Nonprofit and Voluntary Sector Quarterly, 44*(6), 1086–1106. doi:10.1177/0899764014553639

The Japan Association of Charitable Organizations. (2012). *Current status of general incorporated association and general incorporated foundation*. Retrieved July 24, 2015 from http://www.nopodas.com/contents.asp?code=10001005&idx=100933

The Japan Institute for Labour Policy and Training (JILPT). (2007). Diversity of Revenues and Organizational Autonomy: Impact of Commissioned Projects by the Public Sector (in Japanese). In *Road to Development of Nonprofit Employment: Human Resources, Finance, and Legal Institutions*. Report on Labour Policy Research, No.82. Retrieved April 29, 2015, from http://www.jil.go.jp/institute/reports/2007/082.html

Utz, S., Schultz, F., & Glocka, S. (2013). Crisis communication online: How medium, crisis type and emotions affected public reactions in the Fukushima Daiichi nuclear disaster. *Public Relations Review, 39*(1), 40–46. doi:10.1016/j.pubrev.2012.09.010

Veil, S. R., Buehner, T., & Palenchar, M. J. (2011). A work-in-process literature review: Incorporating social media in risk and crisis communication. *Journal of Contingencies and Crisis Management, 19*(2), 110–122. doi:10.1111/j.1468-5973.2011.00639.x

Waters, R. D., Burnett, E., Lamm, A., & Lucas, J. (2009). Engaging stakeholders through social networking: How nonprofit organizations are using Facebook. *Public Relations Review, 35*(2), 102–106. doi:10.1016/j.pubrev.2009.01.006

Waters, R. D., & Tindall, N. T. J. (2011). Exploring the impact of American news coverage on crisis fundraising: Using media theory to explicate a new model of fundraising communication. *Journal of Nonprofit & Public Sector Marketing, 23*(1), 20–40. doi:10.1080/10495142.2010.494875

Yamamoto, T., Hashimoto, Y., Nakamura, I., Sekiya, N., Ogasawara, M., Chiba, N., Yoshiaki, S., & Takahashi, K. (2012). Information behavior and communication anxiety on Twitter after the Great East Japan Earthquake: Web survey of Twitter user in Kanto Region (in Japanese). *Research Survey Reports in Information Studies (Interfaculty Initiative in Information Studies, the University of Tokyo), 28*, 115-160.

Yamauchi, N. (2000). Japanese nonprofit sector in comparative perspective. *Global Economic Review: Perspectives on East Asian Economies and Industries, 29*(4), 106–128. doi:10.1080/12265080008449808

Yamauchi, N., Shimizu, H., Sokolowski, S. W., & Salamon, L. M. (2004). Japan. In L. M. Salamon & H. K. Anheier (Eds.), *Global Civil Society: Dimension of the Nonprofit Sector* (Vol. 2). West Hartford, CT: Kumarian Press.

Zorn, T. E., Grant, S., & Henderson, A. (2013). Strengthening resource mobilization chains: Developing the social media competencies of community and voluntary organizations in New Zealand. *Voluntas, 24*(3), 666–687. doi:10.100711266-012-9265-1

## ENDNOTES

1 Mixi is a Japanese social networking service where users can communicate with their friends through shared diaries, photos, and games.

2 LINE is an application for mobile phones, smartphones, and tablets where users can chat and make an online call.

3 The survey was conducted as part of "The Private Aid Initiative in the Great East Japan Earthquake" co-organized by the Japan NPO Research Association (JANPORA) and the Japan NPO Center (JNPOC). The project is supported by "Takeda Inochi to Kurashi Saisei Program Grant."

4 Acronyms stand for nonprofit organizations, non-governmental organizations, and community-based organizations, respectively.

5 For overall findings on how nonprofits transmitted information on opportunities for voluntary actions, see Okada and Yamauchi (2014).

6 For a more detailed description of Japanese nonprofit sector in general, see Yamauchi (2000), Yamauchi *et al.*, (2004), and Pekkanen (2006).

7 Analysis presented in this figure only includes organizations who answered that they were engaged in fundraising activities in the aftermath of the disaster.

8 Because the year the organization began its operation and the year of obtaining legal status does not necessarily match, year 2012 (after the 2011 disaster) were used to create this variable for some organizations.

9 Includes "approved" specified nonprofit corporations, which have obtained second round of authorization from the Japanese government for tax deduction for incoming donations.

10 From a discussion at the NPO Research Forum organized by Japan NPO Research Association (JANPORA) at Osaka University on April 20, 2014.

# Chapter 4
# E-Government of Occupational Safety and Health:
## Improvement Prospects for a Developing Nation

**Marcia Nathai-Balkissoon**
*The University of the West Indies — St. Augustine, Trinidad and Tobago*

**K. F. Pun**
*The University of the West Indies — St. Augustine, Trinidad and Tobago*

## ABSTRACT

*Electronic government (e-gov) has not been implemented as extensively in many developing countries as in developed countries, especially in certain fields, such as occupational safety and health (OSH). This chapter considers e-gov that is effected through the websites of leading OSH bodies in a developing country, Trinidad and Tobago, and two developed nations, the USA and UK. Using a content analysis and comparison exercise, OSH e-gov shortcomings and opportunities in T&T are noted. Improvement recommendations include development of a strategy and strategy execution plan to boost stakeholder recognition of the value of the OSH agency and OSH e-gov in T&T; partnership-building to make resources available for OSH e-gov enhancement; enhanced accessibility and utility via a wider range of media formats to users; better stakeholder responsiveness via engagement with social media and better online support; and increased data collection and analysis in order to drive continual improvement.*

## INTRODUCTION

It is estimated that almost a third of the US population is comprised of Millenials, a group of youths and young adults who are always connected (Sewake, 2015) to their devices. As a result, this group may also be called the net generation, electronic generation or digital generation (Shih & Allen, 2006), and they have ushered in a communication age that is increasingly online. This group is smart; they use various devices and social media resources to inform their purchasing and other decisions as well as to actually make their personal and work transactions more efficiently.

DOI: 10.4018/978-1-5225-5966-5.ch004

Indeed, in the past few decades, society as a whole has come to embrace electronic technologies more, so that even older adults have become more digitally competent and more reliant on electronic devices such as smart-phones, laptops, and tablets. In some cases, face-to-face communication has been supplanted by electronic communication as they access social media and online news; upload or download photo, video and audio resources; dash off tweets, blog articles, texts, and emails; post reviews and ratings; and share statuses. Government systems have therefore been increasingly embracing electronic modalities in an effort to reach populations more effectively. Through such e-government or e-gov systems, governments seek to leverage the population's electronic connectivity in order to build their awareness, appreciation, and competence and to encourage sharing of attitudes and access to content (Gil-Garcia, Helbig, & Ojo, 2014).

When it comes to ICT access and use, Losh (2013) reports that a digital divide exists not only due to generation differences, but also due to differences in education, gender, and ethnicity in users. One concern that arises with e-gov systems is the disadvantage potentially created for lower socio-economic brackets, whose constrained access to internet and communication technology (ICT) and lower levels of ICT skill reduce their ability to "access and use ICT to promote well-being and prosperity"(United Nations Department of Economic and Social Affairs [UNDESA], 2014, p. 9). Since developing nations reasonably enjoy lower standards of living than developed nations, these lower socio-economic challenges also apply. Thus, developing nations must aggressively work to bridge their ICT gaps (i.e., updating and leveraging ICT technologies and applications), or there is likely to be a widening economic divide between themselves and the first world, which continues to forge ahead with ICT enhancements (Ndou, 2004).

Over the past several years, The Republic of Trinidad and Tobago (T&T), a developing nation, has actively worked toward e-gov system development and rollout in many areas. A 2014 assessment by Nathai-Balkissoon and Pun (2016) identified several shortcomings in the e-government systems for Occupational Safety and Health (OSH) Management. Their view was that OSH had not been a high-priority area, even if the International Labour Organisation [ILO] (2009) recognised it as a critical field of practice for developing companies. With respect to T&T, OSH has an important role to support the efforts of government and industry to diversify the economy from oil and gas, develop more small and medium companies (Nathai-Balkissoon, Maharaj, Guerrero, Mahabir, & Dialsingh, 2017), and support international and regional efforts to provide decent work (ILO, 2017; United Nations Development Programme, 2017). E-gov systems have already proven their utility in boosting safety: social safety in Brazil, food safety in the USA, fisherman safety in T&T (UNDESA, 2014; 2016), and it remains to be seen whether T&T's OSH e-gov system has advanced significantly since the aforementioned 2014 assessment.

In T&T, e-gov has also begun to expand to include OSH matters but more is needed to be truly effective. Updating the work from Nathai-Balkissoon and Pun's assessment, this chapter reports a content analysis that compares the 2017 incarnation of T&T's OSH e-gov site with those of the United States of America (US) and United Kingdom (UK) and suggests how some of the recognised initiatives may be used for T&T's case. The focus is on answering the following research questions:

1. What approaches are used on primary OSH websites of the UK and the US, two of the world's leading OSH and e-government nations, to enable strong OSH e-government?
2. How does T&T's primary OSH website compare to those of the UK and the US?
3. How should the T&T OSH website be enhanced to practice better OSH e-government?

# LITERATURE REVIEW

## E-Government

### Definition of E-Gov

E-gov is typically defined according to its purpose, but which purpose may vary widely. The World Bank (2011, para.1) provides the following definition:

*E-Government' refers to the use by government agencies of information technologies (such as Wide Area Networks, the Internet, and mobile computing) that have the ability to transform relations with citizens, businesses, and other arms of government. These technologies can serve a variety of different ends: better delivery of government services to citizens, improved interactions with business and industry, citizen empowerment through access to information, or more efficient government management.*

Though several years have passed since this World Bank definition, e-government seems to have remained focused on similar themes, though there may be more elements of social media and direct interaction with citizens than ever before. According to the United Nations UNDESA (2016), these are the international trends that are now emerging: significantly more countries are using e-government platforms to make services more accessible to the public, to make their public institutions "more inclusive, effective, accountable and transparent" (p. 2) in line with the 2030 Agenda for Sustainable Development, and in particular Sustainable Development Goal 9, and to boost ICT and wireless access to everyone (and especially to those in developing countries).

### Areas of Focus of E-Gov

According to the Accenture Institute for Health and Public Service Value (2009), e-gov strategies may be:

1. **Outcome-Focused:** Seeking to bring about social and economic conditions, improving public service efficiency and effectiveness, or gathering customer feedback (see ECOSOC (2015) which highlights the need to study the effects of policies on sustainable development outcomes),
2. **Balance-Focused:** Seeking to measure and ensure reach and accessibility across target sectors or citizen profiles (see UNDESA (2016) reports recommending that information should be comprehensive and balanced so that stakeholders are able to make informed decisions and so that progress takes place across all outcome areas, to maximise synergy),
3. **Engagement-Focused:** Providing networking and education tools to build user connectivity and learning (this was set out by the United Nations General Assembly (2015) in UNDESA (2016)), and
4. **Accountability-Focused:** Enhancing transparency by enabling users to share experiences, results, or track complaints to resolution. This is in line with SDG 16, which calls for institutional accountability among other things. Populations are increasingly having input on the goals and targets to be set and reported upon by governments, and open government data and statistical reports are often made available via e-gov systems (Open Data for Development Network, 2017).

The UNDESA (2014) and the US Department of Labor [USDOL] (n.d.) focus heavily on serving stakeholders with priority placed on such e-gov-to-stakeholder communication types as G2B (government to business), G2C (government to citizens), and G2G (government to government). Other recognised e-gov interactions include G2N (government to NGOs) and G2E (government to employees) (Fang, 2002). ICT enables sustainable development by improving coordination, communication and collaboration in diverse fields (Zelenika & Pearce, 2013). Even as internet-enabled technologies become more pervasive, it is notable that various electronic technologies such as the television, radio, telephone and Short Message Service (SMS) text messaging listed by Boujarwah (2006) still play notable roles in e-gov operations. Government Information Systems (GIS), the Internet of Things (IoT) and open data are some aspects of the newer technological advancements that have the potential to boost accountability and fight corruption, though there is also a need to ensure that data is trustworthy and safe (Liu and Lin, 2012; Gathungu and Mungai, 2013; Levy and Johns, 2016; Mayernik, 2017).

When addressing the issue of engagement, accessibility is a prime consideration. Sutton (2017) highlights that, beyond developing an aesthetically-pleasing presence that meets user needs, websites should pay special attention to accessibility for disabled populations especially when safety matters are being addressed, not only for reasons of convenience but also in order to proactively manage crisis situations.

## E-Gov in T&T

In T&T, the National ICT Company Limited (iGovTT) has been tasked to roll out e-gov services and connect key stakeholders (Government of the Republic of Trinidad and Tobago [GORTT], 2011). GORTT (2012, p. 5) has spoken of "the transformative potential of ICTs and the Internet". This derives partly from the potential for enhanced knowledge management, by bringing pertinent and updated information to stakeholders and promoting individual, group, and even organisational learning (Pemberton & Stonehouse, 2000; Pun & Nathai-Balkissoon, 2011). The country's e-gov outreach includes a TTConnect government portal for all ministries, internet service available at schools and national libraries, GovNeTT intranet connecting government to all Ministries, and a single electronic window (SEW) for lodging trade and transport documents via one electronic access point (GORTT, 2011).

T&T ranked 91st of 193 countries on the UNDESA (2014) e-government development index (EGDI) survey, but two years later its efforts to strengthen its e-gov systems were propelling it forward in world rankings so that its rank charged ahead by 21 places, propelling it into the high EGDI bracket (UNDESA, 2016). T&T's EGDI score was 0.5780 (rank 70) compared to 0.9193 (rank 1) for the UK and 0.8420 (rank 12) for the US. T&T's component scores all increased in 2016 compared to 2014: online service (0.5290 from 0.3307), telecommunication infrastructure (0.4973 from 0.4543) and human capital (0.7077 from 0.6945).

In 2014, T&T was among the top 10 small island developing states (SIDS), but it lagged four smaller Caribbean nations, namely Barbados, Antigua and Bermuda, St. Kitts and Nevis, and Grenada. By 2016, Barbados outperformed T&T in two of the three EGDI components, namely telecommunication infrastructure and human capital, but T&T was second only to Barbados in the region. The online service component was T&T's second strongest component, but it was important, as it considered citizen empowerment, online communication and transactions. If OSH e-gov improved in these areas, it may have been a contributing element toward the improved T&T ranking, though this was not specified in the EGDI report.

## Importance of OSH E-Gov

If not properly addressed, OSH has severe and costly implications for society, government, and businesses (European Agency for Safety and Health at Work [EU-OSHA], 2014; Elsler, Takala, & Remes, 2017). Indeed, the ILO estimates that 3.9% of global GDP is lost as a result of work-related injuries and illnesses (Safety and Health Practitioner, 2017), and Elsler, Takala, & Remes (2017) caution that the cost of work-related accidents and illnesses is proportionally higher for less-developed countries. While OSH may be perceived as a technical field, its practice is critical to promote the safety of all people. Good workplace conditions, like those that may be achieved through proper OSH implementation, yield significant economic gains (EU-OSHA, 2010; Schwab, 2013). Moreover, the ILO (2009) points out that there is a moral imperative to use resources efficiently and to protect workers by properly implementing OSH.

Safety legislation, coupled with supporting guidelines, codes of practice and standards are commonly used worldwide to establish minimum practices and conditions for safety in the workplace. In T&T, the legislation is referred to as "The Occupational Safety and Health Act (2004), as amended (2006)" (the OSH Act) (GORTT, 2004; 2006). T&T's safety practitioners have noted that safety management system implementation varies from sector to sector, and industries are often extrinsically motivated to comply with safety legislation. Extrinsic motivators include, but are not limited to, the modern need to meet tender requirements or win contracts (Energy Chamber of Trinidad and Tobago, 2007) and the time-honoured concern of avoiding sanctions for non-compliance (Gleason & Barnum, 1978). On the other hand, safety management systems may be weaker in some industries, and reasons for this can include unavailability or inaccessibility of expertise/guidance as a result of lower resource availability (Surienty, Hong, & Hung, 2011).

There is a need, therefore, for OSH e-gov systems that sensitise stakeholders and make resources available to support national OSH development (Nathai-Balkissoon & Pun, 2016).

## THE METHOD

In the first decade of the 2000s, many studies and papers were published that focused on evaluating e-government websites that served as central portals to a wide range of government services. However, in the second decade, this type of work has declined as general e-gov portals are more commonplace and the guidelines and expertise may by now be well established. Less focus has been placed on evaluating e-government websites dedicated to narrower functions such as Occupational Safety and Health Administration, which is the focus of this chapter. Since little recent guidance is available to carry out an evaluation, some earlier evaluations are used to guide the exercise addressed in this chapter.

E--gov websites may be evaluated by qualitatively observing and quantitatively measuring the sites' performance. Among the areas typically evaluated are outcomes, balance, engagement, and accountability (Accenture Institute for Health and Public Service Value, 2009). The Australian National Audit Office (2004) evaluated website efficiency and effectiveness by looking at costs, benefits, service delivery, productivity, and return on investment measures. It considered issues like user visit patterns, site traffic data, accessibility, usability, information accuracy and usefulness, and stakeholder satisfaction to assess effectiveness. Included in these issues would be the use of websites, databases, videos, audio clips, and social media such as Twitter and Facebook.

Quantitative data judgements are beyond the scope of the work reported in this chapter, since the focus is on observing how various structural and content elements are being incorporated into the selected websites to promote OSH using e-gov modes. The focus is trained on the uses made of electronic media to ensure site usability (Granizo, Yanez, Ramirez, & Machado, 2011) and accessibility (Abanumy, Al-Badi, & Mayhew, 2005).

### Areas of Focus

In this chapter, a simple content analysis approach is used, allowing consideration of elements such as content, intent, messages, and context in order to make judgments about the information sources (Krippendorff, 2004). The judgements made are intended to highlight the similarities and differences between the OSH e-gov site of a developing nation (T&T) and two developed nation sites (the UK and the US). Specifically, the OSH websites' usability and accessibility were evaluated according to three considerations, namely accessibility and support information, provision of technical content for stakeholders, and range and availability of electronic media resources. Figure 1 outlines the sub-elements under the three areas evaluated.

### Information Sources

The US OSHA 30-hour general certificate and UK NEBOSH general certificate are among the most popular OSH qualification programmes pursued in T&T, perhaps because many of the country's multinational companies are headquartered in those two nations. In addition, as mentioned earlier, both the UK and the US are highly ranked internationally in the UNDESA's (2016) EGDI. For these reasons, this chapter is structured around comparing the OSH e-gov approaches of the TTOSHA website with those used by the main OSH website of these two nations.

### Steps Followed

The actual evaluation followed four main steps, namely evaluation of the UK website, evaluation of the US website, evaluation of the T&T website, and lastly comparison of the T&T website elements to those of the UK and US. The comparison was used to recommend how T&T OSH e-gov could be improved, and to propose further work prospects. Figure 2 provides a summary of the steps followed in the evaluation.

## FINDINGS

### UK OSH E-Gov

The major OSH legislation in the UK, the Health and Safety at Work (HSW) Act, was implemented in 1974. OSH legislation enforcement, development, and review, as well as some research and statistics generation are performed by the Health and Safety Executive. The UKHSE website (HSE, n.d.), located at www.hse.gov.uk, is briefly evaluated in this section.

*Figure 1. The e-government considerations used to evaluate OSH websites in this study*
*Source: Nathai-Balkissoon & Pun (2016).*

1. Accessibility and Support Information including:
    - Metadata Elements (Site Map/Index/Website Organisation Map/Online glossary)
    - Frequently Asked Questions (FAQ)/Help page/Search feature)
    - Website Accessibility (Catering to Special Needs Users/Inclusiveness/Languages/browser selection/Look and feel of website)
    - Usability (Feedback Gathering/Complaint Filing)
    - Privacy (Registration/Sign-up programmes/confidentiality statements)
    - About Us (History/Background/Focus/Contact Information/National Call Centre)
    - Job vacancies listings/job boards

2. Provision of Technical Content for Stakeholders including:
    - Targeting Stakeholder Categories
    - Treatment of At-Risk Groups
    - Page Links to Law and Regulations
    - Dataset Access/Query Facilities
    - Training Information and Programmes
    - Links to download Free Publications
    - Links to Publications for Purchase
    - Links to other government/non-government bodies in field of OSH
    - Consultations

3. Range and Availability of Electronic Media Resources including:
    - Website URL and Name
    - Sharing/Social media (Facebook/YouTube/Twitter/Google+/Blog/Mobile app/ Rich Site Summary (RSS) feeds)
    - e-newsletters/ e-magazines
    - Posters, PDF documents, and PPT Slideshows
    - Audio recordings/audio podcasts
    - Video recordings/video podcasts
    - Web-based training/virtual seminars
    - A What's New page/Trending topics
    - Currency (Updates)
    - Online Contests

## Accessibility and Support

The UKHSE site has a deceptively simple appearance with attractive images on every page and only six main tabs (Home/News/Guidance/About You/About HSE/Contact HSE) separating the content. It is very intricately designed, making broad and deep information freely available to users. Hovering over a tab activates a drop down menu listing several subtopics which the user may select. At the bottom of the homepage runs a ribbon from which support information may also be accessed, including a detailed site map that lists subsections under each tab heading, an A to Z index of topics, and an acronym listing. There are both a search bar at the top of every webpage and a search link built into every page footer ribbon. Additionally, there are search links within some webpages. The "News" dropdown menu appeals

*Figure 2. The study approach*

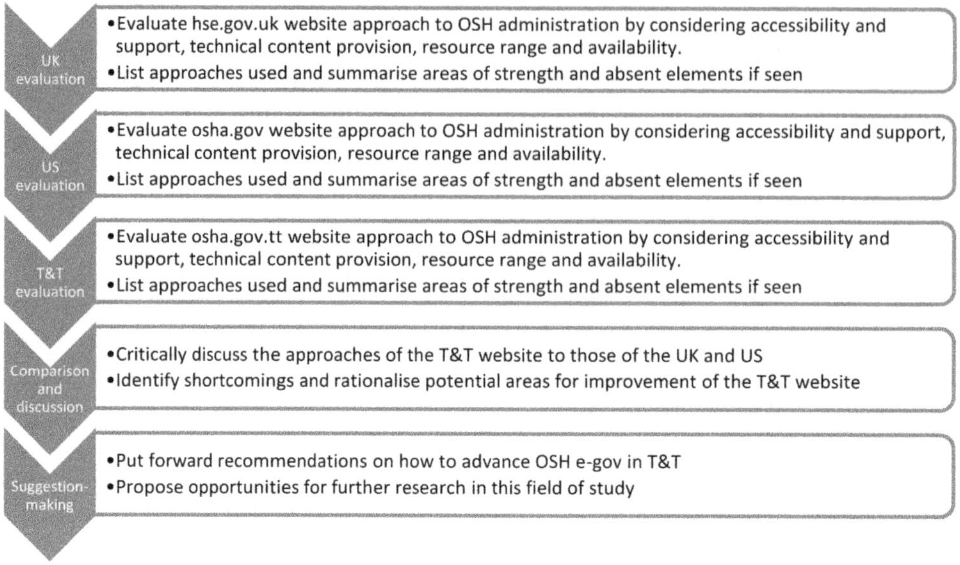


to modern access modalities, allowing users to subscribe to e-bulletins and RSS feeds, providing HSE press office links, and archiving HSE press releases. Two features (the "Chair's Blog" and "Health and Safety Myths") are inactive, but remain available as archives via the "News" dropdown menu.

In the "Guidance" webpage, search boxes allow content to be accessed by Industry or Topic. Convenient access to information is also facilitated with a "Frequently asked questions" (FAQ) page and two panels titled "For businesses…" and "For workers…".

Meeting the needs of users with disabilities is an obvious priority for the UKHSE. An "Accessibility" tab is prominently placed at the top right of the homepage, and repeated at the bottom right for good measure. The visually impaired and others are able to vary text size, colour schemes, navigate using keyboard instead of mouse, and access captions or transcripts for many videos. There are also tips on improving accessibility when using various browsers. The HSE's Accessibility Policy is shared together with sites such as the BBC's "My Web My Way" (BBC, 2014) and the Web Accessibility Initiative (World Wide Web Consortium, 2012), to provide guidance on how to make the best use of accessibility options for users with communication challenges. The site also allows users to optimise content for viewing on mobile devices. While the website is available in English, the footer bar includes a tool leading the user to information created in 19 other languages. Besides, the site is open access and only requires an e-mail address if a user wants to subscribe for free updates. There is an "About You" panel that appears to the left of the "Accessibility" page. It provides general information that users may seek, such as copyright and disclaimer statements.

A special effort has been made to simplify the process of giving feedback throughout the site; on each page there is a "Rate this page" tool that a user could use to award between zero and five stars to any webpage within the site. This is immediately followed with the option to select a reason for the rating given by choosing from among five options that present themselves. The HSE also seems to value open data sharing, since it makes its website usage statistics readily available as well. The UKHSE site actively encourages user feedback, with a section of the "Contact HSE" page supporting lodging of complaints about HSE services. The complaints handling procedure is also outlined on the webpage. Also, reporting concerns about OSH in the workplace is possible via several online forms.

The "About HSE" webpage provides information about HSE history, work focus, strategy and plans, board and senior management, organisation structure, stakeholder collaborations, and annual reports. Clicking on the "Contact HSE" tab opens a main webpage organised into several boxes, many with attractive graphics related to one of a series of reasons to contact HSE and providing links for reporting and other communications. There is also a "Careers" section that details individual vacancies, and "HSE Jobs eBulletin" updates can be accessed through e-mail updates. The "Ways to contact HSE" link shares telephone contact information and allows use of an online advice form, but an email contact was not readily seen.

## Provision of Technical Content for Stakeholders

The site targets workers, employers, and other audience groups through "Are you…" and "How to…" drop down links in the "About you" tab. In the "Guidance" tab, sample risk assessments, interactive tools, and templates provide help that fits SME industry profiles. User targeting is also evident from the provision of materials about protection of at-risk groups, specifically children, young workers, expectant or new mothers, and those at risk of infection. Users are able to access legislation and related content via the website. The "About HSE" tab includes links to all Acts owned and enforced by the HSE, and legislation explanations, news, and supporting information are shared via additional links. Approved Codes of Practice and guidelines to aid stakeholders in complying with statutory requirements are also shared in the "HSE's work" panel, via the "Legislation" link.

A "Statistics" page is available within the "About HSE" page. The links within this page allow users to access annual UK statistics summary reports, search for data, graphs, and reports by topic. In 2014, a "HandS-On" Statistics Data Tool was available for injury and ill health data access and manipulation, but this could not be located in this 2017 review. The HSE also provides a "Shared Research" link on the page, inviting sponsorship and other collaboration to conduct research projects on important health and safety themes. Technical materials abound on the site, and are mainly available through the "Resources" tab. Users may download PDF brochures providing information about duties, as well as implementation guidelines. Links to Government, legal, publication, statistics collection, IOSH and EU-OSHA websites are also provided at various points.

## Range and Availability of Electronic Media Resources

The HSE site incorporates several electronic media types. HSE site content (e.g., RSS feeds) is compatible with and accessible via several mobile apps. In terms of HSE-created apps, only one (that supports land use planning) seems to have been rolled out to date. HSE news may also be received by Twitter, e-mail, and third party mobile apps. Sharing of content takes place via the HSE Press Office Twitter account "@H_S_E", and users may also e-mail and print content. The HSE Chair no longer appears to have an operational blog.

Users would find it easy to stay abreast of changes in the field and new materials being shared if they visit the "What's new in free leaflets" page (available via the path "Guidance>Resources>What's new in free leaflets") or subscribe to any of scores of e-bulletins based on user categories, industries, topics, resource types, news, and other selections. E-bulletins are available by e-mail, podcast, RSS, or SMS text message to share breaking news and core OSH material by industry category or topic, and even statistics. Archived and current newsletters, leaflets and news feeds are also available by RSS. Links in the "News" tab provide access to press releases and regional press releases.

Some critical leaflets and the health and safety law general information poster are also available in MP3 audio format and are referred to as "Talking Leaflets." Short "WorkSmart" videos have been developed as part of safety campaigns; these and several longer videos are available to tell stories, share first-person perspectives, and create big impact on the viewer. A health and safety law poster, several hazard-recognition and mitigation posters, PowerPoint slideshows and pdf publications are all available for free download. The HSE also makes available a guideline book called the "Health and Safety Toolbox", which may be physically purchased or downloaded free of charge. It is supplemented with free e-learning materials through "the health and safety toolbox microsite." The site uses "How Do I?" and "I work in..." prompts to customise material to users' drop-down menu responses. Many case studies, publications, and research outcomes are shared through the website to highlight poor as well as good practices, and to enhance user understanding and learning.

## US OSH E-Gov

In the US, OSH legislation is headed up by an Occupational Safety and Health Act, which was passed in 1970. Through it, the USOSHA has functioned as the agency responsible for enforcement, outreach and several other duties related to OSH. Subordinate to the USDOL, USOSHA uses several electronic manifestations, including its website www.osha.gov (OSHA, n.d.), to support its e-gov efforts.

### Accessibility and Support

The USOSHA site has a busy design and is full of content that is largely structured across nine tabs (About OSHA/Workers/Employers/Regulations/Enforcement/Topics/News & Publications/Data/ Training). There is now the ability to hover over tabs to preview subsections as is the case with the UKHSE site, and clicking on a subsection link loads various webpages directly. As this site is very comprehensive and wide-ranging, the focus in this section is to point out some of the main features of the USOSHA site.

While there is no site map, there is an A to Z index of topics. Users may perform searches using a search box at top right of every webpage or, via the "Topics" tab, they may access the site's searchable "Safety and Health Topics Pages". Finally, convenient access to popular query responses is supported through the "Topics" FAQ page, which is also available in the ribbon at the bottom of each webpage. The "Workers" tab also provides a link to "Worker FAQs". At the top left of all FAQ pages, users are given additional options to "Search OSHA" and "Ask OSHA". The USOSHA homepage makes use of a large and prominent image carousel that features four of USOSHA's highest priority, current issues. In a season where heat stroke and extreme stormy weather both challenged the US, two of the carousel issues were dedicated to heat safety and hurricanes. The other two issues were the proposed amendment of a standard and the site's new ability to support electronic reporting of injuries and illnesses. Hovering over an image indicator button pauses the image rotation, allowing the user to review the image at leisure.

The USOSHA site boosts accessibility to users by allowing viewing in either English or Spanish and also provides a few documents in up to 12 other languages. Transcripts are available for many audio and video documents. The site's accessibility notice directs users to the DOL webmaster's email to obtain help with any problems experienced while using assistive devices such as a screen- or Braille-reader. A link to the Freedom of Information Act is also included at the bottom of the page, committing to provide all information requested in writing, subject to certain named, legislated exceptions. No sign in or registration is required to use the site, and only an e-mail address is needed if subscribing to receive free updates.

The "About OSHA" webpage provides plenty of useful information, including mission, organization structure, leadership, and strategy of the USDOL and/or OSHA. On the page, there is a "Contact Us" link that provides e-mail, phone, and postal contact details. A myriad of ways to connect with USOSHA are listed as well, including Facebook, twitter, YouTube, Instagram, Flickr, RSS feeds, and newsletter subscriptions by email. Finally, a "Careers" link redirects to a page of DOL job opportunities. USOSHA provides many options for users to give feedback and lodge complaints. Users who wish to lodge a complaint are specifically instructed to phone OSHA directly. There are also links to report broken hyperlinks and make quality correction requests within the "Contact Us" webpage.

Excellent support is also provided for users who wish to share OSH-related reports. The "Employers" and "Contact Us" tabs allow injuries, illnesses, and fatalities to be reported via phone, fax, or an online form. The "Workers" tab and "Contact Us" tabs provide email, online, and phone/fax routes for workers seeking to file safety and health complaints or even whistle-blower complaints. USOSHA prominently outlines its commitment to workers experiencing employer retaliation after filing a complaint.

It is admirable that USOSHA boosts material usability by presenting a wide range of data and information. Links take users to sites that provide raw/original sources of data, fact sheets, statistics reports, and even visualisations that range from charts, graphs, tables, and even maps in html and pdf formats.

## Provision of Technical Content for Stakeholders

The USOSHA website focuses primarily on workers and employers, and also provides material that would be of use to those performing training and consultancy roles. On-site consultation is available free of charge, especially for small and medium enterprises (SMEs) seeking OSH compliance help, and an interactive US map is provided to help employers locate their local consultation offices. There is also a QuickStart compliance assistance tool that focuses on the employer groups of most concern to OSHA – small businesses, general industry, construction, and health care. At-risk groups are the focus of materials provided to address protection of young workers, pregnant women, and those at risk of exposure to bloodborne pathogens and violence.

In terms of legislation and related documentation, the website included links to the OSH Act, Federal Regulations information, and the full range of OSHA Standards. The site encourages public consultation by placing a link to items that are "Open for comment". Via the "Data" tab, downloadable data packets are available by year, and work-related injury and illness data are reported according to various focal areas (e.g. industry, state, and year). Statistics links sometimes connect the user to other government sites, such as the Bureau of Labour Statistics and the US Census Bureau, putting original data and statistics at user fingertips.

Free OSHA and other training materials are available through links provided. Additionally, there are several free subject-specific web-based training tools and checklists. The USOSHA site points users to several USOSHA-administered training programmes, and best-practice information is also shared for OSH trainers to improve their effectiveness. Detailed html and/or pdf publications are downloadable on a wide range of topics and there are also a few downloadable e-books. "New Items" and "Hot Topics" are given prominent blocks on the "Publications" page and there is also a "What's New" page under the

"News & Publications" tab. The publication listing is searchable and users may order for publications online, by phone, or by mail, if hard copies are desired.

Though not easily located on the site, a search revealed a page that features OSHA international collaborations up to 2015, and links to international organisations such as the ILO, EU-OSHA, and the World Health Organisation (WHO). Hyperlinks are provided to main USDOL and other US government websites, campaign partner sites (e.g. NIOSH), and OSHA training institute education centres.

### Range and Availability of Electronic Media Resources

RSS Feeds are available for users who want updates from the Federal Register, interpretations of regulations, news releases and the free QuickTakes newsletter. This newsletter is also available by e-mail. The website's "What's new" page and Twitter account highlight the latest updates and a "News Releases" page provides releases sorted by topic, and fully searchable within the page.

The site's resources support training and awareness, too, using scores of free, high quality items that are available for download via the "Training" and "Publications" webpages. The materials ranged from very impressive training videos (real-life and animated), photos, pictograms, newsletters, slideshows, forms, reports, text documents, and brochures to laminatable wallet cards and QuickCards, bulletins, posters, transcripts, e-books, booklets, and even bookmarks. Electronic materials included an extensive array of mp4, pdf, html, mp3, gif, eps, jpg/jpeg, epub, mobi, ppt, doc and xls formats.

## T&T OSH E-Gov

TTOSHA is the national focal point for OSH in T&T. In T&T, there exists a single access point at www.ttconnect.gov.tt to provide e-gov services to the public. The Ministry of Labour and Small Enterprise Development links to TTOSHA, its subordinate agency, through a "Become OSHA Compliant" link on its www.molsmed.gov.tt website. The eGovernment approaches of the TTOSHA site www.osha.gov.tt (Occupational Safety and Health Authority and Agency, 2011) are evaluated in the next section.

### Accessibility and Support

The TTOSHA website content is only available in English and is freely accessible by any users. Hovering over some of the site's nine tabs (Home/About Us/OSHA Services/Enforcement/Legal Requirements/News and Events/Careers/ Contact Us/Resources) activates drop-down menus, while clicking on some tabs opens webpages not included in the drop-down menu. On the homepage, a five-image carousel draws attention just below the main menu bar. The image topics are Refusal to Work (which leads to a one-page document), Request for Proposals (which leads to a page that is also available under the main menu tab "OSHA Services", Job Vacancies (connecting to the "Careers" main menu page), and Protect Yourself at Work followed by Safety and Health (both of which do not redirect the user beyond the homepage). The carousel includes five indicator buttons, but there is no way to pause the carousel. The page does not appear to be updated regularly, as half of the homepage is dedicated to promoting the National OSH Week, which passed over four months ago.

No specific resources have been included to enhance accessibility for different user needs. To find information, users must browse the content or use the search box at the top right of every webpage. There are no FAQ, index, site map, rating tool, feedback link, or online feedback form, but there are OSHA telephone and fax numbers as well as a telephone hotline. Also, there are no e-mail addresses listed on the site so a user wishing to contact TTOSHA can only do so by phone, fax, or in person.

The "About Us" page gives an overview of the focus and functions of both the OSH Authority and its enforcement arm, the OSH Agency. This section presents brief value, vision, and mission statements, and lists executive-level office holders. An entire tab is dedicated to careers, although there are no drop-down items. Copyright, terms of use, and privacy information are located via the webpage footer. Also, a ticker tape runs across the base of the homepage. It features links to some interesting OSH magazine articles available at www.ohsonline.com.

Close to the bottom of the homepage, four pictographs (titled Health & Safety, Hotline, Safety Corner, and Tenders) are prominently placed, though two contain no useful information and do not redirect elsewhere. One pictograph shares TTOSHA's hotline number, and the last redirects to the Request for Proposals page available via the main menu bar and the image carousel (both also on the homepage). It is notable that one of the proposals requested was for development of the TTOSHA website.

## Provision of Technical Content for Stakeholders

Under "Enforcement", webpages reflected OSH Act duties and/or rights of four stakeholder categories, namely employers, occupiers, employees, and the final group, importers, designers, and suppliers. No materials specifically focusing on at risk groups were available on the site. In "Legal Requirements", an OSH Act link leads to a short piece about the act and hyperlinks to a few older regulations that are still in force. There is no link to allow users to find and read the OSH Act itself, but excerpts are available under "Resources" to inform users of requirements related to accidents, major construction work, occupational disease, and injury. Clicking the "Resources" tab opens a page that provides links to local and foreign stakeholders as well as the websites of other OSH institutions and related organisations.

Other than the 10 brochures available for download (two others are shown but not downloadable) within the "Resources" tab, there are no training-related materials available. The site has no e-commerce capability, nor does it offer material for purchase in any other way. There is a noticeable absence of statistics on the site, as well. While webpages (namely OSHA Accidents, OSHA Inspections, OSHA Inspections Breakdown, and OSHA Activities) are reserved under the Resources>Research and Data link, these have remained empty since at least 2014. Besides, clicking on the "Resources" tab brings up a page titled "Stakeholders" with links to local, regional and international stakeholder websites. Some additional technical resources may be located by users who take the time to look for them.

## Range and Availability of Electronic Media Resources

There are limited resource types in use on the website. Social media buttons are notably absent from the site and TTOSHA does not appear to yet have a presence of its own on social media sites, blogs, mobile apps, or e-newsletters. An RSS icon does appear at the bottom of the homepage within the ticker tape, but this RSS feed links to articles from another organisation, the OHS online magazine. The only available documents are 10 of the 12 brochures mentioned before, and they come in one of either png or pdf formats. Audio and video files, posters, slideshows, and web-based training materials are not yet available on the site either. A search for various file formats did not reveal any other materials as being available on the site.

A "News and Events" tab leads to a calendar, a short "News and Events" page, and a photo gallery. The calendar is unmarked for every month of 2017, the last news piece advertised the National OSH Week that passed over four months ago, and the photos appear dated, several reflecting the culture of the organisation and T&T, rather than OSH matters. The website does not allow subscription to updates or news.

## COMPARING T&T'S WEBSITE TO THE UK AND US WEBSITES

It would be reasonably expected that given their significantly longer years of experience with developing and using their own OSH e-gov systems, as well as their greater resource bases, the UK and US OSH e-gov websites would be considerably more advanced than that of T&T. Thus, value can be derived by critically examining the gap between the TTOSHA site and the other two, in order to identify what improvements could be effected. The TTOSHA website is functional, and undoubtedly offers a beneficial service to stakeholders who use it. However, it is much more basic than the UKHSE and USOSHA websites. In terms of accessibility and utility, both the UK and the US sites appear much more user-oriented and performance-driven than the T&T site, as discussed in this section.

TTOSHA should be aiming to provide its stakeholders with convenient access to useful, relevant information. Currently, even some of the most basic information remains absent from or significantly lacking on the site. Although some improvements to TTOSHA have been noted since 2014, in comparison to the UKHSE site, TTOSHA still uses few pictures to boost site appeal, and too many tabs are being used to span the limited offerings currently available on the site. Further, TTOSHA has not stepped up enough to capture the attention of its stakeholders and prove its relevance/value to them; resource searchability, regular news updates/advisories/press releases and social media modalities are severely lacking, and OSH events are not regularly scheduled and advertised.

According to the HSE (2003), guidelines are necessary to help users interpret and comply with legislative requirements and to give them technical advice that might make legislated requirements better understood. While the TTOSHA site makes some guidelines available as free brochures, these are too limited in topic scope and number to adequately meet stakeholder needs. TTOSHA does not provide users with sufficient information about the OSH Act, interpretations of the intent and mandates of the OSH Act, and standards, codes of practice, or enough guidelines to assist users with understanding and complying with the OSH Act's requirements. Perhaps most surprising is the absence of a link to the OSH Act, even though TTOSHA is the lead body responsible for OSH in T&T. It is not clear why this is so, since the country maintains a hyperlinked repository of all of its laws within its legal affairs website (Ministry of Legal Affairs, 2013). In terms of materials targeted to various stakeholder groups, there are only 10 downloadable brochures and there is no facility for filtering of information depending on the type of user visiting the TTOSHA site.

In comparison, the UKHSE and/or USOSHA provide such a breadth of materials (e.g. legislation, standards, codes of practice, interactive tools, books, videos, audio files, slideshows, pictures, bookmarks, summary cards, maps, tables, graphs, and charts) that there is no doubt that the needs of workers (and especially at-risk groups like young workers and pregnant women), employers, and trainers are more than adequately supported. Choices abound so the developed-nation users can access answers or locate resources using a search bar, site map, index, glossary, or FAQ pages.

Considering that some of today's trends include a convenience mentality and technology assimilation into everyday life, the range of media files shared on the TTOSHA site is far too limited; only pdf and png files were available. TTOSHA must be cognisant of the fact that a large portion of the T&T population are digital natives: tech-savvy users who remain ever-connected via social media and other online modalities (Prensky, 2001; Palfrey & Gasser, 2008). They are likely to be accessing much of their information and connecting with others through their mobile devices rather than face-to-face. Building a culture of safety is critical for the long-term well-being of the workforce (McTernan, Dollard, Tuckey, & Vandenberg, 2016) and the economic stability of the country (EU-OSHA, 2010), and so TTOSHA needs to build lasting connections, especially with the country's younger workers. TTOSHA has no social media accounts, although these may be created at no cost and in short time. In comparison, UKHSE and USOSHA users are able to download files of different types, tap into options available via social media like YouTube, Twitter, Facebook, and email/RSS, and obtain resources by printing immediately or ordering right off the site, for convenience. No mobile apps have been created to enhance TTOSHA's connectivity with the T&T population, though it should be noted that apps would be more time-consuming and costly to create as they must be planned and created as original works. Also it is interesting to note that the three apps that were observed in use by USOSHA in 2014 appear to have fallen out of common use now. Also, if TTOSHA seeks to build a pro-safety culture, it is important that at least some of its materials reflect cultural elements from T&T. This will not be achieved if the only subscribable materials are sourced from developed nations, and no original articles are created by TTOSHA itself.

Tailoring the TTOSHA site to the needs of users also speaks the issue of accessibility for persons with disabilities. The UKHSE has done an excellent job of this, and the USOSHA has also adequately focused on this area, not only designing the site to boost accessibility, but also providing users with ways of reporting and obtaining help with any challenges they may face while using the sites. However, the TTOSHA site does not highlight the extent to which it has considered access by users with disabilities. Given that there is an increasing international focus on equal access for all persons without exception – consider Sustainable Development Goal 10 which targets reduction of inequality, including for persons with disabilities (United Nations, 2017) – this is an area where TTOSHA must do more. The site's lack of special accessibility features would significantly limit communication-challenged users' options to tweak the site's appearance and modes of use, give positive and negative feedback and receive TTOSHA responses online. Also, with only phone and fax contacts provided, and no online feedback or complaint tool available, users may not perceive sufficient interest from TTOSHA in supporting user needs. Ultimately, TTOSHA should be seeking to build pervasive and deep user relationships. According to Maxwell and Carboni (2017), increased social engagement can come about when organisations enable effective two-way communication.

Responsiveness and currency also sets the developed-nation sites apart from the TTOSHA site. According to Vikas (2017), ICT is increasingly being intertwined with on-site operations to notify populations of imminent threats and keep them informed about emergency response actions. The TTOSHA site could have been used in a similar way to the USOSHA site to bring updates related to floods, storms, and hurricanes during the hurricane season. Another concern was the impression that the TTOSHA site is infrequently updated, so that irrelevant information may remain too long on the site, or content may be absent for too long from the site. For example, the site should not be advertising National OSH week many months after the event has passed, and the links within the Data and Statistics tab should not have been allowed to lie fallow for years without either removing the time-wasting links or ensuring that the links would lead to some relevant resources.

Additionally, no materials are available for sale online and the site's lack of e-commerce capability is another way in which it contrasts with the other two sites evaluated in this chapter. As T&T becomes even more resource-constrained in the face of a declining economy (Sorias, 2015), agencies such as OSHA will face greater and greater challenges to do much with little. Generating income for itself is one option that TTOSHA should explore, and selling resources via the TTOSHA site should be the first step in that direction.

Finally, the site does not focus enough on strategy and performance. The site provides a good overview of TTOSHA organisation and roles but little information about its strategies or objective details of its approaches and achievements. Of note, some of the site content reflects a need for TTOSHA to clearly establish what it wants to achieve through the TTOSHA site, relocate photos not related to OSH to an intranet or offsite archive, and regularly update site content so that past events do not remain central themes. These shortcomings erode the picture of competence that should consistently be painted by TTOSHA. TTOSHA clearly intends to focus on OSH statistics since its site already includes research and data links, but the raw data and informational reports that abound on the UK and US sites are still totally absent on the TTOSHA site. As Podgorski (2015) points out, lagging and leading safety indicators have critical roles to play in OSH management. If TTOSHA wants stakeholders to adopt values including accountability, traceability, and currency, then its site offerings must consistently model these.

It is notable that both the UK and the US sites have been in existence for decades longer than the TTOSHA site, and the OSH Act has only been in existence for some 10 years in comparison to the UK's and US' Acts which have been in existence for almost 50 years. Both the UK and the US are technologically advanced countries, given their developed-nation status. Some may believe that the limitations of the TTOSHA site should be accepted simply because of the understandable challenges faced by TTOSHA. This should never be the case, lest the site's lagging state become permanent.

## RECOMMENDATIONS TO IMPROVE T&T OSH E-GOV

It is clear from the discussed shortcomings and opportunities that OSH e-gov should be improved in the TTOSHA context. The following recommendations, while geared towards T&T and TTOSHA, could also inform other developing nations who seek to enhance the structure and effectiveness of their own OSH e-gov systems.

### Develop a Comprehensive TTOSHA Strategy and Strategy Execution Plan

TTOSHA will be hard-pressed to achieve excellence unless it takes the time to define its values, understand the pros and cons of its current position, craft its long-term strategy, and plan how to roll out that strategy. TTOSHA's e-gov approach must be set within this broader strategy and should play a prominent role. Establishing a list of priorities informed by a consideration of costs and benefits must lead to the development of a phased implementation approach to be faithfully rolled out. This approach will help TTOSHA to convert an overwhelming list to one that is logical and achievable over time.

## Take Stock of TTOSHA Resource Limitations and Create Partnerships to Bolster Resources

As TTOSHA plans its approach to improve OSH e-gov, the issue of limited resources must be proactively addressed. Currently, resource shortages seem to constrain the agency's ability to create materials, or perform outreach, consultations, inspections and enforcement as much as it would like. Partnering with NGOs, private sector companies, manufacturers' associations, consultants and trainers, auditors, and other regional and international OSH bodies could prove advantageous. Such partnerships could help TTOSHA to develop a network of experts who could provide useful services to support its work. It could deepen society's recognition of and respect for TTOSHA's purpose. It could facilitate sharing of resources, such as training videos and reports that OSHA could share on its website. Also, collaborations could enhance goodwill and trust, and boost buy-in to OSHA's message.

## Boost OSHA's Visibility by Promoting Its Value Proposition

TTOSHA needs to establish itself as the go-to body for individuals and organisations that need to report on OSH occurrences or to obtain OSH guidance or resources. The response of employers and workers to TTOSHA has been lukewarm, perhaps because they have not been able to see any advantages to strengthening ties with the agency. The fact is that certain OSH bodies such as the USOSHA, UKOSHA and even EU-OSHA have become highly relevant to stakeholders. To follow suit, TTOSHA must sensitise stakeholders about why OSH is ethically and economically relevant, shine a light on its offerings and mandates, and underscore its role in voluntary compliance work as well as enforcement efforts.

The agency must use the TTOSHA website to its advantage in carrying out this work. Press releases and news articles must be regularly crafted and visibly posted on the site. Periods of intensive focus on certain industries might be advertised on the homepage, so that companies are encouraged to keep their OSH systems compliant with the legislation. Notices of legal action taken in cases of non-compliance, photos and reports of safety excellence, and safety datasets and statistical reports should be conspicuously available and constantly updated to promote a philosophy of natural justice. Stakeholder partnerships should be developed, leveraged, and publicised to enhance TTOSHA's reach and impact.

## Embrace the Digital Age

As Hood & Margetts recognised since 2007, in this digital age there must be increased reliance on modern technology. TTOSHA's success will depend in part on its effective use of its website and other digital media to connect with, engage, and serve its stakeholders. It must become highly creative and responsive in an age where many users expect service providers to cater to every customer need with customisation and excellent levels of responsiveness. As TTOSHA add social media elements to its e-gov approach, it would be important to gauge the success of each new addition. Only those that prove valuable should be retained; there is no need to jump on the bandwagon with every new tool that becomes popular. It is far more important to maintain a current and relevant presence for each of TTOSHA's selected social media faces.

## Ensure That TTOSHA's E-Gov Presence Is Relevant, Current, and of High Quality

TTTOSHA's website should be full of content that serves the needs of its stakeholders. To be relevant, TTOSHA must identify who its stakeholders are, as well as what the needs of each stakeholder group would be. Certainly workers and employers must be considered, but there would be certain industries (e.g. construction, small and medium enterprises) that would be more at-risk or more resource-strapped than others, just as there would be certain worker groups (e.g. lone workers, pregnant women, young workers) who would be placed at greater risk. As a minimum, support materials on the TTOSHA website should be varied in format (in addition to brochures/booklets, there should be videos, audio files, photos, guidelines, and analytical reports at the very least) to appeal to different user needs and learning styles and in type (pdf, jpeg, ppt, doc, xls, html, mp3, mp4, and epub are among the very commonly used file types) to offer choice. The website should also encourage users to send feedback in real time, for example by including links so user can lodge complaints, suggestions and even accident/injury reports at the click of a button.

Website content should be regularly updated so that outdated content is removed and older information gives way to interesting new content that keeps users interested in returning to obtain more insights or learn more. Dated content will lead to waning user interest, and less interaction with the site.

Also there must be a focus on applying high quality standards to everything that is posted on the site and to the website's design itself. Resources should contain no errors, and there should be prompt corrective action if an error is seen. The website should have no redundancy and there should be no dead links; these would erode user confidence in the agency itself. A high quality agency must be reflected in high quality operations, even those that are digital in nature.

## Focus on Data Collection and Measurement

Data management and analytics must play a huge role in TTOSHA's operations to set targets and track performance of its e-gov system. In line with recommendations from Chen and Hsieh (2014), TTOSHA must determine what it wishes to measure, what sources of data it will use, who might be partners in this undertaking, how to guard against security and privacy risks, and how reporting should be structured. Also, since insightful and responsible data management would have a major impact on the effectiveness of TTOSHA, it should be a priority to recruit a skilled and ethical specialist who would be dedicated to this work. A focus on performance and measurement is also critical since TTOSHA must set the standard that users would be expected to emulate. Podgorski (2015) explains the role of both leading and lagging performance indicators, and TTOSHA should craft an indicator dashboard to report on its achievements and targets.

## Guard Against a Digital Divide

Liptrott (2016) cautions that if socio-economic challenges prevent people from developing IT skills, this can hinder their ability to equally access digital resources. Similarly, if computers or internet access are unavailable or less available, the phenomenon of a digital divide will manifest itself, effectively disempowering certain subsets of the population. Thus it is critical that TTOSHA takes action to push against these challenges, through means that could include the creation of local wi-fi hotspots (e.g. in community centres) and/or use of OSH caravans that travel the country to interact with and connect with communities. Also TTOSHA should ensure that users with disabilities are adequately supported, as groups like them may be more at risk for occupational injury and illness than many others.

### Develop an Improvement Focus

TTOSHA's e-gov approach, no matter how well planned, will have to be adjusted over time. Embedding continual improvement within the approach to website maintenance will be critical so that the website design and content can be improved incrementally over time. Small changes may not be noticeable when considered individually, but over time, many small changes can deliver meaningful value. In this regard, it is important to encourage online and offline feedback to allow for stakeholder critique and suggestions regarding the website and materials. Feedback from TTOSHA's employees would be especially valuable, given their knowledge of the agency's purpose and challenges.

### Aggressively Support OSH Compliance in T&T

Achieving OSH compliance would be a high priority for TTOSHA, so its e-gov approach must aggressively support this. TTOSHA must ensure that its website reflects its philosophy about how to go about the business of boosting compliance. TTOSHA must consider whether T&T's safety culture is one that responds better to encouraging compliance, whether it would only step up when strict enforcement and sanctions are instituted, or whether some well-defined middle ground is to obtain. If certain industries approach OSH compliance with a laissez-faire attitude, TTOSHA may need to consider using a contingency model: stricter approaches used for industries that are less intrinsically motivated to comply, and more trusting approaches used for industries that prove themselves to be committed to compliance.

## FUTURE RESEARCH DIRECTIONS

Only qualitative data was used in conducting this study. Sourcing quantitative data about user demographics, usability, accessibility, and user needs could provide insight into the validity of existing site design and the efficiency of site performance. Insight from stakeholder complaints and suggestions would also lead to design improvements focused on improving OSH e-gov effectiveness. Specific to T&T, the collection and analysis of these data would bring about a deeper understanding of the impact of OSH e-gov, and would be instructive in planning further development of the TTOSHA website and other e-gov tools.

The developed-nation evaluation focused on only two OSH e-gov websites. A wider review and content analysis based on additional international OSH governmental and non-governmental websites could also be beneficial. A broader study may recognise additional e-gov best-practices to emulate. Evaluating how practices vary in first- and third-world settings could also enhance appreciation of how practices may vary in different cultures.

While e-gov is popularly studied, only limited research happens within the OSH e-gov sub-field. More research about design and application of OSH e-gov systems is warranted, as this would identify and share varying thinking and approaches in the field. Of particular relevance would be studies that look at the use of mobile systems in OSH e-gov, as populations of most countries are increasingly connecting to webpages and mobile apps for information, communication, and entertainment.

Partnering between TTOSHA and higher education institutions can be beneficial to both parties, as the latter can analyse rich data already held by the former, saving TTOSHA from having to hire analysts, and reducing costs and research timelines for the researchers. In addition to data analysis, researchers with writing competencies may be able to help create training and outreach resources for the TTOSHA site.

## CONCLUSION

Work is becoming inherently more risky to worker safety and health, particularly as complex mechanisation increases and people juggle more distractions, work faster, and produce more. As populations grow and resource availability is constrained, the government is rolling out more modern IT-enabled means of connecting with citizens and providing public service access. This study has recognised that, notwithstanding admirable levels of e-government advancement in T&T in recent years, OSH e-government has remained stunted. This shortcoming limits the population's ability to access OSH information, improve OSH practice, and build a symbiotic relationship with TTOSHA.

This study supports advancement of TTOSHA's work. It has evaluated several features of two developed-nation OSH e-gov websites, identifying how value is delivered to workers, employers, and other stakeholders. With these best practices in mind, recommendations for achieving OSH e-gov excellence have been made to TTOSHA. These especially take into account the need for TTOSHA to modernise its approach, clearly define its purpose and values, and develop/tailor/share resources to promote and enhance OSH competence, commitment, and involvement of various stakeholder groups. Developing and maintaining a sustainable OSH e-gov presence would be a very involved task, but a proper roll-out as a phased project would add immediate value.

This work could inform efforts of government and other local OSH organisations seeking to craft a meaningful electronic presence. It could enhance understanding and provide support to employers, employees, employee representatives, and the wider public, weaving good OSH practice into everyday living. Further, the chapter provides good insight into developed-nation OSH e-gov practices to ICT practitioners as well as developing-nation governments seeking to improve their own OSH e-gov systems. Finally, this work has pointed out the need for further study in this area and proposed some ideas for deepening research that can enhance understanding and practice in the field of OSH e-government in developed and developing nation contexts.

## REFERENCES

Abanumy, A., Al-Badi, A., & Mayhew, P. (2005). E-government website accessibility: In-depth evaluation of Saudi Arabia and Oman. *The Electronic Journal of E-Government*, *3*(3), 99–106.

Accenture Institute for Health and Public Service Value. (2009). *From e-government to e-governance: Using new technologies to strengthen relationships with citizens*. Accenture.

Australian National Audit Office. (2004). *Measuring the efficiency and effectiveness of e-government.* Audit Report No. 26, 2004-2005. Canberra, Australia: ANAO.

BBC. (2014). *My web my way – Making the web easier to use.* Retrieved August 14, 2014, from http://www.bbc.co.uk/accessibility/

Boujarwah, A. (2006). E-government in Kuwait: From vision to reality. Proceedings of iiWAS2006.

Chen, Y., & Hsieh, T. (2014). Big data for digital government: Opportunities, challenges, and strategies. *International Journal of Public Administration in the Digital Age, 1*(1), 1–14. doi:10.4018/ijpada.2014010101

ECOSOC, United Nations Economic and Social Council. (2015). *Report of the Secretary-General. Strengthening and Building Institutions for Policy Integration in the Post-2015 Era.* E/2015/69.

Elsler, D., Takala, J., & Remes, J. (2017). *An international comparison of the cost of work-related accidents and illnesses.* Luxembourg: Publications Office of the European Union. Retrieved September 11, 2017, from https://osha.europa.eu/sites/default/files/publications/documents/international_comparison-of_costs_work_related_accidents.pdf

Energy Chamber of Trinidad and Tobago. (2007). *STOW contractor guidance manual.* Point Lisas, Trinidad: Energy Chamber. Retrieved August 24, 2014, from http://www.stowtt.info/downloads/STOW%20Guidance%20Manual%20v9-Feb2013.pdf

European Agency for Safety and Health at Work. (2010). *Mainstreaming OSH into business management.* Luxembourg: Office for Official Publications of the European Communities. Retrieved August 14, 2014, from https://osha.europa.eu/en/publications/reports/mainstreaming_osh_business

European Agency for Safety and Health at Work. (2014). *Estimating the cost of accidents and ill health at work: A review of methodologies.* Luxembourg: Publications Office of the European Union. Retrieved August 14, 2014, from https://osha.europa.eu/en/publications/reports/estimating-the-costs-of-accidents-and-ill-health-at-work

Fang, Z. (2002). E-government in digital era: Concept, practice, and development. *International Journal of the Computer, the Internet and Management, 10*(2), 1-22.

Gathungu, J., & Mungai, A. N. (2013). Contextual Factors Affecting E-Government Strategy Implementation and Its Impact on Public Sector Performance in Kenya. *Journal of Arts and Humanities, 1*(1), 143–157. doi:10.18533/journal.v1i1.14

Gil-Garcia, J. R., Helbig, N., & Ojo, A. (2014). Being smart: Emerging technologies and innovation in the public sector. *Government Information Quarterly, 31*(Supp. 1), I1–I8. doi:10.1016/j.giq.2014.09.001

Gleason, J. M., & Barnum, D. T. (1978). Effectiveness of OSHA sanctions in influencing employer behavior: Single and multi-period decision models. *Accident; Analysis and Prevention, 10*(1), 35–49. doi:10.1016/0001-4575(78)90006-4

Government of the Republic of Trinidad and Tobago. (2004). *The occupational safety and health act (2004).* Retrieved November 1, 2011, from http://www.ttparliament.org/legislations/a2004-01.pdf

Government of the Republic of Trinidad and Tobago. (2006). *The occupational safety and health (amendment) act (2006).* Retrieved November 1, 2011, from http://www.ttparliament.org/legislations/a2006-03.pdf

Government of the Republic of Trinidad and Tobago. (2011). *Innovation for lasting prosperity: Medium term policy framework 2011-2014.* Port of Spain: Ministry of Planning and the Economy. Retrieved August 24, 2014, from http://finance.gov.tt/wp-content/uploads/2013/11/Medium-Term-Policy-Framework-2011-14.pdf

Government of the Republic of Trinidad and Tobago. (2012). *National cyber security strategy.* Port of Spain: Inter Ministerial Committee For Cyber Security. Retrieved August 24, 2014, from http://www.nationalsecurity.gov.tt/Portals/0/Pdf%20Files/National_Cyber_Security%20Strategy_Final.pdf

Granizo, C. J., Yanez, P. L., Ramirez, D. P., & Machado, P. C. (2011). Usability in e-government sites. *Eighth International Conference on Information Technology: New Generations (ITNG)*, 453-458.

Health and Safety Executive. (2003). *Health and safety regulation: a short guide.* Leaflet HSC13 (Rev. 1). Retrieved September 18, 2017, from http://www.hse.gov.uk/pubns/hsc13.pdf

Health and Safety Executive. (n.d.). *Health and safety executive.* Retrieved August 15, 2014, from www.hse.gov.uk

Hood, C. C., & Margetts, H. Z. (2007). *The tools of government in the digital age.* Houndmills, UK: Palgrave Macmillan. doi:10.1007/978-1-137-06154-6

International Labour Organisation. (2009). *Guidelines on occupational safety and health management systems: ILO-OSH 2001* (2nd ed.). Geneva, Switzerland: ILO.

International Labour Organisation. (2017). *Decent Work.* Retrieved September 28, 2017, from http://www.ilo.org/global/topics/decent-work/lang--en/index.htm

Krippendorff, K. (2004). *Content analysis: An introduction to its methodology* (2nd ed.). Thousand Oaks, CA: Sage.

Levy, K. E. C., & Johns, D. M. (2016). When open data is a Trojan Horse: The weaponization of transparency in science and governance. *Big Data and Society*, *3*(1), 1–6. doi:10.1177/2053951715621568

Liptrott, M. (2016). Tackling the Digital Divide: The Shift from Access to Capacity. *International Journal of Public Administration in the Digital Age*, *3*(1), 70–84. doi:10.4018/IJPADA.2016010105

Liu, J., & Lin, B. (2012). Government auditing and corruption control: Evidence from China's provincial panel data. *China Journal of Accounting Research*, *5*(2), 163–186. doi:10.1016/j.cjar.2012.01.002

Losh, S. C. (2013). American digital divides: Generation, education, gender, and ethnicity in American digital divides. In Digital Literacy: Concepts, Methodologies, Tools, and Applications (pp. 932-958). IGI Global. doi:10.4018/978-1-4666-1852-7.ch048

Maxwell, S. P., & Carboni, J. L. (2017). Civic engagement through social media: Strategic stakeholder management by high-asset foundations. *International Journal of Public Administration in the Digital Age*, *4*(1), 35–48. doi:10.4018/IJPADA.2017010103

Mayernik, M. S. (2017). Open Data: Accountability and Transparency. *Big Data and Society*, *4*(2), 1–5. doi:10.1177/2053951717718853

McTernan, W. P., Dollard, M. F., Tuckey, M. R., & Vandenberg, R. J. (2016). Beneath the surface: An exploration of remoteness and work stress in the mines. In Psychosocial Factors at Work in the Asia Pacific: From Theory to Practice (pp. 341-358). Springer International. doi:10.1007/978-3-319-44400-0

Ministry of Legal Affairs. (2013). *Alphabetical list of revised laws.* Retrieved August 24, 2014, from http://www.legalaffairs.gov.tt/Laws_listing.html

Nathai-Balkissoon, M., Maharaj, C., Guerrero, R., Mahabir, R., & Dialsingh, I. (2017). *Pilot development of innovation scales for beverage manufacturing companies in a developing country.* Cogent Business and Management. doi:10.1080/23311975.2017.1379214

Nathai-Balkissoon, M., & Pun, K. F. (2011). A holistic model and research agenda for organisational learning in manufacturing. *World Journal of Entrepreneurship, Management and Sustainable Development, 7*(1), 27–38. doi:10.1108/20425961201000028

Nathai-Balkissoon, M., & Pun, K. F. (2016). OSH at Trinidad and Tobago's fingertips: Learning from first-world OSH website approaches. *International Journal of Public Administration in the Digital Age, 3*(3), 57–72. doi:10.4018/IJPADA.2016070104

Ndou, V. (2004). E-government for developing countries: Opportunities and challenges. *The Electronic Journal on Information Systems in Developing Countries, 18*(1), 1–24. doi:10.1002/j.1681-4835.2004.tb00117.x

Occupational Safety and Health Administration. (n.d.). *Occupational safety & health administration.* Retrieved August 15, 2014 from www.osha.gov

Occupational Safety and Health Authority and Agency. (2011). *OSHA.* Retrieved September 17, 2017, from www.osha.gov.tt

Open Data for Development Network. (2017). *Open Data For Development: Building An Inclusive Data Revolution. Annual Report 2016.* International Development Research Centre. Retrieved December 19, 2017, from http://od4d.net/wp-content/uploads/2017/05/Annual-repor-2016_Web.pdf

Palfrey, J. G., & Gasser, U. (2008). *Born digital: Understanding the first generation of digital natives.* New York: Basic Books.

Pemberton, J. D., & Stonehouse, G. H. (2000). Organisational learning and knowledge assets: An essential partnership. *The Learning Organization, 7*(4), 184–193. doi:10.1108/09696470010342351

Podgórski, D. (2015). Measuring operational performance of OSH management system – A demonstration of AHP-based selection of leading key performance indicators. *Safety Science, 73*, 146–166. doi:10.1016/j.ssci.2014.11.018

Prensky, M. (2001). Digital natives, digital immigrants part 1. *On the Horizon, 9*(5), 1–6. doi:10.1108/10748120110424816

Pun, K. F., & Nathai-Balkissoon, M. (2011). Integrating knowledge management into organisational learning: A review of concepts and models. *The Learning Organization, 18*(3), 203–223. doi:10.1108/09696471111123261

Safety and Health Practitioner. (2017). *Poor OSH costing world roughly €2680bn a year*. Retrieved from https://www.shponline.co.uk/poor-osh-costing-world-roughly-e2680bn-year

Schwab, K. (Ed.). (2013). *The global competitiveness report 2013-2014: Full data edition.* World Economic Forum. Retrieved September 11, 2017, from http://www3.weforum.org/docs/WEF_GlobalCompetitivenessReport_2013-14.pdf

Sewake, G. (2015). *The Business of Connecting Through Technology: Millenials*. Published March 12, 2015 online. Retrieved December 19, 2017, from https://extension.unh.edu/articles/Business-Connecting-through-Technology-Millennials

Shih, W., & Allen, M. (2006). Working with generation-D: Adopting and adapting to cultural learning and change. *Library Management*, *28*(1/2), 89–100. doi:10.1108/01435120710723572

Sorias, L. (2015, May 13). Diversification, labour solution needed to fix the economy. *Trinidad Express*. Retrieved from http://www.trinidadexpress.com/article/20150513/business/150519865

Surienty, L., Hong, K. T., & Hung, D. K. M. (2011). Occupational safety and health (OSH) in SMEs in Malaysia: A preliminary investigation. *Journal of Global Entrepreneurship*, *1*(1), 65–75.

Sutton, H. (2017). Follow five steps to create elegant and accessible design. *Disability Compliance for Higher Education, 22*(6), 5-5. doi:10.1002/dhe.30259

United Nations. (2017). *Goal 10: Reduce inequality within and among countries.* Retrieved September 17, 2017, from http://www.un.org/sustainabledevelopment/inequality/

United Nations Department of Economic and Social Affairs. (2014). *UN e-government survey 2014: E-government for the future we want.* Retrieved August 7, 2014, from http://unpan3.un.org/egovkb/Reports/UN-E-Government-Survey-2014

United Nations Department of Economic and Social Affairs. (2016). *UN e-government survey 2016: E-government in support of sustainable development.* Retrieved September 11, 2017, from http://workspace.unpan.org/sites/Internet/Documents/UNPAN97453.pdf

United Nations Development Programme. (2017). *Decent work and economic growth.* Retrieved September 17, 2017, from http://www.undp.org/content/undp/en/home/sustainable-development-goals/goal-8-decent-work-and-economic-growth.html

United Nations General Assembly. (2015). *Outcome document of the high-level meeting of the General Assembly on the overall review of the implementation of the outcomes of the World Summit on the Information Society.* A/RES/70/125.

United States Department of Labor. (n.d.). *U.S. department of labor e-government strategic plan.* Retrieved August 7, 2014, from http://www.dol.gov/_sec/e_government_plan/p41-43_appendixe.htm

Vikas, V. (2017). ICT and disaster management: A study of the social media use in 2015 Chennai City floods. *International Journal of Public Administration in the Digital Age*, *4*(3), 29–41. doi:10.4018/IJPADA.2017070103

World Bank. (2011). *Definition of e-government.* Retrieved March 9, 2014, from http://web.worldbank.org/WBSITE/EXTERNAL/TOPICS/EXTINFORMATIONANDCOMMUNICATIONANDTECHNOLOGIES/EXTEGOVERNMENT/0,contentMDK:20507153~menuPK:702592~pagePK:148956~piPK:216618~theSitePK:702586,00.html

World Wide Web Consortium. (2012). *Web Accessibility Initiative.* Retrieved September 17, 2017, from https://www.w3.org/WAI/changedesign#skip

Zelenika, I., & Pearce, J. M. (2013). The Internet and other ICTs as tools and catalysts for sustainable development: Innovation for 21st century. *Information Development*, *29*(3), 217–232. doi:10.1177/0266666912465742

## KEY TERMS AND DEFINITIONS

**E-Government:** The use of electronic technology, more commonly called information technology to connect government agencies to stakeholders in order to help government meet its goals related to service delivery, interaction, information sharing, and other aspects of governance.

**Image Carousel:** A website navigation option that shows a set of pictures in sequence, with further levels of information being revealed about clicked images if they are attached to hyperlinks.

**Menu:** An array of options offered to users of a website, usually arranged horizontally across the width of the webpage.

**OSH E-Government:** E-government specifically designed for and focused on furthering occupational safety and health aims in a country.

**Ribbon:** A narrow (colored) menu bar that offers page options to users on a website.

**TTOSHA:** An acronym used in the chapter to refer to the primary OSH e-government website of Trinidad and Tobago.

**UKHSE:** An acronym used in the chapter to refer to the primary OSH e-government website of the United Kingdom.

**USOSHA:** An acronym used in the chapter to refer to the primary OSH e-government website of the United States of America.

**Website Effectiveness:** An aspect of website evaluation that could judge elements such as ease of access, ease of use, information utility, and user satisfaction.

**Website Efficiency:** An aspect of website evaluation that could judge elements related to maximizing resource usage, including productivity, return on investment, costs, and benefits.

# Chapter 5
# States' Budget Investments in Technology and Improving Criminal Justice Outcomes

**Deborah Mohammed-Spigner**
*Rutgers University, USA*

**Brian E. Porter**
*Montclair State University, USA*

**Lois W. Warner**
*Rutgers University, USA*

## ABSTRACT

*Investments in criminal justice have been expanding over the decades especially as specific outcomes have been sought to address the issues surrounding crime and public safety. Reducing crime and the rate of imprisonment can both significantly impact public safety and cost savings, as well as address outcomes for the justice-involved population in reducing the rate of return to imprisonment, or recidivism. Lessening sentences for non-violent crimes and expanding drug courts as an alternative to incarceration, along with other major criminal justice reform, have led some states to experience a reduction in crime and prison population. New Jersey, Hawaii, and California have made significant strides to reduce its crime and prison populations and are leaders in achieving major criminal justice reform. This chapter seeks to examine corrections spending for these three leading states that have implemented evidence-based policies and adapted information technology to improve criminal justice outcomes. It will also outline states spending on corrections over the past five years.*

*Whether It's Improving Our Health or Harnessing Clean Energy, Protecting Our Security or Succeeding In the Global Economy, Our Future Depends On Reaffirming America's Role As the World's Engine of Scientific Discovery and Technological Innovation. – President Barack Obama*

DOI: 10.4018/978-1-5225-5966-5.ch005

## BACKGROUND

According to a PEW (2014) study, since 2007 more than half of our nation's states enacted evidence-based policies in an effort to limit prison populations and reduce the rising costs of mass incarceration and high crime levels. Indeed, in 2014, according to the report, the Bureau of Justice Statistics (BJS) reported a combined decrease of more than 15,000 inmates—the second-biggest annual reduction on record—that brought the nation's prison population to its lowest level since 2005 and accompanied a nationwide reduction in crime. Focusing on what works and incorporating policies to reduce imprisonment have led to lower incarceration among the majority of states.

A 2015 study by the Brennan Center for Justice, 23 states reduced their prison populations between 2011 and 2014. In fact, many states with the most dramatic crime drops also shrank their incarcerated populations. All but one of the 23 states (South Dakota) experienced a simultaneous reduction in crime with some states also experiencing crime drops of over 15 percent. Overall however, California, Hawaii and New Jersey had the largest rate of decrease in prison populations and crime rates between 2008 and 2014 (Eisen & Chettair, 2015).

According to a PEW/MacArthur (2014) report, governments make budget and policy choices each year that have long-term effects on both their fiscal futures and the outcomes they deliver for constituents. The report states that using evidence-based practices (EBPs) to inform decisions enables governments to select, fund, and operate public programs more strategically. Fiscal pressures, increasing availability of evidence on what works, federal funding incentives and growing interest from state leaders are some of the factors that the report outlined as influencing the trend in adoption of EBPs. Federal expenditures as well as overall state budgets have increased corrections spending dramatically over the past decades. Since 1985, states expenditures on corrections increased exponentially from $6.7 billion in 1985 to over $56 billion by 2015 (National Association of State Budget Officers, Sentencing Project 2017). To achieve better outcomes however, states have been implementing evidence-based policies and investing in technology to decrease incarceration and crime rates. Examining the budgets for corrections of the three states with the largest reductions in crime and prison populations over the past five years will indicate what are the trends in the states' expenditures on corrections to improve outcomes for the criminal justice populations.

## INTRODUCTION

Increasing costs and limited resources exacerbated the challenges to governments to address rising crime rates and prison population. Consequently, government initiatives focused on strategies that are evidence-based to improve overall performance and outcomes for criminal justice agencies. The Bureau of Justice Assistance's initiatives to improve the performance of policing while reducing costs, or smart policing initiatives (SPI), formulated effective strategies for criminal justice agencies through the adoption of technologies and evidence-based practices to improve outcomes (Bureau of Justice Assistance, n.d.). The BJA documents best practices to inform strategies to improve outcomes and outlines 5 key components of smart policing initiative (SPI). These include:

1. Performance measurement and research partnerships,
2. Outreach and collaboration,

3. Managing organizational change,
4. Strategic targeting, and
5. Making better use of intelligence and other data and information systems. (Bureau of Justice Assistance, n.d.).

The use of information and data are crucial to the SPI. Sharing of real-time data among criminal justice agencies and tracking various criminal justice data increases effectiveness of the policing. Investments in technology, which helps facilitate the sharing of data specifically, and access to information, have become a crucial tool for criminal justice agencies to incorporate more effective practices in order to achieve the goals of reducing crime and recidivism.

Governments have expanded investment in technology overall to improve performance and to enhance overall outcomes, specifically in the service-oriented agencies as health, education and criminal justice. Reforms in government have focused on combining both innovative strategies as well as evidence-based policies to meet increasing constrained budgets and the need for effective and efficient service delivery. In the 2013 budget memorandum, the federal Office of Management and Budget (OMB) outlined guidelines for state and localities that receive funding through both competitive and formula grants to incorporate evidence of effectiveness and build more evaluation into their budget proposals, and as such encouraged federal agencies to prioritize such programs (Budget Memorandum, 2013). The Office of Justice Programs (OJP) leads efforts to use evidence and evaluation to improve programs at the federal, state and local and tribal levels of government across the country. Through its two key evidence-generating components, the Bureau of Justice Statistics (BJS) and the National Institute of Justice (NIJ) statistics and research are used by decision makers at all levels to develop evidence-based policies and programs that respond to emerging criminal justice challenges. OJP's research, evaluation and statistics appropriation provides grants, contracts, and cooperative agreements for research, development and evaluation. It also supports development and dissemination of quality statistical and scientific information. OJP administers the following grants to states criminal justice agencies:

- Byrne Justice Assistance Grants (JAG) for initiatives in body worn cameras and bulletproof vests including smart policing initiatives and training.
- National Criminal History Improvement Program (NCHIP). Administered by BJS, to help states and territories to improve the quality of timeliness and immediate accessibility of criminal history and related records. These records play a vital role in supporting the National Instant Criminal Background Check System (NCIS) and helping federal state, local and tribal law enforcement investigate crime and promote public safety.
- Economic, High-Tech, Cybercrime Prevention which aims to combat economic, high-technology and internal crimes of counterfeiting and piracy. Also supports crime analysis, delivery of evidence-based crime fighting technology, including information sharing systems, software and hardware development, mobile communication solutions to support law enforcement and reentry offender case management systems, through grant, training and technical assistance.

Corrections is now the third largest category of spending in most states, behind education and health care (Mitchell & Leachman, 2014). The rate of expenditures on corrections has been increasing exponentially (Mitchell & Leachman 2014), in part because the federal government incentivized states through funding legislations to adopt more punitive criminal justice policies (Eisen & Chettair, 2015).

An examination of government spending over the past three decades illustrates that expenditures on corrections (state and local) have increased by 324%, triple the rate of increase in education spending ranging as high as 850% in Texas with only two states, Massachusetts and New Hampshire, having higher expenditures on education than corrections over this period (Stullich, Morgan, & Schak, 2016). The report suggests as a result, that states may consider increasing investments in education to address reductions in incarceration rate that will consequently lead to reducing crime and increasing opportunity among at-risk youths as documented in studies cited in the report (Stullich, Morgan, & Schak, 2016).

States can reduce incarceration rates without harming public safety in other ways, such as expanding the use of alternative policies to divert those convicted of low-level felonies and misdemeanors from prison, as well as utilizing alternatives to technical violations of parole/probation that would otherwise result in violators being re-incarcerated (Mitchell and Leachman, 2014). Although the prison populations and crime rates in some states such as New Jersey and California have been falling, the rate of imprisonment still remains high for states like New Jersey which experienced decreasing crime and prison population rates but not similar reductions in the rate of incarceration. According to the authors, incarceration rates are a function of four variables: 1. the crime rate, 2. the ratio of arrests to crimes, 3. the share of offenders sent to prison, and 4. the length of prison sentences. The study emphasized that the drivers of the increase in state incarceration rates over the decades have been both offenders sent to prison and the length of prison sentences which are under policymakers' direct control. As such, reforms aimed at reducing prison populations will need to target these two areas.

Despite the overall decline in incarceration and crime, the United States still leads the developed world with the highest prison population, incarcerating over 25% of the world's total prison population. And, despite advances in practices and innovative technologies employed in the states, there are still many states that have not seen positive trends in reducing prison populations and crime. From 2011 to 2014 there was an overall 1.64% reduction in prison population however, 27 of the states actually saw an increase in prison population. Of the 23 states that experienced a decrease in prison population however, 22 of these also saw a decrease in crime rate (Eisen & Chettiar, 2015).

This study looks at the three states that had the most significant reductions in crime and incarceration, New Jersey, Hawaii and California. While the study is limited in looking at the possible correlation in states' budgets and investment in technologies to produce positive criminal justice outcomes (i.e., reduction recidivism and crime) and implementation of evidence-based policies, the study will examine the three leading states' budgets and spending on corrections over 5 years to show how states spending on corrections, combined with policy changes could reform the criminal justice system and increase public safety.

## EVIDENCE-BASED PRACTICES AND POLICIES, AND THE USE OF TECHNOLOGY

Evidence –based policymaking uses the best available research and information on program results to guide decisions at all stages of the policy process (PEW, 2014). In 2013, federal agencies were given new guidelines to draw on evidence in their budget proposals for budget requests to be backed by evidence and commitment to innovation. However, the guidelines reinforced that determination is not simply whether a program is effective or not as policy development occurs in multiple stages and evidence can add value at every stage (Turner, 2013). According to a PEW (2014) study, more than half of the states enacted evidence-based policies since 2007 to limit prison populations and reduce costs. According to the report, in 2014, the Bureau of Justice Statistics reported a combined of more than 15,000 inmates, the second biggest annual reduction on record, and brought the nation's prison population to its lowest level since 2005 and accompanied by a nationwide reduction in crime (PEW, 2014).

PEW (2014), the PEW-MacArthur Results First Initiative, developed a framework of five key components for governments to follow to adopt a comprehensive system of evidence-based policymaking. Budget development is the second of the five key components that requires incorporation of the review of evidence of effectiveness of public programs into budget and policy decision. To fund more effective programs, government needs to be able to develop a well-functioning performance measurement system. Increasingly, state governments are justifying costs of programs, such as criminal justice reforms, by incorporating evidence-based practices into prison and corrections programs to address public safety concerns and large prison populations that have significant costs to governments and taxpayers. Funding from federal grants specifically has given state governments the ability to invest in technology to support a performance measurement system to adopt evidence-based policymaking.

Criminal justice agencies that receive funding directly or indirectly from Office of Justice Programs (OJP) to enhance research, evaluation, and statistics have sought to improve effective outcomes for corrections through the implementation of innovative practices driven by technologies that have proven to be effective in supporting EB policies. These programs include funding through National Institute of Justice (NIJ) for supporting digital evidence, that will support the development of new technology such as large-scale computer systems and networks to analyze digital evidence, as well as, the Bureau of Justice Statistics (BJS) efforts to provide critical data infrastructure to focus on data-driven, evidence and information-based approaches to crime (Justice, 2017).

Technology can also enhance services which government provides to its citizens and increasingly, all levels of governments have been investing into information technology that can enhance access to services as well as to information that belongs to its citizens. Spending on the development and implementation of modern digital services and technology throughout the federal government has been increasing over the past decade but in recent years, the investment is being made strategically to support overall evidence-based policymaking.

A study that examined specifically the value creation from information technologies in state governments indicated a significantly negative relationship between IT intensity and cost efficiency and that an average of $1 increase per capita IT budget can lead to $4.18 efficiency gains (Pang et al., 2011). The key finding of the study was that more IT spending is associated with greater administrative efficiency and that relationship between IT intensity and cost efficiency endures over a period of years. The state of Michigan for instance, invested $4.6 million in an HR system and estimated up to $28 million in savings over a 5-year period (State of Michigan, 2007 cited in Pang et al, 2011). To adhere to guidelines for funding based on what works and provide more efficient and effective services, governments have been investing in information technologies and IT has played a wider role in improving and innovating administrative processes and public service delivery (Pang et al., 2011, pg. 35).

Research by the National Institute of Corrections (NIC) that provides training to corrections agencies, supports principles of effective offender intervention. NIC highlights 8 principles in its "Evidence-Based Practice" initiative. The principles of effective interventions include measuring outcomes to be able to provide evidence of what works, utilizing risk and needs assessment instruments and, providing measurement feedback for accountability and ultimately improving outcomes. These initiatives require investments in technology for tracking data and sharing information amongst stakeholders.

## Examining Three States

The chapter broadly looks at corrections spending on technology by examining three states that have had positive outcomes in reducing incarceration and crime. Examining the complex multivariate conditions that impact criminal justice outcomes makes it challenging to isolate any one variable such as technology to draw specific conclusions (see Yin, 2003 for applications of case study research). The chapter will examine the three states and the overall trend in expenditures on corrections, budgets and the population changes for these states. States spending on prison and jails have increased about three times more than spending on education over the past three decades (Stullich, Morgan & Schak, 2016). A snapshot of the expenditures on corrections and education in all states over three decades indicated that corrections expenditures grew over 324 percent overall compared to 107 percent for education (Stullich et al, 2016). Hawaii and California were among the 26 states that experienced above 250% increase in expenditures for local and state corrections spending over the three decades. New Jersey similarly had increasing expenditures but overall percentage was slightly below 150% (Stullich, 2016, pg. 6). All three states have achieved major outcomes in decreases in crime and prison rates resulting in achieving the most significant outcomes for reducing prison populations and crime rates leading one to infer that spending on corrections have a positive outcome on public safety. The percentage of spending on corrections by some other states however, were significantly high and some of these also experienced increasing prison population as well. New Mexico saw about 602% change in expenditures in corrections over education over 30 years (up to 2013) (Stullich, 2011, p.6) however, the state didn't experience a negative (decline) change in prison population concurrently. Although the positive change was small, with such a substantial amount of spending, the state failed to experience a drop in its prison population during 2011 to 2014 (Eisen & Chettiar, 2015).

However, state budgets are not growing similarly. Rather, the National Association of State Budget Officers (NASBO) cites that states have been dealing with sluggish overall growth with general fund revenues, growing only 1.8% in 2016 and estimated to be only slightly higher for 2017 (2.4%). There are about 33 states that are seeing general fund revenues coming in below budget projections for 2017 and at least half the states (23) have already made net mid-year budget cuts totaling $4.9 billion for 2017. The overall spending in corrections has been growing, however, spending in other areas as education has declined (Mitchell & Leachman, 2014). State expenditures on corrections overall increased about 750% (1985-2015) according to the State Expenditure Report (cited in The Sentencing Project, Fact Sheet, Trends in US Corrections).

For New Jersey, Hawaii and California and some other states, the past five years of corrections budgets have shown a very slow decline while also experiencing reductions in prison populations, crime rates and imprisonment rates (Eisen & Cullen, n.d.). The following table shows the budgets for the three states over a 5-year period indicating the amount of total budget as well as the amount of percentage and total spending on corrections in these states.

While these three states have all had substantial prison population and crime rate reductions, the percentage of spending on corrections in relation to the states' total budgets decreased slightly over the past 5 years with Hawaii and California having only about -.1% change in spending on corrections while New Jersey had a slightly higher decrease (-.4%) from 2010 to 2016. The states have all had increase in population although New Jersey and Hawaii had only small percentage change. New Jersey had .84% change in population while Hawaii had only a .07% change. California however had a larger percent-

*Table 1. State budgets and corrections expenditures for New Jersey, Hawaii and California from 2014-18*

| | State Budgets | FY 2014 | FY 2015 | FY 2016 | FY 2017 | FY 2018 |
|---|---|---|---|---|---|---|
| NJ | Total | 32,921 | 34,435 | 33,844 | 34,829 | 35,514 |
| | Corrections | 1,084<br>(3.3%) | 1,080<br>(3.1%) | 1,086<br>(3.2%) | 1,061<br>(3.0%) | 1,024<br>(2.9%) |
| CA | Total | 11,758 | 12,081 | 11,855 | 11,926 | 13,472 |
| | Corrections | 249<br>(2.1) | 246<br>(2.0) | 257<br>(2.2) | 262<br>(2.2) | 275<br>(2.0) |
| HI | Total | 145,300 | 156,358 | 167,575 | 170,863 | 183,256 |
| | Corrections | 11,165<br>(7.7%) | 11,972<br>(7.7%) | 12,656<br>(7.6%) | 13,372<br>(7.8%) | 13,869<br>(7.6%) |

Source: NJ: (State of New Jersey, Department of the Treasury, n.d.) CA budget: (State of California, Department of Finance, n.d.) HI budget: (Data Hawaii, n.d.)

age change in population with over a 2% change over this period. The table below shows this change in population for each of the three states.

## SPENDING ON TECHNOLOGY: DATA FOR STATES SPENDING ON INFORMATION TECHNOLOGY

### California

With increasing population, California was one of the states to lead reforms in funding for corrections. In 2009, the state passed the California Community Corrections Performance Incentive Act to reduce its corrections population by providing incentive funding to counties that reduced their criminal justice population leading to the states' saving over $280 million by 2011. During 2009 to 2014, the state's overall violent crime also fell by 13% while property crime fell by 6%. (Eisen & Chettiar, 2015). California therefore has achieved costs savings and curbed spending in corrections despite having a larger increase in population.

### Hawaii

In contrast to California, Hawaii's population has been decreasing but spending in corrections had only a minuscule reduction. Hawaii has been reluctant to embrace (criminal justice) reform (Kaneya, 2016).

*Table 2. States population change: US census bureau*

| States | 2010 Pop | 2016 Pop | Percentage Change |
|---|---|---|---|
| NJ | 8.79 M | 8.95 M | .84% |
| HI | 1.36 M | 1.43 M | .07% |
| CA | 37.3 M | 39.3 M | 2% |

Fortier & Chettiar, 2014.

However, in 2012, Hawaii adopted measures aimed at decreasing its prison population through efforts to have alternatives to incarceration and to further reform the state's criminal justice system. These were not fully adopted and the state has seen a less impact overall in its criminal justice system (Kaneya, 2016). This is in contrast to New Jersey and California that have adopted major reforms in its criminal justice policies.

### New Jersey

The state experienced a significant reduction in prison population leading the state over the period 2011-14 with a 9.5% reduction in incarceration and simultaneously a significant reduction in crime, 20% over this period. Major reforms in the criminal justice system and corrections agencies were adopted by the state during this timeframe including the New Jersey State Parole Board's enhancement of the parole process as well as increase flexibility in the sentencing of low-level drug offenders (Eisen & Chettiar, 2015).

## EXAMINATION

Mass incarceration is one of the nation's most persistent policy issues that impact communities that are poor, with disproportionate minority populations. Fiscal constraints at the state level have imposed additional burdens for states whose budgets have been declining in proportion to spending on corrections. Whilst there is a correlation between investment in IT and overall performance outcomes, when controlled for other factors, investment in IT can lead to more administrative efficiency leading to more saving overall for (state) governments. The literature on states spending in IT specifically to upgrade its corrections system is limited. However, state governments have increasingly adopted more evidence-based practices and policies to meet the demands of the federal government in funding specific criminal justice initiatives including an expansion in the implementation of information technology to support major criminal justice reforms.

Trends in overall IT spending at the federal level indicates that the there has been an upward trend as well from the federal government on IT spending. Over the past 18 years, the amount has doubled, from $45 billion to over $95 billion in total IT spending for both civilian agencies and Department of Defense for development and implementation of modern digital services and technology (Department of Justice budget) The Department's FY2017 Discretionary Budget request totals $29 billion, including $27 billion for federal programs $2 billion for state, local, and tribal assistance programs. The department underscores that the budget reflects the Attorney General's highest priorities and is aligned with the Smart on Crime initiative, introducing a new 21st Century Justice initiative, to efficiently and effectively stop crime and reduce recidivism. Despite advances in overall prison declines, incarceration rates and crime, some states continue to spend more in corrections while achieving little gains in either protecting the public or decreasing the overreliance on incarceration.

## DISCUSSION/CONCLUSION

A concerning problem for criminal justice reform is that high incarceration rates do not necessarily lead to a significant decrease in crime. Therefore, states have been working to reduce both. Eisen and

Cullen of the Brennan Center concluded therefore that the overall efforts in the United States to reduce its prison population, without sacrificing the public safety gains of the last decades varies from state to state. The states that have had positive achievements in reducing both crime and incarceration have varying political and geographic locations. There have been studies conducted of the private sector firms and the relationship between the use of technology and organizational change but no long-term studies specifically in the public sector (Graciano & Heaton, 2010). The expanding use of technology in the criminal justice sector which is information-based, warrants an examination of the impact of technology on implementation of evidence-based practices. There are many factors associated with the use of technology on an agency's productivity and is multifaceted and complicated. However, the chapter looks at the states that have achieved positive outcomes and presented the spending in technology and the simultaneous achievement of reductions in crime and imprisonment. For criminal justice agencies, spending on information and communication technologies is essential for its functioning for inter and intra agency collaboration of sharing data.

## ACKNOWLEDGMENT

The authors would like to acknowledge Nicole E. Sachs, PhD, School of Criminal Justice, Rutgers State University, Newark, NJ

## REFERENCES

Bureau of Justice Assistance. (n.d.). *Smart Policing Initiative Data. Analysis. Solutions.* Retrieved from https://www.bja.gov/Publications/SmartPolicingFS.pdf

Center on Budget and Policy Priorities. (2014). *Changing Priorities: State Criminal Justice Reforms and Investments in Education.* Retrieved from https://www.cbpp.org/research/changing-priorities-state-criminal-justice-reforms-and-investments-in-education

Data Hawaii. (n.d.). *Graph of Federal Expenditures by type.* Retrieved from https://data.hawaii.gov/Economic-Development/Table-9-5-GRAPH-OF-FEDERAL-EXPENDITURES-BY-TYPE/rj4c-efj7

Davis, E. (2016). *Information Technology Demands on State Funded Organizations.* Retrieved from https://www.elliottdavis.com/information-technology-demands-on-state-funded-organizations/

Devaraj, S., & Kohli, R. (2003). Performance Impacts of Information Technology: Is Actual Usage the Missing Link? *Management Science, 49*(3), 273–289. doi:10.1287/mnsc.49.3.273.12736

Eisen, L.-B., & Chettiar, I. (2015). *The Reverse Mass Incarceration.* Brennan Center for Justice. Retrieved from https://www.brennancenter.org/sites/default/files/publications/The_Reverse_Mass_Incarceration_Act%20.pdf

Eisen, L.-B., & Cullen, J. (n.d.). *Update Changes in State Imprisonment.* Brennan Center for Justice. Retrieved October 2017 from https://www.brennancenter.org/sites/default/files/analysis/UpdateChangesinStateImprisonment.pdf

FBI Uniform Crime Reporting Statistics. (n.d.). Retrieved from https://www.ucrdatatool.gov/Search/Crime/State/StatebyState.cfm?NoVariables=Y&CFID=235432167&CFTOKEN=466f51a4d0515b4b-778AD6DC-C10C-8E2E-C12DFFEEB8BEAC7D

Fortier, N. Z., & Chettiar, I. M. (2014). *Success-Oriented Funding: Reforming Federal Criminal*. Retrieved from https://www.brennancenter.org/publication/success-oriented-funding-reforming-federal-criminal-justice-grants

Garicano, L., & Heaton, P. (2010). Information Technology, Organizations, and Productivity in the Public Sector: Evidence from Police Departments. *Journal of Labor Economics*, *28*(1), 167–201. doi:10.1086/649844

Geunjoo, L., & Perry, J. L. (2002). Are Computers Boosting Productivity? A Test of the Paradox in State Governments. *Journal of Public Administration: Research and Theory*, *12*(1), 77–102. doi:10.1093/oxfordjournals.jpart.a003525

Justice. (2017). *Office of Justice Programs (OJP) FY 2017 Budget Request at a Glance*. Retrieved from https://www.justice.gov/jmd/file/822111/download

Kaneya, R. (2016). *Other states are shrinking prison populations – Why not Hawaii?* Honolulu Civil Beat. Council of State Governments Justice Center. Retrieved from www.csgjusticecenter.org

Kohli, R., & Devaraj, S. (2003). Measuring Information Technology Payoff: A Meta-Analysis of Structural Variables in Firm-Level Empirical Research. *Information Systems Research*, *14*(2), 127–145. doi:10.1287/isre.14.2.127.16019

Mathewson, J. W., Jones, F. D., Sklansky, M. S., Perry, J. C., Michelfelder, E. C., Cripe, L., & Kimball, T. R. (2002). Conversion to Digital Technology Improves Efficiency in the Pediatric Echocardiography Laboratory. *Journal of the American Society of Echocardiography*, *15*(12), 1515–1522. doi:10.1067/mje.2002.129498 PMID:12464921

MemorandumB. (2013). Retrieved from https://obamawhitehouse.archives.gov/sites/default/files/omb/memoranda/2013/m-13-17.pdf

Mitchell, M., & Leachman, M. (2014). *Changing Priorities: States Criminal Justice Reforms and Investments in Education*. Center on Budget and Policy Priorities. Policy Futures.

New Jersey Commission on Science and Technology. (2008). *Grants and Initiatives*. New Jersey Technology and Entrepreneur Fellowship Program. Retrieved from http://www.state.nj.us/scitech/programs/

New Jersey State Library. (2017). *Technology Infrastructure Study New Jersey Library Technology Infrastructure Study*. Retrieved from http://www.njstatelib.org/services_for_libraries/resources/technology-infrastructure-study/

New York University School of Law, Brennan Center for Justice. (2015). *The Reverse Mass Incarceration Act*. Retrieved from https://www.brennancenter.org/publication/reverse-mass-incarceration-act

New York University School of Law, Brennan Center for Justice. (2017). *Update on Changes in State Imprisonment*. Retrieved from https://www.brennancenter.org/sites/default/files/analysis/UpdateChangesinStateImprisonment.pdf

Pang, M. F., Tati, A., & Krishnan, M. S. (2011). Information Technology and Administrative Efficiency in U.S. State Governments – A Stochastic Frontier Approach. *Management Information Systems Quarterly, 38*(4), 1079–1102. doi:10.25300/MISQ/2014/38.4.07

Porter, D. R. (1993). Improving Administrative Efficiency through Technology. *New Directions for Adult and Continuing Education, 60*(60), 67–77. doi:10.1002/ace.36719936009

Sandia National Laboratories. (2016). *Comparison of State-Funded Technology Maturation Programs.* Retrieved from http://prod.sandia.gov/techlib/access-control.cgi/2016/1612489.pdf

State of California, Department of Finance. (n.d.). *California State Budget, 2017-2018.* Retrieved from http://www.ebudget.ca.gov/

State of Hawai'i, Department of Budget and Finance. (2016). *The FB 2017-19 Executive Biennium Budget.* Retrieved from https://budget.hawaii.gov/wp-content/uploads/2016/12/FB-17-19-BIB-FINAL-12.15.16.pdf

State of New Jersey, Department of the Treasury. (n.d.). *Appropriations Handbook 2017-2018.* Retrieved from http://www.nj.gov/treasury/omb/publications/18approp/FullApropAct.pdf

State of New Jersey, Office of the Governor. (2016). *NJ State Budget Summary.* Retrieved from http://www.nj.gov/treasury/omb/publications/16bib/BIB.pdf

Stullich, S., Morgan, I., & Schak, O. (2016). *State and Local Expenditures on Corrections and Education.* Retrieved from https://www2.ed.gov/rschstat/eval/other/expenditures-corrections-education/brief.pdf

TechCrunch. (2016). *The Government Technology Pitch.* Retrieved from https://techcrunch.com/contributor/luke-fretwell/

The PEW Charitable Trust. (2014). *Pew-MacArthur Results First Initiative. Evidence-Based Policymaking: A Guide for Effective Government.* Retrieved from http://www.pewtrusts.org/en/research-and-analysis/reports/2014/11/evidence-based-policymaking-a-guide-for-effective-government

The Sentencing Project. (2017). *Fact Sheet: Trends In US Corrections.* Retrieved from: https://sentencingproject.org/wp-content/uploads/2016/01/Trends-in-US-Corrections.pdf

Turner, M. (2013). *It takes a portfolio to make evidence-based policy.* Urban Institute.

University of California. (2008). *Building Administrative Efficiency for the University of California.* Retrieved from http://www.ucop.edu/efficiency/process/reports/building-administrative-efficiency.pdf

U.S. Department of Justice, Bureau of Justice Statistics. (2014). *Prisoners in 2014.* Retrieved from https://www.bjs.gov/content/pub/pdf/p14.pdf

Yin, R. K. (2003). *Case Study Research Design and Methods.* Retrieved from http://www.madeira-edu.pt/LinkClick.aspx?fileticket=Fgm4GJWVTRs%3D&tabid=3004

# APPENDIX

*Figure 1. Change in imprisonment rates by state (2006-2014)*
*Source: U.S. Bureau of Justice Statistics (2014) and Fortier & Chettiar (2014).*

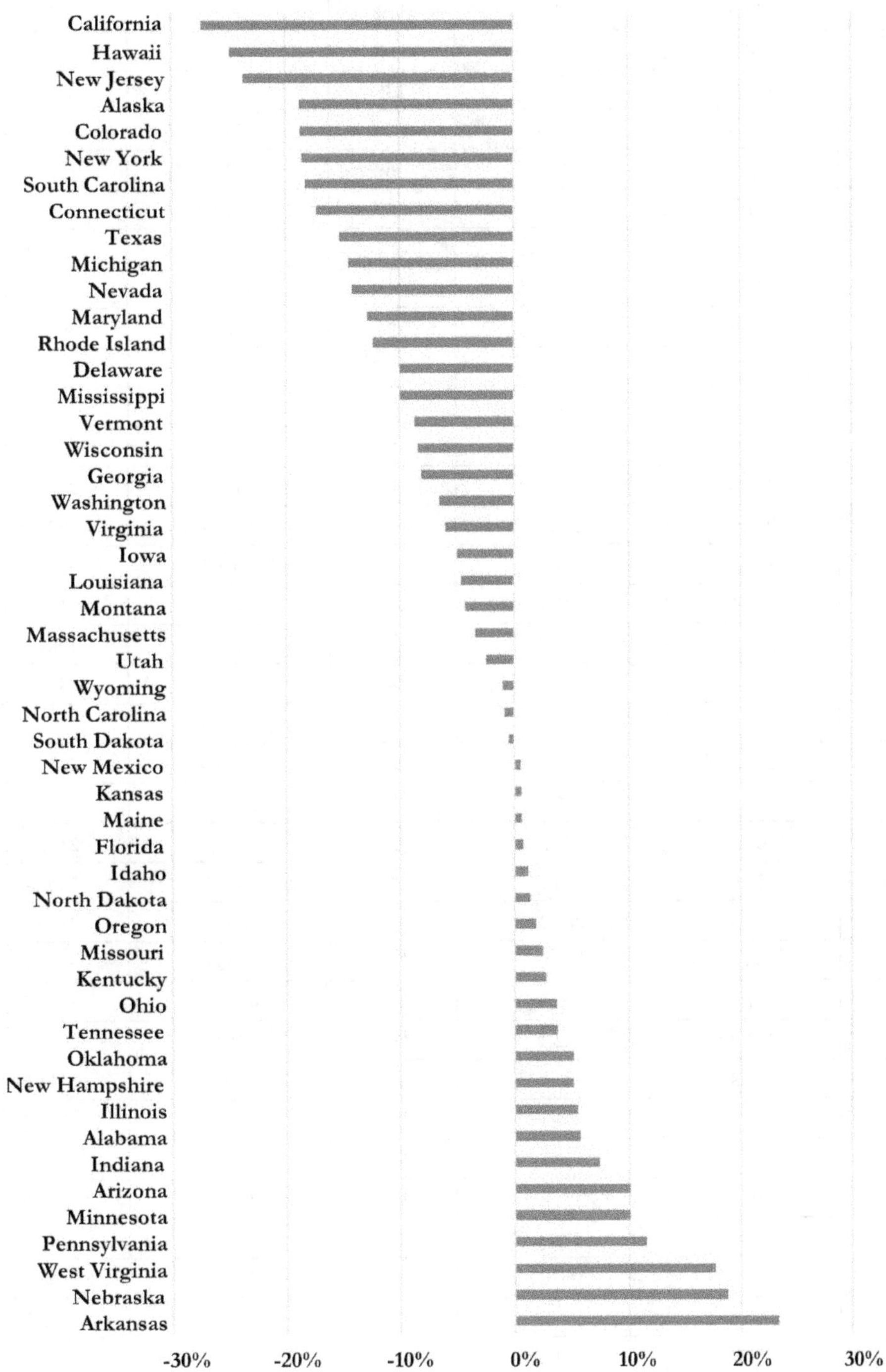

*Table 3. Crime rate per 100,000 residents by state (2006-2014)*

| State | Violent Crime Rate (2006) | Violent Crime Rate (2014) | Percent Change | Crime Rate (2006) | Crime Rate (2014) | Percent Change |
|---|---|---|---|---|---|---|
| Vermont | 117.3 | 81.7 | -30% | 2508.7 | 1606.1 | -36% |
| Maine | 90.2 | 91.3 | 1% | 2637.0 | 2077.8 | -21% |
| New Hampshire | 113.3 | 151.3 | 34% | 2095.2 | 2114.0 | 1% |
| Wyoming | 224.5 | 165.7 | -26% | 3211.0 | 2130.4 | -34% |
| Utah | 191.4 | 166.2 | -13% | 3703.9 | 3044.7 | -18% |
| Virginia | 259.8 | 168.5 | -35% | 2749.1 | 2098.8 | -24% |
| Idaho | 208.3 | 174.9 | -16% | 2604.2 | 2029.7 | -22% |
| Kentucky | 238.9 | 179.0 | -25% | 2840.6 | 2425.9 | -15% |
| Rhode Island | 203.4 | 185.0 | -9% | 2818.0 | 2358.6 | -16% |
| Minnesota | 278.6 | 192.5 | -31% | 3361.1 | 2490.0 | -26% |
| Oregon | 251.7 | 195.6 | -22% | 3976.8 | 3074.7 | -23% |
| Connecticut | 279.9 | 215.2 | -23% | 2866.0 | 2135.6 | -25% |
| North Dakota | 159.5 | 216.6 | 36% | 2260.4 | 2326.9 | 3% |
| Hawaii | 253.2 | 227.9 | -10% | 4473.1 | 3277.9 | -27% |
| Nebraska | 261.3 | 234.5 | -10% | 3621.0 | 2758.0 | -24% |
| Iowa | 256.5 | 237.2 | -8% | 3080.1 | 2330.9 | -24% |
| Ohio | 319.9 | 241.4 | -25% | 4008.1 | 3040.5 | -24% |
| Mississippi | 276.1 | 243.1 | -12% | 3466.4 | 3164.3 | -9% |
| New Jersey | 336.4 | 246.9 | -27% | 2615.2 | 1981.0 | -24% |
| Washington | 305.7 | 247.0 | -19% | 4815.8 | 3953.1 | -18% |
| Colorado | 350.0 | 252.3 | -28% | 3788.4 | 2782.5 | -27% |
| Wisconsin | 263.9 | 261.2 | -1% | 3084.9 | 2349.6 | -24% |
| Montana | 340.5 | 270.8 | -20% | 3197.2 | 2743.7 | -14% |
| South Dakota | 205.4 | 271.5 | 32% | 1971.8 | 2135.3 | 8% |
| West Virginia | 259.0 | 274.7 | 6% | 2895.3 | 2309.4 | -20% |
| Pennsylvania | 413.3 | 284.2 | -31% | 2861.6 | 2215.9 | -23% |
| Kansas | 386.4 | 300.0 | -22% | 4158.4 | 3035.2 | -27% |
| North Carolina | 447.0 | 305.2 | -32% | 4563.2 | 3178.2 | -30% |
| Indiana | 292.9 | 332.2 | 13% | 3742.4 | 2981.6 | -20% |
| Illinois | 509.8 | 337.7 | -34% | 3529.5 | 2413.6 | -32% |
| Georgia | 454.8 | 347.1 | -24% | 4328.3 | 3628.3 | -16% |
| Arizona | 502.8 | 349.7 | -30% | 5277.0 | 3547.2 | -33% |
| New York | 418.8 | 354.3 | -15% | 2483.3 | 2072.5 | -17% |
| Massachusetts | 473.0 | 359.0 | -24% | 2864.4 | 2216.1 | -23% |
| Oklahoma | 458.7 | 360.2 | -21% | 4083.2 | 3350.9 | -18% |
| Texas | 481.4 | 363.6 | -24% | 4564.5 | 3383.0 | -26% |
| Michigan | 511.4 | 364.0 | -29% | 3736.5 | 2407.9 | -36% |

*continued on following page*

*Table 3. Continued*

| State | Violent Crime Rate (2006) | Violent Crime Rate (2014) | Percent Change | Crime Rate (2006) | Crime Rate (2014) | Percent Change |
|---|---|---|---|---|---|---|
| California | 508.1 | 366.4 | -28% | 3689.9 | 2807.5 | -24% |
| Alabama | 389.4 | 386.1 | -1% | 4330.4 | 3563.7 | -18% |
| Missouri | 515.7 | 403.7 | -22% | 4349.7 | 3310.2 | -24% |
| Maryland | 657.7 | 419.0 | -36% | 4138.7 | 2926.5 | -29% |
| Arkansas | 505.6 | 420.7 | -17% | 4491.1 | 3758.7 | -16% |
| Delaware | 652.2 | 447.8 | -31% | 4128.5 | 3429.8 | -17% |
| South Carolina | 728.7 | 454.9 | -38% | 5003.2 | 3915.2 | -22% |
| Louisiana | 684.2 | 485.2 | -29% | 4765.0 | 3944.0 | -17% |
| Florida | 680.6 | 497.4 | -27% | 4666.9 | 3912.9 | -16% |
| New Mexico | 599.8 | 526.7 | -12% | 4488.1 | 4069.0 | -9% |
| Alaska | 611.6 | 531.1 | -13% | 4189.7 | 3291.2 | -21% |
| Tennessee | 726.1 | 569.8 | -22% | 4863.7 | 3630.3 | -25% |
| Nevada | 705.1 | 587.8 | -17% | 4805.9 | 3213.2 | -33% |

Source: F.B.I. Uniform Crime Reports (n.d.); (Chart sorted by 2014 violent crime.). Eisen, Lauren-Brooke and Cullen, James. 2015. Changes in State Imprisonment. Brennan Center for Justice. Mitchell, Michael and Leachman, Michael. 2014. Changing Priorities: State Criminal Justice Reforms and Investments in Education. Center on Budget and Policy Priorities.

*Figure 2. Corrections spending has grown much faster than education spending*
*Source: CBPP analysis data from National Association of State Budget Officers. Changing Priorities: State Criminal Justice Reforms and Investments in Education. Center on Budget and Policy Priorities (Mitchell & Michael, 2014)*

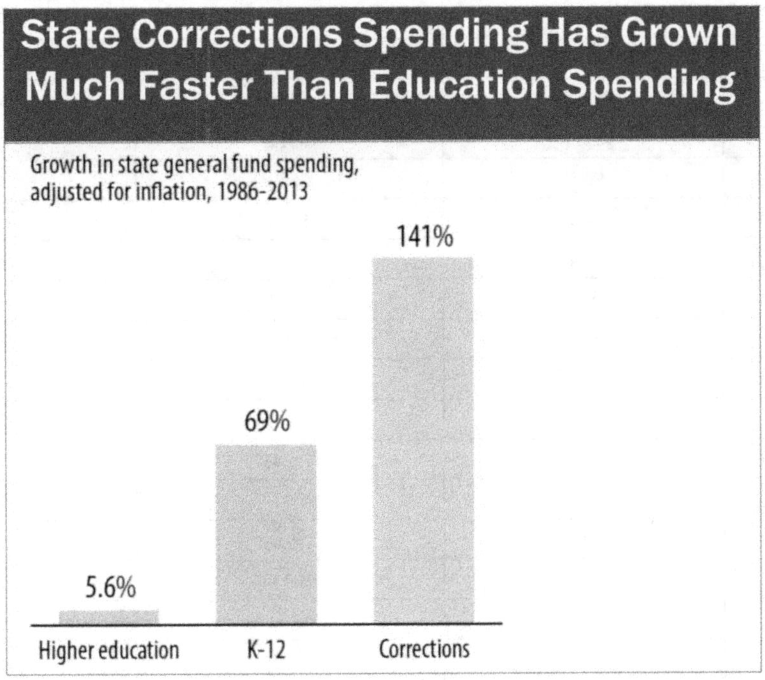

*Table 4. State corrections spending has risen significantly since 1986 (in millions of dollars)*

| | Fiscal Year 1986 (in 2013$'s) | Fiscal Year 2013* | Difference |
|---|---|---|---|
| Alabama | $270 | $460 | $190 |
| Alaska | $166 | $349 | $183 |
| Arizona | $347 | $965 | $618 |
| Arkansas | $81 | $385 | $304 |
| California | $3,329 | $8,618 | $5,289 |
| Colorado | $130 | $670 | $540 |
| Connecticut | $225 | $642 | $417 |
| Delaware | $100 | $265 | $165 |
| Florida | $772 | $2,316 | $1,544 |
| Georgia | $449 | $1,467 | $1,018 |
| Hawaii | $79 | $218 | $139 |
| Idaho | $32 | $213 | $181 |
| llinois | $782 | $1,295 | $513 |
| Indiana | $296 | $687 | $391 |
| Iowa | $155 | $362 | $207 |
| Kansas | $151 | $354 | $203 |
| Kentucky | $196 | $558 | $362 |
| Louisiana | $389 | $713 | $324 |
| Maine | $74 | $133 | $59 |
| Maryland | $780 | $1,313 | $533 |
| Massachusetts | $353 | $1,261 | $908 |
| Michigan | $836 | $2,064 | $1,228 |
| Minnesota | $185 | $469 | $284 |
| Mississippi | $117 | $312 | $195 |
| Missouri | $204 | $589 | $385 |
| Montana | $45 | $178 | $133 |
| Nebraska | $74 | $198 | $124 |
| Nevada | $96 | $247 | $151 |
| New Hampshire | $32 | $95 | $63 |
| New Jersey | $670 | $1,511 | $841 |
| New Mexico | $140 | $266 | $126 |
| New York | $2,762 | $2,918 | $156 |
| North Carolina | $538 | $1,717 | $1,179 |
| North Dakota | $17 | $81 | $64 |
| Ohio | $668 | $1,798 | $1,130 |
| Oklahoma | $208** | $459 | $251 |
| Oregon | $196 | $802 | $606 |

*continued on following page*

*Table 4. Continued*

| | Fiscal Year 1986 (in 2013$'s) | Fiscal Year 2013* | Difference |
|---|---|---|---|
| Pennsylvania | $393 | $2,111 | $1,718 |
| Rhode Island | $74 | $185 | $111 |
| South Carolina | $257 | $492 | $235 |
| South Dakota | $28 | $85 | $57 |
| Tennessee | $472 | $880 | $408 |
| Texas | $872 | $3,191 | $2,319 |
| Utah | $115 | $239 | $124 |
| Vermont | $34 | $131 | $97 |
| Virginia | $940** | $1,174 | $234 |
| Washington | $344 | $913** | $569 |
| West Virginia | $45 | $219 | $174 |
| Wisconsin | $279 | $1,138 | $859 |
| Wyoming | $30 | $123 | $93 |
| | | Total Spending Increase: | $28,006 |

Source: CBPP analysis Data from National Association of State Budget Officers.

FY 2013 spending levels are estimates collected by the National Association of State Budget Officers. Actual state spending levels may differ.

*Oklahoma data reflect corrections spending in FY 1987; Virginia data reflect FY 1990; Washington State data reflect FY 2012.

# Chapter 6
# The eXtensible Business Reporting Language:
## A Digital Tool to Enhance Public Sector Accountability

**Michela Soverchia**
*University of Macerata, Italy*

**Andrea Fradeani**
*University of Macerata, Italy*

## ABSTRACT

*This chapter offers a theoretical analysis related to the eXtensible business reporting language (XBRL), a freely available computer language that has become the de facto standard for digital financial reporting. The aim is to deepen the role that XBRL could play within the public sector, which is partially different from its role in corporate reporting. Literature about that topic is lacking, and this research topic seems to be particularly relevant: considering the strong need for information transparency in government, strengthened by the financial crisis, XBRL could be a useful digital tool to push and improve governments' accountability and transparency. Finally, the authors briefly present the Italian case: after the experimental period conducted by the Court of Auditors from 2013 to 2015, and since the end of 2016, XBRL has been the mandatory format for submitting the financial statements of all public entities to the Italian Ministry of Economy and Finance.*

## INTRODUCTION

In recent decades, the public sector has been involved in many modernization processes worldwide concerning several organizational, managerial, and financial aspects in an effort to recover efficiency and effectiveness as well as improve public transparency and accountability. Within these processes, technology plays a significant role. In the early 2000s, the e-government phenomenon exploded, leading to the use of new digital technologies, in particular Information and Communication Technologies

DOI: 10.4018/978-1-5225-5966-5.ch006

(ICTs), which are used to improve government processes and to deliver public services (Aikins, 2012; Walther et al., 2016).

The lack of financial transparency and accountability is assumed to be one of the main causes of the financial crisis that began in 2008. Governments have been called on to reinforce their own credibility, rebuilding the trust of the citizen taxpayers, markets, and investors (Sapienza & Zingales, 2012). The recent negative events have made clear the importance of the governmental role in financial reporting and identified a compelling and urgent need for governments to address seriously and rapidly the quality improvement of their whole public financial management systems in order to protect both the public interest and government bond investors. There are widespread calls for more rigorous and transparent financial reporting systems that will improve government decision-making and accountability, enhance global fiscal stability and sustainability, and support the ability of monitoring and meeting government commitments now and in the future. Governments should provide clear, consistent, and comprehensive information regarding the economic and financial consequences of their political decisions.

Furthermore, raising funds through debt markets and considering that banks and private investors hold governments' debt, there is a strong demand for financial transparency and accountability from the public sector just like that expected from the private sector, along with comparability. Governments definitely have a public interest obligation to investors and potential investors to provide timely, detailed, and reliable information concerning their financial performance and positions.

In other words, the financial crisis has clearly demonstrated that the lack of transparency in government financial reporting is a real threat to economic, political, and social stability. Within this context, the focus of this chapter is on the eXtensible Business Reporting Language (XBRL), which is the markup language of business financial reporting that is used all over the world. In particular, the aim of this study is to conduct a theoretical analysis concerning the role that XBRL could play within public sector financial reporting. At the moment, in different countries (e.g., Australia, Belgium, Brazil, Canada, Chile, China, Colombia, Denmark, France, Germany, India, Indonesia, Israel, Italy, Japan, Luxembourg, Mexico, Peru, Singapore, South Korea, Spain, Sweden, United Arab Emirates, United Kingdom, and United States), XBRL is either mandatory or voluntarily adopted for different kinds of financial and regulatory reporting (i.e., filing required by prudential and securities regulators, business registers, and tax authorities) over all business sectors. It is considered a means to improve transparency, effectiveness, and timeliness of financial reports and to achieve efficiencies, as some recent theoretical and empirical studies point out (Hodge et al., 2004; Roohani et al., 2009; Chen, 2012; Debreceny et al., 2010; Yoon et al., 2011; Perdana et al., 2014; Birt et al., 2017; Cong et al., 2017; Liu et al., 2017).

However, the same is not true for public entities and their financial reporting. Literature about that topic is *lacking* (Abdolmohammadi et al., 2002; Rezaee & Turner, 2002; Ball, 2007; Kull & Abraham, 2008; Chen, 2013; Mousa, 2013; Soverchia, 2015; Bonollo, 2017; Fradeani et al., in press), and the following research topic seems to be particularly relevant: considering the strong need for governments' information transparency strengthened by the financial crisis, XBRL could be a useful digital tool to push and improve governments' accountability, information transparency, and comparability. As for corporate reporting, using XBRL could also help prevent or avoid future crises (Karamagioli et al., 2014; Anthopoulos & Siozos, 2015).

## BACKGROUND

Innovation is one of the key drivers of economic growth (Verspagen, 2005) and an important element in determining the competitiveness of nations and regions (Porter, 1990), especially in times of financial crisis (Hausman & Wesley, 2014; Petrakis et al., 2015). The positive effects resulting from the implementation of innovations, including those in the ICT field, are produced both in companies that improve their performances and in governments that improve quality and quantity of services provided and, therefore, public value (Moore, 1995, 2005).

The e-government phenomenon that exploded in the early 2000s (Jaeger, 2003; Yildiz, 2007) concerns the ICTs used by governments in carrying out their functions and in management through communications with citizens to simplify procedures and improve the usability of information and services, making delivery activities faster and more efficient. Therefore, e-government refers less to government computerization in the strict sense and more to the implementation of ICTs in producing and delivering products and services for various public-sector stakeholders (individuals, families, businesses, and other public organizations).

In some countries, especially those in continental Europe, there has been a substantial time coincidence between the implementation of significant changes within government and the availability of new ICT tools. The need for coordination and harmonization resulting from the reforms inspired by the principles of subsidiarity, federalism, and devolution has found a strategic resource in ICTs to facilitate the information exchange at an internal level (within the single public entity), at an intra-sectorial level (within the overall public sector), and in the external environment.

ICTs, therefore, not only affect the organizational structure of a single public entity but also the whole public sector, strengthening the interrelationships and interdependencies between the various actors. Accompanied by normative and regulatory changes, ICTs encourage the creation of a governance model based on inter-institutional collaboration and on public, private, and nonprofit cooperation through the development of network systems between different actors (Milward & Provan, 2001; Goldsmith & Eggers, 2004).

In brief, the e-government phenomenon cannot be described without focusing the analysis on the networks that e-government enables to be created or improved. These networks result from different relations that are qualified by three main key elements. The first key element is the object, referring to the relation contents of the interaction, tangible or intangible, strictly related to the needs supporting the creation of the relation: these relations may have money, services, and so on as object information. The second element refers to the subjects, which are the actors between relations that are built up: e-government, in fact, not only concerns the public entity's relations with the end user but also the entire process of services production and delivery. In this regard, interactions may be of different kinds between the public administration and

- Another public administration (at the local, regional, national, supra-international level),
- Businesses (private firms, for profit, or nonprofit), and
- Citizens (individually or organized, as end users of public services).

The third element is instrumental and concerns tools, which are the means and technologies used to support these interactions. ICTs, however, should not be relegated to a mere instrumental role because they change the channels of access to information and services, impacting in different ways on the relations referred to above and, ultimately, on the internal and external decision-making processes.

Obviously, the three identified elements are linked with each other and mutually interrelated; therefore, improvements in speed, efficiency, effectiveness, and relation quality depend on their consistency, which results in improved quality and quantity of services provided and functions carried out. Then, the network's governance model also plays a very important role (Mintzberg, 1996). These interactions, in fact, may have different intensities characterized by a variable degree of interdependence between public entities and other stakeholders.

Many scholars identify the changes in these kinds of relations as a transition from government to governance, providing for the abandonment of relationships based purely on hierarchical patterns. These patterns are considered inadequate to solve the problems that characterize the current socioeconomic scenarios with new forms of collaboration and cooperation between public and private actors.

On one hand, this development finds indispensable support in ICTs, promoting the achievement of the objectives with the processes of modernization given above, such as operational efficiency, simplification, transparency, and accountability. These innovative forms of governance also need new information and monitoring tools, which cannot disregard the use of new ICTs. Appropriate reporting models should be defined to enable the consolidation of public expenditures and the results and outcomes achieved for the benefit of the overall community.

Theoretical and empirical research shows that there is an increasing participation of stakeholders in government actions and policies. Government cooperates progressively with other actors in policy networks and public-private partnerships, and information arrangements should reflect and follow these patterns of relations between governments and other actors, public and private, and regarding financial information as well.

## WHAT IS XBRL?

XBRL is a freely available computer language designed to code and communicate business data so that computers can directly manage that data. Created by Charles Hoffman at the end of the 1990s and then developed by XBRL International (Kernan, 2009), the language has had a fast broad adoption and has become the de facto standard for digital financial reporting (Kernan, 2008; Enachi & Andone, 2015).

As a human language, XBRL needs the interaction between a "grammar" (i.e., the specifications) and a "dictionary" (i.e., the taxonomy). The specifications, and their additional modules, are made directly by XBRL International and are common to all implementations of the language: they define the basic IT rules, derived from the eXtensible Markup Language (XML), to code business data. The taxonomy, on the other hand, varies depending on the type of report to describe; this set of concepts, attributes, and relationships can be used to describe the information and allow concrete encoding. In the case of financial statements, the taxonomy depends on the set of accounting principles adopted; therefore, we have several taxonomies made by local jurisdictions (e.g., IFRS Taxonomy by IASB, US GAAP Financial Reporting Taxonomy by FASB, and ITA GAAP Taxonomy by XBRL Italy).

Instead of treating data in a static way, as a block of text—as happens in a standard Internet page or in a printed document—XBRL provides a computer-readable tag so that each individual item of data

*Figure 1. How XBRL works*

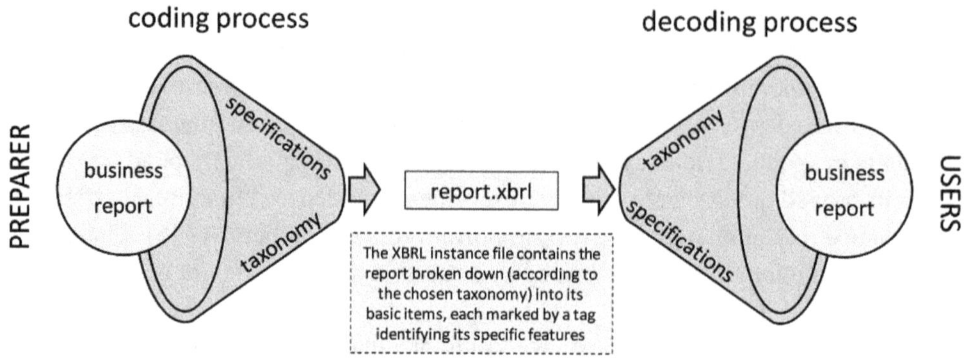


is electronically and uniquely identifiable (like bar codes). Financial reports become systems of alphanumeric values that can be directly processed, and thus they are dynamic and adaptable to the needs of the user of the transmitted information (Debreceny et al., 2009). In short, XBRL eliminates the need for repeated data entry, comparison, transferal, and submission, thus streamlining the process for collecting and reporting financial information, and saving costs in time, resources, and risk of error. Thanks to XBRL, users of financial data, such as investors, analysts, regulators, and financial institutions, can receive, find, compare, and analyze data much more rapidly, efficiently, and interactively.

XBRL's strength is in the ability to distinguish the structure from the content with reference to a specific document. XBRL follows that with the ability to reprocess the information immediately without having to go through printing or rekeying, provided that sender and receiver are equipped with homogeneous software for encoding and decoding data. XBRL is an open standard; no royalties are paid for its use.

The data coding does not affect the mode of representation and allows expressing financial reports in a uniform file format characterized by extensibility, flexibility, interoperability between heterogeneous information systems, and overall transmission via the web. This type of digital and open standard significantly mitigates the trade-off of "richness vs. reach," allowing the production of rich, high-quality information that can be spread among a very high number of recipients via the Internet (Evans & Wurster, 2000).

To benefit from XBRL's potential, the existence of a complete, standardized, and shared taxonomy appears to be a prerequisite. This has to be reconciled with the difficulties arising from such incomparability of information contained in financial statements, especially if prepared in accordance with accounting standards that do not contemplate rigid financial documents, such as International Accounting Standards (IAS)/International Financial Reporting Standards (IFRS) and International Public Sector Accounting Standards (IPSAS). Therefore, taxonomy definition is a complex and delicate operation because it affects the effective disclosure of financial documents (Bovee et al., 2002; Debreceny et al, 2010; Debreceny et al, 2011; Valentinetti & Rea, 2013; Fradeani et al., 2017; Panizzolo et al., 2017).

## XBRL AND PUBLIC SECTOR FINANCIAL DISCLOSURE: THE FINANCIAL REPORTING SUPPLY CHAIN

Information produced by public and private organizations (governments, firms, and nonprofit entities) is designed to support decision-making processes of several stakeholders. The exponential ability to store, process, and disseminate vast amounts of information that characterizes modern technologies is one of the main drivers contributing to the emergence of the knowledge economy.

As for financial accounting, governments have many differences compared to other kinds of organizations, mainly private firms. They are generally required to prepare a budget, according to the law. Moreover, in addition to the diversity of accounts and statements, accounting methods and systems used in governments are often different: think about the traditional cash accounting based on the single entry method, which is different compared to accrual accounting and the double entry method.

Consequently, determining who is interested in government financial information is a very important issue in order to realize who could benefit from the governmental use of XBRL. All subjects having direct and indirect relationships with government could benefit from XBRL.

A public entity transforms inputs into outputs, delivering services and creating public value:

- First, there are actors with which government has direct economic and financial transactions, that is, subjects providing inputs (suppliers: taxpayers, banks, businesses, and other public entities that supplied the additional premium [AP] of money and specific inputs) and subjects getting outputs, who consume public services (users: citizens, businesses, and other public entities).
- Second, there are some actors with which the public entity has no direct transactions, but they are still interested in its financial information to support their decision-making processes, for example, other public entities for controlling and benchmarking purposes, and community members living and working in that region because the outcomes derived from public activities improves the social and economic conditions.

XBRL is particularly useful for reusing data and manipulating and displaying financial information in different ways and for different purposes, according to various user needs. These XBRL features make it a highly appropriate digital standard in contexts where different entities need to share the same information and when an entity has to provide the same information to several other subjects. Those situations are very common for government entities, as different reporting relationships link the various administrative levels of the government. Often, a certain public entity must provide the same information to several other public entities (e.g., ministries), but at specific times and in different ways (sizes, means of transmission). Just as often, some information provided to a particular office will be shared with others. Public entities have reporting obligations with different subjects (other entities) with redundant data entry processes because the objects (pieces of information) are sometimes the same but have to be provided in different times, methods, and formats. In these cases, XBRL could help public entities meet the reporting requirements better. In summary, each public entity has numerous reporting obligations that are often marked by insertion and processing redundancy of the same data and that involve the use of substantial resources (human, financial, time) to meet the entity's needs while not strictly being related to achieving its institutional goals.

The reporting activity, which is typically a supporting activity, may represent a possible area of improved efficiency by saving resources that could be devoted to improving the quality and quantity of the public services provided. Despite the undoubted importance of the reporting activity, it is evident that the underlying processes have no value in themselves, but are valued only because they lead to an outcome, represented by the quality and quantity size of produced and disseminated information.

The introduction of XBRL can help streamline and simplify the government reporting processes by reusing the information, both with reference to the subject to whom it is addressed and with regard to how that subject needs the information, according to its specific purposes and user needs. As an interoperable language, in fact, XBRL allows display customization and information processing, which quickly safeguards the government's integrity.

XBRL is structured so that financial data is part of a financial reporting supply chain that refers to the people and processes involved in the preparation, approval, audit, analysis, and use of financial reports (IFAC, 2008). Such a chain highlights the different activities of the financial reporting process, from information production to dissemination and disclosure, involving both the internal and external subjects (Brown & Willis, 2003).

Figure 2 represents a model of the government financial reporting supply chain. Considering a certain accounting model (accounting rules and standards, accounting systems), with levels of increasing intensity, XBRL could go through the various stages of financial information production to improve efficiency, in terms of time and resources consumed by various activities, and to improve effectiveness to benefit various categories of stakeholders involved in the process itself.

The figure shows that all the elements characterizing the relationships that have been discussed for e-government can be traced. The object is the information production process, that is, all the activities concerning the process of producing and delivering government financial information. The accounting framework is not an activity, but it has to be put at the beginning of the chain because it is the frame in which these activities can be realized. Whereas the instrumental element is XBRL and all its technical components (specifications, taxonomies, instance documents, and software), the subjective dimension refers to the various actors involved in each accounting and reporting activity (information relationships on which XBRL can have an impact), that is, internal and external communication.

As mentioned, XBRL refers to the production of reports for external users, so those external actors engaged in forms of control required by law may be primarily interested. XBRL could be used as a digital standard by which to encode and transmit official financial reports, likely to other public entities. Consider, for example, financial controls carried out by the European Court of Auditors, which sometimes

*Figure 2. The government financial reporting supply chain*

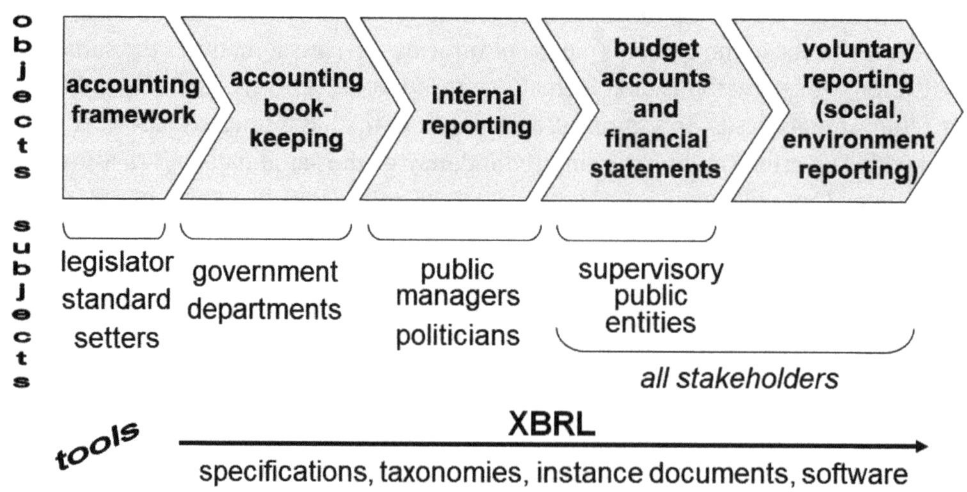

requires the whole budget accounts and financial statements but other times only requires some sets of financial data, referring to specific categories of expenditures. These individuals could get data in their databases without retyping the figures in which they are interested; in other words, they could use the databases in real time, for example, to calculate specific ratios for each public entity, for a part of the public sector, and so on. In addition, the ability to process a huge amount of data in real time allows the use of continuous auditing technologies to control the quality of economic-financial information and to detect any abnormalities or fraud quickly (Rezaee et al., 2002; Flowerday et al., 2005, 2006).

XBRL implementation could help get government financial information—financial statements, budget accounts, and eventual voluntary reporting, such as social and environment reporting—in a rapid and economic way by strongly improving government financial transparency and comparability for all interested people, both for other public institutions (e.g., the European Union or other public bodies who have to control government performances) and for citizens, businesses, media, workers, analysts, and so on. This could improve government levels of transparency and accountability, which are key elements for public trust (Dawes et al., 2009).

## THE CASE OF ITALY

Italy is one of the first nations to make mandatory the adoption of XBRL for the private sector in a large scale. Since 2009, unlisted companies (around 1 million) have been required to submit their financial statements (at the beginning, only the face statements and then the notes to the financial statements) to the Business Register in XBRL format (Avallone et al., 2016; Fradeani et al., 2016).

However, the use of XBRL in the public sector has had a longer and more complex course. The first experimentation started in 2013 in the context of the public administration reform launched previously in 2009 and also thanks to the pushing role of the Court of Auditors. This represents an important body for the Italian public administration because it is in charge of controlling and reporting to Parliament the revenues and expenditures of the public administration.

The first experimental implementation of XBRL in the Italian public sector concerns a particular auditing activity of the Court of Auditors, that is, the one referring to the national entities receiving contributions from the State under Law 259 of 1958. These entities represent a small number of subjects, about 220, which adopt different accounting systems; they are not only public entities but also companies that adopt both Italian and international accounting principles. From 2013, experimentally, these entities could submit their financial statements through the Sistema Informatico Controllo Enti (SICE) (Information System for the Control of Central Public Bodies), in the XBRL format. The most interesting aspect, perhaps, is the fact that the Court of Auditors has provided different taxonomies depending on the type of financial statements and activity of the institution: for a specific taxonomy of the financial statements of public entities, there was another one for the financial statements prepared in accordance with the Italian generally accepted accounting principles (GAAP) (the same that is mandatory for submitting the financial statements of private companies to the Business Register), in accordance to the IFRS (a customized model of the IASB's IFRS taxonomy, differentiated for banks), and for the insurance companies. This experimental period has allowed the Court of Auditors to conduct more sophisticated investigations in a much shorter time, enabling the group to focus more on auditing and analyzing the available data.

The success of the initiative has prompted the Court of Auditors not only to adopt XBRL starting from 2016 as one of the formats through which to fulfill the requirement for submitting the financial statements in the SICE platform (along with specific Microsoft Excel files or manual insertions in the online portal) but also to launch the more ambitious Sistema Monitoraggio ARmonizzazione Territoriale (SMART) project (Local Government Harmonized Monitoring Control System). It concerned the use of XBRL to collect financial statements and the relative detailed accounting data produced by more than 8,000 Italian local governments (20 regions, 110 provinces, and about 8,000 municipalities). The project's objectives included the acquisition of financial statements of local government entities in a digital, editable format to dematerialize the information flows by replacing paper-based submission obligations of accounting data with the telematics one. The project's main objective was to improve the procedures for receiving data without burdening the activities of local governments and, through its cognitive component, to strengthen analysis instruments, investigation, and control, including the business intelligence tools, which allow a quicker comparison of homogeneous accounting items of different entities belonging to the same sector. Altogether, the associated benefit is the growth of the overall knowledge system on public finance for supporting the Court of Auditors' activities.

However, the SMART project has never really worked. The wide adoption of XBRL in the private sector and the success of SICE have led the Italian Ministry of Economy and Finance, in particular the State General Accounting Department (thanks also to the support and experience gained by the Court of Auditors), to launch a new system for collecting the financial statements of the entire Italian public administrations called Banca Dati Amministrazioni Pubbliche – Bilanci Armonizzati (BDAP) (Public Administration Database – Harmonized Budgets and Accounts).

The adoption of the BDAP system also represents a major innovation on an international level. Starting from May 2016, XBRL became the mandatory format for all the Italian public administrations (20 regions, 110 provinces, and 8,000 municipalities, plus local companies controlled by these entities) for submitting their financial statements to the State General Accounting Department. The system provides a single point of access (i.e., "one-stop shop") for data filing (http://www.bdap.tesoro.it) and, above all, is mainly imagined to benefit the citizens who can control the economic-financial data of the Italian public administration via the web in an interactive mode.

The financial statements submission will be made with reference to local entities reporting on the traditional modified cash accounting system through the three available taxonomies: the first related to the budget, the second to the management report, and the third to the consolidated financial statements. As for the financial reports of entities adopting financial accounting, they will use the XBRL taxonomy that already exists for filing the financial statements of private companies (Italian GAAP taxonomy) to the Italian Business Register without further implementations or changes. Furthermore, the accounting documents sent by public entities will undergo a series of checks (blocking and nonblocking controls) to verify the quality and consistency of the reported data.

Because the project was launched just one year ago, it is still not possible currently to assess its results and understand whether the XBRL adoption within the Italian public administration has led to the expected benefits, as highlighted by the literature (Fradeani et al., in press).

## CONCLUSION

The internationalization and integration of socioeconomic scenarios have involved a growing need for information required for making choices. XBRL seems to intercept some of the most pressing needs of the global market: timeliness, accuracy and interoperability of information concerning financial business communication, and costs saving. Reducing administrative burdens is one of the main reasons for choosing XBRL for firms' financial statements. Such savings, in fact, can be achieved along different paths: eliminating or simplifying the rules, using new technologies, or using a combination of the two options.

In this chapter, the role of XBRL within governmental financial reporting has been analyzed from a theoretical point of view. XBRL may help simplify and streamline the relationships between different public entities. The resulting benefits from its use, such as improved controls, will be much greater when a higher number of organizations linked by reporting relationships adopt it. Furthermore, facilitating the exchange of financial information between different levels of public hierarchy may also improve consolidated financial reports.

Another aspect of interest is that XBRL can achieve a standardization of retention and archiving data aimed at a greater comparability over time and space, as well as at a significant flexibility in the presentation of information to the outside, improving accessibility by the various stakeholders. Hence, the use of XBRL could help improve the comparability of economic and financial documents, increase government transparency and accountability, and strengthen its legitimacy. The Italian case, even though the results are still to be assessed, seems to be going in that direction: the BDAP system aims to represent, similar to the idea of a one-stop shop, the central database that collects the financial statements of all the Italian public administrations, making them available not only to the governing bodies but also to the citizens via a web interface for interactive viewing.

Furthermore, as a digital and open standard that requires standardizing the syntactic and semantic information that will feed into the reports, XBRL can assist and encourage the process of governmental accounting systems harmonization and simplification at both the national and international level.

In the Italian case, when the entity adopts Italian accounting principles or IFRS, the choice is available to use standard taxonomies already adopted by the private sector (ITA GAAP) or derived from the international ones (IFRS taxonomy).

Although this chapter is focused on the public sector, the real challenge ahead concerns the realization of a full use of XBRL, without distinction between the public or private nature of its user. In fact, today this distinction is becoming less clear and ambiguous in part because of the widespread forms of collaboration and partnership between public and private organizations that have been mentioned. The success of XBRL will be determined by the scale of its adoption (Doolin & Troshani, 2007).

Finally, it is important to remember that the ICT tools and digital standards cannot be expected to change by default in a mechanistic way because they should be included in a highly dynamic and complex context as that of a public or private socioeconomic organization. The potentials of technology may be canceled or at least severely curtailed if the subjects for which it makes available a higher qualitative and quantitative level of information cannot or do not have the will to use them. Despite the fundamental importance of technologies within government, the central and decisive role of humans is unavoidable.

XBRL can be called a discontinuous innovation, and bureaucratic organizations such as governments may be unable to deal with it effectively (Bessant, 2005); they need real and solid support from politicians and top management.

Considering the strong need for governments' information transparency caused by the fiscal crisis, XBRL could be a useful digital standard to push and improve governments' accountability, transparency, and comparability, as well as a method to prevent or avoid future crises.

This issue needs further specific research because the role of XBRL within governmental financial reporting is somewhat different from the role of XBRL in corporate disclosure. In addition, different levels of government have different reporting obligations within nations and without.

The analysis conducted in this article is predominantly theoretical, as the Italian case—one of the first cases worldwide of this large-scale mandatory adoption of XBRL for the public entities—is too recent to assess the related results. This topic needs to be strengthened by empirical studies concerning projects that are taking place within government or other public sector entities in order to test and verify the actual and effective contribution that XBRL can make to the public sector.

## REFERENCES

Abdolmohammadi, M., Harris, J., & Smith, K. (2002). Government financial reporting on the Internet: The potential revolutionary effects of XBRL. *Journal of Government Financial Management*, *51*(2), 24–31.

Aikins, S. K. (Ed.). (2012). *Managing E-Government Projects: Concepts, Issues, and Best Practices*. Hershey, PA: IGI Global. doi:10.4018/978-1-4666-0086-7

Anthopoulos, L. G., & Siozos, P. (2015). Can IT Innovation become a Tool against Fiscal Crisis?: Findings from Europe. *International Journal of Public Administration in the Digital Age*, *2*(1), 39–55. doi:10.4018/ijpada.2015010103

Avallone, F., Ramassa, P., & Roncagliolo, E. (2016). XBRL Extension to the Financial Statement Notes: Field-based Evidence on Unlisted Companies. *The International Journal of Digital Accounting Research*, *16*, 61–84.

Ball, C. (2007). Better information better management. *Journal of Government Financial Management*, *56*(2), 16–19.

Bessant, J. (2005). Enabling continuous and discontinuous innovation: Learning from the private sector. *Public Money & Management*, *25*(1), 35–42.

Birt, J. L., Muthusamy, K., & Bir, P. (2017). XBRL and the Qualitative Characteristics of Useful Financial Information. *Accounting Research Journal*, *30*(1), 107–126. doi:10.1108/ARJ-11-2014-0105

Bonollo, E. (2017). XBRL Adoption in Public Organizations: Criticalities and Perspectives. In K. Corsi, N. Castellano, R. Lamboglia, & D. Mancini (Eds.), *Reshaping Accounting and Management Control Systems. Lecture Notes in Information Systems and Organisation* (pp. 317–330). Cham, Switzerland: Springer. doi:10.1007/978-3-319-49538-5_21

Bovee, M., Ettredge, M. L., Srivastava, R. P., & Vasarhelyi, M. A. (2002). Does the year 2000 XBRL taxonomy accommodate current business financial-reporting practice? *Journal of Information Systems*, *16*(2), 165–182. doi:10.2308/jis.2002.16.2.165

Brown, F., & Willis, M. (2003). XBRL: Revolutionizing the corporate reporting supply chain. *Financial Executive*, *19*(3), 70–71.

Chen, Y. C. (2012). A comparative study of e-government XBRL implementations: The potential of improving information transparency and efficiency. *Government Information Quarterly*, *29*(4), 553–563. doi:10.1016/j.giq.2012.05.009

Chen, Y. C. (2013). Improving transparency in the financial Sector: e-Government XBRL implementation in the United States. *Public Performance & Management Review*, *37*(2), 241–262. doi:10.2753/PMR1530-9576370203

Cong, Y., Du, H., & Vasarhelyi, M. A. (2017). Are XBRL Files Being Accessed? Evidence from the SEC EDGAR Log File Data Set. *Journal of Information Systems*, isys-51885. doi:10.2308/isys-51885

Dawes, S. S., Cresswell, A. M., & Pardo, T. A. (2009). From "need to know" to "need to share": Tangled problems, information boundaries, and the building of public sector knowledge networks. *Public Administration Review*, *69*(3), 392–402. doi:10.1111/j.1540-6210.2009.01987_2.x

Debreceny, R., Farewell, S., Piechocki, M., Felden, C., & Gräning, A. (2010). Does it add up? Early evidence on the data quality of XBRL filings to the SEC. *Journal of Accounting and Public Policy*, *29*(3), 296–306. doi:10.1016/j.jaccpubpol.2010.04.001

Debreceny, R., Felden, C., Ochocki, B., Piechocki, M., & Piechocki, M. (2009). *XBRL for Interactive Data. Engineering the Information Value Chain*. Heidelberg, Germany: Springer. doi:10.1007/978-3-642-01437-6

Debreceny, R. S., Farewell, S. M., Piechocki, M., Felden, C., Gräning, A., & d'Eri, A. (2011). Flex or break? Extensions in XBRL disclosures to the SEC. *Accounting Horizons*, *25*(4), 631–657. doi:10.2308/acch-50068

Doolin, B., & Troshani, I. (2007). Organizational adoption of XBRL. *Electronic Markets*, *17*(3), 199–209. doi:10.1080/10196780701503195

Enachi, M., & Andone, I. I. (2015). The Progress of XBRL in Europe – Projects, Users and Prospects. *Procedia Economics and Finance*, *20*, 185–192. doi:10.1016/S2212-5671(15)00064-7

Flowerday, S., Blundell, A. W., & Von Solms, R. (2006). Continuous auditing technologies and models: A discussion. *Computers & Security*, *25*(5), 325–331. doi:10.1016/j.cose.2006.06.004

Flowerday, S., & Von Solms, R. (2005). Continuous auditing: Verifying information integrity and providing assurances for financial reports. *Computer Fraud & Security*, *2005*(7), 12–16. doi:10.1016/S1361-3723(05)70232-3

Fradeani, A., Panizzolo, D., & Metushi, E. (2016). Financial Reporting in XBRL: First Evidence on Financial Statement Notes of Italian Unlisted Companies. *The International Journal of Digital Accounting Research*, *16*, 85–115.

Fradeani, A., Regoliosi, C., D'Eri, A., & Campanari, F. (2017). Implementation of Mandatory IFRS Financial Disclosures in a Voluntary Format: Evidence from the Italian XBRL Project. In K. Corsi, N. Castellano, R. Lamboglia, & D. Mancini (Eds.), *Reshaping Accounting and Management Control Systems. Lecture Notes in Information Systems and Organisation* (pp. 331–347). Cham, Switzerland: Springer. doi:10.1007/978-3-319-49538-5_22

Fradeani, A., Soverchia, M., & Metushi, E. (in press). Digital Governmental Financial Reporting: First Evidence from Italy. In R. Lamboglia, A. Cardoni, R. P. Dameri, & D. Mancini (Eds.), *Network, Smart and Open. Three Keywords for Information Systems Innovation*. Cham, Switzerland: Springer. doi:10.1007/978-3-319-62636-9_14

Goldsmith, S., & Eggers, W. D. (2004). *Governing by Network: The New Shape of the Public Sector*. Washington, DC: Brookings Institution Press.

Hausman, A., & Johnston, W. J. (2014). The role of innovation in driving the economy: Lessons from the global financial crisis. *Journal of Business Research*, *67*(1), 2720–2726. doi:10.1016/j.jbusres.2013.03.021

Hodge, F. D., Kennedy, J. J., & Maines, L. A. (2004). Does search-facilitating technology improve the transparency of financial reporting? *The Accounting Review*, *79*(3), 687–703. doi:10.2308/accr.2004.79.3.687

IFAC. (2008). *Financial reporting supply chain. Current perspectives and directions*. New York, NY: IFAC.

Jaeger, P. T. (2003). The endless wire: E-government as global phenomenon. *Government Information Quarterly*, *20*(4), 323–331. doi:10.1016/j.giq.2003.08.003

Karamagioli, E., Staiou, E. R., & Gouscos, D. (2014). Government Spending Transparency on the Internet: An Assessment of Greek Bottom-Up Initiatives over the Diavgeia Project. *International Journal of Public Administration in the Digital Age*, *1*(1), 39–55. doi:10.4018/ijpada.2014010103

Kernan, K. (2008). XBRL around the world. *Journal of Accountancy*, *206*(4), 62–66.

Kernan, K. (2009). *XBRL. The Story of Our New Language*. New York, NY: American Institute of Certified Public Accountants.

Kull, J., & Abraham, C. (2008). XBRL and public sector financial reporting. *Journal of Government Financial Management*, *57*(2), 28–37.

Liu, C., Luo, X. R., & Wang, F. L. (2017). An empirical investigation on the impact of XBRL adoption on information asymmetry: Evidence from Europe. *Decision Support Systems*, *93*, 42–50. doi:10.1016/j.dss.2016.09.004

Milward, H. B., & Provan, K. G. (2001). Do Networks Really Work? A Framework for Evaluating Public-Sector Organizational Networks. *Public Administration Review*, *61*(4), 414–423. doi:10.1111/0033-3352.00045

Mintzberg, H. (1996). Managing Government, Governing Management. *Harvard Business Review, 74*(3), 75–83.

Moore, M. H. (1995). *Creating public value: Strategic management in government.* Cambridge, MA: Harvard University Press.

Moore, M. H. (2005). Break-Through Innovations and Continuous Improvement: Two Different Models of Innovative Processes in the Public Sector. *Public Money & Management, 25*(1), 43–50.

Mousa, R. (2013). E-Government adoption in the UK: XBRL project. *International Journal of Electronic Government Research, 9*(2), 101–119. doi:10.4018/jegr.2013040106

Panizzolo, D., Fradeani, A., & Metushi, E. (2017). Financial Reporting Practices of Italian SMEs: Why Do They Disclose More? *The International Journal of Digital Accounting Research, 17*, 111–137. doi:10.4192/1577-8517-v17_5

Perdana, A., Robb, A., & Rohde, F. (2014). An integrative review and synthesis of XBRL research in academic journals. *Journal of Information Systems, 29*(1), 115–153. doi:10.2308/isys-50884

Petrakis, P. E., Kostis, P. C., & Valsamis, D. G. (2015). Innovation and competitiveness: Culture as a long-term strategic instrument during the European Great Recession. *Journal of Business Research, 68*(7), 1436–1438. doi:10.1016/j.jbusres.2015.01.029

Philip, E., & Wurster, T. S. (1999). *Blown to bits: how the new economics of information transforms strategy.* Boston, MA: Harvard Business School Press.

Porter, M. E. (1990). The competitive advantage of nations. *Harvard Business Review, 68*(2), 73–93.

Rezaee, Z., Sharbatoghlie, A., Elam, R., & McMickle, P. L. (2002). Continuous auditing: Building automated auditing capability. *Auditing, 21*(1), 147–163. doi:10.2308/aud.2002.21.1.147

Rezaee, Z., & Turner, J. L. (2002). XBRL-based financial reporting: Challenges and opportunities for government accountants. *Journal of Government Financial Management, 51*(2), 16–22.

Roohani, S., Furusho, Y., & Koizumi, M. (2009). XBRL: Improving transparency and monitoring functions of corporate governance. *International Journal of Disclosure and Governance, 6*(4), 355–369. doi:10.1057/jdg.2009.17

Sapienza, P., & Zingales, L. (2012). A Trust Crisis. *International Review of Finance, 12*(2), 123–131. doi:10.1111/j.1468-2443.2012.01152.x

Soverchia, M. (2015). How Can Technology Improve Government Financial Transparency? The Answer of the eXtensible Business Reporting Language (XBRL). *International Journal of Public Administration in the Digital Age, 2*(1), 24–38. doi:10.4018/ijpada.2015010102

Valentinetti, D., & Rea, M. A. (2013). XBRL for financial reporting: Evidence on Italian GAAP versus IFRS. *Accounting Perspectives, 12*(3), 237–259. doi:10.1111/1911-3838.12008

Verspagen, B. (2005). Innovation and Economic Growth. In J. Fagerberg, D. C. Mowery, & R. R. Nelson (Eds.), *The Oxford Handbook of Innovation*. Oxford, UK: Oxford University Press.

Walther, F., Vogt, S., & Kabst, R. (2016). A Strategic Foresight about Future Public Service Developments from the Citizens' Perspective. *International Journal of Public Administration in the Digital Age*, *3*(1), 19–42. doi:10.4018/IJPADA.2016010102

Yildiz, M. (2007). E-government research: Reviewing the literature, limitations, and ways forward. *Government Information Quarterly*, *24*(3), 646–665. doi:10.1016/j.giq.2007.01.002

Yoon, H., Zo, H., & Ciganek, A. P. (2011). Does XBRL adoption reduce information asymmetry? *Journal of Business Research*, *64*(2), 157–163. doi:10.1016/j.jbusres.2010.01.008

# Chapter 7
# How to Migrate Citizens Online and Reduce Traffic on Traditional Channels Through Multichannel Management:
## A Case Study of Cross-Organizational Collaboration Surrounding a Mandatory Self-Service Application

**Christian Østergaard Madsen**
*ITU, Denmark*

**Pernille Kræmmergaard**
*Digitaliseringsinstituttet, Denmark*

## ABSTRACT

*E-government channels are a key to achieving economic savings from public digitization. Citizens tend to use multiple channels in a service encounter and often use e-government channels as a supplement instead of replacing traditional channels. There is a lack of knowledge regarding how government organizations apply findings from user studies to migrate citizens online while reducing traffic through traditional channels. The authors present a case study on how public authorities collaborate to create a multichannel strategy for an online application for single parents. After the multichannel strategy was implemented, there was an increase in the use of the application and a reduction in telephone calls. The authors wrote this chapter to contribute to channel choice and multichannel management literature.*

DOI: 10.4018/978-1-5225-5966-5.ch007

## INTRODUCTION

E-government is promoted as a means to increase the effectiveness and efficiency of public authorities as well as citizen satisfaction (Chadwick & May, 2003; Ho, 2002; Layne & Lee, 2001). As e-government channels generally have lower transactions costs than traditional channels, citizens' migration from traditional channels towards e-government channels is regarded as key to achieving savings (The Danish Government, 2011). However, literature reviews of the e-government field show that the papers studied lack practical recommendations on how to achieve these benefits (Heeks & Bailur, 2007; Hofmann, Räckers, & Becker, 2012; Madsen, Berger, & Phythian, 2014).

The channel choice (CC) and multichannel management (MCM) branches of e-government examine how citizens and employees choose communication channels in a public service encounter and how government organizations can migrate citizens towards the most efficient channels (Ebbers, Pieterson, & Noordman, 2008; Kernaghan, 2013; Pieterson, 2010; Pieterson, Ebbers, & Madsen, 2017; van den Boer, Arendsen, & Pieterson, 2016). The majority of CC and e-government adoption studies are conducted in settings where citizens have a choice of channels. These studies typically revolve around increasing the adoption rates of digital channels. There are few studies in mandatory settings where citizens have already adopted e-government channels. Thus, the continued use of traditional channels among those who have adopted e-government channels remain unexplained (Ebbers, Jansen, & van Deursen, 2016; Madsen & Kræmmergaard, 2015a; Reddick & Anthopoulos, 2014). Although strategies to fully integrate government organizations' channels have been suggested (Pieterson, 2010; Wirtz & Langer, 2016), they remain theoretical. Conducting a MCM strategy in practice is complicated, especially when the channels involved are managed by several organizations (Kernaghan, 2009, 2013; Roy, 2009). There is a lack of knowledge and practical recommendations for how such cross-organizational collaborations can be conducted. Therefore, scholars have called for case studies of successful MCM projects (Janssen & Kuk, 2010; Kernaghan, 2013; Mundy, Umer, & Foster, 2011; Wirtz & Langer, 2016), and qualitative studies of citizens' combined use of traditional and e-government channels (Ebbers, Jansen, Pieterson, & van de Wijngaert, 2015; Ebbers et al., 2016; Schmidthuber & Hilgers, 2017). This paper addresses these gaps by answering the following research question; *how can public authorities successfully implement a mandatory channel strategy, to increase citizens' use of e-government channels and simultaneously reduce the use of traditional channels?*

This paper presents a longitudinal case study (Yin, 2014) of a cross-organizational collaboration surrounding a mandatory online self-service application. The authors conduct a study among a group of citizens who have largely adopted the e-government channel. Thereby they analyze multichannel government-to-citizen (G2C) interaction occurring in a post-adoption environment and how government organizations can conduct multichannel management in such settings.

The next section contains a description of the case and its setting. Then follows a presentation of existing literature on CC and MCM to position the paper, illustrating the relevance of the research question and expected contributions. Next, the authors present methods for data collection and analysis, before turning to a discussion of the findings in relation to CC and MCM literature, and contributions to research and practioners. The final section presents concluding remarks, limitations, and recommendations for future studies.

## CASE DESCRIPTION

### The Creation of Udbetaling Danmark

The authority Udbetaling Danmark (UDK) (Payments Denmark) was established by the Danish Government and Local Government Denmark in 2012. UDK is administrated by the Danish Pensions fund *Arbejdsmarkedes Tillægspension* (Labour Market Supplementary Pension) (ATP). UDK administers 27 billion Euros annually within five public benefits areas previously administrated locally by the Danish municipalities. With the establishment of UDK, caseworkers were transferred from the 98 Danish municipalities to five major national UDK centers. One of these centers is co-located with ATP headquarters, where the collaboration took place.

According to UDK's business case, UDK was expected to save 40 million Euro annually through centralization, increased digitization and use of self-service applications after a two year implementation period (ATP, 2011). In 2016, the Danish National Audit Office found that UDK had successfully met this goal (The Danish National Audit Office, 2016). An additional 40 million Euros is expected to be saved through the public procurement of the new IT-systems for UDK. In ATP's digitization strategy, citizen oriented service processes are prioritized according to:

1. No-touch solutions (full automation)
2. Citizens' use of e-government channels (websites and online self-service applications)
3. Interaction through traditional channels (mainly calls)

In line with these priorities and the Danish e-government strategy (see Box 1), citizens are expected to use a web-portal to get information and for conducting transactions with UDK. Citizen-initiated contacts to UDK are mostly conducted on the telephone, while digital post and traditional letters are secondary channels. Counter turn-ups are possible, but rare due to the physical location of UDK.

### The Danish E-Government Strategy 2011-2015

Denmark is regarded as one of the leading countries in regards to e-government adoption (European Commission, 2015). It has a population with high level of ICT skills which generally has good access to broadband and frequently use a wide array of online services (Danish Business Authority 2014; Statistics Denmark 2014). The Danish e-government strategy 2011-2015 (The Danish Government, 2011) aims to increase digitization in the public sector. The components, which support this digitization, are under the authority of the Agency for Digitization, but are outsourced to private companies. Among the citizen-oriented components are:

- **NemID (EasyID):** A national identification system, which citizens use to identify themselves for online interaction with public authorities and private companies, especially banks.
- **NemKonto (Easy Account):** A bank account which is assigned for payments from the public sector. All citizens and companies in Denmark are required to have a NemKonto.

- **Borger.Dk (Citizen.Dk):** A one stop service portal that grants citizens access to services from local and national government agencies. The Agency for Digitization administers Borger.dk, but other public authorities have sub-sections on the portal where they publish their own content. The websites for the benefits UDK administers are located at Borger.dk.
- **Digital Post:** An e-mail system, which replaces traditional letters from public authorities and private companies. In November 2014, digital post became mandatory, and Danish authorities stopped sending traditional letters to the extent possible. Digital post is accessible through Borger.dk and the privately run e-Boks, and requires the user to login with NemID.
- **Mandatory Online Self-Service Applications:** According to the strategy, 80 percent of all requests from citizens within 35 areas (including those of UDK) shall take place via self-service applications in 2015. Citizens are expected to use e-government channels instead of calling or visiting a caseworker. Those who are incapable of using these channels can call, or get help at Borgerservice, local service centers run by the municipalities.

## Family Benefits and the 2013 Single Parent's Declaration

'Family benefits' is an umbrella term for benefits, which parents with children under the age of 18 living with them are legally entitled to. Single parents can get additional benefits as long as they are not living with other adults under marriage-like conditions. To retain these additional benefits single parents are required by law to declare themselves single annually, and to notify UDK if they are no longer single. When the local municipalities administrated family benefits, they used a paper form for the declaration. UDK had an online application developed for this task. In 2013, UDK sent letters concerning the single's declaration to 119.000 single parents[1]. Half of these were sent as digital post while the remaining half was traditional letters. The recipients had to locate the application at Borger.dk, log in using NemID, and declare if they were still single. Those without NemID could call UDK and request a paper form. After five weeks, UDK sent a notification using traditional letters and digital post to those that had not responded. After the second deadline, non-responders were regarded as not being single anymore and lost their benefits. Viewed solely in terms of adoption rates, the mandatory e-government strategy was successful as 98 percent of all those who responded used the online application.

## Challenges to the 2013 Declaration

From an organizational point of view, there were two challenges to the 2013 declaration. The first concerned a surge in calls related to the declaration. Before the letters were sent calls to UDK's family benefit division averaged 6.000 per week (see Figure 1). In the two weeks after the letters were sent incoming calls rose to 19.000 and 13.000 respectively. The second challenge concern citizens who were used to getting information from public authorities through traditional letters, and missed the notifications sent as digital post. Those who did not respond subsequently lost their benefits. In December 2013, the Social Board of Appeals ruled that UDK should have informed the single parents about the change in channels and that those who had lost their benefits should have their cases re-evaluated.

*Figure 1. Citizen-initiated interactions with UDK's family benefit division 2012-2013*

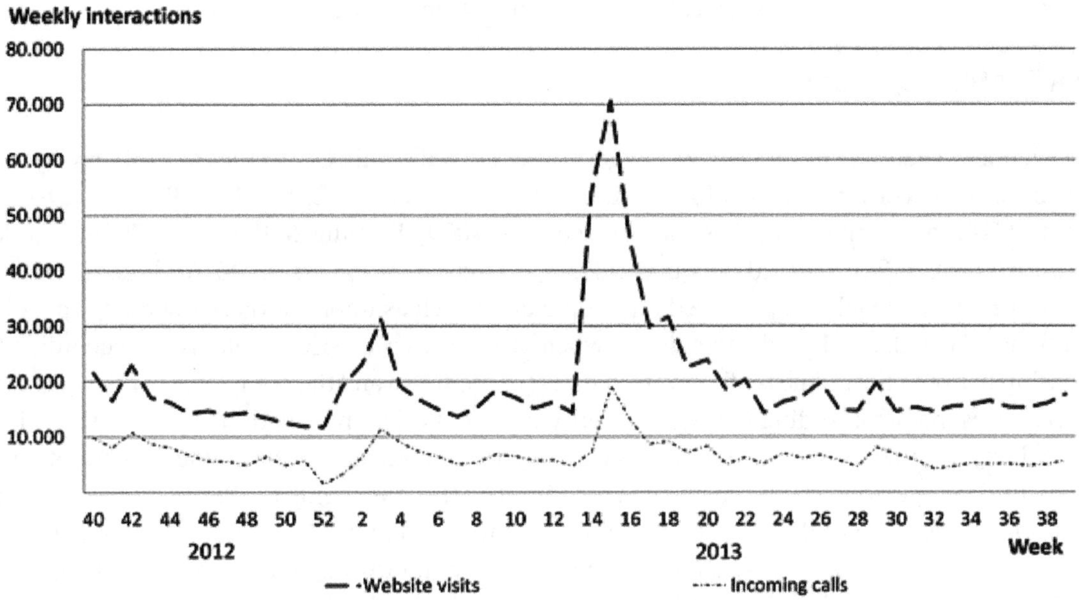


## CHANNEL CHOICE AND MULTICHANNEL MANAGEMENT

### Channel Choice Studies

With the diffusion of the Internet and the digitization of the public sector, citizens have new communication forms (channels) to interact with public authorities. CC studies in e-government study the processes surrounding citizens' or employees choice of channels for interacting with public authorities (Ebbers et al., 2015, 2016; Kernaghan, 2013; Madsen & Kræmmergaard, 2015a; Pieterson, 2010; Reddick & Anthopoulos, 2014; Schmidthuber & Hilgers, 2017; van den Boer et al., 2016). Multichannel management mostly take place at the organizational level, and concern how government organizations can integrate channels and migrate citizens from traditional towards more cost efficient channels, especially e-government channels, where citizens interact with an online system instead of a case worker (Ebbers et al., 2008; Madsen & Kræmmergaard, 2015a; Wirtz & Langer, 2016).

Reddick and Anthopolous (2014) divide channels for citizen interaction with government into three groups: traditional channels (face-to-face meetings, telephone calls, and surface mail), e-government channels (e-mail and websites), and new digital media (text messaging, mobile apps and social media). The authors regard online self-service applications as part of the e-government channels. At the individual transaction level, and investment costs notwithstanding, interaction through e-government channels is cheaper to administer for public authorities than communication through traditional channels. Increased efficiency through lower transaction costs are therefore used as arguments for online migration (Kernaghan, 2013; The Danish Government, 2011). Reaping the economic benefits of this migration, however, is a challenge. CC studies have found that e-government channels supplement rather than replace other channels, and citizens often have several interactions and use several channels per service encounter (Ebbers et al., 2016; Madsen & Kræmmergaard, 2015b, 2016; Pieterson & Ebbers,

2008; Reddick & Turner, 2012). This shows the importance of regarding the entire service encounter rather than a single transaction when calculating savings from online migration.

## Media Richness Theory

Media Richness Theory (MRT) (Daft, & Lengel, 1986) is used within CC studies to explain why citizens and businesses use certain channels for specific tasks (Barth & Veit, 2011; Boer, Pieterson, Arendsen, & Groot, 2014; Pieterson, 2010; Pieterson & Teerling, 2009; Teerling & Pieterson, 2010; van de Wijngaert, Pieterson, & Teerling, 2011; van den Boer, Arendsen, & Pieterson, 2016). Findings show that the e-government channels are preferred for simple tasks such as information searches, but people turn to traditional channels, such as the telephone, when problems arise. MRT explains CC according to the relationship between the richness of a given channel (or medium) and the complexity of the task at hand. MRT classifies media according to their "capacity to process rich information" (Daft & Lengel, 1986, p.560), which is explained by "the medium's capacity for immediate feedback, the number of cues and channels utilized, personalization and language variety" (Daft & Lengel, 1986, p.560). Face-to-face conversation is regarded as the richest communication form, followed by telephone conversations, and finally documents. Tasks are classified according to the ambiguity and uncertainty (absence) of the information to be processed. Tasks with high ambiguity require media that offer instant feedback and rich information, such as telephone or face-to-face conversations. In these cases, what is needed is not more information, but a decision on how something is supposed to be understood. If a task is well understood, but one lacks information, this can effectively be provided through text. Through this classification, MRT offers an explanation of why static websites with text can replace letters, as the level of richness and the lack feedback is roughly the same in the two channels. The telephone provides instant feedback and cannot be replaced by websites unless these present similar feedback through voice or text chat.

## Criticism of Medium Richness Theory

MRT has been criticized for its fixed classifications of media from several perspectives (Cai & Jun, 2015; Carlson & Zmud, 1999; Markus, 1994; Ngwenyama & Lee, 1997). Critics have mentioned that computers and the internet offer a variety of communication forms, which can be both rich and poor (Cai & Jun, 2015). The computer is a meta-medium, which can emulate most previous media forms, and convey text, images, sound and offer both synchronous or asynchronous communication (Kay & Goldberg, 1977). Thus, an organizations' governance and implementation of a medium influence the medium's richness, rather than merely its inherent characteristics (Cai & Jun, 2015). Markus (1994) and Ngwenyama and Lee (1997) argue that media choice is a social, rather than an individual process. They recommend that scholars apply social influence theories to study media choice. The criticism of MRT has led to new theories being applied to study media and CC. According to the Channel Expansion Theory people's experience, with the medium, communication partners, topic and context, influence their perception of media richness, and choice of channels (Carlson & Zmud, 1999). This theory has been successfully applied by CC scholars (Pieterson, Teerling, & Ebbers, 2008). In spite of the criticism, MRT remains the most frequently applied theoretical framework for CC studies (Madsen & Kræmmergaard, 2015a). Moreover, even studies that do not apply MRT directly find that the nature of an interaction and task complexity influence CC (Madsen & Kræmmergaard, 2015b, 2016; Reddick, 2010; Reddick & Turner, 2012; Reddick & Anthopoulos, 2014).

The findings reported in previous CC literature mostly relate to the choice of a single channel for individual tasks, not entire service encounters where there can be an interplay across channels (Madsen & Kræmmergaard, 2015a). Rebound effects of channel migration such as inquiries through traditional channels concerning online transactions have rarely been studied in a digital public administration context (Madsen & Kræmmergaard, 2015a). Finally, there is a lack of knowledge of G2C interaction in a mandatory environment (Ebbers et al., 2016). CC scholars call for more studies on these topics, and recommend the use of qualitative methods, such as interviews and focus group discussions, to study these gaps (Ebbers et al., 2015; Pieterson, 2010; Reddick & Turner, 2012; Reddick & Anthopoulos, 2014).

## Multichannel Management Studies

At the organizational level, MCM focuses on public authorities' vertical and horizontal integration of channels, and how citizens can be migrated from traditional to e-government channels. Field experiments show that integrating channels, increasing the quality of e-government channels, and communicating clearly about these channels are effective channel management instruments (Pieterson & Teerling, 2009; Teerling & Pieterson, 2010). These studies contribute to CC and MCM literature, but still focus on single tasks and individual channels. The gap in empirical studies of entire service encounters and cross-channel interplay also exists at the organizational level. Therefore, Teerling and Pieterson (2011) request longitudinal studies of the effects of MCM instruments.

MCM requires that information is coordinated across multiple channels, which are typically controlled by different sections or organizations (Pieterson, 2010). Thus, both inter- and cross-organizational collaborations are required for successful channel integration. Kernaghan (2013) finds a lack of empirical MCM studies, and requests detailed case studies of cross-organizational collaboration. He also suggests that public organizations apply transaction data for MCM purposes.

Wirtz and Langer present a framework for an integrated channel strategy which combines services and on- and offline channels (Wirtz & Langer, 2016), and offer suggestions for how public organizations can manage new channels and services through expansion and diversification. Their framework is theoretically grounded in the concept of strategic diversification and based on a systematic analysis, which includes the various channels' capacities. However, Wirtz and Langer do not test their model empirically, nor do they present primary empirical data. Therefore, they call for empirical studies, which present applied multichannel management strategies, empirical data on channel mixes and have been demonstrated to create customer value.

## Knowledge Gaps and Contributions to CC and MCM Studies

To sum up, valuable contributions have been made in the CC and MCM fields, but several knowledge gaps remain. At the individual level there is a lack of knowledge of the interplay that takes place across channels related to entire service encounters, and why citizens who have adopted e-government channels keep using traditional channels. At the organizational level there is a lack of studies of cross-organizational MCM collaboration. Finally, there is the matter of connecting these levels in practice. How can public organizations collect information on citizens' multichannel behavior, and turn this information into a successful MCM strategy? How can the channels available to an organization be applied to address the needs of citizens? And how will channel traffic be affected if such a multichannel strategy is carried out? This paper addresses the identified gaps and answer these questions through a detailed longitudinal case study of a cross-organizational collaboration. At the theoretical level the case study presents explanations of why citizens who have adopted e-government channels continue to use traditional channels. Further, the authors demonstrate that reducing information ambiguity and uncertainty can influence CC, and citizens need for communication altogether. Finally, the authors develop a multichannel strategy based on this principle.

## METHOD

Case studies are relevant as a research strategy for answering 'how' and why' types of research questions, and when an extensive in-depth description of some social phenomenon is required (Yin, 2014, p.4). Further, case studies can be appropriate when dealing with longitudinal or unusual events "over which a researcher has little or no control" (Yin, 2014, p.14). The case study presented here contains an embedded study of why citizens' called UDK regarding the service encounter. The 2013 single parents' declaration represents an extreme case. It was successful in terms of adoption rates, but unsuccessful if one regards the surge in calls and citizen satisfaction. This contrast emphasizes the importance of including contextual information and studying the interplay and total traffic across channels, rather than the isolated use of one channel.

To strengthen the validity of the case study the authors collected multiple and convergent sources of data (Yin, 2014, p.121). The longitudinal case study can be divided into four stages: (1) the 2013 single parents declaration, (2) the improvement of the 2014 single parents' declaration, (3) the 2014 single parents' declaration, (4) the 2015 single parents' declaration. Different types of data were collected at each stage (see Table 1). Standard qualitative methods such as focus group discussions, individual interviews, and observations, were applied to collect data on single parents' perception of the declaration process (Blaikie, 2012; Krueger, 1994). Physical artifacts such as the self-service application itself and UDK's letters were also included.

This case study data was classified and analyzed in two steps. First, the data was classified through open coding using the software Atlas.TI to find to the problems which caused single parents to call UDK (Friese, 2012; Strauss & Corbin, 1990). These problems were analyzed to find solutions for how the uncertainties that caused calls could be reduced. Minutes from meetings, e-mails and personal notes were used to document the collaboration. Statistics on calls and use of the self-service application allow for a comparison from 2013 to 2014, and from 2014 to 2015. Table 1 presents the case study data.

## IMPROVING THE SINGLE PARENT'S DECLARATION

This section presents the collaborative efforts to integrate channels and reduce calls in chronological order following stages two and three outlined above.

### Stage 1: Identifying Problems Related to the 2013 Declaration

In February 2014, ATP established a cross-organizational group to solve several technical and administrative problems regarding the single parent's declaration. The group consisted of six employees from ATP, and two from UDK. The employees from ATP included the manager for family benefits and five

*Table 1. Case study data*

| Stage | Evidence Type | Source | Time Frame |
|---|---|---|---|
| 1. | Documentation | Call statistics to UDK family benefits, statistics on use of the self-service application | Spring 2013 |
| | Interview | Five focus group discussions with 28 single parents who receive family benefits | |
| | Physical artifacts | Website, self-service application, letters | |
| 2. | Participant observation | Active participation in meetings regarding 2014 single parents declaration | Spring – Summer 2014 |
| | Letter testing | Presentation of new letters to single parents to ensure that the letters are easy to understand | |
| | Interview | Interviews with single parents from focus group discussions and additional letter testing | |
| 3. | Documentation | Call statistics to UDK family benefits, classification of calls, statistics on use of the self-service application | Fall 2014 – Jan 2015 |
| | Physical artifacts | Website, self-service application, letters, receipts | |
| | Documentation | ATP's and UDK's Newsletters on collaboration | |
| | Participant observation | Participation in evaluation meeting | |
| 4. | Documentation | Call statistics to UDK family benefits, classification of calls, statistics on use of the self-service application | Fall 2015 – Dec 2015 |

others responsible for the technical aspect of the self-service application, communication, legal requirements, and contact with the IT suppliers and the Agency for Digitization. A call section manager and a representative of the caseworkers represented UDK.

The three primary reasons for calls concerned navigation, receipts and attempts of declaration on via the telephone. A fourth problem concerned the single parents who had missed their digital post, as previously mentioned. In 2013, no system existed for classifying calls to UDK. Knowledge of why people were calling was gained through UDK employees and qualitative user studies. These studies suggested that part of the solution to reducing calls was to improve communication, especially the content of the letter. The application itself was described as being easy to use, and many approved of it becoming digital, as they could complete the task at home when they wanted to. A few mentioned the lack of support for mobile platforms. This was not a critical issue, but it would make the process more convenient. Those who read digital post on a tablet or smartphone could reply instantly if the self-service application supported these platforms.

Navigation on the portal Borger.dk was repeatedly mentioned as problematic. One explanation was the respondents' low frequency for visiting Borger.dk. The management of family benefits is mostly automated, and the respondents only visited the website when something was wrong, or a change in their lives affected their benefit eligibility. The 2013 single's declaration was the first that relied upon an online self-service application, so the respondents had to learn how to find and use it. The 2013 letter did not specify where at Borger.dk the application was located. The family benefits subpages did not contain links to the application, meaning that only visitors who entered through the front page saw the link. During a focus group discussion, two participants mention this problem.

**Sten (M47):** The blue line on the floor was missing, like in the hospital, where are we going?
**Tanja (F41):** I had to call them for guidance [on how to find the declaration].

Lack of feedback created uncertainty if the declaration process was successfully completed. When the 2013 declaration was completed an image appeared saying: "The declaration has been sent to Udbetaling Danmark and will be processed". No receipt was offered, and there were no options to save or print the image. Poor communication enhanced this uncertainty. Several respondents picked up on the ambiguity in the application's text which read: *"the declaration was sent to UDK"* not *"received by UDK"*. This caused many to call to make sure the task was solved.

**Tom (M45):** Well I think the problem was that once you've sent it, you don't get any confirmation that it has been received. (...) I don't know, is it okay or not? (...) It would better if you got a confirmation saying it has been received.

The 2013 letter contained instructions to go to Borger.dk, but many called to declare themselves single. The callers were instructed to use the self-service application. Those that lacked NemID were sent a physical form, those without Internet access were instructed to go to a civil center or local library and use the computers there.

Many calls regarded several of these issues. Typically, a citizen would sit in front of her computer, call UDK for directions to the self-service application, fill in the information, and then get a confirmation that UDK had received the declaration before hanging up. Others would call repeatedly, first requesting the location of the application and then asking for a receipt.

## Stage 2: The Efforts Taken to Improve the 2014 Declaration

The group set out to improve the communication across all channels to guide citizens towards the online application, and reduce calls. The changes made can be divided into two groups; improvements of the information presented, which are summarized in Table 2, and the addition of new channels to the single declaration process, which are summarized in Table 3.

The letters regarding the single's declaration were re-written from scratch. An effort was made to write the letter from the citizens' point-of-view, and to be as explicit as possible about what the citizen had to do, how this was to be done, and when the task was completed. Several iterations of the letters were written in an attempt to reduce any uncertainties or ambiguities. Changes were also made to the form of the letter; the font size was increased, bullet points were used for instructions, and headlines formulated as questions from the citizen to UDK such as *"What do I have to do?"* were added in bold text to structure the letter. Text regarding legal requirements was moved from the first to the second page of the letter to enhance clarity. The changes concerned:

- **Call to Action:** A new headline instructing the citizens to declare if they are still single.
- **Navigation:** Instructions and a short URL for how to access and use the online application.
- **Receipt:** A section on what the application says when the declaration process is completed and UDK has received the declaration, to let the citizens know that their task is done.

*Table 2. Channel specific solutions related to poor communication*

| Problem | Solution | | |
|---|---|---|---|
| | Letter | Website | Online Application |
| Citizens missing declaration | | Links on front page and family benefit subpages to the application | |
| Navigation | Short URL to the application | Links on front page and family benefit subpages to the application | |
| Attempts to declare on phone | Text specifying that declarations have to be done online, and not on phone | | |
| Uncertainty regarding completion of task | Describes what the application says when task is completed | FAQ explaining how to get a receipt | Receipt page<br>Improved text<br>Print & save option |

*Table 3. The addition of new channels to the 2014 single declaration process*

| Problem | Solution | | |
|---|---|---|---|
| | Telephone | Digital Post | Traditional Mail |
| Citizens missing declaration | Message for incoming callers | | Notifications sent after first deadline |
| Navigation | Message for incoming callers | | |
| Attempts to declare on phone | Message for incoming callers | | |
| Uncertainty of task completion | | Receipt sent upon task completion | |

- **Consequences of Non-Action:** A section explaining what happens if citizens do not respond within the given deadline.
- **Instructions on Calling:** A section explaining that citizens could call UDK about the application, but which specified that they could not call to declare themselves single.

Similar changes were made to the letters for those who missed the first deadline, and to non-responders. The letters were tested at ATP by four single parents who worked at ATP or were relatives of ATP employees, and again during the first author's follow up-interviews in the homes of four single parents. The purpose of the tests was to ensure that the participants understood what was required of them, where the self-service application was located, and when the task was completed. The single parents preferred the new letters and appreciated the changes in both text and form. After the tests a few minor adjustments were made; the instructions were written in bullet points, and the respondents were informed that they needed NemID to login. The authors asked a participant to compare the 2013 and 2014 letters:

Sanne (F45): But this one [2014] has a nice guide in it, which tells me what to do, right? This one [the 2013 letter] just told me to go digitally to Borger.dk, and where I was messing about, right? (...) This one [2013] seems like somebody has just quickly written it and sent it. While this one [2014] seems more worked through than this one [2013]. (...) The text is bigger, that also matters.

The image and link to the application from 2013 were reused at the front page of Borger.dk in 2014. In addition, every subpage on the family benefit section at Borger.dk was updated with links to the application. An employee from the Agency for Digitization's division of borger.dk was on stand-by after the letters were sent, in case any sudden changes had to be made to Borger.dk.

The self-service application underwent several changes to make it compliant to the Agency for Digitization's guidelines, and make it accessible from mobile devices and Mac computers. The wording was harmonized to correspond with the letter. Changes were made to the page shown after declaration is completed to provide immediate feedback and ensure that the task is completed. The text read: "UDK has received your declaration and will process it. You are not supposed to do anything else". An option to save or print receipts was also added.

To create awareness and guide citizens towards the online application, an automated message was played to incoming calls to UDK's family benefit division saying that declarations should be done online and informing about the location of the self-service application through a short URL. Following the experiences from 2013 and the rulings of the Social Board of Appeals it was decided that for the 2014 declaration notifications for those who had missed the first deadline was sent by traditional letter, rather than digital post. Further, upon completion all those who had signed up for digital post would receive a receipt stating that UDK had received their declaration.

## Stage 3: Channel Traffic for the 2014 Single Parent's Declaration

In 2014, 81 percent of the single parents received the letter concerning the single parents' declaration as digital post compared to roughly 50 percent in 2013. The 2014 declaration process followed a similar schedule to 2013. The declaration period was divided into two periods. After the first six weeks (Window 1) a notification letter was sent to non-responders. Three weeks after this (Window 2) the online application was closed.

Table 4 shows the declarations sent through the online application and on paper. As the amounts of respondents differ, the declarations are shown in percentages to allow for comparison. There was an increase in both response rate and response speed from 2013 to 2014. Figure 2 shows the daily (left axis) and accumulated (right axis) response rates in 2014. Comparable data for 2013 are not available.

Almost one third of the single parents who received the letter as digital post (nearly a quarter of all the recipients) responded the same day as digital post was sent. Several factors can have contributed to the faster reply rates compared to 2013; a larger share of the single parents received the letter as digital post, the letters contained links to the declaration, and in 2014 it was possible to access the application

*Table 4. Declarations sent via the online self-service application and on paper 2013-2015*

| Year | Online Window 1 | Online Window 2 | Online Total | Paper Total | Response Rate Total | Respondents |
|---|---|---|---|---|---|---|
| 2013 | 69% | 11% | 80% | 2% | 82% | 119.000 |
| 2014 | 87% | 8% | 95% | 1% | 96% | 122.000 |
| 2015 | 86% | 8% | 95% | n.a. | n.a. | 123.000 |
| Change 2013 - '14 | 26% | - 27% | 19% | - 50% | 17% | 2% |
| Change 2014 - '15 | - 1% | 0% | 0% | n.a. | n.a. | 1% |

*Figure 2. Response rate for the 2014 single parents' declaration*

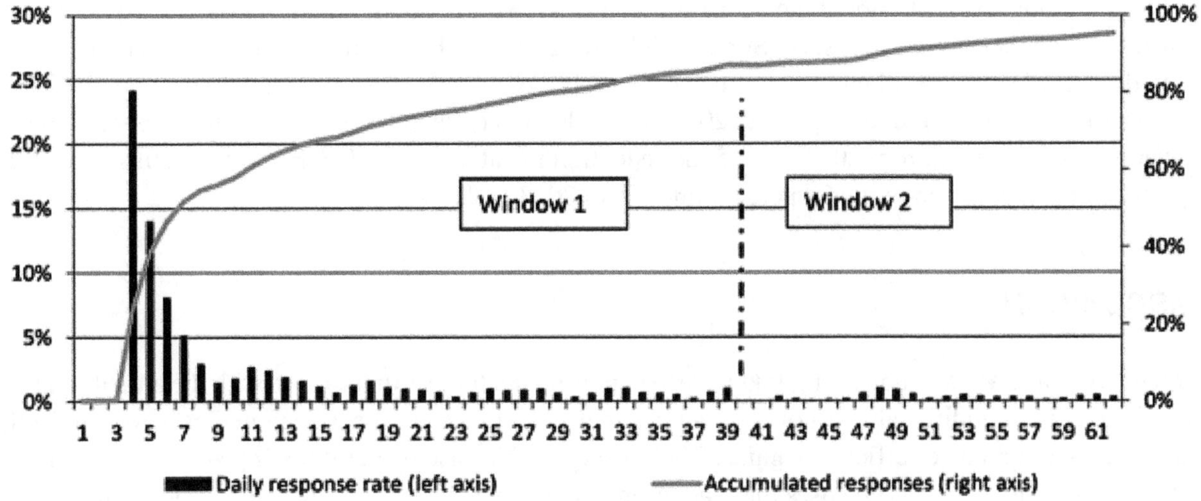


using Apple platforms and mobile devices. Learning is also a likely factor, as this was the second year the declaration was conducted online.

Table 5 presents incoming calls to UDK's family benefit division from 2013 to 2015. From 2013 to 2014, the amount of incoming calls fell by nearly 40 percent. The drop-in calls were biggest in the first declaration period, especially in the first two weeks after UDK sent the letters. Incoming calls fell by 66 percent compared to 2013. This is especially interesting as two thirds of all single parents used the self-service application during these two weeks in 2014. The head of UDK's family benefit section estimated that one third of the calls received in April 2013 concerned the single's declaration. According to the call classification system, this dropped to approximately 10 percent in October 2014. Although a direct comparison to 2013 is not possible, there seems to have been a decrease both in the total amount of calls, and in the share of calls on the declaration.

## Stage 4: Channel Traffic for the 2015 Single Parent's Declaration

Between 2014 and 2015, no major changes were implemented regarding the single parents' declaration, and the same overall schedule was followed. The transition towards digital post continued. In 2015, UDK sent 97 percent of the letters informing the single parents of the declaration using digital post, compared to 81 percent in 2014.

*Table 5. Calls to UDK family benefit division during declaration period*

| Year | Calls Window 1 | Calls Window 2 | Calls in Total |
|---|---|---|---|
| 2013 | 64.000 | 20.000 | 84.000 |
| 2014 | 37.000 | 15.000 | 52.000 |
| 2015 | 31.000 | 12.000 | 43.000 |
| Change 2013 - 2014 | - 42% | - 25% | - 38% |
| Change 2014 - 2015 | -17% | - 15% | -16% |

However, inspired by experiences from the Netherlands, it was decided to send the digital post informing the single parent's about the declaration on a Saturday in 2015. This was done to promote self-service among the single parents. By Sunday night, roughly one third of the declarations were received, even though UDK's family benefit section call center is closed during the weekend. In general, the 2015 response rates were similar to those from 2014. The reduction in telephone calls continued, but at a much lower rate than earlier. From 2014 – 2015 the reduction in calls to the UDK Family benefit section fell by 16 percent, compared to the 38 percent drop from 2013 to 2014.

## DISCUSSION

Previous CC and MCM studies have taken place in non-mandatory settings, often with the aim of migrating citizens from traditional to e-government channels. Migration has been regarded as a goal in itself, based on assumptions of efficiency gains. The novelty of this case is that it takes place in a mandatory setting, where almost everyone uses the e-government channel. This allows the authors to change focus from adoption to post-adoption processes. Moreover, new primary data on channel traffic is presented to document a multichannel user journey combining analog and digital channels.

Mandatory e-government is a powerful tool to achieve high adoption rates. However, increased use of e-government channels does not ensure efficiency gains, as many keep using traditional channels. Poor communication surrounding e-government channels can create rebound effects in the shape of increased information requests via traditional channels. The case demonstrates that user involvement, harmonization and simplification of language, the utilization of e-government channels' interactive features, and integrating channels through links and automated messages are powerful instruments for call reduction and improved user satisfaction.

Transaction data show that the Internet has become the primary channel for single parents' interaction with UDK. The telephone has become a secondary channel, which is used when problems arise. This is interesting as previous studies (Kernaghan, 2013; Lamberti, Benedetti, & Chen, 2014; Pieterson & Ebbers, 2008; Reddick, 2010) found that traditional channels were used by a higher share of the population than e-government channels. This difference may be explained by the change in setting; the study takes place in a country where e-government channels are mandatory, several years after most of the previous studies were conducted and concerns a simple task. Moreover, most Danes have access to broadband, the population has one of the highest levels of IT-skills in Europe (European Commission, 2015), and the public digital infrastructure which UDK relies upon has been implemented. This foundation was an advantage as it allowed for improving an existing infrastructure rather than developing new solutions, e.g. most participants knew that interaction with public authorities took place at Borger.dk. Improving the existing application and its surrounding communication is a smaller task than creating a new application and awareness of it from scratch.

The migration was not voluntary; e-government channels are mandatory for citizens' interaction with public authorities in Denmark related to 35 areas. The participants did not object to the digitization of the single's declaration, in fact, many approved of it. They complained about having to declare themselves single annually and the communication surrounding the self-service application. However, Danish parents, single or not, with children living at home, generally have higher access to IT and better IT skills than the general population (Statistics Denmark, 2014). It is uncertain whether the lack of resistance to digitization is generalizable to other benefit areas such as pensions, where the recipients have lower IT skills. More complicated tasks might also be met with more resistance.

Although the majority used the self-service application in 2013, this did not stop calling. As suggested by CC scholars (Reddick and Turner 2012; Teerling and Pieterson 2010) qualitative methods were used to gain insights from the citizens' point-of-view into why they were calling. Three primary issues were identified; navigation, knowing when the task was completed, and attempts to circumvent the mandatory requirement. Figure 3 illustrates the cross channel behavior. UDK sent a letter to single parents concerning the annual single's declaration. Lack of information, missing feedback, and ambiguous wording caused calls, as shown in the grey boxes.

The cross-organizational collaboration attempted to reduce calls for the 2014 declaration by addressing these issues. The efforts undertaken concern the improvement of communication on existing channels, and adding new channels to the overall service encounter. Communication efforts were developed based on empirical data to increase the use of e-government channels while constraining the use of the telephone. Channel integration and migration were achieved by harmonizing the language and increasing references across channels. The letters were tested repeatedly to weed out any ambiguities. The improvements concerned both the quality and the quantity of the communication. A final aspect concerns better utilization of the interactive features of the e-government channels by presenting a receipt to the single parents upon completion of the task. Some of these improvements, such as improved texts in letters are relatively cheap to implement, whereas others such as the redesign of the self-service application are more costly. However, the case demonstrates that reducing traffic to one channel (the telephone) entails increased costs on other channels (e-government and digital post).

According to MRT people choose communication form based on their information needs (Daft, & Lengel, 1986). The case shows that it is possible to reduce the need for communication by presenting the required information up front and reducing its ambiguity. The three issues were repeatedly addressed across several channels to make sure the single parents received the information. Figure 4 presents a pre-emptive channel positioning strategy; an effort to reduce calls by addressing issues known to cause calls through improved mass communication.

*Figure 3. Causes of calls regarding the 2013 declaration*

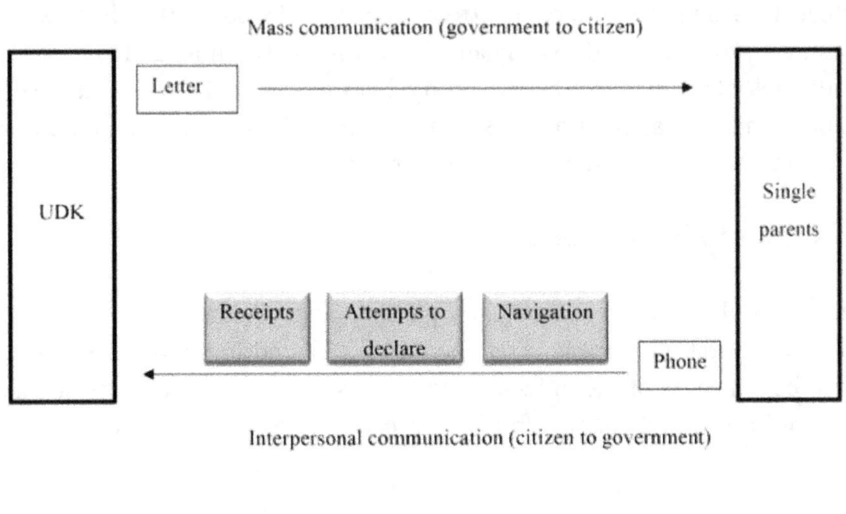

*Figure 4. The pre-emptive strategy employed to reduce calls regarding the 2014 declaration*

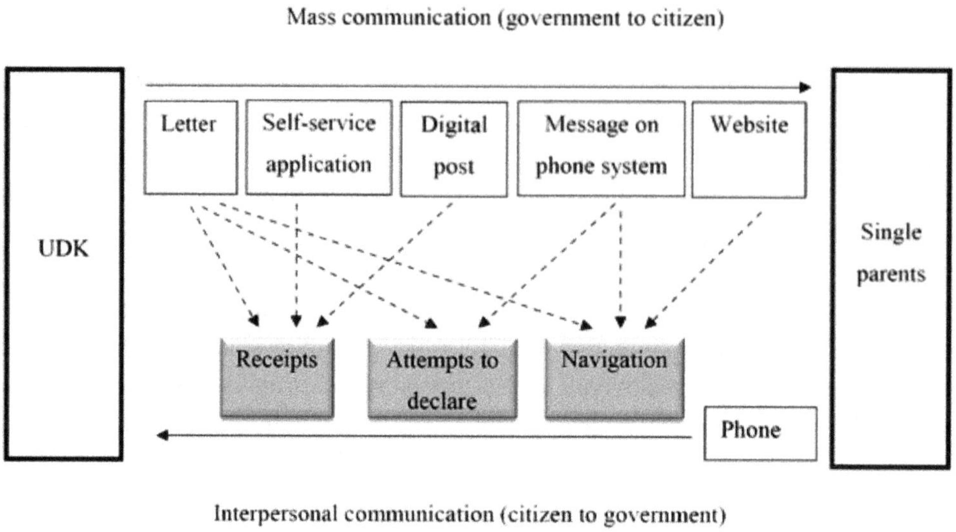


The substantial reduction in calls regarding the single's declaration and the responses to the improved letters indicate that the strategy was successful. However, UDK still received calls regarding the issues addressed in the multichannel strategy. Further, even though efforts were made to make the letters easy to understand, people still interpret texts differently. Finally, some have difficulty reading or have another native language than Danish. Thus, telephone requests cannot be entirely removed, no matter how simple the task is. There will always be complicated or unforeseen cases where citizens need to call, and where calling might be the most efficient. Thus, there is a limit to the amount of call reduction possible. Following previous CC studies, it likely depends on both the users and the tasks in question.

For the single parents, the overall task remained the same from 2014 to 2015. No major changes were made to the self-service application or surrounding communication, and most of the recipients were the same. The development from 2014 to 2015 may give an indication of the share of reduced calls (approximately 15 percent) that may be attributed to the single parents' learning how to use the digital self-service application. Comparing the large drop in calls from 2013 to 2014 to the minor drop from 2014 to 2015 suggests that new empirical user studies and additional changes are needed to significantly reduce calls further. This is in line with results from other MCM studies, which show that channel management is an iterative process (van de Wijngaert, Pieterson, & Teerling, 2011).

This case study took place in a mandatory setting, but the authors believe that the efforts could produce results in non-mandatory settings as well, and in both public and private organizations. Therefore, the following recommendations to practitioners are offered.

## Recommendations to Practitioners

All involved parties should make an agreement regarding costs and revenue sharing before embarking on a multichannel collaboration. Caseworkers should be included in multichannel projects. They have vital insights into the concerns of the citizens, and their cooperation is required to ensure the validity of call classification. Concerning channel traffic, this case demonstrates the necessity of measuring the total volume of traffic across channels, not just the e-government channels. Collecting channel traffic data needs more attention in a cross-organizational setting, where actions taken by one organization can have large consequences for traffic on channels managed by other organizations. It is also important to classify incoming calls according to topic, and to conduct user studies to supplement this quantitative data with qualitative studies that offer explanations to citizens' channel behavior. Once the most frequent call topics are identified, the next step is to address them in the outbound communication. As this case study demonstrates, such an iterative strategy can lead to a significant reduction in calls.

Public authorities can apply links (short urls preferably) and automated messages to guide citizens from traditional to e-government channels. It is important to harmonize wording and use the same terms for key concepts across all channels to reduce uncertainties and create a coherent experience. Wording in written communication can be improved by explaining tasks from the citizens' point of view rather than the organizations'. It should emphasize what citizens are required to do, and how and where to do it. E-government channels can provide instant feedback and receipts to ensure that citizens know when they have completed their tasks. Finally, user tests should cover the entire service encounter and the surrounding communication across all channels, rather than merely the self-service application in isolation. For citizens, finding the self-service application can be a large part of their service encounter, which makes it vital to test this area as well.

## CONCLUSION, LIMITATIONS, AND FUTURE STUDIES

The authors initially asked how a government organization can successfully increase the use of e-government channels and simultaneously reduce the use of traditional channels. A longitudinal case study of UDK and the cross-organizational collaboration undertaken surrounding a mandatory online self-service application has been presented to answer this question.

The authors found that the mandatory migration of citizens towards e-government channels can create rebound effects, in the shape of information requests through traditional channels. Cross- and inter-organizational collaboration was required to reduce these requests as several organizations controlled the channels involved. The continued use of the telephone in relation to the single parents' declaration was related to poor surrounding communication, not the use of the application in itself. Through qualitative user studies and case worker involvement three causes of calls were identified. An effort was made to pre-empt further calls by improving the communication concerning these issues, and by including new channels in the service encounter. The aim was to create a seamless process and reduce the ambiguity and uncertainty that had previously caused calls. The 40 percent drop in calls from 2013 to 2014 and the increase in both the reply rate and speed indicate that the efforts have been successful. However, from 2014 to 2015 no major changes were implemented and the drop in calls did not continue at the same rate. This demonstrates the necessity of continuous user studies, and that MCM is an ongoing iterative process.

At the theoretical level the findings contribute to CC studies by suggesting that reducing information ambiguity and uncertainty, not only affects channel choice, but can reduce the need for communication altogether. Another important finding is that public agencies are not monoliths, and MCM might entail additional costs to one section or organization, to achieve savings elsewhere.

There are particular circumstances to the study presented here. It is a single case study, regarding a simple task, for a highly skilled group of citizens in a mandatory setting. Furthermore, the channels surrounding the single's declaration are managed by different organizations, which affect the statistical data collection. Some statistical systems did not exist in 2013, while others have been affected by actions of other parties. As many of the single parents had carried out the same task the previous year it is likely that some of the reduction were caused by learning. The technical improvements to the application probably also influenced the reduction in calls. Due to the changes being implemented simultaneously and in a live setting, and lack of comparable data, it is not possible to isolate or determine their individual effects. However, the data from 2015 may provide a rough estimate of the effects of learning on channel traffic.

## Future Studies

Efficiency gains do not come from increased use of e-government channels in itself, but from an overall reduction in traffic, especially on traditional channels. Thus, CC and MCM studies should cover the entire service encounter and information presented across all channels, not just the isolated e-government channel. In relation to MRT, the case suggests, that a digital channel's level of richness is not fixed, but can be increased both by implementing interactive features and by changing the tone in the content provided from a traditional bureaucratic to a citizen oriented style. Future studies could test each improvement in isolation to determine their effect.

This case took place in a country where e-government channels are mandatory, and with a target group with high IT-skills. Studies from other countries, with different services, target groups or organizations, and non-mandatory channels, may allow for greater analytical generalization, and contribute to moving the field further forwards.

## REFERENCES

ATP. (2011). *Sådan etablerer vi Udbetaling Danmark.* Retrieved from http://www.penst.dk/~/media/PST/Files/Publikationer/2011/Saedan-etablerer-vi-udbetaling-danmark.ashx

Barth, M., & Veit, D. (2011). *Electronic Service Delivery in the Public Sector: Understanding the Variance of Citizens' Resistance. In Proceedings of the 44th Hawaii International Conference on System Sciences (HICSS-44).* Kauai, HI: IEEE Computer Society Conference Publishing Services. Retrieved from http://doi.ieeecomputersociety.org/10.1109/HICSS.2011.181

Blaikie, N. (2012). Designing Social Research. *Polity.*

Cai, S., & Jun, M. (2015). Relationship between Information Richness and Exchange Outcomes: Moderating Effects of Media Richness and Governance Mechanisms. *International Journal of Information Systems and Supply Chain Management*, *8*(1), 1–21. doi:10.4018/ijisscm.2015010101

Carlson, J. R., & Zmud, R. W. (1999). Channel expansion theory and the experiential nature of media richness perceptions. *Academy of Management Journal*, *42*(2), 153–170. doi:10.2307/257090

Chadwick, A., & May, C. (2003). Interaction between States and Citizens in the Age of the Internet: "e-Government" in the United States, Britain, and the European Union. *Governance: An International Journal of Policy, Administration and Institutions*, *16*(2), 271–300. doi:10.1111/1468-0491.00216

Daft, R. L., & Lengel, R. H. (1986). Organizational Information Requirements, Media Richness and Structural Design. *Management Science*, *32*(5), 554–571. doi:10.1287/mnsc.32.5.554

Danish Business Authority. (2014). *Bredbåndskortlægning 2013*. Retrieved from http://erhvervsstyrelsen.dk/file/444481/bredbaandskortlaegning-2013.pdf

Ebbers, W. E., Jansen, M. G. M., Pieterson, W. J., & van de Wijngaert, L. A. L. (2015). Facts and feelings: The role of rational and irrational factors in citizens' channel choices. *Government Information Quarterly*. doi:10.1016/j.giq.2016.06.001

Ebbers, W. E., Jansen, M. G. M., & van Deursen, A. J. A. M. (2016). Impact of the digital divide on e-government: Expanding from channel choice to channel usage. *Government Information Quarterly*, *33*(4), 685–692. doi:10.1016/j.giq.2016.08.007

Ebbers, W. E., Pieterson, W. J., & Noordman, H. N. N. (2008). Electronic government: Rethinking channel management strategies. *Government Information Quarterly*, *25*(2), 181–201. doi:10.1016/j.giq.2006.11.003

European Commission. (2014). *Digital Agenda Scoreboard 2014 – Denmark Page 1 of 7*. Retrieved from https://ec.europa.eu/digital-agenda/en/scoreboard/denmark

Friese, S. (2012). *Qualitative data analysis with Atlas.ti*. SAGE Publications.

Heeks, R., & Bailur, S. (2007). Analyzing e-government research: Perspectives, philosophies, theories, methods, and practice. *Government Information Quarterly*, *24*(2), 243–265. doi:10.1016/j.giq.2006.06.005

Ho, A. T. (2002). Reinventing Local Governments and the E-Government Initiative. *Public Administration Review*. doi:10.1111/0033-3352.00197

Hofmann, S., Räckers, M., & Becker, J. (2012). Identifying Factors of E-Government Acceptance – A Literature Review. In *33rd International Conference on Information Systems (ICIS 2012)* (pp. 1–10). Orlando, FL: Academic Press.

Janssen, M., & Kuk, G. (2010). Critical success factors for multi-channel service delivery (MCSD). *16th Americas Conference on Information Systems 2010, AMCIS 2010, 3*, 2179–2187. Retrieved from http://www.scopus.com/inward/record.url?eid=2-s2.0-84870334398&partnerID=40&md5=edd94692f8ff3cea55e579edf8fd2216

Kay, A., & Goldberg, A. (1977). Personal Dynamic Media. *Computer*, *10*(3), 31–41. doi:10.1109/C-M.1977.217672

Kernaghan, K. (2009). Moving towards integrated public governance: Improving service delivery through community engagement. *International Review of Administrative Sciences*, *75*(2), 239–254. doi:10.1177/0020852309104174

Kernaghan, K. (2013). Changing channels: Managing channel integration and migration in public organizations. *Canadian Public Administration*, *56*(1), 121–141. doi:10.1111/capa.12006

Krueger, R. A. (1994). *Focus Groups. A Practical Guide for Applied Research*. Sage Publications.

Lamberti, L., Benedetti, M., & Chen, S. (2014). Benefits sought by citizens and channel attitudes for multichannel payment services: Evidence from Italy. *Government Information Quarterly*, *31*(4), 596–609. doi:10.1016/j.giq.2014.03.002

Layne, K., & Lee, J. (2001). Developing fully functional E-government: A four stage model. *Government Information Quarterly*, *18*(2), 122–136. doi:10.1016/S0740-624X(01)00066-1

Madsen, C. Ø., Berger, J., & Phythian, M. (2014). The Development in Leading e-Government Articles 2001-2010: Definitions, Perspectives, Scope, Research Philosophies, Methods and Recommendations: An Update of Heeks and Bailur. In M. Janssen, H. J. Scholl, M. A. Wimmer, & F. Bannister (Eds.), *Electronic Government: Proceedings of the 13th IFIP WG 8.5 International Conference, EGOV 2014* (Vol. 8653, pp. 17–34). Dublin, Ireland: LNCS Springer. 10.1007/BF03251472

Madsen, C. Ø., & Kræmmergaard, P. (2015a). Channel Choice: A Literature Review. In Tambouris, Janssen, Schol, Wimmer, & Tarabanis (Eds.), *Electronic Government: Proceedings of the 14th IFIP WG 8,5 International Conference, EGOV 2015*. Thessaloniki, Greece: LNCS Springer. 10.1007/978-3-319-22479-4_1

Madsen, C. Ø., & Kræmmergaard, P. (2015b). The efficiency of freedom. Single parents' domestication of mandatory e-government. *Government Information Quarterly*, *32*(4), 380–388. doi:10.1016/j.giq.2015.09.008

Madsen, C. Ø., & Kræmmergaard, P. (2016). Warm Experts in the age of Mandatory e-Government: Interaction Among Danish Single Parents Regarding Online Application for Public Benefits. *Electronic Journal of E-Government, 14*(1), 87–98. Retrieved from http://www.ejeg.com/issue/download.html?idArticle=447

Markus, M. L. (1994). Electronic Mail as the Medium of Managerial Choice. *Organization Science*, *5*(4), 502–527. doi:10.1287/orsc.5.4.502

Mundy, D., Umer, Q., & Foster, A. (2011). Examining the Potential for Channel Shift in the UK Through Multiple Lenses Independent Researcher, UK. *Electronic Journal of E-Government*, *9*(2), 203–213.

Ngwenyama, O. K., & Lee, A. S. (1997). Communication Richness in Electronic Mail. Critical Social Theory and The Contextuality of Meaning. *Management Information Systems Quarterly*, *21*(2), 145–167. doi:10.2307/249417

Pieterson, W. (2010). Citizens and Service Channels: Channel Choice and Channel Management Implications. *International Journal of Electronic Government Research*, *6*(2), 37–53. doi:10.4018/jegr.2010040103

Pieterson, W., & Ebbers, W. E. (2008). The use of service channels by citizens in the Netherlands: Implications for multi-channel management. *International Review of Administrative Sciences*, *74*(1), 95–110. doi:10.1177/0020852307085736

Pieterson, W., Ebbers, W. E., & Madsen, C. Ø. (2017). New Channels, New Possibilities: A Typology and Classification of Social Robots and Their Role in Multi-channel Public Service Delivery. In *International conference on Electronic Government* (pp. 47–59). Springer Berlin/Heidelberg. 10.1007/978-3-319-64677-0_5

Pieterson, W., & Teerling, M. (2009). Channel Integration in Governmental Service Delivery: The Effects on Citizen Behavior and Perceptions. *Electronic Government: Proceedings of the 8th [IFIP WG 8.5] International Conference, EGOV 2009*, *5693*(2007), 222–233. 10.1007/978-3-642-03516-6

Pieterson, W., Teerling, M., & Ebbers, W. E. (2008). Channel Perceptions and Usage: Beyond Media Richness Factors. In M. A. Wimmer, H. J. Scholl, & E. Ferro (Eds.), *Electronic Government 7th International Conference, EGOV 2008, Turin, Italy, August 31-September 5, 2008, proceedings* (Vol. 5184/2008, pp. 219–230). Berlin: Springer. 10.1007/978-3-540-85204-9_19

Reddick, C. (2005). Citizen-Initiated Contacts with Government: Comparing Phones and Websites. *Journal of E-Government, 2*(1), 27–53. doi:10.1300/J399v02n01_03

Reddick, C. (2010). Comparing citizens' use of e-government to alternative service channels. *International Journal of Electronic Government Research, 6*(June), 54–67. doi:10.4018/jegr.2010040104

Reddick, C., & Anthopoulos, L. (2014). Interactions with e-government, new digital media and traditional channel choices: citizen-initiated factors. *Transforming Government: People. Process and Policy, 8*(3), 398–419. doi:10.1108/TG-01-2014-0001

Reddick, C., & Turner, M. (2012). Channel choice and public service delivery in Canada: Comparing e-government to traditional service delivery. *Government Information Quarterly, 29*(1), 1–11. doi:10.1016/j.giq.2011.03.005

Roy, J. (2009). E-government and integrated service delivery in Canada: The Province of Nova Scotia as a case study. *International Journal of Electronic Governance, 2*(2/3), 223–238. doi:10.1504/IJEG.2009.029131

Schmidthuber, L., & Hilgers, D. (2017). Browse or Brush? An Exploration of Citizen-Government Interaction in the Municipal Realm. *Proceedings of the 50th Hawaii International Conference on System Science (HICSS-50).*

Statistics Denmark. (2014). *Annual ICT Household Survey 2014*. Author.

Strauss, A. L., & Corbin, J. M. (1990). Open coding. In *Basics of qualitative research: Grounded theory procedures and techniques* (pp. 101–121). SAGE Publications.

Teerling, M., & Pieterson, W. (2010). Multichannel marketing: An experiment on guiding citizens to the electronic channels. *Government Information Quarterly, 27*(1), 98–107. doi:10.1016/j.giq.2009.08.003

Teerling, M., & Pieterson, W. (2011). How to improve e-government use: An empirical examination of multichannel marketing instruments. *Information Polity, 16*(2), 171–187. doi:10.3233/IP-2011-0213

The Danish Government. (2011). *The Danish National E-government Strategy*. Author.

The Danish Government, Danish Regions, & Local Government Denmark. (2011). *The Digital Path to Future Welfare eGovernment Strategy 2011-2015*. Author.

The Danish National Audit Office. (2016). *Rigsrevisionens notat om beretning om etablering af Udbetaling Danmark*. Retrieved from http://www.rigsrevisionen.dk/media/2104270/305-16.pdf

van de Wijngaert, L., Pieterson, W., & Teerling, M. (2011). Influencing citizen behavior: Experiences from multichannel marketing pilot projects. *International Journal of Information Management, 31*(5), 415–419. doi:10.1016/j.ijinfomgt.2010.12.009

van den Boer, Y., Arendsen, R., & Pieterson, W. (2016). In search of information: Investigating source and channel choices in business-to-government service interactions. *Government Information Quarterly, 33*(1), 40–52. doi:10.1016/j.giq.2015.11.010

Van den Boer, Y., Pieterson, W., Arendsen, R., & De Groot, M. (2014). Source and Channel Choices in Business-to-Government Service Interactions: A Vignette Study. *Electronic Government: Proceedings of the 13th IFIP WG 8.5 International Conference, EGOV 2014*. Retrieved from http://link.springer.com/chapter/10.1007/978-3-662-44426-9_10

Wirtz, B. W., & Langer, P. F. (2016). Public Multichannel Management – an Integrated Framework of Off- and Online Multichannel Government Services. *Public Organization Review*. doi:10.100711115-016-0356-0

Yin, R. K. (2014). Case study Research design and methods. *Sage (Atlanta, Ga.).*

## ENDNOTE

1 For reasons of simplicity, all numerical data have been approximated in the following.

# Chapter 8
# The Impact of Digital Health on Traditional Healthcare Systems and Doctor-Patient Relationships:
## The Case Study of Singapore

**Ching Yuen Luk**
*Nanyang Technological University, Singapore*

## ABSTRACT

*This chapter uses a historical perspective to examine the development trajectory of digital health in Singapore since 1980 and the impact of digital health on the current health care system and doctor-patient relationship. It shows that digital health is able to transform a fragmented and provider-centric health care system into a more integrated and patient-centric health care system. Besides, it improves the operational efficiency of health care providers, reduces administrative costs and turnaround time, and empowers patients to contribute in treatment decisions. It shows that the development of digital health requires the government to have strong political will and long-term commitment to support and promote the use of digital health to its full potential and engage stakeholders in the policy making process so that such policy can suit the special needs of stakeholders.*

## BACKGROUND

Health and ICTs are closely linked (World Health Organization, 2005a, p.2). Health is increasingly seen as both a driver for and beneficiary of ICT development (World Health Organization, 2005a, p.2). Health care providers' heightened interest in enhancing the patient experience while facing a shortage of trained health personnel and patients' heightened expectation of high quality of medical care are two key factors that drive the adoption and innovation of ICT in health care. Meanwhile, advances in ICT over the past few decades have brought lots of benefits to patients and health care providers, including

DOI: 10.4018/978-1-5225-5966-5.ch008

patients' improved access to medical care, better quality of care, increased productivity in health care delivery systems, and economy and efficiency of care (Dzenowagis, 2009, p.14). With the emergence of the Internet and web-based technologies, the health care sector is further revolutionised that there are faster and more efficient ways to disseminate health-related information, diagnose, treat and prevent diseases and perform physical exams and surgeries. It is undeniable that ICTs have played an important role in modernizing and reforming health care systems.

Digital health, in the broadest sense, refers to the use of information and communication technologies (ICTs), such as computers, the Internet, multimedia, and mobile phones, to provide four key functions in a timely manner: (1) collect, process, analyse, store, retrieve, share, exchange and manage clinical information and data; (2) provide patients with consultation, prescription, rehabilitation, booking and managing medical appointment or referral services; (3) make health-related information and resources more accessible to patients and the general public; and (4) provide non-clinical services such as medical education, clinical research, provider training and administrative meetings. E-health encompasses a wide range of systems or services, including e-health portals, electronic health records (EHRs), telehealth, robotics and mobile health (m-health). E-health is believed to bring lots of benefits to different types of stakeholders. For health care providers and health care professionals, e-health can enhance operational efficiency, facilitate exchange of clinical information, data and knowledge, facilitate better and more effective communications, enable more evidence-based decision making, improve diagnostic accuracy and safety, service delivery and productivity in health care, and strengthen coordination and collaboration among hospitals and health care professionals. For patients, e-health can increase their engagement and empowerment, reduce waiting and travel time, and receive more personalized medical care. Specifically, elderly patients, patients with physical disabilities and those who live in remote areas can benefit from e-health (World Health Organization, 2004, p.2) because they can have real-time communication and interaction with medical professionals. For the general public, e-health can improve health literacy and health outcomes at both an individual and a societal level, increase their awareness of disease outbreaks and emergencies (Wilson & Brownstein, 2009, p.829), and help them make better decisions about their health and that of family members. Different types of stakeholders hold similar thoughts that e-health plays a promising role in improving the quality of health care.

Since the early 2000s, e-health has attracted considerable international attention. In December 2003, the topic of e-health was discussed at First Phase of the World Summit on the Information Society (WSIS) (World Summit on the Information Society, 2003, p.8). The Geneva Plan of Action, which was agreed at the 2003 WSIS, identified e-health as one of the important areas of activity that required collaborative efforts of health professionals, governments, other agencies and international organizations to promote knowledge building and deployment in medicine and public health, facilitate access to local and international health-related information, extend the reach of medical care and medical assistance to vulnerable populations and those who lived in remote and undeserved areas through the use of ICTs (World Summit on the Information Society, 2003, p.8). Recognizing the potential impacts of ICTs on health care, the Fifty-eighth World Health Assembly in May 2005 adopted a resolution establishing an E-Health Strategy for World Health Organization (WHO) (World Health Organization, 2017) while at the same time calling upon Member States to draw up "a long-term strategic plan for developing and implementing eHealth services in the various areas of the health sector" (World Health Organization, 2005b, p.121) and "endeavour to reach communities, including vulnerable groups, with eHealth services appropriate to their needs" (World Health Organization, 2005b, p.121). The WHO believed that "[t]he strengthening of health systems through eHealth reinforces fundamental human rights by improving equity, solidarity, quality of life and quality of care" (World Health Organization, 2004, p.1). In the same year, the WHO established a facility called Global Observatory for eHealth (GOe), which was responsible for examining e-health capacity in Member States (World Health Organization, 2006, p.4) and "providing Member States with strategic information and guidance on effective practices, policies and standards in eHealth" (World Health Organization, 2006, p.5). Since then, e-health initiatives have been "pursued in various ways and to various degrees across countries and continents" (Gurak and Hudson, 2006, p.30).

## THE DEVELOPMENT TRAJECTORY OF DIGITAL HEALTH IN SINGAPORE

Being Member State of the WHO, Singapore is one of the world's most connected countries with an advanced information and communication infrastructure. This is attributed to the determined and unremitting efforts of the Singaporean government to excel and innovate in e-government initiatives in order to modernize public administration, provide more customer-oriented services, and accelerate economic and social development. Singapore's e-government has gone through different stages of development over time. It has evolved in tandem with each national Infocomm Plan (Ministry of Finance and Infocomm Development Authority of Singapore, 2006, p.12). While e-government Master Plans were launched to set strategies for transforming the government sector, the national Infocomm Plans were launched to set strategies for transforming the business sector and society (Ministry of Finance and Infocomm Development Authority of Singapore, 2006, p.12). Since 1980, the government has launched five e-government Master Plans (GovTech, 2016), which are supported by six national Infocomm Plans (Chua, 2012, p.44; Tan et al., 2013, p.2). These national Infocomm Plans were: The National Computerization Plan (1980-1985), The National IT Plan (1986-1991), and A Vision of an Intelligent Island: The IT2000 Report (1992-1999), Infocomm 21 (2000-2003), Connected Singapore (2003-2006), and Intelligent Nation 2015 (iN2015) (Ministry of Finance and Infocomm Development Authority of Singapore, 2006). Over time, the government has been able to utilize ICT to establish an integrated network that links the entire civil service and helps government ministries establish relationship with the business sector and the general public. The nation has also become more connected when Singapore ONE (a.k.a. One Network for Everyone) was launched in July 1997 to deliver a variety of interactive, multimedia applications and services directly to workplace, school or home through a nation-wide high speed, high capacity broadband network (Ministry of Finance and Infocomm Development Authority of Singapore, 2003; Infocomm Media Development Authority, 2016a; Tan, 2002, p.661). The establishment of a technological infrastructure backbone facilitates the development and use of digital health in Singapore.

### The Development of MediNet

Digital health in Singapore has evolved over time and its development trajectory follows the direction laid down in some e-government Master Plans and national Infocomm Plans. Being the first e-government Master Plan, the Civil Service Computerisation Programme (CSCP) from 1980 to 1985 focused on transforming the civil service from a labour intensive, paper-based work environment into a capital-intensive, computerized and automated work environment by using computing tools (Tan et al., 2013, pp.2-3). In 1984, computerization was introduced in the Ministry of Health (MOH) to improve operations of the hospitals and clinics (Ministry of Communications & Information, 1990a, p.2). From 1986 to 1991, the focus of the CSCP was on establishing data hubs to facilitate information sharing across public agencies

(Ng, 2011, p.115; Tan et al., 2013, p.7) and making public sector information accessible and one-stop services available to the outside world by merging computers and communication technologies (Tan et al., 2013, p.5). This led to the development of a national medical network in the nation. In February 1989, the MOH and the National Computer Board (NCB), which was "a statutory board under the Ministry of Finance" (Michaelis, 1996, p.91), "jointly organised a feasibility and requirements study of a national medical network for Singapore, called MediNet" (Ministry of Communications & Information, 1989, p.2). More than 50 leaders and professionals from both the public and private health care sectors contributed to this feasibility study (Ministry of Communications & Information, 1989, p.2). After the study was completed in October 1989, the MOH decided to form partnership with the Singapore Network Services Pte Ltd (SNS) to jointly develop and operate MediNet (Ministry of Communications & Information, 1989, pp.2-3) and develop plans for the phased implementation of MediNet (Ministry of Communications & Information, 1990a, pp.2-3). The advantage of forming partnership with SNS was that the time and cost taken to develop and operate MediNet could be minimized by captialising on the existing network infrastructure of SNS (Ministry of Communications & Information, 1989, p.3). It was because SNS since 1989 had already operated Singapore's TradeNet, which was an electronic data interchange system that linked the trading community with all relevant government agencies (National Library Board of Singapore, 1989). It was believed that MediNet could bring lots of benefits to the health care community. Firstly, MediNet could increase connectivity among the health care community because this integrated computer network linked hospitals, clinics, medical practitioners, drug suppliers, and researchers with the MOH and other relevant government agencies (Ministry of Communications & Information, 1989, p.3). Secondly, it could "improve health surveillance" (Ministry of Communications & Information, 1990a, p.2) and facilitate "the planning, control, financing and delivery of health care services" (Ministry of Communications & Information, 1990a, p.1) because health data could be collected quickly and more efficiently via MediNet (Ministry of Communications & Information, 1990a, p.2). Thirdly, it could improve the efficiency of information management because the cost and turnaround time for preparing, transmitting and processing health information would decrease (Ministry of Communications & Information, 1989, pp.1-2). Fourthly, it could provide a better service for health care recipients because health information could be accessed in an accurate and timely manner and at a faster pace (Ministry of Communications & Information, 1989, pp.1-2). Fifthly, it could increase the productivity of doctors because the amount of paperwork would decrease (Ministry of Communications & Information, 1989, p.1) and doctors could spend more time on patient care and medical research (Ministry of Communications & Information, 1990a, p.2).

In 1990, the Central Claims Processing System (CCPS) became the first application of MediNet (Michaelis, 1996, p.90; Ministry of Communications & Information, 1990a, p.3). The CCPS was an automated system that processed Medisave and Catastrophic Illness Insurance claims (Ministry of Communications & Information, 1989, p.2). It could "receive electronic claim forms from the computers of hospitals and other health care providers, pre-process the forms and transmit them to the [Central Provident Fund] CPF Board" (Ministry of Communications & Information, 1989, p.2). The CPF Board could also use the CCPS to transmit all returns and payment advice to the senders of claim forms (Ministry of Communications & Information, 1989, p.2). The CCPS brought some benefits to the health care community. For hospitals and other health care providers, the use of the CCPS helped them save time and money because the turnaround time for the claims approval decreased from one week to hours and their administrative cost of processing claim forms decreased (Ministry of Communications & Information, 1989, pp.2-3). For the MOH and the CPF Board, the CCPS helped "provide comprehensive data for effective monitoring of national health care expenditure and long term planning" (Ministry of Communications & Information, 1989, p.3). For patients, the use of the CCPS brought convenience and efficiency to them because of "shorter waiting time and less form filling" (Ministry of Communications & Information, 1989, p.3). Another function of the CCPS was the provision of an abstract on every inpatient and surgery case, with information on the utilization of health care services, diseases and conditions treated, and procedures and interventions carried out (Emmanuel, 1998, p.13). This could facilitate the analysis on intervention and management outcomes for medical practitioners and implement remedial measures if necessary (Emmanuel, 1998, p.13). The CCPS also collected financial data on hospitals and medical bills that were obtained from day surgery patients and inpatients (Emmanuel, 1998, p.13). This could facilitate the conduct of clinical audit (Emmanuel, 1998, p.13) and planning, monitoring and control of costs.

Being the second application of MediNet, the Physician Data Query (PDQ) System for Cancer was officially launched on September 29, 1990 (Ministry of Communications & Information, 1990b, p.4). The PDQ System provided cancer specialists with an easy access to "a database on the latest state-of-the-art information on the treatment, early detection and diagnosis of each and every cancer" (Ministry of Communications & Information, 1990b, p.4). Such information which was updated monthly enabled cancer specialists to offer the best available cure to their patients (Ministry of Communications & Information, 1990b, p.4). In 1994, another application of MediNet called the National Patient Master Index (NPMI) system was launched (Tan, 1995, p.89). The NPMI system was a first national clinical database that contained three main categories of data, namely patient's biographic, drug allergy and medical alert data (Low and Tan, 2016, p.345). "[I]n the original specifications there were plans to also store discharge summaries, though this was never implemented" (Low and Tan, 2016, p.345). The NPMI system "cater[ed] for the citizens, permanent residents and foreigners who stay[ed] more than 3 months in Singapore" (Tan, 1995, p.89). Regular and updated biographic data was provided by People Data Hub (Tan, 1995, p.90) while a patient's drug allergy and medical alert data was reported or updated by Medical Records Officers based on Hospital Inpatient Discharge Summary Forms prepared by the attending doctors (Tan, 1995, p.90). Both the drug allergy and medical alert modules were available in two versions, namely the 'Standalone' version and 'Integrated' versions (Tan, 1995, p.90). The 'Standalone' version catered for hospitals without an internal drug allergy and medical alert database to enter related data into the NPMI system directly (Tan, 1995, p.90). Meanwhile, the 'Integrated' version catered for hospitals which linked up their internal drug allergy and medical alert database with the NPMI system and hence, data could be automatically transferred from the internal system to the NPMI system (Tan, 1995, p.90). Since medical data were sensitive and highly confidential in nature, all public and private hospitals were allowed to access the NPMI system only after they had signed a Memorandum of Understanding (MOU) with the MOH (Tan, 1995, p.93). Besides, any hospital staff who applied for access to the NPMI system must sign a security declaration to undertake safeguarding of NPMI data (Tan, 1995, p.93). Also, a certifying officer must be appointed by the hospital to approve and manage all NPMI user identification numbers within the hospital (Tan, 1995, p.93). Security measures including patient's signed consent and the National Registration Identification Card (NRIC) were in place to safeguard the NPMI data retrieved (Tan, 1995, pp.92-3). Patient management was facilitated by the launch of the NPMI system because the NPMI system allowed "authorized users faster access to a patient's essential medical data" (Tan, 1995, p.89) and "benefit[ed] the patient for a shorter registration time" (Tan, 1995, p.93). The NPMI system could be considered as the first ancestor of the National Electronic Health Record (NEHR) (Low and Tan, 2016, p.345). In 2006, the NPMI system was migrated to the Critical

Medical Information Store (CMIS) (Low and Tan, 2016, p.345), which was launched in October 2005 to allow bidirectional sharing of drug allergies and medical alert data into Electronic Medical Records (EMRs) (Low and Li, 2015, p.6).

## The Development of the Electronic Medical Record (EMR) System

In 1996, the EMR System was established within local health care institutions to allow doctors to retrieve patient's medical information concurrently and share such information across different departments easily (Infocomm Media Development Authority, 2016b). The EMR initiative was regarded by the NCB as a first step to realize a life-long medical record system for Singapore (Infocomm Media Development Authority, 2016b). The NCB thought that there was an increasing need to aggregate a patient's key medical data that existed in different locations into a longitudinal medical record so that health care providers could retrieve it from anywhere at any time, thereby reducing voluminous paper-based records, avoiding duplicate medical tests, optimizing medical resources and containing costs in the long run (Infocomm Media Development Authority, 2016b). Being two major health care providers or health clusters in Singapore, Singapore Health Services (SingHealth) and National Health Group (NHG) adopted different approaches for their EMR Systems (Sinha et al., 2013, p.259). For SingHealth, a single-instance EMR system that covered the entire cluster was adopted to allow a doctor in any SingHealth institution to access patient's medical information generated by any other SingHealth institution (Lee et al., 2006, p.1). Examples of patient's medical information included "patient's biodata, laboratory investigation results, hospital inpatient discharge summaries and other relevant treatment procedures" (Lim, 2000). For NHG, a Cluster Patient Record Sharing system was adopted to integrate and share patient's medical information across periphery institutions (Lee et al., 2006, p.1; Sinha et al., 2013, p.260). Its patients "only need[ed] to register the first time that they [were] seen at an NHG institution and not at subsequent visits to any other NHG institution" (Lim, 2000). However, the EMR Systems in these two clusters "were essentially independent of each other" (Low and Li, 2015, p.6) that exchange of health data across these two clusters was impossible (Sinha et al., 2013, p.260). In the early 2000s, the government identified the initiative for sharing EMR across clusters (Low and Tan, 2016, p.346). The pilot Electronic Medical Record Exchange (EMRX) system, which was built under the direction of the MOH (Low and Li, 2015, p.6), was launched on 1 April 2004 to allow both clusters to view and share hospital inpatient discharge summaries online (Low and Li, 2015, p.6; Low and Tan, 2016, p.347). Over the year, other digitized records became available in the EMRX system, including allergies, lab, radiology reports and medication (Low and Tan, 2016, p.347). In 2005, a new EMRX which ran on Microsoft Biztalk was launched to make more documents available and extend access to more institutions (Low and Tan, 2016, p.347). In 2006, the new EMRX made immunisation data of Health Promotion Board (HPB) and school health records available and in 2007, the access to EMRX was extended to community hospitals (Low and Tan, 2016, pp.347-8). Nevertheless, major drawbacks of the EMRX were that it was "essentially a document-level exchange" (Sinha et al., 2013, p.264) without any technical compatibility to exchange diagnostic images, such as X-rays, or have disease surveillance, within the EMRX framework (Sinha et al., 2013, p.264; Rowlands, 2012). Besides, it was unable to "apply decision support because of structural and semantic inconsistencies between EMRX documents" (Rowlands, 2012).

## The Development of the National Electronic Health Record (NEHR) System

In 2009, the government initiated a major project to develop a NEHR (Accenture, 2012, p.1), which fell under the National Infocomm Plan known as the Intelligent Nation (iN2015) Masterplan (Liau, 2010; Sinha et al., 2013, p.261). The iN2015 Masterplan was a 10-year plan to transform a provider-centric and fragmented heath care delivery system into a more integrated and patient-centred heath care delivery system via ICT (Infocomm Development Authority of Singapore et al., 2006, p.81). A NEHR system was "envisioned to connect healthcare providers across the continuum of care as well as to the patients in the community" (Healthcare Information and Management Systems Society, 2010, p.69) and fulfill the MOH's vision of 'one Singaporean, one health record' (Ministry of Health, 2010). The NEHR system would be staged across many years (Ministry of Health, 2015a). In 2010, the MOH awarded the contract to an Accenture consortia to implement a first phase of NEHR (Ministry of Health, 2010). With investment of S$176 million (US$128.9 million) (Ministry of Health, 2010; Liau, 2010), the first phase of NEHR was launched in 2011 to provide physicians with "a summary care record for each patient including problem lists, medications, discharge and event summaries, allergies, immunizations, investigations, and procedures" (Accenture, 2012, p.1). Since its implementation, the NEHR system has been progressively enhanced, including "a re-designed user interface and customized care setting views to better support clinical workflows" (Ministry of Health, 2015a) and "data augmentation to expand the breadth of patient centric information to support decision making" (Ministry of Health, 2015a). At present, the NEHR can be accessed by 56 community health care providers, all community hospitals and about 40 per cent of GP clinics (Ministry of Health, 2015a) and "over 760,000 patient record searches are made monthly" (Ministry of Health, 2017a). To encourage faster and wider digitisation of medical records, the government since 2015 has provided more than S$2million to private and Voluntary Welfare Organization (VWO) health care providers through the Centre-Based and Home-Care IT Enablement Programme Fund (Bhunia, 2017a). Implementing the NEHR has several advantages, including "better integration and transfers from acute hospitals to primary care and vice versa" (Low and Li, 2015, p.6) and achieving cost savings and proper disease management because duplicate or unnecessary tests are eliminated and medical errors are reduced (Ministry of Health, 2010).

## The Development of Online Health Portals

While ICT was utilized to improve the operational efficiency of health care providers and facilitate medical information sharing among clinicians, it was also used by the government for health education and promotion (Lim, 2000). Developed by the HPB, an Internet-based health education portal known as HPB Online (http://www.hpb.gov.sg) was launched in April 2001 to provide "both corporate and health information through a variety of static and interactive platforms" (Vijaya et al., 2006, p.8). The portal made use of text, pictures, sounds and video clips to provide different types of services (Vijaya et al., 2006, p.13). Firstly, there were interactive online programmes to promote healthy lifestyle. For example, Info Food Search let users "obtain the energy and nutrient composition of more than 6,000 food items, analyse recipes and assess their daily diet of up to seven days" (Vijaya et al., 2006, p.9). Besides, a number of interactive games were offered by the portal to let users obtain health knowledge in an interesting way (Vijaya et al., 2006, p.9). Secondly, users could download, install and make use of some health care software, such as fitness calculators, from their own computers (Vijaya et al., 2006, p.10). Thirdly, users could obtain different types of health information by reading articles on diseases/

ailments, downloading health education materials, clicking international websites (e.g. the website of WHO) recommended by the portal or submitting queries on health to "Ask An Expert" section, which would be answered by health experts online (Vijaya et al., 2006, p.9). The portal had become more and more popular over time, which was visited by local people and people from Australia, Canada, the United States (US) and the United Kingdom (UK) (Vijaya et al., 2006, p.11). The monthly number of page-views "increased from 100,591 in January 2002 to 390,092 in December 2004" (Vijaya et al., 2006, p.10) and the number of monthly visits "increased markedly from 11,650 in January 2002 to 70,341 in December 2004" (Vijaya et al., 2006, p.10). In 2009, HPB Online was revamped in the following ways to enhance its simplicity and user-friendliness. Firstly, health information was organized according to various target groups, such as youths, older adults, men, women, and health care professionals (Health Promotion Board, 2009a). Secondly, easy-to-use online health tools, such as the BMI calculator, recipe analyser and mobile diet tracker, were provided for users to facilitate personal health management (Health Promotion Board, 2009a). Thirdly, registered users were allowed to personalise their own health page according to their preferences and needs (Health Promotion Board, 2009a). Fourthly, Web 2.0 features such as blogs, forums, vodcasts, podcasts and widgets were incorporated into the portal (Health Promotion Board, 2009b, p.50) to "encourage and link the public in their quest towards a healthier lifestyle" (Health Promotion Board, 2009a).

In late 2013, the HPB conceived the idea of building a one-stop health information and services portal with a mobile application (Chambers, 2015) and started developing the portal in May 2014 (GovTech, 2017). During the design phase, focus group discussions were conducted by HPB to understand what the public would like to have in the portal (Chambers, 2015). Those participated in the focus groups included "parents-to-be; parents of young kids; the health conscious; those diagnosed with a condition; and the recently screened" (Chambers, 2015). In January 2016, the new online portal known as HealthHub was launched. It could be accessed via the Internet (https://www.healthhub.sg) or via "a downloadable mobile app on both iOS and Android devices" (GovTech, 2017). HealthHub provided health data and information drawn from multiple IT systems, including the NEHR System, National Immunisation Registry, School Health System, and School Dental System (GovTech, 2017). HealthHub let users get 24/7 access to health-related content, personalized health records and e-services (e.g. viewing medical appointments and checking lab test results) (GovTech, 2017). It allowed parents to "view their children's health records, such as immunisation records, dental health records and referral letters" (GovTech, 2017). In November 2016, HealthHub extended its service to allow "care receivers to grant designated carers access to their personal medical records and appointments" (Lee, 2016). This feature was believed to "provide convenience and administrative support for about 210,000 regular carers of family members and patients" (Lee, 2016). In order to attract people to use HealthHub and make healthy living more rewarding, HealthHub offered reward points - Healthpoints - to users who shared health articles, events and apps through social media (Chambers, 2015). Healthpoints earned from a certain period of time or accumulated to a certain level could then be converted into NTUC LinkPoints to "offset grocery bills, redeem vouchers and other deals offered by participating partners" (Ministry of Health, 2015b). The launch of HealthHub has attracted lots of users. "As of end January 2017, the HealthHub website has had 8.5 million page views — and over 84,000 Singaporeans have downloaded the app" (GovTech, 2017). Every month, HealthHub "has an average of 530,000 page views" (Ministry of Health, 2017b). HealthHub brought lots of benefits to different segments of the population. It was able to "increase health literacy, encourage the adoption of healthy habits and to nudge Singaporeans to take greater ownership of their own health and wellness" (Ministry of Health, 2015b). In 2016, the performance of HealthHub was highly recognized and thereby winning seven ICT awards, including Mob-Ex Awards, Frost & Sullivan Asia Pacific Best Practices Awards and ASEAN ICT Awards (Health Promotion Board, 2017).

## The Development of Telehealth

To further embrace the benefits of digital transformation, the government in recent years has promoted the innovative use of ICTs to provide integrated and seamless health care services to patients, especially the elderly (Smart Nation Singapore, 2017a). In 2014, the government launched the Smart Nation initiatives, with an aim to use information technology (IT) extensively and systematically to make the economy more productive, people's lives more convenient and sustainable, and society more connected and responsive to people's needs (Lee, 2014). It strived to merge IT into five key domains: transport, home and environment, business productivity, health and enabled ageing, and public sector services (Smart Nation Singapore, 2017b). In the aspect of health and enabled ageing, the government strongly advocated Telehealth, which was the use of ICTs to bring care beyond hospitals to the community (Integrated Health Information Systems, 2017a). Telehealth was adopted to deliver home health, consultation, rehabilitation services, and chronic disease monitoring and management (Smart Nation Singapore, 2017a). From June to November 2014, the Housing and Development Board (HDB) piloted the Smart Elderly Monitoring and Alert System (Semas) in 12 rental flats (Yeo, 2015 March 17). Semas used motion sensors to track everyday activities of the elderly, including an old people's "current location, sleeping patterns, and even the duration spent in the toilet" (Koh, 2015 March 17). It alerted caregivers of the elderly via text messages and alarms when abnormalities such as an unusually long period of inactivity were detected (Yeo, 2015 March 17; Smart Nation Singapore, 2017a). It also came with a portable, wireless panic button which allowed the elderly to send alerts to their caregivers in time of distress (Koh, 2015 March 17; Yeo, 2015 March 17; Smart Nation Singapore, 2017a). After a six-month trial, Semas received positive feedback from households, including comments that Semas was "non-intrusive" (Loh, 2016 April 23), "elder-friendly and easy to use" (Yeo, 2015 March 17). From April 2016, the HDB introduced Semas to about 3,200 households in Singapore (Smart Nation Singapore, 2017a). According to HDB's chief executive officer Cheong Koon Hean, the introduction of Semas "enhance[d] the safety of elderly residents and offer[ed] their children greater peace of mind" (Yeo, 2015 March 17).

In 2016, a pilot mobile app known as Health MarketPlace SG was launched to link up discharged patients with a nurse living or working close to them to provide home nursing services, such as wound dressing and changing patient's urinary catheter (Khalik, 2016 October 21; Chan, 2017 May 30; Toh, 2017 May 30). Singapore General Hospital (SGH) and KK Women's and Children's Hospital (KKH) have been participating in this 'match-a-nurse' pilot, with about 140 nurses from SGH and KKH being on this programme and completing about 75 patient visits (Chan, 2017 May 30). The launch of this mobile app could benefit patients who were bed-bound or wheelchair because they could receive care at home without visiting the hospital frequently (Khalik, 2016 October 21). The mobile app will be further enhanced over the next three years to provide more home care services, "ranging from personal care services, medical transportation, meals-on-wheels and therapist services" (Toh, 2017 May 30).

In April 2017, a Smart Health Video Consultation (SHVC) for healthcare was implemented for selected services at KKH, SGH, Tan Tock Seng Hospital and Institute of Mental Health (IMH) to enable post-discharge patients or patients with mobility issues to consult their doctors at home (Bhunia, 2017b). Examples of selected services at KKH included "follow-up services for paediatric eczema pharmacy consultation, paediatric home care services, lactation consultation, and speech" (Bhunia, 2017b). For other participating hospitals, patients could "communicate with their doctors on issues such as post-stroke needs, communicable diseases and cancer" (Phua, 2017a April 12). SHVC could be accessed via computer or smartphone (Phua, 2017a April 12). It adopted two-factor authentication and end-to-end encryption to ensure security of each video consultation session (Phua, 2017a April 12). With high quality audio and video, the SHVC platform enabled health care professionals to assess patients' conditions more accurately and had video conferencing with multi-disciplinary care teams (Bhunia, 2017b). Besides, it was a cloud-based platform allowing "annotation, file sharing and display of medical reports or images for reference during the consultation" (Bhunia, 2017b). SHVC was expected to benefit both doctors and patients. For doctors, SHVC could help them "monitor patients more regularly than traditional face-to-face appointments" (Phua, 2017a April 12) and "save time travelling to and from nursing homes" (Phua, 2017a April 12). For patients, SHVC enabled patients to rest at home, reduce caregiver absence from work and reduce patient's exposure to communicable diseases (Phua, 2017a April 12).

In May 2017, a national pilot for Smart Health TeleRehab (SHTR) was rolled out to enable patients recovering from conditions such as stroke, falls and fractures, lower limb joint replacements and amputations (Bhunia, 2017c; Integrated Health Information Systems, 2017b; Phua, 2017b May 5) to carry out physiotherapy exercises at home. For patients who were suitable for using SHTR after assessment made by their therapists or doctors (Integrated Health Information Systems, 2017b), they could open an app known as Smart Health TeleRehab on an iPad (Phua, 2017b May 5). After putting on neck and limb sensors, patients accessed video demonstrations of exercises prescribed by their therapists who customized the level of difficulty, exercise angles and the number of repetitions of each exercise (Bhunia, 2017c; Phua, 2017b May 5). Patient's motor movements would then be detected and measured by SHTR with wearable sensors and algorithms (Bhunia, 2017c). Being a user-friendly system, SHTR provided instructions in five languages: English, Mandarin, Bahasa Melayu, Tamil and Tagalog (Bhunia, 2017c). Besides, it contained some useful features to guide patients to complete their exercises, including coloured bars to indicate if patients could achieve desired exercise angle (Phua, 2017b May 5), "countdown timer for hold positions" (Bhunia, 2017c), "a counter for the number of repetitions completed" (Phua, 2017b May 5), and "a star indicator to show how accurately the exercise was completed" (Bhunia, 2017c). After the patient's completion of exercises, SHTR would send a record of the patient's performance to the therapist to review via dash boards (Phua, 2017b May 5). The therapist could quickly review the patient's performance and compliance via Exercise Charts and evaluate seated and standing ability of the patient via Balance Charts (Bhunia, 2017c). Meanwhile, SHTR also contained a video conferencing feature to enable patients to remotely consult their therapists (Integrated Health Information Systems 2017b). At present, SHTR is used by suitable patients of NTUC Health and TOUCH Home Care (Bhunia, 2017c). By the end of 2017, SHRT will be available to suitable patients of 12 other institutions in Singapore (Phua, 2017b May 5). SHTR is expected to bring "greater convenience for patients and increased productivity for therapists and service providers" (Bhunia, 2017c). It can prevent patient's conditions from deteriorating further and help them recover faster by carrying more physiotherapy exercises and thereby requiring fewer therapy sessions (Phua, 2017b May 5).

In late 2017, a Vital Signs Monitoring (VSM) System will be launched to facilitate home-based chronic disease management (Ministry of Health, 2016). The VSM System will allow health care personnel to remotely and regularly monitor vital signs such as the weight, blood pressure and blood glucose of patients with heart or pulmonary diseases, diabetes and hypertension (TODAY 2017 May 30; Ministry of Health, 2017a). It will enable patients to get more timely advice and intervention online without scheduling an appointment with physicians at hospitals (TODAY, 2017 May 30; Ministry of Health, 2017a).

## THE IMPACT OF DIGITAL HEALTH ON TRADITIONAL HEALTH CARE SYSTEM AND DOCTOR-PATIENT RELATIONSHIP

A historical review of the development trajectory of digital health in Singapore since the 1980s shows that the government has made unremitting efforts to develop and implement different digital health programmes. After over three decades of development, digital health is able to transform a provider-centric and fragmented health care system into a more integrated and patient-centric health care system. Digital health not only increases internal connectivity among medical, supportive and administrative departments in a hospital, but also increases external connectivity among local and overseas medical practitioners and researchers, different hospitals, clinics and other relevant government agencies. With digital health, the operational efficiency of health care providers is greatly improved. The administrative costs and turnaround time for preparing, transmitting and processing health information decrease. Health data can be collected and retrieved in a more accurate, efficient and timely manner. The productivity of doctors increases due to the reduction of voluminous paperwork, duplicate medical tests and medical errors. With digital health, the delivery of health care services has become more customer-oriented. Repeated form filing when visiting different hospitals can be avoided. There is shorter waiting time. Travelling time and costs can also be saved via Telehealth.

Over the past few years, several international surveys on digital health have indicated that most of the doctors and patients in Singapore have positive views on adopting and utilizing digital health. In late 2012, Accenture conducted an online survey of 3,700 doctors' adoption, utilization and attitudes toward health care information technology (IT) across eight countries: Singapore, the US, the UK, Canada, France, Germany, Spain and Australia (Accenture, 2013). The survey found that there was an increase in health care IT and health information exchange (HIE) adoption among primary and secondary care doctors in Singapore from 2011 and 2012 (Accenture, 2013, p.5). In Singapore, the number of doctors electronically entering patient notes either during or after consultations increased from 41 percent in 2011 to 52 percent in 2012 while the number of doctors having electronic access to clinical data about patients who were seen by different health organizations also increased from 32 percent in 2011 to 49 percent in 2012 (Accenture, 2013, p.3). When comparing with other countries surveyed, Singapore showed the largest increase in doctors electronically receiving clinical results that populated patients' EMR (40 percent) and the largest increase in doctors electronically sending prescription to pharmacies (36 percent) from 2011 to 2012 (Accenture, 2013, pp.1-2). In 2015, Accenture conducted a survey of 2,619 doctors' attitude toward health care IT across six countries: Singapore, the US, the UK, Norway, Australia and Brazil (Accenture, 2015). The survey found that of all the countries surveyed, Singapore had the highest percentage of doctors thinking that they were more proficient using EMRs in their clinical practices in 2015 than they were in 2013 (86 percent) (Accenture, 2015, p.16). Besides, Singapore had the lowest percentage of doctors finding their organizations' EMR systems hard to use (42 percent) (Accenture, 2015, p.23). In the survey, Singapore had the highest percentage of doctors saying that EMR and HIE had a positive impact on reducing medical errors (88 percent) (Accenture, 2015, p.27). And Singapore had the second highest percentage of doctors saying that EMR and HIE had a positive impact on the quality of treatment decisions (85 percent) and health outcomes for patients (80 percent) (Accenture, 2015, pp.25-6).

In 2014, McKinsey conducted Digital Patient Survey of thousands of patients in Singapore, UK and Germany. The survey found that respondents in Singapore had higher frequency of using electronic channels to get health care services than respondents in the UK and Germany in the last 12 months.

While 55 percent respondents in Singapore used website/online portal to interact with the health system (e.g. doctors, hospitals, pharmacies) for at least three times and above, only 49.5 percent respondents in the UK and 34 percent respondents in Germany did so (Biesdorf and Niedermann, 2014). While 48 percent respondents in Singapore used smartphone apps to interact with the health system for at least three times and above, only about 22 percent respondents in the UK and about 9 percent respondents in Germany did so (Biesdorf and Niedermann, 2014). The use of email to interact with the health system was popular in these three places. However, the percentage of respondents using email to interact with the health system for at least three times and above was higher in Singapore (38 percent) than the UK (34 percent) and Germany (31 percent) (Biesdorf and Niedermann, 2014). Nevertheless, respondents in these three places still used tradition channel to obtain health care service. In Singapore, about 22 percent respondents obtained services through health care branch for at least three times and above in the last 12 months while 16 percent respondents in Germany and 43 percent respondents in the UK did so (Biesdorf and Niedermann, 2014). In the 2014 McKinsey's Digital Patient Survey, respondents in Singapore ranked three criteria that could increase their frequency of using online services, which were increased awareness of online services, wider range of value-added services, and width/clarity of information available (Biesdorf and Niedermann, 2014).

In 2016, Accenture conducted health care innovation and transformation survey of 2,250 citizens in Singapore, Japan and Australia. The survey showed that the percentage of citizens' technology confidence in Singapore (60 percent) was lower than that of in Australia (75 percent), but was much higher than that of in Japan (36 percent) (Accenture, 2016a, p.14). In the survey, Singapore had the highest percentage of citizens feeling positive about technology replacing traditional health care services (54 percent), compared with 49 percent in Japan and 41 percent in Australia (Accenture, 2016a, p.15). Besides, Singapore had the highest percentage of citizens considering the use of a virtual assistant in improving their health, compared with 65 percent in Australia and 59 percent in Japan (Accenture, 2016a, p.23). Also, citizens in Singapore showed the greatest willingness to pay for a home health-monitoring kit if such kit allowed them to have faster access to treatment (57 percent), allowed doctors to better manage their health (50 percent), allowed them to be involved in their own health care plans (44 percent), allowed them to accumulate 'reward points' for healthy lifestyle choices (48 percent) and entitled them to discount on gym membership, health coaching and healthy food (42 percent) (Accenture, 2016a, p.21). The survey showed that citizens in Singapore had confidence in and greater openness to the adoption of health care technology to obtain better quality of medical care and they would adopt health care technology more if there were rewards and incentives, such as 'reward points' and discount.

In 2016, Accenture conducted another survey of 935 Singaporean consumers on patient engagement. The survey showed that over half of the respondents had positive views on digital health. In the survey, 57 percent of respondents wanted their primary doctors to have full access to their electronic health records (EHRs) and 90 percent of respondents agreed that they received better care when doctors could access and used their EHRs (Accenture, 2016b, pp.3-4). Besides, 66 percent of respondents believed that the benefits of accessing electronic medical information outweighed the risk of privacy intrusion, compared to 53 percent in 2014 (Accenture, 2016b, p.4). Also, 63 percent of respondents believed that health care technology was important to manage their health (Accenture, 2016b, p.7). Among respondents who said that health care technology was important, 39 percent of them believed that it helped them better understand their condition(s) and medication(s) and 31 percent believed that it helped save time (Accenture, 2016b, p.7). From the above, it showed that many respondents saw the benefits of digital health. Nevertheless, the survey found that most of the respondents still valued the traditional, in-person visits, with 72 percent of respondents preferring traditional over virtual visits (Accenture, 2016b, p.8). While respondents thought that traditional and virtual visits had their own advantage, over half of the respondents surveyed thought that traditional, in-person visits was better than virtual visits in terms of providing quality care to patients (64 percent), diagnosing problems faster (55 percent) and engaging patients in their health/health care decisions (53 percent) (Accenture, 2016b, p.8). But respondents thought that virtual visits was better than traditional, in-person visits in terms of money and time, with over half of the respondents thinking that virtual visits could reduce medical costs to patients (58 percent) and accommodate patients' schedules (56 percent), and 41 percent of them thinking that virtual visits could provide timely care to patients (Accenture, 2016b, p.8). Another finding of this survey was that older Singaporeans aged 55 years and above had positive attitude about digital health and many of them used digital health tools. In this survey, there was a total number of 935 Singaporean consumers, of which 93 percent aged 55 years and above (Accenture, 2016c, p.8). Among these older Singaporeans, the majority of them (84 percent) considered technology to be "somewhat" or "very important" to managing health (Accenture, 2016c, p.5). Websites (56 percent) and mobile apps (40 percent) were top two digital health tools used by older Singaporeans to manage their health care (Accenture, 2016c, p.4). Only 20 percent of older Singaporeans surveyed used EHRs to manage their health care (Accenture, 2016c, p.4). The survey also found that the majority of older Singaporeans would choose a health care provider who offered email or text reminders for preventive or follow-up care (83 percent) and online appointment management (82 percent) (Accenture, 2016c, p.5). The survey showed that older Singaporeans would choose a health care provider who could utilize IT to provide value-added services for them.

The survey results show that while respondents recognize the benefits brought by digital health, many of them think that the traditional, in-person visit still has existence values. Indeed, the government has no intention to use digital health to replace traditional, face-to-face medical care. Instead, digital health is served as an alternative channel to deliver health care services and patients have freedom to choose whether they want to seek medical care through a traditional or digital channel. With digital health, doctors are better informed with a patient's medical condition through accessing the EMR online and thereby making better treatment decisions. For patients, digital health serves as a convenient channel for patients to communicate with the doctors. Patients in Singapore were more active in using website or online portal to interact with doctors, hospitals and pharmacies. There is no doubt that digital health facilitates the communication between doctors and patients by breaking down the physical and time boundaries. Emails can be used for non-urgent enquiries and served as a reminder for follow-up care or online appointment management. But in-person visits are still preferred for urgent or serious illnesses. At this stage, digital health has unavoidably brought some changes to doctor-patient relationship. It is because digital health empowers patients to contribute in treatment decisions when patients have greater accessibility of online information about their medical conditions (Robinson, 2013, p.79). Traditionally, there is an inherent power imbalance in a doctor-patient relationship (Nimmon and Stenfors-Hayes, 2016, p.114). Doctors were in position of power in the doctor-patient relationship because of their medical training and credentials (Nimmon and Stenfors-Hayes, 2016, p.114). They had "an inherent responsibility to act in the patient's best interest" (Nimmon and Stenfors-Hayes, 2016, p.114) when making decision about medical treatment. Patients put their trust in doctors and seldom challenged a doctor's decision because they were not equipped with the professional medical knowledge like that of the doctors. With digital health, however, doctors are no longer the only source of information patients can rely on (Lim, 2000). Communication is no longer just "a unidirectional flow of information from health professional to patient" (Robinson, 2013, p.79) because patients have become more well-informed through browsing information on the Internet or HealthHub. Patients become more active in having dialogue with doctors and it becomes more common that information flows back from patients to doctors (Robinson, 2013, p.79). With digital health, patients want to "play a bigger role in managing their own health" (Lim, 2000). In Singapore, some patients would discuss Internet information with their doctors when seeking medical care at clinics (Lim, 2000). If patients obtain online information from a valid source and interpret the information accurately, they may be able to ask the right questions when seeing doctors. Communication gaps can be bridged and doctors can communicate with patients more easily because patients are equipped with some medical knowledge online. However, if patients obtain irrelevant information and interpret such information inaccurately, they may ask inappropriate questions when seeing doctors. This may lead to a time-consuming and less efficient consultation and harm doctor-patient relationship. However, based on the existing survey results, doctors and patients seem to be positive about the impact of digital health on doctor-patient relationship.

## IMPLICATIONS OF DIGITAL HEALTH IN SINGAPORE FOR OTHER COUNTRIES

The development of digital health is an ongoing process. It requires political leaders to have strong political will and long-term commitment to create conditions for the continuous development of digital health and support and promote the use of digital health to its full potential. In Singapore, the government incorporates the idea of developing digital health into the nation's IT strategic plans. It facilitates the development of digital health by building a robust technological infrastructure backbone. Recognizing that the development and advancement of the use of telemedicine involves heavy financial investment and substantial research and development (R&D), the government since 1991 has made sustained effort to increase its financial commitment to research and innovation. It invested S$2 billion in the National Technology Plan (1991-1995) (National Research Foundation, 2017a), which was Singapore's first directed and definitive 5-year science and technology plan to boost R&D activities (Agency for Science, Technology and Research, 2011, p.2). In 2016, the government invested S$19 billion for its sixth 5-year plan known as Research Innovation Enterprise 2020 Plan (RIE2020), with Health and Biomedical Sciences being one of the major strategic thrusts (National Research Foundation, 2017a). Under the RIE2020, S$4 billion was allocated to the strategic thrust of Health and Biomedical Sciences (National Research Foundation, 2017a), with part of the funding being used to support research on transforming and enhancing the efficiency of health services delivery, such as digital delivery of health services (National Research Foundation, 2017b). To further increase its financial commitment to research and innovation, the government in 2014 established the National Health Innovation Centre Singapore, which provided "the publicly-funded clinical research sector of Singapore with translational funding and strategic guidance to accelerate healthcare innovation" (National Health Innovation Centre Singapore, 2015). In May 2017, the government invested S$150 million into a national programme called AI.SG, with a target to come up with 100 artificial intelligence projects to provide solutions in the field of health care, finance and city management solutions over the next five years (Jamal, 2017). One of the national-scale projects was about building an intelligent platform that would allow patients with diabetes to monitor and manage their medical conditions from home (Loke, 2017). The fiscal incentives provided by publicly funded R&D not only boost the quantity and quality of research on digital health, but also encourage researchers, experts and industry to devote themselves to generating new knowledge and turning it into new products that can improve the operational efficiency of health care delivery and the lives and wellbeing of people. Apart from providing financial support to R&D, the government also "work[ed] closely with the private sector to promote health tech innovation" (Greene, 2016). For example, EDBI, the corporate investment arm of the Economic Development Board partnered with Royal Philips to seek effective use of telehealth so that patients could be empowered with greater responsibility over their health (Lawrence, 2016). They jointly invested in digital health companies that worked on population health management tools, with EDBI using its local and regional stakeholder connections in Asia to aid these companies and Royal Philips offering mentorship to them (Lawrence, 2016). The advantage of public and private sector collaboration is that bringing in technical expertise from the private sector can supplement limited public sector capabilities. Bringing the complementing skills of public and private sectors together helps give a boost to the digital health business and industry.

The development of digital health is also facilitated by the provision of a clear legal and regulatory framework. Over the past few years, the Singaporean government and professional organizations have promulgated regulation and issued guidelines in order to govern the delivery of digital health services. There are lots of stakeholders in the health care community, including medical practitioners, nurses, health workers, pharmacists, physiotherapists, hospital administrators, and patients. To better assess the impacts of regulation on affected parties, balance the opposing interests and ensure compliance, the government actively sought the opinions of stakeholders by conducting public consultation or bringing in experts or representatives from professional bodies during the regulatory process. It made sure that the public was adequately informed and sufficient time was given to the public to give useful feedback to the government. Public consultation can increase public awareness of digital health and lead to a higher level of acceptance of the legislation. Besides, there is an improved understanding among stakeholders of their rights and responsibilities under the legislation. It helps increase compliance rate and reduce the cost of enforcement. For example, after conducting three rounds of public consultation, the government promulgated Personal Data Protection Act 2012 (PDPA) to govern the access to and collection, use, disclosure and care of personal data stored in electronic and non-electronic forms (Personal Data Protection Commission, 2017). PDPA, which complemented sector-specific legislative and regulatory frameworks and came into operation in July 2014 (Personal Data Protection Commission, 2017), introduced an additional layer of obligations for healthcare institutions to put in place reasonable security arrangements to safeguard patient data, especially when such data was transferred from one health care provider to another and from Singapore to overseas (Yeo and Gaw, 2013, p.2). Another example is that the MOH in January 2015 issued National Telemedicine Guidelines (NTG) to establish the initial strategic direction for Telemedicine in Singapore (Ministry of Health, 2015c, p.8). NTG was developed with the guidance of the National Telemedicine Advisory Committee (NTAC), which comprised leading Telemedicine practitioners of Singapore and representatives from professional bodies such as Academy of Medicine, Singapore (AMS) and College of Family Physicians (Ministry of Health, 2015c, p.8). In the development of NTG, references were made to international precedents, including the US, Canada, Australia and Japan (Ministry of Health, 2015c, p.8). This helped ensure that NTG met international standards and thereby increasing public confidence. NTG aimed to provide health care providers with a holistic approach to execute the appropriate delivery of Telemedicine services through the domains of 'Clinical Standards and Outcomes', 'Human Resources', 'Organisational', and 'Technology and Equipment' and outline principles to address the safety of both health care providers and patients (Ministry of Health, 2015d, p.1). In September 2016, Singapore Medical Council published the latest version of Ethical Code and Ethical Guidelines (ECEG). In the section of Good Clinical Care, ECEG stated that the idea of providing Telemedicine responsibly required medical practitioners to "provide the same quality and standard of care as in-person medical care" (Singapore Medical Council, 2016, p.19). Medical practitioners should have sufficient information and training to manage patients through telemedicine, provide telemedicine only with patient's knowledge and consent, and ensure confidentiality of patient's personal data shared electronically (Singapore Medical Council, 2016, p.19). In late 2016, the Health Sciences Authority (HSA), which was a statutory board of the MOH to regulate health products, conducted public consultation on proposed regulatory guidelines for Telehealth devices (Health Sciences Authority, 2017a). In August 2017, the HAS issued Regulatory Guidelines for Telehealth Devices, which applied to Telehealth products, including hardware devices, software and mobile applications (Health Sciences Authority, 2017b, p.6). The Guidelines provided "clarity on the types of Telehealth Products that [were] regulated as medical devices, as well as its current regulatory approach and requirements for such Telehealth Products" (Health Sciences Authority, 2017c).

Recognizing that it is important to protect the privacy of individuals and data security online, the government has taken some security measures to protect patients' health care data online. The NRIC system, which "is used extensively in Singapore, for verification of identity and other transactions" (Woon, 2014, p.212), is used to safeguard the retrieval of NPMI data. Another security measure is the use of Singapore Personal Access (or SingPass). SingPass, which was launched in 2003, "is the online equivalent of the identity card" (Central Provident Fund Board, 2003). It "is a gateway to hundreds of digital services offered by more than 60 government agencies" (Singapore Personal Access, 2017). It is "automatically issued to Singaporeans who register for their identity cards at the age of 15" (Central Provident Fund Board, 2003). With SingPass, users only have to remember one password when transacting with government agencies online (Central Provident Fund Board, 2003; Singapore Personal Access, 2017). They can use SingPass to access HealthHub and their medical records. Since the use of SingPass is simple and convenient (Central Provident Fund Board, 2003), it makes citizens feel safe and encourages them to use digital health. Other measures to encourage citizens to use digital health services and networks are providing incentives and customer-oriented, value-added services for the users. The case study of Singapore shows that the government boosted the user rate of HealthHub by offering reward points to users to redeem vouchers and offset grocery bills and providing customer-oriented, value-added services through introducing one-stop health information and services portal, 24/7 access to health-related content, interactive online programmes, easy-to-use online health tools and website personalization. It shows that customer-orientation, user-friendliness, and ease of use are essential components to enhance users' personal digital experience and increase public acceptance to use digital health networks and services.

From the above, the case study of Singapore shows that there are lots of factors shaping the successful development and implementation of digital health. These include strong political will and long-term commitment of political leaders, a robust technological infrastructure backbone, the government's continuous financial commitment to R&D, the provision of a clear legal and regulatory framework, convenient and easy-to-use security measures, and a user-friendly, customer-centric design of digital health portal and services. The case study of Singapore shows that the development of digital health is not simply a technological issue. It involves lots of inputs from the government and stakeholder engagement. The government plays an important role in facilitating the development of digital health. The government acts as a service provider, financier, regulator and facilitator. Meanwhile, health care providers, in response to the government's digital health initiatives, utilize digital health in different ways. Patients and the general public, gradually shows an increased interest in using digital health to improve their health and take ownership of their health. Singapore has a centralized political system. The ruling party's long reign of paternalism and ruling elites' adoption of a top-down model of policy making (Luk, 2014, p.92) facilitate the development digital health policy. In many countries, the development of digital health is still in its infancy and the idea of digital health is still very new. To let the idea of digital health take hold and being endorsed by the general public and stakeholders in the health care community, the government and political leaders must have strong political will and commitment to create conditions for the development and advancement of digital health and engage stakeholders in the policy making process so that such policy can be tailored to suit the expectations and special needs of stakeholders. Another important thing is that the government and political leaders are able to link digital health to some positive impacts, such as customer-orientation, better quality of care and shortened waiting time, thereby enhancing the psychological readiness and confidence in using digital health.

## FUTURE RESEARCH DIRECTIONS

At present, there is still the lack of study on digital health in Singapore. Under the 2014 Smart Nation initiatives, Telehealth has been strongly advocated by the government. Different pilot Telehealth programmes are rolled out in phases and they are under regular review. It is expected that Telehealth programmes can be extended to benefit more segments of population. Future research directions can evaluate the outcomes of these Telehealth programmes and examine users' perspective on these Telehealth programmes. It can examine whether the implementation of digital health helps solve the challenges caused by ageing population. Comparative studies on digital health between Singapore and other countries can also be conducted in order to examine whether cross-national differences lead to different design and application of digital health.

## CONCLUSION

To conclude, the government in Singapore has made unremitting efforts to develop digital health and promote the use of it. The development of digital health is an ongoing process that requires regular reviews. It requires strong political will and long-term commitment of the government and stakeholder engagement so that digital health can be utilized to its full potential and meet the expectations and special needs of users. Looking forward, it is anticipated that digital health can play an important role in tackling the increasing health care needs caused by rapidly ageing population.

## REFERENCES

Accenture. (2012). *Accenture Works with Singapore to Implement Its National Electronic Health Record System*. Retrieved September 11, 2017, from https://www.accenture.com/t20160510T050818__w__/us-en/_acnmedia/Accenture/Conversion-Assets/DotCom/Documents/Global/PDF/Industries_11/Accenture-Works-Singapore-Implement-NEHR-System.pdf

Accenture. (2013). *The Digital Doctor is "In": Accenture Eight-Country Survey of Doctors Shows Significant Increase in Healthcare IT Usage*. Retrieved September 20, 2017, from https://www.accenture.com/t20150708T033736__w__/us-en/_acnmedia/Accenture/Conversion-Assets/DotCom/Documents/Global/PDF/Industries_11/Accenture-Digital-Doctor-Is-In.pdf

Accenture. (2015). *Doctors Survey 2015: Six-Country Report*. Retrieved September 22, 2017, from https://www.accenture.com/_acnmedia/Accenture/Conversion-Assets/DotCom/Documents/Global/PDF/Dualpub_22/Accenture-Global-Report-Acn-Doctors-Study-SG.pdf

Accenture. (2016a). *Accenture Asia-Pacific Healthcare Innovation and Transformation Survey*. Retrieved September 22, 2017, from https://www.accenture.com/t00010101T000000Z__w__/au-en/_acnmedia/PDF-17/Accenture-Health-Transformation-Survey-Full-Report.pdf

Accenture. (2016b). *Singaporean Patients Embrace Digital Health*. Retrieved September 20, 2017, from https://www.accenture.com/t20160627T034015Z__w__/sg-en/_acnmedia/PDF-22/Accenture-Digital-Health-Consumer-Survey-Research-Brief-Singapore.pdf

Accenture. (2016c). *Silver Surfers: Older Singaporeans Are Making Waves in Digital Health*. Retrieved September 27, from https://www.accenture.com/t20170314T215209__w__/sg-en/_acnmedia/PDF-46/Accenture-Health-Silver-Surfers-in-Singapore.pdf

Agency for Science, Technology and Research. (2011). *Science, Technology & Enterprise Plan 2015*. Retrieved September 30, 2017, from http://www.a-star.edu.sg/portals/0/media/otherpubs/step2015_1jun.pdf

Bhunia, P. (2017a). *3 'Ds' Supporting 3 'B's - Objectives and Principles of Singapore's Health IT Master Plan*. Retrieved September 15, 2017, from http://www.opengovasia.com/articles/7649-ds-supporting-3-bs---objectives-and-principles-of-singapores-health-it-master-plan

Bhunia, P. (2017b). *Consult Your Doctor from Anywhere: National Rollout of Smart Health Video Consultation in Singapore*. Retrieved September 15, 2017, from http://www.opengovasia.com/articles/7506-consult-your-doctor-from-anywhere-national-rollout-of-smart-health-video-consultation-in-singapore

Bhunia, P. (2017c). *National Pilot of Smart Health TeleRehab in Singapore for Remote Access to Rehabilitation Services*. Retrieved September 15, 2017, from http://www.opengovasia.com/articles/7590-national-pilot-of-smart-health-telerehab-solution-being-implemented-in-singapore

Biesdorf, S., & Niedermann, F. (2014). *Healthcare's Digital Future*. Retrieved September 18, 2017, from http://www.mckinsey.com/industries/healthcare-systems-and-services/our-insights/healthcares-digital-future

Central Provident Fund Board. (2003). *SingPass: One PASSWORD for E-Services*. Retrieved October 11, 2017, from https://www.imda.gov.sg/about/newsroom/archived/ida/media-releases/2003/20061106191925

Chambers, J. (2015). *How We Built It... Singapore HealthHub*. Retrieved September 13, 2017, from https://govinsider.asia/smart-gov/how-we-built-it-singapore-health-hub/

Chan, L. E. (2017 May 30). *MOH to Ramp up Use of Apps, Robotics to Improve Home Care: Health Minister. Channel NewsAsia*. Retrieved September 15, 2017, from http://www.channelnewsasia.com/news/singapore/moh-to-ramp-up-use-of-apps-robotics-to-improve-home-care-health-8894250

Chua, J. (2012). The e-Transformation Journey of Singapore. In N.K. Hanna & P.T. Knight (Eds.), National Strategies to Harness Information Technology, Innovation, Technology and Knowledge Management (pp. 41-76). New York, NY: Springer Science +Business Media, LLC. doi:10.1007/978-1-4614-2086-6_2

Dzenowagis, J. (2009). Bridging the Digital Divide: Linking Health and ICT Policy. In R. Wootton, N.G. Patil, R.E. Scott, & K. Ho (Eds.), Telehealth in the Developing World (pp. 9-26). Royal Society of Medicine Press, IDRC.

Emmanuel, S. C. (1998). Information and Research for Decision-makers. *World Health Forum*, *19*, 12–14. PMID:9610236

GovTech. (2016). *eGov Master Plan*. Retrieved August 30, 2017, from https://www.tech.gov.sg/About-Us/Corporate-Publications/eGov-Masterplan

GovTech. (2017). *A Healthy Hub at Your Fingertips*. Retrieved September 13, 2017, from https://www.tech.gov.sg/TechNews/DigitalGov/2017/04/27/07/08/A-healthy-hub-at-your-fingertips

Greene, W. (2016). *Health Tech Innovation Blooms in Singapore*. Retrieved September 29, 2017, from http://techonomy.com/2016/04/health-tech-innovation-blooms-in-singapore/

Gurak, L. J., & Hudson, B. L. (2006). E-health: beyond Internet search. In M. Murero & R. E. Rice (Eds.), *The Internet and Health Care: Theory, Research, and Practice* (pp. 29–48). Mahwah, NJ: Lawrence Erlbaum Associates.

Health Promotion Board. (2009a). *New HPB Online Your One-stop Health Information Portal*. Retrieved September 13, 2017, from https://www.hpb.gov.sg/article/new-'hpb-online'---your-one-stop-health-information-portal

Health Promotion Board. (2009b). *Health Promotion Board Annual Report 2008/2009*. Retrieved September 13, 2017, from https://www.hpb.gov.sg/docs/default-source/annual-reports/hpb-annual-report-2009.pdf?sfvrsn=2

Health Promotion Board. (2017). *Our Awards*. Retrieved September 13, 2017, from https://www.hpb.gov.sg/about/awards

Health Sciences Authority. (2017a). *Consultation on Proposed Regulatory Guidelines for Telehealth Devices*. Retrieved September 29, 2017, from http://www.hsa.gov.sg/content/hsa/en/News_Events/Public_Consultation1/consultationtelehealthdevices.html

Health Sciences Authority. (2017b). *Regulatory Guidelines for Telehealth Devices*. Retrieved September 29, 2017, from http://www.hsa.gov.sg/content/dam/HSA/HPRG/Medical_Devices/Updates_and_Safety_reporting/Regulatory_Updates/Telehealth%20Guideline%20-%20Aug%202017.pdf

Health Sciences Authority. (2017c). *Regulatory Updates*. Retrieved September 29, 2017, from http://www.hsa.gov.sg/content/hsa/en/Health_Products_Regulation/Medical_Devices/Regulatory_Updates.html

Healthcare Information and Management Systems Society. (2010). *Electronic Health Records: A Global Perspective* (2nd ed.). Retrieved September 11, 2017, from http://web.pdx.edu/~nwallace/GHS/EHRP2.pdf

Infocomm Development Authority of Singapore, Singapore Computer Society, & Singapore Infocomm Technology Federation (2006). *Innovation, Integration, Internationalisation: Report by the iN2015 Steering Committee*. Retrieved September 11, 2017, from http://unpan1.un.org/intradoc/groups/public/documents/unpan/unpan032993.pdf

Infocomm Media Development Authority. (2016a). *Five Government Networks Upgraded to Support the Government Information Infrastructure and Singapore ONE*. Retrieved August 30, 2017, from https://www.imda.gov.sg/about/newsroom/archived/ida/media-releases/1997/20050726122310

Infocomm Media Development Authority. (2016b). *Using IT to Support Quality and Affordable Healthcare*. Retrieved September 8, 2017, from https://www.imda.gov.sg/about/newsroom/archived/ida/media-releases/1996/20050726150709

Integrated Health Information Systems. (2017a). *Healthcare Consultations Move Online in Singapore's First National Implementation of Smart Health Video Consultation for Healthcare*. Retrieved September 15, 2017, from https://www.ihis.com.sg/Latest_News/Media_Releases/Pages/Healthcare-Consultations-Move-Online-in-Singapore%E2%80%99s-First-National-Implementation-of-VC.aspx

Integrated Health Information Systems. (2017b). *Smart Health TeleRehab to Improve Patient Access to Rehabilitation Services and Productivity for Therapists*. Retrieved September 15, 2017, from https://www.ihis.com.sg/Latest_News/Media_Releases/Pages/Smart-Health-TeleRehab.aspx

Jamal, A. (2017). *Singapore's New Mission to Build AI Capabilities*. Retrieved September 29, 2017, from http://www.connectedtoindia.com/singapores-new-mission-to-build-ai-capabilities-1366.html

Khalik, S. (2016 October 21). *'Bid' to Care under Match-A-Nurse*. Retrieved September 15, 2017, from http://www.straitstimes.com/singapore/health/bid-to-care-under-match-a-nurse

Koh, V. (2015 March 17). *HDB Completes Trial of Smart Elderly Monitoring and Alert System. TODAY*. Retrieved September 14, 2017, from http://www.todayonline.com/singapore/hdb-completes-semas-test-bed

Lawrence, S. (2016). *Philips, Singapore to Jointly Invest in Population Health Management Companies Targeting Asia*. Retrieved September 29, 2017, from http://www.fiercebiotech.com/medical-devices/philips-singapore-to-jointly-invest-population-health-management-companies

Lee, C. E., Lim, B. K., & Tan, P. C. S. (2006). *Singapore HIT Case Study*. Retrieved September 8, 2017, from http://pacifichealthsummit.org/downloads/HITCaseStudies/Economy/SingaporeHIT.pdf

Lee, D. (2016). *HealthHub: A Holistic Way for S'poreans to Manage Health*. Retrieved September 13, 2017, from http://www.todayonline.com/voices/healthhub-holistic-way-sporeans-manage-health

Lee, H. L. (2014). *Transcript of Speech by Prime Minister Lee Hsien Loong at Smart Nation Launch, 24 November 2014*. Retrieved September 14, 2017, from https://www.smartnation.sg/happenings/speeches/smart-nation-launch

Liau, Y. Q. (2010). *Standards Important for S'pore E-healthcare*. Retrieved September 11, 2017, from http://www.zdnet.com/article/standards-important-for-spore-e-healthcare/

Lim, H. K. (2000). *Second Ministry Of Health IT Seminar*. Retrieved September 11, 2017, from https://www.moh.gov.sg/content/moh_web/home/pressRoom/speeches_d/2000/second_ministry_of_health_IT_seminar.html

Loh, C. J. (2016 April 23). *Smart Devices Trial Extended to 3,200 Households in Yuhua*. Retrieved September 14, 2017, from http://www.channelnewsasia.com/news/singapore/smart-devices-trial-extended-to-3-200-households-in-yuhua-8086356

Loke, K. F. (2017). *Singapore's Artificial Intelligence Capabilities to Get S$150m Boost*. Retrieved September 29, 2017, from http://www.channelnewsasia.com/news/singapore/singapore-s-artificial-intelligence-capabilities-to-get-s-150m-8813174

Low, C. O., & Li, D. (2015). Challenges of Transformation on Our Healthcare IT Journey. *SMA News*, *47*(5), 5-7. Retrieved September 8, 2017, from https://www.sma.org.sg/UploadedImg/files/Publications%20-%20SMA%20News/4705/Full%20PDF.pdf

Low, C. O., & Tan, P. (2016). Our IT Journey: One Patient-One Record. In C. E. Lee & K. Satku (Eds.), *Singapore's Health Care System: What 50 Years Have Achieved* (pp. 337–350). World Scientific. doi:10.1142/9789814696067_0027

Luk, S. (2014). *Health Insurance Reforms in Asia*. Abingdon, UK: Routledge.

Michaelis, A. R. (1996). Information Bureaucracy: Australia and Singapore Compared. *Interdisciplinary Science Reviews*, *21*(2), 89–93. doi:10.1179/isr.1996.21.2.89

Ministry of Communications & Information. (1989). *Speech by Dr. Tay Eng Soon, Senior Minister of State for Education, at the Opening of MEDINFO '89 Singapore at the Raffles City Convention Centre on Sunday, 10 December 1989, at 1.30 PM*. Retrieved September 3, 2017, from http://www.nas.gov.sg/archivesonline/data/pdfdoc/tes19891210s.pdf

Ministry of Communications & Information. (1990a). *Speech by Mr. Yeo Cheow Tong, AG Minister for Health at the Launching of MediNet on 22 October 1990 at 4 PM at Ministry of Health Auditorium, College of Medicine Building*. Retrieved September 3, 2017, from http://www.nas.gov.sg/archivesonline/data/pdfdoc/yct19901022s.pdf

Ministry of Communications & Information. (1990b). *Address by Acting Minister for Health, Mr. Yeo Cheow Tong at the Opening of the National Cancer Education Programme at the Mandarin Hotel on Saturday, 29 September 1990 at 2.00 PM*. Retrieved September 6, 2017, from http://www.nas.gov.sg/archivesonline/data/pdfdoc/yct19900929s.pdf

Ministry of Finance, & Infocomm Development Authority of Singapore (2003). *Singapore E-government*. Retrieved August 31, 2017, from https://www.tech.gov.sg/-/media/GovTech/About-us/Corporate-Publications/eGov/eGap-II.pdf?la=en

Ministry of Finance, & Infocomm Development Authority of Singapore (2006). *iGov2010: From Integrating Service to Integrating Government*. Retrieved August 31, 2017, from https://www.tech.gov.sg/-/media/GovTech/About-us/Corporate-Publications/eGov/iGov.pdf?la=en

Ministry of Health. (2010). *Contract to Implement Singapore's National Electronic Health Record (Phase 1) Awarded*. Retrieved September 11, 2017, from https://www.moh.gov.sg/content/moh_web/home/pressRoom/pressRoomItemRelease/2010/Contract_to_Implement_Singapore_National_Electronic_Health_Record_Phase_1_Awarded.html

Ministry of Health. (2015a). *Future Phase of NEHR*. Retrieved September 11, 2017, from https://www.moh.gov.sg/content/moh_web/home/pressRoom/Parliamentary_QA/2015/future-phase-of-nehr.html

Ministry of Health. (2015b). *One-stop Health Information and Services Portal Provides Access to Key Medical Records and Health Content*. Retrieved September 13, 2017, from https://www.moh.gov.sg/content/moh_web/home/pressRoom/pressRoomItemRelease/2015/one-stop-health-information-and-services-portal-provides-access-.html

Ministry of Health. (2015c). *National Telemedicine Guidelines*. Retrieved September 28, 2017, from https://www.moh.gov.sg/content/dam/moh_web/Publications/Guidelines/MOH%20Cir%2006_2015_30Jan15_Telemedicine%20Guidelines%20rev.pdf

Ministry of Health. (2015d). *MOH National Telemedicine Guidelines: Summary Card*. Retrieved September 28, 2017, from https://www.moh.gov.sg/content/dam/moh_web/Publications/Guidelines/MOH%20Cir%2006_2015_30Jan15_Telemedicine%20Summary.pdf

Ministry of Health. (2016). *Speech by Mr Gan Kim Yong, Minister for Health, at Home Nursing Foundation's "Futurescape: Home Healthcare – Local and International Perspectives" Conference, 20 August 2016*. Retrieved September 15, 2017, from https://www.moh.gov.sg/content/moh_web/home/pressRoom/speeches_d/2016/speech-by-mr-gan-kim-yong--minister-for-health--at-home-nursing-.html

Ministry of Health. (2017a). *Speech by Mr Gan Kim Yong, Minister for Health, at the National Health IT Summit 2017, 30 May 2017*. Retrieved September 15, 2017, from https://www.moh.gov.sg/content/moh_web/home/pressRoom/speeches_d/2017/speech-by-mr-gan-kim-yong--minister-for-health--at-the-national-.html

Ministry of Health. (2017b). *HealthHub*. Retrieved September 15, 2017, from https://www.moh.gov.sg/content/moh_web/home/pressRoom/Parliamentary_QA/2017/healthhub.html

National Health Innovation Centre Singapore. (2015). *Accelerating Healthcare Innovation*. Retrieved September 29, 2017, from https://nhic.sg/

National Library Board of Singapore. (1989). *TradeNet is Officially Launched*. Retrieved September 4, 2017, from http://eresources.nlb.gov.sg/history/events/8db3ea66-c99a-41a0-bd9a-b6300d1a4454

National Research Foundation. (2017a). *RIE2020 Plan*. September 29, 2017, from https://www.nrf.gov.sg/rie2020

National Research Foundation. (2017b). *Health and Biomedical Sciences*. September 29, 2017, from https://www.nrf.gov.sg/rie2020/health-and-biomedical-sciences

Ng, P. T. (2011). Embracing Emerging Technologies: The Case of the Singapore Intelligent Nation 2015 Vision. In P. O. de Pablos, W. B. Lee, & J. Zhao (Eds.), *Regional Innovation Systems and Sustainable Development: Emerging Technologies* (pp. 115–123). Hershey, PA: IGI Global. doi:10.4018/978-1-61692-846-9.ch008

Nimmon, L., & Stenfors-Hayes, T. (2016). The "Handling" of Power in the Physician-patient Encounter: Perceptions from Experienced Physicians. *BMC Medical Education*, *16*(1), 114. doi:10.118612909-016-0634-0 PMID:27091146

Personal Data Protection Commission. (2017). *Legislation and Guidelines: Overview*. Retrieved September 29, 2017, from https://www.pdpc.gov.sg/legislation-and-guidelines

Phua, R. (2017a April 12). *National Video Consultation Platform to Allow Patients to 'See' Doctors from Home*. Retrieved September 15, 2017, from http://www.channelnewsasia.com/news/singapore/national-video-consultation-platform-to-allow-patients-to-see-do-8701218

Phua, R. (2017b May 5). *Undergoing Physiotherapy Exercises from Home Now a Reality for Patients*. Retrieved September 15, 2017, from http://www.channelnewsasia.com/news/singapore/undergoing-physiotherapy-exercises-from-home-now-a-reality-for-8821356

Robinson, L. (2013). Is Digital Health Technology Empowering Patients? *Journal of Medical Radiation Sciences*, *60*(3), 79–80. doi:10.1002/jmrs.20 PMID:26229613

Rowlands, D. (2012). *National eHealth Record Systems – The Singapore Experience*. Retrieved September 11, 2017, from https://www.pulseitmagazine.com.au/index.php?option=com_content&view=article&id=1139:guest-editorial-national-ehealth-record-systems-the-singapore-experience&catid=16:australian-ehealth&Itemid=327

Singapore Medical Council. (2016). *Ethical Code and Ethical Guidelines*. Retrieved September 29, 2017, from http://www.healthprofessionals.gov.sg/content/dam/hprof/smc/docs/guidelines/2016%20SMC%20Ethical%20Code%20and%20Ethical%20Guidelines%20-%20(13Sep16).pdf

Singapore Personal Access. (2017). *Frequently Asked Questions*. Retrieved October 11, 2017, from http://www.ifaq.gov.sg/SINGPASS/apps/fcd_faqmain.aspx#FAQ_130407

Sinha, P.K., Sunder, G., Bendale, P., Mantri, M., & Dande, A. (2013). *Electronic Health Record: Standards, Coding Systems, Frameworks and Infrastructure*. Wiley-IEEE.

Smart Nation Singapore. (2017a). *Telehealth: Integrated and Seamless Healthcare Services at Home*. Retrieved September 14, 2017, from https://www.smartnation.sg/initiatives/Health/telehealth-integrated-and-seamless-healthcare-services-at-home

Smart Nation Singapore. (2017b). *Enablers*. Retrieved September 14, 2017, from https://www.smartnation.sg/about-smart-nation/enablers

Tan, B., Ling, P. S., & Cha, V. (2013). The Evolution of Singapore's Infocomm Plans: Singapore's E-government Journey from 1980 to 2007. In G. Pan (Ed.), *Dynamics of Governing IT Innovation in Singapore: A Case Book* (pp. 1–39). World Scientific. doi:10.1142/9789814417839_0001

Tan, C. H. (2002). *Singapore Financial and Business Sourcebook* (2nd ed.). Singapore: Singapore University Press.

Tan, L. T. (1995). National Patient Master Index in Singapore. *International Journal of Bio-Medical Computing, 40*(2), 89–93. doi:10.1016/0020-7101(95)01130-7 PMID:8847128

TODAY. (2017 May 30). *Healthcare Sector to Ride Digital Revolution Intelligently*. Retrieved September 15, 2017, from https://www.gov.sg/news/content/today-online-healthcare-sector-to-ride-digital-revolution-intelligently

Toh, E. M. (2017, May 30). From Wearable Sensors to Robots, Home Care to Get Tech Boost. *TODAY*. Retrieved September 15, 2017, from http://www.todayonline.com/singapore/healthcare-sector-ride-digital-revolution-intelligently-gan-kim-yong

Vijaya, K., Chan, S. P., Ho, H. P. C., Lim, Y. Y. L., & Lim, R. (2006). HPB Online: An Electronic Health Education Portal in Singapore. *Singapore Medical Journal, 47*(1), 8–13. PMID:16397714

Wilson, K., & Brownstein, J. S. (2009). Early Detection of Disease Outbreaks Using the Internet. *Canadian Medical Association Journal, 180*(8), 829–831. doi:10.1503/cmaj.1090215 PMID:19364791

Woon, B. (2014). Singapore: Health Database in an IT Society. Japan Medical Association Journal. 57(4), 212-5.

World Health Organization. (2004). *eHealth: Report by Secretariat*. Retrieved August 25, 2017, from http://www.who.int/healthacademy/media/en/eHealth_EB-en.pdf?ua=1

World Health Organization. (2005a). *Connecting for Health: Global Vision, Local Insight*. Retrieved August 25, 2017, from http://www.who.int/ehealth/publications/WSISReport_Connecting_for_Health.pdf

World Health Organization. (2005b). *eHealth*. Retrieved August 25, 2017, from http://apps.who.int/iris/bitstream/10665/20378/1/WHA58_28-en.pdf?ua=1

World Health Organization. (2006). *eHealth Tools & Services: Needs of the Member States*. Retrieved August 25, 2017, from http://apps.who.int/iris/bitstream/10665/69226/1/WHO_EHL_06.1_eng.pdf

World Health Organization. (2017). *eHealth Resolution*. Retrieved August 25, 2017, from http://www.who.int/healthacademy/news/en/

World Summit on the Information Society. (2003). *Plan of Action*. Retrieved August 25, 2017, from https://www.itu.int/dms_pub/itu-s/md/03/wsis/doc/S03-WSIS-DOC-0005!!PDF-E.pdf

Yeo, S. J. (2015 March 17). *HDB Elderly Alert System Well-received in Test-bed. Straits Times*. Retrieved September 14, 2017, from http://www.straitstimes.com/singapore/housing/hdb-elderly-alert-system-well-received-in-test-bed

Yeo, T., & Gaw, B. (2013). *Developments in Singapore's Healthcare Regulatory Landscape*. Retrieved September 29, 2017, from http://www.drewnapier.com/DrewASPX/media/assets/Publications/Drew-Napier-ALB-Nov-Life-Sciences-issue-Developments-in-Singapore-s-Healthcare-Regulatory-Landscape.pdf

## KEY TERMS AND DEFINITIONS

**HealthHub:** A one-stop portal introduced by the Singaporean government to allow users to have 24/7 access to personal health records and health-related information.

**MediNet:** An integrated computer network introduced by the Singaporean government to link the health care community with all relevant government agencies.

**National Electronic Health Record:** A patient data exchange system that allows medical practitioners to have access to a patient's health record so that more accurate treatment decisions can be made for their patients.

**Personal Data Protection Act:** A legislation promulgated in Singapore in 2012 to govern the access to and collection, use and disclosure of electronic and non-electronic personal data.

**SingPass:** A security measure that is used in Singapore for verification of identity when people have online transaction with government agencies.

**Smart Elderly Monitoring and Alert System:** A sensor system that tracks daily activities of the elderly in their homes and alert their caregivers via text messages if abnormalities are detected.

**Smart Nation:** An initiative launched by the Singaporean government in 2014 to solve problems, create more opportunities and make society more connected through the extensive use of information technology.

**Telehealth:** The use of information and communication technologies to obtain health care services remotely.

# Chapter 9
# The Evolution of Self-Organized Social Solidarity (SoSS) Initiatives in Greece and Their Relationship to Online Media:
## A Longitudinal Research

**Eleni-Revekka Staiou**
*National and Kapodistrian University of Athens, Greece*

**Dimitris Gouscos**
*National and Kapodistrian University of Athens, Greece*

## ABSTRACT

*Since the beginning of the economic crisis in Greece, the first impacts were felt on standards of everyday living. Citizens felt the urge to self-organize and take action based on their own strengths as the only practical solution to fill in the gaps left by the state's absence of intervention. Rooted in the country's economic crisis, Greek citizens' self-organized social solidarity (SoSS) initiatives have been focused on acting and innovating rather than protesting. Examples of such initiatives are social grocery stores, alternative currencies, time banks, neighborhood groups for sanitation and general caretaking, assistance to students in primary/secondary education to name a few. The main objective of this chapter is to show the evolution of SoSS initiatives through a longitudinal research for the period 2014-2016. A second objective is to present the relationship between these initiatives and the online media: How did they use the internet and the social media for their communication for the same period of time? Finally, the authors will attempt an assessment of their operation so far, with data obtained from updating the platform Organosi 2.0, in the summer of 2017.*

DOI: 10.4018/978-1-5225-5966-5.ch009

## INTRODUCTION

Since 2009, when the economic crisis in Greece became more evident, many changes occurred in the country, one of them being the further development of civil society. The State had (and still has) severe problems in generating funds and helping its citizens at the same time. The combination of high taxes and low or no income at all created a new reality for most people and new needs emerged in everyday life.

In the beginning, civil society tried to protest through strikes and demonstrations, but soon realized that this was not the right way of acting since it led to no practical effects. People decided to act and in many neighborhoods the so-called "people assemblies" were formed, with indignant citizens discussing the problems and the deficiencies of the state and proposing solutions.

However, the problems of society and citizens were far more serious and required action. Therefore, citizens started to self-organize in order to solve as many problems they could. Several problems were crucial for survival (e.g. food). Further to this, many other aspects of everyday life which were dependent on the state, began to become independent from bureaucracy and public-sector organizations (e.g. neighborhood sanitation or student lessons). Therefore, a number of self-organized social solidarity (SoSS) initiatives have emerged. Some of the initiatives have been inspired by organizations abroad (e.g. systems for alternative currencies). Most initiatives do not have the need of state support to function. Even those that do, are kept alive through the help of citizens.

So, in Greece, in a way, a new kind of citizen was created, what according to Bang (2010) should be called "Everyday maker". This citizen creates politics in his everyday life. He is not an activist, nor is he organized in a political party, he does not belong to an organization and he is much more flexible. He focuses on specific goals and he is not meant to be politically successful or to influence others. He does not like professional politicians, but he prefers to solve his own problems, in practical ways, and asks for the help of the system only when it is necessary. Before, according to Soritopoulos and Karamagioli (2005) civil society in Greece was "*relatively underdeveloped and poorly organized [...], comparatively weak*". There were many initiatives, but Greek civil society was still influenced by political parties. Even the non-governmental organizations created at times in Greece were, in fact, lobbying groups in relation to political parties (Tsaliki, 2010).

A first objective of this article is to define these initiatives that emerged in Greece during the crisis and to show their evolution in the period 2014-2016, ending with the stage they are in, in 2017. The second objective is to study their use of the Internet and online media for communication with renewed statistics from the original 2014 survey.

For both these objectives, our discussion departs from a brief contextualization of our work within the broader agenda of technology- and organization-related issues for IT use by voluntary non-profit and non-governmental organizations. This discussion is useful to keep in mind, as our presentation moves on to the landscape of self-organized social solidarity initiatives in Greece.

## LITERATURE REVIEW

### IT and Internet Use by Civil Society Organizations

Many different types of organizations can be found in civil society that are likely to differ considerably from one another in terms of the ways they use information technology and arrange their internal structure and organizational relations. Some well-known (Saeed et al, 2008) such types of organizations include community-based organizations, non-governmental organizations (NGOs), activist groups, think tanks, cultural groups as well as informal citizens organizations and cooperatives.

In recent years, the number of these organizations is constantly growing due to the fact that the problems which societies and citizens face are also growing at a fast pace. At the same time, information technology advancements offer a multitude of new possibilities for organizing and communicating that until a few years ago were not available at all, or at least not for lay people with no specialized technical knowledge.

The expectation that civil society organizations will take advantage of information technology to operate more efficiently has been much discussed in the literature, with information technology collectively referring to tools such as websites, information systems and strategies that would help civil society organizations get organized and communicate (Merkel et al, 2007). According to early literature, when a civil society organization finds the information system or technology that suits its needs, it can stand out from other similar organizations by becoming more efficient and increasing its reputation, which in turn means that it can attract more volunteers (Klemz et al, 2003). On top of that, such an organization can stand better chances to attract funding, train volunteers who want to join it, create online and offline communities and improve its external and internal communication (Klemz et al, 2003, Spencer, 2002).

In reality, however, this virtuous circle is not so easy or straightforward to activate. According to Boeder (2002), the websites related to civil society organizations most often have to do with e-commerce, auctions, fundraising, philanthropy and donor services, knowledge and capacity building, volunteering and services, social advocacy and events. In order to develop and communicate these activities with the help of information technology, civil society organizations typically need to undergo through three successive phases of technology usage: experimental retrieval, broadcast power and, finally, interactive dialogue. In the so-called experimental retrieval phase, organizations start to use e-mail as a communication tool and then proceed to creating a website. In the next phase (broadcast power) they use the internet as an online brochure with the main objective to give information about their actions. Only in the third phase of interactive dialogue can organizations actually proceed to enacting a dialogue with their audience (Spencer, 2002).

Although technology advancements and the advent of Web 2.0 and social media seem to put the linearity of this phased approach of IT usage in doubt, such linear patterns of change still exist in the evolution and operation of today's civil society organizations, essentially due to the fact that, at the bottom line, these patterns do not have to do with the capabilities of information technology itself. Probably, the single most important factor for such a linear progress towards using information technology in a more interactive intention, is the need for the mindset of the people comprising an organization to progress accordingly from a one-way message broadcasting-based approach to a more open discussion-based approach. This mentality shift, which lies at the roots of our perception about information technology and the opportunities that it offers, could then effectively allow the members of an organization to identify the capabilities of information technology as a tool for engaging audiences in dialogues.

This view is in line with more recent research that shows that, while civil society organizations use e-mail and the internet for general communication, they tend not to rely on the internet to organize campaigns or online meetings, neither do they have the same readiness to use more social technologies such as blogs and wikis (Saeed et al, 2008). The paradox, here, is that while the internet and information technologies can seem particularly useful to civil society organizations, the latter do not seem to use these tools as expected. In fact, many civil society organizations claim to understand how much these tools could help, but at the same time they face many problems when it comes to implementation of similar projects.

One reason for this is that as much as information technologies become more and more simple to use, one of the major technology-related problems that persist for civil society organizations is that they lack dedicated qualified personnel to set up and operate projects based on new IT tools. Most organizations rely on volunteers, who either lack the experience or do not stay enough time with the organization in order to develop such a project. In some cases volunteers can set an IT system up and running and then leave, with nobody else in their place able to continue their work (Merkel et al, 2007; Voida, 2011; Voida et al, 2011).

The lack of money necessary for access to technology is yet another problem, referring to access to both knowhow and equipment. Many civil society organizations do not have the money to hire an IT professional on a permanent basis. Many such organizations, at the same time, also lack the necessary IT (computing, telecoms, peripheral) equipment and need to rely on volunteers that can work mainly with their home equipment (Merkel et al, 2007, Voida, 2011).

Apart from these more practical technology-related problems, there are some more subtle organization-related issues that civil society organizations trying to effectively use IT need to consider. In order for any organization to successfully integrate technology, it should define its objectives, identify its target audience and establish a focus on the ways in which this audience will be approached. For civil society organizations, in particular, this need becomes even more important in light of the fact that the audience of such an organization is not merely a passive group of listeners; on the contrary, it is a pool of potential volunteers that can develop the intention to get involved and contribute to the projects of this organization. These potential volunteers represent the single greatest strength of a civil society organization, making up a community that operates as the ultimate source from which such an organization can draw what it needs to become successful (Spencer, 2002). Still, in order to develop and retain such a community, civil society organizations need to be shape-shifters in their patterns of work and technology usage, since they have to constantly follow the changes that happen in their surroundings (Voida, 2011).

## Social Media Use by Civil Society Organizations

Despite all the problems, the use of the internet by Civil Society Organizations brings a lot of profits and on a practical level. It is an effective way of achieving their goals at a low cost (Soon, 2013). The knowledge, they have access to, is wide and until previously it was under the "ownership" of governments or other interests. They have access to a much larger audience with greater ease and their communication is easier with the flow of information being continuous on both sides. Two-way communication is a feature of the Internet, and in particular of the social media (May, 2002).

Mainly, the use of the Internet and the social media, by the Civil Society Organizations is summarized in 6 functions: providing information, enhancing actions and mobilizing, promoting interaction and dialogue, creating collateral relationships, creative expression and finding funding and resources (Vozab, 2012). They use them for communication and interaction with volunteers and their sponsors, citizens' education on the issues they deal with, and general information on what they do, to organize actions and defend their principles (Waters et al., 2009, Johnson Center, 2012, Rahman et al., 2014). According to a 2015 survey, most organizations have websites and e-mail, and they provide a great deal of support for printed media and events. In conjunction with the above, they also use social media, but not at such a high frequency as one would expect. It is important to note that CSOs have no communication plans for organized communication. Official plan has only the 25% of them, while unofficial, about half of them (59%) (Nonprofit Marketing Guide, 2015).

However, it should be noted that it is not at all easy to use social media and they are not everything they look at first glance. For example, social media may not be completely free to use. It's free to make an account and have a basic use, but when the organization goes to business use some money may be required, even if it's against this logic-of-payment. Also, no one can guarantee that this will make it easier for younger generations to be approached, or donors and volunteers will be gathered (Ogden and Starita, 2009). Competition is great, and everyone is required to prove they are different and better than others who claim the same things (Suart, 2012).

Social media have a special place in communication strategies, especially for Civil Society organizations, with some relying only on them.

For the use of social media there are 5 principles to be followed. First, CSOs should listen to their audience, listen to what it says, see if there are elements that are not understandable in order to correct them. The second principle is that the CSO should discuss with its audience, as the two-way discussion is crucial on social media in relation to the first generation of the internet. Then it must have an active presence in the ever-evolving environment and support those who support it. Finally, it should encourage citizens to participate actively in what they do, as they depend on them (Regan, 2011).

People who manage social media play an important role. They should be people who will be well aware of the organization, who will be willing to spend time on handling and maintaining them (James, 2013b). These people should have creative thinking and writing skills, they should have experience, photo and video editing skills and basic programming skills. They should be flexible and able to do many things at the same time, take initiatives and be able to build a community (Nonprofit Tech for Good, 2014b).

Of course, it is extremely difficult to find a single person with all these characteristics and that is why the obligations are often shared by more people. This also contributes to the need for several hours a week update all media, which makes the situation even more difficult. If the CSO maintains a blog, it takes about 4 hours a week to write articles and publish them. For Facebook it takes another 4 hours, as for Twitter. Smaller networks need less time, but all media cumulatively generate a lot of workload (Nonprofit Tech for Good, 2014a).

The content of social media is particular. Multimedia is the big advantage, as videos and photos can be added to the posts to help communicate the message in a more straightforward way (Next Principles, 2012). But the rest of the content is special as it has to be written in a specific way, in the "language" of social media, it should contain elements that interest the public to read them (Ventureneer, 2010). The storytelling method makes the subject much more impressive and easy to understand, especially if this story has some practical and useful meaning. Discussion in the context of social media and the creation of contacts facilitates the sharing of stories and, consequently, the communication of the desired message, which is even more important if it is authentic and not fake in an effort to impress everyone (Pitman, 2013, James, 2013a).

Whatever the power of social media, the organization of communication is a very basic component in order to be able a communication plan to succeed. Also, in many cases, social media, by themselves, are not capable of success, they must be combined with other channels of communication and face to face interaction (Mansfield, 2014).

The self-organized social solidarity initiatives presented in the rest of the paper may seem, at least in theory, to avoid some of the problems mentioned in the above discussion, mostly due to their flat and completely volunteer-based structure. Whether these initiatives will be able to better respond to such problems or not will largely depend upon the extent to which their self-organized structure may avoid decision bottlenecks and allow more people to informally learn from each other in a peer-to-peer fashion for making better use of the low-cost and simple-to-use capabilities that IT and social media offer.

## Self-Organized Social Solidarity (SoSS) Initiatives in Greece

### Organosi 2.0 Platform

A first-level mapping and categorization of self-organized social solidarity initiatives in Greece has been attempted through the Organosi 2.0 platform (http://organosi20.gr) (Organosi, or *οργάνωση* in Greek, standing for organization) based on their thematic scope (e.g. clothing, food etc.) and locality of action (e.g. urban vs. rural, local vs. regional vs. national). Mapping SoSS initiatives in Greece is quite difficult because many such initiatives do not have an online presence. A large percentage use the internet just like traditional media i.e. only for publicity rather than for "organizing". Communicating with a SoSS initiative could prove tricky because many such initiatives do not answer to emails or respond to comments on social media.

The Organosi 2.0 platform began its operation in December 2011, with the aim to collect information on a single website for as many as possible current SoSS initiatives. The Organosi 2.0 website is freely accessible to everyone. In fact, Organosi 2.0 operates as a meta-index for these initiatives so that they can be easily found by people in need.

The SoSS initiatives indexed in the Organosi 2.0 platform have three common characteristics, which also operate as criteria for inclusion:

*Figure 1. Snapshot of the Organosi 2.0 website (in Greek)*

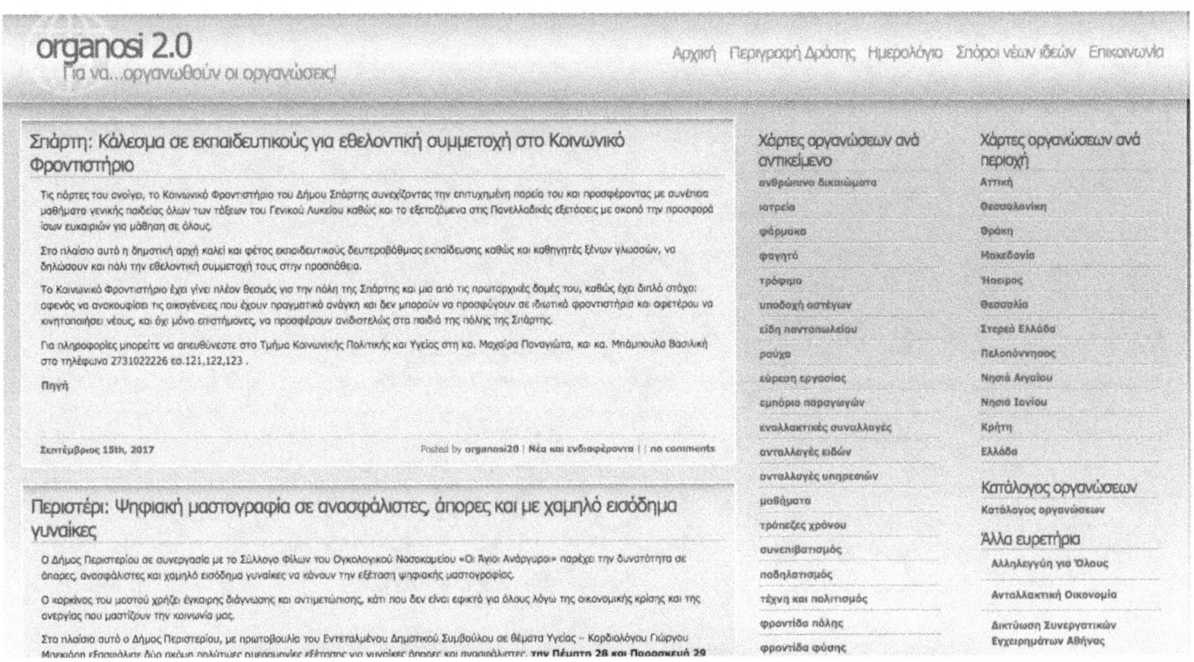

1. They try to cover a gap in the services provided by the state. They are initiatives which provide services that ought to be offered or even supported by the state, if conditions were better.
2. They act. Their actions and involvement in society is practical and tangible. They take action and provide services.
3. They do not discriminate. Initiatives that show any kind of discrimination (political, religious or any other) are not included in the platform.

Organosi 2.0 does not adopt nor evaluate the ideas of SoSS initiatives included in the online platform. This evaluation may be made by site visitors through the comments and rating facilities that exists for every post.

It must be noted here that official NGOs (Non-Governmental Organizations) are not included in the Organosi 2.0 platform although they may be created by citizens. The reason for this is two-fold. Firstly, the number of NGOs in Greece is currently close to 6,000 and it is difficult to confirm which of there are still active. Secondly, and most importantly, during the past years many NGOs in Greece have been accused as "ghost" organizations, formed only for the sake of taking grants from the state. Therefore,

*Figure 2. Snapshot of the main categories index (in Greek)*

*Figure 3. The geographical mapping of SoSS initiatives listed in the Organosi 2.0 platform all over Greece*

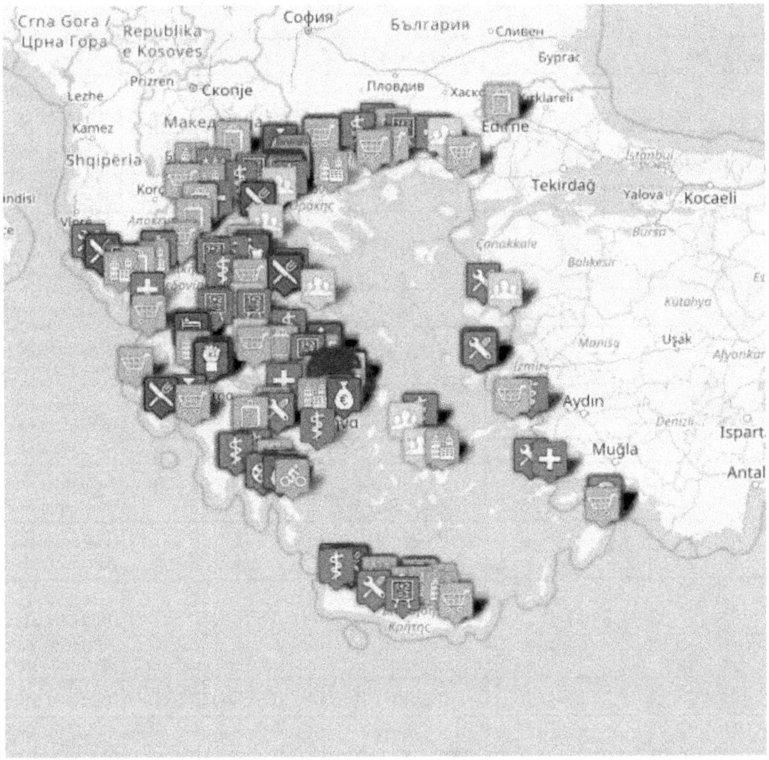


due to these problems, it has been considered better not to include NGOs in the platform, even though there are some that provide very useful services.

It should also be noted that in this sample neither social enterprises have been included. This type of organization, which is a characteristic one of the social economy, is not included in the sample as in recent years there has been a rapid increase in the establishment of such enterprises in Greece and we were not been able to control all of them for inclusion into Organosi 2.0. Exceptions are self-organizations that at some stage of their operation have become formal (either social enterprises or non-governmental organizations).

## Thematic and Geographical Area of Activity of SoSS Initiatives

As of March 2014, the Organosi 2.0 index includes 371 SoSS initiatives and by January 2016 the number increased to 563 initiatives. There are two different mappings provided by the Organosi 2.0 platform, one by the thematic type and one by the geographical area of activity of the SoSS initiatives listed[1]. Table 1 presents the thematic mapping of SoSS initiatives. In 2014 included 19 different types of initiatives but in 2016 we had 21 different categories.

In 2014, the most populated thematic categories of the above regard everyday problems (food, medication, doctors), but initiatives focused on the exchange of time, items and services are encountered at a quite high percentage as well, since they enable people to obtain items and save time at no cost. On top of that, there are categories for initiatives that are not tackling practical or survival problems, but still they give their members a sense of belonging and take action instead of the state.

*Table 1. Thematic types of SoSS initiatives currently listed on the Organosi 2.0 website (multiple thematic types recorded for each initiative)*

| Thematic Type | # Initiatives (2014) | # Initiatives (2016) | Description |
|---|---|---|---|
| human rights | 4/371 | 7/563 | self-organized initiatives about human rights, i.e. against racism |
| infirmaries | 41/371 | 52/563 | volunteer doctors offering their services to people who cannot afford or are not covered to visit doctors or public hospitals |
| medication | 29/371 | 64/563 | citizens and pharmacists offering medication to people who need them and cannot afford to buy them |
| cooked food | 7/371 | 34/563 | volunteers cooking and offering food for free |
| canned food | 83/371 | 106/563 | volunteers offering and gathering canned food for low-income or unemployed people |
| groceries | 83/371 | 106/563 | volunteers offering and gathering grocery goods, detergents, household appliances etc. for low-income or unemployed people |
| clothing | 33/371 | 45/563 | volunteers offering and gathering clothes for low-income or unemployed people |
| bypassing middlemen in trade | 16/371 | 20/563 | producers selling their products to consumers without the intervention of middlemen |
| alternative currencies/exchanges | 33/371 | 58/563 | groups of people using alternative (non-official) currencies instead of the Euro, or employing direct exchanges without money involved, during transactions |
| exchanging items | 36/371 | 40/563 | groups of people exchanging used items |
| exchanging services | 28/371 | 29/563 | groups of people exchanging services |
| lessons | 54/371 | 76/563 | volunteers giving lessons to students/adults who cannot afford to pay for them |
| time banks | 12/371 | 32/563 | groups of people exchanging their time to help each other |
| carpooling | 8/371 | 8/563 | people sharing the same schedule, their cars as well as travel expenses |
| bicyclism | 7/371 | 8/563 | groups of people sharing the same interest about bicycles and organizing events to promote the use of bicycles over other means of transport |
| art and culture | 7/371 | 12/563 | groups of people sharing the same interest about art and culture and organizing free-entrance artistic and cultural events and workshops |
| city care | 32/371 | 50/563 | groups of people taking action to make the city they live in more clean and beautiful |
| nature care | 4/371 | 11/563 | groups of people taking action to keep nature (parks, forests, beaches and other sites) clean |
| miscellaneous | 15/371 | 21/563 | self-organized social solidarity initiatives whose thematic scope does not fit in the categories above |
| homeless reception | -- | 10/563 | Facilities for the Homeless (sleep, personal care, etc.) |
| Job finding | -- | 9/563 | Services to help the unemployed to find a job |

In 2016, the highest rates continue to occur in essentials such as food and medicine, but we observe that lessons have increased, a fact directly linked to Greek education, where students need help, especially before the exams for the university. Interestingly, there are two new categories that have been added and have to do directly with the Greek society: Reception for the homeless, which shows how much the number of the homeless has increased, especially in urban centers and, job centers, which is entirely justified by the high rates of unemployment all over Greece. Chart 1 shows the comparison between 2014 and 2016:

The second mapping has to do with the geographical area of activity of each initiative. A great part (approx. 1 out of 3) of the SoSS initiatives currently listed are active in the Attica region, both in 2014 and in 2016. Athens, as the capital of Greece and the most populated urban center in the country, is the single city gathering most SoSS initiatives. Many of these are initiatives with national scope (approx. 10%).

*Figure 4. Comparison of 2014 and 2016 populations of SoSS initiatives, broken down by thematic scope*

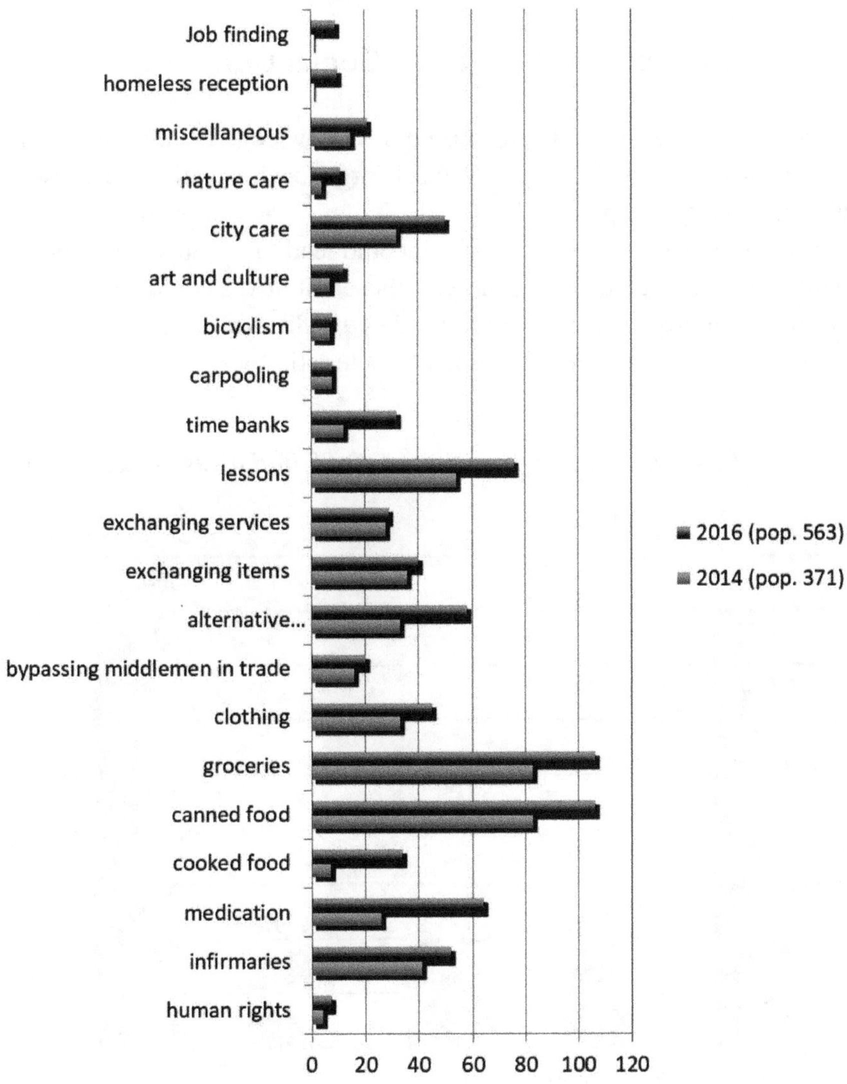

In 2014, in a total of 371 initiatives, the overall geographical distribution of the initiatives includes categories about Salonica, the capital of Northern Greece (30 initiatives), Thrace, Macedonia and Epirus regions in Northern Greece (10, 29 and 8 initiatives, respectively), Thessaly, Sterea Ellada and Peloponnese regions in Central Greece (19, 21 and 37 initiatives, respectively), Aegean islands in Eastern Greece (23 initiatives), Ionian islands in Western Greece (11 initiatives), Crete island in Southern Greece (33 initiatives).

In 2016, in a total of 563 initiatives, the corresponding numbers are: Attica 208 initiatives, Salonica 45 initiatives, Thrace 10 initiatives, Macedonia 41 initiatives, Epirus 16 initiatives, Thessaly 27 initiatives, Sterea Ellada 30 initiatives, Peloponnese 51 initiatives, Aegean Islands 32 initiatives, Ionian Islands 16 initiatives, Crete 49 initiatives and with national scope 40 initiatives.

Most initiatives are based in smaller or larger urban centers, but many initiatives seem to work better in small communities/neighborhoods, where people know each other and can meet offline.

Many of these SoSS initiatives are very active and have a great number of engaged members. However, some of them seem becoming inactive after their initial breakthrough faded out. Most of the initiatives have some sort of online presence through a website or social media accounts.

## Attempting to Classify SoSS Initiatives as Social Constructs

The effort to define the term self-organization combines knowledge from various disciplines, because the term itself is complex. A classification for the self-organized initiatives discussed above would be extremely useful theoretically and practically. Firstly, it could gather the characteristics of these initiatives with the greatest possible completeness, which could lead to a comparison between the initiatives under study and other social constructs. Secondly, if these initiatives could be classified based on their characteristics, it might be possible to predict how they might evolve, drawing conclusions from the evolution of other social constructs with the same characteristics.

*Figure 5. Comparison of 2014 and 2016 populations of SoSS initiatives, broken down by geographical distribution*

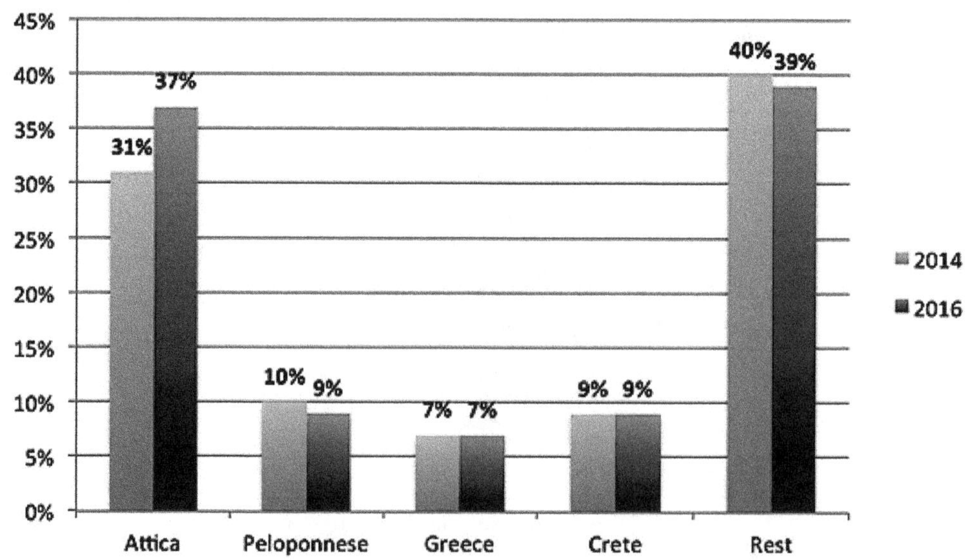

These self-organized initiatives are largely exhibiting characteristics of their own, as well as features influenced by the environment in which they were created and enacted and by the actions and the relationships formed between their members. All these, in combination, lead to a complex definition. This definition could blend elements from sociology, organizational theory, social economy and even management.

It is almost impossible for a single closed-form definition to be created for all the initiatives that have been included in the Organosi 2.0 website. Depending on the purpose of each such initiative, respective characteristics may differ significantly. In many cases, the definitions may be completely different from one to the other, so there is no use in giving a completely closed formal definition without flexibility. The objective is more to formulate some sort of open-ended umbrella definition, broad enough to include many possible features and cover many initiatives.

## Civil Society Organizations

Sociology offers many definitions and descriptions of social constructs that might coincide with or even subsume citizens' self-organized initiatives. According to the literature, the terms more related to the phenomenon of self-organization seem to be those of civil society, community, social movements, social enterprises and solidaristic forms of production and services, groups and organizations. While they may not have all the characteristics required, self-organized initiatives, depending on their nature, more or less relate to at least one of these constructs.

Exploring the concept of civil society in Makridimitris (2006), it can be seen that the state is quite the opposite of civil society. The state is criticized as dysfunctional, making everything difficult for its citizens rather than assisting and protecting them. Civil Society, on the other hand, is an arena of collective action around common interests, purposes and values. Its relationship with the state and the market is dynamic, changing over time and in different contexts (Henderson & Vercseg, 2010, p. 16). Civil Society includes, among others, people's organizations, cooperatives, human rights groups, neighborhood or community coalitions as well as grass-roots movements. CSOs (Civil Society Organizations) express the interests of people. They are organized by citizens that are united by common needs, interests and values and are mobilized into many types of activities (Makridimitris 2006).

## Communities

Social organization and the sharing of values are two basic characteristics of community as cited in Castells (2002) among other aspects, such as mutual interests and common needs. Castells refers to communities as networks of interpersonal ties that provide socialization, support, information, a sense of belonging and social identity. A community has to fulfill five functions in order to exist (Henderson & Vercseg, 2010, p. 20):

1. **Socialization:** The community implants certain values into its members
2. **Economic Wealth:** The community ensures the livelihoods of its members
3. **Social Participation:** Fulfilling the general need for socialization
4. **Social Control:** Demands that members should observe certain community values
5. **Mutual Support:** Community members carry out tasks that are too big or too urgent to be handled by an individual alone.

## Social Movements

Another very common definition used is that of social movements. By referring to social movements, a collective effort is meant to promote a common interest or a common goal realization outside the sphere of established institutions. The dividing line between a social movement and a formal organization is not always clear because when the movements become permanent they obtain bureaucratic characteristics. There are movements of transformation, reform, redemption and alteration (Giddens, 2002). Most social movements are defensive rather than offensive and tend to be temporary. Despite this fact, they can be very important actors during social transformation (Frank & Fuentes, 1987).

## Groups

One definition which seems theoretically close to self-organized initiatives is that of groups. A group can be meant as a formation of two or more people who are associated with a relatively fixed shape of social interaction and have a common sense of unity. "*It is a collection of individuals who are engaged in a specific type of mutually oriented activity (or set of interconnected activities), entry to which occurs according to one or more criteria of membership*" (Verdon, 1981 in Hechter, 1988, p. 16). A group of people is not the same as a mass or a category or a corporation of people. But the common experiences of people who fall under the same categories and the same social position may be the basis for the creation of social movements or political action (Hughes & Kroehler, 2007).

The above four terms (civil society, community, social movement and group) share several common characteristics and, in some cases, complement each other.

## Organizations

One more term, which seems to be a possible fit for self-organized initiatives, is that of organization. In many cases, the term refers to a formal, perhaps bureaucratic, organization, which does not fit with the initiatives of citizens that are under study here. In Hughes & Kroehler (2007), formal organizations are considered as groups which have been created ad hoc to achieve specific goals. Formal organizations are divided into voluntary organizations, coercive and utilitarian. In Giddens (2002), an organization is a large group of people, structured in an impersonal way and pursuing specific purposes.

## Social Economy

In recent years, a so-called Third Sector has been developed, the other two being the Public and Private Sectors. This Third Sector includes, among others, civil initiatives to meet needs for goods and services that cannot be offered by public or private entities (Klimi-Kaminari & Papageorgiou, 2010). Within this Third Sector operates the so-called Social Economy, which is made up of social enterprises and organizations. It is a sector that lays the emphasis on people rather than money, and on satisfying social needs rather than profit needs (Julia & Chaves, 2012).

Social Economy is a term that appeared in the literature around 1830. The most recent definition of its features emerged in 2002, within the Social Economy Charter. According to this Charter, a Social Economy formation (mostly a Social Enterprise) follows 7 principles (Chaves & Monzón, 2012, p. 8):

1. The primacy of the individual and the social objective over capital
2. Voluntary and open membership
3. Democratic control by the membership
4. The combination of the interests of members/users and/or the general interest
5. The defense and application of the principle of solidarity and responsibility
6. Autonomous management and independence from public authorities
7. The essential surplus is used to carry out sustainable development objectives, services of interest to members or of general interest.

Social enterprises (Klimi-Kaminari & Papageorgiou, 2010) have the following characteristics:

1. Absence of profit incentives
2. Free participation
3. Democratic administration
4. Independence from government.

## Solidarity Economy

Solidarity is an essential component of all of the constructs briefly discussed above. According to the literature, there are four forms of solidarity: (a) attraction, which is the primary ties of affection between people; (b) loyalty, when a group member cares about the unity of the group; (c) identification, the feeling of belonging to the group; and (d) association, which transcends established group identities and distinctions (Komter, 2005, p. 115).

The term Solidarity Economy refers to heterogeneous forms of grassroots activities that allow for the participation of formerly oppressed social actors (Primavera, 2010). Solidarity Economy is a movement of movements, as Miller says (2010). It is an open process, an invitation. It is not a finished model of economic organization but rather an ongoing process of economic organizing, an active process of collective vision (Miller, 2010, p. 3). All the initiatives within a solidarity economy have four characteristics (Dacheux & Goujon, 2011, p. 206):

1. Productive activity is linked to social needs rather than profit
2. The producing of the goods and services is based on the participation of people (men and women)
3. Social networks are built (locally, nationally and internationally) and based on consensus and cooperation
4. Initiatives work for the democratic regulation of economic activity.

In conclusion, the name proposed for these initiatives is Self-Organized Social Solidarity Initiatives (SoSS initiatives) as it brings together their key features: they are self-organized by citizens for the citizens and for the society and their aim is solidarity (Staiou and Gouscos, 2014). Particular importance should be given to the part of self-organization, as the structure of these initiatives is such that the effects of their actions influence and reshape their structure (Fuchs, 2003).

Many of the features we encounter in the abovementioned categories are repeated and link not only to the initiatives being studied but also in between categories. We notice that some terms such as volunteering or the social and solidarity economy or non-profit organizations or the third sector are "umbrella terms" that include many of the other terms.

The initiatives that have been studied have some characteristics of all the social structures mentioned, but none of them fully coincide.

The characteristics of the initiatives are that they begin from citizens, are linked to common interests, values and needs, and want to offer support, solidarity and generally achieve common goals. The members interact, socialize and feel mutual trust. They are independent from the state, apart from official institutions, they are self-governing, and decisions are made through democratic processes. In some of them, horizontal direct democracy operates with assemblies making decisions. They do not have profits and the problems they want to solve are gaps left by the state. Participation is free and voluntary and there is no pay in the sense of work-salary (Staiou, 2017).

An important difference between the SoSS initiatives and other similar initiatives in the Third Sector or the Solidarity Economy, is that they are not formal, legal entities. Some become formal along the way to managing revenue and expenses, but most do not want to be formal. This feature automatically separates them from NGOs. In addition, SoSSs initiatives do not manage money to make a profit. They offer services but do not exchange money in the sense that they sell items or services. This separates them from Social Enterprises, which, although they do not have profits that go to the owners, they sell their services, and the resulting surplus is invested again in the enterprise (Staiou, 2017).

However, one might argue that SoSSs are merely voluntary organizations. The commonality with voluntary organizations is that all people involved in SoSS initiatives are not rewarded with money for the service they offer and are there because they want it themselves and are not forced by someone else. However, while volunteer organizations do not have a profit from their participation, the participant in SoSS initiatives may use the same service offered to someone else in the same context. He who helps some of his fellow humans can at the same time receive help under the same terms. This does not exist in volunteerism. In SoSS Initiatives, participants have the same needs and problems, so they self-organize in their effort to overcome them with the help of the other, so both sides have a profit (not in the sense of money) (Staiou, 2017).

## A SURVEY ON SoSS INITIATIVES IN GREECE

### Purpose of the Survey and Research Questions

Following the mapping of self-organized social solidarity initiatives in Greece on the Organosi 2.0 website, it has been possible to launch a survey on their operational features and, more specifically, on their preferred media mix for communication. The main purpose of this survey has been to investigate whether the SoSS initiatives in question use at a significant extent the Internet and social media to communicate with people. To this end, the listing process of these initiatives on the Organosi 2.0 platform includes documenting their coordinates on any media (digital and traditional) which can be used for contacting them. On the basis of this information, a questionnaire-based survey has tried to look deeper into the patterns in which SoSS initiatives actually use these media in practice.

In 2014, the three following research questions have been formulated:

**[RQ1]:** *In which way, to which ends, and to what extent, do the self-organized social solidarity initiatives under study use online media and exploit their capabilities?*

**[RQ2]:** *Can online media effectively compare to traditional media and face-to-face contact as preferred modes of communication for self-organized social solidarity initiatives?*

**[RQ3]:** *Is there an eventual positive impact of the use of online social media and social networks on the development of self-organized social solidarity initiatives?*

Below, we'll compare the results with the ones from the 2016 data collection.

## Population of the Survey

The survey population originated from the SoSS initiatives already included on the Organosi 2.0 website.

For the first research question, in 2014, all 371 initiatives currently listed on the Organosi 2.0 platform were addressed. In 2016, the number increased to 563 initiatives.

For the second and third research questions, only the initiatives claiming to use the internet in some form (email, web, social media) were addressed (157 initiatives, approx. 40% of the entire population). In the 2016 data collection, this number increased to 291 initiatives, approx. 52% of a population of 563.

A set of 57 initiatives (approx. 15% of the population) have responded to the survey till March 2013. By the end of the survey we had a total of 90 complete questionnaires, approx. 16% of the population.

## Data Collection Processes and Tools

The collection of qualitative data for the first research question (RQ1 – use of online media) was made via desktop online research. It was investigated whether these initiatives maintained websites/webpages and profiles on social media (Staiou and Gouscos 2014).

For the second and third research question (RQ2 – effective use of online vs. traditional media, RQ3 – eventual positive impact of using online media) the data obtained was both quantitative and qualitative and resulted from sending out and collecting a short questionnaire with 3 questions addressed to the participant initiatives:

- What are your main ways of approaching people that may be interested in discovering your work and participating in your activity?
- As soon as someone claims to be interested in your work, what are the main ways in which your contact is maintained?
- By what criteria do you judge the success of your communication activities? What do you need to achieve in order to believe that you communicate well?

# FINDINGS

## Findings on the First Research Question

**[RQ1]:** *In which way, to which ends, and to what extent, do the self-organized social solidarity initiatives under study use online media and exploit their capabilities?*

Driven by the data obtained with respect to the first research question, it has been possible to identify four different categories of SoSS initiatives regarding the media mix they use for communication: Web 0.0, Web1.0, Web2.0 and Web1.0-Web 2.0. The Web 0.0 category includes initiatives that do not use the Internet at all; they work offline, whereas they have some online references from third parties, mostly in the form of information releases, without however engaging in online activities themselves. The Web1.0 category includes initiatives using websites, without simultaneous use of social media. The Web2.0 category, on the other hand, includes initiatives following an inverse media mix, i.e. initiatives using social media, without simultaneous use of a website. Finally, initiatives classified in the Web1.0-Web2.0 category make use of websites and social media at the same time.

In 2014, most of the initiatives of the survey population (176 out of 371 initiatives, approx. 50%) fall in the first category (Web 0.0) as to their communication media mix. They do not have online presence and they rely on offline communication and third-party references in order to become known to the public and to the people who may need their services. The second biggest percentage is that of Web 1.0-Web 2.0 initiatives (83/371 initiatives, 22%). A higher percentage for this category would have been expected on the intuitive premise that, from the moment that such an initiative uses the Internet, it could equally well use social media as well. Despite this fact, there is an almost equal number of initiatives which continue to use only a website (81/371 initiatives, 22% of the population), falling in the Web 1.0 category. Last but not least, there is a small portion of initiatives (31 out of 371 initiatives, something less than 10%) which use exclusively social media. In many cases, these are initiatives that do not just communicate, but have been formed through, online social networks like Facebook or other social media platforms like wikis.

In 2016 these percentages remained almost the same, always in line with the larger sample of the survey. In the first category, Web 0.0, we have 272/563 initiatives, 48% of the population. In the category Web 1.0 we have 105 initiatives (19%), in the category Web 2.0 60 initiatives (11%) and in the category Web 1.0-2.0 126 initiatives (22%). One can easily observe that the percentages do not change much, even in a larger population, which proves that the original results were in the right track. The majority of the initiatives still prefer offline communication, building on networks of trust and interpersonal contact.

A second point which is equally interesting has to do with the individual media that are used for communication, with some statistics that can help highlight the media that SoSS initiatives prefer, possibly because of their ease of use.

The numbers in 2014 were quite interesting. Despite the use of new media, 242/371 initiatives (approx. 65%) also prefer a more conventional way of communication like the telephone and face-to-face contact (via a postal address which can be detected easily and allow people to pay visits and meet in person). Second on this list comes the web (167/371, approx. 45%), followed by the email (144/371, approx. 40%). Among the three popular social networks, Facebook, Twitter and You Tube, the most popular by far is Facebook (111/371 initiatives using it, 30% of the survey population), probably because it combines many facilities like messaging, photos, documents etc. Twitter is far behind (41/371 initiatives, approx. 10%) and You Tube has a marginal share, with only 15 initiatives (less than 5% of the survey population) using it.

In 2016, the percentages are almost the same. 385 initiatives (out of 563, 68%) use a phone number and postal address. 231 initiatives (41%) have a website, 211 (37%) have an email address, 183 (33%) use Facebook, 53 (9%) use Twitter and only 23 initiatives (4%) use YouTube. The evidence continues to show that, despite the use of the internet and social media, the most "conventional" media, such as telephone

*Figure 6. Comparison of the media mix used by SoSS initiatives, 2014 and 2016*

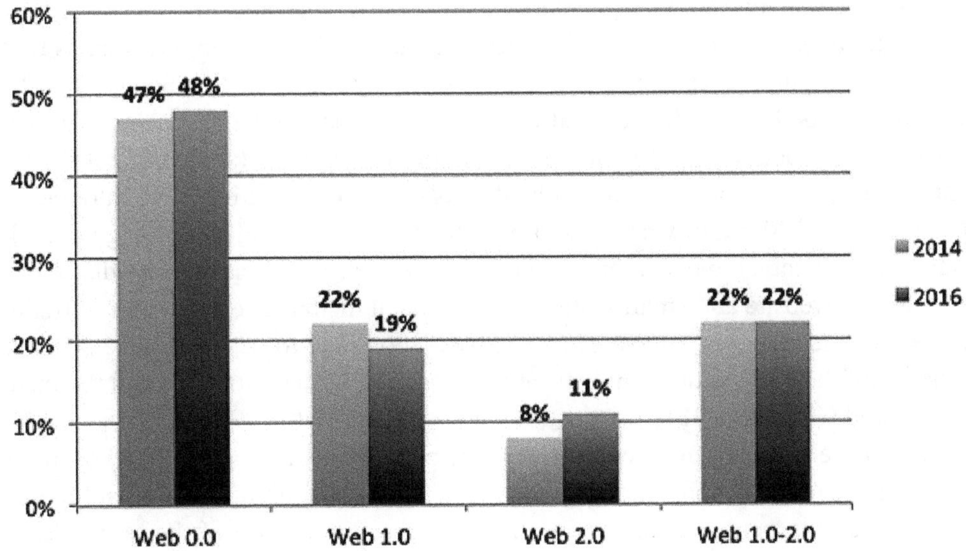


*Figure 7. Comparison of the media used by SoSS initiatives, for 2014 and 2016*

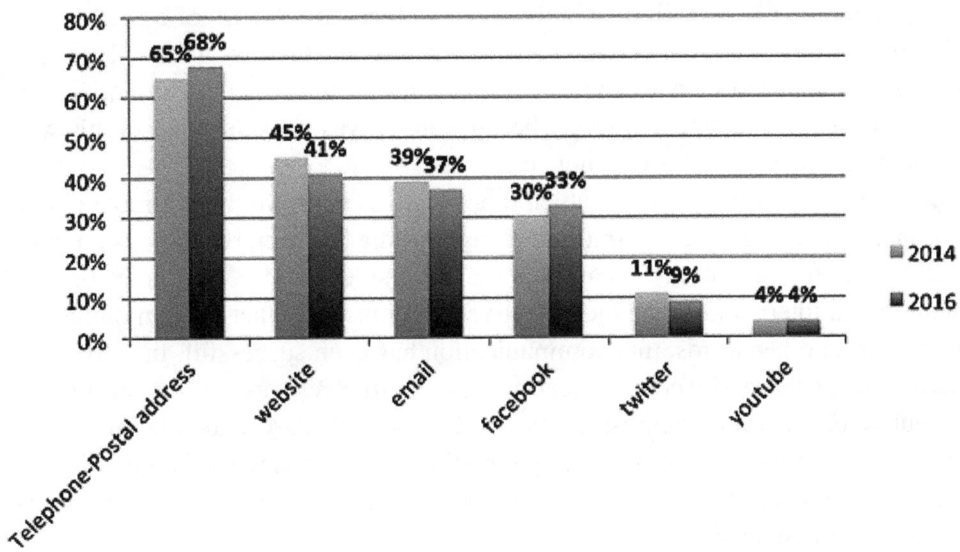


and email, win the confidence of the initiatives. This, to a great extent, also has to do with the small societies in which the initiatives under study are active, where interpersonal contact has a dominant role.

## Findings on the Second Research Question

**[RQ2]:** *Can online media effectively compare to traditional media and face-to-face contact as preferred modes of communication for self-organized social solidarity initiatitves?*

In 2014, all of the 57 SoSS initiatives that responded to the questionnaire of the survey use the Internet and social media to communicate with people, to get in contact and inform about their actions for the first time, and/or to maintain contact and follow-up from face-to-face meetings. As far as first contact is concerned, out of the 57 initiatives that responded to the survey questionnaire, no less than 24 initiatives (some 40% of the respondents) indicated that they use traditional media to reach out to people and to inform them about their actions. On top of that, a total of 36 initiatives (some 60% of the respondents) reported that they rely on personal contact with citizens prior to integrating them into the community.

In 2016, in a total of 90 questionnaires and initiatives, these percentages change slightly. 21% say they use interpersonal contact to reach their audience, 31% use traditional mass media, 20% use simple internet tools such as website and email while 28% use social media. The high rates of traditional mass media, such as local newspapers or posters and banners, continue to be impressive. This is to further strengthen the belief that the relationship between the location of the initiatives and the media they use is strong (Staiou and Gouscos, 2014).

In the second phase of maintaining contact with the public, only 5 (approx. 10%) of these initiatives claimed to continue to use traditional media. In contrast, the number of initiatives that report to continue giving importance to interpersonal contact increases to 38 (approx. 67% of the respondents, i.e. 2 out of the 3 initiatives that have responded). In the second phase of the survey these percentages change. Only 5% now use traditional mass media, while interpersonal contact rates are rising, reaching close to 36%. Simple online tools have high rates as well, 35%, while the percentage of social media remains at the same level, at about 26%. Key figures in these percentages are the use of e-mail, a tool they use at a rate of 26%, but also meetings between members of initiatives, that reach 12%. These data influence the final percentages and also show to a great extent the logic with which the initiatives use the media. Interpersonal contact is a predominant target because initiatives consider that, in this way, the much-needed trust between their members is being cultivated.

Finally, concerning the criteria along which the initiatives perceive the desirable outcomes of their communication activities, coverage by traditional mass media has been reported as an indicator of successful communication policy in just 1 case. On the other side, 36 (60%) of the respondent initiatives believe that sustained interpersonal contact effectively demonstrates that the communication effort has not been wasted or, in other words, that communication has been successful. In 2016, one of the most important indicators of successful communication for the initiatives was the large participation of members and the public in general in their assemblies and in the calls they made for various actions (60%). Important for the initiatives was also whether the public understands what the initiative is doing, what its purpose is (17%). It is interesting that only 10% consider successful communication the solution the problem of action/communication.

## Findings on the Third Research Question

**[RQ3]:** *Is there an eventual positive impact of the use of online social media and social networks on the development of self-organized social solidarity initiatives?*

The quantitative data on the use of internet and online media by the initiatives (in both 2014 and 2016) allow to claim that these media can at least be expected to:

1. Eliminate communication costs, as well as space and time barriers (esp. in the case of asynchronous online communication, based on message sending/posting), and
2. Make it easier to get in touch with the people who are the driving power of each community.

In this sense, online media can be expected to eliminate traditional communication barriers, and thus facilitate the communication processes of SoSS initiatives and also eliminate corresponding cost, space and time barriers to their operation and potential development.

However, it has not been possible to identify findings as to whether this elimination of development barriers actually results in more and/or faster development, by attracting more participants, engaging in more activities and the like. This is an important question which calls for further research and it has to do with the way in which the initiatives themselves are organized and what their goals are.

## ANALYSIS AND INTERPRETATION OF THE FINDINGS

### Effect of Thematic Scope on the Use of Online Media

A more detailed analysis of the findings presented above shows that they have to do to a large extent with the thematic scope of the SoSS initiatives under consideration. Regarding the first research question, almost all categories are shown to have a web presence except for infirmaries, medication, canned food and groceries. The latter categories exhibit a zero web presence and all of their contact information comes from third references. This can be assumed to follow from the fact that these services correspond to "hard" everyday needs pertinent to health and practical survival, which are mostly felt by people of lower socio-economic status and higher ages, i.e. by population groups traditionally under-represented in online access. A second explanation for this could be the fact that these needs are at the same time much more personal and thus difficult to express openly, which also relates to the mode of operation of many such initiatives; many groceries, for instance, serve their beneficiaries in a completely anonymous way, requiring no personal data for registration of beneficiaries and the like, exactly in order not to exclude any people in need who would restrain, for social reasons, from revealing their identity.

It is important to note here that the vast majority of these initiatives are supported by the municipalities concerned. This means that a great deal of the communication is through the official communication channels of the municipalities themselves. To a large extent, the use of social media is not considered necessary as the beneficiaries are informed through the structures of the municipalities.

### Persistent Need for Using Local Media and Interpersonal Contact

Most of the SoSS initiatives who have responded to the survey report using new online media (Internet, social media) side-by-side with local traditional media (e.g. local newspapers, and the like) to inform citizens about what they do. Coverage by local media becomes even more important, in fact, for initiatives operating in small towns or neighborhoods.

Apart from that, a sizable proportion of the respondent initiatives are using open presentations for their actions to become known to the community or even open meetings where everyone is invited to attend.

Follow-up of initial communication is made through the Internet, using email and social media, but at the same time the role of sustained interpersonal contact becomes more important. Many of the initiatives report that they maintain contact with their members via telephone, through group meetings, as well as through participation in the various voluntary activities organized. In fact, although in most cases, the respondent initiatives are using the Internet and some of the opportunities of online media, in the end they always prefer face-to-face communication and interaction. Website traffic statistics are not considered to play such an important role as they cannot reflect, in the respondents' opinion, real participation. The latter tend to believe that a community strengthens further when members meet and exchange opinions and ideas in person.

This persistent need for the use of local media and interpersonal contact can be explained, in our view, from a number of reasons. Firstly, concerning local traditional media, it can be assumed to follow from the fact that, in contexts where local public spaces already exist, initiatives and stories absent from these local spaces find it inevitably hard to connect with the local community; this entails the need for all such initiatives, including the SoSS initiatives under study, to also communicate themselves through local media, not only to reach the local audience, but also in order to effectively tap on the local sense of identity and belonging.

The need for sustained interpersonal contact, on the other hand, can be assumed to follow both from practical and from psychological reasons. Practical reasons include the need for active members to collaborate on issues that are too unstructured/contradictory to be effectively discussed online, as well as the need for active members to physically participate and collaborate in the context of offline activities. Psychological reasons, on the other side, may have to do with the fact that people change, their priorities change, and subsequently trust and commitment are difficult to be taken for granted on the long term. Indeed, the trust- and commitment-building required for active participation in such initiatives is never a finished result, but rather an ongoing process which needs to be continually renewed.

## Common and Varying Perceptions for "Good" Communication

The responses collected through the survey as to how "good" communication is perceived and assessed were, beyond some common points, varied depending on the thematic scope of the respondent initiatives.

At a first, but somewhat superficial level, most initiatives tend to assess quality of their communication activity by looking at the visitors' statistics, the number of members or the number of ads displayed on their websites.

At a second, more thoughtful level, what seems to worry respondent initiatives is the real participation of people in their actions, as well as participation in their physical meetings on a more regular basis. This seems to be an important criterion used to determine whether communication is successful. This criterion, in our view, may be assumed to play a more crucial role for initiatives whose thematic scope is more demanding in terms of physical presence and offering of tangible goods (e.g. infirmaries, groceries).

Another criterion cited for good communication is to receive criticism, new ideas and suggestions on the actions of the initiative, showing that participants are effectively dealing with what the initiative does with a commitment that gets them in the process of thinking how this initiative could go further. This criterion, in our view, may be assumed to play an important role particularly for initiatives whose thematic scope is more open-ended, offering itself to new ideas and possibilities for action (e.g. city care initiatives).

Last but not least, one more criterion cited as important by initiatives such as those operating exchange communities or alternative currencies is that people successfully understand the philosophy of what these initiatives actually do. This dimension of effective communication can be assumed to play an important role in SoSS initiatives whose thematic scope contradicts some fundamental principles of traditional socio-economic organization, as for instance the concept of the price (as opposed to the value) of goods, and money-based exchanges.

As a general point following from the above, all respondent SoSS initiatives seem to consider communication as an integral part of their core effort. As a result, their objectives and criteria for what constitutes good communication are no less than the top-level objectives and criteria they set for their overall success.

These are conclusions that are confirmed by both phases of the survey in 2014 and 2016, even more in a larger sample of research.

## THE EVOLUTION OF SoSS INITIATIVES

Over the years, the update of the Organosi 2.0 continued normally, even after the official end of the research. In July 2017, all the initiatives that had been included so far on the website were re-examined to see how many are still active and to have a clue, albeit faint, for their development.

It should be noted that this audited population is not exactly the same as the 563 initiatives that constituted the initial population, but it can give us an idea of how these initiatives have evolved over the years.

The first data from July 2017 show that only 54% of the initiatives remain active. In an initial analysis of the data, we see that initiatives that continue to operate, and constantly added new ones, are those that have to do with the main needs of everyday life (canned food, cooked food, medicine, doctors, lessons). However, the initiatives that the overwhelming majority of them have stopped operating are those that had proposed a different, alternative way of living and everyday life, such as alternative currencies, items and service exchanges, time banks and carpooling.

A first reading of these results may indicate two things: On the one hand, the burden has fallen to the day-to-day needs of citizens, which is perfectly reasonable in the context of the economic crisis that Greece is still experiencing. On the other hand, perhaps this alternative way of thinking and everyday life has not convinced the ordinary citizens and has failed to function in Greek reality.

Another important factor that should be taken into account, in further study of these data, is that many of the initiatives that continue to exist have taken a more formal, legal form. Self-organizations have been forced to become Non-Governmental Organizations or Social Enterprises in order to be able to manage any revenue or expenses.

Also, initiatives that have been helped (either by human resources or premises) by official bodies, such as local municipalities, are still active. Initiatives supported by municipalities continue to be set up and run, well organized and continuously meeting the needs of their citizens.

Organizations that rely only or mainly on self-organization seemed to be unable to respond to reality. There are some that are still active, but they are few and, in some cases, they have changed their thematic reference, doing other things than the ones they did in the first years of their operation. An important factor that may have played a role in their evolution is that they depend on volunteers whose presence is not permanent. Also, the role of self-organizing and decision-making (many of these self-organizations used assemblies for their decisions) may also have played a role. In some initiatives it worked but in others it seemed to create problems and delays.

These elements should be extensively analyzed in the future in order to produce much more concrete results and there may also be a link to the communication habits of the initiatives.

## CONCLUDING REMARKS

As discussed in the above, the Internet and social media are used by a large percentage of self-organized social solidarity initiatives all over Greece. Most of these initiatives use online media for communicating their activities, without the explicit objective to create communities. This is mostly left at the level of interpersonal contacts which, despite their restrictions in terms of time and space, are still considered as a necessary means for community- and commitment-building.

Eventually it appears that, to a large extent, social media are currently being used by SoSS initiatives in Greece in ways similar to traditional media, i.e. for one-way information provision, building on their usability and user base. This practice of not exploiting more capabilities online, such as for instance the opportunity for creating communities through online social networks, inevitably leaves some potential untapped.

Last but not least, notwithstanding any other factors, some of the SoSS initiatives of the survey population are currently undergoing transformations at the institutional level. Some initiatives like social groceries are currently passing from the hands of self-organized groups to those of municipalities and local administration. Still others, especially certain ones that have successfully responded to pressing problems, transform into Non-Governmental Organizations, in an effort to better manage their income and expenses.

There are a number of directions for further research based on the work reported in this article. Such a direction is definitely the analysis of the results from July 2017. How is this course of these initiatives justified and how can it be linked to the media they use? It would also be interesting to study the new forms of initiatives that are emerging in Greece, such as work collectives and social enterprises, and to record the differences that exist in relation to the self-organized initiatives that have been studied so far.

## REFERENCES

Bang, H. (2010). Between everyday makers and expert citizens. In Public Management in the Postmodern Era: Challenges and Prospects (pp. 163-192). Cheltenham, UK: Edward Elgar Publishing.

Boeder, P. (2002, July). Non-Profits on E: How non-profit organizations are using the internet for communication, fundraising, and community building. *First Monday*, *7*(7). doi:10.5210/fm.v7i7.969

Castells, M. (2002). *The Internet Galaxy. Reflections on the Internet, Business and Society*. Oxford, UK: Oxford University Press. doi:10.1093/acprof:oso/9780199255771.001.0001

Chaves, R., & Monzòn, J. L. (2012). Beyond the crisis: The social economy, prop of a new model of sustainable economic development. *Service Business*, *6*(1), 5–26. doi:10.100711628-011-0125-7

Dacheux, E., & Goujon, D. (2011). The solidarity economy: An alternative development strategy? *International Social Science Journal*, *62*(203-204), 205–215. doi:10.1111/j.1468-2451.2011.01804.x

Frank, A. G., & Fuentes, M. (1987). Nine Theses on Social Movements. *Economic and Political Weekly*, *22*(35), 1503-1507+1509-1510. Available online at: http://www.jstor.org/stable/4377447

Fuchs, C. (2003). Structuration Theory and Self-organization. *Systemic Practice and Action Research*, *16*(2), 133–167. doi:10.1023/A:1022889627100

Giddens, A. (2002). *Sociology*. Athens: Gutenberg. (in Greek)

Hechter, M. (1988). *Principles of Group Solidarity*. University of California Press.

Henderson, P., & Vercseg, I. (2010). *Community Development and Civil Society. Making Connections in the European context*. Bristol, UK: Polity Press.

Hughes, M., & Kroehler, C. J. (2007). *Sociology. The basic concepts*. Athens: Kritiki. (in Greek)

James, J. (2013a). *8 tips for effectively using social media for social change*. Available online at: http://www.impatientoptimists.org/Posts/2013/03/8-Simple-Strategies-to-Effectively-Use-Social-Media-for-Social-Change

James, J. (2013b). *5 experts share top social media advice for Nonprofits*. Available online at: http://www.impatientoptimists.org/Posts/2013/04/Experts-Share-Top-Social-Media-Advice-for-Nonprofits

Johnson Center. (2012). *Nonprofit Organizations and social media*. Available online at: https://www.mnaonline.org/CMDocs/MNA/Research/Nonprofit%20Organizations%20and%20Social%20Media,%20Feb%202012.pdf

Julià, J. F., & Chaves, R. (2012). Introduction: Social economy, a third sector in a plural people-oriented economy. *Service Business*, *6*(1), 1–4. doi:10.100711628-011-0130-x

Klemz, J., Simon, G., & Kumar, A. (2003). *IS planning in Non-Profit organizations: an exploratory study*. Available online at: http://iacis.org/iis/2003/KlemzSimonKumar.pdf

Klimi-Kaminari, O., & Papageorgiou, K. L. (2010). *Social economy. A first approach*. Athens: Ellinoekdotiki. (in Greek)

Komter, A. (2005). *Social Solidarity and the Gift*. Cambridge, UK: Cambridge University Press.

Makridimitris, A. (2006). *State and Civil Society*. Athens: Metamesonikties Ekdoseis. (in Greek)

Mansfield, H. (2014). *12 steps to launching a social media strategy for your NGO*. Webinar Notes, 22/07/2014.

May, C. (2002). *The Information Society. A sceptical view*. Blackwell Publishing.

Merkel, C., Farooq, U., Xiao, L., Ganoe, C., Rosson, M. B., & Carrol, J. M. (2007). Managing technology use and learning in nonprofit community organizations: Methodological challenges and opportunities. *CHIMIT 2007*.

Miller, E. (2010). Solidarity Economy: Key Concepts and Issues. In E. Kawano & ... (Eds.), *Solidarity Economy I: Building Alternatives for People and Planet*. Amherst, MA: Center for Popular Economics. Available online at http://www.communityeconomies.org/site/assets/media/Ethan_Miller/Miller_Solidarity_Economy_Key_Issues_2010.pdf

Next Principles. (2012). *Media tips for Non Profit Organizations.* Available online at: https://nextprinciples.com/social-media-tips-for-non-profit-organizations/

Non Profit Marketing Guide. (2015). *2015 Nonprofit Communications Trends Report.* Available online at: http://www.nonprofitmarketingguide.com/freemembers/2015NonprofitCommunicationsTrends.pdf

Nonprofit Tech for Good. (2014a). *How much time mobile and social media require*. Available online at: http://www.nptechforgood.com/2014/05/18/how-much-time-mobile-and-social-media-require/

Nonprofit Tech for Good. (2014b). *10 Must-Have skills for Nonprofit New Media Managers*. Available online at: http://www.nptechforgood.com/2014/07/14/10-must-have-skills-for-nonprofit-new-media-managers/

Ogden, T. N., & Starita, L. (2009). *Social Networking and Mid-Size Non-Profits: What's the Use?* Available online at: http://philanthropyaction.com/documents/Social_Networks_and_Mid-Size_Non-Profits.pdf

Pitman, M. A. (2013). *21 social media tips for Nonprofits from top experts*. Available online at: http://fundraisingcoach.com/2013/05/06/21-social-media-tips-for-nonprofits-from-top-experts/

Primavera, H. (2010). Social currencies and solidarity economy: An enduring bond of common good. *Working USA*, *13*(1), 41–59. doi:10.1111/j.1743-4580.2010.00272.x

Rahman, M. A., Raihan, A., & Nakka, R. (2014, October-December). Emerging Information Technology and Knowledge Management Capacity for Nonprofit Organizations. *International Journal of Public Administration in the Digital Age*, *1*(4), 52–69. doi:10.4018/ijpada.2014100104

Regan, T. T. J. (2011). *Social media as a branding tool for non-profit organisations*. BA in marketing & management communications, Aarhus School of Business, May 2011. Available online at: http://pure.au.dk/portal/files/38823160/36294202.pdf

Saeed, S., Rohde, M., & Wulf, V. (2008). A framework towards IT appropriation in voluntary organizations. *International Journal of Knowledge and Learning*, *4*(5), 438–451. doi:10.1504/IJKL.2008.022062

Soon, C. (2013). Net technologies, net gain: An institutional and micro-structural approach to understanding technology use for collective action. CeDEM13.Conference for E-Democracy and Open Government, 229-240.

Sotiropoulos, A. D., & Karamagioli, E. (2005). *Greek Civil Society: The Long road to maturity*. Oxford, UK: Oxford University Press. Available online at http://www.civicus.org/new/media/CSI_Greece_Executive_Summary.pdf

Spencer, T. (2002, August). The potential of the internet for Non-Profit organizations. *First Monday*, *7*(8). doi:10.5210/fm.v7i8.976

Staiou, E. R. (2017). *From electronic governance and the participatory web to self-organised social solidarity initiatives and their digital communication policy: the Greek case* (Doctoral Thesis). Available online in Greek: https://www.didaktorika.gr/eadd/handle/10442/40314?locale=en)

Staiou, E. R., & Gouscos, D. (2014, October-December). Self-organized social solidarity (SoSS) initiatives in Greece: Exploring their scope and their relationship to online media. *International Journal of Public Administration in the Digital Age*, *1*(4), 21–43. doi:10.4018/ijpada.2014100102

Suart, J. C. (2012). *A guide to the changes sweeping non-profit marketing and communications.* Available online at: http://volunteeralberta.ab.ca/varc/wp-content/documents/The_Revolution:_A_Guide_to_the_Changes_Sweeping_Non-profit_Marketing_and_Communications_09-10-2012_05.59.59.pdf

Tsaliki, L. (2010). Technologies of Political Mobilization and Civil Society in Greece. *Convergence (London)*, *16*(2), 151–161. doi:10.1177/1354856509357675

Ventureneer. (2010). *Nonprofits and Social Media: It ain't optional.* Available online at: http://ventureneer.com/node/2285

Voida, A. (2011). *Shapeshifters in the voluntary sector: Exploring the human-centered-computing challenges of nonprofit organizations.* Available online at: http://amy.voida.com/Site/Whats_New/Entries/2011/11/10_Reflections_on_Voluntary_Sector_Research_in_the_Nov_Dec_Issue_of_Interactions_files/shapeshifters-interactions.pdf

Voida, A., Harmon, E., & Al-Ani, B. (2011). Homebrew databases: Complexities of everyday information management in nonprofit organizations. In *Proceedings of the SIGCHI Conference on Human Factors in Computing Systems.* (p. 915-924). New York, NY: ACM. 10.1145/1978942.1979078

Vozab, D. (2012). *Communication models of civil society organizations in Croatia. Observatorio (OBS*) Journal.*

Waters, R. D., Burnett, E., Lamm, A., & Lucas, J. (2009). Engaging stakeholders through social networking: How nonprofit organizations are using facebook. *Public Relations Review*, *35*(2), 102–106. doi:10.1016/j.pubrev.2009.01.006

## ENDNOTE

1 The lists and maps available can be found in http://organosi20.gr (in Greek).

# Chapter 10
# Motivational Factors and Barriers for Technology-Driven Governance:
## An Indian Perspective

**Ankit Dhamija**
*Amity University Gurgaon, India*

**Deepika Dhamija**
*Amity University Gurgaon, India*

## ABSTRACT

*The world today is witnessing unprecedented changes in every walk of life. Most of these changes can be attributed to advancements in information and communication technologies (ICT). It is because of ICT only, the trade between various economies, the education, physical movement, and everything else that can be thought of, takes place. Governments of today have realized that in this digital era, traditional methods of remaining connected with its citizens are not going to be sufficient. Therefore, they must come up with innovative measures to find out ways of providing government services to citizens through digital means. When governments adopt ICT to achieve this, it is called e-governance. This chapter will touch upon what e-governance is all about, the state of e-governance, the successful e-governance implementations, and the barriers and constraints that prevent the adoption of an e-governance platform. The chapter has an Indian context due to the unprecedented change in India's economy and e-governance implementation.*

## INTRODUCTION

Utilizing technology for governance is the need of today as it allows the government to showcase their agendas, policies, processes and services to citizens in a transparent manner. Governments are using Information and Communication Technologies to simplify and make their systems more efficient as it is critical for transformation to make the delivery of government services more effective across various

DOI: 10.4018/978-1-5225-5966-5.ch010

government domains. Governments of today's connected world have become a lot more proactive and technologies driven then they were a decade ago. The reasons for this transformation can be attributed to the accessibility to internet, affordable smart handheld devices and social media platforms which have motivated governments to utilize this medium to remain connected with its citizens and make them feel that they are being taken care off well. Running after government officials from one office to another for getting approvals, sanctions and signatures & stamps are things of the past. Thanks to IT, now the governments are making all of their systems online so that the citizens are benefitted, time and money is saved and processes become smooth and are streamlined. Thus, it can be said that governments, with the help of Information & Communication Technology are moving towards e-governance.

## BACKGROUND AND LITERATURE REVIEW

The history of e-governance can be attributed to early 1990s and it is directly related to development of Information Technology. To gain an insight about the way e-governance has evolved over past two decades, this term can be seen and understood as "before 1990's and after 1990's".

### E-Governance Evolution

Table 1 provides insights about the emergence of e-governance in US Federal Government, where before 1990s, the potential of e-governance was not realized and Information Technology in governance was being used only as a cost saving option by utilizing it in only the backend processes. The focus was on minimizing the cost in IT investments and maximizing the efficiency and economy. However, the focus shifted towards projects that offer "services to the citizens" during late 1990s where various government

*Table 1. Evolution of e-governance*

| Before 1990s | After 1990s |
|---|---|
| • Used to automate backroom operations<br>• Less emphasis on automating customer facing functions (Information Dissemination or Service Delivery)<br>• Using IT only to save money in backroom operations<br>• Systems created on "least cost basis" | • Emphasizing IT projects that offered "Service to the Citizens"<br>• Improving Service Delivery through technology.<br>• FirstGov.gov website- official US gateway to all government information.<br>• Various organizations and departments- NSF, CEG, OMB initiated e-governance initiatives.<br>• Private Sector saw e-business opportunities<br>• Academics saw opportunities for research & teaching.<br>• Public sector saw opportunities for revenue generation.<br>• Focus shifted to emphasize data & service integration to support economy & efficiency rather than service delivery. |

bodies like National Science Foundation (NSF), Council of Excellence in Government (CEG), National Research Council (NRC) and Office of Management & Budget (OMB) initiated various projects that kick started the e-governance in US.

The Federal Government administration conducted a National Performance Review or Reengineering Government that emphasized IT enabled government and very first initiative taken was on improving service delivery through technology. The result of this initiative was the FirstGov.gov website that was made online and which had every information related to government. Thereafter, NSF and CEG created a group of practitioners and researchers in public policy and public administration to create an agenda for digital government research. Then, NRC conducted a study to inspect the impact of government's investments in IT. All such efforts were signaling towards a major paradigm shift in governance and every sector saw its growth opportunities with it. The Private sector saw its growth through e-business; the public sector was able to see revenue generation due to the growth of Private Sector; academics saw growth opportunities in teaching & research and so on.

Even the change in administration in 2001 didn't affected e-governance initiatives and it remained a prime focus of the new government too where it created Office of Management & Budget (OMB) that expanded the e-governance initiatives further. Initiatives like Internal Revenue Service's (IRS's) Free File initiative that offered free tax preparation and e-filing services to selected taxpayers, Business Gateway initiative that provided all the information and compliances that businesses have to follow, e-vital initiative that enabled communication between centre and state governments and facilitate data exchange.

Thus, it is evident that the world's largest economy also adopted e-governance slowly and steadily, after understanding its importance and set an example for the rest of the world. Soon after, the governments across the world started moving towards e-governance.

So many definitions of e-governance have been proposed by researchers where Osborne and Gaebler, (1992) defined e-Government as "The government's use of technology, in particular, web-based Internet applications to enhance access and delivery of government services to citizens, business partners, employees and other government entities. It is a way for governments to use the new technologies to provide people with more convenient access to government information and services, to improve the quality of the services and to provide greater opportunities to participate in our democratic institutions and processes."

M Backus (2001), in his report " E-Governance and Developing Countries" defined e-governance as the application of *electronic means* in (1) the *interaction* between *government* and citizens and government and businesses, as well as (2) in internal *government operations* to simplify and improve democratic, government and business aspects of Governance.

The World Bank, (2012) define E-Government as "The use by government agencies of information technologies (such as Wide Area Networks, the Internet, and mobile computing) that have the ability to transform relations with citizens, businesses, and other arms of government. These technologies can serve a variety of different ends: better delivery of government services to citizens, improved interactions with business and industry, citizen empowerment through access to information, or more efficient government management. The resulting benefits can be less corruption, increased transparency, greater convenience, revenue growth, and/or cost reductions."

The reason of choosing definitions from three different decades is to emphasize the fact that governments across the world have been using technology in some form or the other in past decades. Whatever technology was available, it was utilized by governments in their public service delivery, engaging citizens and to support government operations.

The first definition emphasized the use of web based internet applications, the second one focused on the interaction between governments, citizens & businesses and the third definition brought more technology in governance in the form of mobile computing etc. Thus, it is evident that during past three decades, since when Internet Boom started, the governments have been trying to utilize ICT to deliver public services, make things transparent and to connect with citizens.

According to the Research Report No 3 (2001), e-governance model is based on three target groups-governments, citizens and business groups. Thus the following three e-governance models exist:

- **G2C:** Government to Citizen:
- **G2B:** Government to Businesses
- **G2G:** Government to Government

Figure 1 depicts the way various e-governance models interact and communicate with each other. Citizens may interact with the government through government portals; central and state governments may interact electronically regarding creation and implementation of various welfare policies, conducting live discussion forums etc; governments may interact with business firms and NGOs in the form of business tenders that may be issued or auctioned online, and business firms participate in it. On careful observation in Figure 1, it can be seen that all the arrows are two sided, which means e-governance allows two-way communication among these three groups like governments may ask citizens to fill out some data on its portal like for population verification, id verification etc; local government may write to the centre and business firms may contact government regarding any issues they face in government implemented policies.

Thus, e-governance model allows for a three-way communication which is essential for its successful implementation.

Gartner (2000), an international e-business research consultancy firm, formulated a four-phase e-governance maturity model.

- **Early 90's Information Phase:** A Presence
- **Mid 90's Interaction Phase:** An Intake process
- **Present Transaction Phase:** A Complete transaction
- **Future Transformation Phase:** Integration and organizational changes

*Figure 1. Interactions among various E-Governance models*
*Source: Research Report: E-Governance & Developing Countries (2001).*

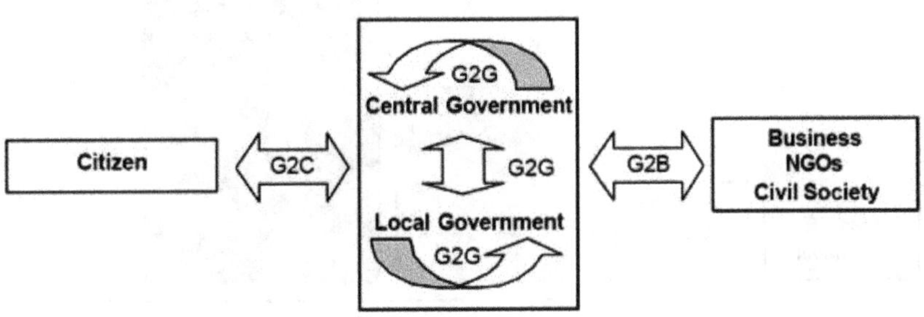

In each of the four phases of Figure 2, the delivery of online services and use of ICTs in government operations serve one or more of the aspects of e-governance: democracy, government, business.

In the first Information phase, e-governance is about providing basic information to citizens and businesses through its web presence. The government is able to provide its information electronically.

In the second Interaction phase, citizens and businesses may interact with government through emails; have access to various forms, documents and reports on government portal.

In the third Transaction phase, e-governance takes a more complex shape in the form of availability of online services like filing income tax returns, paying fee for various services like passport, visa, birth/ death certificates etc online, online voting and so on.

In the fourth Transformation phase, the e-governance is expected to reach at the pinnacle of complexity and providing the best possible services to customers where all information system gets integrated, governments may be contacted through single point of contact and existence of personal accounts for citizens and businesses.

Now, the e-governance initiatives were being implemented by governments across the world and in 2001, first E-Government index was created to analyze the progress being in e-governance. In a report "Benchmarking E-government: Assessing the Progress of UN Member States" by S A Ronaghan (2002), an E-government Index based on several parameters was created and it covered North, Central & South America, Middle East, Europe, Asia, The Caribbean and Africa.

The figure 3 above categorizes nations according to high, medium, minimal and deficient e-governance index where USA stood first in High EGI and India stood in Minimal category in 2001. The report followed the following benchmarks to create the index: services, dynamic website presence, support for online transactions, citizens involvement through discussion groups etc.

Till date, a total of nine e-governance surveys have been conducted by United Nations with the latest one conducted in 2016 which will be in focus in the next section.

## Present E-Governance Scenario Globally

E-governance has taken a huge leap from 2001 to 2017, mostly due to advancements in Information and Communication Technologies in the form of high speed internet connections, availability of high bandwidth now, low cost handheld devices and the intent of governments worldwide to be specific. In the

*Figure 2. E-Governance maturity models*
*Source: Gartner (2000).*

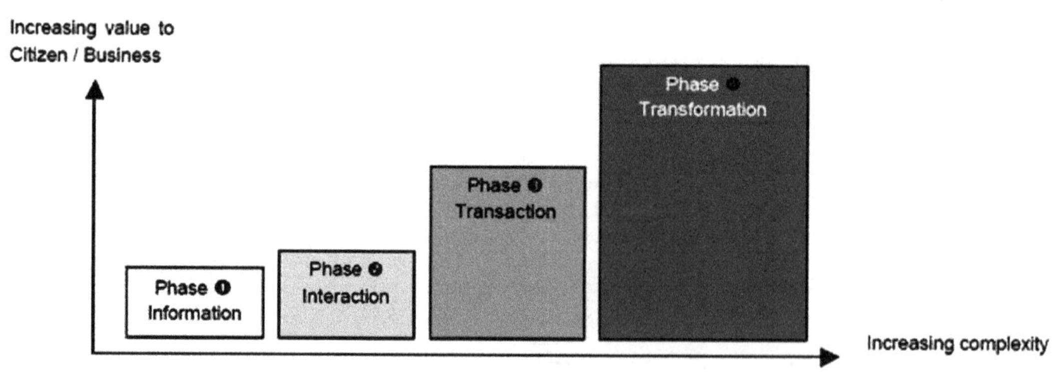

*Figure 3. E-Governance index 2001*
*Source: Research Report: E-Governance & Developing Countries (2001).*

| High E-gov Capacity 2.00 - 3.25 | | Medium E-gov Capacity 1.60 - 1.99 | | Minimal E-gov Capacity 1.00 - 1.59 | | Deficient E-gov Capacity Below 1.00 | |
|---|---|---|---|---|---|---|---|
| USA | 3.11 | Poland | 1.96 | Armenia | 1.59 | Cameroon | 0.99 |
| Australia | 2.60 | Venezuela | 1.92 | Brunei | 1.59 | Cent African Rep. | 0.98 |
| New Zealand | 2.59 | Russian Fed. | 1.89 | South Africa | 1.56 | Ghana | 0.98 |
| Singapore | 2.58 | Colombia | 1.88 | Paraguay | 1.50 | Nepal | 0.94 |
| Norway | 2.55 | Latvia | 1.88 | Cuba | 1.49 | Thailand | 0.94 |
| Canada | 2.52 | Saudi Arabia | 1.86 | Philippines | 1.44 | Congo | 0.94 |
| UK | 2.52 | Turkey | 1.83 | Costa Rica | 1.42 | Maldives | 0.93 |
| Netherlands | 2.51 | Qatar | 1.81 | Panama | 1.38 | Sri Lanka | 0.92 |
| Denmark | 2.47 | Lithuania | 1.81 | Nicaragua | 1.35 | Mauritania | 0.91 |
| Germany | 2.46 | Ukraine | 1.80 | Djibouti | 1.35 | Bangladesh | 0.90 |
| Sweden | 2.45 | Bahamas | 1.79 | Dominican Rep. | 1.34 | Kenya | 0.90 |
| Belgium | 2.39 | Hungary | 1.79 | Trinidad & Tobago | 1.34 | Laos | 0.88 |
| Finland | 2.33 | Greece | 1.77 | Indonesia | 1.34 | Angola | 0.85 |
| France | 2.33 | Jordan | 1.75 | Jamaica | 1.31 | Haiti | 0.84 |
| Rep of Korea | 2.30 | Bolivia | 1.73 | Iran | 1.31 | Mauritius | 0.84 |
| Spain | 2.30 | Egypt | 1.73 | Azerbaijan | 1.30 | Tanzania | 0.83 |
| Israel | 2.26 | Slovakia | 1.71 | India | 1.29 | Senegal | 0.80 |
| Brazil | 2.24 | Slovenia | 1.66 | Kazakhstan | 1.28 | Madagascar | 0.79 |
| Italy | 2.21 | Mongolia | 1.64 | Belize | 1.26 | Zimbabwe | 0.76 |
| Luxembourg | 2.20 | Oman | 1.64 | Barbados | 1.25 | Burkina Faso | 0.75 |
| Unit. Arab Emir. | 2.17 | Ecuador | 1.63 | Guyana | 1.22 | Zambia | 0.75 |
| Mexico | 2.16 | Suriname | 1.63 | Honduras | 1.20 | Mozambique | 0.71 |
| Ireland | 2.16 | Malaysia | 1.63 | El Salvador | 1.19 | Sierra Leone | 0.68 |
| Portugal | 2.15 | Romania | 1.63 | Guatemala | 1.17 | Cambodia | 0.67 |
| Austria | 2.14 | Belarus | 1.62 | Gabon | 1.17 | Comoros | 0.65 |
| Kuwait | 2.12 | Peru | 1.60 | Turkmenistan | 1.15 | Guinea | 0.65 |
| Japan | 2.12 | | | Uzbekistan | 1.10 | Namibia | 0.65 |
| Malta | 2.11 | | | Vietnam | 1.10 | Togo | 0.65 |
| Iceland | 2.10 | | | Samoa (Western) | 1.09 | Gambia | 0.64 |
| Czech Republic | 2.09 | | | Cote d'Ivoire | 1.05 | Malawi | 0.64 |
| Argentina | 2.09 | | | China | 1.04 | Mali | 0.62 |
| Estonia | 2.05 | | | Pakistan | 1.04 | Ethiopia | 0.57 |
| Bahrain | 2.04 | | | Nigeria | 1.02 | Chad | 0.55 |
| Uruguay | 2.03 | | | Kyrgyzstan | 1.01 | Niger | 0.53 |
| Chile | 2.03 | | | Botswana | 1.01 | Uganda | 0.46 |
| Lebanon | 2.00 | | | Tajikistan | 1.00 | | |

*2016 United Nations E-Government Survey*, a positive trend is visible towards e-governance at a global level where governments across the world are aiming at improving the relationship between people, making public services delivery more effective, accessible and responsive to people's needs and increasing participation in decision making and making public institutions more transparent and accountable.

Figure 4 shows the E-Government Development Index (EGDI) which is a weighted average of normalised scores on the three most important dimensions of e-government, namely: scope and quality of online services (Online Service Index, OSI), status of the development of telecommunication infrastructure (Telecommunication Infrastructure Index, TII) and inherent human capital (Human Capital Index, HCI). In year 2016, it was found that there are more countries with very-high-EGDI values (i.e., EGDI values greater than 0.75). 29 countries scored "very-high-EGDI" values in 2016. The above trend signals that more & more economies are advancing towards higher levels of e-government. They are responding to people's increasingly varied and complex needs, as well as the persistent call for new, better and faster

*Figure 4. E-Governance development index 2016*
*Source: Research Report: United Nations E-Governance Survey (2016).*

| Very-High-EGDI (Greater than 0.75) | High-EGDI (Between 0.50 and 0.75) | | Middle-EGDI (Between 0.25 and 0.50) | | Low-EGDI (Less than 0.25) |
|---|---|---|---|---|---|
| Australia | Albania | Mauritius | Algeria | Lesotho | Afghanistan |
| Austria | Andorra | Mexico | Angola | Libyan Arab Jamahiriya | Benin |
| Bahrain | Argentina | Monaco | Antigua and Barbuda (-) | Maldives | Burkina Faso |
| Belgium | Armenia | Mongolia | Bangladesh | Marshall Islands | Burundi |
| Canada | Azerbaijan | Montenegro | Belize | Micronesia (Federated States of) | Central African Republic |
| Denmark | Bahamas (+) | Morocco | Bhutan | Namibia | Chad |
| Estonia | Barbados | Oman | Bolivia | Nauru | Comoros |
| Finland | Belarus | Peru | Botswana | Nepal (+) | Congo (-) |
| France | Bosnia and Herzegovina (+) | Philippines (+) | Cambodia | Nicaragua | Côte d'Ivoire |
| Germany | Brazil | Poland | Cameroon | Nigeria | Democratic Republic of Congo |
| Iceland | Brunei Darus-salam | Portugal | Cape Verde | Pakistan | Djibouti |
| Ireland | Bulgaria | Qatar | Cuba | Palau | Equatorial Guinea |
| Israel | Chile | Republic of Moldova | DPR of Korea | Panama | Eritrea |
| Italy | China | Romania | Dominica | Paraguay | Gambia |
| Japan | Colombia | Russian Federation | Dominican Republic | Rwanda | Guinea |
| Lithuania (+) | Costa Rica | Saint Kitts and Nevis (+) | Egypt (-) | Saint Lucia | Guinea-Bissau |
| Luxembourg | Croatia | San Marino | El Salvador | St Vincent & the Grenadines | Haiti |
| Netherlands | Cyprus | Saudi Arabia | Ethiopia | Samoa | Liberia |
| New Zealand | Czech Republic | Serbia | Fiji (-) | Senegal | Madagascar (-) |
| Norway | Ecuador | Seychelles | Gabon | Sudan | Malawi |
| Republic of Korea | Georgia | Slovakia | Ghana | Suriname | Mali |
| Singapore | Greece | South Africa (+) | Guatemala | Swaziland | Mauritania |
| Slovenia (+) | Grenada | Sri Lanka | Guyana | Syrian Arab Republic | Mozambique |
| Spain | Hungary | Thailand (+) | Honduras | Tajikistan | Myanmar |
| Sweden | Jordan | TFYR of Macedonia | India | Timor-Leste | Niger |
| Switzerland (+) | Kazakhstan | Trinidad and Tobago (+) | Indonesia | Togo (+) | Papua New Guinea |
| United Arab Emirates (+) | Kuwait | Tunisia | Iran (Islamic Republic of) | Tonga | Sao Tome and Principe |
| United Kingdom | Latvia | Turkey | Iraq | Turkmenistan | Sierra Leone |
| United States of America | Lebanon (+) | Ukraine | Jamaica | Tuvalu | Solomon Islands |
| | Liechtenstein | Uruguay | Kenya | Uganda | Somalia |
| | Malaysia | Uzbekistan (+) | Kiribati | United Republic of Tanzania | South Sudan |
| | Malta | Venezuela | Kyrgyzstan | Vanuatu | Yemen (-) |
| | | Viet Nam (+) | Lao People's PR | Zambia (+) | |
| Australia | | | | Zimbabwe | |

public services. There is also growing recognition of e-government to support sustainable development in the three dimensions – economic growth, social inclusion and environmental protection.

## Online Services Index

The online services component of the E-Government Development Index (EGDI) is a composite indicator measuring the use of ICT by governments to deliver public services at national level. As per the 2016 EGDI, the highest performing countries in OSI include 15 countries from Europe, 8 from Asia and 6 from the Americas. These countries stand out, among other reasons, for adopting innovative approaches to transform public sector and the delivery of services. Highlighted in Figure 5, among the 32 top performing countries (OSI from 0.75 to 1), the United Kingdom of Great Britain and Northern Ireland ranks first in online service delivery in 2016, followed closely by Australia.

*Figure 5. Countries with best OSI index*
*Source: 2016 EGDI Index.*

| Country | Online Service Index (OSI) |
|---|---|
| United Kingdom of Great Britain & Northern Island | 1 |
| Australia | 0.9783 |
| Singapore | 0.9710 |
| Canada | 0.9565 |
| Republic of Korea | 0.9420 |
| Finland | 0.9420 |
| New Zealand | 0.9420 |
| France | 0.9420 |
| Netherlands | 0.9275 |
| United States of America | 0.9275 |
| Austria | 0.9130 |
| Spain | 0.9130 |
| Estonia | 0.8913 |
| United Arab Emirates | 0.8913 |
| Sweden | 0.8768 |
| Japan | 0.8768 |
| Italy | 0.8696 |
| Israel | 0.8623 |
| Slovenia | 0.8478 |
| Mexico | 0.8478 |
| Germany | 0.8406 |
| Lithuania | 0.8261 |
| Bahrain | 0.8261 |
| Serbia | 0.8188 |
| Norway | 0.8043 |
| Malta | 0.7971 |
| Columbia | 0.7899 |
| Denmark | 0.7754 |
| Uruguay | 0.7754 |
| Chile | 0.7754 |
| China | 0.7681 |
| Kazakhstan | 0.7681 |

## Telecommunication Infrastructure Index, TII

The Telecommunication Infrastructure Index (TII) is composed of five indicators: (i) estimated internet users per 100 inhabitants; (ii) number of main fixed telephone lines per 100 inhabitants; (iii) number of mobile subscribers per 100 inhabitants; (iv) number of wireless broadband subscriptions per 100 inhabitants; and (v) number of fixed broadband subscriptions per 100 inhabitants. The data was taken from International Telecommunication Union. As per 2016 EGDI, Monaco had the best TII as 1 followed by Singapore(0.84), Japan & Denmark (0.82) and Luxembourg & Sweden (0.81).

## Human Capital Index (HCI)

The Human Capital Index (HCI) consists of four components, namely: (i) adult literacy rate; (ii) the combined primary, secondary and tertiary gross enrolment ratio; (iii) expected years of schooling; and (iv) average years of schooling. As per 2016 EGDI, Belgium had the best TII as 0.97 followed by UK, New Zealand & Finland (0.94), Sweden & Ireland (0.92) and Netherland (0.91).

## BEST E-GOVERNANCE INITIATIVES: GLOBALLY

In this section, the best practices adopted and measures undertaken by the top governments across the world are highlighted.

### United Kingdom of Great Britain and Northern Ireland

According to the 2016 Online Service Index, UK stood first in the online service delivery. That happened because it adopted e-governance very early and it invested in establishing the needed technical infrastructure, created secure government websites, ensuring safe user authentication etc. They focused primarily on adopting new technologies that ensure that service progression went from simply publishing information to offering basic interactions, (e.g., e-forms), to full transactional capability (e.g., filing and processing tax returns, welfare benefits, passports, etc.) and to a more complete transformation and reform of public sector online operations and public service delivery.

It introduced Chief Information Officers (CIOs) Council between the e-Government Unit of the Cabinet Office and the Office of Government Commerce to transform online service delivery and make it citizens centered, self-service, accessible and enabling.

### Australia

Australia stood at second position in 2016 E-Government Index with a 0.9783 EGDI. A report from Australian Government states that one in eight Australians aged 14 and over look up government information and services online, which equates to about 324 million searches a year. The reason behind this can be attributed to categorized and organized web content on the Australian government website. It has just six main menus, separated at a distance with each menu except the "Home", has sub menus which are well organized too. The "Information and Services" menu is the one having most of the options including pages for payments, IT, public safety, jobs, health, money, transport, education, immigration, travel, culture etc. Each of these sub menus opens up to specific pages where all information is accessible very easily.

The stand-out part of the website is "myGov" menu (See Figure 6) that is accessible only after a citizen signs in to their account and thereafter they can search for jobs, avail taxation services, medical facilities, health records etc. Thus, from a single website, the Australian citizens can access wide variety of services that are delivered in a seamless manner and that have made Australia number two in worldwide rankings.

### Singapore

The first Asian Country ranked third with a 0.9710 EGDI index is Singapore. The first look of its official government portal doesn't give the user an out of the world experience and one gets an impression that its not what is expected out of a third ranked website but when you access it for a minute, browse through its menu, then you realize that it's a wonderfully maintained website and the highlight of it is the eServices submenu under Resources. Clicking on eServices takes the user to a "CitizenConnect" page where all the Singaporean citizen services and the agencies providing these services are listed.

*Figure 6. Australian Government's MyGov Portal Snapshot*
*Source: Official website of Australia Government.*

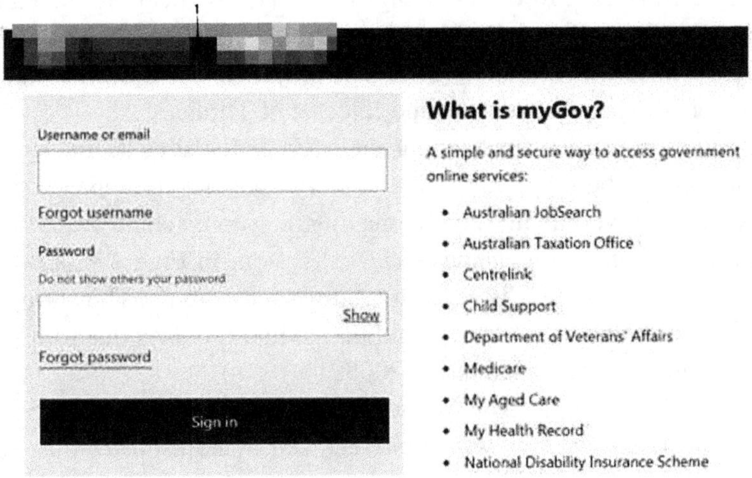


Also, as can be seen in Figure 7, a big search box at the top allows searching for any service in a quick manner. For example the Central Provident Fund Board (CPFB) service link takes the user to its own website that has all the provisions to access its related information. Similarly, Ministry of Manpower link takes you to its website where e-services regarding work passes & permits, workplace safety and health, employment practices, various e-forms and details about employment agencies can be found. The biggest highlight is the availability of around 550 e-services under various departments that can be availed without any hassles.

The usage of SINGPASS feature makes sure that a single common password is used by users to access all the e-services. Some of their initiatives are listed below:

*Figure 7. Citizen Connect website of Singapore government*
*Source: Singapore Government website.*

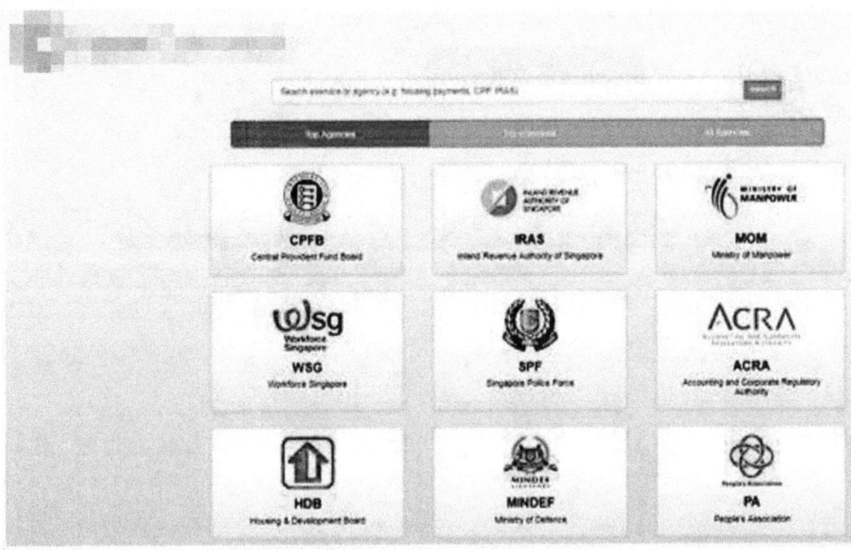

- The most recent development in Singaporean e-governance initiatives is the GovTech which has transformed the delivery of government's digital services by keeping the end users at the centre of each process. GovTech, along with the Prime Minister Office (PMO) implemented the Smart Nation and Digital Government Office (SNDGO) project to build Smart Nation Infrastructure by deploying new technologies like sensors and Internet of Things.
- The TradeExchange Project is transforming the trade & logistics sector by establishing uninterrupted inter connections between various regulatory agencies and ensuring smooth interactions among businesses and government; thereby making the supply chain system a much efficient one.
- The OBLS (Online Business Licensing Services) system in Figure 8, an e-government service that allows businesses to apply for licenses in a simplified manner. The entrepreneurs are required to fill a single form online which is processed in maximum 8 days due to which it received a UN Public Service Award for e-Government in 2005.
- Through the REACH (Reaching Everyone for Active Citizenry @ Home) portal, the government engages citizens in policy making where citizens can make use of blogs, social networks, and online chats to communicate their ideas to the government.

Thus, from the examples of above mentioned economies, it is evident that the leaders in e-governance have become leaders because they invested in it, streamlined the processes and brought every service online and engaged the users in policy making which ultimately won government the trust and support of its citizens.

## Present E-Governance Scenario: Indian Perspective

E-governance in India started in 1987 with the launch of NICNET- the national Satellite based Computer Network. Thereafter, the DISNIC (District Information System of the National Informatics Centre) programme ensured that all district offices are computerized. Thereafter, as the innovations in ICT and telecommunications saw a steep rise, e-governance in India started to take a huge leap.

The Indian E-Government Index as per the report of United Nations E-Government survey 2003 was 0.259. Fast forward to 2016, in the latest survey, India stood at 107$^{th}$ rank out of 193 countries with

*Figure 8. Snapshot of OBLS of Singapore government*
*Source: Singapore Government website.*

0.4637 EGDI. Out of this, the Online Service component (OSI) is the one which has been growing the most with Human Capital component (HCI) second and Telecommunication infrastructure (TII) at the last. This leads to the understanding that the e-services are there in abundance but the government lacks in providing the adequate telecommunication infrastructure for all these services.

Most of the e-governance initiatives by Indian Government makes use of one common parameter i.e. Aadhar Number. It's a unique twelve digit number allotted to every citizen by the government and it has been linked to most of the government's services i.e. Bank Accounts, Mobile Numbers, Gas connections and many others. The objective is to keep track of each person's activity so that government's social welfare schemes are not misused and reach to every common man of the country.

The section below covers some of the meaningful e-governance initiatives in India that have made the systems transparent to users and convenient to access the desired information:

## 1. Haryana Government's Department of Social Justice and Empowerment, Haryana

The first case from Indian Perspective in e-governance is about the e-governance initiatives of Department of Social Justice and Empowerment of Haryana Government. This website is all about the status of how various pension schemes of Haryana Government are working, who all are the beneficiaries

*Figure 9. E-Governance development index 2016*
*Source: United Nations Government website.*

| Rank | Country | EGDI Level | EGDI | Online Service Component | Telecomm. Infrastructure Component | Human Capital Component |
|---|---|---|---|---|---|---|
| 50 | Czech Republic | High | 0.6454 | 0.4783 | 0.5952 | 0.8627 |
| 153 | Democratic People's Republic of Korea | Medium | 0.2801 | 0.0217 | 0.0363 | 0.7822 |
| 180 | Democratic Republic of the Congo | Low | 0.1876 | 0.0870 | 0.0788 | 0.3970 |
| 9 | Denmark | Very high | 0.8510 | 0.7754 | 0.8247 | 0.9530 |
| 187 | Djibouti | Low | 0.1337 | 0.0217 | 0.0698 | 0.3095 |
| 109 | Dominica | Medium | 0.4577 | 0.3043 | 0.4305 | 0.6384 |
| 98 | Dominican Republic | Medium | 0.4914 | 0.5072 | 0.2992 | 0.6676 |
| 74 | Ecuador | High | 0.5625 | 0.6304 | 0.3438 | 0.7134 |
| 108 | Egypt | Medium | 0.4594 | 0.4710 | 0.3025 | 0.6048 |
| 104 | El Salvador | Medium | 0.4718 | 0.4855 | 0.3265 | 0.6035 |
| 165 | Equatorial Guinea | Low | 0.2403 | 0.0797 | 0.1237 | 0.5174 |
| 190 | Eritrea | Low | 0.0902 | 0.0217 | 0.0000 | 0.2487 |
| 13 | Estonia | Very high | 0.8334 | 0.8913 | 0.7329 | 0.8761 |
| 157 | Ethiopia | Medium | 0.2666 | 0.5290 | 0.0495 | 0.2212 |
| 96 | Fiji | Medium | 0.4989 | 0.4130 | 0.3326 | 0.7509 |
| 5 | Finland | Very high | 0.8817 | 0.9420 | 0.7590 | 0.9440 |
| 10 | France | Very high | 0.8456 | 0.9420 | 0.7502 | 0.8445 |
| 129 | Gabon | Medium | 0.3584 | 0.1522 | 0.3068 | 0.6162 |
| 167 | Gambia | Low | 0.2396 | 0.1957 | 0.1959 | 0.3274 |
| 61 | Georgia | High | 0.6108 | 0.6377 | 0.4184 | 0.7763 |
| 15 | Germany | Very high | 0.8210 | 0.8406 | 0.7342 | 0.8882 |
| 120 | Ghana | Medium | 0.4181 | 0.4493 | 0.2594 | 0.5458 |
| 43 | Greece | High | 0.6910 | 0.5797 | 0.6032 | 0.8901 |
| 88 | Grenada | High | 0.5168 | 0.3696 | 0.3988 | 0.7820 |
| 102 | Guatemala | Medium | 0.4790 | 0.6667 | 0.2358 | 0.5345 |
| 189 | Guinea | Low | 0.1226 | 0.0870 | 0.0906 | 0.1903 |
| 181 | Guinea-Bissau | Low | 0.1818 | 0.1087 | 0.0828 | 0.3538 |
| 126 | Guyana | Medium | 0.3651 | 0.2826 | 0.2432 | 0.5694 |
| 178 | Haiti | Low | 0.1931 | 0.1667 | 0.1004 | 0.3124 |
| 127 | Honduras | Medium | 0.3611 | 0.3116 | 0.2008 | 0.5709 |
| 46 | Hungary | High | 0.6745 | 0.6304 | 0.5615 | 0.8317 |
| 27 | Iceland | Very high | 0.7662 | 0.6232 | 0.7814 | 0.8940 |
| 107 | India | Medium | 0.4637 | 0.7464 | 0.1430 | 0.5019 |
| 116 | Indonesia | Medium | 0.4478 | 0.3623 | 0.3016 | 0.6796 |

under which scheme, details about various concessional schemes, provision to file a Right to Information (RTI) and many other things.

This is a prime example of e-governance is because of the sensitivity of the matter i.e. the Pension Schemes of the Government. Pension is a right to the citizens who belong to old age group, widows and disabled people. Traditionally, the pension records were managed manually where accounts may be forged, also the pensions were distributed in hand of individuals and signatures were taken. The chances of forgery exist there also. Figure 10 displays the home page of the website.

To curtail the issues mentioned above, the government made an attempt to computerize all these records, created a website, did a fresh enrollment for all eligible citizens under various schemes for the whole state and uploaded all the data on its website. The biggest reform that was introduced was linking of every pension account with a bank account in which the pension amount will be deposited directly every month. Thus, the cash disbursement was eliminated totally and the pension came with direct bank transfer (DBT) of pension account holder. Thus, this move helped the needy people of whole state and brought transparency in the whole process.

Also, the website has a feature where pension holders can see and access their account information, when the pension was credited (Figure 11). New enrollment can also be done online and account updating has also been provisioned for. Also, any user can see district wise, area wise, municipality wise and area wise details of the pension account holders.

## 2. Education Ministry and UGC's Online Student Grievance Redressal Portal

The second case is about the launch of a students' grievance redressal portal by University Grants Commission (UGC) that has helped students a lot (Figure 12). UGC works under education ministry of central government and is the sole authority to decide and create the reforms and guidelines to be followed by the universities and colleges across country. There have been cases where universities & institutions were not following the prescribed guidelines in admissions, facilities offered etc and the complaints from students were not answered or heard.

*Figure 10. Website Snapshot of Department of Social Justice and Empowerment, Haryana*
*Source: Official Website.*

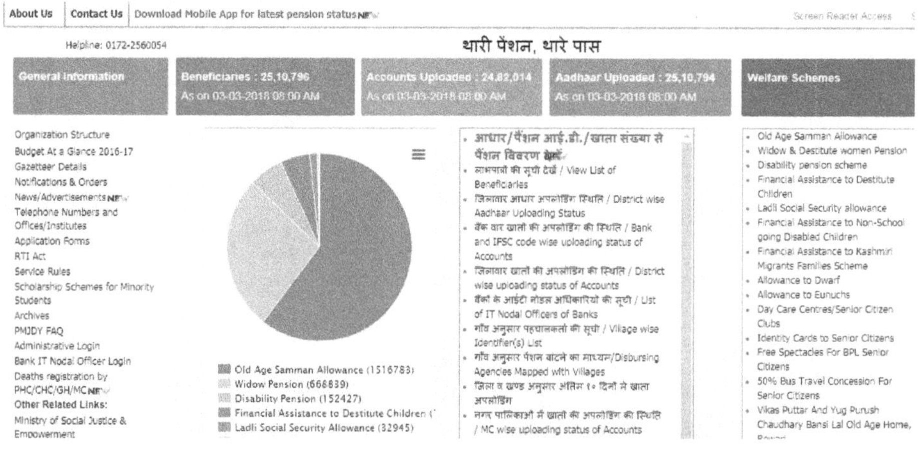

*Figure 11. Website Snapshot of Department of Social Justice and Empowerment, Haryana*
*Source: Official Website.*

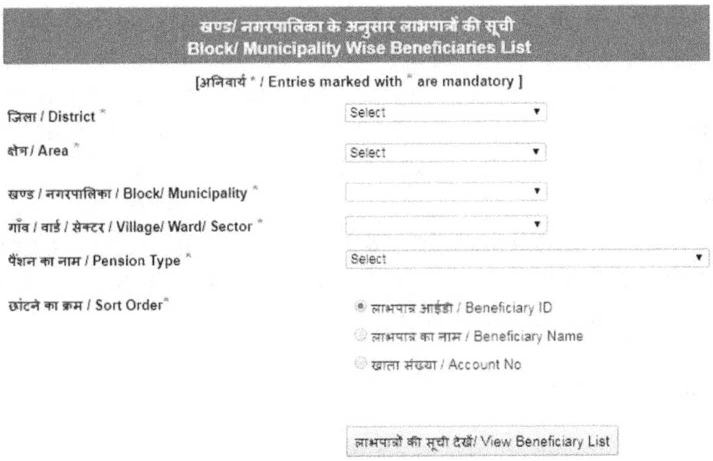


*Figure 12. Website snapshot of UGC's online student grievance redressal portal*
*Source: Official Website.*

This grievance redressal portal has equipped all students with a means to send their complaints and grievances about various aspects to the universities. To post a complaint, students are required to create an account on the website. Thereafter they are redirected to the grievance posting page where the complaint can be written. Then the university or college name is to be selected and finally the application gets submitted. The highlight of this portal is that it's mandatory for all universities to appoint a Nodal Officer to whom this complaint or grievance will reach. This officer is generally the Registrar of the institution. The complaint must be addressed and reply must be sent to the concerned student applicant within 15 days. Failing to which, the student again has the option to ping the University for a Suitable Reply. Thus, it's a two way mechanism where UGC has given facility to students also and is making sure that the complaints are addressed and resolved.

## 3. "Mann ki Baat" Initiative by Prime Minister

The third case is about the "Mann ki Baat" sessions- the monthly, interactive sessions by the Prime Minister where he utilizes Radio, TV, FM, all news channels, Internet to brief the public about the recent developments in all fields, shares his observations on the areas that are concerning him, the praise to the extraordinary work done by individuals and any other issue or development that needs to be talked about. This initiative has a very positive impact on the citizens and they feel as if they are connected to the Prime Minister in person.

Utilizing the technology further, all these "Mann ki baat" sessions get uploaded on the official website of Prime Minister and also available on the mobile app too. This is an excellent effort to reach out to the masses that connects him to the public strongly.

## 4. DigiLocker Facility to Keep Documents Safe

The last but not the least e-governance reform introduced in India is the digitization of essential official documents that include educational qualification documents, all government id proofs like passport, aadhar card, voter id, driving licenses etc. DigiLocker is the online platform (Figure 13) where all such documents can be uploaded on the cloud server and they remain safe in government's custody. The benefits of keeping documents in DigiLocker is that the citizens are exempted to carry these documents physically thus reducing the risk of losing them while on the move. During any checking by security officials, one can show these documents in their DigiLocker accounts or through its mobile app too. Another advantage is that through this service, the people can get documents from various issuers also and get them verified by requesters too. This is a great convenience to citizens as carrying these important documents in hard copy was always a risky affair but thanks to DigiLocker, the problem is gone now.

Apart from the initiatives mentioned above, there are so many other noteworthy initiatives and reforms taken by Indian Government to incorporate technology into its functioning. These are listed below:

- Simplification of the process of Filing Income Tax Returns.
- Computerization and online delivery of Land Records.

*Figure 13. Digilocker Website Snapshot*
*Source: Official Website.*

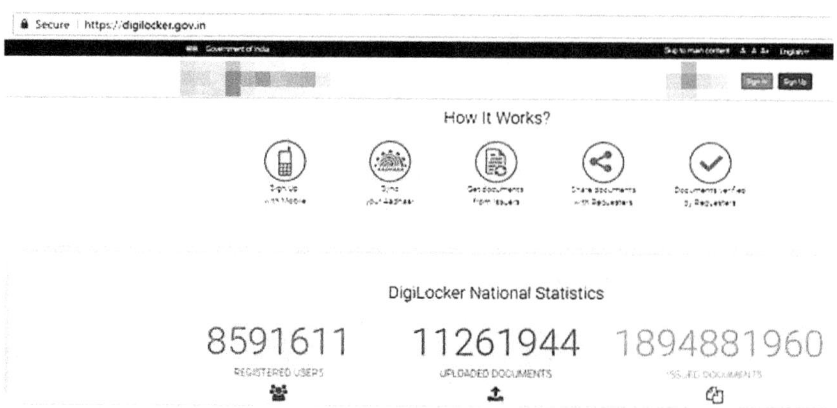

- E-Sewa project to facilitate online payments of utility bills.
- MyGov.in platform where citizens can interact with government.
- Ebasta, an ebook platform where e-books of all classes can be freely downloaded.
- Admission to professional colleges through Common Entrance Tests (CET).
- E-Kranti project to deliver services of Digital India Programme.
- E-Mandi portal to make procurement of agricultural products smoother and provide competitive remuneration.
- E-Hospital- The Online Registration System to take appointments of patients.

## Motivational Factors and Barriers for E-Governance

No doubt, e-governance is increasing globally; and with the advancements in technology, the governments worldwide are leveraging its benefits and utilizing it to the maximum to make their processes transparent and easily accessible. On the one hand governments are using ICT to improve their efficiency, service delivery that is helping them in their economic development too but, at the same time, disparities remain within and among countries. Lack of access to technology, poverty and inequality prevent people from fully taking advantage of the potential of ICTs and e-government for sustainable development. For ICTs to truly transform the public sector into an instrument of sustainable development efficiency in service delivery must be also coupled with social equity and ensuring that all people can access quality services.

Such efforts are vital to making sure that the sustainable development goals are at the centre of all government policies and of public management and that no one is left behind.

## CONCLUSION

In this chapter, the authors touched upon basics of e-governance and how it has grown till date worldwide. Various forms in which e-governance is conducted are presented and a global as well as Indian

*Table 2. Motivational factors and barriers for E-Governance*

| Motivational Factors for E-Governance | Barriers to E-Governance |
|---|---|
| Improved Efficiency | Organizational or Staff resistance to |
| | Technology |
| Improved Services | Lack of Public Support |
| Builds Citizens' Trust in Government | Lack of Support from Policy makers |
| Enhances Transparency & Accountability | Lack of access to Technology |
| Reduces Corruption | Insufficient Bandwidth |
| Promotes Economic Development | Poverty |
| Technological Advancements | Illiteracy |
| | Security & Privacy Issues |
| | Questionable Return on Investment on e- |
| | governance |

perspective of e-governance is highlighted. Few cases of the countries utilizing e-governance are discussed. Thereafter, some of the best e-governance initiatives in Indian Context are given. Finally, the motivational factors and barriers to e-governance are presented.

To conclude, it can be said that every economy in this world has understood the importance of e-governance and they are trying to utilize it to provide better services to their citizens. However, there is no doubt that barring a few, most of the economies are still far behind to truly leverage its benefits. But with the intent to serve the citizens, the governments worldwide are on a path to achieve this mammoth task. For this, a holistic approach has to be adopted in order to understand the needs of the citizens, the capabilities of government organizations, their processes and structures and based on these, the technology-based solution would have to be devised.

## REFERENCES

Backus, M. (2001). *E-Governance and Developing Countries*. Retrieved October 17, 2017 from https://publicadministration.un.org/egovkb/Data-Center

Baum, C. H. (n.d.). *A D Maio Gartner's Four Phases of E-Government Model*. Retrieved October 11, 2017 from https://www.gartner.com/doc/317292/gartners-phases-egovernment-model

Council for Excellence in Government. (n.d.). *E-Government: The Next American Revolution*. Retrieved November 10, 2017 from http://www.excelgov.org/index.php?keyword=a432c10480be99

Dawes, S. S., Bloniarz, P. A., Kelly, K. L., & Fletcher, P. D. (1999). *Some Assembly Required: Building a Digital Government for the 21st Century*. Center for Technology in Government University at Albany, State University of New York.

Hongbo, W. U. (2016). *United Nations E-Government Survey 2016*. Retrieved October 13, 2017 from https://publicadministration.un.org/egovkb/en-us/Reports/UN-E-Government-Survey-2016

National Research Council. (2000). *Information Technology Research, Innovation, and E-Government*. Washington, DC: National Academy Press.

Office of Management and Budget. (2002). *E-Government Strategy: Simplified Delivery of Services to Citizens*. Washington, DC: Executive Office of the President.

Official DigiLocker Website of Indian Government. (n.d.). Retrieved September 27, 2017 from https://digilocker.gov.in/

Official Website of Australia Government. (n.d.a). Retrieved October 7, 2017 from http://www.australia.gov.au/

Official Website of Australia Government. (n.d.b). Retrieved October 7, 2017 from https://my.gov.au/LoginServices/main/login?execution=e1s1

Official Website of FirstGov.gov. (n.d.a). Retrieved October 3, 2017 from http://firstgov.gov/About.shtml

Official Website of FirstGov.gov. (n.d.b). *About FirstGov.gov*. Retrieved October 3, 2017 from http://web.archive.org/web/20060707043959re_/firstgov.gov/About.shtml

Official Website of Prime Minister of India. (n.d.). Retrieved September 27, 2017 from https://www.narendramodi.in/mann-ki-baat

Official Website of Singapore Government. (n.d.a). Retrieved October 7, 2017 from https://www.gov.sg/

Official Website of Singapore Government. (n.d.b). Retrieved October 7, 2017 from http://ccc.ecitizen.gov.sg/

Official Website of Singapore Government. (n.d.c). Retrieved from October 7, 2017 https://www.cpf.gov.sg/

Official Website of Social Justice and Empowerment of Haryana Government. (n.d.). Retrieved September 27, 2017 from http://socialjusticehry.gov.in/

Official Website of UGC. (n.d.). Retrieved September 27, 2017 from https://www.ugc.ac.in/grievance/

Osborne, D., & Gaebler, T. (1992). *Reinventing Government: How the Entrepreneurial Spirit is transforming the Public Sector.* Addison-Wesley. Retrieved October 8, 2017 from https://publicadministration.un.org/egovkb/Portals/egovkb/Documents/un/English.pdf

Ronaghan, S. A. (2002). *Benchmarking E-government: A Global Perspective. Assessing the Progress of the UN Member States.* United Nations. Retrieved October 8, 2017 from https://publicadministration.un.org/egovkb/Portals/egovkb/Documents/un/English.pdf

# Chapter 11
# A Central Asian View of E-Government Services Adoption:
## Citizens' Trust and Intention to Use E-Services

**Rita Ismailova**
*Kyrgyz-Turkish Manas University, Kyrgyzstan*

**Gulshat Muhametjanova**
*Kyrgyz-Turkish Manas University, Kyrgyzstan*

**Bahtiyar Kurambayev**
*KIMEP University, Kazakhstan*

## ABSTRACT

*Results of survey from a snowball convenient sample of Kyrgyz respondents (N = 216) showed that employees of private sector are more likely to use government websites than those of government employees themselves and level of knowledge about security issues directly related to intention to use of Kyrgyz government websites. Specifically, higher level of knowledge about security issues leads less likely to use government websites. Factors such as ease of use and usefulness, relative advantage of using web sites, and compatibility with respondents' lifestyle have also great impact on intention to use government web sites. Image, given by using internet technologies to communicate with government also has a direct relation on people's intention. The findings also suggest about the gender role in if and under circumstances men and women tend to use government websites. The findings are explained via the investigation of diffusion of innovation model and technology acceptance model in relation to use of government websites in the context of Kyrgyz Republic.*

DOI: 10.4018/978-1-5225-5966-5.ch011

## INTRODUCTION

Growing internet penetration in wider developing countries including in Central Asia has heightened the need for examination of electronic government and e-government services and how such services lead to efficiency in the public sector. For example, there are studies about factors that influence consumer adoption of e-government services in the United Arab Emirates (Rodrigues, Sarahdeen & Balasubramanian, 2016), use of e-government services in various contexts and countries such as Turkey (Kurfali, Arifoglu, Tokdemir & Pacin, 2017), Jordan (Zawaideh, 2017), Estonia (Bjorklund, 2016), Thailand (Gunawong & Gao, 2017), Indonesia (Choi, Park, Rho, & Zo, 2016), Pakistan (Rehman, Kamal, & Esichaikul, 2016), India (Kumar, Sachan, & Mukherjee, 2017) as well as comparative study of the United States and the United Kingdom (Carter, Weerakkody, Philips & Dwivedi, 2016), comparative study of the democratic and non-democratic countries (Stier, 2015) just to name a few. However, Kyrgyzstan and other countries in Central Asian region still remain under-reported or lacking in scholar studies (Freedman & Shafer, 2012) in part because internet and other new communication technologies are at their nascent stages in the region. Assuming that internet is relatively new to the region, Freedman and Shafer (2012) argue that "there is no shortage of potential research [in wider Central Asia]…, given globalization and the rapid changes in communications technologies, such efforts would be particularly timely" (p. 124). To fill this gap, the study focuses on examination of seven research questions related to e-government services in the context of Central Asian Kyrgyz Republic. Specifically, this chapter examines citizens' intention to use government websites based on their perceived usefulness and ease of use.

### Contextualization/Background on Kyrgyzstan

It is important to understand the context of Kyrgyzstan. Kyrgyzstan gained its independence from Soviet Union in 1991. It has about six million of population and currently, approximately 35% of Kyrgyzstan population has access to the Internet (International Telecommunications Union, 2016; Freedom House, 2017). But the number of internet users is gradually increasing because Internet companies have grown in capital Bishkek city over the years, and now there are local internet chains whose computer equipment is virtually world class (DeYoung, 2010). Kyrgyz government has actively started connecting all educational institutions of the country to internet and opening free public wifi spots across the country. Furthermore, private transportation companies in major cities are offering free wifi connections on public transportations increasing availability of internet connection to wider population at little or no costs. And, a special internet club provides internet access for people with disabilities in Bishkek capital city (Gazeta.kg, October 22, 2015). In spite of the low internet penetration rate in the Kyrgyz Republic compared to the developed countries, young people especially students in higher education institutions are using Internet very frequently. They access internet though lab PCs, laptops, but mostly through cell phones (Muhametjanova & Çagiltay, 2012).

In recent months, there has been an increasing interest in Kyrgyz government to increase e-government services both to its own citizens and foreigners as well. For example, a new recently launched e-services portal include application for a newly introduced biometric passport, request and obtain for a criminal and non-criminal record certification, apply for and obtain marriage certificate, vehicle and property registration services and people can also pay taxes and other state services fee online. Also, Kyrgyz government introduced electronic visa for foreigners wishing to visit the country for a short-term and facilitated electronic registration of such foreign citizens in the country. Other major areas of e-government push by the Kyrgyz government include internet banking, electronic healthcare records, e-commerce, digital services in social and education sphere, citizen complaints, business investment and stimulating the development of local digital content online (Tazacom.kg, 2017). In other words, Kyrgyz government wants to become a digital nation by 2040 according to recently accepted National Sustainable Development Strategy titled "Taza Koom" (Smart Nation) by integrating information and communication technology to everyday life.

However, the government of the Kyrgyz Republic currently has 55 government web sites listed on the State Information Resources List of the Kyrgyz Republic at the web site of the government - www.okmot.kg. The number is expected to grow because of Kyrgyz government's push to move toward more e-government. These current available web sites do not form e-government in the way it was defined in the literature, mostly they are of an informative nature. In the literature, e-government concept includes E-Government Development Index (EGDI) as a composite indicator measuring the use of ICT by government to deliver public services (UN, 2014). Another element of e-government includes E-Participation Index. It is used to assess the quality and usefulness of information and services provided by a country's government for the purpose of engaging its citizens in public policy issues (Palvia & Sharma, 2007).

## LITERATURE REVIEW

Plethora literature exists on understanding under what circumstances citizens tend to use e-government services and under what conditions they refrain from using them. Scholars (Al-Adawi, Yousafzai, & Pallister, 2005) proposed a conceptual model of e-government adoption by citizens and this model included four determinants. Specifically, this model included perceived usefulness, perceived ease of use, trust, and perceived risk were included in the proposed model. The first two determinants such as perceived usefulness, the perceived ease of use were initially borrowed from earlier studies (Davis, Bagozzi, & Warshaw, 1989). The model proposed by Al-Adawi and her colleagues were adopted in various contexts around the world. For example, Carter and Belanger (2005) examined government to citizen (G2C) web sites adoption in the United States. They argued that people's willingness to use e-government services depended on easiness of use of these online e-government services and on the perceived compatibility with their lifestyle. The study also argued that reliability and security of the internet played a role in it. In addition, trustworthiness of state government agencies also plays a key role for users to accept online services of government (Welch, Hinnant, & Moon, 2005). Another study examined most critical factors influencing citizens' trust in respect of the adoption of e-government, for example, trust to government, and trust in the internet (Alzahrani, Al-Karaghouili & Weerakkody, 2017). These scholars outlined different types of trust such as knowledge-based trust, institution-based trust, calculative-based trust, relation-based trust, personal-based trust, cognitive-based trust, and disposition to trust. Beyond trust factor, other studies examined if other criteria played a role in whether citizens adopt e-government services including perceived image and relative advantages of using them. Kumar, Sachan, Mukherjee (2017) examined qualitatively how citizens value e-government services.

The outcomes of e-government development have varied across countries. Some countries are successful while others may fail to accomplish their set goals by introducing e-government services depending on numerous factors. Because developing countries generally have a poorer context than developed countries, they confront many challenges in e-government implementations (Choi, Park, Rho & Zo, 2016) because these different countries have different contexts including differences in institutions, regulatory frameworks, the leadership, planning, management, and many other reasons. Choi et al. argue that careful assessment in such developing countries (such as in Kyrgyzstan as this country is the focus of this work) are important before, during and after the project to avoid partial or complete failure. These scholars assessed strategy, technology, organization and people and environment. Aladwani (2016) examined whether corruption could be a source of e-government projects failure in developing countries. There was a research undertaken to examine political factors in e-government performance (Stier, 2015) and Elbahnasawy (2014) examined the impact of how e-government and internet adoption on curbing corruption. An existing literature suggests that 60% to 85% of all e-government implementation attempts in developing countries end up with failure (Mates, Lechner, Rieger, & Pekna, 2013) and scholars explain common reasons for failure include design-reality gaps, ineffective project management and unrealistic planning (Anthopoulos, Reddick, Giannakidou & Mavridis, 2016). It is well known that countries may have different political, cultural and socio-economical context but trust is universal factor in the adoption of e-government (Carter & Weerakkody, 2008).

Unlike the United States where internet penetration is relatively higher than most countries in the world, Zhao and Khan (2013) argued that people's perceived ease of use (PEOU) and trust to Internet does not affect people intention to use e-government services in the United Arab Emirates, while trust to government does. Awan (2008) undertook similar study to evaluate government to business (G2B) websites and suggested that G2B web sites are easy to use, but due to security concerns people in business refrain from conducting online transactions and use the government portals mainly for other type of online services. Akman, Yazici, Mishra and Arifoglu (2015) examined whether demographic factors play a role in predicting people's intention to use e-government services. They argued gender and education of respondents have a significant impact on the active use of e-government portals, as well as on the type of information searched in these web pages and type of e-government services used by them. Elsewhere in Asia, study concluded that quality, appeal, efficiency and personalization of e-government was significantly related to the e-government functionality factors (Rahardjo, Michandani, & Joshi, 2007). Rahardjo et al. undertook sampling in Indonesia. In Taiwain, scholars argued that three factors – perceived usefulness, perceived ease of use, and computer self-efficacy have the direct influence on the intention to use government web pages in Taiwan, with computer literacy rate being the least significant predictor (Wangpipatwong, Chutimaskul, & Papasratorn, 2008). In Romania, the key factors influencing the willingness of citizens to use government web portals are privacy concerns, followed by quality of services and their usefulness, while demographic factors such as gender and education level do not affect respondents' intention to use e-government (Colesca, 2009). In other related study by Colesca and Dobrica (2008), the study found the key factor influencing the usage via the perceived easiness and usefulness was defined as the level of education. The comparison of citizens' attitude toward e-government between Australian and New Zealand citizens was examined by Gauld, Goldfinch, and Horsburgh (2010). They argued that majority of respondents were reluctant to use some of the transactional e-government measures, and less than half of respondents had even visited a government websites.

## E-Government in Central Asian Countries

Since this study focuses on the context of Kyrgyzstan where little scholarly research has been done. It is logical to focus on such country because the implementation of e-government is at its early stage, and so far government web portal are being gradually developed and very few people have access to and use internet. One recent publication focused on Central Asian Kazakhstan. The study examined whether

Kazakhstan government's e-government approach as an anti-corruption strategy in the country (Sheryazdanova & Butterfield, 2017). Maerz (2016) examined how e-government in autocracies is used as a seemingly democratic pattern of legitimation. Specifically, Maerz qualitatively assessed about differences of e-government in Uzbekistan, Kazakhstan and Russia suggesting that non-competitive regimes create their web presences primarily for an international audience. Specifically focusing on Kyrgyz Republic, Brimkulov and Baryktabasov (2014) undertook one of the first studies in the country and analyzed governmental web sites on public service delivery. They said there was lack of cooperation between the government bodies, lack of sufficient incentives for civil servants and corruption, and weak knowledge of citizens about the value of e-government.

Overview of the United Nations E-Government Survey for the period of 2003-2014 shows that the position of the Kyrgyz Republic in the global ranking of e-government is decreasing; it was at 66th position in 2004, then it came down to 101-th place out of 193 in 2014 (UN, 2014). But it is ranked in 97$^{th}$ among 193 countries in the world suggesting that Kyrgyzstan has a long way to catch up with the rest of the world. According to some scholars (Brimkulov & Baryktabasov, 2014; Johnson & Kolko, 2010), this dropdown from early 2000s is mainly due to political instability in the country, as well as low citizens' activity, which are the main obstacles for development of the e-government in the Kyrgyz Republic. Kyrgyzstan faced two coups in 2005 and 2010 years, in which presidents in both revolutions had to flee the county to seek asylum in foreign countries. Ismailova (2017) argued that problems with building e-government in Kyrgyzstan are mainly related to legislation, as well as the lack of qualified specialists, particularly in the field of information security.

## MAIN FOCUS OF THE CHAPTER

In this study, authors measured the citizens' intention to use government web sites in the context of Kyrgyz Republic based on how they perceive these web sites, their lifestyle and trust to government and to internet. Also, this study measured the computer literacy rate and information security awareness rate. As an instrument of the analysis, the quantitative questionnaires were used during March 2016. The questions were adopted from previous studies (Carter & Bélanger, 2005), and some questions were

*Table 1. E-government Development Index, E-participation Index and World Ranking for Kyrgyz Republic*

| Year | E-Government Development Index | E-Participation Index | World Rank |
|---|---|---|---|
| 2003 | 0.327 | 0.034 | 110 |
| 2004 | 0.4468 | 0.15 | 66 |
| 2005 | 0.4417 | 0.1587 | 76 |
| 2008 | 0.4195 | 0.1364 | 102 |
| 2010 | 0.4417 | 0.4286 | 91 |
| 2012 | 0.4879 | 0.2895 | 99 |
| 2014 | 0.4657 | 0.4118 | 101 |
| 2016 | 0.4969 | 0.5932 | 97 |

modified and add to meet this study's objectives. Overall, this study proposed the following research questions originated from recent literature:

**RQ-1:** Does perceived usefulness of sites impact citizen's intention to use government web sites (Perceived usefulness)

**RQ-2:** Does perceived ease of use of sites impact citizen's intention to use government web sites (Perceived ease of use)

**RQ-3:** Does perceived image given by use of sites impact citizen's intention to use government web sites (Perceived image)

**RQ-4:** Does perceived relative advantage of using sites impact citizen's intention to use government web sites (Perceived relative advantage)

**RQ-5:** Does perceived compatibility of internet usage with their lifestyle impact citizen's intention to use government web sites (Perceived compatibility)

**RQ-6:** Does trust in the internet impact citizen's intention to use government web sites (Perceived trustworthiness of the internet)

**RQ-7:** Does trust in state government agencies impact citizen's intention to use government web sites (Perceived trustworthiness of state government)

In the scope of this study employees of government and commercial organizations and other eligible respondents were approached to voluntarily participate in this research. No one under 18 years of old were invited to participate in this study. Questionnaires were distributed both online (via social networks) and in paper based form. Participants completed the survey questionnaire in Russian language as Russian is the official language of Kyrgyzstan along with Kyrgyz language. Thus, the total sample comprised of 216 respondents of age between 19 and 62. In this sample approximately 42% of respondents are male and 58% of female respondents. According to National Statistics Committee (NSC, 2015), in the Kyrgyz Republic 49% of population are male and 51% of population are female. In Bishkek city, where the questionnaires were distributed, this proportion is roughly 47% male and 53% female, thus, the gender rate in this study mostly represents the country as a whole.

The questionnaire included for a total of 56 questions inclusive of six demographic questions like, age, gender, etc. The general computer literacy rate is measured using six questions of three point Likert type (1 = poor knowledge, 2 = average knowledge, 3 = good knowledge). There are 15 questions on Technology acceptance mode (questions to measure Use intentions - USE, Perceived usefulness - PU and Perceived ease of use - PEOU, five statements each). 15 questions on Diffusion of Innovation (5 statements on Relative advantage (RA), 5 statements on Image (IM) and 4 statements on Compatibility (CT)) and, in the final part of this section, Trustworthiness statements were asked, including questions on the trust of the internet (TRUS_I – consists of 3 statements) and questions on the trust to state government (TRUS_S, which includes 4 statements). Seven questions were asked on frequency of occurrence of different cybercrime events (FoC) (1 = never happens, 2 = happens sometimes, 3 = happens often).

# FINDINGS

## Demographic Overview

The analysis of questionnaire revealed that among respondents almost 96% have a personal computer, while an internet penetration rate among the sampled respondents is 85% (the previous research on having personal computer and internet penetration in the Kyrgyz Republic showed that approximately 74% of respondents had personal computers, an internet penetration rate was 55%). As it is shown in Table 2, the participants are mostly between 19-29 years old.

The reliability analysis of user data showed that overall Cronbach's Alpha based on standardized items is .724, where the highest result is for trust variable - .859. Thus, the data can be considered reliable.

## Demographic Profile on Intention to Use E-Government

### Impact of Gender on Intention to Use E-Government

T-test on the impact of gender of respondents on their intention to use government web sites shows that there is statistically significant difference between males (M = 2.68, $SD = .37$) and females ($M = 2.49$, $SD = .49$) on intention to use e-government; $t\,(214) = 3.14$, $p < 0.05$. According to results, men seem to be more willing to use web sites that women.

### Impact of Occupation on Intention to Use E-Government

T-test on impact of respondents' occupation on their intention to use governmental web sites shows that there is statistically significant difference between those who work for government ($M = 2.53$, $SD = .50$) and in private sector ($M = 2.62$, $SD = .38$) on intention to use e-government; $t\,(214) = -1.40$, $p < 0.05$, with employees of private sector being more active in using government web sites.

*Table 2. Demographic profile of respondents*

| Category | Sub-Categories | Percentages % | Frequency |
|---|---|---|---|
| Gender | Male<br>Female | 41.66<br>58.34 | 90<br>126 |
| Age | 19-29 years<br>30-39 years<br>40-59 years<br>Over 50 years | 57.0<br>32.0<br>8.8<br>2.2 | 123<br>69<br>19<br>5 |
| Have home computer | Yes<br>No | 95.8<br>4.2 | 207<br>9 |
| Internet Access | Yes<br>No | 85.2<br>14.8 | 184<br>32 |

## Impact of Computer Literacy Rate and Cybercrime Awareness Rate on Intention to Use E-Government

Literacy rates for given sample were calculated using questions on knowledge of application software to measure the computer literacy rate and frequency of occurrence of different cybercrime events for and information security awareness rate. ANOVA test on influence of computer literacy rate on intention to use indicated that this rate does not impact the respondents' use government websites with $p > 0.05$. The test on how much cybercrime awareness rate influences respondents' intention to use government websites was conducted. Results of one-way ANOVA show that there is a statistical significant difference between 3 groups (with low, moderate and high literacy rates) on intension to use e-government; $F(2, 213) = 5.29, p < 0.05$. Respondents from group 1 with lower rate of cybercrime awareness ($M$ = 2.84, $SD$ = .29) have higher means than those in group 3 - who have the highest rate of awareness ($M$ = 2.5, $SD$= .53).

## Impact of Trustworthiness on Intention to Use E-Government

Authors tested the impact of respondents' trust to government on their use of websites. Based on questionnaire, the respondents were divided into 3 groups, with the group 1 showing lowest rate of trust and group 3 showing highest rate of trust to government. Results of One-way ANOVA show that there is a statistical significant difference between 3 groups on intension to use e-government; $F(2,213) = 20.09$, $p < 0.05$. Respondents from group 1 with lower rate of trust to government ($M$ = 2.18, $SD$ = .54) have lower intention to use e-government, while those in group 3 - who have highest rate of trust ($M$ = 2.76, $SD$ = .38).

*Table 3. ANOVA of respondents' intention to use government websites in terms of their cybercrime awareness rate*

| Use Intentions | Sum of Squares | df | Mean Square | F | Sig. |
|---|---|---|---|---|---|
| Between Groups | 2.094 | 2 | 1.047 | 5.291 | .006 |
| Within Groups | 42.140 | 213 | .198 | | |
| Total | 44.233 | 215 | | | |

*Table 4. ANOVA of respondents' intention to use government websites in terms of their rate of trust to government*

| Use Intentions | Sum of Squares | df | Mean Square | F | Sig. |
|---|---|---|---|---|---|
| Between Groups | 7.021 | 2 | 3.510 | 20.093 | .000 |
| Within Groups | 37.212 | 213 | .175 | | |
| Total | 44.233 | 215 | | | |
| Between Groups | 5.352 | 2 | 2.676 | 14.658 | .000 |
| Within Groups | 38.882 | 213 | .183 | | |
| Total | 44.233 | 215 | | | |

Since trust to internet, especially in a country with given type of "internetization", authors test the impact of respondents' trust to internet technologies on their use of websites. For this test again the group 1 showed lowest rate of trust and group 3 showed highest rate of trust to internet. Results of one-way ANOVA show that there is a statistical significant difference between 3 groups on intension to use e-government; $F$ (2,213) = 14.66, $p < 0.05$. Respondents from group 1 with lower rate of trust to internet ($M$ = 2.26, $SD$ = .53) have lower intention to use e-government, while those in group 3 who have highest rate of trust ($M$ = 2.74, $SD$ = .41).

## Impact of Diffusion of Innovation on Intention to Use E-Government

Diffusion of innovation (DOI) model consists of questions revealing compatibility of technology with respondents' life style, relative advantage and complexity of using technology, as well as respondents' perception of technology usage as an indicator of their social status.

For the compatibility in the first group the following results were obtained: $M$ = 2.17, $SD$ = .54, in the second group $M$ = 2.61, $SD$ = .432 and in the third group $M$ = 2.78, $SD$ = .18, which shows that there is a difference between intension to use government websites of respondents' who do not use in their daily life.

Similarly, those who see relative advantage in using technology tend to use it to communicate with government as well: ($M$ = 1.4, $SD$ = .00) – the first group ($M$ = 2.47, $SD$ = .41) – the second group, ($M$ = 2.76, $SD$ = .41) – the third group. People who think that using websites increase their social status also show high interest in using it. Respondents from group 1 with lower rate of perceived Social Profile ($M$ = 2.43, $SD$ = .48) have lower intention to use government web sites, while those in group 3 - who have highest rate of perceived Social Profile ($M$ = 2.47, $SD$ = .50).

Results of one-way ANOVA show that there is a statistical significant difference between 3 groups on intension to use e-government for all factors: for the factor Image – $F$ (2,213) = 4.13, $p < 0.05$; for the factor Compatibility - $F$ (2,213) = 13.09, $p < 0.05$ for the factor Relative Advantage - $F$ (2,213) = 25.48, and $p < 0.05$.

*Table 5. ANOVA of respondents' intention to use government websites in terms of DOI*

| | | Sum of Squares | df | Mean Square | F | Sig. |
|---|---|---|---|---|---|---|
| Image | Between Groups | 1.651 | 2 | .825 | 4.129 | .017 |
| | Within Groups | 42.582 | 213 | .200 | | |
| | Total | 44.233 | 215 | | | |
| Compatibility | Between Groups | 4.841 | 2 | 2.421 | 13.088 | .000 |
| | Within Groups | 39.392 | 213 | .185 | | |
| | Total | 44.233 | 215 | | | |
| Relative Advantage | Between Groups | 8.541 | 2 | 4.270 | 25.484 | .000 |
| | Within Groups | 35.693 | 213 | .168 | | |
| | Total | 44.233 | 215 | | | |

## Impact of Technology Acceptance Model on Intention to Use E-Government

Analysis on the impact of technology acceptance model on intention to use e-government reveals that citizens who think that government web-sites are easy to use are more willing to use government web sites: the mean and standard deviation for the first group in the Perceived Ease of Use (PEU) questions are ($M$ = 1.24, $SD$ = .22), for the second group – ($M$ = 2.55, $SD$ = .43), and for the third group – ($M$ = 2.84, $SD$ = .16). In addition, people who think that sites are useful show more intension to use government web-sites: Perceived Usefulness (PU) results are ($M$ = 1.223, $SD$ = *.18)* – for group 1, ($M$ = 2.58, $SD$ = .40) – for group 2, and ($M$ = 2.78, $SD$ = .25) – for group 3.

Results of one-way ANOVA show that there is a statistical significant difference between 3 groups on intension to use e-government for all factors: for the factor PEU – $F(2,213) = 38.11$, $p < 0.05$; for the factor PU – $F(2,213) = 51.25$, $p < 0.05$.

## SOLUTIONS AND RECOMMENDATIONS

Kyrgyz Republic is still at the beginning of e-government establishment and currently in the State Information Resources List of the Kyrgyz Republic there are 55 web sites listed but the number is increasing. In this work, authors examined whether the target users for government online services - citizens, are ready and willing to use e-government, and what criteria determine the readiness of citizens to use e-government services. This issue became important in the light of recent collection of biometrical date in the Kyrgyz Republic and transition to e-voting system, since participation in election depends, along with other factors, on the citizen's perception of e-government as well. Overall, Kyrgyz government is introducing a range of new e-services in replacement of traditional paper-based services.

The data for this research was collected via survey questionnaires. In the sample used in this work 96% of respondents had a personal computer at home, and 85% of them were connected to Internet. These rates have major role in estimating citizens' behavior and their perception of government web sites as a part of general perception of computerization and, let's call it "internetization" in KR. One more factor that should be taken into account is that in the Kyrgyz Republic there are two languages in use – Kyrgyz language in the status of the state language, and Russian – in the status of official language. Although in the big cities there is a high level of knowledge of both languages, in the countryside Russian is used rarely. However the review of government web sites showed that only 26% of them have full Kyrgyz version, which also have impact on the citizen's intention to use the web sites.

*Table 6. ANOVA of respondents' intention to use government websites in terms of TAM*

| | | Sum of Squares | df | Mean Square | F | Sig. |
|---|---|---|---|---|---|---|
| PEU | Between Groups | 11.657 | 2 | 5.828 | 38.109 | .000 |
| | Within Groups | 32.576 | 213 | .153 | | |
| | Total | 44.233 | 215 | | | |
| PU | Between Groups | 14.372 | 2 | 7.186 | 51.256 | .000 |
| | Within Groups | 29.862 | 213 | .140 | | |
| | Total | 44.233 | 215 | | | |

In addition, the analysis revealed some obvious results such as those respondents with lower rate of cybercrime awareness are more willing to use e-government, while those with higher rate of awareness have lower desire to use it. It suggests that people who are not aware of cybercrime are open to use e-governments, while those who are aware of risks are not willing to use it because of potential and real risks. As it was mentioned above, government web sites in the Kyrgyz Republic offer no more than generic information about government and its programs at the moment. Nevertheless, security awareness was found to be a statistically significant factor influencing the willingness of people to use government web sites. Same results are obtained for factor Compatibility and Relative Advantage, meaning that people for whom using internet technologies fit their lifestyle and who see relative advantage in using it prefer to use government web sites to search information. Unlike results, obtained in similar studies elsewhere, for Kyrgyz people the image given by use of internet technologies is an important factor to use government web sites. Thus, all diffusion of innovation factors are important for Kyrgyz society and have impact on their intention to refer to government web sites.

Characteristics of web sites such as usability and usefulness of information available there on the websites are also important for people to use these web sites. In this work perceived of ease of use and perceived usefulness played significant role in intension to use government web sites in Kyrgyz society. As for trustworthiness, respondents with lower rate of trust to government have lower intensions to use e-government, while those with higher rate of trust have higher intension to use it. Furthermore, people who trust to internet are more likely to use it, while those who do not trust internet, are reluctant to use e-government. This result reaffirms the existence of correlation between security awareness of citizens and their willingness to use government online services.

However, the results of this research on the impact of technology acceptance model on intention to use shows that quality of government web sites still considered to be not high enough for users. As it was mentioned in (Brimkulov & Baryktabasov, 2014) research, governmental web sites face the problem of lack of cooperation between the government bodies, lack of sufficient incentives for civil servants and corruption and low knowledge of citizens about the value of e-government. In addition, more effort is needed for government web sites in the Kyrgyz Republic to improve accessibility, usability and security (Ismailova, 2017).

According to National Statistics Committee, in 2013, only 2% (i.e., 80 out of 4200) of government agencies are connected to Government computer network; 6% (263 out of 4200) of government agencies and companies have web sites and less than half of them have a content in Kyrgyz language (NSC, 2015).

It is believed that these services will further develop into complete e-government system. The citizens' perception of government web sites will certainly be reflected into their perception of e-government as well. In order for e-government in the Kyrgyz Republic to work effectively and be useful and based on results of this work, it is suggested the following steps to be made to increase the popularity of government websites and services provided online:

- Increase the quality of government web sites
- Increase the quality of information in government web sites
- Pay more attention to the availability of web site versions in both Kyrgyz and Russian Language at least

In 2013 the number of employees that use information and communication technologies has made 106 thousand (which is 3% of working age population) according to National Statistics Committee. Therefore, along with the increase of the web sites quality, it is necessary to

- Increase computer literacy rate in the country
- Increase awareness of citizens about government web sites and online services

Without these steps, government web sites in the Kyrgyz Republic risk to become web sites providing information and oriented toward the international development community rather than to the local population of the country. So far, government web sites in the Kyrgyz Republic still need great efforts to improve ease of use and the relative advantage of using web sites, and gain citizen's trust.

## Limitations

Several limitations need to be noted. First, the study was conducted in Russian language and having Kyrgyz language service might have yielded a more meaning and different result. Second limitation is that this study predominantly consisted of government employees and members of local organizations. It is important to reach out to ordinary citizens especially outside of Bishkek capital city and how they view e-government services. Perhaps, this is something that could be pursuit in future studies. Another weakness is that this study focuses on Kyrgyzstan as a case study but involving other countries in the region of Central Asia would contribute to wider body of knowledge about how e-government and e-government services might bring efficiency in public sector.

## REFERENCES

Akman, I., Yazici, A., Mishra, A., & Arifoglu, A. (2005). E-Government: A global view and an empirical evaluation of some attributes of citizens. *Government Information Quarterly*, *22*(2), 239–257. doi:10.1016/j.giq.2004.12.001

Al-Adawi, Z., Yousafzai, S., & Pallister, J. (2005, September). Conceptual model of citizen adoption of e-government. In *The Second International Conference on Innovations in Information Technology (IIT'05)* (pp. 1-10). Academic Press.

Aladwani, A. (2016). Corruption as a source of e-Government projects failure in developing countries: A theoretical exposition. *International Journal of Information Management*, *36*(1), 105–112. doi:10.1016/j.ijinfomgt.2015.10.005

Alzahrani, L., Al-Karaghouili, W., & Weerakkody, V. (2017). Analyzing the critical factors influencing trust in-government adoption from citizens' perspective: A systematic review and a conceptual framework. *Information Business Review*, *26*(1), 164–175. doi:10.1016/j.ibusrev.2016.06.004

Anthopoulos, L., Reddick, C., Giannakidou, I., & Mavridis, N. (2016). Why e-government projects fail? An analysis of the Healthcare.gov website. *Government Information Quarterly*, *33*(1), 161–173. doi:10.1016/j.giq.2015.07.003

Awan, M. A. (2008). Dubai e-government: An evaluation of G2B websites. *Journal of Internet Commerce*, *6*(3), 115–129. doi:10.1300/J179v06n03_06

Bjorklund, F. (2016). E-government and moral citizenship: The case of Estonia. *Citizenship Studies*, *20*(6-7), 914–931. doi:10.1080/13621025.2016.1213222

Brimkulov, U., & Baryktabasov, K. (2014). Public Transactional e-Services through Government Web Sites in Kyrgyzstan. *Electronic. Journal of E-Government*, *12*(1).

Carter, L., & Bélanger, F. (2005). The utilization of e-government services: Citizen trust, innovation and acceptance factors*. *Information Systems Journal*, *15*(1), 5–25. doi:10.1111/j.1365-2575.2005.00183.x

Carter, L., Weerakkody, V., Philips, B., & Dwivedi, Y. (2016). Citizen Adoption of E-Government Services: Exploring Citizen Perceptions of Online Services in the United States and United Kingdom. *Information Systems Management*, *33*(2), 124–140. doi:10.1080/10580530.2016.1155948

Carter, L., & Weerakkody, W. (2008). E-government adoption: A cultural comparison. *Information Systems Frontiers*, *10*(4), 473–482. doi:10.100710796-008-9103-6

Choi, H., Park, M. J., Rho, J. J., & Zo, H. (2016). Rethinking the assessment of e-government implementation in developing countries from the perspective of the design-reality gap: Applications in the Indonesian e-procurement system. *Telecommunications Policy*, *40*(7), 644–660. doi:10.1016/j.telpol.2016.03.002

Colesca, S. E. (2009). Increasing e-trust: A solution to minimize risk in e-government adoption. *Journal of Applied Quantitative Methods*, *4*(1), 31–44.

Colesca, S. E., & Dobrica, L. (2008). Adoption and use of e-government services: The case of Romania. *Journal of Applied Research and Technology*, *6*(03).

Davis, F. D., Bagozzi, R. P., & Warshaw, P. R. (1989). User acceptance of computer technology: A comparison of two theoretical models. *Management Science*, *35*(8), 982–1003. doi:10.1287/mnsc.35.8.982

DeYoung, A. (2010). *Lost in Transition: redefining students and universities in the contemporary Kyrgyz Republic*. Charlotte, NC: Information Age Publishing.

Elbahnasawy, N. (2014). E-government, Internet Adoption, and Corruption: An Empirical Investigation. *World Development*, *57*, 114–126. doi:10.1016/j.worlddev.2013.12.005

Freedman, E., & Shafer, R. (2012). Advancing a Comprehensive Research Agenda for Central Asian Mass Media. *Media Asia*, *39*(3), 119–126. doi:10.1080/01296612.2012.11689927

Freedom House. (2017). *Freedom on the Net*. Available https://freedomhouse.org/report/freedom-net/2016/kyrgyzstan

Gauld, R., Goldfinch, S., & Horsburgh, S. (2010). Do they want it? Do they use it? The 'Demand-Side'of e-Government in Australia and New Zealand. *Government Information Quarterly*, *27*(2), 177–186. doi:10.1016/j.giq.2009.12.002

Gazeta.kg. (2015). *В Бишкеке открылся информационно-образовательный центр для людей с ограниченными возможностями здоровья*. Retrieved on March 5, 2016, from http://www.gazeta.kg/news/kyrgyzstan/society/32463-v-bishkekeotkrylsya-informacionno-obrazovatelnyy-centr-dlya-lyudey-s-ogranichennymivozmozhnostyami-zdorovya.html

Gunawong, P., & Gao, P. (2017). Understanding e-government failure in the developing country context: A process-oriented study. *Information Technology for Development*, *23*(1), 153–178. doi:10.1080/02681102.2016.1269713

International Telecommunications Union. (2017). *Asia: Marketing Research, Internet Usage, Population Statistics and Facebook Information*. Available at http://www.internetworldstats.com/asia.htm

Ismailova, R. (2017). Web site accessibility, usability and security: A survey of government web sites in Kyrgyz Republic. *Universal Access in the Information Society*, *16*(1), 257–264. doi:10.100710209-015-0446-8

Janenova, S., & Kim, S. (2016). Innovating Public Service Delivery in Transitional Countries: The Case of One Stop Shops in Kazakhstan. *International Journal of Public Administration*, *39*(4), 322–333. doi:10.1080/01900692.2015.1064445

Kumar, R., Sachan, A., & Mukherjee, A. (2017). Qualitative approach to determine user experience of e-government services. *Computers in Human Behavior*, *71*, 299–306. doi:10.1016/j.chb.2017.02.023

Kurfali, M., Arifoglu, A., Tokdemir, G., & Pacin, Y. (2017). Adoption of e-government services in Turkey. *Computers in Human Behavior*, *66*, 168–178. doi:10.1016/j.chb.2016.09.041

Maerz, S. (2016). The electronic face of authoritarianism: E-government as a tool for gaining legitimacy in competitive and non-competitive regimes. *Government Information Quarterly*, *33*(4), 725–735. doi:10.1016/j.giq.2016.08.008

Mates, P., Lechner, T., Rieger, P., & Pekna, J. (2013). Toward e-government project assessment: European approach. *Preliminary Communication*, *31*(1), 103–125.

Muhametjanova, G., & Çagiltay, K. (2012, July). Students' and Instructors' Perceptions on Use of Information and Communication Technologies during Instruction in a Kyrgyzstan University. In *Advanced Learning Technologies (ICALT), 2012 IEEE 12th International Conference on* (pp. 500-502). IEEE.

Palvia, S. C. J., & Sharma, S. S. (2007). E-government and e-governance: definitions/domain framework and status around the world. In *International Conference on E-governance*. Available at http://www.iceg.net/2007/books/1/1_369.pdf

Rahardjo, E., Mirchandani, D., & Joshi, K. (2007). E-government functionality and website features: A case study of Indonesia. *Journal of Global Information Technology Management*, *10*(1), 31–50. doi:10.1080/1097198X.2007.10856437

Rehman, M., Kamal, M., & Esichaikul, V. (2016). Adoption of e-Government Services in Pakistan: A Comparative Study Between Online and Offline Users. *Information Systems Management*, *33*(3), 248–267. doi:10.1080/10580530.2016.1188570

Rodrigues, G., Sarabdeen, J. & Balasubramanian, S. (2016). *Factors that Influence Consumer Adoption of E-government Services in the UAE: A UTAUT Model Perspective*. Academic Press.

Sheryazdanova, G., & Butterfield, J. (2017). E-government as an anti-corruption strategy in Kazakhstan. *Journal of Information Technology & Politics*, *14*(1), 83–94. doi:10.1080/19331681.2016.1275998

Stier, S. (2015). Political determinants of e-government performance revisited: Comparing democracies and autocracies. *Government Information Quarterly*, *32*(3), 270–278. doi:10.1016/j.giq.2015.05.004

Wangpipatwong, S., Chutimaskul, W., & Papasratorn, B. (2008). Understanding citizen's continuance intention to use e-government website: A composite view of technology acceptance model and computer self-efficacy. *The Electronic Journal of E-Government, 6*(1), 55-64.

Welch, E. W., Hinnant, C. C., & Moon, M. J. (2005). Linking citizen satisfaction with e-government and trust in government. *Journal of Public Administration: Research and Theory*, *3*(15), 371–391.

Zawaideh, F. (2017). Acceptance of E-Government Services among Jordanian Citizen. *International Journal of Recent Advances in Multidisciplinary Research*, *4*(2), 2348–2351.

Zhao, F., & Khan, M. S. (2013). An Empirical Study of E-Government Service Adoption: Culture and Behavioral Intention. *International Journal of Public Administration*, *36*(10), 710–722. doi:10.1080/01900692.2013.791314

## KEY TERMS AND DEFINITIONS

**Central Asia:** The region of five countries of former Soviet Union. The countries are Kazakhstan, Kyrgyzstan, Tajikistan, Turkmenistan, and Uzbekistan.

**E-Government:** The use of new information and communication technologies to provide people, businesses, and organizations about government services, programs and information.

**Taza Koom (Smart Nation):** The Kyrgyz government national strategy program until 2040 to move toward to digital nation. The set goals include becoming digital nation with developed information society and ensuring full access of citizens to information, digital infrastructure and digital services.

**Technology Acceptance Model:** A general model that describes peoples' acceptance of information technology based on their individual perception. This model may be outdated in the developed world but it is of current interest where new communication technologies are only appearing at a massive scale.

# Chapter 12
# Mobile Governance for Affordability and Profitability/Feasibility

**Vinay Sharma**
*Indian Institute of Technology Roorkee, India*

**Anita Sengar**
*University of Petroleum and Energy Studies, India*

## ABSTRACT

*The chapter expresses the extent of the application of "e" and mobile mode for governance along with the extent to which, this application can be uplifted through building up the case around the healthcare system and changing market scenario in rural areas because of the researches which the authors/proponents of this chapter have been conducting. The premise that emerges in the chapter has evolved through the primary interaction with the concerned population. The findings suggest that the rural people of India opine and desire for better healthcare services and market scenario through alternative means, they are willing to pay for the services, they have opined positively and they wish to be involved in the market development scenario wherein E-governance and m-governance has emerged to be an important mode.*

## INTRODUCTION

This chapter expresses the extent of the application of 'E' and Mobile mode for governance along with the extent to which, this application can be uplifted through building up the case around the 'Health Care' system and 'Changing Market Scenario' in rural areas because of the researches which the authors/proponents of this chapter have been conducting.

The chapter highlights the aspects of

- E-Governance and Citizen Trust
- E-Governance and Digital Divide and
- Mobile Government

DOI: 10.4018/978-1-5225-5966-5.ch012

The premise of the preceding elements and propositions those emerge as cases and examples in the chapter has evolved through the primary interaction longitudinally pursued through Reflexive Research Approach.

The findings suggest that:

1. The rural people of India opine and desire for better 'Health Care' Services and Market Scenario through alternative means,
2. They are willing to pay for the services,
3. They have opined positively and are willing for suitable Health –Insurance cover and
4. They wish to be involved in the market development scenario.

## Importance of 'E' and 'M' Governance

The important point to be noticed here is that not only 'E' and 'M' Governance has provided impetus to the above aspects but also has become a mode of delivery for the same. Further, it is interesting to find out that how they (the population concerned) are adopting 'E' and 'M' in their daily lives and subsequently how Governance is getting inclined towards these modes and further how the said modes may be foreseen to enhance the intensity and capacity of Governance especially for the domains chosen for demonstrative purposes in this proposed chapter?

The evidences are suggestive of an association as expressed below:

Development of Association of Health Care to other Business Opportunities or vice versa through Mobile Governance

- As in the case of ITC's E-Choupal (https://www.echoupal.com) and many other interventions along with the adoption of Mobile Communication by the rural population, where the said organizations propelling their interventions are supplementing their ICTs (Information and Communication Technologies) based business activities with the 'Health Care' activities.
- Here, begins an extensive usage and spread of Health Insurance Propositions further propelling the market development, further triggering the process towards other areas that, if strategically is complimented with objective Governance as in the case of a massive demonetization exercise in India.

## SUMMARY OF THE CHAPTER

## The Basic Model

### An Integrative Model

Integrating the perspective of the findings of the researches as suggested above, the role of 'E' and 'M' Governance and Market Development in the Rural Areas of India and the similar countries, this research work puts forward a model/a proposition based on the premise of 'Affordability for the Poor & Profitability/feasibility for the Provider' (This model was presented at Network of Asia-Pacific Schools and

Institutes of Public Administration and Governance (NAPSIPAG) Annual Conference 2005 BEIJING, PRC, 5-7 DECEMBER 2005) and is published as a book with the same name.

This model argues on the following major aspects:

1. The Private Health Care Providers; with the perspective of feasibility and profitability and The State with the perspective of the sustainability of the level of its services and infrastructure should be looking at the 'Size' of the market (rural and the poor population) and not at the buying capacity as a fundamental aspect in the case of highly populated developing and the underdeveloped nations.
2. Technology 'E' and 'M' modes can play an extensive and a very positive role in the Health Care provision and disbursement to the Rural Poor.
3. Health services are the human right of the masses and should be seen as a social responsibility by the marketer (the private health care providers) along with being seen as a business opportunity, on the one hand and on the other hand as the central most aspect of a broader and overall social development.
4. The proposition is also suggestive of the fact that, by looking at the size of the market as an asset, we can compliment the same with strategic generation of buying power i.e. by 'creating buying power' (with the perspective of co-creation of value) (Prahalad, 2005).

So as to:

*Provide a stable solution for the health care problems to the poor and the rural population at their doorsteps through commercial health care providers and others, without sacrificing the commercial feasibility or viability of the resources invested by them.*

The core concept here asks for the solution of the following problems:

1. How to enhance (maximize) the levels of usage of the present Health Care Services infrastructure (which includes Human Resources also)?
2. How to motivate the commercial (large or small) health care providers (organizations) to spread over into seemingly less lucrative rural & poor markets?
3. How to develop a universally acceptable and financially viable business proposition for such a situation and the people involved?

The basic need is for a model to be generated in this regard mainly involving commercial organizations because of the reasons such as:

1. Being the commercial motive involved positive results can be expected.
2. The major issue is of replicating the model and this definitely is expected when commercial organizations are involved, as it is a major characteristic of money to replicate.

But, why would commercial healthcare providers provide their services (which involve substantial costs) to the people who cannot afford the same? OR why they would enter into a MARKET i.e. serve the population, which at least seemingly, does not assure financial feasibility?

In addition, the answer is that this market is associated with the huge population however poor but has access to the most basic and huge resources of agriculture and other rural produce and labor and the huge 'size' of this market supports the logic of a Business Proposition.

Henceforth, the evolved strategic model, which broadly is based primarily on the development of 'human will' through the support of clear vision and precise objectives emphasizes on the role of 'E' and 'M' modes of Governance.

The said model comprises of five strategic elements in the form of sequential steps, wherein, two of the strategies are based on the basis of the marketing logic & feasibility and two of them are based and supported by the fundamental aspects of the generation of buying power and integrating the same with providing the health care services with profitability/feasibility and subsequently reaping the benefits of business development and the market development.

But, the very first step would be the infusion of technology in the present system with the perspective of generating commitment and credibility through information Technology.

## IMPORTANCE OF THE THIRD STAGE OF THE PROPOSED MODEL

This Chapter focuses on the third stage of the model suggested and published, (Sharma, 2009)

The third step, which is primarily based on the effective and the strategic distribution of services also emphasizes on the integration of some other business propositions and the services specifically relevant to the rural and the poor population of India and similar nations. Here, also as and when the MNC's are perceived to effectively look towards the markets mentioned as profitable business propositions, the usage of Information technology would become an effective part of the success of this third step. Though, the insurance factor can well be spread from the initial most phase, but its effectiveness may be strengthened if it is introduced along with the second and the third steps, when perceivably the strategic activation of all the forces involved in the provision of 'Health Care to the Rural and the Poor' of India is already done. For example, ITC's E-Choupal (ITC Portal, n.d.a) may go ahead with such a proposition.

### The Execution Strategy (Relevance of 'E' and 'M' Governance)

Here, the suggestion is that keeping in mind the requirement for the replicability factor, these steps may be bifurcated into self-reliant separate profit generating businesses at the peak of their development.

One more important factor that this study strongly recommends is the role of women in all the steps beginning from the execution level to the levels of strategic management, as time and again females have proven themselves and their roles in the social development. They have also proved to be the binding forces in the development of such models of social values and importance. This fact is duly endorsed by the organizations like UNICEF with the perspective that the financial independence of the mother is directly proportional to the development of the child.

### A Clue About the Practical Implementation of the Proposition

A Prospective Association of ITC's e-Choupal (ITC Portal, n.d.a; ITC Portal, n.db) with the Health Care and Rural Market System:

*Figure 1. The Model: 'Affordability for the Poor and Profitability/Feasibility for the Provider'*

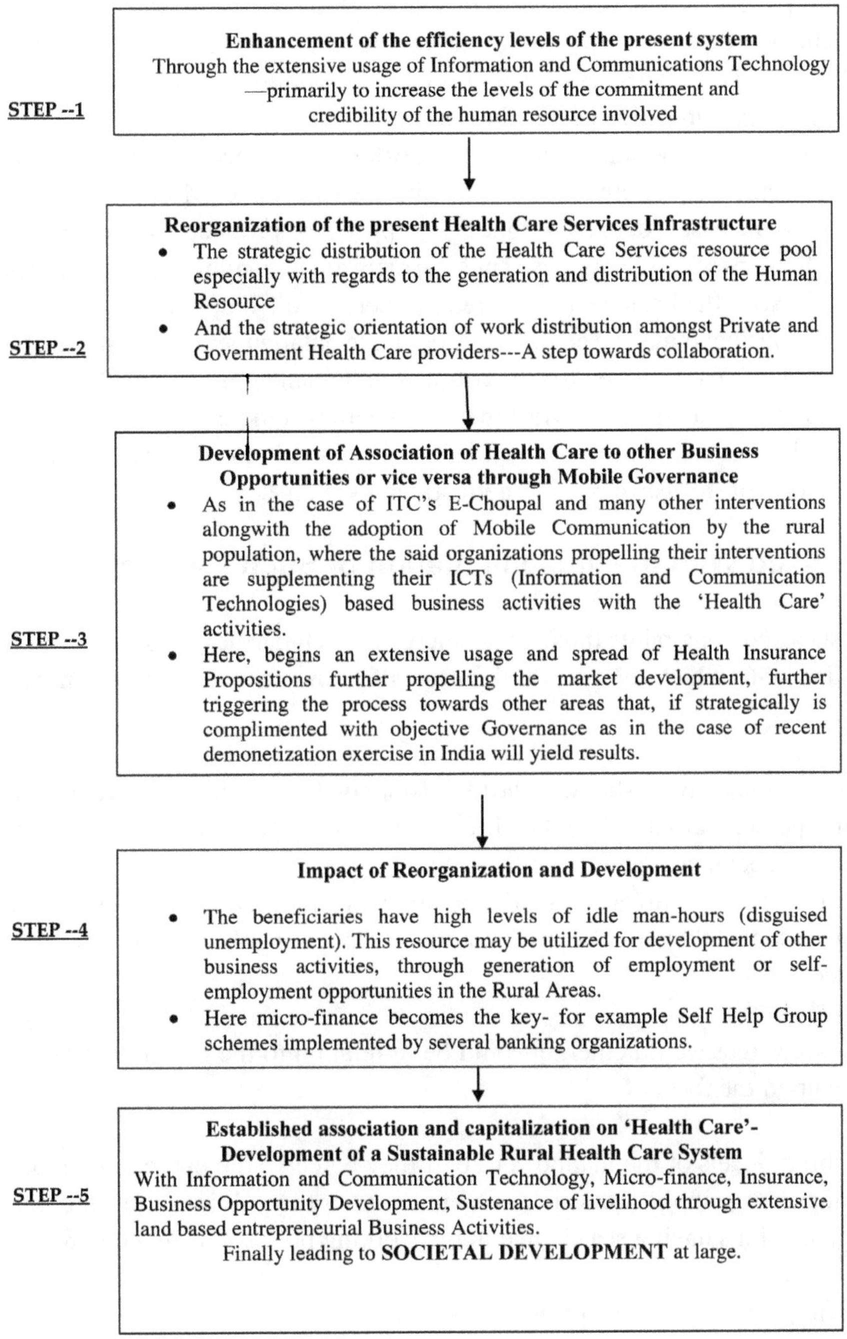


Here, comes the role of Information Technology based organization like ITC's e-Choupal. ITC is one of India's foremost private sector companies with a market capitalization of over US $ 7.5 billion and a turnover of US $ 2.6 billion. The Company's 'e-Choupal' initiative is enabling Indian agriculture significantly enhance its competitiveness by empowering Indian farmers through the power of the Internet.

This transformational strategy, which has already become the subject matter of a case study at Harvard Business School, is expected to progressively create for ITC a huge rural distribution infrastructure, significantly enhancing the Company's marketing reach. Presently – More than 5500 Choupals are serving over 3 million farmers and villagers across 30000 villages (adding 6 a day) out of which Uttar Pradesh has more than 1700 kiosks installed in its villages.

ITC is also exploring collaborating with banks to offer farmers access to credit, insurance, and other services that are not currently offered or are prohibitively expensive. Moreover, farmers are beginning to suggest—and in some cases, demand—that ITC supply new products or services or expand into additional crops, such as onions and potatoes. Thus, farmers are becoming a source of product and service innovation for ITC. Now, the basic factor and requirement is to fill up the gaps in the Health Care Services, which, on the one hand may be achieved through the enlargement of the infrastructure and human resource requiring lot of fixed and recurring costs and redundancy of resource base. While on the other hand a partnership of the Health Care Machinery and Rural Markets with ITC may give a reasonable raise in the profitability of the company, also fulfilling its new-found objective of 'co- creation of value' through multiplication of the usage of their network and systems.

## Issues Associated With the Implementation of Such a Model

The expected issues and constraints those may emerge in such partnerships:

Foreseen issues, with which the proposed partnerships may expectedly be confronted with, would emerge in terms of:

1. Difference in the Objectives, Missions and the Visions of the government and the private organizations.
2. Cultural and perceptual barriers related to the acceptability of the beneficiaries towards private institutions and social changes accompanying the same.
3. Social structure, as the politically and the socially powerful people would be required to be adaptive of the changes so that they may be instrumental in replicating the process once the associations are implemented.

Some of the issues that would emerge would be in relation to the facilitators of the process. These issues may come up in the form of:

- The adaptability levels of the manpower i.e. if they perceive the process to be beneficial for them and adapt the change in the working environment after the public institutions get associated with private organizations having sea change in the working philosophy and environment as compared to theirs.
- The prevalent problems of corruption in the state.

## MAGIC OF 'E' AND 'M' GOVERNANCE (EXAMPLES AND CASELETS)

### 1. Kumbh: The Biggest Congregations on Earth—How Do They Do It?

Imagine around 25 – 30 Million people at one place at one time near the river Ganges in an area of not more than 5000 acres.

This is a glimpse of Kumbh Mela, which happens at four different places in India after a cycle of 12 years wherein total influx of people during a period of 20 days is around 70 -100 Million.

We as authors and researchers have been visiting these congregations regularly and it seems like magic because of two major reasons:

- All of the visitors are uninvited and visit randomly wherein demographic segregation does not play any role.
- The people must reach at the designated places to take a dip in the rivers during a particular time period on *one particular day*.

Therefore, however one makes the arrangements and bring in a mechanism to manage the gathering wherein people when go to take a dip in the river may have to walk in beelines for hours.

There are several possibilities especially, in terms of:

- Health Care and
- Market Development

Any infection may breakout and may take a shape of an epidemic and on the other side, there is a possibility of Integrated Marketing Communication, Data Collection and even Sales because people stay in the surroundings and a rotational influx of millions of people is there.

Since the year 2001, the usage of 'E' and 'M' Governance in sequence has started in such congregations, which has helped the people, the Government as well as the marketers.

In 2001 (Also refer to "*Motivation absorbs Magnitude*" by Sharma, Vinay, 2009) wherein one of the authors visited and camped in the Kumbh Mela of Allahabad (The Largest Congregation of people at one place at one time since the times immemorial) it was for the first time that the usage of 'E' mode started for Governance purposes and especially for Health Care purposes through Telemedicine wherein not only patients were recorded electronically but also were catered through telemedicine from distant specialty hospitals.

Numbers may speak for themselves and the inception of 'E' mode can open up large possibilities as we can understand for example when millions gather then thousands are at least catered to. Further Management of such congregations have now been catered to with 'M' Governance also along with an important development wherein several companies have started using electronic devices and kiosks for catering to the visit-based needs of the consumers while simultaneously generating a data base of the visitors.

## 2. Forest Bio-Residue Energy Generation and 'M' Governance

Around 100000 Tons of Pine Leaves are shed on the floor of North Western Himalayas in India every year. This is a huge repository renewable energy. One of the authors of this chapter along with a researcher who also is a Forest Department Government Officer catered to this problem through the development of a value chain through the development of a Machine for producing the forest bio-residue briquettes (Joshi, Sharma, Mittal, 2015) also see other papers as referred in Bibliography list of this chapter.

Everything seemed to be in place even the Government support came in terms of policy augmentation wherein the pine needles were freed from the conservation policy, but the bigger deal was to manage this value chain and here came in 'E' and 'M' mode.

Concurrently when this chapter is being written today on 31st of October 2017, Mobile and Internet based interventions, which have now been developed by a team lead by one of the authors, are being introduced through a project to establish the massive business proposition and the proposed value chain. The quantum result in terms of the alternative energy, generated, carbon credits earned, socio-economic changes brought and the GDP contribution at large would be substantial enough to be noticed and imitated globally.

## 3. Education and 'M' Governance

Another project which one of the authors is about to steer though is usual education accessibility enhancement but is unique and has achieved is structural capability through Mobile and Internet interventions.

Management Education in India has predominantly been supported by the literature, examples and models developed elsewhere especially USA and Europe except of the components, which are now complimenting the thought process and the literature recently in terms of examples or scriptural theories now being acknowledged in terms of managerial fundamentals.

Exploring the need of the disbursement of management education with relevance and in understandable terms and language a project of converting the literature and text in the local languages and delivering it to the students by the trained faculty while strengthening the process through 'M' and 'E' modes is to be initiated. This project and process would take some time and seems at a proposition stage but the prospective magnitude holds a large promise especially when Indian economy is gearing itself up for next manufacturing and market development movement and would be requiring millions of entrepreneurial managers.

## 4. Rural Market Development and 'M' Governance

Having worked in and for rural markets in India for several years wherein a definition of rural marketing has been proposed in one of their researches,

*Rural Marketing is values based strategic approach to cumulative, inclusive upliftment of the rural markets cumulatively addressing this market as a different segment while keeping the social fabric of this market intact and addressing this segment through basic products and services required at first. (Sengar, 2015)*

The authors have realized that the future of marketing lead by INNOVATIVE DIGITAL GOVERNANCE lies in the rural areas wherein countries like India have large part of their populations belonging to the rural areas (In India it is to the levels of around 650 Million). Therefore, authors have continuously been collecting data and have been observing and consulting with the organizations focused on rural areas, which suggests that 'M' Governance and 'M' marketing is the future.

In recent years, Government of India The government had introduced many programs that will help digitizing the whole nation. These are providing technology enabled solutions such as setting optical fiber cable, availability of affordable devices, linking subsidies and other facilities with these initiatives and providing appropriate training to develop relevant skills to use all services related to E-governance and m-governance. Some of these initiatives (Deloitte, 2015) are explained in the following section.

## Pradhan Mantri Jandhan Yojana (PMJDY)

The basic objective of this scheme was to empower Indians by opening bank accounts and providing them debit cards and accidental insurance coverage. More than 100 million RuPay cards were distributed. In order to increase adoption rate of these RuPay debit cards, handheld PoS devices were distributed specifically in rural areas.

## Direct Benefit Transfer (DBT)

The basic objective of this scheme was to transfer directly into the accounts of consumers, in order to reduce the malpractices, adulteration and pilferage. Bank accounts of these consumers were also attached with Aadhar number for effective operation of the scheme.

## JAM Trinity (Jan-Dhan-Aadhar-Mobile Trinity)

Government of India made it mandatory to link three identification numbers of Indian citizens. These are Jan Dhan bank account number, Aadhar number and mobile number. The basic objective was to make cashless society, transfer of government benefits directly to citizen accounts and removal of leakages of any form.

## Smart Cities

Indian government's objective is to develop 100 smart cities by the end of year 2022. Smart cities are equipped with public infrastructure, advanced communication facilities, internet connections, CCTV cameras for making life easier for public and it will facilitate government in e-governance as well as mobile governance. Many countries like France, Germany, UK, US, Spain are assisting technically in development of many of smart cities in India by adopting them. In smart cities, technology will be extensively used to monitor all-important areas of development such as education, health, traffic, energy, crime etc. Government is trying to develop these cities in PPPs (Public-Private-Partnership) mode.

### DigiLocker

DigiLocker service provides the facility to store important documents of citizens such as Pan Card, driving license, Voter ID card, educational certificates. Every citizen can store data upto 10MB and this storage space is linked to their Aadhar number. Although security of these documents is very important. These DigiLockers has helped in reducing the paper work and reduction in processing time. It is an important aid in e-governance and m-governance.

### Wi-Fi Hotspots

Government of India has taken this initiative to establish Wi-Fi Hotspots throughout the country by collaborating with BSNL. This will help in establishing good interconnectivity across country and enable smooth operation of all the initiatives related to e-governance and m-governance. These Wi-Fi Hotspots are already operational at locations like metro stations, railway stations, airports etc.

### E-Hospital

E-Hospital, a very important step to ease using hospital services in India. The Department of Electronics and Information Technology directly manage this initiative. It has an online registration system that provides which access to several hospitals in India. It provides facilities ranging from registrations, appointments, fee payment, online reports, blood availability etc. This initiative will better hospital management.

### Skill India Initiative

To make e-governance and m-governance most effective and making its implementation easier, there was a need to make people digitally aware and there was a need to educate people regarding technical knowhow for using these services. Government of India launched Skill India initiative whose objective was to prepare skilled workforce.

### National Optical Fiber Network (NOFN)

Another important initiative by the government of India is to develop National Optical Fiber Network (NOFN) to make India digital and make implementation of e-governance and m-governance easier and affordable to mass population in India that resides in rural areas. Government is developing a high-speed digital highway, which is world's largest rural broadband project using optical fiber that will connect all 250,000-gram panchayats of the country.

## HOW IS THE PROCESS TO BE IMPLEMENTED SUCCESSFULLY? THE SECRET LIES IN PUBLIC PRIVATE SPIRITUAL PARTNERSHIP AND CO-CREATION OF VALUE

Public Private Spiritual Partnership and Co-Creation of Value will be instrumental in achieving Trust and overcoming Digital Divide.

Public Private Spiritual Partnership or PPSP is a proposition proposed by one of the authors in relation to the Health Care Provision to the Rural-Poor Population of the World (Please refer to Sharma, n.d.c).

The proposition is self-explanatory in terms of how the required level of synergy would be achieved to realize the results in self – replicable mode, which desirably would achieve Co-Creation of Value as also suggested by Prahalad.

## REFERENCES

Deloitte. (2015). *E-governance and Digital India Empowering Indian Citizens through Technology*. Retrieved from https://www2.deloitte.com/content/dam/Deloitte/in/Documents/technology-media-telecommunications/in-tmt-empowering-indian-citizens-through-technology-noexp.pdf

ITC Portal. (n.d.a). *ITC Enduring Value*. Retrieved from http://www.itcportal.com

ITC Portal. (n.d.b). *Echoupal Frameset*. Retrieved from http://www.itcportal.com/sets/ echoupal_frameset.htm

Joshi, K. K., & Sharma, V. (2013). *Concrete heaps to carpet green through peoples participation. In Success Stories in Mountain Ecosystem Management* (pp. 34–42). Thimpu, Bhutan: SAARC Forestry Center.

Joshi, K. K., & Sharma, V. (2014). A study on Passages to global climate change financing: Funding for a greener Earth. *Indian Forester*.

Joshi, K.K., & Sharma, V. (2014). Challenges in community based forest bio residue resource utilization for bio briquetting in the Western Himalayan region of Uttarakhand. *SAARC Forestry Journal 2014*.

Joshi, K.K., & Sharma, V. (2014). Genesis of people's perception of forest fires in Western Himalayan region of Uttarakhand, India: Causes and Remedies. *Journal of Trade Science*.

Joshi, K. K., & Sharma, V. (2014). Mitigating land disaster through community involvement and righteous practices in Himalayan region of Uttarakhand, India. In *Strategic Disaster Risk Management in Asia*. Singapore: Springer.

Joshi, K. K., Sharma, V., & Mittal, S. (2015). Social entrepreneurship through forest bio residue briquetting: An approach to mitigate forest fires in Pine areas of Western Himalaya, India. *Renewable & Sustainable Energy Reviews*, *51*, 1338–1344. doi:10.1016/j.rser.2015.07.057

Prahalad, C. K. (2005). *The fortune at the bottom of the pyramid: Eradicating poverty through profits*. Pearson Education.

Sengar, A. (2015). *A study on evolving perspectives of rural marketing* (Unpublished doctoral dissertation). Indian Institute of Technology, Roorkee, India.

Sharma, V. (2009). Motivation absorbs Magnitude. *Chinese Public Administration Review*, *6*(1/2), 1–8. doi:10.22140/cpar.v6i1/2.82

Sharma, V. (2009). *Affordability For The Poor And Profitability For The Provider: Provision of Health for the Rural and the Poor Population of the world with special reference to Uttar Pradesh in India.* VDM Verlag.

Sharma, V. (n.d.a). *Enhancing the reach of the Health-Care with the perspective of Affordability for the Poor & Profitability for the Provider A Proposition with special reference to Uttar Pradesh- A State in India.* Health Care for the Poor in Asia Workshop in Network of Asia-Pacific Schools and Institutes of Public Administration and Governance (NAPSIPAG) Annual Conference 2005, Beijing, China.

Sharma, V. (n.d.b). *Innovations in Public Service and Rural market Development in India to achieve a Harmonious Society.* Innovations in governance and public service to achieve a harmonious society workshop in Network of Asia-Pacific Schools and Institutes of Public Administration and Governance (NAPSIPAG) Annual Conference 2005, Beijing, China.

Sharma, V. (n.d.c). *Health for All Through Affordability and Profitability With Public Spiritual Partnership.* Retrieved from http://www.napsipag.org/PDF/VINAY%20SHARMA.pdf

Sharma V., Joshi K., & Agrawal R. (2014). Empowering Women through Social Entrepreneurship. *Indian Management- The Journal of AIMA, 53*(4), 58-63.

Sharma, V., Joshi, K., & Agrawal, R. (2015). *Mobility for aspirations while aspiring for not moving----Understanding aspirations and mobility of the Forest users and the dwellers of the North-Western Himalayan region of India.* Paper presented at the annual conference of the HDCA, Tokyo, Japan.

Sharma, V., Mishra, H. S., Joshi, K. K., & Agrawal, R. (2016). *Disasters, Diversity, Disparity, Discrimination and Vulnerability.* Paper presented at the annual conference of the HDCA, Tokyo, Japan.

# Chapter 13
# Embodiment and Gameplay: Situating the User in Crowdsourced Information Production

**Karin Hansson**
*Stockholm University, Sweden*

**Love Ekenberg**
*International Institute for Applied Systems Analysis, Austria & Stockholm University, Sweden*

## ABSTRACT

*Distributed decision making with several stakeholders has various facets. On one hand, it enables significant opportunities for fast and efficient information provision, in particular when various structuring frameworks are provided. On the other hand, there are several problems regarding the reliability and consistency of the data produced in social media contexts as well as with the frameworks themselves. Online collaborative data production systems where crowd feedbacks are aggregated and mediated are easily affected by group biases. There are also several credibility and verification issues as the representativeness of the participants normally is difficult or impossible to determine. This chapter discusses the handling of user data in tools for crowd sourced data production and suggests a framework for describing the socio-technical setting for the production of data, and thereby the detectability of bias patterns in collaborative information production.*

## INTRODUCTION

There seems to be an ever-growing demand for fair participatory processes and participation has become an important part of research and design processes, where the basic idea is to decentralize the control to various and inclusive groups of stakeholders. The idea is that, thereby, the democratic decision making in the development of more participatory and innovative governments will more or less automatically be strengthened (cf., eg., Hansson, Belkacem & Ekenberg, 2014, Ekenberg et al, 2017). To facilitate this, there are various IT-based platforms, such as voting systems, communication platforms, and various crowd-sourcing techniques aiming at facilitating various features of participation and transparency.

DOI: 10.4018/978-1-5225-5966-5.ch013

However, the success of all these methods has, in general, been quite limited to communication platforms, whereas tools for more analytical and deliberate support to a substantial participatory democracy have not seldom failed quite miserably.

The core idea of deliberative and participatory processes is that a broad public engagement and influence is important for understanding the issues at hand and that the transparency of the processes behind public decision making will provide a better and more trustworthy result. This general idea is supposed to be of high significant within both semi-public and public spheres and that the support from, e.g., social media platforms, further augmented with various structuring features and reputation mechanisms for analysing and verifying information, would provide a fundamental change to more hierarchical decision processes. The dream of an open government thus envisions transparent and deliberative processes, where the civil society can participate in the collection and analytical phases as well as in the actual decisions. These ideas have been explored more thoroughly by a multitude of researchers and practitioners, such as, (Heeks & Bailur, 2007; Roy, 2003; Yildiz, 2007). More recently, more elaborate ideas of fundamental institutional transformations have also appeared, where the fundamental idea is to investigate whether different social media platforms, rather that dedicated tools, more effectively can support participatory democracy and, equally importantly, create a more instrumental meaning to concepts such as e-government, e-participation and open data, cf., e.g., (Bright, J. and Margetts, H. 2016; Sinclair et al, 2017; Alarabiat et al, 2016)). An interesting and related question here is to what extent participation at all can be stimulated by some specific tools, or whether there are other mechanisms that are more dominant. Most informed or semi-informed people have ideas of democracy, transparency, fairness, equity, and so on, but in many cases in very vague terms. Concepts like these are of course constructs, and there are no unifying ideas regarding what participation and deliberation actually mean in relation to them, which of course is a further complicating factor when trying to understand to what extent various tools adequately represent what is going on and what they are actually support for.

We will not try to define these concepts herein. Sufficient for us is to assume that they include some inclusive and participatory aspects together with some degree of transparency when it comes to decision-making in different forms and that there are also decision-making bodies, such as governments, that can be more informed and effective at all. Transparency here seems to be crucial due to its obvious relation to trust, but also important when it comes to understanding the whole information process, why, e.g., Bannister and Connolly (2011) suggest that transparency in the online contexts not only should be about data, but also include the information and decision processes involved, i.e., who is behind the information as well as where, when, how and why it was produced. Regarding the participatory and decentralized components, some authors claim that these, except for strengthen the democratic processes per se, also can be a more sustainable and dynamical way of general governance, maintained through broad participation without a central authority, where larger groups can stipulate the agenda and the content as well as measure its quality. (See, e.g. Fung 2013; Parasie & Dagiral 2012.)

Some also claims some positive effects of that networked publics' are performed, shared and reproduced online by crowds of participants, where trust and mutual recognition is central, contrary to more traditional public spheres controlled by centralized gatekeepers (Hansson, 2015a). These networked publics can be used for establishing public archives and providing alternative decentralized sources of data, enabling different, and sometimes more reliable, data validation in the forms of different discussion forms, motivating mechanisms and voting systems, or mixes thereof, for extending communication modalities through, e.g., linking, liking, blogging, digging, and tweeting. The evaluation of information can also be facilitated by the creation of new value systems using various forms of reputation mechanisms for validation content rather than, more traditionally, using the legitimacy of conventional institutional frameworks (Hansson, Karlström, et al., 2013). Well-known examples of the latter include Wikipedia, where, usually, a larger group of participants produce and validate the data, or news services such as Digg where extended networks assist the participants in identifying the most interesting things to read and watch. Such reputation mechanisms can also be extended with more elaborated methods, such as more extended ranking support, pro-contra-lists, decision analytical support and so on (cf., e.g., Kivinuke et al, 2011; Danielson et al, 2014; Mihai et al, 2015). IT-based solutions can also be included for "alternative fact" detection and spread as well as for more automatic reliability mechanisms (eg Kaligotla et al, 2015; Kumar and Geethakumari, 2014); Karlova & Fisher, 2012). Not the least within the area of emergency management and catastrophic events (Hughes & Palen, 2012; Spiro et al., 2012). These trends of course increase when the use of various media is becoming more widespread in societies and leads to transformational governments, in the sense of (Irani, Elliman, & Jackson, 2007; Irani, Love, & Jones, 2008; King & Cotterill, 2007; Lindblad-Gidlund & Nygren, 2011; Veenstra, Klievink, & Janssen, 2011), as well as a related concept of open government and associated technologies (Hansson, Belkacem, & Ekenberg, 2014; Janssen, Charalabidis, & Zuiderwijk, 2012; Linders, 2012; Maier-rabler & Huber, 2011; Nam, 2012). The baseline here is that not only should the information and methods be accessible by default, but also being interoperable and open for reuse and analysis, by government agencies, the private sector and other relevant entities, such as the complicated "general public". In these contexts, collaborative information sharing and deliberative discussions, ever increasingly prevailing in social media on platforms, such as micro-blogs, social networks, photo and video sharing sites as well as wikis, are put forward as means for creating a more innovative and collaborative public sector and, in extension, more deliberative and participatory systems. The ever-expanding trends are of course generally positive, but there are severe complications due to the usual technological barriers, lack of security, privacy and trust, lack of resources, digital divide, group phenomena, biases, poor management among other things, and the ambitions with more participatory governments are often not fulfilled. The various complications thus result in severe problems when it comes to the actual participation and strongly delimit the representativeness of the people that are participating at all. As an example, geo-mapping tools such as OpenStreetMap are subject to a large demographic bias with significantly more males contributing (Neis and Zielstra, 2014; Stephens, 2013). In these negotiation games, there are always actors that are more successful than others in making their perspectives the dominant ones. Similarly, the social games on Wikipedia's many discussion forums are difficult to handle and are very much educational biased. Thus, we must somehow clarify such games without restricting them and find support mechanisms for otherwise underprivileged groups. Otherwise, democracy in a more elaborated sense is impossible.

To illuminate this a bit further, the remaining article provides an overview of how tools for crowd sourced data production are dealing with the inequality and representativeness issues, and discusses some ideas of how patterns of bias in collaborative information production online can become more transparent and avoidable. We also provide a theoretical framework for analyzing some popular tools for crowd sourced information production in this context. Thereafter, we suggest how to visualize patterns of bias in crowd sourced information production.

## THE ISSUE OF EQUAL REPRESENTATION

Collaborative digital platforms have been in use for at least two decades and have been quite extensively explored. Except for the more well-known and popular tools like Flickr and YouTube, Facebook, LinkedIn, or Twitter, there are e.g., SeeClickFix (Richman, 2010) and FixMyStreet (Ibid), for identifying neighbourhood issues and Ushahidi (Gao & Barbier, 2011) for collecting eyewitness reports of violence; Peer-to-Patent (Jian, 2010) to open the patent examination process Ballotpedia (n.d.), OpenCongress (n.d.), or more innovative like Diplopedia (Bronk & Smith, 2010), Intellipedia (Ben Eli & Hutchins, 2010), GCpedia (Fyfe & Crookall, 2010) and MyUniversity (n.d.). Crowdsourced or Volunteered Geographic Information (VGI) is also used to manage disasters like floods and fires. An overview of the area shows that the prevailing media for sharing VGI was found to be social media (i.e. Twitter, Facebook, Youtube) and mobile devices. Other platforms for VGI include Ushaidi, OpenStreetMap, Google MapMaker, Waze and Wikimapia. All these different platforms have in common are that they encompass components for deliberative discussions, in one way or another, and have thus a potential for supporting various facets of a more participatory government.

However, such information production online is essentially unequal as participants basically always are representing specific groups, contexts, experiences and opinions. As, e.g., (Dawes, 2008) points out, the main focus of e-government is usually merely on enhanced public services and improved government operations, while how to support transformations of governments to more open and interactive operating modalities is given considerably less attention; something that fundamentally obstructs a rapid and efficient transition to an inclusion of systematical open and participatory mechanisms in the general governance. The ambitions with a more participatory government are therefore often not fulfilled, which has repetedly been pointed out by several authors, such as (Rana, Dwivedi, & Williams, 2013) and (Hansson, Belkacem & Ekenberg, 2014). One particularly disturbing issue in this context is that there is a lack of systematic strategies for handling differences and representativeness in participatory information practices, why there are still many open problems to be resolved. This is nothing particular for digital media, but an effect of structural issues that must be addressed beyond specific technologies:

*In short, when the epistemologies, vocabularies, and categories of data structures do not or cannot encompass the experiences, knowledge claims, and identities of some social groups or places, this produces their under-representation in digital data. (Elwood, 2008, p. 6)*

The issue here is that in a more deliberative democracy, where citizens' participation is important in decision-making, people have unequal possibilities and incentives to actually participate. Online communication creates new possibilities for a more participatory regime at the same time as inequalities often are reinforced. Much focus has been on inequalities in access to the Internet, the so called "digital divide" excluding groups of people from the possibilities to participate in online activities. The communication technology also enables a differentiation between people on a larger scale, due to differences in digital literacy based on social and cultural preferences. There is a social divide between rich and poor within each nation, both in access and in the way Internet is used (Freschi, 2009; Norris, 2001), and there is a digital production-gap that correlates with socioeconomic status (Dutta-Bergman, 2005; Schradie, 2011; Sui et al., n.d.), language (Mocanu et al., 2013), as well as with gender (Elwood, 2008; Min, 2010). The relational nature of information production and dissemination in networked media makes peoples' situated social network central for information production, determining their information and communication range. Studies of young people's internet practices also show the importance of identity and recognition when it comes to information consumption and production online (Ahn, 2012; Hansson, 2015b; Ito et al., 2009).

Thus, the digital differentiation makes the problem with lack of, or at least unequal, representation in participation even more polarized and various aspects of this have been discussed, e.g., in (Abu-Shanab et al., 2010; Al-rashidi and London, 2010; Aman and Kasimin, 2011; Choudrie et al., 2005; Duggan et al., 2015; Elsheikh and Cullen, 2008; Mbarika and Byrd, 2009; Sang et al., 2009). Furthermore, processes of identification shapes networked publics and similar, reproduce and strengthen differences online (Hansson, Verhagen, et al., 2013; Hansson, 2015b). A public can just as well be a mob and the usual problems regarding participation are consequently even more frequent in virtual as in other social contexts as online participation demands a high level of digital literacy that not only is about education but to have access to the right social networks. A large issue here is thus that networked publics can thus be 'echo chambers' where people's opinions are reinforced by like-minded (Sunstein, 2001), and where this homogeneity is reinforced by information 'filter-bubbles' that mainly present information based on earlier searches (Pariser, 2011). To address these tendencies, new technologies have been researched and developed in different areas to promote deliberative publics where different opinions can meet such as e.g. (Faridani et al., 2010; Mankoff et al., 2011; Munson and Resnick, 2010; Oh et al., 2009; Park et al., 2009). However, these technologies are most often based on a simplified deliberative democratic ideal, where deep conflicts and dominating discourses are ignored. To support the transformation of government and a sustainable information production the problem with echo chambers and filter bubbles and lack of heterogeneity and representativeness in the development of data in online settings needs to be better addressed, analyzed and systematized.

Another significant issue concerns data reliability in networked publics online. This is usually based on aggregation of trustworthiness from multiple sources and the question of who produces the data becomes more complicated when it's a loose network of actors that are behind. In an overview of recent trends in VGI research Neis and Zielstra (2014) suggests a focus on questions about credibility and trust, with a focus on the contributor. Thus, identifying new methods to compute trust and contributor reputation is important in addition to the cultural context of the contributor (Ibid). Another neglected area is the interpretation of the data in VGI contexts; the conceptual quality of the vocabularies and ontologies used to understand and describe geographic information (Ballatore and Zipf, 2015). Furthermore, as (Mashhadi et al., 2015) shows in their OpenStreetMap study, social factors as population density, decentralization and poverty correlates with information completeness, why it for example is problematic that the age in the typical user generated context is rather low. Especially FaceBook, OpenStreetMap and Wikipedia have a very young user base (Steinmann et al., 2013). Wikipedia editors and OpenStreetMap contributors are simply not very representative citizens (Ibid).

## A THEORETICAL FRAMEWORK ACKNOWLEDGING INEQUALITIES ONLINE

Unequal digital representation can mean a lot of things: Inequalities in Internet access; Inequalities due to differences in digital literacy; and Inequalities within groups due to different modalities, structuring norms and accumulated reputation. Furthermore, inequalities are not only something that exists between groups, but also within groups. It can for example be about differences in types of equipment and modalities (Spante et al., 2006) or it can be about discrimination due to structuring norms about gender, race, or other discriminating factors (Hansson, 2015a). It can also be due to participants' own action and other participants' reactions on these actions, which also generates a certain social reputation that accumulates over time (Hansson, Verhagen, et al., 2013). In any case, to interpret crowd produced online data accurately, these inequalities have to be part of the "data" and to better understand the perspectives as well as the antagonisms between perspectives and groups, represented in the information produced in a specific context, it is important to describe the inequalities within and between online crowds; How these crowds are embodied in material production of data and how value is accumulated through practices.

In our earlier overviews of groupware for online collaborative information production we could not find tools that supported the ambition to describe the inequalities within and between online crowds (Hansson, Belkacem & Ekenberg, 2014; Hansson, Karlström, et al., 2013). To find ways forward it is therefore interesting to first investigate the potentials in different available tools for making the processes of inequalities more transparent, and here, we will try to explain these inequalities with a focus on representation online.

Representation online is not only about the distribution of means to access information and to have contact with right networks of people, but also how actual bodies are represented online in the form of data mirroring various experiences, what can be called *embodiment*. With the concept of embodiment we point to how culturally defined structures and norms are performed and materialized as well as situated in a certain context and individual experience. The technical constrains, mechanisms, and rules for action, in different collaborative tools also create certain locally constrained economies, what can be called *gameplays* in this context, more or less explicitly structure the participants' actions. Gameplay is the interaction that is formalized by the rules of a game, motivated by game challenges in form of different activities that help players to level up and get a "score" (Adams & Rollings, 2007). The data produced with the help of different collaborative tools can thus be understood as an embodiment of culturally defined structures, norms and motives, which also are structured by the gameplay of the tool. Below we discuss some of the more popular tools asking questions about embodiment and gameplay under the following discourse:

- **Embodiment:** How are participants' bodies structured in relation to norms and material conditions: Does the tool collect and visualize belonging to categories; data about the user such as gender, race, location and age? What does it take in terms of social and cultural capital to participate? Are there means to measure social network or describing educational levels?
- **Gameplay:** How is participant activity described in the tool? How are values and rankings accumulated, constructed and exchanged? For instance, is reputation counted for in the system or used as part of the interface? Is activity and "likes" measured and made transparent? Is some sort of reputation mechanism described?

The discussion is based on a study of the actual interfaces and how they gather information on their user base, complemented with available literature and documentation. We have chosen the more popular tools in the English-speaking sphere for crowd sourced information gathering, tools where focus is on a specific task rather on the social network in itself such as: Wikipedia, Twitter, OpenStreetMap, Waze, and Wikimapia. These tools are also interesting to compare as they represent different types of attitudes to crowd sourced information production; from the more open attitude to quality assessment in Wikipedia and OpenStreetMap where contributors also are the ones deciding on quality, to the more predefined framework Wikimapia or Waze contributors have to adapt to.

In Table 1, we have summarized available categories to define the data contributors. Our intention here is not to define an exhaustive and exact set of categories, but rather to highlight available meta-data that can be useful as a way of defining user demographics. Instead our purpose is primarily to separate between embodiment and gameplay, where embodiment signifies the situated perspective of the user belonging to a certain material reality. Gameplay is the rules for acting on the platform.

As we have chosen to look at tools for crowd sourced information gathering rather than social network platforms, the focus is not so much on user profile appearance. Embodiment indicators such as age and gender are for example asked for only by two systems and only displayed as part of the public profile by Wikimapia. There is thus not much data available that can help the users to position contributors as belonging to a certain perspective or group, and none of the platforms make user statistics available that are simple to overview. Even though there is a possibility to add a photo, this type of data (if it at all is available and meaningful) is difficult to systematize and aggregate statistically. For example, a profile page for a Wikipedia user is a blank page without predefined categories where it is up to the user to define themselves (see Figure 1).

However, self-reported pre-categorized data might be erroneous anyway and there are other ways to correct the information provided. For instance, in Twitter, gender, age, language and location is possible to understand through the API through a combination of looking at user language, IP-addresses, relations and usage (Malhotra, 2014; Underwood, 2012). There is an extensive amount of research on

*Table 1. Summary of interface analysis looking at what data (1) contributors are submitting and if this data also is publicly (2) available, in tools for crowd sourced data production*

| | Wikipedia | Twitter | OSM | Waze | Wikimapia | Yelp | Instagram | Youtube | Pinterest | Reddit | Flickr |
|---|---|---|---|---|---|---|---|---|---|---|---|
| **Embodiment: User Profile Data That Can Help to Indicate Structuring Norms and Literacy** | | | | | | | | | | | |
| Name | | 1 | | 1 | | 2 | 1 | 2 | 2 | | 2 |
| User name | 2 | 2 | 2 | 2 | 2 | 2 | 2 | 2 | 2 | 2 | 2 |
| Profile photo | | 2 | 2 | | 2 | 2 | 2 | 2 | 2 | 2 | 2 |
| Gender | | | | | 2 | 1 | 1 | 1 | 1 | | |
| Age | | | | | 2 | 1 | | 1 | 1 | | |
| Language | | | | | | 1 | | | 1 | | |
| Race | | | | | | | | | | | |
| Work | | | | | | | | 1 | | | |
| Education | | | | | | | | 1 | | | |
| Location | | 2 | 2 | 2 | 2 | 2 | | 1 | 1 | | |
| E-mail | | 1 | 1 | 1 | 1 | 1 | 1 | 1 | 1 | 1 | 1 |
| Phone | | 1 | | | 1 | 1 | 1 | 1 | | | 1 |
| Network | | 2 | 2 | 1 | | 2 | 2 | 2 | 2 | | 2 |
| **Gameplay Indicators and Tools** | | | | | | | | | | | |
| Activity | 2 | 2 | 2 | 1 | | 2 | 2 | 2 | 2 | 2 | 2 |
| Discussion | 2 | 2 | 2 | 1 | 2 | 2 | 2 | 2 | 2 | 2 | 2 |
| Voting | | 2 | 2 | 2 | 2 | 2 | 1 | 1 | 2 | 2 | 2 |
| Followers | | 2 | | | | 2 | 2 | 2 | 2 | 1 | 2 |

*Figure 1. Wikipedia editor home page*

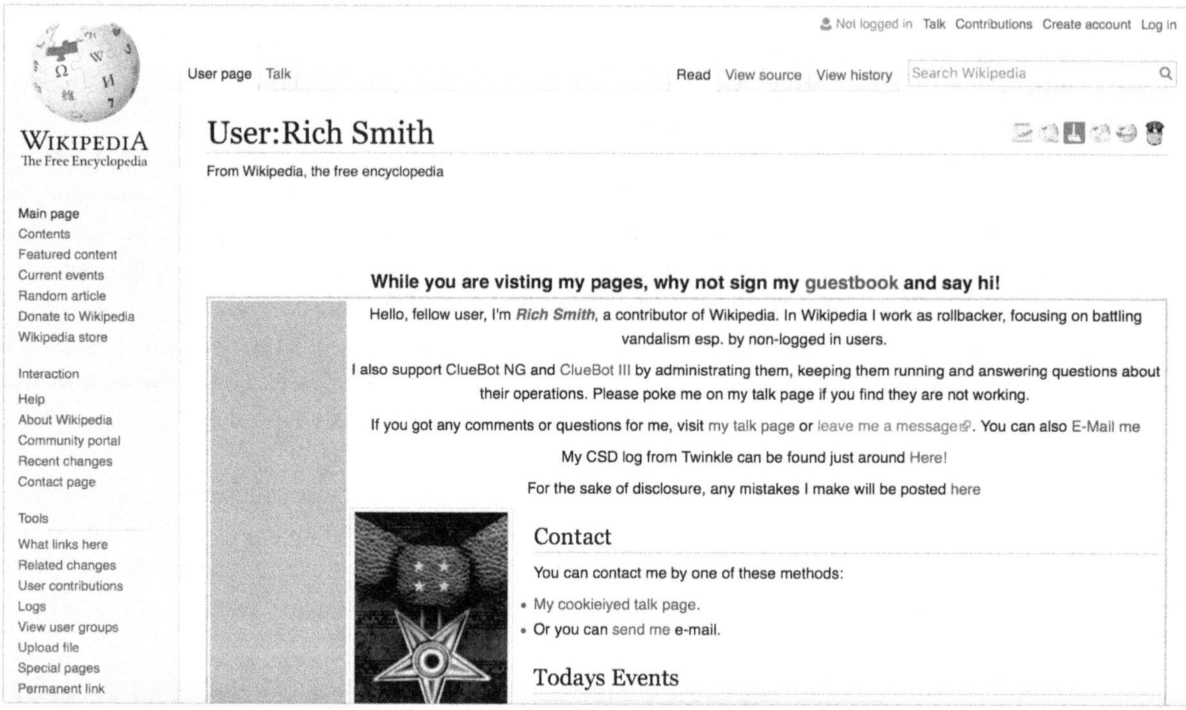


the best ways of doing this, such as (Culotta et al., 2015), but the accuracy of this is highly debated (Adnan et al., 2014; Burger et al., 2011; Hargittai, 2015; Harris, n.d.; Mislove et al., 2011; Sloan et al., 2013). None of the tools visualize any indications of the type of participants' literacies. The only tool that gathers information on social and cultural capital indicators, such as education and work, is YouTube, which takes the data from Google's general profile management system. However, this data is not made publicly available on the platform. Location is, on the other hand, something that is gathered and publicly available in several of the tools. This is not surprising as many of these are about collaborative mapping. Only one tool, the collaborative street mapping tool Waze, are using location as a part of the contributors' permission level restricting editing to areas where the users actually have been located.

In some of the tools, the user can provide a text description, but there are no categorizations of interest, age or education. User identity is foremost defined by user followers or friends and by those the user follows or are friend with, which is public in Twitter and OpenStreetMap, where user relations and activities define the user. Thus, despite the lack of self-reported demographic data, investigating the user relations and interests could be used to determine group identity and educational level of the users. Geolocation is another way of determining where the users are living and working, which then can be compared to available demographic information on the area.[1]

Regarding gameplay indicators, most of these systems we have looked at gather and sometimes also display information on the users, activities and discussions. Several applications visualize activities of the users, but previous activities are usually not used by the system to provide special privileges. Instead the reputation mechanisms seem to be purely social and sometimes used as arguments in discussions with other users rather than for informing reputation mechanisms. Often the activities are divided into multiple categories. OpenStreetMap, for example, collects users "Edits", "Map Notes", "Traces", "Send Message", "Diary", "Comments" and "Friends", which makes the information a bit difficult to overview and interpret for new users. But usually just a curated part of the user data is promotet, such as for example Pinterest, where the user metrics "pins" and "followers" are on display on top of the page (See figure 2). Waze is an exception in that user activity is not directly publicly available. It is instead simplified and translated to a score providing a higher gamification level as a way of motivating contributions to the system (See figure 3). Here, users are earning points to level up from one role to another, from "Baby" to "Royalty". Some tools utilize forms of user rankings for example by giving "likes", or showing various metrics, such as visits to the users' profile, mentions user names, number of new followers/friends, and similar. The standard Twitter interface displays followers and the amount of tweets and as an additional service, the users get access to more extended analytics. This information is also important when assigning credibility ranks. A trustworthy Twitter user might not be the one with the largest group of followers, on the contrary a study of influence on Twitter showed that that credibility rather is about showing sign of being in mutual relationships than having many followers (Bakshy et al., 2011).

There are also potential methods for evaluating reputation more than just counting followers or re-tweets. For example, users' sharing activity can be used as a way to position this user in a social context. Likewise can the social neighbourhood of users and topic popularity be other properties used as measurements of reputation or influence (Han et al., 2014). Based on studies on twitter during crisis situations, Castillo et al. (2013) suggest a method to measure credibility based on the characteristics of the users that propagate the information in combination with the reactions that certain topics generate and types of external sources mentioned. These types of reputation mechanisms can be especially useful in crisis situation when there is a limited access to other trustworthy information sources or when they are entirely absent (Castillo et al., 2011).

*Figure 2. Pinterest user page*

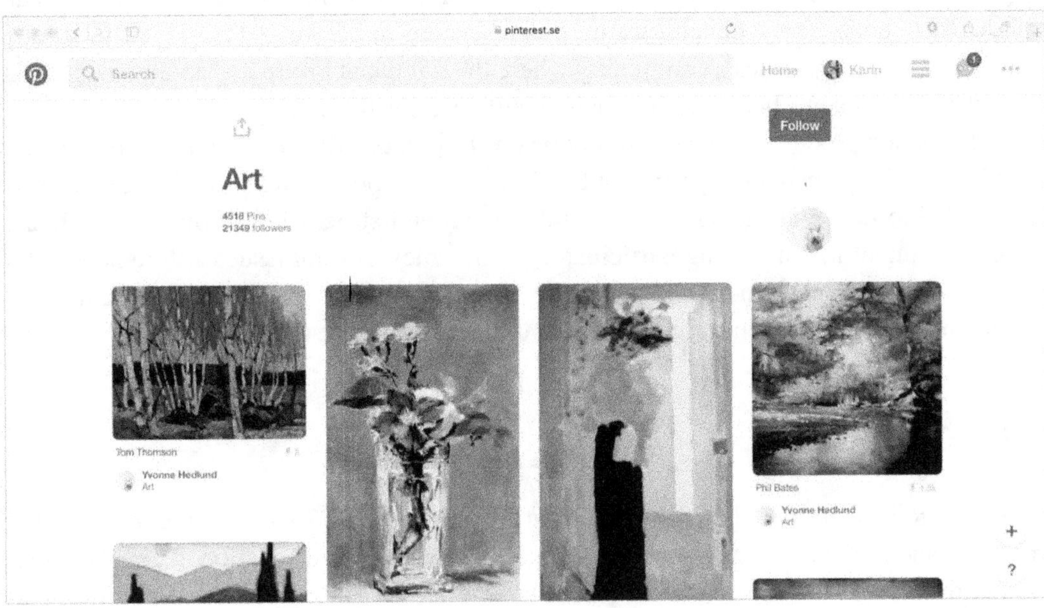

*Figure 3. Waze mobile application interface showing private scoreboard and public profile information*

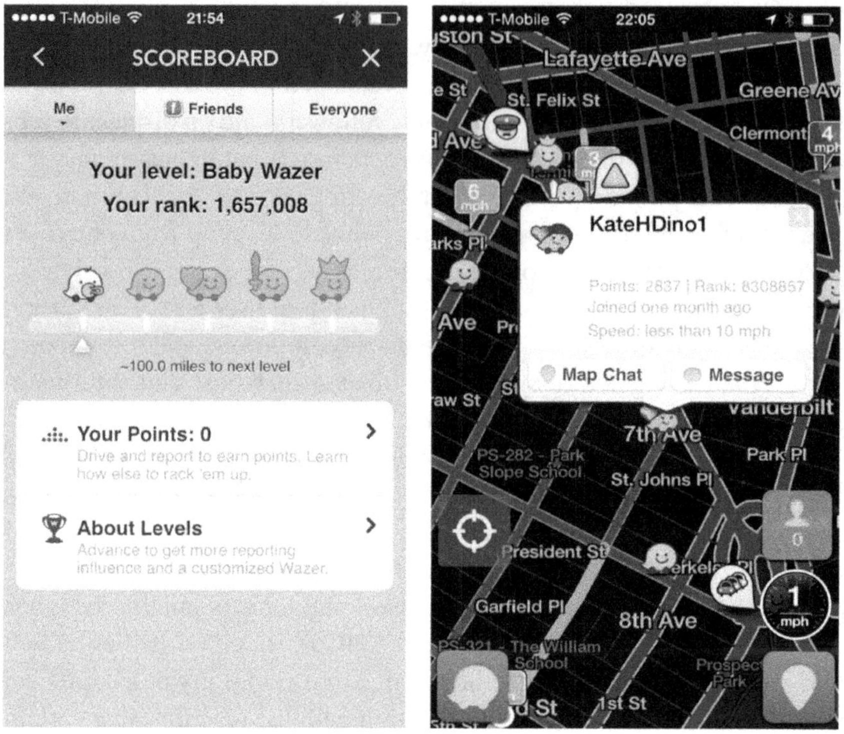


Time is in general an obvious asset here. People with a lot of time to spend online usually get a higher impact. A gameplay can also favor certain more specific behaviors. Qualitative data from the process of introducing new categories in OpenStreetMap illustrates this in that the gameplay requires a certain amount of votes before a new category can become introduced. This might make it difficult for, e.g., minority groups to suggest changes. For example, "strip club" and "brothel" have existed as categories in OpenStreetMap since 2009 but "childcare" was not voted in before 2011 and not without protests (Stephens, 2013), which indicates a community where the dominant group had an interest in institutions for sexualization of women's bodies rather than in child care institutions.

Again, information production and consumption online polarize the factors already prevalent in other contexts. It is essentially unequal as participants primarily are representing specific groups, experiences and opinions due to different modalities, societal context and structuring norms. For utilizing social media as an instrument for enhancing participatory democracy, several issues still remain to be solved when it comes to representativeness and the above analysis, in terms of gamification and embodiment processes, intends to highlight some crucial problems inherent in these media and their societal interplay.

## CONCLUSION

One central question when it comes to distributed participation is to find a reasonable concept of deliberative democracy and relate it to a reasonable notion of equity and representation. There are here several practical and theoretical issues on how to obtain large-scale citizen involvement and transparency in public participatory decision making, and an actual understanding of these decision processes is usually far from clear. When conceptualising participation in relation to representativeness and engagement, it is basically impossible to understand which are the true "public" preferences involved and to elicit and utilise these involves several complications when trying to achieve a more analytical and transparent decision making. We have therefore discussed some prevailing principles, methods and tools for crowd sourced data production and have suggested a new framework for increasing the transparency, and detectability of bias patterns in collaborative information production. In this framework we use the concept *embodiment* to describe the situated perspective of the user belonging to a certain material reality in, and the concept *gameplay* to describe the technical measurements for acting on the platform.

Openly defined platforms such as Wikipedia and OpenStreetMap are interesting contexts for developing forms of democracy that are networked rather than constrained to a predefined authority. The core idea here is that the community controls itself, and thus both decide the context and the contributors. However, research also shows that mechanisms excluding certain groups and voices are especially prevalent in the decision processes on these so called open platforms and are reproducing the inequalities between different groups and identities. Especially geo-mapping tools such as OpenStreetMap are subject to a large demographic bias (Neis and Zielstra, 2014; Stephens, 2013). In these negotiation games, there are always actors that are more successful than others in making their perspectives the dominant ones, but unlike the gamificated environment of, for example, Waze, social games on Wikipedia's many discussion forums are trickier to master and are not accessible to everyone. However, if we can somehow clarify the game without restricting it, the data produced within these types of peer-to-peer created contexts can become easier to interpret and use in meaningful ways, also from a governing perspective.

These popular platforms for crowd produced information does not emphasize the *embodiment* of this production in terms of elaborated user profiles or by making user statistics easier available. However, by investigating user activity we can find other means to retrieve data on gender, age, language and location, in particular by combining it with, geolocation and demographic data as well as user relations and interests. In connection with mechanisms for visualizing reputation this can be a way of making the *gameplay* of the tool more explicit to create more transparent and equal information production and decision processes. By combining data indicating embodiment with data indicating gameplay we provide a framework for describing data production that acknowledge the inequalities in these processes and uses this information as a knowledge base.

Most of these systems gathers and sometimes also displays information on users' activity and discussions but seldom in a way that is easy to overview and understand. Instead the process of gaining higher status is complicated and not very transparent. As a contrast one system uses a gamification as a way to motivate contributions, but on the other hand this is not one of the more open systems and the game-rules are predefined.

Relational metrics like profile visits, number of followers or citations are maybe most important when judging credibility. Users' sharing activity, characteristics of the users, and the reactions on actions, are other properties that can be used as measurements of reputation.

Obviously, there are plenty of methods available that could make crowd-produced information easier to understand. This without creating detailed control mechanisms, but just using available data. But the accuracy depends on the combination of different retrieval mechanisms for data, research methodology, and the actual context.

This overview of the handling of user profile data and contributor activity provides a framework for analyzing data production processes in terms of embodiment and gameplay. This can create a better understanding of the quality of the data in crowd produced environments. This can especially be interesting in contexts were tools for aggregated trustworthiness is developed as a way to support a more decentralized participatory government, and as an alternative when public institutions can't provide trustworthy information. If we can connect gameplay metrics with user data indicating embodiment the production of data can become more transparent, and can also be a way to explore ways to strengthen democracy in networked publics.

## REFERENCES


Abu-Shanab, E., Al-Rub, S. A., & Md Nor, K. (2010). Obstacles Facing the Adoption of E-Government Services in Jordan. *Journal of E-Governance*, *33*(1), 35–47.

Adnan, M., Lima, A., Rossi, L., Veluru, S., Longley, P., Musolesi, M., & Rajarajan, M. (2014). The uncertainty of identity toolset : Analysing digital traces for user profiling. In *Proceedings of the 7th International Conference on Security of Information and Networks* (p. 254). ACM. 10.1145/2659651.2659741

Ahn, J. (2012). Teenagers and social network sites : Do off-line inequalities predict their online social networks? *First Monday*, *17*(1), 1–14. doi:10.5210/fm.v17i1.3752

Al-Khalifa, H. S., & Al-Eidan, R. M. (2011). An experimental system for measuring the credibility of news content in Twitter. *International Journal of Web Information Systems Vol.*, *7*(2), 130–151. doi:10.1108/17440081111141772

Al-Rashidi, H., & London, W. (2010). Examining Internal Challenges to E-Government Implementation from System Users Perspective. In *European and Mediterranean Conference on Information Systems* (*Vol. 2010*). Abu Dhabi, UAE: Academic Press.

Alarabiat, A., Soares, D. S., & Estevez, E. (2016). Electronic Participation with a Special Reference to Social Media - A Literature Review. In E. Tambouris & ... (Eds.), Lecture Notes in Computer Science: Vol. 9821. *Electronic Participation. ePart 2016*. Cham: Springer. doi:10.1007/978-3-319-45074-2_4

Aman, A., & Kasimin, H. (2011). E-procurement implementation: a case of Malaysia government. *Transforming Government: People, Process and Policy*, *5*(4), 330–344.

Ames, M. G., Go, J., Kaye, J. J., Spasojevic, M., Road, P. M., & Alto, P. (2011). Understanding Technology Choices and Values through Social Class. In CSCW 2011 Proceedings (pp. 55–64). Academic Press. doi:10.1145/1958824.1958834

Bakshy, E., Hofman, J., Mason, W., & Watts, D. (2011). Everyone's an influencer: quantifying influence on twitter. *Proceedings of the Fourth ACM International Conference on Web Search and Data Mining SE - WSDM '11*, 65–74. 10.1145/1935826.1935845

Ballatore, A., & Zipf, A. (2015). A Conceptual Quality Framework for Volunteered Geographic Information. In *COSIT 2015 Conference on Spatial Information Theory XII October 12-16, 2015, Lecture Notes in Computer Science*. eScholarship University of California. 10.1007/978-3-319-23374-1_5

Bannister, F., & Connolly, R. (2011). The Trouble with Transparency : A Critical View of Openness in e- Government. *Policy and Internet, 3*(1), 158–187. doi:10.2202/1944-2866.1076

boyd, d. (2011). White Flight in Networked Publics ? How Race and Class Shaped American Teen Engagement with MySpace and Facebook. In L. Nakamura & P. A. Chow (Eds.), *Race After The Internet* (pp. 203–222). Routledge.

Bright, J., & Margetts, H. (2016). Big Data and Public Policy: Can It Succeed Where E-Participation Has Failed? *Policy and Internet, 8*(3), 218–224. doi:10.1002/poi3.130

Burger, J. D., Henderson, J., Kim, G., & Zarrella, G. (2011). Discriminating gender on Twitter. In *Proceedings of the 2011 Conference on Empirical Methods in Natural Language Processing* (*Vol. 146*, pp. 1301–1309). Academic Press.

Castillo, C., Mendoza, M., & Poblete, B. (2011). Information credibility on twitter. In *Proceedings of the 20th international conference on World wide web - WWW '11* (p. 675). Academic Press. 10.1145/1963405.1963500

Castillo, C., Mendoza, M., Poblete, B., & Authors, F. (2013). Predicting information credibility in time-sensitive social media. *Internet Research, 23*(5), 560–588. doi:10.1108/IntR-05-2012-0095

Choudrie, J., Weerakkody, V., & Jones, S. (2005). Realising e-government in the UK: rural and urban challenges: Journal of Enterprise Information Management: Vol 18, No 5. *Journal of Enterprise Information Management, 18*(5), 568–585. doi:10.1108/17410390510624016

Crutcher, M., & Zook, M. (2009). Placemarks and waterlines: Racialized cyberscapes in post-Katrina Google Earth. *Geoforum, Elsevier Ltd, 40*(4), 523–534. doi:10.1016/j.geoforum.2009.01.003

Culotta, A., Ravi, N. K., & Cutler, J. (2015). Predicting the Demographics of Twitter Users from Website Traffic Data. In *Proceedings of the Twenty-Ninth AAAI Conference on Artificial Intelligence* (pp. 72–78). Academic Press.

Danielson, M., Ekenberg, L., Larsson, A., & Riabacke, M. (2014). Weighting Under Ambiguous Preferences and Imprecise Differences in a Cardinal Rank Ordering Process. *International Journal of Computational Intelligence Systems, 7*(1), 105–112. doi:10.1080/18756891.2014.853954

Duggan, M., Ellison, N. B., Lampe, C., Lenhart, A., & Madden, M. (2015). Demographics of Key Social Networking Platforms. *Pew Research Center*. Retrieved July 8, 2015, from http://www.pewinternet.org/2015/01/09/demographics-of-key-social-networking-platforms-2/

Dutta-Bergman, M. J. (2005). Access to the internet in the context of community participation and community satisfaction. *New Media & Society, 7*(1), 89–109. doi:10.1177/1461444805049146

Edelmann, N., & Cruickshank, P. (2012). In A. Manoharan & M. Holzer (Eds.), *E-Governance and Civic Engagement: Factors and Determinants of E-Democracy* (pp. 338–361). Hershey, PA: IGI Global Publishing. doi:10.4018/978-1-61350-083-5.ch017

Ekenberg, L., Hansson, K., Danielson, M., & Cars, G. (2017). *Deliberation, Representation and Equity: Research Approaches, Tools and Algorithms for Participatory Processes*. Open Book Publishers. doi:10.11647/OBP.0108

Elsheikh, Y., & Cullen, A. (2008). e-Government in Jordan: challenges and opportunities. *Transforming Government: People, Process and Policy, 2*(2).

Elwood, S. (2008). Volunteered geographic information: Future research directions motivated by critical, participatory, and feminist GIS. *GeoJournal, 72*(3-4), 173–183. doi:10.100710708-008-9186-0

Faridani, S., Bitton, E., Ryokai, K., & Goldberg, K. (2010). Opinion space: Opinion space: a scalable tool for browsing online comments. In *Proceedings of the 28th international conference on Human factors in computing systems - CHI '10* (p. 1175). New York: ACM Press. 10.1145/1753326.1753502

Freschi, A. C. (2009). eParticipation in the institutional domain: a review of research: analytical report on eParticipation research from an administration and political perspective in six European countries (A. C. Freschi, R. Medaglia, & J. Nørbjerg, Eds.). DEMO-Net Consortium.

Fung, A. (2013). Infotopia: Unleashing the Democratic Power of Transparency. *Politics & Society, 41*(2), 183–212.

Han, H., Nakawatase, H., & Oyama, K. (2014). Evaluating credibility of interest reflection on Twitter. *International Journal of Web Information Systems, 10*(4), 343–362. doi:10.1108/IJWIS-04-2014-0019

Hansson, K. (2015a). *Accommodating differences: Power, belonging, and representation online*. Stockholm University.

Hansson, K. (2015b). Controlling singularity: The role of online communication for young visual artists' identity management. *First Monday, 20*(5). doi:10.5210/fm.v20i5.5626

Hansson, K., Belkacem, K., & Ekenberg, L. (2014, December). Open government and democracy: A research review. *Social Science Computer Review*.

Hansson, K., Karlström, P., Larsson, A., & Verhagen, H. (2013). Reputation, inequality and meeting techniques: Visualising user hierarchy. *Computational & Mathematical Organization Theory, 20*(2), 155–175. doi:10.100710588-013-9165-y

Hansson, K., Verhagen, H., Karlström, P., & Larsson, A. (2013). Reputation and Online Communication : Visualizing Reputational Power to Promote Collaborative Discussions Abstract. In *HICSS-46 - Hawaii International Conference on System Sciences* (p. 11). Academic Press.

Hargittai, E. (2015). Is Bigger Always Better? Potential Biases of Big Data Derived from Social Network Sites. *The Annals of the American Academy of Political and Social Science, 659*(1), 63–76. doi:10.1177/0002716215570866

Harris, J. (n.d.). Gender, Twitter, and the Value of Taking Things Apart - Learning - Source: An OpenNews project. *Source: Journalism code and the people who make it*. Retrieved July 7, 2015, from https://source.opennews.org/en-US/learning/gender-twitter-and-value-taking-things-apart/

Hughes, A. L., & Palen, L. (2012). The Evolving Role of the Public Information Officer: An Examination of Social Media in Emergency Management. *Journal of Homeland Security and Emergency Management, 9*(1). doi:10.1515/1547-7355.1976

Ito, M., Baumer, S., Bittanti, M., Boyd, D., Cody, R., Herr-Stephenson, B., … Tripp, L. (2009). Hanging Out, Messing Around, and Geeking Out: Kids Living and Learning with New Media. MIT Press.

John Sinclair, A., & Timothy, J. (2017). Peirson-Smith & Morrissa Boerchers, Environmental assessments in the Internet age: The role of e-governance and social media in creating platforms for meaningful participation. *Impact Assessment and Project Appraisal, 35*(2). doi:10.1080/14615517.2016.1251697

Kaligotla, C., Yücesan, E., & Chick, S. E. (2015). An agent based model of spread of competing rumors through online interactions on social media. *WSC '15 Proceedings of the 2015 Winter Simulation Conference*, 3985-3996.

Karlova, N. A., & Fisher, K. E. (2012). "Plz RT": A social diffusion model of misinformation and disinformation for understanding human information behaviour. *Proceedings of the ISIC2012 (Tokyo).*

Kivunike, F., Ekenberg, L., Danielson, M., & Tusubira, F. (2011). Perceptions of the Role of ICT on Quality of Life in Rural Communities in Uganda. *Information Technology for Development, 17*(1), 61–80. doi:10.1080/02681102.2010.511698

Malhotra, N. (2014). Introducing language targeting. *Twitter*. Retrieved June 9, 2015, from https://blog.twitter.com/2014/introducing-language-targeting

Mankoff, J., Kuksenok, K., Kiesler, S., Rode, J. A., & Waldman, K. (2011). Competing online viewpoints and models of chronic illness. In *Proceedings of the 2011 annual conference on Human factors in computing systems - CHI '11* (p. 589). New York: ACM Press. 10.1145/1978942.1979027

Mashhadi, A., Quattrone, G., & Capra, L. (2015). The Impact of Society on Volunteered Geographic Information: The case of OpenStreetMap. In J. Jokar, A. Universit, & A. Z. Universit (Eds.), *OpenStreetMap in GIScience Experiences, Research, and Applications* (pp. 125–141). Springer. doi:10.1007/978-3-319-14280-7_7

Mbarika, V. W., & Byrd, T. A. (2009). An Exploratory Study of Strategies to Improve Africa's Least Developed Economies; Telecommunications Infrastructure: The Stakeholders Speak. *IEEE Transactions on Engineering Management, 56*(2), 312–328. doi:10.1109/TEM.2009.2013826

Mihai, A., Marincea, A., & Ekenberg, L. (2015). A MCDM Analysis of the Roşia Montană Gold Mining Project. *Sustainability, 2015*(7), 7261–7288. doi:10.3390u7067261

Min, S.-J. (2010). From the digital divide to the democratic Ddivide: Internet skills, political interest, and the second-level digital divide in political Internet use. *Journal of Information Technology & Politics, 7*(1), 22–35. doi:10.1080/19331680903109402

Mislove, A., Lehmann, S., Ahn, Y., Onnela, J., & Rosenquist, J. N. (2011). Understanding the Demographics of Twitter Users. *Artificial Intelligence*, 554–557.

Mocanu, D., Baronchelli, A., Perra, N., Gonçalves, B., Zhang, Q., & Vespignani, A. (2013). The Twitter of Babel: Mapping World Languages through Microblogging Platforms. *PLoS One, 8*(4), 1–9. doi:10.1371/journal.pone.0061981 PMID:23637940

Munson, S. A., & Resnick, P. (2010). Presenting diverse political opinions. In *Proceedings of the 28th international conference on Human factors in computing systems - CHI '10* (p. 1457). New York: ACM Press.

Neis, P., & Zielstra, D. (2014). Recent Developments and Future Trends in Volunteered Geographic Information Research: The Case of OpenStreetMap. *Future Internet*, *6*(1), 76–106. doi:10.3390/fi6010076

Norris, P. (2001). *Digital divide: Civic engagement, information poverty, and the Internet worldwide*. Cambridge, UK: Cambridge University Press. doi:10.1017/CBO9781139164887

Oh, A., Lee, H., & Kim, Y. (2009). User Evaluation of a System for Classifying and Displaying Political Viewpoints of Weblogs. In *Proceedings of the Third International ICWSM Conference* (pp. 282–285). Academic Press.

Parasie, S., & Dagiral, E. (2012). Data-driven journalism and the public good: "Computer-assisted-reporters" and "programmer-journalists" in Chicago. *New Media & Society*, *15*(6), 853–871. doi:10.1177/1461444812463345

Pariser, E. (2011). *The filter bubble: What the Internet is hiding from you*. London: Viking.

Park, S., Kang, S., Chung, S., & Song, J. (2009). NewsCube: Delivering multiple aspects of news to mitigate media bias. In *Proceedings of the 27th international conference on Human factors in computing systems - CHI 09* (p. 443). New York: ACM Press. 10.1145/1518701.1518772

Sang, S., Lee, J., & Lee, J. (2009). E-government adoption in ASEAN: The case of Cambodia. *Internet Research*, *19*(5), 517–534. doi:10.1108/10662240910998869

Schradie, J. (2011). The digital production gap: The digital divide and Web 2.0 collide. *Poetics*, *39*(2), 145–168. doi:10.1016/j.poetic.2011.02.003

Sloan, L., Morgan, J., Housley, W., Williams, M., Edwards, A., Burnap, P., & Rana, O. (2013). Knowing the Tweeters: Deriving Sociologically Relevant Demographics from Twitter. *Sociological Research Online*, *18*(3), 1–11. doi:10.5153ro.3001

Spante, M., Axelsson, A.-S., & Schroeder, R. (2006). The Good Inequality: Supporting Group-Work in Shared Virtual Environments. In R. Schroeder & A.-S. Axelsson (Eds.), *Avatars at Work and Play* (Vol. 34, pp. 151–166). Berlin: Springer-Verlag. doi:10.1007/1-4020-3898-4_7

Spiro, E. S., Fitzhugh, S., Sutton, J., Pierski, N., Greczek, M., & Butts, C. T. (2012). Rumoring during extreme events. In *Proceedings of the 3rd Annual ACM Web Science Conference on - WebSci '12* (pp. 275–283). New York: ACM Press. 10.1145/2380718.2380754

Steinmann, R., Häusler, E., Klettner, S., Schmidt, M., & Lin, Y. (2013). Gender Dimensions in UGC and VGI: A Desk-Based Study. *Proceeding of GI_Forum 2013 – Creating the GISociety*, 355–364.

Stephens, M. (2013). Gender and the GeoWeb: Divisions in the production of user-generated cartographic information. *GeoJournal*, *78*(6), 981–996. doi:10.100710708-013-9492-z

Sui, D., Goodchild, M., & Elwood, S. (n.d.). *Volunteered Geographic Information, the Exa fl ood, and the Growing Digital Divide*. Academic Press.

Sunstein, C. R. (2001). *Republic.com*. Princeton, NJ: Princeton University Press.

Underwood, A. (2012). Gender targeting for Promoted Products now available. *Twitter*. Retrieved June 9, 2015, from https://blog.twitter.com/2012/gender-targeting-for-promoted-products-now-available

## ENDNOTE

1 Regarding these types of methods, Mislove et al (2011), for example, shows a bias in the Twitter population relative to the U.S. population, indicating that entire regions of the U.S. are underrepresented on Twitter. The result indicates that social and cultural capital are important for Twitter activity, why a higher education and an urban type of social network can, as in other contexts, have significant advantages.

# Chapter 14
# Friending and Funding Through Facebook:
## Social Media Use of Regional Nonprofit Organizations

**Debika Sihi**
*Southwestern University, USA*

## ABSTRACT

*Social media may be leveraged as a cost-effective way for nonprofit organizations (1) to share information and (2) as a platform for fundraising. This is especially true for regional nonprofit organizations which may have less dedicated resources for marketing and fundraising. This chapter has two main objectives. First, the impacts of regional nonprofit organizations' leadership and strategic emphasis on the use of social media for information transmission is examined. Insights are gained from leadership at 121 nonprofits and through analysis of 377 days of Facebook data for seven nonprofit organizations. The second objective of this work is to examine regional nonprofit organizations' use of social media for crowdfunding or raising donations through a network of social media followers. The Facebook pages of 647 regional nonprofits are examined, and insights are gained from key staff members at 10 organizations.*

## INTRODUCTION

Social media is "a group of Internet-based applications that build on the ideological and technological foundations of Web 2.0, and that allow the creation and exchange of user generated content" (Kaplan & Haenlein, 2010). Social media offers a viable platform for information dissemination, engagement, and fundraising for nonprofits. This is especially true of regional nonprofit organizations which may have less dedicated resources for marketing and fundraising. This chapter addresses two objectives:

DOI: 10.4018/978-1-5225-5966-5.ch014

1. To examine the impacts of leadership and strategic emphasis on the use of social media for information transmission for regional nonprofit organizations
2. To analyze the adoption of social media tools for crowdfunding (fundraising through a network of social media followers) for regional nonprofit organizations.

The majority of studies on social media and nonprofits, to date, have focused on large, national nonprofits featured in lists like the Nonprofit 100 Times, the list of the 100 largest non-educational U.S. nonprofit organizations (Nah and Saxton, 2012) and the Forbes National Charity seal program (Curtis et al., 2010). These studies provide valuable insights which are applicable to nonprofit organizations that typically have large operating budgets and staff. This chapter emphasizes nonprofit organizations which serve a regional audience. In doing so, it extends the literature on nonprofits and social media as it offers a lens into social media usage by smaller entities which are likely to have less financial and human resources. For example, the American Society for the Prevention of Cruelty to Animals (ASPCA) had total revenues of $117, 222,668, 18 directors, and 853 staff members in 2013. Comparatively, the Hill Country Animal League SPCA (in Central Texas) has total revenues of $1,037,651, 7 directors, and 28 employees in the same year. These differences are likely to impact not only the adoption of relatively new technologies like social media but also how social media is used.

A national organization clearly has many spheres of leadership and influence. However, for regional organizations, the footprints of the executive director and board of directors are likely to be imprinted in most strategic aspects of the nonprofit, including its marketing and communications strategy. Thus, Section I of this chapter examines the impacts of two elements of leadership on information dissemination through social media: (1) the career background of the executive director and the (2) level of influence the board of directors. Executive director background and board influence have previously not been studied in this context. In addition, two strategic factors are analyzed: (3) an organization's customer orientation, for nonprofits, this is an organization's focus on its constituents and (4) the financial allocations towards social media.

Section II of this chapter highlights the use of social media followers for fundraising. Regional nonprofit organizations may have less resources to host fundraising events or engage in expensive donor focused campaigns. Social media offers a vehicle for crowdfunding through which a regional nonprofit is able to expand its fundraising reach through social media followers and their connections.

Each section of the chapter provides a literature overview and research hypotheses/questions, a detailed description of the data and analysis methods utilized, and then offers implications of the results. The chapter concludes with a combined section of limitations and future directions for research.

## SOCIAL MEDIA AS A PLATFORM FOR INFORMATION TRANSMISSION

Social media provides a viable platform for sharing information. A large number of supporters can be reached through a single post or update. The following sections provide a review of relevant literature and then outline hypotheses related to regional nonprofit organizations' use of social media for information transmission.

## Nonprofit Organizations' Use of Social Media to Share Information

Nonprofit organizations use social media across a variety of platforms. A content analysis of the most popular videos on the top 100 nonprofit YouTube channels finds that such videos are primarily used to inform users about organizational missions and programs (Waters and Jones, 2011). The authors note that of the 100 organizations, 97 had built-in comment features enabled, which allowed users to comment and ask questions about a video. However, only 25 organizations actually responded to comments or questions posted by viewers, suggesting a lack of engagement. Lovejoy, Waters, and Saxton (2012) analyzed the Tweets of 73 non-profit organizations. They determined that rather than use Twitter as a platform for dialogue and engagement with users, most of the organizations simply used the Tweets as a way to disseminate information. Similarly, an analysis of 275 nonprofit profiles on Facebook (Waters, et al., 2009) shows that most organizations share information such as external links to news stories, pictures, and discussion board posts which garner little interaction with users. A consistent lack of dialog is also found among environmental nonprofits (Bortree and Seltzer, 2009; Greenberg and MacAulay, 2009) and among nonprofit human services organizations which primarily use social media to promote organizations and services (Young 2017). Maxwell and Carboni (2017) find that while private and corporation foundations utilize social media more than community foundations, they are less likely to utilize call to actions to engage their users. Overall, this suggests that nonprofit organizations primarily utilize social media for information sharing rather than a two-way dialogue with supporters.

Despite underutilizing the engagement capabilities of social media, using it as a "push" marketing outlet still offers benefits. Effective use of informational processes can be leveraged as a strategic competitive advantage (Levitt & March, 1988). Nonprofit organizations can use such platforms to share information about organizations' needs, events, and milestones, keeping volunteers, donors, and staff up to date. Informational transmission is often conceptualized as the degree to which information is disseminated to users within an organization (Kohli & Jaworski, 1990). However, in this context, social media may be used for both internal and external communication of information. Therefore, no distinction is made between internal and external dissemination.

Researchers have explored various drivers of social media adoption by nonprofit organizations. Nah and Saxton (2012) find that organizations which center on program service revenues, rather than grants and donations, are more likely to adopt and use social media, specifically Facebook and Twitter. These organizations have strategies focused on "market-like transactions with clients." They also find that organizations "with a substantial website presence" are more likely to adopt and use social media because they already have a technologically savvy user base. In terms of leadership, the size of the board impacts the frequency of an organization's Facebook updates. The authors posit that a larger board is indicative of more ties outside the organization which initiates greater use of social media to maintain those ties. Organizations with clearly defined public relations departments are also more likely to use social media (Curtis et al., 2010) since a clearly defined organizational unit can take ownership of such initiatives. This research builds on the existing work by examining other leadership and strategic factors which may impact nonprofit organizations' use of social media.

## Impacts of Leadership, Customer Orientation, and Social Media Investments on Social Media Use

The leadership of a nonprofit organization is typically comprised of the executive director and board of directors. In a principal-agent framework (Fama & Jensen, 1983; Miller, 2002), an executive director is the principal in charge of the day to day operations of a nonprofit organization and its overall strategy. Prior work suggests the leadership of an organization impacts whether technology is effectively used in the organization (Berlinger & Te'eni, 1999) and that managerial decisions impact how effectively social media is used by nonprofit organizations (Hu & Shi, 2017). Extending this view, an executive director's characteristics are likely to influence the use of technology in strategic efforts including the use of social media to share information. A study by the global consulting firm Grant Thornton (Jackson, 2014) finds that senior management often lack the background and expertise to guide effective social media strategy. A 2014 study (Callanan et al., 2014) of almost 200 nonprofit leaders found that "chronic underinvestment in leadership development within the U.S. social sector, accompanied by 25 percent growth in the number of nonprofit organizations in the past decade, has opened a gap between demands on leaders and their ability to meet those needs." Thus, it is plausible that an executive director of a nonprofit organization, who has spent the majority of his/her career in the nonprofit sector, may not have participated in the same level of social media training as an individual with more experience in the for-profit sector. In the for-profit sector, social media training is more prevalent due to less time and budgetary constraints. For example, in many large companies like Dell, Adidas, and Sprint, social media training is now mandatory (Meister, 2012). In addition, in 2010, large companies spent a little over $562,000 on internal social media development (Leonard, 2013). Therefore, it is hypothesized that a nonprofit which has an executive director with more corporate (for-profit) experience will be more likely to utilize social media for information transmission, as he/she will be better equipped to do so.

**H1:** Nonprofits with executive directors who have more experience in the for-profit sector will utilize social media more for information transmission.

The level of influence exerted by board members in an organization is also likely to affect social media usage. A board of directors monitors an organization's management and can influence the strategic decision making (Fama and Jensen, 1983). In nonprofit organizations, board members may directly impact strategy. For example, Harlan and Saidel (1994) find that board members are highly engaged in initiating and maintaining relationships with state governments. At the regional level, where nonprofits are often hindered with smaller staffs and budgets, board members are likely to leverage their external ties to aid organizational missions (e.g., volunteerism). Social media provides a cost effective medium to maintain these ties. The size of a nonprofit's board of directors affects its use of social media since larger boards offer more members who can utilize social media to maintain external ties (Nah and Saxton, 2012). While a larger board offers more individuals who may utilize social media, an influential board may be comprised of individuals who use social media more to promote the organization. Due to their larger role, board members who have greater influence are more likely to be committed to the organization and thus, more likely to use social media to share information about the organization.

**H2:** Nonprofits with more influential boards will utilize social media more for information transmission.

Jackson (2014) suggests that organizations which prioritize social media are more likely to use it effectively as a communications tool. Organizational priorities are a result of the overall strategy of the organization. A nonprofit's strategic objectives affect its adoption and use of technology and social media (Hackler and Saxton, 2007; Nah and Saxton, 2012). Organizations which are constituency focused are likely to prioritize channels (social media) through which to connect to their "customers" or constituents. Customer orientation is "the set of beliefs that puts the customer's interest first, while not excluding those of all other stakeholders" (Deshpandé, Farley, and Webster, Jr., 1993). While nonprofits do not have "customers" in the traditional business sense, they do have constituents who depend on them for services and aid. Therefore, in this project, customer orientation is defined as the set of beliefs which puts the organization's constituents' interests first. A constituency focused nonprofit is likely to engage in strategies to provide constituents with necessary organizational information (Kohli and Jaworski, 1990). In addition, given the popularity of social media among individual users (e.g., Pew Research, 2014), a customer-oriented organization will likely try to utilize popular communications mediums.

**H3:** Nonprofits with higher customer orientation will utilize social media more for information transmission.

Finally, while the creation of a social media site (e.g., Facebook page) is largely free, many aspects of using social media, such as promoting posts or measuring engagement across platforms, require financial investment. For-profit organizations have become more effective in their use of social media through spending on social media initiatives (Leonard, 2013). Therefore, it is possible that nonprofits (which typically have more limited resources) which allocate funds towards social media, also consider it a priority. However, social media is a relatively new communications channel for most organizations. There may be institutional pressures to spend on social media because of its "newness" and popularity. Nonprofits may spend on social media initiatives due to a need to maintain legitimacy with other organizations (DiMaggio and Powell, 1983) rather than actually utilize it as a communications tool. This is reflective of companies which initially allocated money towards corporate social responsibility (CSR) efforts without really devising a strategy around such efforts, a practice coined "checkbook philanthropy" (Bertels and Peloza, 2008). It is possible that nonprofits which spend more on social media actually use social media less. Their spending is viewed as sufficient investment towards social media, essentially a trade-off in time investment for financial investment. Thus, dual hypotheses are posed.

**H4a:** Nonprofits with higher spending on social media development will utilize social media more for information transmission

**H4b:** Nonprofits with higher spending on social media development will utilize social media less for information transmission

## RESEARCH METHOD

### Analytical Methods

Detail on executive director background, board influence, customer orientation, and spending on social media is not uniformly and publicly available. Thus, a survey was used to collect this information from contacts at regional nonprofit organizations. Assessments on the use of social media for information transmission were also gathered. To test the hypotheses, the data was analyzed using regression analysis. The survey sample, measures, and analysis are outlined below. While survey data is useful in gaining deep insights from organizational members, self-report data can be susceptible to respondent biases such as self-presentation bias (since each of the respondents is affiliated with the organization on which he/she reported) and common method bias (Donaldson and Vallone, 2002). Thus, a secondary test of the hypotheses is conducted through cases studies of four dyads of the regional nonprofit organizations. Facebook post data is used as a secondary measure of information transmission. This analysis is described in detail following the discussion of the survey and regression analysis.

## Survey Data

The Austin, Texas metropolitan area has more nonprofits per capita than any other major metropolitan area in Texas and the southwestern United States (Kouri and Edward, 2013). The majority of these organizations are regional in nature, meaning their service areas are limited to the Central Texas region or a subsection of that region. A database of regional nonprofits was compiled using two public directories of nonprofits in the Central Texas area. First, organization names were gathered from the Greenlights member organization directory. Greenlights is an organization dedicated to fostering nonprofit leadership and success. These names were cross-listed with the list of nonprofits on the "I Live Here, I Give Here" website. "I Live Here, I Give Here" provides a directory of Central Texas nonprofits so donors can donate locally. The resultant list of nonprofits was then used to examine each organization webpage for contact information, specifically staff member e-mail addresses. An online survey was sent to employees, with deliverable e-mail addresses, at 230 organizations in the Central Texas area. The survey was sent using an online questionnaire due to ease of response. Insights were gained directly from individuals in leadership level positions (i.e., individuals with the sufficient knowledge about the nonprofit's operations and strategic initiatives). The survey was only sent to organizations which have staff members (some organizations only have a board of directors) since questions about the board of directors are included in the survey. The survey was sent to a marketing director, if possible, as this individual is most likely to have intimate knowledge about the nonprofit's social media usage. However, given the size of the organizations (based on the response sample: 37 staff members on average), in many cases, the organizational development director was also responsible for communications and marketing. In such instances, the development director was sent the survey. The survey was not sent to executive directors of organizations because there are questions about the executive director included in the survey.

230 surveys were e-mailed to the contacts in two separate collections. 121 responses were collected for a response rate of 52.6%. Survey response rates in organizational studies are 35.7% with a standard deviation of 18.8% (e.g., Baruch and Holtom, 2008). Prior studies of nonprofit organizations have response rates around 20% (e.g., Curtis et al., 2010), suggesting the response rate for this survey falls within acceptable levels. To ensure honesty and accuracy in response, the respondents were assured of confidentiality. Finally, to motivate participation, a whitepaper with study results was offered upon completion of this project, and a small amount was donated to a university scholarship fund for each completed survey.

The final sample includes a cross-section of nonprofits in a variety of areas. The sample is comprised of nonprofits with a focus on Health (15%), Social Services (15%), Human Services (14%), Arts (13%), and Education (12%). The remainder of the organizations operate in various domains. A full categorization of all the organizations in this sample is provided in Figure 1. The sample is representative of the composition of nonprofit organizations found in earlier studies. For example, Waters et al.'s (2009) sample of 275 nonprofits had a similar composition: Health (17%), Human Services (14%), Arts (12%), Education (18%), and the remainder in public benefit and religious organizations.

## Measures

Measures were adapted from prior research, whenever available, and new measures were developed when necessary. To develop the measures, 16 nonprofit marketing directors and development directors were interviewed to ensure that the terminology was interpreted in a consistent manner to that intended. A pilot survey was also conducted with contacts from a separate group of nonprofit organizations. All the measures are provided in Appendix A. Reliability statistics (Cronbach's alpha), descriptive statistics, and correlations for all the measures are included in Table 1 and Table 2. Reliability statistics are above or just around 0.70, as prescribed by Nunnally and Bernstein (1967). In addition, the survey responses were divided into "early" (n=93) and "late" responders (n=28) based on the length of time it took a survey participant to respond from when he/she received the e-mail with the survey link (Armstrong and Overton, 1977). The means and variances of all the measures were compared. There were no significant differences between the two responder groups, suggesting that non-response bias is unlikely to distort the findings of the analysis. In addition, no significant differences were found in responses between the first (n=76) and second collections (n=45).

*Figure 1.*

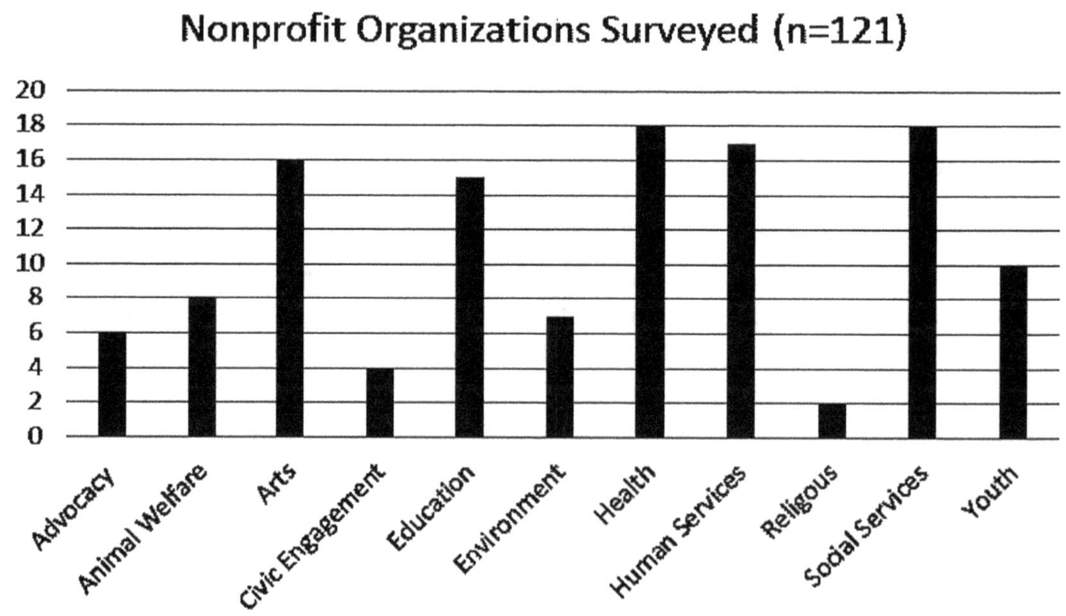

*Table 1. Summary of survey measures*

| Measures | Number of Items | Description | Cronbach's Alpha | Mean (Std. Dev) | Source |
|---|---|---|---|---|---|
| **Independent** | | | | | |
| Exec Director Background | 3 | Executive director's experience in the nonprofit sector | 0.756 | 5.33 (1.43) | Created |
| Board Influence | 4 | Influence of board members in the nonprofit's strategic decision making | 0.894 | 5.74 (1.14) | Created |
| Customer Orientation | 8 | Organizational focus and emphasis on main constituency served | 0.847 | 5.83 (0.914) | Deshpandé, Farley, Webster Jr. 1993 |
| Social Media Spending ($) | Directly reported | Total annual social media spending in 2014 | - | 2,929 (8,901) | - |
| **Dependent** | | | | | |
| Information Transmission | 4 | Social media use to disseminate information to internal and external stakeholders | 0.699 | 4.89 (1.34) | Moorman 1995 |
| **Control** | | | | | |
| Board Size | Directly reported | Number of members on the board of directors | - | 13.24 (9.66) | Nah and Saxton 2012 |
| Proportion of Millennial Staff | - | Number of paid staff members under 33 / Number of total paid staff members | - | 0.716 (0.299) | Created |
| Organization Size | Directly reported | Number of paid staff members | - | 37 (12.54) | Pugh et al. 1969 |
| National Affiliation | Indicator Variable | Indicates whether the organization is affiliated with a national charity | - | 0.0579 (0.234) | - |

*Table 2. Correlation matrix of measures (n=121)*

| Variable | 1 | 2 | 3 | 4 | 5 | 6 | 7 | 8 | 9 |
|---|---|---|---|---|---|---|---|---|---|
| 1. Information Transmission | 1.000 | | | | | | | | |
| 2. Exec Director Background | -0.178* | 1.000 | | | | | | | |
| 3. Board Influence | 0.235** | 0.020 | 1.000 | | | | | | |
| 4. Customer Orientation | 0.016 | 0.137 | 0.312** | 1.000 | | | | | |
| 5. Social Media Spending | -0.333** | 0.027 | -0.057 | -0.080 | 1.000 | | | | |
| 6. Board Size | -0.025 | -0.047 | 0.057 | 0.131 | 0.168* | 1.000 | | | |
| 7. Proportion of Millennial Staff | -0.021 | 0.089 | -0.165* | -0.013 | 0.018 | -0.095 | 1.000 | | |
| 8. Organization Size | -0.168* | 0.182* | -0.107 | 0.137 | 0.038 | -0.026 | -0.005 | 1.000 | |
| 9. National Affiliation | 0.171* | -0.122 | 0.082 | 0.085 | -0.077 | -0.028 | 0.060 | -0.030 | 1.000 |

*=p<0.10, **=p<0.05

## Executive Director Background and Board Influence

The measure for executive director background was created using three items which gauge an executive director's background in the nonprofit sector. Respondents rated their agreement with an item using a 7 point Likert scale. The measure for board influence was created using four items which assess the importance of board members' influence in the nonprofit organization. Respondents again utilized a 7 point Likert rating scale.

## Customer Orientation and Social Media Spending

Customer orientation was operationalized using 8 (of the 9) items from Deshpandé, Farley, and Webster Jr. (1993). These items were modified to reflect a constituency focus, rather than a traditional customer focus since this project examines nonprofit organizations. Respondents used a 7 point Likert rating scale to indicate their agreement with the statements.

## Information Transmission

Items for the information transmission measure were adapted from Moorman (1995) to specifically gauge information dissemination using social media. Four items were used for the measure, and respondents used a 7 point rating scale, consistent with Moorman (1995), to provide agreement with each statement/item. In addition to this measure of information transmission, respondents were asked to list the main uses of social media for their organizations. 93.4% of the organizations use social media as a way to "share information" about their organization. 76% of the organizations use it as a way to "promote volunteerism." The responses indicate that, similar to national nonprofits (e.g., Waters et al., 2009), information transmission is an important and primary use of social media for regional nonprofits.

## Control Variables

Prior research (Nah and Saxton, 2012) indicates that board size impacts the use of social media for national nonprofit organizations. Thus, the number of board members was included in the model as a control variable. The number of board members was measured using a single item. Survey respondents indicated the number of board members as a whole number. The proportion of staff members who are millennials was also included as a control variable. Millennials are individuals born between 1982 and 2000 (Howe and Strauss, 2000) and are referred to as the "Net Generation." They have spent the majority of their developmental years using the Internet and digital technologies. Thus, millennials are likely to be more adept (compared to other generations) in using social media for distributing information. In addition, a higher proportion of millennial staff members reduces the likelihood of organizational inertia, and new practices, such as social media use, are more likely to be adopted (e.g., Baron, Hannan, and Burton, 2001). Respondents were asked to provide that total number of paid staff members in their organizations. They were also asked to estimate the number of paid staff members under age 33 (represented individuals born in 1982 and after at the time of data collection). The proportion of millennial staff members was calculated as the ratio of paid staff members under age 33 to the total number of paid staff members. Number of paid staff members was also included as a control variable in the model since larger organizations may have greater resources to dedicate towards social media usage. Organizational size is commonly measured as number of employees in social science research (e.g., Pugh et al., 1969). The sample of organizations in this study included regional nonprofit organizations which tend to be more limited in terms of organizational scope and resources compared to national nonprofits. However, it is possible that affiliates of national organizations (e.g., Easter Seals of Texas) may have greater resources available to them given their connections to large, national organizations. This may result in more advanced marketing practices, including the use of social media. Thus, an alternate model is tested in which a control variable for nationally affiliated organizations is included.

## Results and Case Studies

The impacts of executive director background, board influence, customer orientation, and social media spending on information transmission (through social media) were estimated using ordinary least squares regression (OLS). Control variables for board size, proportion of millennial employees, and organization size were also included in the model. Although Likert rating scales were used, which are technically ordinal in nature, prior work (e.g., Lubke and Muthén, 2004) indicates that parametric tests can be performed with Likert scales when a larger scale (7 point versus 5 point) is used, and the interval between scale points is perceived as approximately equal (continuous) (Grace-Martin, 2008; Robson, 2002). A 7 point scale was used for the Likert scales in this study. In addition, during the measure refinement process, the 16 nonprofit marketing directors were asked select questions about the scale intervals which indicated consistency. For example, the marketing directors were asked how they interpreted the scale 1 (Very Strongly Disagree) to 7 (Very Strongly Agree) for the information transmission item which stated "My nonprofit uses social media for sharing information about its initiatives to donors." 14 of the 16 directors viewed 1 (Very Strongly Disagree) to 7 (Very Strongly Agree) as weekly posts targeting donors where a 1 would be indicative of 1 post in a week and 7 would reflect 7 posts in a week (one per day). The results of the main regression and two alternate models are included in Table 3 and discussed below.

Model 1 includes the independent variables of interest (executive director background, board influence, customer orientation, and social media spending) as well as the control variables. This model accounts for 20.1% of the variance in information transmission via social media. The results indicate the executive directors with more for-profit (less nonprofit) background enhance information transmission via social media (b= -0.142, p<.10), supporting Hypothesis 1. Greater board involvement also increases information transmission (b=0.269, p<.05) via social media while no effect for customer orientation is found (b= -0.071, ns). Thus, Hypothesis 2 is supported but Hypothesis 3 is not. Greater spending on social media results in significantly (b= -.00005, p<.05) less information transmission via social media, supporting Hypothesis 4b.

Model 2 adds a variable for nationally affiliated organization. Nationally affiliated organizations comprise of 5.79% of the sample. An F-test indicates no significant improvement (F(1, 112)=1.79, p=0.184) by adding a national affiliation indicator in the model.

The results of the regression analysis suggest that an executive with greater for-profit (corporate) background, greater board influence, and less direct spending on social media enhance information transmission via social media. The hypotheses are further tested using a secondary source of the dependent measure to provide greater support for these conclusions.

*Table 3. Regression of information transmission through social media on executive director background, board influence, customer orientation, and social media spending*

| | Model 1 Coefficient (Std. Error) | Model 2 |
|---|---|---|
| Executive Director Background | -0.142 (0.080)* | -0.129 (0.080) |
| Board Influence | 0.269 (0.107)** | 0.262 (0.107)** |
| Customer Orientation | -0.071 (0.134) | -0.084 (0.134) |
| Social Media Spending | -0.00005 (0.00001)** | -0.00005 (0.00001)** |
| Board Size | 0.002 (0.012) | 0.002 (0.012) |
| Proportion of Millennial Staff | 0.010 (0.039) | 0.010 (0.039) |
| Organization Size | -0.0004 (0.0003) | -0.0004 (0.0003) |
| National Affiliation | - | 0.653 (0.488) |
| Overall Significance | F(7, 113) = 4.07; Prob > F = 0.0005 | F(8, 112) = 3.81; Prob > F = 0.0005 |
| $R^2$ | 0.201 | .214 |
| $R^2$ change from Model 1 | - | 0.013 |
| Adjusted $R^2$ | 0.152 | 0.158 |
| n | 121 | 121 |

*=p<0.10, **=p<0.05

## Case Studies

A secondary measure of information transmission was created using 377 days of Facebook page data for 4 dyads of organizations. Daily page administrator (the nonprofit organization) Facebook posts were utilized as the measure of information transmission. Then each of the variables in the model were compared to construct dyads based on similarity of characteristics. While exact matchings were not realistically possible, the values of each of the variables are aligned to the greatest extent possible within the sample of organizations. For example, the data sample was stratified by variable, and the values for Organizations 1 and 2 (Case Study 1) are in the same quartile of results for all variables except for executive director background where they fall in the top and bottom quartile, respectively. This process was used to create dyads to isolate the impact of each independent variable on information transmission (via social media). Dyads were not constructed based on similarity in nonprofit category (e.g., health versus animal welfare) as prior literature does not indicate any significant difference in social media use for information sharing based on such categories. Table 4 provides the values of each of the variables.

### *Case Study 1: Executive Director Background*

Organization 1 provides housing support to individuals afflicted with serious illnesses. Organization 2 is provides financial aid to individuals and organizations. These organizations are very similar except that Organization 1 has an executive director with largely a nonprofit background (executive director background=6.33), and the executive director at Organization 2 has a background outside of the nonprofit sector (executive director background=2.33). The number of daily administrator posts was significantly

*Table 4. Dyads of organizations compared*

| | Executive Director Background | Board Influence | Customer Orientation | Social Media Spending | Number of Directors | Proportion of Millennial Staff Members | Organization Size |
|---|---|---|---|---|---|---|---|
| Organization 1 | **6.33** | 4.25 | 6.0 | $475 | 8 | 17% | 30 |
| Organization 2 | **2.33** | 4.0 | 6.25 | $400 | 8 | 13% | 24 |
| Organization 3 | 6.0 | **7.0** | 5.5 | $25 | 5 | 60% | 5 |
| Organization 4 | 6.33 | **1.5** | 5.63 | $25 | 6 | 60% | 5 |
| Organization 5 | 5.67 | 5.0 | **6.75** | **$500** | 7 | 33% | 6 |
| Organization 6 | 5.33 | 5.25 | **2.0** | $500 | 6 | 43% | 7 |
| Organization 7 | 5.0 | 5.0 | 7.0 | **$35,000** | 6 | 20% | 5 |

(p<.05) higher for Organization 2 (1.86 average posts per day) compared to Organization 1 (0.54 posts per day). Figure 2 provides a comparison of the two organizations administrator posts over the 377 day time period analyzed. Organization 1 is represented by the darkly shaded bars in the figure, and Organization 2 is shown by the lightly shaded bars.

## Case Study 2: Board Influence

Organization 3 is focused on animal welfare. Organization 4 provides aid for homeless populations. These organizations are largely similar except that Organization 3 has very high board influence (board influence rating=7.0; in the top quartile of ratings from survey data), and Organization 4 has a very low board influence rating (board influence rating 1.5; in the bottom quartile of ratings from survey data). The number of daily administrator posts was significantly higher (p<.05) for Organization 3 (average of

*Figure 2.*

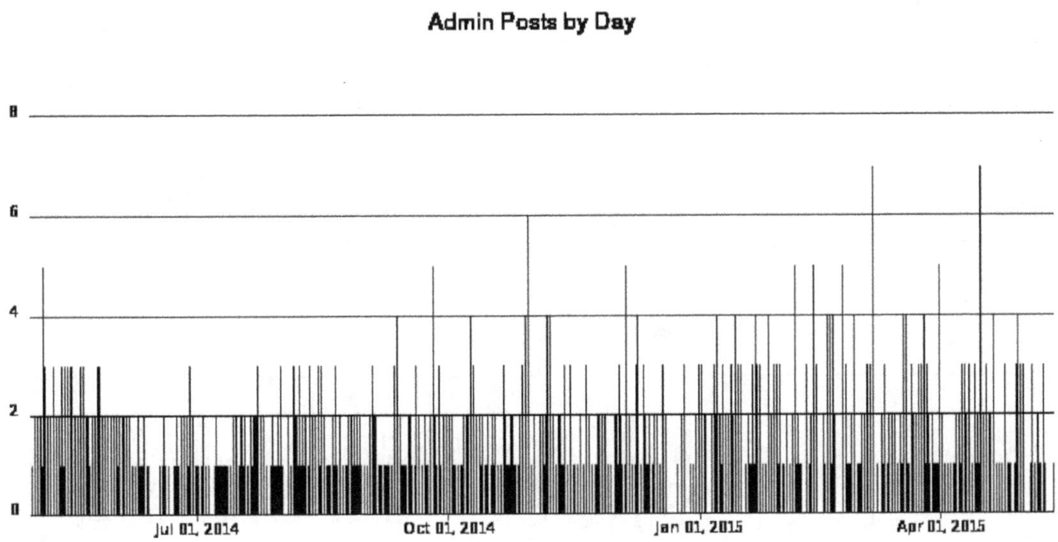

2.18 posts per day) compared to Organization 4 (average of 0.46 posts per day). In Figure 3, Organization 3 is represented by the lightly shaded bars in the graph, and Organization 4 is shown by the darkly shaded bars.

### Case Study 3: Customer Orientation

Organization 5 provides social services to youths. Organization 6 is a youth oriented, religious organization. These organizations are similar except that Organization 5 has very high customer orientation (customer orientation rating=6.75; in the top quartile of ratings from survey data), and Organization 6 has a very low customer orientation rating (customer orientation rating=2.0; in the bottom quartile of ratings from survey data). The number of daily administrator posts was significantly higher ($p<.05$) for Organization 5 (average of 1.12 posts per day) compared to Organization 6 (average of 0.17 posts per day). There was an outlier in the data (one day, when Organization 5 posted 22 times). The analysis was conducted after removing this data point, and the results remained consistent. In Figure 4, Organization 5 is represented by the light colored bars on the graph, and Organization 6 is the shown by the dark bars.

### Case Study 4: Social Media Spending

Organization 7 is focused on the arts. Given their similarities, Organization 7 was compared to Organization 5. The largest difference between these two organizations is the difference in social media spending. Organization 7 spent $35,000 in social media spending in 2014 while Organization 5 spent $500. In the 377 day period analyzed, Organization 7 did not post any content on its Facebook page, compared to Organization 5 which posted, on average, 1.12 posts a day.

The case studies indicate that executive directors with more experience in the for-profit sector, greater board influence, and greater customer orientation generate greater information transmission via Facebook.

*Figure 3.*

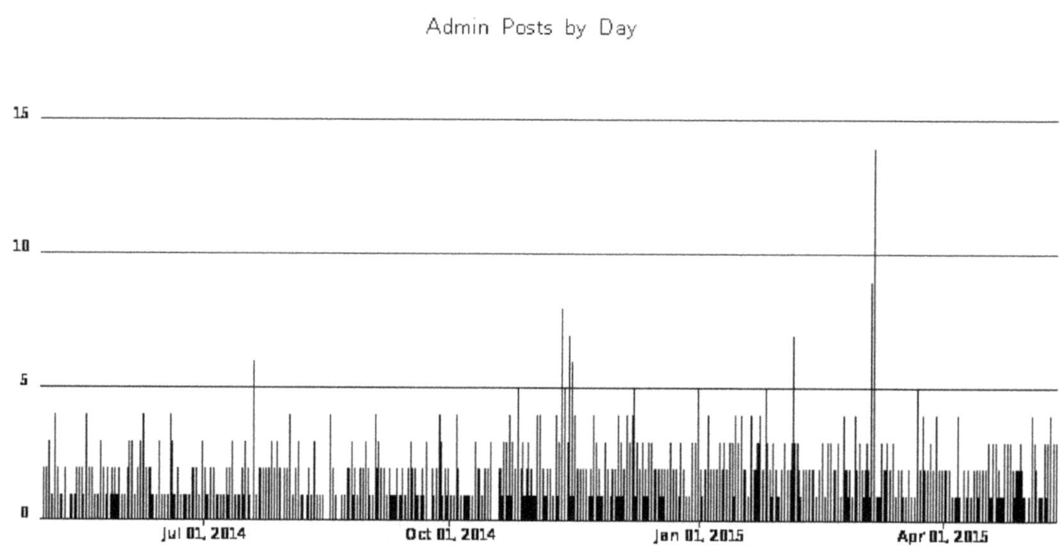

*Figure 4.*

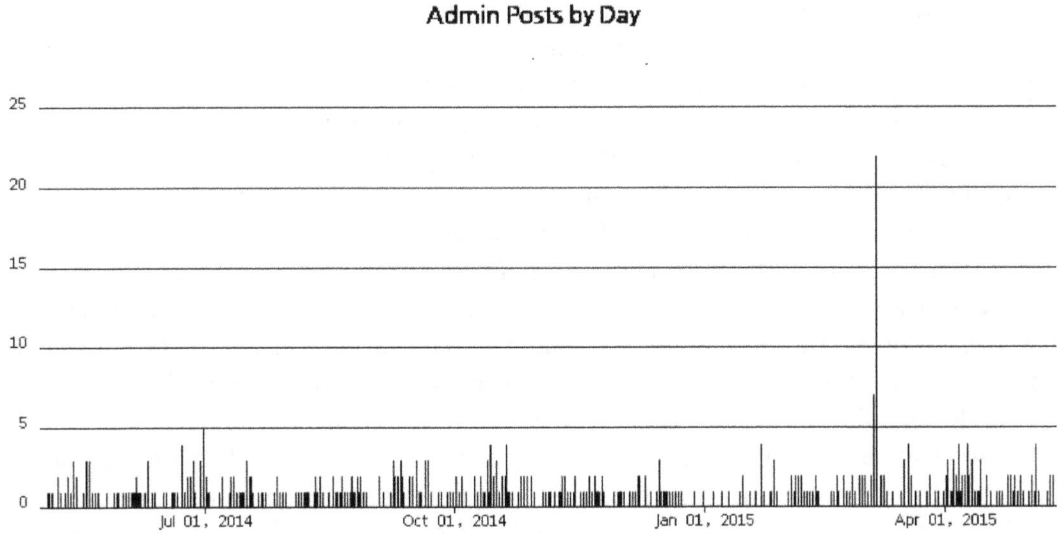


Greater spending on social media produces less information transmission via Facebook. Other than the result related to customer orientation, these results are consistent with the findings in the regression analysis. All the results are discussed in more detail in the following section.

## DISCUSSION AND IMPLICATIONS

Regression analysis of the survey data and case study 1 suggest that organizations which have executive directors with more experience in the for-profit sector engage in greater information transmission through social media compared to organizations with directors who have less corporate background. Executive directors who spend more time in the corporate sector are likely to have received more in-depth training on social media (e.g., Meister, 2012) which they can utilize in their leadership roles in nonprofit organizations. This offers a new criterion for consideration when regional nonprofits hire an executive director. Organizations which are trying to advance their communications strategy through social media may consider candidates who have experience working in the corporate sector. In addition, it may be beneficial to include more interview questions gauging a candidate's social media training and experience. Given the growing popularity of social media (Pew Research, 2014), effectively using such channels is a necessity for the communications strategies of all organizations, including nonprofits.

An influential board of directors also enhances the use of social media for information transmission. Board members often act as liaisons between a nonprofit and external organizations (Harlan and Saidel, 1994), and an influential board of directors is more likely to share information about the organization with these external ties. Social media offers board members an effective outlet through which to disseminate organizational information. In order to fully leverage the external associations of board members and to provide them a forum through which to do so, nonprofits may consider (1) enhancing the role of board members in the organization and (2) providing them with training related to social media. This may not only increase the social media presence of an organization, but also garner greater external awareness. However, separation between managerial and board functions is an important aspect of governance (Fama and Jensen, 1983), so organizations must maintain some distinction between duties. For example, the board may offer suggestions on content for social media while organizational staff actually shares the content since they are more closely connected to the organization's operations.

The results of the regression analysis and case study 3 produced conflicting results, rendering the impact of customer orientation on information transmission (via social media) inconclusive. It is possible that the relationship between customer orientation and information transmission is contingent on the nature of the posts, which is beyond on the scope of this research, but offers a fruitful area for further investigation. In case study 3, Organization 5's posts mainly consisted of reminders for upcoming fundraising events. Customer oriented nonprofits may use social media more for communicating information for fundraising or donor specific initiatives. More research is required to provide definitive results.

Interestingly, organizations which spend less on social media annually actually utilize it more for information transmission. A limitation to this finding may be that social media spending was based on spending data from one year, which may not be reflective of past years. However, it is plausible that in the case of social media spending "less may be more." Organizations which have less money to spend on social media may actually be more intentional and strategic in how they utilize social media since they do not have large, financial resources dedicated to such efforts. Follow up interviews were conducted with organizational contacts at nonprofits which spent a considerable amount on social media ($10,000 or higher annually) but had low information transmission via such platforms. Their insights suggest that often organizations spend a large amount on new software, social media analytics systems, or social media management systems. However, once purchased, there is often no time to take advantage of such assets due to higher order organizational objectives (i.e., more central to the organizational mission). Organizational members feel as though they are utilizing social media, due to the financial investment, when in fact they are spending and not implementing. It may be useful for nonprofits to outline a strategic plan with specific individuals responsible for implementation of social media efforts before such large investments are made. The negative consequences of such large, under-utilized investments may have disproportionally greater long-term effects for regional organizations compared to national organizations, which have much greater operating budgets to "cushion" such losses.

## SOCIAL MEDIA AS A PLATFORM FOR CROWDFUNDING

Social media offers a viable platform for fundraising. By connecting organizations to an online network or crowd of potential donors and fundraisers, crowdfunding provides a way to raise funds through many people. The idea is that many small donations accumulate to a substantial amount of funds raised. The following sections provide a review of relevant literature and then outline research questions related to regional nonprofit organizations' use of social media for crowdfunding.

### Crowdfunding Overview

Crowdfunding is a variant of crowdsourcing (Howe, 2006) which is utilizing a "crowd" or many individuals to accomplish a tasks or set of tasks. Specifically, crowdfunding allows an individual or organization to raise funds through many small contributions rather than a few large investments. There are different types of crowdfunding (Outlaw, 2013). Rewards based crowdfunding offers contributors perks or rewards for their contribution. Equity crowdfunding provides contributors equity or ownership shares in an organization in exchange for an investment. In lending crowdfunding, crowd members lend a small amount of money to an individual or an organization which they are paid back over time with interest. Royalty crowdfunding offers crowd members a certain revenue percentage once the project they invest in is earning a return. Most relevant to this work, donation crowdfunding simply offers opportunities to give to an organization or cause without anything promised in return. The motivation for giving is a donor's interest or affinity with the cause supported by the organization.

The ability to crowdfund online or through mobile applications has spurred an increase in its use as a fundraising tool. Two of the most popular crowdfunding sites are Kickstarter and Indiegogo. These sites allow organizations or individuals to launch an online fundraising campaign in exchange for a fee from the funds raised. Kickstarter launched in April 2009 with a focus on funding creative projects. This includes projects which fall into one the following categories: art, comics, crafts, dance, design, fashion, film and video, food, games, journalism, music, photography, publishing, technology, and theater. Since its launch, over 14 million people have funded a project on Kickstarter and over $3 billion has been pledged (Kickstarter, 2017). Indiegogo launched in 2007 with a mission to help entrepreneurs make "ideas come to life" and allows for funding of a wide range of projects. Between 2008-2015, over $800 million was raised for projects through Indiegogo (Indiegogo, 2015). In October 2015, Indiegogo launched the Generosity site so nonprofit organizations could set up crowdfunding campaigns without having to pay any fees. Other crowdfunding platforms, aimed specifically at nonprofit organizations, include Razoo, Crowdrise, and FirstGiving and have stimulated growth in the crowdfunding efforts by nonprofits.

Social media has historically been used as platform for *promoting* crowdfunding campaigns. Okada, Ishida, and Yamauchi (2017) find that social media use before and after disaster situations results in more donations since information about relief needs and giving can be shared easily. Posts on Facebook, Twitter, and other social media sites can provide website links to fundraising campaign webpages, similar to e-mail notifications about a campaign. These posts have the advantage of being integrated within a supporter's social media news feed compared to an e-mail which must be actively opened. In this manner, social media serves as a way to share information about the campaign rather than directly fundraise through a platform.

Options to directly donate within social media platforms are also becoming available. Facebook developed two fundraising call to action (CTA) features for its platform. They added a "Donate Now" CTA in 2015. This allows the "crowd" of followers on Facebook to donate without having to leave the social media platform. Then in 2016, the "Create a Fundraiser" CTA was added so that followers could fundraise on behalf of the organization. This offers a different mechanism because donors contribute to the campaign of a friend or connection who is acting as an agent of the organization. Nonprofit organizations may apply (nonprofit status is verified by Facebook) to add these call to actions to their Facebook page. Similar to other crowdfunding platforms, Facebook charges a fee on donations collected through their platform which ranges between 5-5.75% depending on whether the nonprofit uses the Facebook Payments systems or Network for Good's Advised Fund to collect the donations. Given the variety of crowdfunding platforms available, the following section describes the research to date on crowdfunding by nonprofit organizations.

## Nonprofit Organizations' Use of Crowdfunding

Nonprofits may be more successful in crowdfunding campaigns than for-profit ventures due to donors' perceptions that such campaigns have greater positive community impacts (Belleflamme, Lambert, and Schwienbacher, 2013). Nonprofit organizations are motivated to engage in crowdfunding as a viable means of development to quickly raise funds and generate awareness for their organization (Gerber and Hui, 2013). However, running an effective crowdfunding campaign requires developing a deep understanding of an organization's social network, motivating members of the network to donate or advocate the campaign, and growing the network to maximize crowdfunding efforts (Hui, Gerber, and Gergle, 2014). Large crowds or networks may be easier to leverage for donations. In addition, organizations must understand the nature of campaigns which motivate their supporters to not only give but also advocate the cause online.

From the donor perspective, there are varied motivations for donating to a crowdfunding campaign. A field study of campaigns hosted on the crowdfunding platform Razoo suggests that donors are motivated to give based on fundraising outcomes or targets when the campaign is for a nonprofit organization (Gleasure and Feller, 2016). However, when the campaign is for an individual fundraiser, they (donors) are influenced by what the authors describe as "interaction-related factors" such as the level of dialogue around a campaign which stimulates hedonic benefits and "warm glow" from giving. In addition, the virality (how often the content is shared) of a campaign on social media may trigger social norms which enhance giving (Lee- Won, Abo, Na, and White, 2016). In a study of social media (Facebook) based crowdfunding efforts by the 100 largest nonprofits in the United States, Saxton and Wang (2014) find the size of social networks and category of the cause impact crowdfunding success. Organizations with larger social networks are able to leverage those networks to garner greater donations. In addition, donors to online crowdfunding campaigns may be predisposed to give to specific categories of causes. Health related causes generated the most donations presumably because of the immediate needs that are typically connected to these fundraising campaigns.

Overall, the literature suggests that the effectiveness of crowdfunding campaigns may vary by the size of the organization and the organizational cause. Organizations with smaller social networks may focus on trying to expand their crowdfunding efforts beyond their immediate followers (to expand reach and donations garnered). Organizations with campaigns for causes with less immediate needs may find activating their network around a campaign to be more challenging.

This work extends the existing literature by examining the use of social media for crowdfunding by regional nonprofit organizations. Specific attention is given to an organization's social network size and primary cause of the organization. The use of crowdfunding may be especially attractive to regional nonprofits due to more constrained (compared to national nonprofit organizations) resources for fundraising and because such platforms offer the additional benefit of expanding the viral reach of a campaign. Given the exploratory nature of this section of the chapter (due in part to the recency of nonprofit crowdfunding through social media) broad research questions are posted rather than formal hypotheses.

**R1:** How are regional organizations which vary in social network size utilizing social media for crowdfunding?

**R2:** How are regional organizations which vary by cause utilizing social media for crowdfunding?

# RESEARCH METHOD

## Analytical Methods

The research questions required a context in which social media tools are being leveraged by regional nonprofit organizations to crowdfund. Saxton and Wang (2014) utilized Facebook Causes to examine giving through social media at the national nonprofit level. Building on that work, data is collected on the presence of the "Donate Now" and "Create a Fundraiser" call to actions on the Facebook pages of regional nonprofit organizations. The "Create a Fundraiser" CTA goes one step beyond fundraising from an organization's social network of followers by allowing individuals in the network to act as agents on behalf of the organization. This may trigger both personal (i.e., a donor wants to help support a friend in fundraising efforts) and cause related motivations for donors. Therefore, further insights were gathered from representatives at 10 of the regional nonprofit organizations to gain deeper perspectives about their use of this relatively new feature.

## Analysis of Data From Facebook Pages

The Central Texas area was again selected for examination due to the high concentration of regional nonprofit organizations in the area. This time the databases of local nonprofit organizations were examined to find organizations which had a Facebook page since this is necessary to analyze the use of the two fundraising CTA features. This resulted in a list of 647 organizations with Facebook pages. The sample included a cross-section of nonprofits affiliated with a variety of causes: Social Services (16%), Arts (13%), Youth (13%), Education (11%), and Human Services (10%). The remainder of the organizations operate in various domains. A full categorization of all the organizations in this sample is provided in Figure 5.

*Figure 5.*

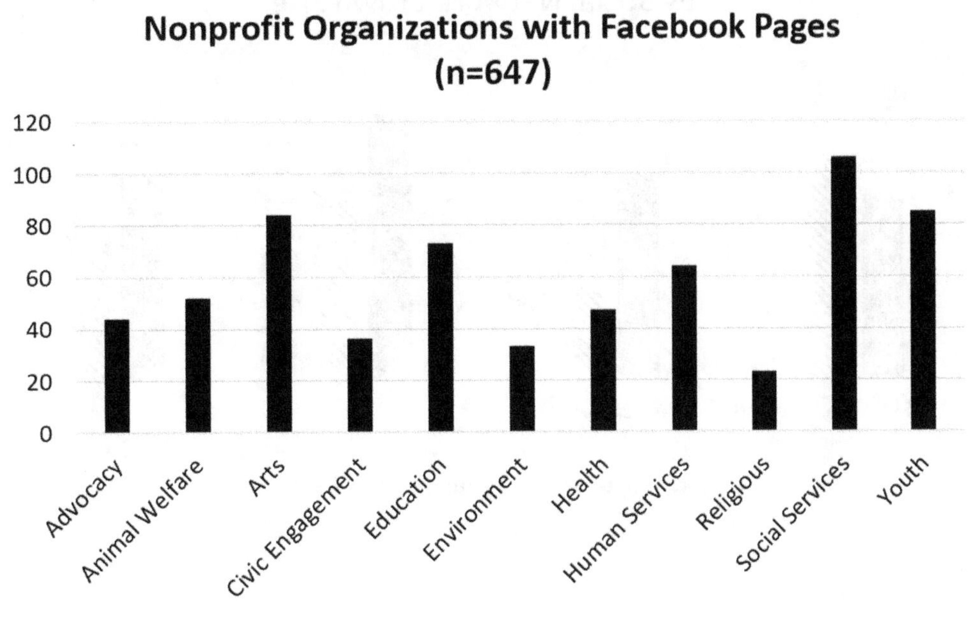

Each page was then examined within a two day window (to account for any dramatic fluctuations in Facebook activity or the number of followers) to determine whether the organization was had: (1) a "Donate Now" call to action on their Facebook page, (2) a "Create a Fundraiser" call to action on their Facebook page, (3) both "Donate Now" and 'Create a Fundraiser" call to actions on their Facebook page, or (4) neither call to actions on their Facebook page. The number of social media users who "Liked" the page was also recorded. The number of "Likes" is representative of the size of an organization's social media crowd network.

## Results From Facebook Page Analysis

Nearly half 49.92% of the regional nonprofits in the sample have the "Donate" CTA on their Facebook pages. 42.50% have the "Create Fundraiser" CTA. The sample was stratified based on the size of the social media crowd network. The sample was divided into quartiles based on the median number of likes (7,912 Likes). Addressing Research question 1 (R1), analysis revealed that the "Donate" button was more frequently present on the Facebook pages of organizations in all the quartiles except for the quartile with the lowest number of "Likes" (bottom 25% quartile). For these organizations with small social network crowds, the "Create a Fundraiser" button was present on more (8% more) pages. The patterns across the quartiles (by organization social media crowd network size) is provided in Figure 6.

To investigate Research question 2 (R2). The sample was then divided based on categories of social causes with which the organizations were affiliated. The "Donate" CTA was used by more than half of the organizations in the: Health, Animal Welfare, Social Services, Human Services, Religious, and Youth categories. Almost 70% of the organizations in the Health category have the "Donate" CTA on their Facebook page. Although used less overall, the "Create a Fundraiser CTA" was present on the Face-

*Figure 6.*

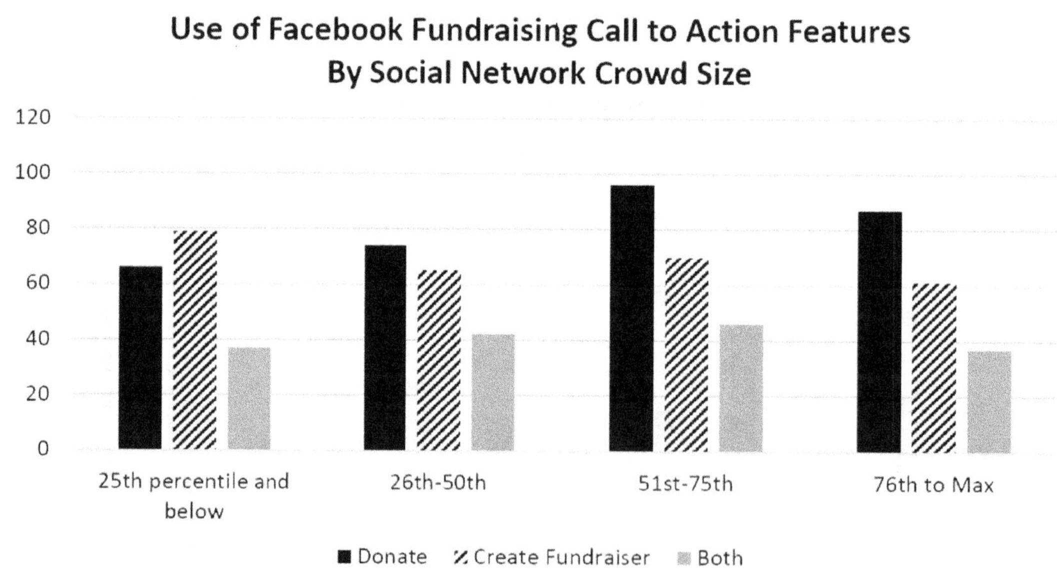

book pages of over 40% of the organizations in the Advocacy, Youth, Social Services, Animal Welfare, Health, and Civic Engagement categories. Almost 70% of the organizations in the Advocacy category included the "Create a Fundraiser" CTA on their page. Less than 40% of the Organizations which fell into the Arts and Environment categories included either CTA. The patterns across the organizations (by cause type) are provided in Figure 7.

## Insights From Representatives at Regional Nonprofit Organizations

The "Create a Fundraiser" CTA is Facebook's newest feature for fundraising at the time this research was conducted. To better understand the use of this feature, insights were gathered from staff members at 10 regional nonprofit organizations located in Central Texas. The representatives covered a range of different causes (arts, civic engagement, youth, advocacy, health, environment, social services, and human services). All of the representatives were affiliated with nonprofits with a "Create a Fundraiser" CTA located on their Facebook page. They were asked about the success of this feature as a fundraising tool. Many of the respondents indicated they had not yet utilized the feature on their page. There were two main reasons for this: (1) Facebook's approval process (as a nonprofit organization) took several weeks to a few months, so some of the nonprofits had just added the CTA added to their Facebook page and (2) many organizations had existing platforms they utilized for crowdfunding (e.g., Crowdrise). Interestingly, several of the staff members from different organizations explained that they were actually dissuading supporters from using the feature because it was logistically difficult to collect funds from Facebook, and it disconnected the donors from the actual organizations since it was done via Facebook's platform. Also, donor information is difficult to extract from Facebook. Key insights from the staff members are provided in Table 5.

*Figure 7.*

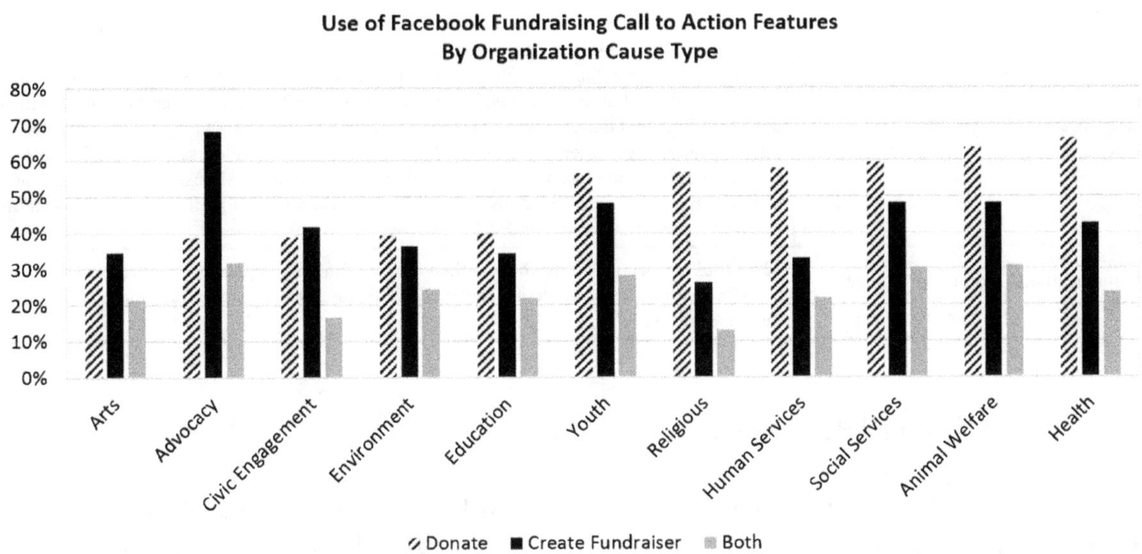

*Table 5. Insights from key staff members are regional nonprofit organizations*

| Staff Members From Regional Nonprofits-Organization Cause | Insights About Facebook "Create Fundraiser" CTA |
|---|---|
| Community Outreach Manager-Arts | "Though this is a function that is on our Facebook page, we have not used it yet." |
| Director of Development-Civic Engagement | "Third party online fundraising is not something that we do a great deal here… Crowdfunding has a place in the development pantheon but it will never replace or be as large as traditional fundraising methods for the typical nonprofit, and, therefore, many do not spend a great deal of time promoting it…There are some excellent examples of where this type of fundraising works, but what happens with this type of giving is that they are giving to the person asking and not necessarily building a relationship with the agency, which is what the agency truly wants. It seems to work best for national organizations and with fundraising that is attached to some kind of athletic event." |
| Director of Development-Youth | "We actually have never done any fundraising through Facebook. We only just recently even went through the steps of verifying our nonprofit status on their platform. Historically, we have used Crowdrise as our place to create and manage peer-to-peer fundraisers. Obviously, our peer-to-peer fundraisers have used Facebook to advertise their Crowdrise pages and we've been pretty successful. But we are wondering if the more integrated platform that Facebook fundraising directly can provide would be more successful." |
| Central Texas Area Director- Advocacy | "We actually discourage our supporters from using this feature, as it becomes a logistical headache to process the funds in a way that ensures they stay with the local chapter. Our primary method of fundraising is peer-to-peer fundraising through events. This is all housed through a system called DonorDrive, which automatically divvies up funds based on the individual chapter associated with that location." |
| Development and Communications Manager- Health | "It has been successful but we are now detreating people from using it because it doesn't give us the information we need. Ex. The mailing and contact information, besides the name, of the donor." |
| VP of Marketing and Communications-Youth | "Honestly, in the 2.5 years I have been here I have never had anyone use the 'Create a Fundraiser' button on our Facebook page. So, this feature hasn't really done anything for us unless it has given someone an idea about fundraising that they have pursued without clicking through Facebook." |
| Development Associate-Environment | "We have actually never used that function." |
| Vice President of Development-Social Services | "We have barely even used the FB donation function and have only received a few gifts from it." |
| Marketing and Programs Manager-Advocacy | "We include the fundraiser option on our FB page in case there is anyone interested in starting one, but we don't actively promote it because we prefer to raise money where we can keep track of the donors better and build a relationship with them. We have had a few small donations here and there come from FB in the spring of this year, but again, we have had little interaction with them because we don't know their email address or FB profile name. So I'd say this feature has been successful in that we have done almost nothing to promote it and have received some donations from it! But for now we don't plan to engage in recruiting people to create fundraisers on FB for us." |
| Communications Coordinator-Human Services | "This tool has been used maybe less than a dozen times by supporters since it became available. At this time, we do not rely on these feature as a source for developing funds for the organization." |

## DISCUSSION AND IMPLICATIONS

The results suggest that regional nonprofit organizations with the smallest social networks (the bottom quartile of Facebook likes in the data sample) utilize the "Create a Fundraiser" more other organizations. It is presumed that because their immediate networks are small, the "Create a Fundraiser" CTA offers these organizations a way to simultaneously garner donations and expand their social network via their current followers. This may offer a viable and cost effective way for small regional nonprofit organizations to fundraise as well as enhance brand awareness about their organizations.

Similar to the finding in Saxton and Wang's (2014) research, there appears to be an "immediacy" effect in that organizations which are linked to causes which may have immediate donor needs (e.g., related to health care or animal welfare) tend to use social media tools more than organizations affiliated with causes which may have less time sensitive campaigns. Thus, given the real time nature of social media, crowdfunding is likely to be most effective for nonprofit campaigns with short timelines that require immediate action. Nonprofit organizations with longer campaigns (e.g., funding for a museum program) may consider testing whether dividing a longer campaign into a series of smaller fundraising targets with more immediate objectives results in more successful crowdfunding results through social media.

Finally, the insights gathered from the staff of various regional nonprofits indicated that Facebook CTA features, specifically the "Create a Fundraiser" CTA, was very much still used as a supplementary element to overall fundraising efforts. In addition, because social media created an added layer between the organization and donors, many viewed this as an impediment to building long term connections with donors.

## LIMITATIONS AND FUTURE RESEARCH

Overall, this chapter focused on two uses of social media by regional nonprofit organizations: information transmission and fundraising. The results of the data analysis extend knowledge on social media as a tool for marketing and fundraising for regional nonprofit organizations. However there are limitations to this work and opportunities exists for future research.

Facebook was the only social media platform examined in this work. Future work examining other platforms would be worthy of investigation. For example, Twitter offers users a way to donate to a charity using a hashtag (Keady, 2015).

This chapter also focused on two uses of social media: information transmission and fundraising. However, there are other ways nonprofits can use social media including polling supporters to better understand their needs and wants, encouraging dialogue among users and the organization, and even as a way to build brand awareness and gain credibility. These offer fruitful areas for future research. In addition, the feedback from representatives at the regional nonprofit organizations indicated that crowdfunding through social media is still ancillary to other fundraising efforts. It would be interesting to see if this pattern remains after a few years or if social media becomes a more primary fundraising tool.

Finally, the sample of organizations in this chapter where located in Central Texas around the Austin, Texas area. Austin is a technological hub (Athwal, 2015) in the United States so the organizations in this area may be more technologically savvy due to migration of employees from the technology sector and from being located in a technology embracing culture. Thus, future research in a different region may prove fruitful in identifying environmental and cultural factors which affect social media use by regional nonprofit organizations.

## REFERENCES


Armstrong, J. S., & Overton, T. S. (1977). Estimating nonresponse bias in mail surveys. *JMR, Journal of Marketing Research, 14*(3), 396–402. doi:10.2307/3150783

Athwal, N. (2015). 5 Cities Poised to be the next Silicon Valley tech hub. *Forbes*. Retrieved from: http://www.forbes.com/sites/navathwal/2015/02/12/5-markets-poised-to-be-the-next-silicon-valley-for-real-estate/

Baron, J. N., Hannan, M. T., & Burton, M. D. (2001). Labor pains: Change in organizational models and employee turnover in young, high-tech firms. *American Journal of Sociology, 106*(4), 960–1012. doi:10.1086/320296

Baruch, Y., & Holtom, B. C. (2008). Survey response rate levels and trends in organizational research. *Human Relations, 61*(8), 1139–1160. doi:10.1177/0018726708094863

Belleflamme, P., Lambert, T., & Schwienbacher, A. (2013). Individual crowdfunding practices. *Venture Capital, 15*(4), 313–333. doi:10.1080/13691066.2013.785151

Berlinger, L. R., & Te'eni, D. (1999). Leaders' attitudes and computer use in religious congregations. *Nonprofit Management & Leadership, 9*(4), 399–412. doi:10.1002/nml.9405

Bertels, S., & Peloza, J. (2008). Running just to stand still? Managing CSR reputation in an era of ratcheting expectations. *Corporate Reputation Review, 11*(1), 56–72. doi:10.1057/crr.2008.1

Bortree, D. S., & Seltzer, T. (2009). Dialogic strategies and outcomes: An analysis of environmental advocacy groups' Facebook profiles. *Public Relations Review, 35*(3), 317–319. doi:10.1016/j.pubrev.2009.05.002

Callanan, L., Gardner, N., Mendonca, L., & Scott, D. (2014). *What social-sector leader needs to succeed.* McKinsey & Company Insights & Publications. Retrieved from: http://www.mckinsey.com/insights/social_sector/what_social_sector_leaders_need_to_succeed

Curtis, L., Edwards, C., Fraser, K. L., Gudelsky, S., Holmquist, J., Thornton, K., & Sweetser, K. D. (2010). Adoption of social media for public relations by nonprofit organizations. *Public Relations Review, 36*(1), 90–92. doi:10.1016/j.pubrev.2009.10.003

Deshpandé, R., Farley, J. U., & Webster, F. E. Jr. (1993). Corporate culture, customer orientation, and innovativeness in Japanese firms: A quadrad analysis. *Journal of Marketing, 57*(1), 23–37. doi:10.2307/1252055

DiMaggio, P. J., & Powell, W. W. (1983). The iron cage revisited: Institutional isomorphism and collective rationality in organizational fields. *American Sociological Review, 48*(2), 147–160. doi:10.2307/2095101

Donaldson, S. I., & Grant-Vallone, E. J. (2002). Understanding self-report bias in organizational behavior research. *Journal of Business and Psychology, 17*(2), 245–260. doi:10.1023/A:1019637632584

Fama, E. F., & Jensen, M. C. (1983). Separation of ownership and control. *The Journal of Law & Economics, 26*(2), 301–325. doi:10.1086/467037

Gerber, E. M., & Hui, J. (2013). Crowdfunding: Motivations and deterrents for participation. *ACM Transactions on Computer-Human Interaction, 20*(6), 34. doi:10.1145/2530540

Gleasure, R., & Feller, J. (2016). Does heart or head rule donor behaviors in charitable crowdfunding markets? *International Journal of Electronic Commerce, 20*(4), 499–524. doi:10.1080/10864415.2016.1171975

Grace-Martin, K. (2008). Can Likert scale data ever be continuous. *Article Alley*. Retrieved from: http://www.theanalysisfactor.com/can-likert-scale-data-ever-be-continuous/

Greenberg, J., & MacAulay. (2009). NPO 2.0? Exploring the web presence of environmental nonprofit organizations in Canada. *Global Media Journal-Canadian Edition, 2*(1), 63-88.

Hackler, D., & Saxton, G. D. (2007). The strategic use of information technology by nonprofit organizations: Increasing capacity and untapped potential. *Public Administration Review, 67*(3), 474–487. doi:10.1111/j.1540-6210.2007.00730.x

Harlan, S. L., & Saidel, J. R. (1994). Board members' influence on the government-nonprofit relationship. *Nonprofit Management & Leadership, 5*(2), 173–196. doi:10.1002/nml.4130050206 PMID:10140720

Howe, J. (2006). The rise of crowdsourcing. *Wired Magazine, 14*(6), 1-4.

Howe, N., & Strauss, W. (2000). *Millennials rising: The next great generation*. New York: Vintage.

Hu, Q., & Shi, W. (2017). Understanding nonprofit organizations' use of social networking sites: An examination of management factors. *International Journal of Public Administration in the Digital Age, 4*(1), 19–34. doi:10.4018/IJPADA.2017010102

Hui, J. S., Gerber, E. M., & Gergle, D. (2014). Understanding and leveraging social networks for crowdfunding: opportunities and challenges. In *Proceedings of the 2014 conference on Designing interactive systems* (pp. 677-680). ACM. 10.1145/2598510.2598539

Indiegogo. (2015). *Indiegogo's 2015 Year in Review: Crowdfunding Statistics*. Retrieved from: https://go.indiegogo.com/blog/2015/12/2015-crowdfunding-infographic-statistics-tech-film-social.html

Jackson, D. (2014). Growing communities: How charity leaders govern social media globally to thrive online. *Grant Thornon*. Retrieved from: http://www.grantthornton.global/Insights/Articles/Growing-Communities

Kaplan, A. M., & Haenlein, M. (2010). Users of the world, unite! The challenges and opportunities of Social Media. *Business Horizons, 53*(1), 59–68. doi:10.1016/j.bushor.2009.09.003

Keady, C. (2015). #Donate allows you to easily give to charity through Twitter hashtags. *Huffington Post*. Retrieved from: http://www.huffingtonpost.com/2015/04/17/donate-charity-social-media-platform_n_7089280.html

Kickstarter. (2017). *About us*. Retrieved from: https://www.kickstarter.com/about

Kohli, A. K., & Jaworski, B. J. (1990). Market orientation: The construct, research propositions, and managerial implications. *Journal of Marketing, 54*(2), 1–18. doi:10.2307/1251866

Kouri, M., & Edward, D. (2013). Does Central Texas have too many nonprofits. *Greenlights for Nonprofit Success*. Retrieved from: http://www.greenlights.org/

Lee-Won, R. J., Abo, M. M., Na, K., & White, T. N. (2016). More than numbers: Effects of social media virality metrics on intention to help unknown others in the context of bone marrow donation. *Cyberpsychology, Behavior, and Social Networking*, *19*(6), 404–411. doi:10.1089/cyber.2016.0080 PMID:27327068

Leonard, H. (2013). Big business pouring money into social tools. *Business Insider.* Retrieved from: http://www.businessinsider.com/companies-investing-in-social-2013-4

Levitt, B., & March, J. G. (1988). Organizational learning. *Annual Review of Sociology*, *14*(1), 319–340. doi:10.1146/annurev.so.14.080188.001535

Lovejoy, K., Waters, R. D., & Saxton, G. D. (2012). Engaging stakeholders through Twitter: How nonprofit organizations are getting more out of 140 characters or less. *Public Relations Review*, *38*(2), 313–318. doi:10.1016/j.pubrev.2012.01.005

Lubke, G. H., & Muthén, B. O. (2004). Applying multigroup confirmatory factor models for continuous outcomes to Likert scale data complicates meaningful group comparisons. *Structural Equation Modeling*, *11*(4), 514–534. doi:10.120715328007sem1104_2

Maxwell, S. P., & Carboni, J. L. (2017). Civic engagement through social media: Strategic stakeholder management by high-asset foundations. *International Journal of Public Administration in the Digital Age*, *4*(1), 35–48. doi:10.4018/IJPADA.2017010103

Meister, J. (2012). Social media training is now mandatory: five ways to make sure your company does it right. *Forbes*. Retrieved from: http://www.forbes.com/sites/jeannemeister/2012/10/31/social-media-training-is-now-mandatory/

Miller, J. L. (2002). The board as a monitor of organizational activity: The applicability of agency theory to nonprofit boards. *Nonprofit Management & Leadership*, *12*(4), 429–450. doi:10.1002/nml.12407

Moorman, C. (1995). Organizational market information processes: Cultural antecedents and new product outcomes. *JMR, Journal of Marketing Research*, *32*(3), 318–335. doi:10.2307/3151984

Nah, S., & Saxton, G. D. (2012). Modeling the adoption and use of social media by nonprofit organizations. *New Media & Society*.

Nunnally, J., & Bernstein, I. H. (1967). *Psychometric theory*. New York: McGraw-Hill Book Company.

Okada, A., Ishida, Y., & Yamauchi, N. (2017). Effectiveness of social media in disaster fundraising: Mobilizing the public towards voluntary actions. *International Journal of Public Administration in the Digital Age*, *4*(1), 49–68. doi:10.4018/IJPADA.2017010104

Outlaw, S. (2013). Which Type of Crowdfunding is best for you? *Entrepeneur*. Retrieved from: https://www.entrepreneur.com/article/228524

Pew Research. (2014). *Social media fact sheet*. Retrieved from: http://www.pewinternet.org/fact-sheet/social-media/

Pugh, D. S., Hickson, D. J., Hinings, C. R., & Turner, C. (1969). The context of organization structures. *Administrative Science Quarterly*, *14*(1), 91–114. doi:10.2307/2391366

Robson, C. (2002). *Real world research*. Oxford, UK: Blackwell Publishing.

Saxton, G. D., & Wang, L. (2014). The social network effect: The determinants of giving through social media. *Nonprofit and Voluntary Sector Quarterly*, *43*(5), 850–868. doi:10.1177/0899764013485159

Waters, R. D., Burnett, E., Lamm, A., & Lucas, J. (2009). Engaging stakeholders through social networking: How nonprofit organizations are using Facebook. *Public Relations Review*, *35*(2), 102–106. doi:10.1016/j.pubrev.2009.01.006

Waters, R. D., & Jones, P. M. (2011). Using video to build an organization's identity and brand: A content analysis of nonprofit organizations' YouTube videos. *Journal of Nonprofit & Public Sector Marketing*, *23*(3), 248–268. doi:10.1080/10495142.2011.594779

Young, J. A. (2017). Facebook, Twitter, and blogs: The adoption and utilization of social media in nonprofit human service organizations. *Human Service Organizations, Management, Leadership & Governance*, *41*(1), 44–57. doi:10.1080/23303131.2016.1192574

## APPENDIX

### Nonprofit Social Media Strategy Survey Items

Respondents were asked to read the statements below and then indicate his/her agreement with the statement.

1= Very Strongly Disagree
2= Strongly Disagree
3=Disagree
4=Neutral
5=Agree
6=Strongly Agree
7=Very Strongly Agree

#### Executive Director Background (Created)

1. The executive director of my nonprofit has work experience primarily in the nonprofit sector.
2. The executive director of my nonprofit has been involved in the nonprofit sector for a long (more than five years) time.
3. The executive director of my nonprofit has little experience in the private (for-profit) sector.

#### Board Influence (Created)

1. The board of directors is involved in strategic planning for my nonprofit.
2. The board for directors has a strong voice (i.e., their opinions matter) at my nonprofit.
3. The board of directors is involved in budgetary decision making for my nonprofit.
4. The board of directors plays an important role in my nonprofit.

#### Customer Orientation (Adapted From Deshpandé, Farley, and Webster Jr., 1993)

* "Constituents" were defined for respondents as individuals who utilize or benefit from the services provided by the nonprofit organization

1. My nonprofit has regular or routine measures of service to its constituents
2. The services offered by my nonprofit are based on reliable market and constituent information.
3. The nonprofit is aware and familiar with the services provided by similar nonprofits.
4. My nonprofit has a strong sense of how our constituents value our services.
5. We are more constituent focused than other, similar non-profits.
6. Our constituents' needs always come first.
7. The services provided by my nonprofit are the best offered for this type of service.
8. I believe this non-profit exists primarily to service its constituency.

## Information Transmission (Adapted From Moorman, 1995)

1. My nonprofit uses social media for internally (within the organization) sharing information.
2. My nonprofit uses social media for sharing information about its initiatives to donors.
3. My nonprofit uses social media for sharing information about its volunteer opportunities to volunteers.
4. My nonprofit employs people who are willing to share information through social media.

The following questions did not involve a rating scale but were directly answered by respondents.

## Board Size

1. How many directors are on your nonprofit's board of directors?

## Proportion of Millennial Staff Members and Organization Size

1. How many paid staff members work at your nonprofit?
2. How many staff members are under 33 years old (your best estimate)?

## Social Media Spending

1. What was your nonprofit's spending towards social media efforts/development in 2014? (answer in dollars)

## Use of Social Media

1. What are the main uses of social media by your nonprofit?

# Compilation of References


Abanumy, A., Al-Badi, A., & Mayhew, P. (2005). E-government website accessibility: In-depth evaluation of Saudi Arabia and Oman. *The Electronic Journal of E-Government, 3*(3), 99–106.

Abdolmohammadi, M., Harris, J., & Smith, K. (2002). Government financial reporting on the Internet: The potential revolutionary effects of XBRL. *Journal of Government Financial Management, 51*(2), 24–31.

Abu-Shanab, E., Al-Rub, S. A., & Md Nor, K. (2010). Obstacles Facing the Adoption of E-Government Services in Jordan. *Journal of E-Governance, 33*(1), 35–47.

Accenture Institute for Health and Public Service Value. (2009). *From e-government to e-governance: Using new technologies to strengthen relationships with citizens*. Accenture.

Accenture. (2012). *Accenture Works with Singapore to Implement Its National Electronic Health Record System*. Retrieved September 11, 2017, from https://www.accenture.com/t20160510T050818__w__/us-en/_acnmedia/Accenture/Conversion-Assets/DotCom/Documents/Global/PDF/Industries_11/Accenture-Works-Singapore-Implement-NEHR-System.pdf

Accenture. (2013). *The Digital Doctor is "In": Accenture Eight-Country Survey of Doctors Shows Significant Increase in Healthcare IT Usage*. Retrieved September 20, 2017, from https://www.accenture.com/t20150708T033736__w__/us-en/_acnmedia/Accenture/Conversion-Assets/DotCom/Documents/Global/PDF/Industries_11/Accenture-Digital-Doctor-Is-In.pdf

Accenture. (2015). *Doctors Survey 2015: Six-Country Report*. Retrieved September 22, 2017, from https://www.accenture.com/_acnmedia/Accenture/Conversion-Assets/DotCom/Documents/Global/PDF/Dualpub_22/Accenture-Global-Report-Acn-Doctors-Study-SG.pdf

Accenture. (2016a). *Accenture Asia-Pacific Healthcare Innovation and Transformation Survey*. Retrieved September 22, 2017, from https://www.accenture.com/t00010101T000000Z__w__/au-en/_acnmedia/PDF-17/Accenture-Health-Transformation-Survey-Full-Report.pdf

Accenture. (2016b). *Singaporean Patients Embrace Digital Health*. Retrieved September 20, 2017, from https://www.accenture.com/t20160627T034015Z__w__/sg-en/_acnmedia/PDF-22/Accenture-Digital-Health-Consumer-Survey-Research-Brief-Singapore.pdf

Accenture. (2016c). *Silver Surfers: Older Singaporeans Are Making Waves in Digital Health*. Retrieved September 27, from https://www.accenture.com/t20170314T215209__w__/sg-en/_acnmedia/PDF-46/Accenture-Health-Silver-Surfers-in-Singapore.pdf

Adler, S., & Carpenter, H. (2015). Peer-to-peer fundraising success: paws with a cause. In H. Asencio & R. Sun (Eds.), *Cases on Strategic Social Media Utilization in the Nonprofit Sector*. Hershey, PA: Information Science Reference. doi:10.4018/978-1-4666-8188-0.ch002

Adnan, M., Lima, A., Rossi, L., Veluru, S., Longley, P., Musolesi, M., & Rajarajan, M. (2014). The uncertainty of identity toolset : Analysing digital traces for user profiling. In *Proceedings of the 7th International Conference on Security of Information and Networks* (p. 254). ACM. 10.1145/2659651.2659741

Agency for Science, Technology and Research. (2011). *Science, Technology & Enterprise Plan 2015*. Retrieved September 30, 2017, from http://www.a-star.edu.sg/portals/0/media/otherpubs/step2015_1jun.pdf

Ahn, J. (2012). Teenagers and social network sites : Do off-line inequalities predict their online social networks? *First Monday*, *17*(1), 1–14. doi:10.5210/fm.v17i1.3752

Aikins, S. K. (Ed.). (2012). *Managing E-Government Projects: Concepts, Issues, and Best Practices*. Hershey, PA: IGI Global. doi:10.4018/978-1-4666-0086-7

Akman, I., Yazici, A., Mishra, A., & Arifoglu, A. (2005). E-Government: A global view and an empirical evaluation of some attributes of citizens. *Government Information Quarterly*, *22*(2), 239–257. doi:10.1016/j.giq.2004.12.001

Al-Adawi, Z., Yousafzai, S., & Pallister, J. (2005, September). Conceptual model of citizen adoption of e-government. In *The Second International Conference on Innovations in Information Technology (IIT'05)* (pp. 1-10). Academic Press.

Aladwani, A. (2016). Corruption as a source of e-Government projects failure in developing countries: A theoretical exposition. *International Journal of Information Management*, *36*(1), 105–112. doi:10.1016/j.ijinfomgt.2015.10.005

Alalwan, J., & Thomas, M. (2011). *Designing ERM Ontology to Evaluate Records Management System*. Paper presented at the System Sciences (HICSS), 2011 44th Hawaii International Conference on. 10.1109/HICSS.2011.149

Alalwan, J. A., Thomas, M. A., & Weistroffer, H. R. (2014). Decision support capabilities of enterprise content management systems: An empirical investigation. *Decision Support Systems*, *68*, 39–48. doi:10.1016/j.dss.2014.09.002

Alan, A., Soskis, B., & Toepler, S. (2012). *Public Philanthropic Partnerships in the U.S.: A Literature Review of Recent Experiences*. Washington, DC: Council on Foundations.

Alarabiat, A., Soares, D. S., & Estevez, E. (2016). Electronic Participation with a Special Reference to Social Media - A Literature Review. In E. Tambouris & ... (Eds.), Lecture Notes in Computer Science: Vol. 9821. *Electronic Participation. ePart 2016*. Cham: Springer. doi:10.1007/978-3-319-45074-2_4

Alberta, G. o. (2004). *Managing Web Content: applying the information management framework to web resources*. Government of Alberta.

Al-Khalifa, H. S., & Al-Eidan, R. M. (2011). An experimental system for measuring the credibility of news content in Twitter. *International Journal of Web Information Systems Vol.*, *7*(2), 130–151. doi:10.1108/17440081111141772

Almarabeh, T., & AbuAli, A. (2010). A general framework for e-government: Definition maturity challenges, opportunities, and success. *European Journal of Scientific Research*, *39*(1), 29–42.

Al-Rashidi, H., & London, W. (2010). Examining Internal Challenges to E-Government Implementation from System Users Perspective. In *European and Mediterranean Conference on Information Systems* (*Vol. 2010*). Abu Dhabi, UAE: Academic Press.

Al-Sebie, M. (2014). Organizational challenges facing integrating e-government systems: an empirical study. *European Scientific Journal, 10*(10).

Álvarez Sabucedo, L. M., Anido Rifón, L. E., Corradini, F., Polzonetti, A., & Re, B. (2010). Knowledge-based platform for eGovernment agents: A Web-based solution using semantic technologies. *Expert Systems with Applications*, *37*(5), 3647–3656. doi:10.1016/j.eswa.2009.10.026

Alzahrani, L., Al-Karaghouili, W., & Weerakkody, V. (2017). Analyzing the critical factors influencing trust in-government adoption from citizens' perspective: A systematic review and a conceptual framework. *Information Business Review, 26*(1), 164–175. doi:10.1016/j.ibusrev.2016.06.004

Aman, A., & Kasimin, H. (2011). E-procurement implementation: a case of Malaysia government. *Transforming Government: People, Process and Policy, 5*(4), 330–344.

Ames, M. G., Go, J., Kaye, J. J., Spasojevic, M., Road, P. M., & Alto, P. (2011). Understanding Technology Choices and Values through Social Class. In CSCW 2011 Proceedings (pp. 55–64). Academic Press. doi:10.1145/1958824.1958834

Anheier, H. (2005). *Nonprofit Organizations: Theory, Management and Policy*. New York: Routledge.

Anthopoulos, L. G., & Siozos, P. (2015). Can IT Innovation become a Tool against Fiscal Crisis?: Findings from Europe. *International Journal of Public Administration in the Digital Age, 2*(1), 39–55. doi:10.4018/ijpada.2015010103

Anthopoulos, L., Reddick, C., Giannakidou, I., & Mavridis, N. (2016). Why e-government projects fail? An analysis of the Healthcare.gov website. *Government Information Quarterly, 33*(1), 161–173. doi:10.1016/j.giq.2015.07.003

Armstrong, J. S., & Overton, T. S. (1977). Estimating nonresponse bias in mail surveys. *JMR, Journal of Marketing Research, 14*(3), 396–402. doi:10.2307/3150783

Athwal, N. (2015). 5 Cities Poised to be the next Silicon Valley tech hub. *Forbes*. Retrieved from: http://www.forbes.com/sites/navathwal/2015/02/12/5-markets-poised-to-be-the-next-silicon-valley-for-real-estate/

ATP. (2011). *Sådan etablerer vi Udbetaling Danmark*. Retrieved from http://www.penst.dk/~/media/PST/Files/Publikationer/2011/Saedan-etablerer-vi-udbetaling-danmark.ashx

Auger, G. A. (2013). Fostering democracy through social media: Evaluating diametrically opposed nonprofit advocacy organizations' use of Facebook, Twitter, and YouTube. *Public Relations Review, 39*(4), 369–376. DOI: 10.1016/j.pubrev.2013.07.013

Auger, G. A. (2010). Using dialogic website design to encourage effective grantor –grantee Relationships. *Prism, 7*(2). http://praxis.massey.ac.nz/prism_on-line_journ.html

Auger, G. A. (2014). Rhetorical framing: Examining the message structure of nonprofit organizations on Twitter. *International Journal of Nonprofit and Voluntary Sector Marketing, 19*(4), 239–249. doi:10.1002/nvsm.1499

Austin, L., Liu, B. F., & Jin, Y. (2012). How audiences seek out crisis information: Exploring the social-mediated crisis communication model. *Journal of Applied Communication Research, 40*(2), 188–207. doi:10.1080/00909882.2012.654498

Australia, G. o. (2013). *Protective Security Framework: Securing government business*. Academic Press.

Australian National Audit Office. (2004). *Measuring the efficiency and effectiveness of e-government*. Audit Report No. 26, 2004-2005. Canberra, Australia: ANAO.

Avallone, F., Ramassa, P., & Roncagliolo, E. (2016). XBRL Extension to the Financial Statement Notes: Field-based Evidence on Unlisted Companies. *The International Journal of Digital Accounting Research, 16*, 61–84.

Awan, M. A. (2008). Dubai e-government: An evaluation of G2B websites. *Journal of Internet Commerce, 6*(3), 115–129. doi:10.1300/J179v06n03_06

Backus, M. (2001). *E-Governance and Developing Countries*. Retrieved October 17, 2017 from https://publicadministration.un.org/egovkb/Data-Center

Baker, T., Bechhofer, S., Isaac, A., Miles, A., Schreiber, G., & Summers, E. (2013). Key choices in the design of Simple Knowledge Organization System (SKOS). *Journal of Web Semantics*, *20*, 35–49. doi:10.1016/j.websem.2013.05.001

Bak, J., Jedrzejek, C., & Falkowski, M. (2009). *Usage of the Jess engine, rules and ontology to query a relational database. In Rule Interchange and Applications* (pp. 216–230). Springer.

Bakshy, E., Hofman, J., Mason, W., & Watts, D. (2011). Everyone's an influencer: quantifying influence on twitter. *Proceedings of the Fourth ACM International Conference on Web Search and Data Mining SE - WSDM '11*, 65–74. 10.1145/1935826.1935845

Ballatore, A., & Zipf, A. (2015). A Conceptual Quality Framework for Volunteered Geographic Information. In *COSIT 2015 Conference on Spatial Information Theory XII October 12-16, 2015, Lecture Notes in Computer Science*. eScholarship University of California. 10.1007/978-3-319-23374-1_5

Ball, C. (2007). Better information better management. *Journal of Government Financial Management*, *56*(2), 16–19.

Bang, H. (2010). Between everyday makers and expert citizens. In Public Management in the Postmodern Era: Challenges and Prospects (pp. 163-192). Cheltenham, UK: Edward Elgar Publishing.

Bannister, F., & Connolly, R. (2011). The Trouble with Transparency : A Critical View of Openness in e- Government. *Policy and Internet*, *3*(1), 158–187. doi:10.2202/1944-2866.1076

Baron, J. N., Hannan, M. T., & Burton, M. D. (2001). Labor pains: Change in organizational models and employee turnover in young, high-tech firms. *American Journal of Sociology*, *106*(4), 960–1012. doi:10.1086/320296

Barth, M., & Veit, D. (2011). *Electronic Service Delivery in the Public Sector: Understanding the Variance of Citizens' Resistance. In Proceedings of the 44th Hawaii International Conference on System Sciences (HICSS-44)*. Kauai, HI: IEEE Computer Society Conference Publishing Services. Retrieved from http://doi.ieeecomputersociety.org/10.1109/HICSS.2011.181

Baruch, Y., & Holtom, B. C. (2008). Survey response rate levels and trends in organizational research. *Human Relations*, *61*(8), 1139–1160. doi:10.1177/0018726708094863

Baum, C. H. (n.d.). *A D Maio Gartner's Four Phases of E-Government Model*. Retrieved October 11, 2017 from https://www.gartner.com/doc/317292/gartners-phases-egovernment-model

BBC. (2014). *My web my way – Making the web easier to use*. Retrieved August 14, 2014, from http://www.bbc.co.uk/accessibility/

Beimel, D., & Peleg, M. (2011). Using OWL and SWRL to represent and reason with situation-based access control policies. *Data & Knowledge Engineering*, *70*(6), 596–615. doi:10.1016/j.datak.2011.03.006

Belleflamme, P., Lambert, T., & Schwienbacher, A. (2013). Individual crowdfunding practices. *Venture Capital*, *15*(4), 313–333. doi:10.1080/13691066.2013.785151

Bennett, S. (2014). 86% of charities and nonprofits use Twitter, 71% say social useful for donations. *Social Times*. Retrieved August 5, 2015 from http://www.adweek.com/socialtimes/charity-nonprofit-social-media-study/499579

Bera, P., Burton-Jones, A., & Wand, Y. (2011). Guidelines for designing visual ontologies to support knowledge identification. *Management Information Systems Quarterly*, *35*(4), 883–908. doi:10.2307/41409965

Berlinger, L. R., & Te'eni, D. (1999). Leaders' attitudes and computer use in religious congregations. *Nonprofit Management & Leadership*, *9*(4), 399–412. doi:10.1002/nml.9405

Bertels, S., & Peloza, J. (2008). Running just to stand still? Managing CSR reputation in an era of ratcheting expectations. *Corporate Reputation Review*, *11*(1), 56–72. doi:10.1057/crr.2008.1

Bessant, J. (2005). Enabling continuous and discontinuous innovation: Learning from the private sector. *Public Money & Management*, *25*(1), 35–42.

Bhunia, P. (2017a). *3 'Ds' Supporting 3 'B's - Objectives and Principles of Singapore's Health IT Master Plan*. Retrieved September 15, 2017, from http://www.opengovasia.com/articles/7649-ds-supporting-3-bs---objectives-and-principles-of-singapores-health-it-master-plan

Bhunia, P. (2017b). *Consult Your Doctor from Anywhere: National Rollout of Smart Health Video Consultation in Singapore*. Retrieved September 15, 2017, from http://www.opengovasia.com/articles/7506-consult-your-doctor-from-anywhere-national-rollout-of-smart-health-video-consultation-in-singapore

Bhunia, P. (2017c). *National Pilot of Smart Health TeleRehab in Singapore for Remote Access to Rehabilitation Services*. Retrieved September 15, 2017, from http://www.opengovasia.com/articles/7590-national-pilot-of-smart-health-telerehab-solution-being-implemented-in-singapore

Biesdorf, S., & Niedermann, F. (2014). *Healthcare's Digital Future*. Retrieved September 18, 2017, from http://www.mckinsey.com/industries/healthcare-systems-and-services/our-insights/healthcares-digital-future

Birt, J. L., Muthusamy, K., & Bir, P. (2017). XBRL and the Qualitative Characteristics of Useful Financial Information. *Accounting Research Journal*, *30*(1), 107–126. doi:10.1108/ARJ-11-2014-0105

Bjorklund, F. (2016). E-government and moral citizenship: The case of Estonia. *Citizenship Studies*, *20*(6-7), 914–931. doi:10.1080/13621025.2016.1213222

Blaikie, N. (2012). Designing Social Research. *Polity*.

Boeder, P. (2002, July). Non-Profits on E: How non-profit organizations are using the internet for communication, fundraising, and community building. *First Monday*, *7*(7). doi:10.5210/fm.v7i7.969

Bonollo, E. (2017). XBRL Adoption in Public Organizations: Criticalities and Perspectives. In K. Corsi, N. Castellano, R. Lamboglia, & D. Mancini (Eds.), *Reshaping Accounting and Management Control Systems. Lecture Notes in Information Systems and Organisation* (pp. 317–330). Cham, Switzerland: Springer. doi:10.1007/978-3-319-49538-5_21

Bortree, D., & Seltzer, T. (2009). Dialogic strategies and outcomes: An analysis of environmental advocacy groups' Facebook profiles. *Public Relations Review*, *35*, 317-319. 10.1016/j.pubrev.2009.05.002

Bouamrane, M.-M., Rector, A., & Hurrell, M. (2009). *A hybrid architecture for a preoperative decision support system using a rule engine and a reasoner on a clinical ontology. In Web Reasoning and Rule Systems* (pp. 242–253). Springer.

Boujarwah, A. (2006). E-government in Kuwait: From vision to reality. Proceedings of iiWAS2006.

Bovee, M., Ettredge, M. L., Srivastava, R. P., & Vasarhelyi, M. A. (2002). Does the year 2000 XBRL taxonomy accommodate current business financial-reporting practice*? Journal of Information Systems*, *16*(2), 165–182. doi:10.2308/jis.2002.16.2.165

boyd, d. (2011). White Flight in Networked Publics ? How Race and Class Shaped American Teen Engagement with MySpace and Facebook. In L. Nakamura & P. A. Chow (Eds.), *Race After The Internet* (pp. 203–222). Routledge.

Brengarth, L. B., Mujkic, E., & Millar, M. A. (2015). Social media in crisis: how social media created a npo and relief during a wildfire crisis. In H. Asencio & R. Sun (Eds.), *Cases on Strategic Social Media Utilization in the Nonprofit Sector*. Hershey, PA: Information Science Reference. doi:10.4018/978-1-4666-8188-0.ch001

Bright, J., & Margetts, H. (2016). Big Data and Public Policy: Can It Succeed Where E-Participation Has Failed? *Policy and Internet*, *8*(3), 218–224. doi:10.1002/poi3.130

Brimkulov, U., & Baryktabasov, K. (2014). Public Transactional e-Services through Government Web Sites in Kyrgyzstan. *Electronic. Journal of E-Government*, *12*(1).

Briones, R. L., Kuch, B., Liu, B. F., & Jin, Y. (2011). Keeping up with the digital age: How the American Red Cross uses social media to build relationships. *Public Relations Review*, *37*(1), 37–43. doi:10.1016/j.pubrev.2010.12.006

Brown, F., & Willis, M. (2003). XBRL: Revolutionizing the corporate reporting supply chain. *Financial Executive*, *19*(3), 70–71.

Bureau of Justice Assistance. (n.d.). *Smart Policing Initiative Data. Analysis. Solutions.* Retrieved from https://www.bja.gov/Publications/SmartPolicingFS.pdf

Burger, J. D., Henderson, J., Kim, G., & Zarrella, G. (2011). Discriminating gender on Twitter. In *Proceedings of the 2011 Conference on Empirical Methods in Natural Language Processing* (*Vol. 146*, pp. 1301–1309). Academic Press.

Bürger, T. (2015). Use of digital advocacy by German nonprofit foundations on Facebook. *Public Relations Review*, *41*(4), 523–525. doi:10.1016/j.pubrev.2015.07.007

Burt, E., & Taylor, J. (2003). New technologies, embedded values, and strategic change: Evidence from the U.K. voluntary sector. *Nonprofit and Voluntary Sector Quarterly*, *32*(1), 115–127. doi:10.1177/0899764002250009

Cabinet Office of Japan. (2011). *White Paper Disaster Management* (in Japanese). Retrieved February 23, 2015, from http://www.bousai.go.jp/kaigirep/hakusho/h23/index.htm

Cabinet Office of Japan. (2012). *Survey on disaster volunteer activities on the Great East Japan Earthquake* (in Japanese). Retrieved September 10, 2014, from http://www.bousai.go.jp/kyoiku/volunteer/pdf/120625jittaichousa.pdf

Cabinet Office of Japan. (2015). *2014 Survey on specified nonprofit corporations and citizens' social contributions* (in Japanese). Retrieved July 24, 2015 from https://www.npo-homepage.go.jp/uploads/h26_shimin_chousa_all.pdf

Cai, S., & Jun, M. (2015). Relationship between Information Richness and Exchange Outcomes: Moderating Effects of Media Richness and Governance Mechanisms. *International Journal of Information Systems and Supply Chain Management*, *8*(1), 1–21. doi:10.4018/ijisscm.2015010101

Callanan, L., Gardner, N., Mendonca, L., & Scott, D. (2014). *What social-sector leader needs to succeed.* McKinsey & Company Insights & Publications. Retrieved from: http://www.mckinsey.com/insights/social_sector/what_social_sector_leaders_need_to_succeed

Carboni, J. L., & Maxwell, S. P. (2015). Effective social media engagement for nonprofits: What matters? *Journal of Nonprofit and Public Affairs*, *1*(1), 18–28. doi:10.20899/jpna.1.1.18-28

Carboni, J. L., McNeely, C. L., & Maxwell, S. P. (2014). Community Engagement as a Predictor of Higher Education Matriculation. In T. Bryer (Ed.), *National service and volunteerism: Achieving impact in our communities*. Lanham, MD: Lexington Books.

Carlson, J. R., & Zmud, R. W. (1999). Channel expansion theory and the experiential nature of media richness perceptions. *Academy of Management Journal*, *42*(2), 153–170. doi:10.2307/257090

Carter, L., & Bélanger, F. (2005). The utilization of e-government services: Citizen trust, innovation and acceptance factors*. *Information Systems Journal*, *15*(1), 5–25. doi:10.1111/j.1365-2575.2005.00183.x

Carter, L., Weerakkody, V., Philips, B., & Dwivedi, Y. (2016). Citizen Adoption of E-Government Services: Exploring Citizen Perceptions of Online Services in the United States and United Kingdom. *Information Systems Management, 33*(2), 124–140. doi:10.1080/10580530.2016.1155948

Carter, L., & Weerakkody, W. (2008). E-government adoption: A cultural comparison. *Information Systems Frontiers, 10*(4), 473–482. doi:10.100710796-008-9103-6

Castells, M. (2002). *The Internet Galaxy. Reflections on the Internet, Business and Society*. Oxford, UK: Oxford University Press. doi:10.1093/acprof:oso/9780199255771.001.0001

Castillo, C., Mendoza, M., & Poblete, B. (2011). Information credibility on twitter. In *Proceedings of the 20th international conference on World wide web - WWW '11* (p. 675). Academic Press. 10.1145/1963405.1963500

Castillo, C., Mendoza, M., Poblete, B., & Authors, F. (2013). Predicting information credibility in time-sensitive social media. *Internet Research, 23*(5), 560–588. doi:10.1108/IntR-05-2012-0095

Center on Budget and Policy Priorities. (2014). *Changing Priorities: State Criminal Justice Reforms and Investments in Education.* Retrieved from https://www.cbpp.org/research/changing-priorities-state-criminal-justice-reforms-and-investments-in-education

Central Provident Fund Board. (2003). *SingPass: One PASSWORD for E-Services*. Retrieved October 11, 2017, from https://www.imda.gov.sg/about/newsroom/archived/ida/media-releases/2003/20061106191925

Chadwick, A., & May, C. (2003). Interaction between States and Citizens in the Age of the Internet: "e-Government" in the United States, Britain, and the European Union. *Governance: An International Journal of Policy, Administration and Institutions, 16*(2), 271–300. doi:10.1111/1468-0491.00216

Chambers, J. (2015). *How We Built It... Singapore HealthHub*. Retrieved September 13, 2017, from https://govinsider.asia/smart-gov/how-we-built-it-singapore-health-hub/

Chan, L. E. (2017 May 30). *MOH to Ramp up Use of Apps, Robotics to Improve Home Care: Health Minister. Channel NewsAsia*. Retrieved September 15, 2017, from http://www.channelnewsasia.com/news/singapore/moh-to-ramp-up-use-of-apps-robotics-to-improve-home-care-health-8894250

Charles Stewart Mott Foundation. (2015). *Funding interests*. Retrieved from http://www.mott.org/FundingInterests/programs/civilsociety/us July 14, 2015.

Chaves, R., & Monzòn, J. L. (2012). Beyond the crisis: The social economy, prop of a new model of sustainable economic development. *Service Business, 6*(1), 5–26. doi:10.100711628-011-0125-7

Chen, H. L. (2004). *An intelligent broker architecture for pervasive context-aware systems* (PhD Dissertation). University of Maryland, Baltimore County.

Chen, Y. C. (2012). A comparative study of e-government XBRL implementations: The potential of improving information transparency and efficiency. *Government Information Quarterly, 29*(4), 553–563. doi:10.1016/j.giq.2012.05.009

Chen, Y. C. (2013). Improving transparency in the financial Sector: e-Government XBRL implementation in the United States. *Public Performance & Management Review, 37*(2), 241–262. doi:10.2753/PMR1530-9576370203

Chen, Y., & Hsieh, T. (2014). Big data for digital government: Opportunities, challenges, and strategies. *International Journal of Public Administration in the Digital Age, 1*(1), 1–14. doi:10.4018/ijpada.2014010101

Chen, Y.-J. (2010). Development of a method for ontology-based empirical knowledge representation and reasoning. *Decision Support Systems, 50*(1), 1–20. doi:10.1016/j.dss.2010.02.010

Choi, H., Park, M. J., Rho, J. J., & Zo, H. (2016). Rethinking the assessment of e-government implementation in developing countries from the perspective of the design-reality gap: Applications in the Indonesian e-procurement system. *Telecommunications Policy*, *40*(7), 644–660. doi:10.1016/j.telpol.2016.03.002

Choudrie, J., Weerakkody, V., & Jones, S. (2005). Realising e-government in the UK: rural and urban challenges: Journal of Enterprise Information Management: Vol 18, No 5. *Journal of Enterprise Information Management*, *18*(5), 568–585. doi:10.1108/17410390510624016

Chua, J. (2012). The e-Transformation Journey of Singapore. In N.K. Hanna & P.T. Knight (Eds.), National Strategies to Harness Information Technology, Innovation, Technology and Knowledge Management (pp. 41-76). New York, NY: Springer Science +Business Media, LLC. doi:10.1007/978-1-4614-2086-6_2

Colesca, S. E. (2009). Increasing e-trust: A solution to minimize risk in e-government adoption. *Journal of Applied Quantitative Methods*, *4*(1), 31–44.

Colesca, S. E., & Dobrica, L. (2008). Adoption and use of e-government services: The case of Romania. *Journal of Applied Research and Technology*, *6*(03).

Cong, Y., Du, H., & Vasarhelyi, M. A. (2017). Are XBRL Files Being Accessed? Evidence from the SEC EDGAR Log File Data Set. *Journal of Information Systems*, isys-51885. doi:10.2308/isys-51885

Council for Excellence in Government. (n.d.). *E-Government: The Next American Revolution*. Retrieved November 10, 2017 from http://www.excelgov.org/index.php?keyword=a432c10480be99

Council on Foundations. (2011). *Community foundations: Snapshots of public-philanthropic partnerships*. Washington, DC: Council on Foundations.

Council on Foundations. (2015). *Public-Private Partnerships*. Retrieved from http://www.cof.org/content/public-philanthropic-partnerships

Cruce, T. M., & Moore, J. V. III. (2012). Community Service during the Frist Year of College: What is the Role of Past Behavior? *Journal of College Student Development*, *53*(3), 399–417. doi:10.1353/csd.2012.0038

Crutcher, M., & Zook, M. (2009). Placemarks and waterlines: Racialized cyberscapes in post-Katrina Google Earth. *Geoforum, Elsevier Ltd*, *40*(4), 523–534. doi:10.1016/j.geoforum.2009.01.003

Culotta, A., Ravi, N. K., & Cutler, J. (2015). Predicting the Demographics of Twitter Users from Website Traffic Data. In *Proceedings of the Twenty-Ninth AAAI Conference on Artificial Intelligence* (pp. 72–78). Academic Press.

Curtis, L., Edwards, C., Fraser, K. L., Gudelsky, S., Holmquist, J., Thornton, K., & Sweetser, K. D. (2010). Adoption of social media for public relations by nonprofit organizations. *Public Relations Review*, *36*(1), 90–92. doi:10.1016/j.pubrev.2009.10.003

Dacheux, E., & Goujon, D. (2011). The solidarity economy: An alternative development strategy? *International Social Science Journal*, *62*(203-204), 205–215. doi:10.1111/j.1468-2451.2011.01804.x

Daft, R. L., & Lengel, R. H. (1986). Organizational Information Requirements, Media Richness and Structural Design. *Management Science*, *32*(5), 554–571. doi:10.1287/mnsc.32.5.554

Danielson, M., Ekenberg, L., Larsson, A., & Riabacke, M. (2014). Weighting Under Ambiguous Preferences and Imprecise Differences in a Cardinal Rank Ordering Process. *International Journal of Computational Intelligence Systems*, *7*(1), 105–112. doi:10.1080/18756891.2014.853954

Danish Business Authority. (2014). *Bredbåndskortlægning 2013*. Retrieved from http://erhvervsstyrelsen.dk/file/444481/bredbaandskortlaegning-2013.pdf

Data Hawaii. (n.d.). *Graph of Federal Expenditures by type*. Retrieved from https://data.hawaii.gov/Economic-Development/Table-9-5-GRAPH-OF-FEDERAL-EXPENDITURES-BY-TYPE/rj4c-efj7

Davis, E. (2016). *Information Technology Demands on State Funded Organizations*. Retrieved from https://www.elliottdavis.com/information-technology-demands-on-state-funded-organizations/

Davis, F. D., Bagozzi, R. P., & Warshaw, P. R. (1989). User acceptance of computer technology: A comparison of two theoretical models. *Management Science*, *35*(8), 982–1003. doi:10.1287/mnsc.35.8.982

Dawes, S. S., Bloniarz, P. A., Kelly, K. L., & Fletcher, P. D. (1999). *Some Assembly Required: Building a Digital Government for the 21st Century*. Center for Technology in Government University at Albany, State University of New York.

Dawes, S. S., Cresswell, A. M., & Pardo, T. A. (2009). From "need to know" to "need to share": Tangled problems, information boundaries, and the building of public sector knowledge networks. *Public Administration Review*, *69*(3), 392–402. doi:10.1111/j.1540-6210.2009.01987_2.x

Dawes, S. S., Pardo, T. A., & DiCaterino, A. (1999). Crossing the threshold: Practical foundations for government services on the World Wide Web. *Journal of the American Society for Information Science*, *50*(4), 346–353. doi:

Debreceny, R. S., Farewell, S. M., Piechocki, M., Felden, C., Gräning, A., & d'Eri, A. (2011). Flex or break? Extensions in XBRL disclosures to the SEC. *Accounting Horizons*, *25*(4), 631–657. doi:10.2308/acch-50068

Debreceny, R., Farewell, S., Piechocki, M., Felden, C., & Gräning, A. (2010). Does it add up? Early evidence on the data quality of XBRL filings to the SEC. *Journal of Accounting and Public Policy*, *29*(3), 296–306. doi:10.1016/j.jaccpubpol.2010.04.001

Debreceny, R., Felden, C., Ochocki, B., Piechocki, M., & Piechocki, M. (2009). *XBRL for Interactive Data. Engineering the Information Value Chain*. Heidelberg, Germany: Springer. doi:10.1007/978-3-642-01437-6

Deloitte. (2015). *E-governance and Digital India Empowering Indian Citizens through Technology*. Retrieved from https://www2.deloitte.com/content/dam/Deloitte/in/Documents/technology-media-telecommunications/in-tmt-empowering-indian-citizens-through-technology-noexp.pdf

Deshpandé, R., Farley, J. U., & Webster, F. E. Jr. (1993). Corporate culture, customer orientation, and innovativeness in Japanese firms: A quadrad analysis. *Journal of Marketing*, *57*(1), 23–37. doi:10.2307/1252055

Devaraj, S., & Kohli, R. (2003). Performance Impacts of Information Technology: Is Actual Usage the Missing Link? *Management Science*, *49*(3), 273–289. doi:10.1287/mnsc.49.3.273.12736

DeYoung, A. (2010). *Lost in Transition: redefining students and universities in the contemporary Kyrgyz Republic*. Charlotte, NC: Information Age Publishing.

DiMaggio, P. J., & Powell, W. W. (1983). The iron cage revisited: Institutional isomorphism and collective rationality in organizational fields. *American Sociological Review*, *48*(2), 147–160. doi:10.2307/2095101

Ding, Y., & Foo, S. (2002). Ontology research and development. Part 1-a review of ontology generation. *Journal of Information Science*, *28*(2), 123–136.

Donaldson, S. I., & Grant-Vallone, E. J. (2002). Understanding self-report bias in organizational behavior research. *Journal of Business and Psychology*, *17*(2), 245–260. doi:10.1023/A:1019637632584

Doolin, B., & Troshani, I. (2007). Organizational adoption of XBRL. *Electronic Markets, 17*(3), 199–209. doi:10.1080/10196780701503195

Dozier, D. M., Grunig, L. A., & Grunig, J. E. (1995). Manager's guide to excellence in public relations and communication management. Mahwah, NJ: Lawrence Erlbaum Associates, Inc.

Duan-Barnett, N., Wangelin, J., & Lamm, H. (2012). Models of Social Change: Community Foundations and Agenda Setting. *The Foundation Review*, *4*(4), 7. doi:10.4087/FOUNDATIONREVIEW-D-12-00030.1

Duggan, M., Ellison, N. B., Lampe, C., Lenhart, A., & Madden, M. (2015). Demographics of Key Social Networking Platforms. *Pew Research Center*. Retrieved July 8, 2015, from http://www.pewinternet.org/2015/01/09/demographics-of-key-social-networking-platforms-2/

Du, J., & Zhou, L. (2012). Improving financial data quality using ontologies. *Decision Support Systems*, *54*(1), 7686. doi:10.1016/j.dss.2012.04.016

Dutta-Bergman, M. J. (2005). Access to the internet in the context of community participation and community satisfaction. *New Media & Society*, *7*(1), 89–109. doi:10.1177/1461444805049146

Dzenowagis, J. (2009). Bridging the Digital Divide: Linking Health and ICT Policy. In R. Wootton, N.G. Patil, R.E. Scott, & K. Ho (Eds.), Telehealth in the Developing World (pp. 9-26). Royal Society of Medicine Press, IDRC.

Ebbers, W. E., Jansen, M. G. M., Pieterson, W. J., & van de Wijngaert, L. A. L. (2015). Facts and feelings: The role of rational and irrational factors in citizens' channel choices. *Government Information Quarterly*. doi:10.1016/j.giq.2016.06.001

Ebbers, W. E., Jansen, M. G. M., & van Deursen, A. J. A. M. (2016). Impact of the digital divide on e-government: Expanding from channel choice to channel usage. *Government Information Quarterly*, *33*(4), 685–692. doi:10.1016/j.giq.2016.08.007

Ebbers, W. E., Pieterson, W. J., & Noordman, H. N. N. (2008). Electronic government: Rethinking channel management strategies. *Government Information Quarterly*, *25*(2), 181–201. doi:10.1016/j.giq.2006.11.003

ECOSOC, United Nations Economic and Social Council. (2015). *Report of the Secretary-General. Strengthening and Building Institutions for Policy Integration in the Post-2015 Era*. E/2015/69.

Edelmann, N., & Cruickshank, P. (2012). In A. Manoharan & M. Holzer (Eds.), *E-Governance and Civic Engagement: Factors and Determinants of E-Democracy* (pp. 338–361). Hershey, PA: IGI Global Publishing. doi:10.4018/978-1-61350-083-5.ch017

Edgington, T., Raghu, T. S., & Vinze, A. (2005). Knowledge Ontology: A Method for Empirical Identification of'AsIs' Contextual Knowledge. *System Sciences, 2005. HICSS'05. Proceedings of the 38th Annual Hawaii International Conference on*. 10.1109/HICSS.2005.377

Ehrlich, T. (2000). *Civic Responsibility and Higher Education*. Phoenix, AZ: Orynx Press.

Eikenberry, A. M. (2012). Social networking, learning, and civic engagement: New relationships between professors and students, public administrators and citizens. *Journal of Public Affairs Education*, *3*(18), 449–466.

Eimhjellen, I., Wollebaek, D., & Stromsnes, K. (2013). Associations online: Barriers for using web-based communication in voluntary organizations. *Voluntas*, *25*(3), 730–753. doi:10.100711266-013-9361-x

Eisen, L.-B., & Chettiar, I. (2015). *The Reverse Mass Incarceration*. Brennan Center for Justice. Retrieved from https://www.brennancenter.org/sites/default/files/publications/The_Reverse_Mass_Incarceration_Act%20.pdf

Eisen, L.-B., & Cullen, J. (n.d.). *Update Changes in State Imprisonment.* Brennan Center for Justice. Retrieved October 2017 from https://www.brennancenter.org/sites/default/files/analysis/UpdateChangesinStateImprisonment.pdf

Ekenberg, L., Hansson, K., Danielson, M., & Cars, G. (2017). *Deliberation, Representation and Equity: Research Approaches, Tools and Algorithms for Participatory Processes.* Open Book Publishers. doi:10.11647/OBP.0108

Elbahnasawy, N. (2014). E-government, Internet Adoption, and Corruption: An Empirical Investigation. *World Development, 57*, 114–126. doi:10.1016/j.worlddev.2013.12.005

Elsheikh, Y., & Cullen, A. (2008). e-Government in Jordan: challenges and opportunities. *Transforming Government: People, Process and Policy, 2*(2).

Elsler, D., Takala, J., & Remes, J. (2017). *An international comparison of the cost of work-related accidents and illnesses.* Luxembourg: Publications Office of the European Union. Retrieved September 11, 2017, from https://osha.europa.eu/sites/default/files/publications/documents/international_comparison-of_costs_work_related_accidents.pdf

Elwood, S. (2008). Volunteered geographic information: Future research directions motivated by critical, participatory, and feminist GIS. *GeoJournal, 72*(3-4), 173–183. doi:10.100710708-008-9186-0

Emmanuel, S. C. (1998). Information and Research for Decision-makers. *World Health Forum, 19*, 12–14. PMID:9610236

Enachi, M., & Andone, I. I. (2015). The Progress of XBRL in Europe – Projects, Users and Prospects. *Procedia Economics and Finance, 20*, 185–192. doi:10.1016/S2212-5671(15)00064-7

Energy Chamber of Trinidad and Tobago. (2007). *STOW contractor guidance manual.* Point Lisas, Trinidad: Energy Chamber. Retrieved August 24, 2014, from http://www.stowtt.info/downloads/STOW%20Guidance%20Manual%20v9-Feb2013.pdf

Eschenfelder, K. R. (2004). Behind the Web site: An inside look at the production of Web-based textual government information. *Government Information Quarterly, 21*(3), 337–358. doi:10.1016/j.giq.2004.04.004

European Agency for Safety and Health at Work. (2010). *Mainstreaming OSH into business management.* Luxembourg: Office for Official Publications of the European Communities. Retrieved August 14, 2014, from https://osha.europa.eu/en/publications/reports/mainstreaming_osh_business

European Agency for Safety and Health at Work. (2014). *Estimating the cost of accidents and ill health at work: A review of methodologies.* Luxembourg: Publications Office of the European Union. Retrieved August 14, 2014, from https://osha.europa.eu/en/publications/reports/estimating-the-costs-of-accidents-and-ill-health-at-work

European Commission. (2014). *Digital Agenda Scoreboard 2014 – Denmark Page 1 of 7.* Retrieved from https://ec.europa.eu/digital-agenda/en/scoreboard/denmark

Facebook. (2015). *How is engagement rate defined?* Retrieved from https://www.facebook.com/help/178043462360087 July 7, 2015.

Falk, S. (2011). The rise of the digital citizen. *Policy Advice and Consulting, 4*(4), 157–161.

Fama, E. F., & Jensen, M. C. (1983). Separation of ownership and control. *The Journal of Law & Economics, 26*(2), 301–325. doi:10.1086/467037

Fang, Z. (2002). E-government in digital era: Concept, practice, and development. *International Journal of the Computer, the Internet and Management, 10*(2), 1-22.

Faridani, S., Bitton, E., Ryokai, K., & Goldberg, K. (2010). Opinion space: Opinion space: a scalable tool for browsing online comments. In *Proceedings of the 28th international conference on Human factors in computing systems - CHI '10* (p. 1175). New York: ACM Press. 10.1145/1753326.1753502

Fauzi, F., & Belkhatir, M. (2013). Multifaceted conceptual image indexing on the world wide web. *Information Processing & Management, 49*(2), 420–440. doi:10.1016/j.ipm.2012.08.001

FBI Uniform Crime Reporting Statistics. (n.d.). Retrieved from https://www.ucrdatatool.gov/Search/Crime/State/StatebyState.cfm?NoVariables=Y&CFID=235432167&CFTOKEN=466f51a4d0515b4b-778AD6DC-C10C-8E2E-C12DFFEEB8BEAC7D

Fernandez, K. M., & Hager, M. A. (2014). Public and private dimensions of grantmaking foundations. *Public Administration Quarterly, 38*(3), 405–439.

Firat, A., Madnick, S. E., & Grosof, B. (2004). *Contextual alignment of ontologies for semantic interoperability.* Social Science Research Network Electronic Paper Collection.

Flowerday, S., Blundell, A. W., & Von Solms, R. (2006). Continuous auditing technologies and models: A discussion. *Computers & Security, 25*(5), 325–331. doi:10.1016/j.cose.2006.06.004

Flowerday, S., & Von Solms, R. (2005). Continuous auditing: Verifying information integrity and providing assurances for financial reports. *Computer Fraud & Security, 2005*(7), 12–16. doi:10.1016/S1361-3723(05)70232-3

Fonou-Dombeu, J. V., & Huisman, M. (2013). *Adaptive search and selection of domain ontologies for reuse on the Semantic Web.* Academic Press.

Forgy, C. L. (1982). Rete: A fast algorithm for the many pattern/many object pattern match problem. *Artificial Intelligence, 19*(1), 17–37. doi:10.1016/0004-3702(82)90020-0

Fortier, N. Z., & Chettiar, I. M. (2014). *Success-Oriented Funding: Reforming Federal Criminal.* Retrieved from https://www.brennancenter.org/publication/success-oriented-funding-reforming-federal-criminal-justice-grants

Foundation Center (2010). *Are Foundation Leaders Using Social Media?* Washington, DC: The Foundation Center.

Foundation Center. (2014). *Foundations Today Tutorials.* Retrieved from http://foundationcenter.org/getstarted/tutorials/ft_tutorial/what.html

Foundation Center. (2014). *Infographic: What's trending with foundations and social media.* Retrieved from http://glasspockets.org/glasspockets-gallery/foundations-and-social-media-infographic#sthash.kj7wkbMv.dpuf

Fountain, J. (2002). *Developing a basic research program for digital government: information, organizations, and governance. National Center for Digital Government, Kennedy School of Government.* Harvard University.

Fountain, J. E. (2004). *Building the virtual state: Information technology and institutional change.* Brookings Institution Press.

Fox, M. S., Barbuceanu, M., & Gruninger, M. (1996). An organisation ontology for enterprise modeling: Preliminary concepts for linking structure and behaviour. *Computers in Industry, 29*(1), 123–134. doi:10.1016/0166-3615(95)00079-8

Fradeani, A., Panizzolo, D., & Metushi, E. (2016). Financial Reporting in XBRL: First Evidence on Financial Statement Notes of Italian Unlisted Companies. *The International Journal of Digital Accounting Research, 16*, 85–115.

Fradeani, A., Regoliosi, C., D'Eri, A., & Campanari, F. (2017). Implementation of Mandatory IFRS Financial Disclosures in a Voluntary Format: Evidence from the Italian XBRL Project. In K. Corsi, N. Castellano, R. Lamboglia, & D. Mancini (Eds.), *Reshaping Accounting and Management Control Systems. Lecture Notes in Information Systems and Organisation* (pp. 331–347). Cham, Switzerland: Springer. doi:10.1007/978-3-319-49538-5_22

Fradeani, A., Soverchia, M., & Metushi, E. (in press). Digital Governmental Financial Reporting: First Evidence from Italy. In R. Lamboglia, A. Cardoni, R. P. Dameri, & D. Mancini (Eds.), *Network, Smart and Open. Three Keywords for Information Systems Innovation*. Cham, Switzerland: Springer. doi:10.1007/978-3-319-62636-9_14

Frank, A. G., & Fuentes, M. (1987). Nine Theses on Social Movements. *Economic and Political Weekly*, *22*(35), 1503-1507+1509-1510. Available online at: http://www.jstor.org/stable/4377447

Freedman, E., & Shafer, R. (2012). Advancing a Comprehensive Research Agenda for Central Asian Mass Media. *Media Asia*, *39*(3), 119–126. doi:10.1080/01296612.2012.11689927

Freedom House. (2017). *Freedom on the Net*. Available https://freedomhouse.org/report/freedom-net/2016/kyrgyzstan

Freeman, R. T., & Yin, H. (2005). Web content management by self-organization. *Neural Networks. IEEE Transactions on*, *16*(5), 1256–1268. PMID:16252831

Freschi, A. C. (2009). eParticipation in the institutional domain: a review of research: analytical report on eParticipation research from an administration and political perspective in six European countries (A. C. Freschi, R. Medaglia, & J. Nørbjerg, Eds.). DEMO-Net Consortium.

Friese, S. (2012). *Qualitative data analysis with Atlas.ti*. SAGE Publications.

Fuchs, C. (2003). Structuration Theory and Self-organization. *Systemic Practice and Action Research*, *16*(2), 133–167. doi:10.1023/A:1022889627100

Fung, A. (2013). Infotopia: Unleashing the Democratic Power of Transparency. *Politics & Society*, *41*(2), 183–212.

Furuholt, B., & Wahid, F. (2008). E-government Challenges and the Role of Political Leadership in Indonesia: the Case of Sragen. *Hawaii International Conference on System Sciences, Proceedings of the 41st Annual*. 10.1109/HICSS.2008.134

Gao, H., Barbier, G., & Goolsby, R. (2011). Harnessing the Crowdsourcing Power of Social Media for Disaster Relief. *Cyber-Physical Social Systems*. Retrieved April 29, 2015 from http://oai.dtic.mil/oai/oai?verb=getRecord&metadataPrefix=html&identifier=ADA581803

Garcia-Crespo, A., Ruiz-Mezcua, B., Lopez-Cuadrado, J. L., & Gonzalez-Carrasco, I. (2011). Semantic model for knowledge representation in e-business. *Knowledge-Based Systems*, *24*(2), 282–296. doi:10.1016/j.knosys.2010.09.006

Garicano, L., & Heaton, P. (2010). Information Technology, Organizations, and Productivity in the Public Sector: Evidence from Police Departments. *Journal of Labor Economics*, *28*(1), 167–201. doi:10.1086/649844

Gathungu, J., & Mungai, A. N. (2013). Contextual Factors Affecting E-Government Strategy Implementation and Its Impact on Public Sector Performance in Kenya. *Journal of Arts and Humanities*, *1*(1), 143–157. doi:10.18533/journal.v1i1.14

Gauld, R., Goldfinch, S., & Horsburgh, S. (2010). Do they want it? Do they use it? The 'Demand-Side'of e-Government in Australia and New Zealand. *Government Information Quarterly*, *27*(2), 177–186. doi:10.1016/j.giq.2009.12.002

Gazeta.kg. (2015). *В Бишкеке открылся информационно-образовательный центр для людей с ограниченными возможностями здоровья*. Retrieved on March 5, 2016, from http://www.gazeta.kg/news/kyrgyzstan/society/32463-v-bishkekeotkrylsya-informacionno-obrazovatelnyy-centr-dlya-lyudey-s-ogranichennymivozmozhnostyami-zdorovya.html

Gerber, E. M., & Hui, J. (2013). Crowdfunding: Motivations and deterrents for participation. *ACM Transactions on Computer-Human Interaction, 20*(6), 34. doi:10.1145/2530540

Geunjoo, L., & Perry, J. L. (2002). Are Computers Boosting Productivity? A Test of the Paradox in State Governments. *Journal of Public Administration: Research and Theory, 12*(1), 77–102. doi:10.1093/oxfordjournals.jpart.a003525

Giddens, A. (2002). *Sociology*. Athens: Gutenberg. (in Greek)

Gil-Garcia, J. R., Helbig, N., & Ojo, A. (2014). Being smart: Emerging technologies and innovation in the public sector. *Government Information Quarterly, 31*(Supp. 1), I1–I8. doi:10.1016/j.giq.2014.09.001

Gil-García, J. R., & Pardo, T. A. (2005). E-government success factors: Mapping practical tools to theoretical foundations. *Government Information Quarterly, 22*(2), 187–216. doi:10.1016/j.giq.2005.02.001

Gleason, J. M., & Barnum, D. T. (1978). Effectiveness of OSHA sanctions in influencing employer behavior: Single and multi-period decision models. *Accident; Analysis and Prevention, 10*(1), 35–49. doi:10.1016/0001-4575(78)90006-4

Gleasure, R., & Feller, J. (2016). Does heart or head rule donor behaviors in charitable crowdfunding markets? *International Journal of Electronic Commerce, 20*(4), 499–524. doi:10.1080/10864415.2016.1171975

Goldsmith, S., & Eggers, W. D. (2004). *Governing by Network: The New Shape of the Public Sector*. Washington, DC: Brookings Institution Press.

Goodwin, S., & Vidgen, R. (2002). Content, content, everywhere... time to stop and think? The process of Web content management. *Computing & Control Engineering Journal, 13*(2), 66–70. doi:10.1049/cce:20020202

Government of the Republic of Trinidad and Tobago. (2004). *The occupational safety and health act (2004)*. Retrieved November 1, 2011, from http://www.ttparliament.org/legislations/a2004-01.pdf

Government of the Republic of Trinidad and Tobago. (2006). *The occupational safety and health (amendment) act (2006)*. Retrieved November 1, 2011, from http://www.ttparliament.org/legislations/a2006-03.pdf

Government of the Republic of Trinidad and Tobago. (2011). *Innovation for lasting prosperity: Medium term policy framework 2011-2014*. Port of Spain: Ministry of Planning and the Economy. Retrieved August 24, 2014, from http://finance.gov.tt/wp-content/uploads/2013/11/Medium-Term-Policy-Framework-2011-14.pdf

Government of the Republic of Trinidad and Tobago. (2012). *National cyber security strategy*. Port of Spain: Inter Ministerial Committee For Cyber Security. Retrieved August 24, 2014, from http://www.nationalsecurity.gov.tt/Portals/0/Pdf%20Files/National_Cyber_Security%20Strategy_Final.pdf

GovTech. (2016). *eGov Master Plan*. Retrieved August 30, 2017, from https://www.tech.gov.sg/About-Us/Corporate-Publications/eGov-Masterplan

GovTech. (2017). *A Healthy Hub at Your Fingertips*. Retrieved September 13, 2017, from https://www.tech.gov.sg/TechNews/DigitalGov/2017/04/27/07/08/A-healthy-hub-at-your-fingertips

Grace-Martin, K. (2008). Can Likert scale data ever be continuous. *Article Alley*. Retrieved from: http://www.theanalysisfactor.com/can-likert-scale-data-ever-be-continuous/

Granizo, C. J., Yanez, P. L., Ramirez, D. P., & Machado, P. C. (2011). Usability in e-government sites. *Eighth International Conference on Information Technology: New Generations (ITNG)*, 453-458.

Greenberg, J., & MacAulay. (2009). NPO 2.0? Exploring the web presence of environmental nonprofit organizations in Canada. *Global Media Journal-Canadian Edition, 2*(1), 63-88.

Greene, W. (2016). *Health Tech Innovation Blooms in Singapore*. Retrieved September 29, 2017, from http://techonomy.com/2016/04/health-tech-innovation-blooms-in-singapore/

Gruber, T. R. (1993). A translation approach to portable ontology specifications. *Knowledge Acquisition, 5*(2), 199220. doi:10.1006/knac.1993.1008

Gunawong, P., & Gao, P. (2017). Understanding e-government failure in the developing country context: A process-oriented study. *Information Technology for Development, 23*(1), 153–178. doi:10.1080/02681102.2016.1269713

Guo, C., & Saxton, G. D. (2014). Tweeting social change: How social media are changing nonprofit advocacy. *Nonprofit and Voluntary Sector Quarterly.*

Guo, C., & Saxton, G. D. (2017). Speaking and being heard: How nonprofit advocacy organizations gain attention on social media. *Nonprofit and Voluntary Sector Quarterly*, 1–22.

Gurak, L. J., & Hudson, B. L. (2006). E-health: beyond Internet search. In M. Murero & R. E. Rice (Eds.), *The Internet and Health Care: Theory, Research, and Practice* (pp. 29–48). Mahwah, NJ: Lawrence Erlbaum Associates.

Hackler, D., & Saxton, G. D. (2007). The strategic use of information technology by nonprofit organizations: Increasing capacity and untapped potential. *Public Administration Review, 67*(3), 474–487. doi:10.1111/j.1540-6210.2007.00730.x

Haddow, G. D., & Haddow, K. S. (2014). *Disaster Communication in a Changing Media World.* Waltham, MA: Elsevier Inc.

Hand, L. C., & Ching, B. D. (2011). "You have one friend request": An exploration of power and citizen engagement in local governments' use of social media. *Administrative Theory & Praxis, 33*(3), 362–382. doi:10.2753/ATP1084-1806330303

Han, H., Nakawatase, H., & Oyama, K. (2014). Evaluating credibility of interest reflection on Twitter. *International Journal of Web Information Systems, 10*(4), 343–362. doi:10.1108/IJWIS-04-2014-0019

Hansson, K., Belkacem, K., & Ekenberg, L. (2014, December). Open government and democracy: A research review. *Social Science Computer Review.*

Hansson, K., Verhagen, H., Karlström, P., & Larsson, A. (2013). Reputation and Online Communication : Visualizing Reputational Power to Promote Collaborative Discussions Abstract. In *HICSS-46 - Hawaii International Conference on System Sciences* (p. 11). Academic Press.

Hansson, K. (2015a). *Accommodating differences: Power, belonging, and representation online*. Stockholm University.

Hansson, K. (2015b). Controlling singularity: The role of online communication for young visual artists' identity management. *First Monday, 20*(5). doi:10.5210/fm.v20i5.5626

Hansson, K., Karlström, P., Larsson, A., & Verhagen, H. (2013). Reputation, inequality and meeting techniques: Visualising user hierarchy. *Computational & Mathematical Organization Theory, 20*(2), 155–175. doi:10.100710588-013-9165-y

Hargittai, E. (2015). Is Bigger Always Better? Potential Biases of Big Data Derived from Social Network Sites. *The Annals of the American Academy of Political and Social Science, 659*(1), 63–76. doi:10.1177/0002716215570866

Harlan, S. L., & Saidel, J. R. (1994). Board members' influence on the government-nonprofit relationship. *Nonprofit Management & Leadership, 5*(2), 173–196. doi:10.1002/nml.4130050206 PMID:10140720

Harris, J. (n.d.). Gender, Twitter, and the Value of Taking Things Apart - Learning - Source: An OpenNews project. *Source: Journalism code and the people who make it.* Retrieved July 7, 2015, from https://source.opennews.org/en-US/learning/gender-twitter-and-value-taking-things-apart/

Hashemi, S., Monfaredi, K., & Masdari, M. (2013). Using cloud computing for e-government: Challenges and benefits. *International Journal of Computer, Information. Systems and Control Engineering*, *7*(9), 596–603.

Hausman, A., & Johnston, W. J. (2014). The role of innovation in driving the economy: Lessons from the global financial crisis. *Journal of Business Research*, *67*(1), 2720–2726. doi:10.1016/j.jbusres.2013.03.021

Health and Safety Executive. (2003). *Health and safety regulation: a short guide.* Leaflet HSC13 (Rev. 1). Retrieved September 18, 2017, from http://www.hse.gov.uk/pubns/hsc13.pdf

Health and Safety Executive. (n.d.). *Health and safety executive.* Retrieved August 15, 2014, from www.hse.gov.uk

Health Promotion Board. (2009a). *New HPB Online Your One-stop Health Information Portal.* Retrieved September 13, 2017, from https://www.hpb.gov.sg/article/new-'hpb-online'---your-one-stop-health-information-portal

Health Promotion Board. (2009b). *Health Promotion Board Annual Report 2008/2009.* Retrieved September 13, 2017, from https://www.hpb.gov.sg/docs/default-source/annual-reports/hpb-annual-report-2009.pdf?sfvrsn=2

Health Promotion Board. (2017). *Our Awards.* Retrieved September 13, 2017, from https://www.hpb.gov.sg/about/awards

Health Sciences Authority. (2017a). *Consultation on Proposed Regulatory Guidelines for Telehealth Devices.* Retrieved September 29, 2017, from http://www.hsa.gov.sg/content/hsa/en/News_Events/Public_Consultation1/consultationtele-healthdevices.html

Health Sciences Authority. (2017b). *Regulatory Guidelines for Telehealth Devices.* Retrieved September 29, 2017, from http://www.hsa.gov.sg/content/dam/HSA/HPRG/Medical_Devices/Updates_and_Safety_reporting/Regulatory_Updates/Telehealth%20Guideline%20-%20Aug%202017.pdf

Health Sciences Authority. (2017c). *Regulatory Updates.* Retrieved September 29, 2017, from http://www.hsa.gov.sg/content/hsa/en/Health_Products_Regulation/Medical_Devices/Regulatory_Updates.html

Healthcare Information and Management Systems Society. (2010). *Electronic Health Records: A Global Perspective* (2nd ed.). Retrieved September 11, 2017, from http://web.pdx.edu/~nwallace/GHS/EHRP2.pdf

Hechter, M. (1988). *Principles of Group Solidarity.* University of California Press.

Hecker, M., Dillon, T. S., & Chang, E. (2008). Privacy ontology support for e-commerce. *IEEE Internet Computing*, *12*(2), 54–61. doi:10.1109/MIC.2008.41

Heeks, R., & Bailur, S. (2007). Analyzing e-government research: Perspectives, philosophies, theories, methods, and practice. *Government Information Quarterly*, *24*(2), 243–265. doi:10.1016/j.giq.2006.06.005

Henderson, P., & Vercseg, I. (2010). *Community Development and Civil Society. Making Connections in the European context.* Bristol, UK: Polity Press.

Henriksson, A., Yi, Y., Frost, B., & Middleton, M. (2007). Evaluation instrument for e-government websites. *Electronic Government, an International Journal, 4*(2), 204-226.

Hernon, P., & Relyea, H. C. (1995). Government publishing: Past to present. *Government Information Quarterly*, *12*(3), 309–330. doi:10.1016/0740-624X(95)90021-7

Ho, A. T. (2002). Reinventing Local Governments and the E-Government Initiative. *Public Administration Review.* doi:10.1111/0033-3352.00197

Hodge, F. D., Kennedy, J. J., & Maines, L. A. (2004). Does search-facilitating technology improve the transparency of financial reporting? *The Accounting Review*, *79*(3), 687–703. doi:10.2308/accr.2004.79.3.687

Hofmann, S., Räckers, M., & Becker, J. (2012). Identifying Factors of E-Government Acceptance – A Literature Review. In *33rd International Conference on Information Systems (ICIS 2012)* (pp. 1–10). Orlando, FL: Academic Press.

Hongbo, W. U. (2016). *United Nations E-Government Survey 2016*. Retrieved October 13, 2017 from https://publicadministration.un.org/egovkb/en-us/Reports/UN-E-Government-Survey-2016

Hood, C. C., & Margetts, H. Z. (2007). *The tools of government in the digital age*. Houndmills, UK: Palgrave Macmillan. doi:10.1007/978-1-137-06154-6

Horridge, M., Knublauch, H., Rector, A., Stevens, R., & Wroe, C. (2004). A practical guide to building OWL ontologies using the Protégé-OWL plugin and CO-ODE Tools. University of Manchester.

Howe, J. (2006). The rise of crowdsourcing. *Wired Magazine, 14*(6), 1-4.

Howe, N., & Strauss, W. (2000). *Millennials rising: The next great generation*. New York: Vintage.

Howto.gov. (2014). *Federal laws and regulations for government websites*. Retrieved from http://www.usa.gov/webcontent/reqs_bestpractices/laws_regs/index.shtml

Hughes, A. L., & Palen, L. (2009). Twitter adoption and use in mass convergence and emergency events. *International Journal of Emergency Management, 6*(3/4), 248–260. doi:10.1504/IJEM.2009.031564

Hughes, A. L., & Palen, L. (2012). The Evolving Role of the Public Information Officer: An Examination of Social Media in Emergency Management. *Journal of Homeland Security and Emergency Management, 9*(1). doi:10.1515/1547-7355.1976

Hughes, M., & Kroehler, C. J. (2007). *Sociology. The basic concepts*. Athens: Kritiki. (in Greek)

Hui, J. S., Gerber, E. M., & Gergle, D. (2014). Understanding and leveraging social networks for crowdfunding: opportunities and challenges. In *Proceedings of the 2014 conference on Designing interactive systems* (pp. 677-680). ACM. 10.1145/2598510.2598539

Hung, C. F. (2005). Exploring types of organization public relationships and their implications for relationship management in public relations. *Journal of Public Relations Research, 17*(4), 393–42. doi:10.12071532754xjprr1704_4

Hu, Q., & Shi, W. (2017). Understanding nonprofit organizations' use of social networking sites: An examination of management factors. *International Journal of Public Administration in the Digital Age, 4*(1), 19–34. doi:10.4018/IJPADA.2017010102

IFAC. (2008). *Financial reporting supply chain. Current perspectives and directions*. New York, NY: IFAC.

Indiegogo. (2015). *Indiegogo's 2015 Year in Review: Crowdfunding Statistics*. Retrieved from: https://go.indiegogo.com/blog/2015/12/2015-crowdfunding-infographic-statistics-tech-film-social.html

Infocomm Development Authority of Singapore, Singapore Computer Society, & Singapore Infocomm Technology Federation (2006). *Innovation, Integration, Internationalisation: Report by the iN2015 Steering Committee*. Retrieved September 11, 2017, from http://unpan1.un.org/intradoc/groups/public/documents/unpan/unpan032993.pdf

Infocomm Media Development Authority. (2016a). *Five Government Networks Upgraded to Support the Government Information Infrastructure and Singapore ONE*. Retrieved August 30, 2017, from https://www.imda.gov.sg/about/newsroom/archived/ida/media-releases/1997/20050726122310

Infocomm Media Development Authority. (2016b). *Using IT to Support Quality and Affordable Healthcare*. Retrieved September 8, 2017, from https://www.imda.gov.sg/about/newsroom/archived/ida/media-releases/1996/20050726150709

Integrated Health Information Systems. (2017a). *Healthcare Consultations Move Online in Singapore's First National Implementation of Smart Health Video Consultation for Healthcare*. Retrieved September 15, 2017, from https://www.ihis.com.sg/Latest_News/Media_Releases/Pages/Healthcare-Consultations-Move-Online-in-Singapore%E2%80%99s-First-National-Implementation-of-VC.aspx

Integrated Health Information Systems. (2017b). *Smart Health TeleRehab to Improve Patient Access to Rehabilitation Services and Productivity for Therapists*. Retrieved September 15, 2017, from https://www.ihis.com.sg/Latest_News/Media_Releases/Pages/Smart-Health-TeleRehab.aspx

International Labour Organisation. (2009). *Guidelines on occupational safety and health management systems: ILO-OSH 2001* (2nd ed.). Geneva, Switzerland: ILO.

International Labour Organisation. (2017). *Decent Work*. Retrieved September 28, 2017, from http://www.ilo.org/global/topics/decent-work/lang--en/index.htm

International Telecommunications Union. (2017). *Asia: Marketing Research, Internet Usage, Population Statistics and Facebook Information*. Available at http://www.internetworldstats.com/asia.htm

Ishida, Y. (2008, January). Financial Basis of Nonprofits Supported by the Society (in Japanese). *Komei*, 52-57.

Ismailova, R. (2017). Web site accessibility, usability and security: A survey of government web sites in Kyrgyz Republic. *Universal Access in the Information Society*, *16*(1), 257–264. doi:10.100710209-015-0446-8

ITC Portal. (n.d.a). *ITC Enduring Value*. Retrieved from http://www.itcportal.com

ITC Portal. (n.d.b). *Echoupal Frameset*. Retrieved from http://www.itcportal.com/sets/ echoupal_frameset.htm

Ito, M., Baumer, S., Bittanti, M., Boyd, D., Cody, R., Herr-Stephenson, B., … Tripp, L. (2009). Hanging Out, Messing Around, and Geeking Out: Kids Living and Learning with New Media. MIT Press.

Jackson, D. (2014). Growing communities: How charity leaders govern social media globally to thrive online. *Grant Thornon*. Retrieved from: http://www.grantthornton.global/Insights/Articles/Growing-Communities

Jaeger, P. T. (2003). The endless wire: E-government as global phenomenon. *Government Information Quarterly*, *20*(4), 323–331. doi:10.1016/j.giq.2003.08.003

Jamal, A. (2017). *Singapore's New Mission to Build AI Capabilities*. Retrieved September 29, 2017, from http://www.connectedtoindia.com/singapores-new-mission-to-build-ai-capabilities-1366.html

James, J. (2013a). *8 tips for effectively using social media for social change*. Available online at: http://www.impatient-optimists.org/Posts/2013/03/8-Simple-Strategies-to-Effectively-Use-Social-Media-for-Social-Change

James, J. (2013b). *5 experts share top social media advice for Nonprofits*. Available online at: http://www.impatientoptimists.org/Posts/2013/04/Experts-Share-Top-Social-Media-Advice-for-Nonprofits

Janenova, S., & Kim, S. (2016). Innovating Public Service Delivery in Transitional Countries: The Case of One Stop Shops in Kazakhstan. *International Journal of Public Administration*, *39*(4), 322–333. doi:10.1080/01900692.2015.1064445

Janssen, M., & Kuk, G. (2010). Critical success factors for multi-channel service delivery (MCSD). *16th Americas Conference on Information Systems 2010, AMCIS 2010, 3*, 2179–2187. Retrieved from http://www.scopus.com/inward/record.url?eid=2-s2.0-84870334398&partnerID=40&md5=edd94692f8ff3cea55e579edf8fd2216

Japan Civil Network for Disaster Relief in the East Japan (JCN). (n.d.). *Profile*. Retrieved July 10, 2014, from http://www.jpn-civil.net/2014/english/about_us/

Japan NPO Research Association (JANPORA). (2012) *Report on awareness survey on donation and volunteering after the Great East Japan Disaster* (in Japanese). Retrieved July 10, 2014 from http://www.osipp.osaka-u.ac.jp/janpora/shinsaitokubetsuproject/seika/seika1208.pdf

Joha, A., & Janssen, M. (2010). *Content management implemented as shared service: a public sector case study. In EGovernment, E-Services and Global Processes* (pp. 138–151). Springer.

John Sinclair, A., & Timothy, J. (2017). Peirson-Smith & Morrissa Boerchers, Environmental assessments in the Internet age: The role of e-governance and social media in creating platforms for meaningful participation. *Impact Assessment and Project Appraisal*, *35*(2). doi:10.1080/14615517.2016.1251697

Johnson Center. (2012). *Nonprofit Organizations and social media.* Available online at: https://www.mnaonline.org/CMDocs/MNA/Research/Nonprofit%20Organizations%20and%20Social%20Media,%20Feb%202012.pdf

Joshi, K.K., & Sharma, V. (2014). Challenges in community based forest bio residue resource utilization for bio briquetting in the Western Himalayan region of Uttarakhand. *SAARC Forestry Journal 2014.*

Joshi, K.K., & Sharma, V. (2014). Genesis of people's perception of forest fires in Western Himalayan region of Uttarakhand, India: Causes and Remedies. *Journal of Trade Science.*

Joshi, K. K., & Sharma, V. (2013). *Concrete heaps to carpet green through peoples participation. In Success Stories in Mountain Ecosystem Management* (pp. 34–42). Thimpu, Bhutan: SAARC Forestry Center.

Joshi, K. K., & Sharma, V. (2014). A study on Passages to global climate change financing: Funding for a greener Earth. *Indian Forester.*

Joshi, K. K., & Sharma, V. (2014). Mitigating land disaster through community involvement and righteous practices in Himalayan region of Uttarakhand, India. In *Strategic Disaster Risk Management in Asia*. Singapore: Springer.

Joshi, K. K., Sharma, V., & Mittal, S. (2015). Social entrepreneurship through forest bio residue briquetting: An approach to mitigate forest fires in Pine areas of Western Himalaya, India. *Renewable & Sustainable Energy Reviews*, *51*, 1338–1344. doi:10.1016/j.rser.2015.07.057

Julià, J. F., & Chaves, R. (2012). Introduction: Social economy, a third sector in a plural people-oriented economy. *Service Business*, *6*(1), 1–4. doi:10.100711628-011-0130-x

Justice. (2017). *Office of Justice Programs (OJP) FY 2017 Budget Request at a Glance*. Retrieved from https://www.justice.gov/jmd/file/822111/download

Jutla, D., & Xu, L. (2004). *Privacy agents and ontology for the semantic web*. Academic Press.

Kaligotla, C., Yücesan, E., & Chick, S. E. (2015). An agent based model of spread of competing rumors through online interactions on social media. *WSC '15 Proceedings of the 2015 Winter Simulation Conference*, 3985-3996.

Kaneya, R. (2016). *Other states are shrinking prison populations – Why not Hawaii?* Honolulu Civil Beat. Council of State Governments Justice Center. Retrieved from www.csgjusticecenter.org

Kaplan, A. M., & Haenlein, M. (2010). Users of the world, unite! The challenges and opportunities of Social Media. *Business Horizons*, *53*(1), 59–68. doi:10.1016/j.bushor.2009.09.003

Kapucu, N. (2007). Non-profit response to catastrophic disasters. *Disaster Prevention and Management*, *16*(4), 551–561. doi:10.1108/09653560710817039

Kapucu, N., Yuldashev, F., & Feldheim, M. A. (2011). Nonprofit organizations in disaster response and management: A network analysis. *European Journal of Economic and Political Studies*, *4*(1), 83–112.

Karamagioli, E., Staiou, E. R., & Gouscos, D. (2014). Government Spending Transparency on the Internet: An Assessment of Greek Bottom-Up Initiatives over the Diavgeia Project. *International Journal of Public Administration in the Digital Age*, *1*(1), 39–55. doi:10.4018/ijpada.2014010103

Karlova, N. A., & Fisher, K. E. (2012). "Plz RT": A social diffusion model of misinformation and disinformation for understanding human information behaviour. *Proceedings of the ISIC2012 (Tokyo)*.

Kawai, T., & Fujishiro, H. (2013). Use of Twitter in the disaster information after the Great East Japan Earthquake. *Corporate Communication Studies*, *17*, 118–128.

Kay, A., & Goldberg, A. (1977). Personal Dynamic Media. *Computer*, *10*(3), 31–41. doi:10.1109/C-M.1977.217672

Keady, C. (2015). #Donate allows you to easily give to charity through Twitter hashtags. *Huffington Post*. Retrieved from: http://www.huffingtonpost.com/2015/04/17/donate-charity-social-media-platform_n_7089280.html

Kent, M., & Taylor, M. (1998). Building dialogic relationships through the World Wide Web. *Public Relations Review*, *24*(3), 321–334. doi:10.1016/S0363-8111(99)80143-X

Kernaghan, K. (2009). Moving towards integrated public governance: Improving service delivery through community engagement. *International Review of Administrative Sciences*, *75*(2), 239–254. doi:10.1177/0020852309104174

Kernaghan, K. (2013). Changing channels: Managing channel integration and migration in public organizations. *Canadian Public Administration*, *56*(1), 121–141. doi:10.1111/capa.12006

Kernan, K. (2008). XBRL around the world. *Journal of Accountancy*, *206*(4), 62–66.

Kernan, K. (2009). *XBRL. The Story of Our New Language*. New York, NY: American Institute of Certified Public Accountants.

Khalik, S. (2016 October 21). *'Bid' to Care under Match-A-Nurse*. Retrieved September 15, 2017, from http://www.straitstimes.com/singapore/health/bid-to-care-under-match-a-nurse

Kickstarter. (2017). *About us*. Retrieved from: https://www.kickstarter.com/about

Kivunike, F., Ekenberg, L., Danielson, M., & Tusubira, F. (2011). Perceptions of the Role of ICT on Quality of Life in Rural Communities in Uganda. *Information Technology for Development*, *17*(1), 61–80. doi:10.1080/02681102.2010.511698

Klemz, J., Simon, G., & Kumar, A. (2003). *IS planning in Non-Profit organizations: an exploratory study*. Available online at: http://iacis.org/iis/2003/KlemzSimonKumar.pdf

Klimi-Kaminari, O., & Papageorgiou, K. L. (2010). *Social economy. A first approach*. Athens: Ellinoekdotiki. (in Greek)

Koh, V. (2015 March 17). *HDB Completes Trial of Smart Elderly Monitoring and Alert System. TODAY*. Retrieved September 14, 2017, from http://www.todayonline.com/singapore/hdb-completes-semas-test-bed

Koh, C. E., Prybutok, V. R., & Zhang, X. (2008). Measuring e-government readiness. *Information & Management*, *45*(8), 540–546. doi:10.1016/j.im.2008.08.005

Kohli, A. K., & Jaworski, B. J. (1990). Market orientation: The construct, research propositions, and managerial implications. *Journal of Marketing*, *54*(2), 1–18. doi:10.2307/1251866

Kohli, R., & Devaraj, S. (2003). Measuring Information Technology Payoff: A Meta-Analysis of Structural Variables in Firm-Level Empirical Research. *Information Systems Research*, *14*(2), 127–145. doi:10.1287/isre.14.2.127.16019

Komter, A. (2005). *Social Solidarity and the Gift*. Cambridge, UK: Cambridge University Press.

Kouri, M., & Edward, D. (2013). Does Central Texas have too many nonprofits. *Greenlights for Nonprofit Success*. Retrieved from: http://www.greenlights.org/

Krippendorff, K. (2004). *Content analysis: An introduction to its methodology* (2nd ed.). Thousand Oaks, CA: Sage.

Krueger, R. A. (1994). *Focus Groups. A Practical Guide for Applied Research*. Sage Publications.

Kull, J., & Abraham, C. (2008). XBRL and public sector financial reporting. *Journal of Government Financial Management*, *57*(2), 28–37.

Kumar, R., Sachan, A., & Mukherjee, A. (2017). Qualitative approach to determine user experience of e-government services. *Computers in Human Behavior*, *71*, 299–306. doi:10.1016/j.chb.2017.02.023

Kurfali, M., Arifoglu, A., Tokdemir, G., & Pacin, Y. (2017). Adoption of e-government services in Turkey. *Computers in Human Behavior*, *66*, 168–178. doi:10.1016/j.chb.2016.09.041

Kuzma, J. M., & Price, C. (2009). Analysis of UK Parliament Web Sites for Disability Accessibility. *Proceedings of the 8th European Conference on Information Warfare and Security*.

Lamberti, L., Benedetti, M., & Chen, S. (2014). Benefits sought by citizens and channel attitudes for multichannel payment services: Evidence from Italy. *Government Information Quarterly*, *31*(4), 596–609. doi:10.1016/j.giq.2014.03.002

Landsbergen, D. Jr, & Wolken, G. Jr. (2001). Realizing the promise: Government information systems and the fourth generation of information technology. *Public Administration Review*, *61*(2), 206–220. doi:10.1111/0033-3352.00023

Lawrence, S. (2016). *Philips, Singapore to Jointly Invest in Population Health Management Companies Targeting Asia*. Retrieved September 29, 2017, from http://www.fiercebiotech.com/medical-devices/philips-singapore-to-jointly-invest-population-health-management-companies

Layne, K., & Lee, J. (2001). Developing fully functional E-government: A four stage model. *Government Information Quarterly*, *18*(2), 122–136. doi:10.1016/S0740-624X(01)00066-1

Ledingham, J. (2003). Explicating relationship management as a general theory of public relations. *Journal of Public Relations Research*, *15*(2), 181–198. doi:10.1207/S1532754XJPRR1502_4

Ledingham, J., & Bruning, S. D. (1998). Relationship management in public relations: Dimensions of an organization-public relationship. *Public Relations Review*, *24*(1), 55–65. doi:10.1016/S0363-8111(98)80020-9

Ledingham, J., & Bruning, S. D. (2000). *Public relations as relationship management: A relational approach to the study and practice of public relations*. Mahwah, NJ: Lawrence Erlbaum & Associates, Inc.

Lee, C. E., Lim, B. K., & Tan, P. C. S. (2006). *Singapore HIT Case Study*. Retrieved September 8, 2017, from http://pacifichealthsummit.org/downloads/HITCaseStudies/Economy/SingaporeHIT.pdf

Lee, D. (2016). *HealthHub: A Holistic Way for S'poreans to Manage Health*. Retrieved September 13, 2017, from http://www.todayonline.com/voices/healthhub-holistic-way-sporeans-manage-health

Lee, H. L. (2014). *Transcript of Speech by Prime Minister Lee Hsien Loong at Smart Nation Launch, 24 November 2014*. Retrieved September 14, 2017, from https://www.smartnation.sg/happenings/speeches/smart-nation-launch

Lee-Won, R. J., Abo, M. M., Na, K., & White, T. N. (2016). More than numbers: Effects of social media virality metrics on intention to help unknown others in the context of bone marrow donation. *Cyberpsychology, Behavior, and Social Networking*, *19*(6), 404–411. doi:10.1089/cyber.2016.0080 PMID:27327068

Lee, Y. H., & Hsieh, G. (2013, April). Does slacktivism hurt activism?: the effects of moral balancing and consistency in online activism. In *Proceedings of the SIGCHI Conference on Human Factors in Computing Systems* (pp. 811-820). ACM. 10.1145/2470654.2470770

Leonard, H. (2013). Big business pouring money into social tools. *Business Insider.* Retrieved from: http://www.businessinsider.com/companies-investing-in-social-2013-4

LePendu, P., & Dou, D. (2011). Using ontology databases for scalable query answering, inconsistency detection, and data integration. *Journal of Intelligent Information Systems*, *37*(2), 217–244. doi:10.100710844-010-0133-4 PMID:22163378

Levitt, B., & March, J. G. (1988). Organizational learning. *Annual Review of Sociology*, *14*(1), 319–340. doi:10.1146/annurev.so.14.080188.001535

Levy, K. E. C., & Johns, D. M. (2016). When open data is a Trojan Horse: The weaponization of transparency in science and governance. *Big Data and Society*, *3*(1), 1–6. doi:10.1177/2053951715621568

Liau, Y. Q. (2010). *Standards Important for S'pore E-healthcare.* Retrieved September 11, 2017, from http://www.zdnet.com/article/standards-important-for-spore-e-healthcare/

Lim, H. K. (2000). *Second Ministry Of Health IT Seminar.* Retrieved September 11, 2017, from https://www.moh.gov.sg/content/moh_web/home/pressRoom/speeches_d/2000/second_ministry_of_health_IT_seminar.html

Lin, F., Fofanah, S. S., & Liang, D. (2011). Assessing citizen adoption of e-Government initiatives in Gambia: A validation of the technology acceptance model in information systems success. *Government Information Quarterly*, *28*(2), 271–279. doi:10.1016/j.giq.2010.09.004

Liptrott, M. (2016). Tackling the Digital Divide: The Shift from Access to Capacity. *International Journal of Public Administration in the Digital Age*, *3*(1), 70–84. doi:10.4018/IJPADA.2016010105

Liu, B. F., Austin, L., & Jin, Y. (2011). How publics respond to crisis communication strategies: The interplay of information form and source. *Public Relations Review*, *37*(4), 345–353. doi:10.1016/j.pubrev.2011.08.004

Liu, C., Luo, X. R., & Wang, F. L. (2017). An empirical investigation on the impact of XBRL adoption on information asymmetry: Evidence from Europe. *Decision Support Systems*, *93*, 42–50. doi:10.1016/j.dss.2016.09.004

Liu, J., & Lin, B. (2012). Government auditing and corruption control: Evidence from China's provincial panel data. *China Journal of Accounting Research*, *5*(2), 163–186. doi:10.1016/j.cjar.2012.01.002

Loh, C. J. (2016 April 23). *Smart Devices Trial Extended to 3,200 Households in Yuhua.* Retrieved September 14, 2017, from http://www.channelnewsasia.com/news/singapore/smart-devices-trial-extended-to-3-200-households-in-yuhua-8086356

Loke, K. F. (2017). *Singapore's Artificial Intelligence Capabilities to Get S$150m Boost.* Retrieved September 29, 2017, from http://www.channelnewsasia.com/news/singapore/singapore-s-artificial-intelligence-capabilities-to-get-s-150m-8813174

Losh, S. C. (2013). American digital divides: Generation, education, gender, and ethnicity in American digital divides. In Digital Literacy: Concepts, Methodologies, Tools, and Applications (pp. 932-958). IGI Global. doi:10.4018/978-1-4666-1852-7.ch048

Lovejoy, K., & Saxton, G. D. (2012). Information, community, and action: How nonprofit organizations use social media. *Journal of Computer-Mediated Communication*, *17*(3), 337–353. doi:10.1111/j.1083-6101.2012.01576.x

Lovejoy, K., Waters, R. D., & Saxton, G. D. (2012). Engaging stakeholders through Twitter: How nonprofit organizations are getting more out of 140 characters or less. *Public Relations Review*, *38*(2), 313–318. doi:10.1016/j.pubrev.2012.01.005

Low, C. O., & Li, D. (2015). Challenges of Transformation on Our Healthcare IT Journey. *SMA News, 47*(5), 5-7. Retrieved September 8, 2017, from https://www.sma.org.sg/UploadedImg/files/Publications%20-%20SMA%20News/4705/Full%20PDF.pdf

Low, C. O., & Tan, P. (2016). Our IT Journey: One Patient-One Record. In C. E. Lee & K. Satku (Eds.), *Singapore's Health Care System: What 50 Years Have Achieved* (pp. 337–350). World Scientific. doi:10.1142/9789814696067_0027

Lubke, G. H., & Muthén, B. O. (2004). Applying multigroup confirmatory factor models for continuous outcomes to Likert scale data complicates meaningful group comparisons. *Structural Equation Modeling, 11*(4), 514–534. doi:10.120715328007sem1104_2

Lucas, E. (2017). Reinventing the rattling tin: How UK charities use Facebook in fundraising. *International Journal of Nonprofit and Voluntary Sector Marketing, 22*(2), e1576. doi:10.1002/nvsm.1576

Luk, S. (2014). *Health Insurance Reforms in Asia*. Abingdon, UK: Routledge.

M+R & NTEN. (2012). *eNonprofit Benchmarks Study: An analysis of online messaging, fundraising, advocacy, social media, and mobile metrics for nonprofit organizations*. Retrieved from http://www.e-benchmarksstudy.com/

M+R & NTEN. (2014). *eNonprofit Benchmarks Study: An analysis of online messaging, fundraising, advocacy, social media, and mobile metrics for nonprofit organizations*. Authors.

M+R & NTEN. (2015). *eNonprofit Benchmarks Study: An analysis of online messaging, fundraising, advocacy, social media, and mobile metrics for nonprofit organizations*. Authors.

Madsen, C. Ø., & Kræmmergaard, P. (2015a). Channel Choice: A Literature Review. In Tambouris, Janssen, Schol, Wimmer, & Tarabanis (Eds.), *Electronic Government: Proceedings of the 14th IFIP WG 8,5 International Conference, EGOV 2015*. Thessaloniki, Greece: LNCS Springer. 10.1007/978-3-319-22479-4_1

Madsen, C. Ø., & Kræmmergaard, P. (2016). Warm Experts in the age of Mandatory e-Government: Interaction Among Danish Single Parents Regarding Online Application for Public Benefits. *Electronic Journal of E-Government, 14*(1), 87–98. Retrieved from http://www.ejeg.com/issue/download.html?idArticle=447

Madsen, C. Ø., Berger, J., & Phythian, M. (2014). The Development in Leading e-Government Articles 2001-2010: Definitions, Perspectives, Scope, Research Philosophies, Methods and Recommendations: An Update of Heeks and Bailur. In M. Janssen, H. J. Scholl, M. A. Wimmer, & F. Bannister (Eds.), *Electronic Government: Proceedings of the 13th IFIP WG 8.5 International Conference, EGOV 2014* (Vol. 8653, pp. 17–34). Dublin, Ireland: LNCS Springer. 10.1007/BF03251472

Madsen, C. Ø., & Kræmmergaard, P. (2015b). The efficiency of freedom. Single parents' domestication of mandatory e-government. *Government Information Quarterly, 32*(4), 380–388. doi:10.1016/j.giq.2015.09.008

Maerz, S. (2016). The electronic face of authoritarianism: E-government as a tool for gaining legitimacy in competitive and non-competitive regimes. *Government Information Quarterly, 33*(4), 725–735. doi:10.1016/j.giq.2016.08.008

Magoutas, B., Halaris, C., & Mentzas, G. (2007). An ontology for the multi-perspective evaluation of quality in e-Government services. Electronic Government, 318-329.

Makridimitris, A. (2006). *State and Civil Society*. Athens: Metamesonikties Ekdoseis. (in Greek)

Ma, L. (2016). What drives the adoption of social media applications by the public sector? Evidence from local health departments. *International Journal of Public Administration in the Digital Age, 4*(3), 76–93. doi:10.4018/IJPADA.2016100106

Malhotra, N. (2014). Introducing language targeting. *Twitter*. Retrieved June 9, 2015, from https://blog.twitter.com/2014/introducing-language-targeting

Mankoff, J., Kuksenok, K., Kiesler, S., Rode, J. A., & Waldman, K. (2011). Competing online viewpoints and models of chronic illness. In *Proceedings of the 2011 annual conference on Human factors in computing systems - CHI '11* (p. 589). New York: ACM Press. 10.1145/1978942.1979027

Mansfield, H. (2014). *12 steps to launching a social media strategy for your NGO.* Webinar Notes, 22/07/2014.

Markus, M. L. (1994). Electronic Mail as the Medium of Managerial Choice. *Organization Science*, *5*(4), 502–527. doi:10.1287/orsc.5.4.502

Mashhadi, A., Quattrone, G., & Capra, L. (2015). The Impact of Society on Volunteered Geographic Information: The case of OpenStreetMap. In J. Jokar, A. Universit, & A. Z. Universit (Eds.), *OpenStreetMap in GIScience Experiences, Research, and Applications* (pp. 125–141). Springer. doi:10.1007/978-3-319-14280-7_7

Mates, P., Lechner, T., Rieger, P., & Pekna, J. (2013). Toward e-government project assessment: European approach. *Preliminary Communication*, *31*(1), 103–125.

Mathewson, J. W., Jones, F. D., Sklansky, M. S., Perry, J. C., Michelfelder, E. C., Cripe, L., & Kimball, T. R. (2002). Conversion to Digital Technology Improves Efficiency in the Pediatric Echocardiography Laboratory. *Journal of the American Society of Echocardiography*, *15*(12), 1515–1522. doi:10.1067/mje.2002.129498 PMID:12464921

Maxwell, S. P., & Carboni, J. L. (2014). Stakeholder communication in Service Implementation Networks: Expanding Relationship Management Theory in the voluntary sector. *International Journal of Nonprofit and Voluntary Sector Marketing*. doi:10.1002/nvsm.1506

Maxwell, S. P., & Carboni, J. L. (2017). Civic engagement through social media: Strategic stakeholder management by high-asset foundations. *International Journal of Public Administration in the Digital Age*, *4*(1), 35–48. doi:10.4018/IJPADA.2017010103

May, C. (2002). *The Information Society. A sceptical view*. Blackwell Publishing.

Mayernik, M. S. (2017). Open Data: Accountability and Transparency. *Big Data and Society*, *4*(2), 1–5. doi:10.1177/2053951717718853

Mayfield, A. (2006). Social media...the hunted can become the hunter. *Public Relations Quarterly*, *52*(4), 9–12.

Mbarika, V. W., & Byrd, T. A. (2009). An Exploratory Study of Strategies to Improve Africa's Least Developed Economies; Telecommunications Infrastructure: The Stakeholders Speak. *IEEE Transactions on Engineering Management*, *56*(2), 312–328. doi:10.1109/TEM.2009.2013826

McTernan, W. P., Dollard, M. F., Tuckey, M. R., & Vandenberg, R. J. (2016). Beneath the surface: An exploration of remoteness and work stress in the mines. In Psychosocial Factors at Work in the Asia Pacific: From Theory to Practice (pp. 341-358). Springer International. doi:10.1007/978-3-319-44400-0

Meister, J. (2012). Social media training is now mandatory: five ways to make sure your company does it right. *Forbes*. Retrieved from: http://www.forbes.com/sites/jeannemeister/2012/10/31/social-media-training-is-now-mandatory/

MemorandumB. (2013). Retrieved from https://obamawhitehouse.archives.gov/sites/default/files/omb/memoranda/2013/m-13-17.pdf

Merkel, C., Farooq, U., Xiao, L., Ganoe, C., Rosson, M. B., & Carrol, J. M. (2007). Managing technology use and learning in nonprofit community organizations: Methodological challenges and opportunities. *CHIMIT 2007*.

Michaelis, A. R. (1996). Information Bureaucracy: Australia and Singapore Compared. *Interdisciplinary Science Reviews*, *21*(2), 89–93. doi:10.1179/isr.1996.21.2.89

Mihai, A., Marincea, A., & Ekenberg, L. (2015). A MCDM Analysis of the Roşia Montană Gold Mining Project. *Sustainability*, *2015*(7), 7261–7288. doi:10.3390u7067261

Miller, E. (2010). Solidarity Economy: Key Concepts and Issues. In E. Kawano & ... (Eds.), *Solidarity Economy I: Building Alternatives for People and Planet.* Amherst, MA: Center for Popular Economics. Available online at http://www.communityeconomies.org/site/assets/media/Ethan_Miller/Miller_Solidarity_Economy_Key_Issues_2010.pdf

Miller, J. L. (2002). The board as a monitor of organizational activity: The applicability of agency theory to nonprofit boards. *Nonprofit Management & Leadership*, *12*(4), 429–450. doi:10.1002/nml.12407

Milward, H. B., & Provan, K. G. (2000). Governing the hollow state. *Journal of Public Administration: Research and Theory*, *10*(2), 359–379. doi:10.1093/oxfordjournals.jpart.a024273

Milward, H. B., & Provan, K. G. (2001). Do Networks Really Work? A Framework for Evaluating Public-Sector Organizational Networks. *Public Administration Review*, *61*(4), 414–423. doi:10.1111/0033-3352.00045

Milward, H. B., & Provan, K. G. (2003). Managing the Hollow State: Collaboration and contracting. *Public Management Review*, *5*(1), 2–18. doi:10.1080/1461667022000028834

Milward, H. B., & Provan, K. G. (2006). *A manager's guide to choosing and using collaborative networks.* IBM Center for the Business of Government.

Minister of Internal Affairs and Communication. (2017). *White Paper Information and Communications in Japan* (in Japanese). Retrieved September 8, 2017 from http://www.soumu.go.jp/johotsusintokei/whitepaper/index.html

Ministry of Communications & Information. (1989). *Speech by Dr. Tay Eng Soon, Senior Minister of State for Education, at the Opening of MEDINFO '89 Singapore at the Raffles City Convention Centre on Sunday, 10 December 1989, at 1.30 PM.* Retrieved September 3, 2017, from http://www.nas.gov.sg/archivesonline/data/pdfdoc/tes19891210s.pdf

Ministry of Communications & Information. (1990a). *Speech by Mr. Yeo Cheow Tong, AG Minister for Health at the Launching of MediNet on 22 October 1990 at 4 PM at Ministry of Health Auditorium, College of Medicine Building.* Retrieved September 3, 2017, from http://www.nas.gov.sg/archivesonline/data/pdfdoc/yct19901022s.pdf

Ministry of Communications & Information. (1990b). *Address by Acting Minister for Health, Mr. Yeo Cheow Tong at the Opening of the National Cancer Education Programme at the Mandarin Hotel on Saturday, 29 September 1990 at 2.00 PM.* Retrieved September 6, 2017, from http://www.nas.gov.sg/archivesonline/data/pdfdoc/yct19900929s.pdf

Ministry of Finance, & Infocomm Development Authority of Singapore (2003). *Singapore E-government.* Retrieved August 31, 2017, from https://www.tech.gov.sg/-/media/GovTech/About-us/Corporate-Publications/eGov/eGap-II.pdf?la=en

Ministry of Finance, & Infocomm Development Authority of Singapore (2006). *iGov2010: From Integrating Service to Integrating Government.* Retrieved August 31, 2017, from https://www.tech.gov.sg/-/media/GovTech/About-us/Corporate-Publications/eGov/iGov.pdf?la=en

Ministry of Health. (2010). *Contract to Implement Singapore's National Electronic Health Record (Phase 1) Awarded.* Retrieved September 11, 2017, from https://www.moh.gov.sg/content/moh_web/home/pressRoom/pressRoomItemRelease/2010/Contract_to_Implement_Singapore_National_Electronic_Health_Record_Phase_1_Awarded.html

Ministry of Health. (2015a). *Future Phase of NEHR.* Retrieved September 11, 2017, from https://www.moh.gov.sg/content/moh_web/home/pressRoom/Parliamentary_QA/2015/future-phase-of-nehr.html

Ministry of Health. (2015b). *One-stop Health Information and Services Portal Provides Access to Key Medical Records and Health Content*. Retrieved September 13, 2017, from https://www.moh.gov.sg/content/moh_web/home/pressRoom/pressRoomItemRelease/2015/one-stop-health-information-and-services-portal-provides-access-.html

Ministry of Health. (2015c). *National Telemedicine Guidelines*. Retrieved September 28, 2017, from https://www.moh.gov.sg/content/dam/moh_web/Publications/Guidelines/MOH%20Cir%2006_2015_30Jan15_Telemedicine%20Guidelines%20rev.pdf

Ministry of Health. (2015d). *MOH National Telemedicine Guidelines: Summary Card*. Retrieved September 28, 2017, from https://www.moh.gov.sg/content/dam/moh_web/Publications/Guidelines/MOH%20Cir%2006_2015_30Jan15_Telemedicine%20Summary.pdf

Ministry of Health. (2016). *Speech by Mr Gan Kim Yong, Minister for Health, at Home Nursing Foundation's "Futurescape: Home Healthcare – Local and International Perspectives" Conference, 20 August 2016*. Retrieved September 15, 2017, from https://www.moh.gov.sg/content/moh_web/home/pressRoom/speeches_d/2016/speech-by-mr-gan-kim-yong--minister-for-health--at-home-nursing-.html

Ministry of Health. (2017a). *Speech by Mr Gan Kim Yong, Minister for Health, at the National Health IT Summit 2017, 30 May 2017*. Retrieved September 15, 2017, from https://www.moh.gov.sg/content/moh_web/home/pressRoom/speeches_d/2017/speech-by-mr-gan-kim-yong--minister-for-health--at-the-national-.html

Ministry of Health. (2017b). *HealthHub*. Retrieved September 15, 2017, from https://www.moh.gov.sg/content/moh_web/home/pressRoom/Parliamentary_QA/2017/healthhub.html

Ministry of Internal Affairs and Communication Statistics Bureau. (2011). *Impact of the Disaster on Results of Household Survey (with two or more people): Shift in Amount of Donation* (in Japanese). Retrieved April 29, 2015 from http://www.stat.go.jp/info/shinsai/pdf/ka1106-2.pdf

Ministry of Internal Affairs and Communication. (2011). *Research on possibilities of next-generation ICT society* (in Japanese). Retrieved April 28, 2015, from http://www.soumu.go.jp/johotsusintokei/linkdata/h23_05_houkoku.pdf

Ministry of Legal Affairs. (2013). *Alphabetical list of revised laws*. Retrieved August 24, 2014, from http://www.legalaffairs.gov.tt/Laws_listing.html

Min, S.-J. (2010). From the digital divide to the democratic Ddivide: Internet skills, political interest, and the second-level digital divide in political Internet use. *Journal of Information Technology & Politics*, *7*(1), 22–35. doi:10.1080/19331680903109402

Mintzberg, H. (1996). Managing Government, Governing Management. *Harvard Business Review*, *74*(3), 75–83.

Mislove, A., Lehmann, S., Ahn, Y., Onnela, J., & Rosenquist, J. N. (2011). Understanding the Demographics of Twitter Users. *Artificial Intelligence*, 554–557.

Mitchell, M., & Leachman, M. (2014). *Changing Priorities: States Criminal Justice Reforms and Investments in Education*. Center on Budget and Policy Priorities. Policy Futures.

Mocanu, D., Baronchelli, A., Perra, N., Gonçalves, B., Zhang, Q., & Vespignani, A. (2013). The Twitter of Babel: Mapping World Languages through Microblogging Platforms. *PLoS One*, *8*(4), 1–9. doi:10.1371/journal.pone.0061981 PMID:23637940

Moore, M. H. (1995). *Creating public value: Strategic management in government*. Cambridge, MA: Harvard University Press.

Moore, M. H. (2005). Break-Through Innovations and Continuous Improvement: Two Different Models of Innovative Processes in the Public Sector. *Public Money & Management*, *25*(1), 43–50.

Moorman, C. (1995). Organizational market information processes: Cultural antecedents and new product outcomes. *JMR, Journal of Marketing Research*, *32*(3), 318–335. doi:10.2307/3151984

Mousa, R. (2013). E-Government adoption in the UK: XBRL project. *International Journal of Electronic Government Research*, *9*(2), 101–119. doi:10.4018/jegr.2013040106

Muhametjanova, G., & Çagiltay, K. (2012, July). Students' and Instructors' Perceptions on Use of Information and Communication Technologies during Instruction in a Kyrgyzstan University. In *Advanced Learning Technologies (ICALT), 2012 IEEE 12th International Conference on* (pp. 500-502). IEEE.

Mundy, D., Umer, Q., & Foster, A. (2011). Examining the Potential for Channel Shift in the UK Through Multiple Lenses Independent Researcher, UK. *Electronic Journal of E-Government*, *9*(2), 203–213.

Munson, S. A., & Resnick, P. (2010). Presenting diverse political opinions. In *Proceedings of the 28th international conference on Human factors in computing systems - CHI '10* (p. 1457). New York: ACM Press.

Muralidharan, S., Rasmussen, L., Patterson, D., & Shin, J. (2011). Hope for Haiti: An analysis of Facebook and Twitter usage during the earthquake relief efforts. *Public Relations Review*, *37*(2), 175–177. doi:10.1016/j.pubrev.2011.01.010

Nah, S., & Saxton, G. E. (2013). Modeling the adoption and use of social media by nonprofit organizations. *New Media & Society*, *15*(2), 294–313. doi:10.1177/1461444812452411

Nathai-Balkissoon, M., Maharaj, C., Guerrero, R., Mahabir, R., & Dialsingh, I. (2017). *Pilot development of innovation scales for beverage manufacturing companies in a developing country*. Cogent Business and Management. doi:10.1080/23311975.2017.1379214

Nathai-Balkissoon, M., & Pun, K. F. (2011). A holistic model and research agenda for organisational learning in manufacturing. *World Journal of Entrepreneurship, Management and Sustainable Development*, *7*(1), 27–38. doi:10.1108/20425961201000028

Nathai-Balkissoon, M., & Pun, K. F. (2016). OSH at Trinidad and Tobago's fingertips: Learning from first-world OSH website approaches. *International Journal of Public Administration in the Digital Age*, *3*(3), 57–72. doi:10.4018/IJPADA.2016070104

National Health Innovation Centre Singapore. (2015). *Accelerating Healthcare Innovation*. Retrieved September 29, 2017, from https://nhic.sg/

National Library Board of Singapore. (1989). *TradeNet is Officially Launched*. Retrieved September 4, 2017, from http://eresources.nlb.gov.sg/history/events/8db3ea66-c99a-41a0-bd9a-b6300d1a4454

National Police Agency of Japan. (2017). *Updated information on victims and policy responses to earthquakes off the coast of Pacific Ocean in northeast Japan* (in Japanese). Retrieved December 13, 2017, from https://www.npa.go.jp/news/other/earthquake2011/pdf/higaijokyo.pdf

National Research Council. (2000). *Information Technology Research, Innovation, and E-Government*. Washington, DC: National Academy Press.

National Research Foundation. (2017a). *RIE2020 Plan*. September 29, 2017, from https://www.nrf.gov.sg/rie2020

National Research Foundation. (2017b). *Health and Biomedical Sciences*. September 29, 2017, from https://www.nrf.gov.sg/rie2020/health-and-biomedical-sciences

Ndou, V. (2004). E-government for developing countries: Opportunities and challenges. *The Electronic Journal on Information Systems in Developing Countries*, *18*(1), 1–24. doi:10.1002/j.1681-4835.2004.tb00117.x

Neis, P., & Zielstra, D. (2014). Recent Developments and Future Trends in Volunteered Geographic Information Research: The Case of OpenStreetMap. *Future Internet*, *6*(1), 76–106. doi:10.3390/fi6010076

New Jersey Commission on Science and Technology. (2008). *Grants and Initiatives*. New Jersey Technology and Entrepreneur Fellowship Program. Retrieved from http://www.state.nj.us/scitech/programs/

New Jersey State Library. (2017). *Technology Infrastructure Study New Jersey Library Technology Infrastructure Study*. Retrieved from http://www.njstatelib.org/services_for_libraries/resources/technology-infrastructure-study/

New York University School of Law, Brennan Center for Justice. (2015). *The Reverse Mass Incarceration Act*. Retrieved from https://www.brennancenter.org/publication/reverse-mass-incarceration-act

New York University School of Law, Brennan Center for Justice. (2017). *Update on Changes in State Imprisonment*. Retrieved from https://www.brennancenter.org/sites/default/files/analysis/UpdateChangesinStateImprisonment.pdf

Next Principles. (2012). *Media tips for Non Profit Organizations*. Available online at: https://nextprinciples.com/social-media-tips-for-non-profit-organizations/

Ng, P. T. (2011). Embracing Emerging Technologies: The Case of the Singapore Intelligent Nation 2015 Vision. In P. O. de Pablos, W. B. Lee, & J. Zhao (Eds.), *Regional Innovation Systems and Sustainable Development: Emerging Technologies* (pp. 115–123). Hershey, PA: IGI Global. doi:10.4018/978-1-61692-846-9.ch008

Ngwenyama, O. K., & Lee, A. S. (1997). Communication Richness in Electronic Mail. Critical Social Theory and The Contextuality of Meaning. *Management Information Systems Quarterly*, *21*(2), 145–167. doi:10.2307/249417

Nimmon, L., & Stenfors-Hayes, T. (2016). The "Handling" of Power in the Physician-patient Encounter: Perceptions from Experienced Physicians. *BMC Medical Education*, *16*(1), 114. doi:10.118612909-016-0634-0 PMID:27091146

Non Profit Marketing Guide. (2015). *2015 Nonprofit Communications Trends Report*. Available online at: http://www.nonprofitmarketingguide.com/freemembers/2015NonprofitCommunicationsTrends.pdf

Nonprofit Tech for Good. (2014a). *How much time mobile and social media require*. Available online at: http://www.nptechforgood.com/2014/05/18/how-much-time-mobile-and-social-media-require/

Nonprofit Tech for Good. (2014b). *10 Must-Have skills for Nonprofit New Media Managers*. Available online at: http://www.nptechforgood.com/2014/07/14/10-must-have-skills-for-nonprofit-new-media-managers/

Norris, P. (2001). *Digital divide: Civic engagement, information poverty, and the Internet worldwide*. Cambridge, UK: Cambridge University Press. doi:10.1017/CBO9781139164887

Nunnally, J., & Bernstein, I. H. (1967). *Psychometric theory*. New York: McGraw-Hill Book Company.

O'Connor, M. J., Shankar, R. D., Nyulas, C., Tu, S. W., & Das, A. K. (2008). *Developing a Web-Based Application using OWL and SWRL*. Paper presented at the AAAI Spring Symposium: AI Meets Business Rules and Process Management.

O'Reilly, T. (2005) *What is Web 2.0? Design patterns and business models for the next generation of software*. Retrieved from http://www.oreilly.com/pub/a/web2/archive/what-is-web-20.html

Obar, J. A. (2014). Canadian advocacy 2.0: An analysis of social media adoption and perceived affordances by advocacy groups looking to advance activism in Canada. *Canadian Journal of Communication*, *39*(2), 211–233. doi:10.22230/cjc.2014v39n2a2678

Obar, J. A., Zube, P., & Lampe, C. (2012). Advocacy 2.0: An analysis of how advocacy groups in the United States perceive and use social media as tools for facilitating civic engagement and collective action. *Journal of Information Policy*, *2*, 1–25. doi:10.5325/jinfopoli.2.2012.0001

Occupational Safety and Health Administration. (n.d.). *Occupational safety & health administration.* Retrieved August 15, 2014 from www.osha.gov

Occupational Safety and Health Authority and Agency. (2011). *OSHA.* Retrieved September 17, 2017, from www.osha.gov.tt

Office of Management and Budget. (2002). *E-Government Strategy: Simplified Delivery of Services to Citizens.* Washington, DC: Executive Office of the President.

Official DigiLocker Website of Indian Government. (n.d.). Retrieved September 27, 2017 from https://digilocker.gov.in/

Official Website of Australia Government. (n.d.a). Retrieved October 7, 2017 from http://www.australia.gov.au/

Official Website of Australia Government. (n.d.b). Retrieved October 7, 2017 from https://my.gov.au/LoginServices/main/login?execution=e1s1

Official Website of FirstGov.gov. (n.d.a). Retrieved October 3, 2017 from http://firstgov.gov/About.shtml

Official Website of FirstGov.gov. (n.d.b). *About FirstGov.gov.* Retrieved October 3, 2017 from http://web.archive.org/web/20060707043959re_/firstgov.gov/About.shtml

Official Website of Prime Minister of India. (n.d.). Retrieved September 27, 2017 from https://www.narendramodi.in/mann-ki-baat

Official Website of Singapore Government. (n.d.a). Retrieved October 7, 2017 from https://www.gov.sg/

Official Website of Singapore Government. (n.d.b). Retrieved October 7, 2017 from http://ccc.ecitizen.gov.sg/

Official Website of Singapore Government. (n.d.c). Retrieved from October 7, 2017 https://www.cpf.gov.sg/

Official Website of Social Justice and Empowerment of Haryana Government. (n.d.). Retrieved September 27, 2017 from http://socialjusticehry.gov.in/

Official Website of UGC. (n.d.). Retrieved September 27, 2017 from https://www.ugc.ac.in/grievance/

Ogden, T. N., & Starita, L. (2009). *Social Networking and Mid-Size Non-Profits: What's the Use?* Available online at: http://philanthropyaction.com/documents/Social_Networks_and_Mid-Size_Non-Profits.pdf

Oh, A., Lee, H., & Kim, Y. (2009). User Evaluation of a System for Classifying and Displaying Political Viewpoints of Weblogs. In *Proceedings of the Third International ICWSM Conference* (pp. 282–285). Academic Press.

Okada, A., & Yamauchi, N. (2014). *Role of information in mobilizing the public towards voluntary actions in times of disaster.* Japan NPO Research Association Discussion Paper Series. Retrieved February 23, 2015, from http://www.osipp.osaka-u.ac.jp/janpora/dparchive/papers/2014004E.pdf

Okada, A., Ishida, Y., & Kikuchi, R. (2016). *"Dialogue" in Social Media: Implications for Strategic Communication of Nonprofits.* Association for Research on Nonprofit Organizations and Voluntary Action (ARNOVA) *45th Annual Conference*, Washington, DC.

Okada, A., Ishida, Y., & Yamauchi, N. (2017). Effectiveness of Social Media in Disaster Fundraising: Mobilizing the Public towards Voluntary Actions. *International Journal of Public Administration in the Digital Age*, *4*(1), 49–68. doi:10.4018/IJPADA.2017010104

Open Data for Development Network. (2017). *Open Data For Development: Building An Inclusive Data Revolution. Annual Report 2016.* International Development Research Centre. Retrieved December 19, 2017, from http://od4d.net/wp-content/uploads/2017/05/Annual-repor-2016_Web.pdf

Osborne, D., & Gaebler, T. (1992). *Reinventing Government: How the Entrepreneurial Spirit is transforming the Public Sector.* Addison-Wesley. Retrieved October 8, 2017 from https://publicadministration.un.org/egovkb/Portals/egovkb/Documents/un/English.pdf

Outlaw, S. (2013). Which Type of Crowdfunding is best for you? *Entrepeneur.* Retrieved from: https://www.entrepreneur.com/article/228524

Palfrey, J. G., & Gasser, U. (2008). *Born digital: Understanding the first generation of digital natives.* New York: Basic Books.

Palvia, S. C. J., & Sharma, S. S. (2007). E-government and e-governance: definitions/domain framework and status around the world. In *International Conference on E-governance.* Available at http://www.iceg.net/2007/books/1/1_369.pdf

Pang, M. F., Tati, A., & Krishnan, M. S. (2011). Information Technology and Administrative Efficiency in U.S. State Governments – A Stochastic Frontier Approach. *Management Information Systems Quarterly, 38*(4), 1079–1102. doi:10.25300/MISQ/2014/38.4.07

Panizzolo, D., Fradeani, A., & Metushi, E. (2017). Financial Reporting Practices of Italian SMEs: Why Do They Disclose More? *The International Journal of Digital Accounting Research, 17*, 111–137. doi:10.4192/1577-8517-v17_5

Parasie, S., & Dagiral, E. (2012). Data-driven journalism and the public good: "Computer-assisted-reporters" and "programmer-journalists" in Chicago. *New Media & Society, 15*(6), 853–871. doi:10.1177/1461444812463345

Pariser, E. (2011). *The filter bubble: What the Internet is hiding from you.* London: Viking.

Park, S., Kang, S., Chung, S., & Song, J. (2009). NewsCube: Delivering multiple aspects of news to mitigate media bias. In *Proceedings of the 27th international conference on Human factors in computing systems - CHI 09* (p. 443). New York: ACM Press. 10.1145/1518701.1518772

Pavlik, J. V. (2001). News framing and new media: digital tools to re-engage an alienated citizenry. In Framing Public Life: Perspectives on Media and Our Understanding of the Social World. Mahwah, NJ: Lawrence Erlbaum Associates, Inc.

Pekkanen, R. (2000). Japan's new politics: The case of the NPO law. *Journal of Japanese Studies, 26*(1), 111–148. doi:10.2307/133393

Pekkanen, R. (2006). *Japan's Dual Civil Society: Members without Advocates.* Stanford, CA: Stanford University Press.

Pemberton, J. D., & Stonehouse, G. H. (2000). Organisational learning and knowledge assets: An essential partnership. *The Learning Organization, 7*(4), 184–193. doi:10.1108/09696470010342351

Perdana, A., Robb, A., & Rohde, F. (2014). An integrative review and synthesis of XBRL research in academic journals. *Journal of Information Systems, 29*(1), 115–153. doi:10.2308/isys-50884

Personal Data Protection Commission. (2017). *Legislation and Guidelines: Overview.* Retrieved September 29, 2017, from https://www.pdpc.gov.sg/legislation-and-guidelines

Petrakis, P. E., Kostis, P. C., & Valsamis, D. G. (2015). Innovation and competitiveness: Culture as a long-term strategic instrument during the European Great Recession. *Journal of Business Research, 68*(7), 1436–1438. doi:10.1016/j.jbusres.2015.01.029

Peuschel, B., & Schäfer, W. (1992). Concepts and implementation of a rule-based process engine. *Proceedings of the 14th international conference on Software engineering.*

Pew Research. (2014). *Social media fact sheet.* Retrieved from: http://www.pewinternet.org/fact-sheet/social-media/

Philip, E., & Wurster, T. S. (1999). *Blown to bits: how the new economics of information transforms strategy.* Boston, MA: Harvard Business School Press.

Phua, R. (2017a April 12). *National Video Consultation Platform to Allow Patients to 'See' Doctors from Home.* Retrieved September 15, 2017, from http://www.channelnewsasia.com/news/singapore/national-video-consultation-platform-to-allow-patients-to-see-do-8701218

Phua, R. (2017b May 5). *Undergoing Physiotherapy Exercises from Home Now a Reality for Patients.* Retrieved September 15, 2017, from http://www.channelnewsasia.com/news/singapore/undergoing-physiotherapy-exercises-from-home-now-a-reality-for-8821356

Pieterson, W., & Teerling, M. (2009). Channel Integration in Governmental Service Delivery: The Effects on Citizen Behavior and Perceptions. *Electronic Government: Proceedings of the 8th [IFIP WG 8.5] International Conference, EGOV 2009, 5693*(2007), 222–233. 10.1007/978-3-642-03516-6

Pieterson, W., Ebbers, W. E., & Madsen, C. Ø. (2017). New Channels, New Possibilities: A Typology and Classification of Social Robots and Their Role in Multi-channel Public Service Delivery. In *International conference on Electronic Government* (pp. 47–59). Springer Berlin/Heidelberg. 10.1007/978-3-319-64677-0_5

Pieterson, W., Teerling, M., & Ebbers, W. E. (2008). Channel Perceptions and Usage: Beyond Media Richness Factors. In M. A. Wimmer, H. J. Scholl, & E. Ferro (Eds.), *Electronic Government 7th International Conference, EGOV 2008, Turin, Italy, August 31-September 5, 2008, proceedings* (Vol. 5184/2008, pp. 219–230). Berlin: Springer. 10.1007/978-3-540-85204-9_19

Pieterson, W. (2010). Citizens and Service Channels: Channel Choice and Channel Management Implications. *International Journal of Electronic Government Research, 6*(2), 37–53. doi:10.4018/jegr.2010040103

Pieterson, W., & Ebbers, W. E. (2008). The use of service channels by citizens in the Netherlands: Implications for multi-channel management. *International Review of Administrative Sciences, 74*(1), 95–110. doi:10.1177/0020852307085736

Pitman, M. A. (2013). *21 social media tips for Nonprofits from top experts.* Available online at: http://fundraisingcoach.com/2013/05/06/21-social-media-tips-for-nonprofits-from-top-experts/

Pletikosa, C. I., & Michahelles, F. (2013). Online engagement factors on Facebook brand pages. *Social Network Analysis and Mining, 3*(4), 843–861. doi:10.100713278-013-0098-8

Podgórski, D. (2015). Measuring operational performance of OSH management system – A demonstration of AHP-based selection of leading key performance indicators. *Safety Science, 73*, 146–166. doi:10.1016/j.ssci.2014.11.018

Porter, D. R. (1993). Improving Administrative Efficiency through Technology. *New Directions for Adult and Continuing Education, 60*(60), 67–77. doi:10.1002/ace.36719936009

Porter, M. E. (1990). The competitive advantage of nations. *Harvard Business Review, 68*(2), 73–93.

Porter, M., & Kramer, M. (1999). Philanthropy's new agenda: Creating value. *Harvard Business Review, 77*(6). PMID:10662001

Prahalad, C. K. (2005). *The fortune at the bottom of the pyramid: Eradicating poverty through profits.* Pearson Education.

Prensky, M. (2001). Digital natives, digital immigrants part 1. *On the Horizon, 9*(5), 1–6. doi:10.1108/10748120110424816

Primavera, H. (2010). Social currencies and solidarity economy: An enduring bond of common good. *Working USA, 13*(1), 41–59. doi:10.1111/j.1743-4580.2010.00272.x

Protégé. (2012). Protégé Editor and Knowledge Acquisition System. Author.

Protégé. (2017). Retrieved from http://protege.stanford.edu/

Pugh, D. S., Hickson, D. J., Hinings, C. R., & Turner, C. (1969). The context of organization structures. *Administrative Science Quarterly, 14*(1), 91–114. doi:10.2307/2391366

Pun, K. F., & Nathai-Balkissoon, M. (2011). Integrating knowledge management into organisational learning: A review of concepts and models. *The Learning Organization, 18*(3), 203–223. doi:10.1108/09696471111123261

Putnam, R. D. (2001). *Bowling Alone*. New York: Simon and Schuster.

Qin, J. (2004). Article. *Management Information Systems Quarterly, 28*(1), 75–105. doi:10.2307/25148625

Qin, J. (2004). *Web content management*. John Wiley & Sons.

Raeth, P., Smolnik, S., Urbach, N., & Zimmer, C. (2009). Towards assessing the success of social software in corporate environments. *AMCIS 2009 Proceedings*. Retrieved from http://aisel.aisnet.org/amcis2009/662

Ragan Communications and NASDAQ. (2013). *Structuring a social media team*. Raglan Communications.

Rahardjo, E., Mirchandani, D., & Joshi, K. (2007). E-government functionality and website features: A case study of Indonesia. *Journal of Global Information Technology Management, 10*(1), 31–50. doi:10.1080/1097198X.2007.10856437

Rahman, M. A., Raihan, A., & Nakka, R. (2014, October-December). Emerging Information Technology and Knowledge Management Capacity for Nonprofit Organizations. *International Journal of Public Administration in the Digital Age, 1*(4), 52–69. doi:10.4018/ijpada.2014100104

Ramaprasad, A., Sánchez-Ortiz, A., & Syn, T. (2015). *An ontology of egovernment.* Paper presented at the International Conference on Electronic Government.

Reddick, C. G., & Aikins, S. K. (2012). Web 2.0 Technologies and Democratic Governance: Political, Policy and Management Implications. New York, NY: Springer.

Reddick, C. (2005). Citizen-Initiated Contacts with Government: Comparing Phones and Websites. *Journal of E-Government, 2*(1), 27–53. doi:10.1300/J399v02n01_03

Reddick, C. (2010). Comparing citizens' use of e-government to alternative service channels. *International Journal of Electronic Government Research, 6*(June), 54–67. doi:10.4018/jegr.2010040104

Reddick, C. G. (2014). Citizens and Mobile Government Adoption: A Comparison of Activities and Uses. *International Journal of Civic Engagement and Social Change, 1*(1), 13–26. doi:10.4018/ijcesc.2014010102

Reddick, C. G., & Ponomariov, B. (2013). The Effect of Individuals' Organization Affiliation on their Internet Donations. *Nonprofit and Voluntary Sector Quarterly, 42*(6), 1197–1223. doi:10.1177/0899764012452670

Reddick, C., & Anthopoulos, L. (2014). Interactions with e-government, new digital media and traditional channel choices: citizen-initiated factors. *Transforming Government: People. Process and Policy, 8*(3), 398–419. doi:10.1108/TG-01-2014-0001

Reddick, C., & Turner, M. (2012). Channel choice and public service delivery in Canada: Comparing e-government to traditional service delivery. *Government Information Quarterly, 29*(1), 1–11. doi:10.1016/j.giq.2011.03.005

Regan, T. T. J. (2011). *Social media as a branding tool for non-profit organisations*. BA in marketing & management communications, Aarhus School of Business, May 2011. Available online at: http://pure.au.dk/portal/files/38823160/36294202.pdf

Rehman, M., Kamal, M., & Esichaikul, V. (2016). Adoption of e-Government Services in Pakistan: A Comparative Study Between Online and Offline Users. *Information Systems Management*, *33*(3), 248–267. doi:10.1080/10580530.2016.1188570

Relyea, H. C. (2002). E-gov: Introduction and overview. *Government Information Quarterly*, *19*(1), 9–35. doi:10.1016/S0740-624X(01)00096-X

Rezaee, Z., Sharbatoghlie, A., Elam, R., & McMickle, P. L. (2002). Continuous auditing: Building automated auditing capability. *Auditing*, *21*(1), 147–163. doi:10.2308/aud.2002.21.1.147

Rezaee, Z., & Turner, J. L. (2002). XBRL-based financial reporting: Challenges and opportunities for government accountants. *Journal of Government Financial Management*, *51*(2), 16–22.

Robinson, L. (2013). Is Digital Health Technology Empowering Patients? *Journal of Medical Radiation Sciences*, *60*(3), 79–80. doi:10.1002/jmrs.20 PMID:26229613

Robson, C. (2002). *Real world research*. Oxford, UK: Blackwell Publishing.

Rocheleau, B. (2000). Prescriptions for Public-Sector Information Management A Review, Analysis, and Critique. *American Review of Public Administration*, *30*(4), 414–435. doi:10.1177/02750740022064759

Rodrigues, G., Sarabdeen, J. & Balasubramanian, S. (2016). *Factors that Influence Consumer Adoption of E-government Services in the UAE: A UTAUT Model Perspective*. Academic Press.

Ronaghan, S. A. (2002). *Benchmarking E-government: A Global Perspective. Assessing the Progress of the UN Member States*. United Nations. Retrieved October 8, 2017 from https://publicadministration.un.org/egovkb/Portals/egovkb/Documents/un/English.pdf

Roohani, S., Furusho, Y., & Koizumi, M. (2009). XBRL: Improving transparency and monitoring functions of corporate governance. *International Journal of Disclosure and Governance*, *6*(4), 355–369. doi:10.1057/jdg.2009.17

Rose, W. R., & Grant, G. G. (2010). Critical issues pertaining to the planning and implementation of e-government initiatives. *Government Information Quarterly*, *27*(1), 26–33. doi:10.1016/j.giq.2009.06.002

Rowlands, D. (2012). *National eHealth Record Systems – The Singapore Experience*. Retrieved September 11, 2017, from https://www.pulseitmagazine.com.au/index.php?option=com_content&view=article&id=1139:guest-editorial-national-ehealth-record-systems-the-singapore-experience&catid=16:australian-ehealth&Itemid=327

Roy, J. (2009). E-government and integrated service delivery in Canada: The Province of Nova Scotia as a case study. *International Journal of Electronic Governance*, *2*(2/3), 223–238. doi:10.1504/IJEG.2009.029131

Saeed, S., Rohde, M., & Wulf, V. (2008). A framework towards IT appropriation in voluntary organizations. *International Journal of Knowledge and Learning*, *4*(5), 438–451. doi:10.1504/IJKL.2008.022062

Safety and Health Practitioner. (2017). *Poor OSH costing world roughly €2680bn a year*. Retrieved from https://www.shponline.co.uk/poor-osh-costing-world-roughly-e2680bn-year

Sandia National Laboratories. (2016). *Comparison of State-Funded Technology Maturation Programs*. Retrieved from http://prod.sandia.gov/techlib/access-control.cgi/2016/1612489.pdf

Sang, S., Lee, J., & Lee, J. (2009). E-government adoption in ASEAN: The case of Cambodia. *Internet Research, 19*(5), 517–534. doi:10.1108/10662240910998869

Santos, J. (2003). E-service quality: A model of virtual service quality dimensions. *Managing Service Quality, 13*(3), 233–246. doi:10.1108/09604520310476490

Santoso, H., Zeniarja, J., Luthfiarta, A., & Wijaya, B. (2016). An Ontological Crawling Approach for Improving Information Aggregation over eGovernment Websites. *Journal of Computational Science, 12*(9), 455–463. doi:10.3844/jcssp.2016.455.463

Sapienza, P., & Zingales, L. (2012). A Trust Crisis. *International Review of Finance, 12*(2), 123–131. doi:10.1111/j.1468-2443.2012.01152.x

Sarantis, D., Charalabidis, Y., & Askounis, D. (2011). A goal-driven management framework for electronic government transformation projects implementation. *Government Information Quarterly, 28*(1), 117–128. doi:10.1016/j.giq.2009.10.006

Saxton, G. D., & Guo, C. (2014). Online stakeholder targeting and the acquisition of social media capital. *International Journal of Nonprofit and Voluntary Sector Marketing, 19*(4), 286–300. doi:10.1002/nvsm.1504

Saxton, G. D., Niyirora, J. N., Guo, C., & Waters, R. D. (2015). # AdvocatingForChange: The Strategic Use of Hashtags in Social Media Advocacy. *Advances in Social Work, 16*(1), 154–169.

Saxton, G. D., & Wang, L. (2014). The social network effect: The determinants of giving through social media. *Nonprofit and Voluntary Sector Quarterly, 43*(5), 850–868. doi:10.1177/0899764013485159

Saxton, G. D., & Waters, R. D. (2014). What do stakeholder like on Facebook? examining public reactions to nonprofit organizations' informational, promotional, and community-building messages. *Journal of Public Relations Research, 26*(3), 280–299. doi:10.1080/1062726X.2014.908721

Schmidthuber, L., & Hilgers, D. (2017). Browse or Brush? An Exploration of Citizen-Government Interaction in the Municipal Realm. *Proceedings of the 50th Hawaii International Conference on System Science (HICSS-50).*

Schradie, J. (2011). The digital production gap: The digital divide and Web 2.0 collide. *Poetics, 39*(2), 145–168. doi:10.1016/j.poetic.2011.02.003

Schultz, F., Utz, S., & Goritz, A. (2011). Is the medium the message? Perceptions of and reactions to crisis communication via twitter, blogs, and traditional media. *Public Relations Review, 37*(1), 20–27. doi:10.1016/j.pubrev.2010.12.001

Schwab, K. (Ed.). (2013). *The global competitiveness report 2013-2014: Full data edition.* World Economic Forum. Retrieved September 11, 2017, from http://www3.weforum.org/docs/WEF_GlobalCompetitivenessReport_2013-14.pdf

Sekiya, N. (2012). The Great East Japan Earthquake and social media [in Japanese]. *Journal of Disaster Information Studies, 12*, 29–36.

Sengar, A. (2015). *A study on evolving perspectives of rural marketing* (Unpublished doctoral dissertation). Indian Institute of Technology, Roorkee, India.

Sewake, G. (2015). *The Business of Connecting Through Technology: Millenials.* Published March 12, 2015 online. Retrieved December 19, 2017, from https://extension.unh.edu/articles/Business-Connecting-through-Technology-Millennials

Sharma V., Joshi K., & Agrawal R. (2014). Empowering Women through Social Entrepreneurship. *Indian Management-The Journal of AIMA, 53*(4), 58-63.

Sharma, V. (n.d.a). *Enhancing the reach of the Health-Care with the perspective of Affordability for the Poor & Profitability for the Provider A Proposition with special reference to Uttar Pradesh- A State in India.* Health Care for the Poor in Asia Workshop in Network of Asia-Pacific Schools and Institutes of Public Administration and Governance (NAPSIPAG) Annual Conference 2005, Beijing, China.

Sharma, V. (n.d.b). *Innovations in Public Service and Rural market Development in India to achieve a Harmonious Society.* Innovations in governance and public service to achieve a harmonious society workshop in Network of Asia-Pacific Schools and Institutes of Public Administration and Governance (NAPSIPAG) Annual Conference 2005, Beijing, China.

Sharma, V. (n.d.c). *Health for All Through Affordability and Profitability With Public Spiritual Partnership.* Retrieved from http://www.napsipag.org/PDF/VINAY%20SHARMA.pdf

Sharma, V., Joshi, K., & Agrawal, R. (2015). *Mobility for aspirations while aspiring for not moving----Understanding aspirations and mobility of the Forest users and the dwellers of the North-Western Himalayan region of India.* Paper presented at the annual conference of the HDCA, Tokyo, Japan.

Sharma, V., Mishra, H. S., Joshi, K. K., & Agrawal, R. (2016). *Disasters, Diversity, Disparity, Discrimination and Vulnerability.* Paper presented at the annual conference of the HDCA, Tokyo, Japan.

Sharma, V. (2009). *Affordability For The Poor And Profitability For The Provider: Provision of Health for the Rural and the Poor Population of the world with special reference to Uttar Pradesh in India.* VDM Verlag.

Sharma, V. (2009). Motivation absorbs Magnitude. *Chinese Public Administration Review, 6*(1/2), 1–8. doi:10.22140/cpar.v6i1/2.82

Sheng, L., & Lingling, L. (2011, November). Application of Ontology in E-Government. In *Management of e-Commerce and e-Government (ICMeCG), 2011 Fifth International Conference on.* IEEE.

Shepherd, E., Stevenson, A., & Flinn, A. (2010). Information governance, records management, and freedom of information: A study of local government authorities in England. *Government Information Quarterly, 27*(4), 337–345. doi:10.1016/j.giq.2010.02.008

Sheryazdanova, G., & Butterfield, J. (2017). E-government as an anti-corruption strategy in Kazakhstan. *Journal of Information Technology & Politics, 14*(1), 83–94. doi:10.1080/19331681.2016.1275998

Shih, W., & Allen, M. (2006). Working with generation-D: Adopting and adapting to cultural learning and change. *Library Management, 28*(1/2), 89–100. doi:10.1108/01435120710723572

Sihi, D. (2017). The influence of leadership and strategic emphasis on social media use of regional nonprofit organizations. *International Journal of Public Administration in the Digital Age, 4*(1), 1–18. doi:10.4018/IJPADA.2017010101

Singapore Medical Council. (2016). *Ethical Code and Ethical Guidelines.* Retrieved September 29, 2017, from http://www.healthprofessionals.gov.sg/content/dam/hprof/smc/docs/guidelines/2016%20SMC%20Ethical%20Code%20and%20Ethical%20Guidelines%20-%20(13Sep16).pdf

Singapore Personal Access. (2017). *Frequently Asked Questions.* Retrieved October 11, 2017, from http://www.ifaq.gov.sg/SINGPASS/apps/fcd_faqmain.aspx#FAQ_130407

Sinha, P.K., Sunder, G., Bendale, P., Mantri, M., & Dande, A. (2013). *Electronic Health Record: Standards, Coding Systems, Frameworks and Infrastructure.* Wiley-IEEE.

Siskos, E., Askounis, D., & Psarras, J. (2014). Multicriteria decision support for global e-government evaluation. *Omega, 46*, 51–63. doi:10.1016/j.omega.2014.02.001

Skocpol, T., & Fiorina, M. (Eds.). (1999). *Civic engagement in American democracy*. Brookings Institution Press.

Sloan, L., Morgan, J., Housley, W., Williams, M., Edwards, A., Burnap, P., & Rana, O. (2013). Knowing the Tweeters: Deriving Sociologically Relevant Demographics from Twitter. *Sociological Research Online*, *18*(3), 1–11. doi:10.5153ro.3001

Smart Nation Singapore. (2017a). *Telehealth: Integrated and Seamless Healthcare Services at Home*. Retrieved September 14, 2017, from https://www.smartnation.sg/initiatives/Health/telehealth-integrated-and-seamless-healthcare-services-at-home

Smart Nation Singapore. (2017b). *Enablers*. Retrieved September 14, 2017, from https://www.smartnation.sg/about-smart-nation/enablers

Smith, A. G. (2001). Applying evaluation criteria to New Zealand government websites. *International Journal of Information Management*, *21*(2), 137–149. doi:10.1016/S0268-4012(01)00006-8

Solnit, R. (2009). *A paradise built in hell: The extraordinary communities that arise in disaster*. New York, NY: Penguin Books.

Soon, C. (2013). Net technologies, net gain: An institutional and micro-structural approach to understanding technology use for collective action. CeDEM13.Conference for E-Democracy and Open Government, 229-240.

Sorias, L. (2015, May 13). Diversification, labour solution needed to fix the economy. *Trinidad Express*. Retrieved from http://www.trinidadexpress.com/article/20150513/business/150519865

Sotiropoulos, A. D., & Karamagioli, E. (2005). *Greek Civil Society: The Long road to maturity*. Oxford, UK: Oxford University Press. Available online at http://www.civicus.org/new/media/CSI_Greece_Executive_Summary.pdf

Souer, J., Honders, P., Versendaal, J., & Brinkkemper, S. (2008). A Framework for Web Content Management System Operations and Maintenance. *Journal of Digital Information Management*, *6*(4), 342–347.

Sourouni, A.-M., Kourlimpinis, G., Mouzakitis, S., & Askounis, D. (2010). Towards the government transformation: An ontology-based government knowledge repository. *Computer Standards & Interfaces*, *32*(1), 44–53. doi:10.1016/j.csi.2009.06.002

Soverchia, M. (2015). How Can Technology Improve Government Financial Transparency? The Answer of the eXtensible Business Reporting Language (XBRL). *International Journal of Public Administration in the Digital Age*, *2*(1), 24–38. doi:10.4018/ijpada.2015010102

Spante, M., Axelsson, A.-S., & Schroeder, R. (2006). The Good Inequality: Supporting Group-Work in Shared Virtual Environments. In R. Schroeder & A.-S. Axelsson (Eds.), *Avatars at Work and Play* (Vol. 34, pp. 151–166). Berlin: Springer-Verlag. doi:10.1007/1-4020-3898-4_7

Spencer, T. (2002, August). The potential of the internet for Non-Profit organizations. *First Monday*, *7*(8). doi:10.5210/fm.v7i8.976

Spiro, E. S., Fitzhugh, S., Sutton, J., Pierski, N., Greczek, M., & Butts, C. T. (2012). Rumoring during extreme events. In *Proceedings of the 3rd Annual ACM Web Science Conference on - WebSci '12* (pp. 275–283). New York: ACM Press. 10.1145/2380718.2380754

Staiou, E. R. (2017). *From electronic governance and the participatory web to self-organised social solidarity initiatives and their digital communication policy: the Greek case* (Doctoral Thesis). Available online in Greek: https://www.didaktorika.gr/eadd/handle/10442/40314?locale=en)

Staiou, E. R., & Gouscos, D. (2014, October-December). Self-organized social solidarity (SoSS) initiatives in Greece: Exploring their scope and their relationship to online media. *International Journal of Public Administration in the Digital Age, 1*(4), 21–43. doi:10.4018/ijpada.2014100102

State of California, Department of Finance. (n.d.). *California State Budget, 2017-2018*. Retrieved from http://www.ebudget.ca.gov/

State of Hawai'i, Department of Budget and Finance. (2016). *The FB 2017-19 Executive Biennium Budget*. Retrieved from https://budget.hawaii.gov/wp-content/uploads/2016/12/FB-17-19-BIB-FINAL-12.15.16.pdf

State of New Jersey, Department of the Treasury. (n.d.). *Appropriations Handbook 2017-2018*. Retrieved from http://www.nj.gov/treasury/omb/publications/18approp/FullAppropAct.pdf

State of New Jersey, Office of the Governor. (2016). *NJ State Budget Summary*. Retrieved from http://www.nj.gov/treasury/omb/publications/16bib/BIB.pdf

Statistics Denmark. (2014). *Annual ICT Household Survey 2014*. Author.

Steinmann, R., Häusler, E., Klettner, S., Schmidt, M., & Lin, Y. (2013). Gender Dimensions in UGC and VGI: A Desk-Based Study. *Proceeding of GI_Forum 2013 – Creating the GISociety*, 355–364.

Stephens, M. (2013). Gender and the GeoWeb: Divisions in the production of user-generated cartographic information. *GeoJournal, 78*(6), 981–996. doi:10.100710708-013-9492-z

Stier, S. (2015). Political determinants of e-government performance revisited: Comparing democracies and autocracies. *Government Information Quarterly, 32*(3), 270–278. doi:10.1016/j.giq.2015.05.004

Strauss, A. L., & Corbin, J. M. (1990). Open coding. In *Basics of qualitative research: Grounded theory procedures and techniques* (pp. 101–121). SAGE Publications.

Stullich, S., Morgan, I., & Schak, O. (2016). *State and Local Expenditures on Corrections and Education*. Retrieved from https://www2.ed.gov/rschstat/eval/other/expenditures-corrections-education/brief.pdf

Suart, J. C. (2012). *A guide to the changes sweeping non-profit marketing and communications*. Available online at: http://volunteeralberta.ab.ca/varc/wp-content/documents/The_Revolution:_A_Guide_to_the_Changes_Sweeping_Non-profit_Marketing_and_Communications_09-10-2012_05.59.59.pdf

Sui, D., Goodchild, M., & Elwood, S. (n.d.). *Volunteered Geographic Information, the Exa fl ood, and the Growing Digital Divide*. Academic Press.

Sunstein, C. R. (2001). *Republic.com*. Princeton, NJ: Princeton University Press.

Surienty, L., Hong, K. T., & Hung, D. K. M. (2011). Occupational safety and health (OSH) in SMEs in Malaysia: A preliminary investigation. *Journal of Global Entrepreneurship, 1*(1), 65–75.

Sutton, H. (2017). Follow five steps to create elegant and accessible design. *Disability Compliance for Higher Education, 22*(6), 5-5. doi:10.1002/dhe.30259

Svensson, P. G., Mahoney, T. Q., & Hambrick, M. E. (2015). Twitter as a communication tool for nonprofits: A study of sport-for-development organizations. *Nonprofit and Voluntary Sector Quarterly, 44*(6), 1086–1106. doi:10.1177/0899764014553639

Sweetser, K. D., & Lariscy, R. W. (2008). Candidates make good friends: An analysis of candidates' uses of Facebook. *International Journal of Strategic Communication, 2*(3), 175–198. doi:10.1080/15531180802178687

Tan, B., Ling, P. S., & Cha, V. (2013). The Evolution of Singapore's Infocomm Plans: Singapore's E-government Journey from 1980 to 2007. In G. Pan (Ed.), *Dynamics of Governing IT Innovation in Singapore: A Case Book* (pp. 1–39). World Scientific. doi:10.1142/9789814417839_0001

Tan, C. H. (2002). *Singapore Financial and Business Sourcebook* (2nd ed.). Singapore: Singapore University Press.

Tan, L. T. (1995). National Patient Master Index in Singapore. *International Journal of Bio-Medical Computing*, *40*(2), 89–93. doi:10.1016/0020-7101(95)01130-7 PMID:8847128

TechCrunch. (2016). *The Government Technology Pitch*. Retrieved from https://techcrunch.com/contributor/luke-fretwell/

Teerling, M., & Pieterson, W. (2010). Multichannel marketing: An experiment on guiding citizens to the electronic channels. *Government Information Quarterly*, *27*(1), 98–107. doi:10.1016/j.giq.2009.08.003

Teerling, M., & Pieterson, W. (2011). How to improve e-government use: An empirical examination of multichannel marketing instruments. *Information Polity*, *16*(2), 171–187. doi:10.3233/IP-2011-0213

The Danish Government, Danish Regions, & Local Government Denmark. (2011). *The Digital Path to Future Welfare eGovernment Strategy 2011-2015*. Author.

The Danish Government. (2011). *The Danish National E-government Strategy*. Author.

The Danish National Audit Office. (2016). *Rigsrevisionens notat om beretning om etablering af Udbetaling Danmark*. Retrieved from http://www.rigsrevisionen.dk/media/2104270/305-16.pdf

The Japan Association of Charitable Organizations. (2012). *Current status of general incorporated association and general incorporated foundation*. Retrieved July 24, 2015 from http://www.nopodas.com/contents.asp?code=10001005&idx=100933

The Japan Institute for Labour Policy and Training (JILPT). (2007). Diversity of Revenues and Organizational Autonomy: Impact of Commissioned Projects by the Public Sector (in Japanese). In *Road to Development of Nonprofit Employment: Human Resources, Finance, and Legal Institutions*. Report on Labour Policy Research, No.82. Retrieved April 29, 2015, from http://www.jil.go.jp/institute/reports/2007/082.html

The PEW Charitable Trust. (2014). *Pew-MacArthur Results First Initiative. Evidence-Based Policymaking: A Guide for Effective Government*. Retrieved from http://www.pewtrusts.org/en/research-and-analysis/reports/2014/11/evidence-based-policymaking-a-guide-for-effective-government

The Sentencing Project. (2017). *Fact Sheet: Trends In US Corrections*. Retrieved from: https://sentencingproject.org/wp-content/uploads/2016/01/Trends-in-US-Corrections.pdf

Thomas, M., & Redmond, R. (2011). A Framework for Analyzing User Interaction in Digital Spaces. In V. Sugumaran (Ed.), Intelligent, Adaptive and Reasoning Technologies: New Developments and Applications (pp. 23-25). Hershey, PA: IGI Global.

Thomas, M., Redmond, R., Yoon, V., & Singh, R. (2005). A semantic approach to monitor business process. *Communications of the ACM*, *48*(12), 55–59. doi:10.1145/1101779.1101809

TODAY. (2017 May 30). *Healthcare Sector to Ride Digital Revolution Intelligently*. Retrieved September 15, 2017, from https://www.gov.sg/news/content/today-online-healthcare-sector-to-ride-digital-revolution-intelligently

Toh, E. M. (2017, May 30). From Wearable Sensors to Robots, Home Care to Get Tech Boost. *TODAY*. Retrieved September 15, 2017, from http://www.todayonline.com/singapore/healthcare-sector-ride-digital-revolution-intelligently-gan-kim-yong

Treem, J. W., & Leonardi, P. M. (2012). Social Media Use in Organizations: Exploring the Affordances of Visibility, Editability, Persistence, and Association. *Communication Yearbook*, *36*, 143-189. Available at SSRN: http://ssrn.com/abstract=2129853

Tsaliki, L. (2010). Technologies of Political Mobilization and Civil Society in Greece. *Convergence (London)*, *16*(2), 151–161. doi:10.1177/1354856509357675

Tsoumas, B., & Gritzalis, D. (2006). *Towards an ontology-based security management.* Paper presented at the Advanced Information Networking and Applications, 2006. AINA 2006. 20th International Conference on. 10.1109/AINA.2006.329

Tummers, L., & Rocco, P. (2015). Serving clients when the server crashes: How frontline workers cope with E-government challenges. *Public Administration Review*, *75*(6), 817–827. doi:10.1111/puar.12379

Turner, M. (2013). *It takes a portfolio to make evidence-based policy*. Urban Institute.

U.S. Department of Justice, Bureau of Justice Statistics. (2014). *Prisoners in 2014*. Retrieved from https://www.bjs.gov/content/pub/pdf/p14.pdf

Underwood, A. (2012). Gender targeting for Promoted Products now available. *Twitter*. Retrieved June 9, 2015, from https://blog.twitter.com/2012/gender-targeting-for-promoted-products-now-available

United Nations Department of Economic and Social Affairs. (2014). *UN e-government survey 2014: E-government for the future we want.* Retrieved August 7, 2014, from http://unpan3.un.org/egovkb/Reports/UN-E-Government-Survey-2014

United Nations Department of Economic and Social Affairs. (2016). *UN e-government survey 2016: E-government in support of sustainable development.* Retrieved September 11, 2017, from http://workspace.unpan.org/sites/Internet/Documents/UNPAN97453.pdf

United Nations Development Programme. (2017). *Decent work and economic growth.* Retrieved September 17, 2017, from http://www.undp.org/content/undp/en/home/sustainable-development-goals/goal-8-decent-work-and-economic-growth.html

United Nations General Assembly. (2015). *Outcome document of the high-level meeting of the General Assembly on the overall review of the implementation of the outcomes of the World Summit on the Information Society.* A/RES/70/125.

United Nations. (2013). *The role of philanthropic organizations in the post-2015 development agenda setting*. New York: United Nations.

United Nations. (2017). *Goal 10: Reduce inequality within and among countries.* Retrieved September 17, 2017, from http://www.un.org/sustainabledevelopment/inequality/

United States Department of Labor. (n.d.). *U.S. department of labor e-government strategic plan.* Retrieved August 7, 2014, from http://www.dol.gov/_sec/e_government_plan/p41-43_appendixe.htm

University of California. (2008). *Building Administrative Efficiency for the University of California.* Retrieved from http://www.ucop.edu/efficiency/process/reports/building-administrative-efficiency.pdf

Utz, S., Schultz, F., & Glocka, S. (2013). Crisis communication online: How medium, crisis type and emotions affected public reactions in the Fukushima Daiichi nuclear disaster. *Public Relations Review*, *39*(1), 40–46. doi:10.1016/j.pubrev.2012.09.010

Valdés, G., Solar, M., Astudillo, H., Iribarren, M., Concha, G., & Visconti, M. (2011). Conception, development and implementation of an e-Government maturity model in public agencies. *Government Information Quarterly*, *28*(2), 176–187. doi:10.1016/j.giq.2010.04.007

Valentinetti, D., & Rea, M. A. (2013). XBRL for financial reporting: Evidence on Italian GAAP versus IFRS. *Accounting Perspectives, 12*(3), 237–259. doi:10.1111/1911-3838.12008

van de Wijngaert, L., Pieterson, W., & Teerling, M. (2011). Influencing citizen behavior: Experiences from multichannel marketing pilot projects. *International Journal of Information Management, 31*(5), 415–419. doi:10.1016/j.ijinfomgt.2010.12.009

Van den Boer, Y., Pieterson, W., Arendsen, R., & De Groot, M. (2014). Source and Channel Choices in Business-to-Government Service Interactions: A Vignette Study. *Electronic Government: Proceedings of the 13th IFIP WG 8.5 International Conference, EGOV 2014*. Retrieved from http://link.springer.com/chapter/10.1007/978-3-662-44426-9_10

van den Boer, Y., Arendsen, R., & Pieterson, W. (2016). In search of information: Investigating source and channel choices in business-to-government service interactions. *Government Information Quarterly, 33*(1), 40–52. doi:10.1016/j.giq.2015.11.010

Van der Aalst, W. M. P., & Kumar, A. (2003). XML–Based Schema Definition for Support of Interorganizational Workflow. *Information Systems Research, 14*(1), 23–46. doi:10.1287/isre.14.1.23.14768

Vandic, D., Van Dam, J.-W., & Frasincar, F. (2012). Faceted product search powered by the Semantic Web. *Decision Support Systems, 53*(3), 425–437. doi:10.1016/j.dss.2012.02.010

Veil, S. R., Buehner, T., & Palenchar, M. J. (2011). A work-in-process literature review: Incorporating social media in risk and crisis communication. *Journal of Contingencies and Crisis Management, 19*(2), 110–122. doi:10.1111/j.1468-5973.2011.00639.x

Ventureneer. (2010). *Nonprofits and Social Media: It ain't optional.* Available online at: http://ventureneer.com/node/2285

Verspagen, B. (2005). Innovation and Economic Growth. In J. Fagerberg, D. C. Mowery, & R. R. Nelson (Eds.), *The Oxford Handbook of Innovation*. Oxford, UK: Oxford University Press.

Vijaya, K., Chan, S. P., Ho, H. P. C., Lim, Y. Y. L., & Lim, R. (2006). HPB Online: An Electronic Health Education Portal in Singapore. *Singapore Medical Journal, 47*(1), 8–13. PMID:16397714

Vikas, V. (2017). ICT and disaster management: A study of the social media use in 2015 Chennai City floods. *International Journal of Public Administration in the Digital Age, 4*(3), 29–41. doi:10.4018/IJPADA.2017070103

Visser, U., Stuckenschmidt, H., Schuster, G., & Vögele, T. (2002). Ontologies for geographic information processing. *Computers & Geosciences, 28*(1), 103–117.

Vogt, S., Förster, B., & Kabst, R. (2014). Social Media and e-Participation: Challenges of Social Media for Managing Public Projects. [IJPADA]. *International Journal of Public Administration in the Digital Age, 1*(3), 85–105. doi:10.4018/ijpada.2014070105

Voida, A. (2011). *Shapeshifters in the voluntary sector: Exploring the human-centered-computing challenges of nonprofit organizations*. Available online at: http://amy.voida.com/Site/Whats_New/Entries/2011/11/10_Reflections_on_Voluntary_Sector_Research_in_the_Nov_Dec_Issue_of_Interactions_files/shapeshifters-interactions.pdf

Voida, A., Harmon, E., & Al-Ani, B. (2011). Homebrew databases: Complexities of everyday information management in nonprofit organizations. In *Proceedings of the SIGCHI Conference on Human Factors in Computing Systems*. (p. 915-924). New York, NY: ACM. 10.1145/1978942.1979078

von Alan, R. H., March, S. T., Park, J., & Ram, S. (2004). Design science in information systems research. *Management Information Systems Quarterly, 28*(1), 75–105.

Vozab, D. (2012). *Communication models of civil society organizations in Croatia. Observatorio (OBS*) Journal.*

Wall Street Journal. (2015). *Buzz, engagement, and reach performances of the Wall Street Journal on social media.* Retrieved from http://www.talkwalker.com/en/academy/academy/industries/media-publishers/social-media-analytics-for-the-wall-street-journal/

Wallace, C. (2012). Can information and communications technology enhance social quality? *The International Journal of Social Quality*, *2*(2), 98–117. doi:10.3167/IJSQ.2012.020207

Walther, F., Vogt, S., & Kabst, R. (2016). A Strategic Foresight about Future Public Service Developments from the Citizens' Perspective. *International Journal of Public Administration in the Digital Age*, *3*(1), 19–42. doi:10.4018/IJPADA.2016010102

Wangpipatwong, S., Chutimaskul, W., & Papasratorn, B. (2008). Understanding citizen's continuance intention to use e-government website: A composite view of technology acceptance model and computer self-efficacy. *The Electronic Journal of E-Government, 6*(1), 55-64.

Waters, R. D. (2008). Applying relationship management theory to the fundraising process for individual donors. *Journal of Communication Management*, *12*(1), 73–87. doi:10.1108/13632540810854244

Waters, R. D. (2009). Measuring stewardship in public relations: A test exploring impact on the fundraising relationship. *Public Relations Review*, *35*(2), 113–119. doi:10.1016/j.pubrev.2009.01.012

Waters, R. D. (2011). Redefining stewardship: Examining how Fortune 100 organizations use stewardship with virtual stakeholders. *Public Relations Review*, *37*(2), 129–136. doi:10.1016/j.pubrev.2011.02.002

Waters, R. D., Burnett, E., Lamm, A., & Lucas, J. (2009). Engaging stakeholders through social networking: How nonprofit organizations are using Facebook. *Public Relations Review*, *35*(2), 102–106. doi:10.1016/j.pubrev.2009.01.006

Waters, R. D., & Feneley, K. L. (2013). Virtual stewardship in the age of new media: Have nonprofit organizations' moved beyond Web 1.0 strategies? *International Journal of Nonprofit and Voluntary Sector Marketing*, *18*(3), 216–230. doi:10.1002/nvsm.1469

Waters, R. D., & Jamal, J. Y. (2011). Tweet, tweet, tweet: A content analysis of nonprofit organizations' Twitter updates. *Public Relations Review*, *37*(3), 321–324. doi:10.1016/j.pubrev.2011.03.002

Waters, R. D., & Jones, P. M. (2011). Using video to build an organization's identity and brand: A content analysis of nonprofit organizations' YouTube videos. *Journal of Nonprofit & Public Sector Marketing*, *23*(3), 248–268. doi:10.1080/10495142.2011.594779

Waters, R. D., & Tindall, N. T. J. (2011). Exploring the impact of American news coverage on crisis fundraising: Using media theory to explicate a new model of fundraising communication. *Journal of Nonprofit & Public Sector Marketing*, *23*(1), 20–40. doi:10.1080/10495142.2010.494875

Weare, C., Loges, W. E., & Oztas, N. (2007). Email effects on the structure of local associations: A social network analysis. *Social Science Quarterly*, *88*(1), 222–243. doi:10.1111/j.1540-6237.2007.00455.x

Weinberger, H., Te'eni, D., & Frank, A. J. (2008). Ontology-based evaluation of organizational memory. *Journal of the American Society for Information Science and Technology*, *59*(9), 1454–1468. doi:10.1002/asi.20859

Welch, E. W., Hinnant, C. C., & Moon, M. J. (2005). Linking citizen satisfaction with e-government and trust in government. *Journal of Public Administration: Research and Theory*, *3*(15), 371–391.

Westcott, S. (2007). Face time: Charities flock to social-networking Web sites to reach out to new people, spark discussion, and help raise money. *The Chronicle of Philanthropy, 19*(7).

Wilson, K., & Brownstein, J. S. (2009). Early Detection of Disease Outbreaks Using the Internet. *Canadian Medical Association Journal, 180*(8), 829–831. doi:10.1503/cmaj.1090215 PMID:19364791

Wimmer, M. A. (2002). A European perspective towards online one-stop government: The eGOV project. *Electronic Commerce Research and Applications, 1*(1), 92–103. doi:10.1016/S1567-4223(02)00008-X

Wirtz, B. W., & Langer, P. F. (2016). Public Multichannel Management – an Integrated Framework of Off- and Online Multichannel Government Services. *Public Organization Review*. doi:10.100711115-016-0356-0

Woon, B. (2014). Singapore: Health Database in an IT Society. Japan Medical Association Journal. 57(4), 212-5.

World Bank. (2011). *Definition of e-government*. Retrieved March 9, 2014, from http://web.worldbank.org/WBSITE/EXTERNAL/TOPICS/EXTINFORMATIONANDCOMMUNICATIONANDTECHNOLOGIES/EXTEGOVERNMENT/0,contentMDK:20507153~menuPK:702592~pagePK:148956~piPK:216618~theSitePK:702586,00.html

World Health Organization. (2004). *eHealth: Report by Secretariat*. Retrieved August 25, 2017, from http://www.who.int/healthacademy/media/en/eHealth_EB-en.pdf?ua=1

World Health Organization. (2005a). *Connecting for Health: Global Vision, Local Insight*. Retrieved August 25, 2017, from http://www.who.int/ehealth/publications/WSISReport_Connecting_for_Health.pdf

World Health Organization. (2005b). *eHealth*. Retrieved August 25, 2017, from http://apps.who.int/iris/bitstream/10665/20378/1/WHA58_28-en.pdf?ua=1

World Health Organization. (2006). *eHealth Tools & Services: Needs of the Member States*. Retrieved August 25, 2017, from http://apps.who.int/iris/bitstream/10665/69226/1/WHO_EHL_06.1_eng.pdf

World Health Organization. (2017). *eHealth Resolution*. Retrieved August 25, 2017, from http://www.who.int/healthacademy/news/en/

World Summit on the Information Society. (2003). *Plan of Action*. Retrieved August 25, 2017, from https://www.itu.int/dms_pub/itu-s/md/03/wsis/doc/S03-WSIS-DOC-0005!!PDF-E.pdf

World Wide Web Consortium. (2012). *Web Accessibility Initiative*. Retrieved September 17, 2017, from https://www.w3.org/WAI/changedesign#skip

Wuthnow, R. (1998). *Loose Connections*. Boston: Harvard University Press.

Yamamoto, T., Hashimoto, Y., Nakamura, I., Sekiya, N., Ogasawara, M., Chiba, N., Yoshiaki, S., & Takahashi, K. (2012). Information behavior and communication anxiety on Twitter after the Great East Japan Earthquake: Web survey of Twitter user in Kanto Region (in Japanese). *Research Survey Reports in Information Studies (Interfaculty Initiative in Information Studies, the University of Tokyo), 28*, 115-160.

Yamauchi, N. (2000). Japanese nonprofit sector in comparative perspective. *Global Economic Review: Perspectives on East Asian Economies and Industries, 29*(4), 106–128. doi:10.1080/12265080008449808

Yamauchi, N., Shimizu, H., Sokolowski, S. W., & Salamon, L. M. (2004). Japan. In L. M. Salamon & H. K. Anheier (Eds.), *Global Civil Society: Dimension of the Nonprofit Sector* (Vol. 2). West Hartford, CT: Kumarian Press.

Yeo, S. J. (2015 March 17). *HDB Elderly Alert System Well-received in Test-bed. Straits Times*. Retrieved September 14, 2017, from http://www.straitstimes.com/singapore/housing/hdb-elderly-alert-system-well-received-in-test-bed

Yeo, T., & Gaw, B. (2013). *Developments in Singapore's Healthcare Regulatory Landscape*. Retrieved September 29, 2017, from http://www.drewnapier.com/DrewASPX/media/assets/Publications/Drew-Napier-ALB-Nov-Life-Sciences-issue-Developments-in-Singapore-s-Healthcare-Regulatory-Landscape.pdf

Yildiz, M. (2007). E-government research: Reviewing the literature, limitations, and ways forward. *Government Information Quarterly*, *24*(3), 646–665. doi:10.1016/j.giq.2007.01.002

Yin, R. K. (2003). *Case Study Research Design and Methods*. Retrieved from http://www.madeira-edu.pt/LinkClick.aspx?fileticket=Fgm4GJWVTRs%3D&tabid=3004

Yin, R. K. (2014). Case study Research design and methods. *Sage (Atlanta, Ga.)*.

Yoon, H., Zo, H., & Ciganek, A. P. (2011). Does XBRL adoption reduce information asymmetry? *Journal of Business Research*, *64*(2), 157–163. doi:10.1016/j.jbusres.2010.01.008

Young, J. A. (2017). Facebook, Twitter, and blogs: The adoption and utilization of social media in nonprofit human service organizations. *Human Service Organizations, Management, Leadership & Governance*, *41*(1), 44–57. doi:10.1080/23303131.2016.1192574

Zawaideh, F. (2017). Acceptance of E-Government Services among Jordanian Citizen. *International Journal of Recent Advances in Multidisciplinary Research*, *4*(2), 2348–2351.

Zelenika, I., & Pearce, J. M. (2013). The Internet and other ICTs as tools and catalysts for sustainable development: Innovation for 21st century. *Information Development*, *29*(3), 217–232. doi:10.1177/0266666912465742

Zhao, F., & Khan, M. S. (2013). An Empirical Study of E-Government Service Adoption: Culture and Behavioral Intention. *International Journal of Public Administration*, *36*(10), 710–722. doi:10.1080/01900692.2013.791314

Zhu, Q., Du, J., & Han, X. (2007). *The establishment and application of evaluation criteria systems for Chinese egovernment websites*. Paper presented at the Wireless Communications, International Conference on Networking and Mobile Computing, 2007. WiCom 2007.

Ziemba, P., Jankowski, J., Wątróbski, J., & Becker, J. (2015). *Knowledge management in website quality evaluation domain. In Computational collective intelligence* (pp. 75–85). Springer. doi:10.1007/978-3-319-24306-1_8

Zorn, T. E., Grant, S., & Henderson, A. (2013). Strengthening resource mobilization chains: Developing the social media competencies of community and voluntary organizations in New Zealand. *Voluntas*, *24*(3), 666–687. doi:10.100711266-012-9265-1

# About the Contributors

**Ankit Dhamija** is working as an Assistant Professor of Information Systems at Amity Business School, Amity University Haryana since Oct'2012. Before that, he has worked with several affiliated institutes of Guru Gobind Singh Indraprastha University, New Delhi and Maharishi Dayanand University, Rohtak. He is a double post graduate in MCA and M.Tech(IT) and a graduate with B.Com (H). Currently he is enrolled as a Ph.D research scholar in Engineering & Technology Department at Amity University Haryana. His areas of interests are Cloud computing security issues, network security and ecommerce payment systems security. During his teaching experience of almost ten years, he has published and presented several research papers and articles in various International Journals and National & International conferences of repute. His next immediate goal is to produce a quality research in his research area of Change Impact Analysis in Software Maintenance. His other areas of interest are Cloud Computing Security, Ecommerce, MIS, Mcommerce, Data Mining, Security issues, epayment, etc.

**Deepika Dhamija** is working as an Assistant Professor at Amity College of Commerce, Amity University Gurgaon. She has more than seven years of teaching experience at both undergraduate and postgraduate level. Her areas of interest are Management Information Systems, e-commerce, Mobile Banking and Software Testing.

**Love Ekenberg**, Ph.D., is a professor of Computer and Systems Sciences, Stockholm University and researcher at the International Institute of Applied Systems Analysis, IIASA, in Austria. He has primarily been investigating risk and decision analysis; i.e., the development of processes, products and methodologies within these areas in various industrial and public sectors.

**Andrea Fradeani**, Ph.D., is Associate Professor of Accounting and Business Administration at the Department of Economics and Law of the University of Macerata (Italy). He teaches courses on Auditing and Financial Accounting and his main research fields concern financial accounting and corporate reporting, International Financial Reporting Standards, internal and external audit, digital accounting, XBRL and reporting information systems. He is author of articles and contributions published in international journals and volumes.

**Dimitris Gouscos,** PhD, is Assistant Professor in the Department of Communication and Media Studies at the National and Kapodistrian University of Athens and a Research Fellow at the Laboratory of New Technologies in Communication, Education and the Mass Media. His research interests include digital communication, electronic governance, social media and digital games. He has worked as a consultant for public sector innovation with UN ESCWA and he is editing-in-chief the International Journal of Electronic Governance.

**Karin Hansson**, Ph.D., is a researcher at the Department of Computer & System Science, Stockholm University. Her research area is online participatory processes, focusing on dynamics of inclusion/exclusion and social validation processes.

**Yu Ishida** is Associate Professor of Miyagi University Faculty of Project Design in Japan. He holds a PhD in International Public Policy from the Osaka University (Osaka, Japan) and Master of Policy Studies from the Kwansei Gakuin University (Hyogo, Japan). His research focuses on voluntary actions and behaviors of nonprofit organizations from an angle of provisioning of public service and management of public finance.

**Pernille Kræmmergaard** is the director of the Digitization Institute, and a former Professor in Information Systems. She holds a Ph.D. and a Master of Science in International Business. Her research focus is on Digital Transformation; e-government, the changing role of the IT organization, the changing role of CIOs and the organizational mindsets required to prosper in dynamic digitalized environments. She has previous published in e.g. Government Information Quarterly, MISQ Executive and has a passion for disseminating theoretical knowledge to practitioners, collaborating with practice and facilitating digital change processes in organizations.

**Sarah Maxwell** is an associate professor in the School of Economic, Political and Policy Sciences, Department of Public Affairs and Social Policy. Her research focuses nonprofit management, social media, and social policy. Dr. Maxwell holds a Ph.D. in public policy from George Mason University.

**Deborah Mohammed-Spigner**, PhD, is currently working as a research scientist in state government for a criminal justice agency and is also the grant specialist and program coordinator for federal grant programs for her agency. She is also adjunct professor of strategic management and organizational development courses within the Public Administration programs at Rutgers and Kean universities, as well as adjunct professor of political science and communications. Many years of experience in the non-profit sector in communications and administration as a government liaison and served as executive director of Common Cause, New Jersey. Her doctoral dissertation focused on Freedom of Information laws and her publications have focused on facilitating citizens' participation in government through transparency and through the expedition of technology. Presented at the Transatlantic Conference on Transparency Research in June on Pay to Play: A Framework to Evaluate Effectivenes.

**Marcia Nathai-Balkissoon** holds a B.Sc. Industrial Engineering and M.Sc Engineering Management and is currently pursuing a Ph.D. Industrial Engineering, with a focus on Occupational Safety and Health Management. Marcia's publications address topics such as Safety and Health Management, Innovation, Knowledge Management, and Teaching and Learning. A Registered Engineer in Trinidad and Tobago, Marcia has memberships in the Association of Professional Engineers of Trinidad and Tobago as well as the Safety Council of Trinidad and Tobago, and is a senior member of the Institute of Industrial and Systems Engineers.

**Aya Okada** is Associate Professor of Kanazawa University Institute of Liberal Arts and Science in Japan. She holds a PhD in Public and International Affairs and Master of International Development from the University of Pittsburgh, as well as an MA in Social Sciences from Hitotsubashi University (Tokyo, Japan). Her research focuses communication process used by nonprofits as they seek to sustain their voluntary support in societies undergoing economic, social, and political change.

**Brian E. Porter** has thirty years as a Corporate Controller. Currently full time faculty at Montclair State University in Management Department in the School of Business, teaching Applied Business Strategy. He has owned and managed e-commerce company. He has also conducted Marketing & Business consulting. Also, he has a wide and diverse range of business experience in Accounting/Finance & Management. Graduated with his MBA from Montclair State University in 2014. He is one of five graduate students selected by Department Chair and professors in Management Department to participate in pilot program to conduct business and market analysis for local businesses. Program became part of graduate school curriculum.

**Christian Østergaard Madsen** is an assistant professor at the IT University of Copenhagen. He holds a Ph.D. from the ITU University of Copenhagen. His research focuses on service design, citizens' channel choice and multichannel management in cross-organizational settings. He has published in Government Information Quarterly, International Journal of Public Administration in the Digital Age, the Electronic Journal of e-Government and conference proceedings for the IFIP Electronic Government conference.

**Kit Fai Pun** is presently Professor of Industrial Engineering of the Faculty of Engineering at The University of the West Indies. He is a Registered Professional Engineer in Australia, Europe, Hong Kong, and The Republic of Trinidad and Tobago. His research interests and activities include industrial engineering, engineering management, quality systems, performance measurement, innovation, and information systems.

**Anita Sengar** is Assistant Professor at Department of Marketing, School of Business, University of Petroleum & Energy studies, Dehradun. She did Ph.D from IIT Roorkee, has been a researcher in the field of rural marketing and qualitative research having 12 research papers to her credit in reputed directories like Springer, Elsevier, Inderceince etc. She has done her B.E. (IT) followed by MBA (Marketing) and has been a gold medalist in academics. She did a project on Co creation in Social Entrepreneurship: Partnering with Copenhagen Business School, Copenhagen, Denmark and FGV, Sao Paulo, Brazil and has also been awarded Noel Deerr Gold Medal Award of the Year 2012–13 at the 71st Annual Convention of STAI at Hyderabad. She has also presented 21 research papers in conferences organized nationally and internationally. She has a teaching experience of more than eight years.

**Vinay Sharma** is currently an Associate Professor at the Department of Management Studies IIT-Roorkee. His research areas include marketing management, rural marketing, advertising and business strategy. He has contributed many research papers, book chapters in top international publications and has presented his research works at several national and international conferences. He teaches courses in marketing management, advertising and business strategy to students of the Masters in Business Administration program at IIT-Roorkee.

**Debika Sihi** is an Assistant Professor of Business at Southwestern University. Her research interests are in digital marketing strategy, and she explores technological innovations and disruptions in the field of marketing. Debika has published works in a variety of peer reviewed marketing and business journals including the *Journal of Marketing Theory and Practice, Industrial Marketing Management, Journal of the Academy of Marketing Science,* Journal of Retailing, and the International Journal of Public Administration in the Digital Age. Debika teaches courses in the areas of digital, strategic, and nonprofit marketing.

**Michela Soverchia**, Ph.D., is Associate Professor of Accounting and Business Administration at the Department of Economics and Law of the University of Macerata (Italy). She teaches courses on Public Sector Accounting and Business Administration and her main research fields concern public administration (with particular reference to public management and governmental budgeting, accounting and financial reporting), accounting history, and circular economy. She is author of articles and contributions published in international journals and volumes.

**Eleni-Revekka Staiou** graduated, in 2007, from National and Kapodistrian University of Athens, Department of Communication and Media Studies and, in 2008, she completed her postgraduate studies in London, UK in London School of Economics and Political Science (LSE), obtaining an MSc in Communication, Information and Society. In February 2017 she received her PhD at the National and Kapodistrian University of Athens, Department of Communication and Mass Media with focus on the Greek solidarity initiatives and their communication via social media. She is a researcher of the Laboratory of New Technologies in Communication, Education and the Mass Media and her research interests are about eParticipation, Social and Solidarity Economy and Web 2.0, with emphasis on social networks and their potential use by individuals, groups and organizations. Also, her focus is on Non-Profit organizations' communication, especially using social media. She is currently working on the Organosi 2.0 (Organizing 2.0) project, a platform for self-organized social solidarity (SoSS) initiatives in Greece.

**Lois M. Warner**, PhD, is an Assistant Professor and Teaching Resources Coordinator, School of Public Affairs and Administration, Rutgers, the State University of New Jersey, Newark. Her research interests include innovations in public administration, multimedia course delivery, and organizational culture. She is an author of several case studies on public sector technology-based innovations in different world regions. She is also a quarterly columnist, PA Times on Teaching with multimedia. Assistant Director, Virtual Museum of Public Service www.vmps.us. She teaches courses on public policy processes, administrative ethics, and the art and culture of public service. Also, she is a member of the Board of American Society for Public Administration, Section on Public Administration Education. Chair-Elect, American Society for Public Administration, Section on Historical, Artistic & Reflective Expression.

**Naoto Yamauchi** is Professor of Public Economics at Osaka University Osaka School of International Public Policy (OSIPP) in Japan. He received a BA from Osaka University, MSc from the London School of Economics, and a PhD from Osaka University. His research focuses empirical analysis of the nonprofit sector, giving and volunteering, social capital, corporate social responsibility and issues on public-private partnership.

# Index

## N



## O



## P



## R



## S



## T



## U



## V



## W



## X

www.ingramcontent.com/pod-product-compliance
Lightning Source LLC
LaVergne TN
LVHW060419300926
849162LV00006B/1472